THE UNCENSORED

∼ *Boris Godunov*

Народъ.

Разметanite, разметanite. ...

За кѣмъ они пришли?

...

Автерю приводятъ въ ... Лужинова —
в самомъ дѣлѣ? — ... !
тревога, суматоха —

Народъ

Взойдемъ! — двери заперты — ...
вижу! — это крики голосовъ — ...
... — ... прода...

(отворяютъ двери;
Мосальскiй входитъ на ...)

Народъ! Марiя Годунова и сынъ её Ѳео-
доръ отравили себя ядомъ. Мы ви-
дѣли ихъ мёртвые трупы (народъ
слушаетъ молча) что жъ вы молчите
кричите, да здравствуй Ц. Димитрiй
Ивановичъ!... Марiя

Да здравствуетъ царь Димитрiй
Ивановичъ!

7 ноября
1825.

Конецъ комедии въ ней же
первая персона царь Борисъ Годуновъ
слава отцу и сыну и св. духу
аминь.

51

Frontispiece. Final page of the original manuscript of Pushkin's *Komediia o tsare Borise i o Grishke Otrep'eve*, dated 7 November 1825. From Institut russkoi literatury (Pushkinskii Dom) RAN, Rukopisnyi otdel, fond 244, opis' 1, No. 891, list 51. Courtesy of the Russian Academy of Sciences.

THE UNCENSORED
Boris Godunov

∽ The Case for Pushkin's Original *Comedy*, with Annotated Text and Translation

Chester Dunning

with Caryl Emerson, Sergei Fomichev, Lidiia Lotman, and Antony Wood

THE UNIVERSITY OF WISCONSIN PRESS

This book was published with the support of Texas A&M University, the Princeton University Committee for Research in the Humanities and Social Sciences, and the Wisconsin Center for Pushkin Studies at the University of Wisconsin–Madison.

The University of Wisconsin Press
1930 Monroe Street
Madison, Wisconsin 53711

www.wisc.edu/wisconsinpress/

3 Henrietta Street
London WC2E 8LU, England

5   4   3   2

Printed in the United States of America

Library of Congress Cataloging-in-Publication Data
Dunning, Chester S. L., 1949–
    The uncensored Boris Godunov : the case for Pushkin's original comedy, with annotated text and translation / Chester Dunning with Caryl Emerson ... [et al.].
        p. cm. – (Publications of the Wisconsin Center for Pushkin Studies)
    Includes bibliographical references and index.
    ISBN 0-299-20760-9 (cloth : alk. paper)
        1. Pushkin, Aleksandr Sergeevich, 1799–1837. Boris Godunov. 2. Boris Fyodorovich Godunov, Czar of Russia, 1551?–1605 – Drama. I. Emerson, Caryl. II. Pushkin, Aleksandr Sergeevich, 1799–1837. Boris Godunov. III. Pushkin, Aleksandr Sergeevich, 1799–1837. Boris Godunov. English. IV. Title. V. Series.
PG3343.B64D86 2005
891.72'3 – dc22
                                                                        2004025636

ISBN 0-299-20764-1 (pbk. : alk. paper)

*Dedicated to the memory of Philip Vellacott,
a great friend and teacher*

Contents

Illustrations

Preface to the First Edition

The purpose of this book is to rescue the original version of Alexander Pushkin's historical drama *Boris Godunov* from obscurity. Long ignored by specialists and virtually unknown to general readers, Pushkin's *Comedy about Tsar Boris and Grishka Otrepiev* was composed in 1824–25 while the "dangerously radical" poet was living in exile on his family's estate. His underappreciated *Comedy* is a provocative and aesthetically appealing play that differs in many ways from the well-known *Boris Godunov* published in 1831. The interdisciplinary team of specialists who prepared this volume contends that Pushkin's *Comedy* is an extremely important text in its own right – one that deserves to take its place in the canon of the great poet's works alongside the more familiar version of his play.

In addition to new scholarship about Pushkin's *Comedy*, this volume presents for the first time an accurate transcription of the original manuscript of *Komediia o Tsare Borise i o Grishke Otrep'eve*. (In the text published here, readers familiar with *Boris Godunov* will find – in addition to the scenes and lines of dialogue omitted from the so-called canonical text – several words and phrases not found in previous editions of the play.) In order to make Pushkin's *Comedy* known to a wider audience, this volume also contains the first English translation of the play. Notes are also provided to help readers understand occasionally obscure references and to demonstrate the remarkable historical accuracy of the original version of Pushkin's daring drama set in early modern Russia's darkest hour, the Time of Troubles (1598–1613).

This book project grew out of an investigation of the circumstances surrounding the composition of *Komediia* conducted by Professors Chester Dunning and Brett Cooke of Texas A&M University. Dunning, a specialist in early modern Russian history, became intrigued by the tragic fate of the earlier and more historically accurate version of Pushkin's play. When Dunning presented his initial research findings at the annual convention of the American Association for the Advancement of Slavic Studies in 1999, his work caught the attention of Professor Caryl Emerson of Princeton University, a leading scholar of nineteenth-century Russian literature. When Dunning and Emerson decided to embark on this book project, they asked Professor Sergei Fomichev of Novgorod State University – a renowned Pushkinist and one of the world's leading authorities on the poet's handwriting – to contribute to the volume. Fomichev suggested adding to the team his colleague Dr. Lidiia Lotman, a highly productive scholar of Russian literature who is the leading researcher at the Institute of Russian Literature (Pushkinskii Dom) of the Russian Academy of Sciences. Finally, when the team received a National Endowment for the Humanities Collaborative Research Grant, it became possible to expand the project to include an English translation of *Komediia* prepared by Antony Wood, an award-winning translator of Pushkin's poetry.

Research for this book was made possible by a grant from the National Endowment for the Humanities, an independent federal agency, and smaller grants from the University Committee on Research in the Humanities and Social Sciences of Princeton University, the Wisconsin Center for Pushkin Studies, and Texas A&M University's Office of the Vice President for Research, Office of the Assistant Provost for International Programs, College of Liberal Arts, Melburn G. Glasscock Center for Humanities Research, and Department of History. Several colleagues went out of their way to encourage our research, to support applications for funding, and to offer valuable assistance and advice during the conceptualization and development of this book project. We are especially indebted to Svetlana Fedotova, Olga Catalena, Ksana Blank, Olga Peters Hasty, Michael Wachtel, David Budgen, Alla Gelich, David Bethea, Stephanie Sandler, Brett Cooke, J. Thomas Shaw, Irene Masing-Delic, Kurt Schultz, Raphael Kadushin, Sheila McMahon Moermond, Steve Salemson, Christopher J. Syrnyk, Don Ostrowski, Walter Kamphoefner, Nancy Livengood, Elizabeth Arndt, Janet G. Tucker, David Chroust, Elise Kimerling Wirtschafter, Svitlana Kobets, and the anonymous referees who were so positive about our National Endowment for the Humanities grant proposal.

We wish to thank the Institute of Russian Literature (Pushkin House) of the Russian Academy of Sciences (Institut russkoi literatury [Pushkinskii Dom] Rossiiskoi Akademii Nauk) for permission to publish the text of *Komediia o Tsare Borise i o Grishke Otrep'eve* and two drawings by Alexander Pushkin. We are grateful to Houghton Library (Harvard University) for permission to publish two seventeenth-century woodcuts. We wish to acknowledge the extremely generous and timely assistance we received from the staff of the Institute of Russian Literature (Pushkinskii Dom), without whose help this project would have been slowed down by months if not years. Similarly, we appreciate the generous assistance we received from the staff of the British Library, without whose help this project would have taken significantly longer to complete. We also wish to acknowledge the valuable assistance we received from the staff of the Russian State Historical Archive (Rossiiskii gosudarstvennyi istoricheskii arkhiv), the Library of the Russian Academy of Sciences (Biblioteka Rossiiskoi Akademii Nauk), the Russian State Library (Rossiiskaia gosudarstvennaia biblioteka), the Russian National Library (Rossiiskaia natsional'naia biblioteka), Bibliothèque Nationale (Paris), Widener and Houghton Libraries (Harvard University), the Library of Congress, the Wisconsin Center for Pushkin Studies, the University of Washington Libraries, Indiana University Libraries (Bloomington), the James Ford Bell Library (University of Minnesota), Angel Books, Texas A&M Research Foundation, and the interlibrary services division of the Sterling C. Evans Library at Texas A&M University.

It would have been impossible to finish this book project without the tireless assistance of the professional staff of the Department of History, Texas A&M University – especially Barbara Dawson, Jude K. Swank, Judy Mattson, Mary Johnson, and Kelly Cook. Equally important has been the highly professional assistance of the staff of The University of Wisconsin Press. Finally, a word of thanks is also in order for Elsie Kersten, Stephen K. Dunning, and Helen Mills who encouraged this project from the very beginning and cheerfully tolerated my obsession with Alexander Pushkin for several years.

Chester S. L. Dunning
College Station, Texas
September 6, 2004

Prefaces to the Paperback Edition

I am grateful for the opportunity to add some prefatory remarks to the paperback edition of our book, which differs from the original in several modest ways: The paperback edition contains four minor (single word) corrections in our chapters, a one-word correction in the play, and a few minor layout corrections in two scenes of the play.

First, I wish to pinpoint when Pushkin started writing his *Comedy about Tsar Boris and Grishka Otrepiev*. It is well known that he completed it on November 7, 1825. Pushkin's earliest notes concerning the play appear in his "Second Masonic Notebook" and date from November 1824.[1] That means he probably started working on the play in November 1824 and took almost exactly a year to write it. Although Pushkin moved sharply away from Nikolai Karamzin's view of Grishka Otrepiev, his grim portrayal of Tsar Ivan IV was strongly influenced by the controversial interpretation of the "terrible tsar" found in volume nine of Karamzin's *History of the Russian State*. In our book I discuss the possible influence of Friedrich Schiller's unfinished play *Demetrius* on Pushkin's *Comedy* (pages 69–73). Since writing that passage, I have done additional research on this topic. Interested readers will find a stronger case for Schiller's influence on Pushkin's play in *Stanford Slavic Studies*, vols. 29–30.[2]

Just as the first edition of our book was about to go to press, my colleague Sergei Fomichev made several minor corrections to the play based upon careful scrutiny of the original manuscript of Pushkin's *Comedy*. Fortunately, we were able to include all those changes in our book.

Nevertheless, I was unable to add a note about one of those changes – until now. In Scene 17 ("The Tsar's Council") Basmanov reassures Tsar Boris that Grishka Otrepiev will soon be captured and brought to Moscow to be displayed "in an iron cage" (page 391). It has been suggested that Pushkin borrowed this striking image from a notorious and widely reported promise made by Marshal Michel Ney to Louis XVIII – to bring Napoleon to the king "in an iron cage." That is possible, but as a child Pushkin may have read about Tamerlane defeating the Ottoman sultan Bayezid I in 1402 and then displaying him in an iron cage for the entertainment of his soldiers. Pushkin may also have read about Ivan the Terrible's grandfather, Grand Prince Ivan III (r. 1462–1505), who reportedly ordered two Polish conspirators to be placed in an iron cage on the frozen Moskva River and then burned to death. But it is more likely that Pushkin mined the history of the Time of Troubles for this image. In 1612, the bloodthirsty and cruel "third false Dmitry" (the so-called Pskov pretender) was captured, paraded for many miles in chains, and then reportedly placed in an iron cage before Moscow for the amusement of the national militia. Upon reflection, however, it seems even more likely that the iron cage reference came from an episode much closer to Pushkin's own lifetime. It is well known that Catherine the Great resorted to using an iron cage. I am not thinking of the apocryphal story about Catherine locking her wig maker in an iron cage to keep her bad hair a secret. Instead, I am referring to the fate of that other famous Russian Pretender, Emelian Pugachev – the cossack chieftain who claimed to be Catherine's unfortunate husband, Tsar Peter III. In 1774, after his powerful rebellion was suppressed, Pugachev was allegedly transported to Moscow for his execution in an iron cage. As noted in our book, Pushkin was keenly interested in Pugachev at the time he wrote his *Comedy;* and soon after becoming historian laureate of Russia he published *Istoriia Pugachevskago bunta* (1834). Good historian that he was, by then his research led him to modify Pugachev's iron cage into the more accurate "closed sledge." Later historians described it as a "wooden cage on wheels." There is a woodcut of that wretched vehicle located in the State Historical Museum in Moscow.[3]

In our book I briefly discuss Pushkin's use of his own family's historical records in developing the characters of the two Pushkins portrayed in his *Comedy* (pages 80, 474 n104, and 480 n126). While conducting research for a biography of Tsar Dmitrii (r. 1605–06), I recently came across a meticulous survey of early seventeenth-century Pushkin family papers preserved in Russian archives. Those records resoundingly confirm that Pushkin did not invent or exaggerate his family's historical rebelliousness or the multiple Siberian exiles associated with that spirit. Those papers also provide intriguing clues about the interesting, itinerant, and politically active Pushkins who lived during the Time of Troubles and were used to construct the character of Afanasy Mikhailovich Pushkin.[4]

Finally, since writing note 202 (page 495), I have learned that Pushkin embedded more "good jokes" than I had thought in Scene 19 ("A Plain Near Novgorod-Seversky"). There a fleeing Russian soldier refers to the Pretender Dmitry's Polish and Ukrainian soldiers as "basurmany," meaning Muslims or infidels. I noted that Pushkin and his intended audience probably heard that term being applied to Napoleon's soldiers in 1812 – a good joke indeed. But I neglected to mention that Pushkin also knew that Tsar Boris initially tried to hide Dmitry's invasion from his own army and that, using the same ruse in 1606, the unpopular usurper Tsar Vasily Shuisky claimed that the enemies his army faced were not Dmitry's supporters but a band of Russia's ancient enemies, the Crimean Tatars – or "basurmany."[5] The depth of Pushkin's knowledge of early modern Russian history and the clever ways he wove that history into his *Comedy* are remarkable.

Chester S. L. Dunning
College Station, Texas
October 2006

~

There is a patron demon of the printed word whose job it is to guarantee that whenever something goes definitively to press, several details – some crucial, others ornamental, still others simply silly mistakes – will elude the author until it is too late. Of the various second thoughts I have had about my chapters since their submission in 2004, two have proved durable enough to deserve mention in this preface to the paperback edition.

The first is an omission I especially regret, since it is in print under my name elsewhere among University of Wisconsin Press books on Pushkin and a fuller discussion of it here would have bolstered our case for the comedic, pan-European sources of Pushkin's *Komediia*.[6] This is the

Rossini connection. In the years preceding his southern exile, Pushkin had become an enthusiastic fan of Italian opera in St. Petersburg. The removal to Odessa in 1823–24, unlike his later house arrest at Mikhailov-skoe, did not deprive the poet of the delights of urban culture. Pushkin attended the theater, such as it was, wherever he was. He loved musical comedy and learned a great deal from it. Boris Tomashevsky, in his essay on Pushkin and Italian opera, makes the case for Pushkin in Odessa having seen a performance of Rossini's 1817 *melodramma* (or *semiseria* opera) *La gazza ladra* / "Soroka-vorovka" / *The Thieving Magpie*. A pivotal moment occurs in Act I, scene 9, where the servant-girl heroine Ninetta volunteers to read aloud an arrest warrant (in this case, against her own father) for the Mayor magistrate who has misplaced his glasses; horrified but quick-witted, Ninetta alters the age (changing forty-eight into twenty-five), the height, the features, and saves a life. Tomashevsky surmises that a year later, in 1825, Pushkin remembered this comic device of a forensic misreading and gave it to his besieged Grigory Otrepiev in the tavern scene.[7] The hypothesis is all the more persuasive since in Italian *melodramma,* which borrows from the French rescue-opera tradition, the virtuous characters conventionally survive and succeed in their goal – but only after an anxious subtext of prisons, unjust death sentences, and political oppression of simple folk by a "manor" or palace always visible on the horizon of the stage. (In Rossini's source play, and in the real-life story on which it was based, Ninetta dies on the gallows.) In Pushkin's *Comedy,* that threatening manor house has become all of Tsar Boris's Russia, to be outwitted by the young, bold, and socially mobile. Grigory's distortion of the "Tsar's Decree" exposes the ineptness of Godunov's illiterate border police and permits the would-be Pretender to escape to a new life. Of course the crude, crafty Varlaam, part *skomorokh* and part monastery bum, catches him out. But the comic-opera episode serves as a loophole that adds buoyancy to the Otrepiev escape story, which in Karamzin is so grim and humorless, so freighted with dishonor and historical disaster.

The second adjustment is more an extension than an omission. It was the happy result of a closer acquaintance with the abandoned 1937 Mey-erhold-Prokofiev production of *Boris Godunov,* part of my preparation for Princeton University's 2007 realization of that project in Antony Wood's translation. Pages 175–81 of the present volume discuss the Mey-erhold connection. While the treatment there is not incorrect, it is (I now think) blurred. Meyerhold devoted two intense stretches of time to Pushkin's play, the first during 1924–25 in the Vakhtangov theatre and then in 1936 with his own company. Rehearsals for both were abandoned. My comments treat Meyerhold's "Boris project" as a seamless arc over these eleven years, drawing on two memoirists, Boris Zakhava (for 1924–25) and Mikhail Sadovsky (for 1936), without differentiating clearly between the two productions. Although common to both was the image of Pimen as a sly, bustling *khlopotun,* an energetic professional writer with a streak of the hoarder and the rebel in him (Meyerhold's inspiration was the septuagenarian Leo Tolstoy, whom he met as a student in Moscow), the two dramatic concepts were not identical. Especially important for the comedic potential of the 1936 production was Meyerhold's insistence on the youth, battle-readiness, and responsiveness of the major players. Perhaps Pimen needs that crutch not only because he's old, but because of a war wound? Meyerhold muses. His campaign against a pious and static *Boris* – against the "declamation and phony emotionalism" of the Pushkin Cult as well as the operatized *Boris* – depended on agility, dissonance, street smarts, even a certain Eurasian *skifstvo* (Scythianism), in which spirit Prokofiev was to compose the eerie, angular untexted choral moaning of the people for the final scenes of the play. As Gladkov recalls Meyerhold saying, the stage should feel like everyone on it has just gotten down from a horse. People are tired, sweaty, but able to revive, charm, and threaten one other anew at a moment's notice, because "all the people in this play are warriors, not clerks with beards and fur coats."[8] Prokofiev's limpid musical-vocal score, with its laments, discordant dreams, and songs of loneliness, provided sobering counterpoint to the re-militarized urgency that Meyerhold was hoping to instill into this production.

The high energy level and genre hybridity of the truncated 1936 production was certainly comedic. But on further consideration, I do not think it would have ended up wholly, or even predominantly, comic. For all the importance of a spritely Pimen and the hilarious outwit-the-cops routine in that Rossini-like episode with the arrest warrant, there was a dark, fated vein in the production that grew over time. It was associated in Meyerhold's mind with Shakespeare's *Hamlet,* another repertory classic with Prokofiev's music, also rehearsed and also not brought to fruition. In memoirs published in 2004, Leonid Agranovich (still alive at ninety-one in 2006, who as a twenty-one-year-old fledgling actor had been cast as Gavrila Pushkin for the 1936 production of *Boris*), recalls how Meyerhold stubbornly championed Pushkin's choice of meter for twenty-three out of his twenty-five *Boris* scenes: blank verse iambic pentameter with caesura. As is well known, Pushkin himself later had reservations about this choice, claiming in a draft preface from 1830 that such a mandatory mid-line pause had "deprived his verse-line of its distinctive variety" and flexibility (see Translator's Preface in the present volume, page 239). According to Agranovich, however, Meyerhold passionately defended what he read as a choppy, breathless, broken, and paranoid line. "Take Pushkin, read him without rushing, strictly observing the caesura – its great music will pierce you," Agranovich recalls the Master saying to his actors. "Don't brush off the caesura – technically you'll gain nothing by it. The caesura! The whole meaning of what's happening is contained in it, the insane temperature, temperament, the beating of the heart, the search for a solution, for a way out, for salvation, your breathing is like gasping for breath . . ."[9] In his memoirs, Gladkov corroborates Meyerhold's constant demand for just such wary, nervous animal energy, interruptable and on its guard, the energy that comes to hunted beasts in their final extremity. "It must be all *staccato*, separate jolts," Gladkov cites Meyerhold. "For correct intonation you need the right irritant" (205).

Meyerhold advised his actors to read at least a few pages of Pushkin every day, before beginning their work. For him, Pushkin was not only a great playwright but also potentially a great stage director. And Meyerhold's overall vision for *Boris*, I now believe, would have been tragicomic. Or rather, he would have taken from comedy its commitment to surprise, irreverence, its concentration on eye-to-eye encounters, its fast conversational pace and high energy level. These priorities are reflected in the half-a-dozen scenes that were most vigorously rehearsed. Pushkin's plans for a comedic arc culminating in the ascension of the Romanovs were not part of Meyerhold's plans for 1936. But the tragic pulse would never fade. As in *Hamlet*, the end we see on stage is meant to signify the end. If there is an arc, it is made of other stuff. In his directives to Prokofiev on the music, Meyerhold specified the final choral number as a "moaning [or drone: *gul*] of the crowd, agitated, threatening [*groznyi*], like the clamor of the sea. One must feel that sooner or later this unorganized crowd will solidify, unify, and begin to struggle against its oppressors, whoever they may be."[10] This is the canonized Belinskian reading of *narod bezmolvstvuet*: the play's finale understood as a holding

pattern, a caesura-like pause without the resumption of meter, a suspended tragedy. But silence can be slack and inertia-driven, a void – or
it can be strategic, with its pulsations temporarily below the auditory bar
but still beating. The latter technique would be one way of grafting
tragedy and comedy. Whether Meyerhold's *Boris Godunov* would have
evolved into a tragicomedy of history, we cannot know.

Caryl Emerson
Princeton, New Jersey
October 2006

Certain characteristics of what was a bipolar "comedic" drama before
being streamlined into a Classical tragedy can cause practical difficulties
in presentation of the text. Pushkin's friends and/or his unofficial censor
spared the editors of the 1831 edition the uneasiness they might have
experienced at the "impurity" of the use of no less than five further
meters along with the basic blank verse pentameter, which enhances the
principle of variety that runs through the 1825 version. In one of the three
scenes in which the meter departs from the iambic pentameter, scene 6,
problems of verse layout were liable to occur in an English translation
that used anything like the original meter (my translation has loose heptameters for Pushkin's octometers); and sure enough, in the first edition
of this book they did. So long are the lines in the Evil Monk scene that
when they run over, it can be hard to tell where one line ends and the
next begins, and runovers may be confused with broken lines. In this
paperback edition, the layout of several verse lines in scene 6, and also in
scene 13, where the lesser problem of differential indentation occurs, has
been corrected.

Pushkin wrote his *Comedy* in highly wrought verse which is also living
speech, and in my translation I have aimed at the same combination. Its
test, of course, will be in the theater. I once heard a director say that
Shakespeare does over half an actor's preparatory work for him simply in
the architecture of his lines. If an actor speaks the lines as they are in the
text (of a good edition!), then he or she will be halfway or more toward
achieving emphases, contrasts, hesitations, climaxes, and relaxations
that make sense, even the sense intended by Shakespeare. It is the same
with Pushkin's subtly crafted speeches, and I have tried to hold onto their
verbal patterns and their structure and dynamic. Though the word has
lost some of its old weight and currency today, I hope that any stage

production will relish and exploit these verbal features to the full, and that this may play its part in the realization of Pushkin's drama in English.

Antony Wood
London, United Kingdom
October 2006

◦~◦

Two of my notes in the original edition of our book need to be updated. In note 22 (page 460) I discuss the ancient cap of Monomakh, one of the crowns worn by the early tsars. According to legend, it had been a gift from a Byzantine emperor to Grand Prince Vladimir Monomakh of Kiev (r. 1113–25). That is extremely unlikely. Although there is still no agreement among scholars about the timing and purpose of this "gift," the cap of Monomakh was probably of fourteenth century Central Asian origin. In note 33 (page 462) I discuss the icon known as the "Holy Virgin of the Don," which was supposedly given as a gift to Grand Prince Dmitry (Donskoi) by the Don cossacks sometime before the Battle of Kulikovo Field in 1380. That is also very unlikely. The legend itself dates from long after the fourteenth century, and its reference to Don cossacks that early appears to be anachronistic.

Lidiia Lotman
St. Petersburg, Russia
October 2006

◦~◦

I wish to apologize to our readers for a one-word transcription error in Pushkin's *Komediia* made while preparing the text for the first edition of *The Uncensored Boris Godunov*. That error (in the "Tavern Scene") has been corrected in the new paperback edition, along with the English translation. See note 97 (pages 473–74).

Sergei Fomichev
St. Petersburg, Russia
October 2006

Notes

1. Pushkin, *Rabochie tetradi,* 4: 44–450b.

2. Dunning, "Did Schiller's *Demetrius* Influence Alexander Pushkin's *Comedy about Tsar Boris and Grishka Otrepiev?*" in "Word, Music, History: A Festschrift for Caryl Emerson," edited by Lazar Fleishman, Gabriella Safran, and Michael Wachtel, *Stanford Slavic Studies* 29–30 (2005): 80–92.

3. Avrich, *Russian Rebels,* 242–43; Pushkin, *The History of Pugachev,* 106; John T. Alexander, *Emperor of the Cossacks: Pugachev and the Frontier Jacquerie of 1773–1775* (Lawrence, KS: Coronado Press, 1973), 189–91.

4. V. I. Koretskii, "Pushkiny v Smutnoe vremia i letopisets iz ikh roda," in V. I. Koretskii, *Istoriia russkogo letopisaniia vtoroi poloviny XVI-nachala XVII v.* (Moscow: Nauka, 1986), 231–65.

5. Dunning, *Russia's First Civil War,* 157–58, 271–72.

6. See Boris Katz and Caryl Emerson, "Pushkin and Music," in *The Pushkin Handbook,* edited by David M. Bethea (Madison: University of Wisconsin Press, 2006), 596.

7. B. Tomashevskii, "Pushkin i ital'ianskaia opera," in *Pushkin i ego sovremenniki. Materialy i issledovaniia,* vyp. 31–32 (Leningrad: AN SSSR, 1927): 49–60.

8. Aleksandr Gladkov, *Meyerhold Speaks, Meyerhold Rehearses,* edited and translated by Alma Law (Amsterdam: Harwood Academic Publishers, 1997), 202.

9. L. D. Agranovich, *Stop-kadr: Meierkhol'd. Vorkuta i drugoe kino* (Moscow: Sovpadenie, 2004), 24 and 28.

10. "Pis'mo V. E. Meierkhol'da k S. S. Prokofievu," appended to V. Gromov, "Zamysel postanovki," in *Tvorcheskoe nasledie V. E. Meierkhol'da,* edited by L. D. Vendrovskaia and A. V. Fevral'skii (Moscow: Vserossiskoe teatral'noe obshchestvo, 1978), 399.

Acknowledgments

The preparation of this volume was made possible in part by a grant from the National Endowment of the Humanities, an independent federal agency.

The authors also wish to acknowledge with gratitude the generous subvention grants from the University Committee on Research in the Humanities and Social Sciences of Princeton University and The Wisconsin Center for Pushkin Studies at the University of Wisconsin–Madison.

THE UNCENSORED

∽ *Boris Godunov*

Introduction

Reconsidering History and Expanding the Canon

~ CARYL EMERSON AND CHESTER DUNNING

Alexander Pushkin considered *Boris Godunov* his finest work. Upon completing it at Mikhailovskoe in November 1825, he wrote glowingly to his friends about the experience: he felt his talent had matured, he could create. By the time the play was approved for publication in 1830, however, this initial enthusiasm had faded. During that year Pushkin drafted several prefaces in which he remembered with nostalgia those moments of creative inspiration now five years distant, recalled with gratitude the approval of a few chosen friends, and confessed his mounting aversion for putting the play before the public for fear it would not be understood. Except for that same narrow circle of friends, the prediction turned out to be true.

From the 1840s onward, the play was published in a bewildering number of variants. But by the early twentieth century, the 1831 version, with one of its omitted scenes restored, had come to be accepted as canonical – even though it was much less successful with its audience than the original text and had been severely stressed by its censors. It is the premise of the present study that the canonical status of the 1831 text should be rethought, and that the 1825 original be allowed to compete with it. This introduction previews some of our reasons, which later chapters will examine in detail.

The two versions were titled, realized, and received in quite different ways. The 1825 *Comedy about Tsar Boris and Grishka Otrepiev*, written in exile, smuggled into the capital, and recited in a thrillingly unpretentious manner by the poet himself at several private gatherings in St. Petersburg, was an immediate aural experience, and a sensation. Pushkin was hailed as a daring radical, in his history and his dramaturgy. By contrast, the 1831 *Boris Godunov,* although not wholly new to the reading public (excerpts had been published in 1827 and 1829), was a silent in-print affair, received in a perfunctory way. It reinforced the opinion that Pushkin not only had passed his prime as a poet but also (some thought) had cast in his lot with opportunistic, perhaps even reactionary, forces. How should we interpret this shift in reception? Was it due to the external political environment – the increasing intensity of the Decembrist movement throughout 1825 as compared with the Polish Uprising of 1830, suppressed by imperial troops – or due rather to internal aesthetic criteria (the poet continued to revise, and not always for the better)? A third route, pursued in chapters 1 through 3, examines the evolution of Pushkin's professional ambitions as a historian in the space between the play's writing and its approval for print. All three levels of inquiry are relevant to the present study. For the path of this play from composition to publication, and from there to canonization, is more oscillating, more arduous, and more biographically significant than has usually been supposed.

Given the far more lethal poet-versus-tsar stories of the Stalinist period, it is easy to forget the brutal mindlessness of censorship under Nicholas I. Creative writers learned to respond with surgical precision to this pressure, cutting into their own work so that it might, at some level, continue to live. At times they just gave up, as Pushkin eventually did with "The Bronze Horseman" (1833), unpublished in his lifetime.[1] But Pushkin persevered with *Boris.* The nature of that perseverance has resisted definitive explanation. Pushkin, of course, did not note down for the benefit of later textologists when a censor's mark infuriated him beyond all remedy and when it triggered a search for alternatives, none as good as his freely composed text, but nevertheless (given who he was) always aesthetically defensible. With a poet of Pushkin's caliber, every act of revision, however initially motivated, projected its own new sense of the whole. So in Pushkin's *Boris* project we are confronted with two versions: an original text that thrilled its author, and a derivative of that text. The vast bulk of scholarly attention has been devoted to the derivative.

The Problem with Versions

There are uncanny parallels between the history of Pushkin's play and the history of Musorgsky's far more famous opera built on it forty-five years later. Both the play and the opera exist in two authorial (authorized) versions. In each instance the first version was unpublished, although it was finished and formally submitted to the relevant state agencies for their approval. When the respective authority rejected the submission – for Pushkin in 1826, it was the censor-surrogate delegated by Tsar Nicholas I; for Musorgsky in 1869, it was the Imperial Theater Directorate – each author returned to the drafting board. Pushkin, already an established and revered poet, turned to the task of revising with extreme reluctance; Musorgsky, an unknown amateur composer, with manifest enthusiasm. In both cases the revised texts, which went public as a book and as an operatic premiere one half-decade after their first failed submissions, received mixed reviews.

In each case, the political and aesthetic climate had changed significantly. Each was judged unplayable or unsingable by the stage norms of the time. Several generations had to pass before the content of these two *Boris Godunov*s stabilized. Pushkin's play was cleared for stage performance only in 1866 and suffered a botched premiere in 1870, in sixteen scenes, to unenthusiastic reviews.[2] Musorgsky's opera, after a gala premiere that utilized sets from the ill-starred Pushkin premiere, faded away from the Russian stage soon after the composer's death – until Fyodor Chaliapin brought it back to life in the 1890s, in a version reorchestrated (and in part rewritten) by Rimsky-Korsakov, one decade after the government had relinquished its monopoly over the theaters of the empire. Although Pushkin's source-text was now considered closet drama, this Musorgsky revival paved the way for the triumph of Diaghilev's opera productions in Paris. In the twentieth century, for most theater-goers, *Boris Godunov* is a story that has always been sung.

In this parallel saga of the eclipse and rebirth of two multi-versioned masterpieces, academic practice has played an important supporting role. As textologists, musicologists and editors worked over the available manuscripts and created an industry worthy of these two works' rising fame, it became accepted practice to refer to the initial version as "preliminary" or "provisional," the second (published) version as "definitive." Taken in their own time, of course, the 1825 and 1869 *Boris Godunov*s were perceived by their authors as finished works. There was nothing "provisional" in Pushkin's mind about the play he read to his friends in the fall of 1826. In this particular, however, the experience of Pushkin and Musorgsky does not coincide: the composer insisted loudly and often that the initial rejection was a blessing and that his opera was much improved by his having been obliged to revise it. Nevertheless, the twentieth century witnessed a number of eminent music historians and opera producers who not only "de-Rimskified" Musorgsky's opera but even argued for the superiority of the bare-bones 1869 initial version, with its thin, ineffective orchestration and half-shouted arias. Such "quests for the original concept" have *not* been the rule, however, with Pushkin's play. Somehow, in the history of Pushkin's dramaturgy, the 1825 original *Boris Godunov* became a draft.

When confronted with several authorial versions of one creative project, certain prejudices seem to take over. First, there is the suspicion that "later is better." In our everyday creative experience, revisions improve things; how much more true of great poets, then, who revise with focus and intelligence beyond our keenest dreams! But in fact a case can be made either way. Very great creative minds might conceive a project as an entirety, commit it to a draft or working notebook, and then dissipate its integrity while responding piecemeal to criticism of its parts. This latter liability is all the more pronounced, of course, when later versions are the result not only of more time and concentration put in by the poet but also of a censor's markings. The most reliable guideline under these circumstances must be authorial intention, to the extent that one can recuperate it. Did the author, repeatedly and over a reasonable stretch of time, try to publish or perform the work in its initial version? Did the author register anger, frustration, and disgust at being prevented from doing so? If the answer is yes, then one must be very careful assigning automatic priority to any later variant, just because it happened to be approved for a public life.

For there is also a tendency to believe that "in print is better." An unpublished work feels unfinished, unvetted, even unborn. In Russia, however, as in other cultures with a long, capricious history of civil and ecclesiastical censorship, there is a powerful counter-tradition: "in print" usually means "official" – tampered-with, compromised – whereas handwritten manuscripts, books "for the drawer," and poems memorized for safekeeping and passed mouth-to-mouth, are authentic and free. Interestingly, this familiar reflex on the part of keepers of the Russian literary legacy has not been much in evidence in the case of critics responding to Pushkin's *Boris Godunov*.

With practicing artists the response was quite different. "Time of Troubles" plays were written by several of Pushkin's friends and competitors, men who remembered the electrifying ending of the 1825 text (altered in the published version), and some of these plays open on precisely that tension-filled final moment of Pushkin's original, presuming their audience's aural memory of it. But Pushkin's play never became a staple of the stage. And in the absence of a robust performance history, sensitive to the input of directors and actors, it is the critics and scholars who create a canonical playtext out of the published record.

Critical industries are not innocent. One version might triumph over its rivals not because the author wished it so, but because it offers a spectacular opportunity for strong literary critics to interpret it. Prime moments of ambiguous ethical potential could be isolated and then expanded, as the political climate required, into whole philosophies of history. Indeed, from the 1830s until well into the Soviet 1970s, one detail belonging exclusively to the 1831 text of *Boris Godunov* held center stage: the final stage direction *narod bezmolvstvuet* (literally, "the people are speechless"). These two words replaced the popular cheer "Long live Tsar Dimitry Ivanovich!" that had ended the stage action of the 1825 original. Did Pushkin adjust his original ending as part of a newly revised design, in response to censorship worries, or according to some other calculation? This question has been exhaustively debated, with inconclusive results.[3] Since the final cheer for Dmitry was not among the lines known to be objectionable to the censor, the "pressure" to remove it must have been subtle, perhaps even preemptively self-applied. And yet, for all its uncertain authorial status, the phrase *narod bezmolvstvuet* – whether read to oneself, acted out, or mouthed silently to the audience – has been allowed to define the play, its author, the virtues of the Russian folk, and the teleological shape of Russian history.

End-driven Interpretations: A Chronological Sampling,
with Commentary

Chapter 1 will examine in detail some influential interpretations of the canonical text. As background to that exercise and to demonstrate how a single stage direction at the end – perhaps not even of the author's free devising – can set the terms of debate for two centuries of readings, we sample here some *Boris* criticism through that famous lens. The *bezmolvstvuet* of 1831 is not the first mention of the people's silence in the final scene. At an earlier point in both versions, after the assembled crowd is informed that Boris's widow, Maria, and son, Feodor, have poisoned themselves and their corpses are on display, a stage direction informs us that *narod v uzhase molchit* (the people are silent in horror). A mute reaction (*narod ... molchit*) to the murder of a reigning royal family is credible and excusable. But Mosalsky, announcing the fate of the Godunovs, is not satisfied with it; he orders the crowd to lend its enthusiastic support to events, commanding them to cheer Dmitry. In 1825, they do cheer – and with vigor. The 1831 text adds a second, significantly different type of silence. They have become speechless, "without utterance," unable (or unwilling) to respond (*bezmolvstvuet*). The power of the verb *bezmolvstvovat'* lies precisely in its expectant, responsive context: something has been spoken, and response to it is withheld. But for how long, in what mood, with what potential, and implying what vision of history? Silence such as this is a critic's paradise for speculation. To lose that marvelous withholding moment would be to make the play far less interesting for many of its readers.

One contribution of the present study will be to reexamine these two ending strategies from the perspective of Pushkin *as an historian*, with special attention to his attitude toward the False Dmitry. In our view, that relation has been grievously understudied and over-aestheticized. It is common practice to assume that Pushkin matured late as a serious historian, only in the early 1830s. It is also often assumed that Pushkin felt a choice had to be made between historical accuracy and symmetrical poetic structure. Such was the view of the Soviet-era Pushkinist Grigory Vinokur, who remarked in a popular essay on *Boris Godunov* published in 1935: "even if we ignore the fact that historical criticism in the twenties stood at a rather low level, Pushkin would have had no use for it at all, because the value and meaning of his tragedy are determined not by the degree of its historical accuracy."[4] Against that received wisdom, we will argue that Pushkin's professional interest in history was of early vintage and accuracy always mattered to him a great deal. Pushkin read sources that made him better informed about the historical Pretender than generations of Pushkinists have been since, and he used this knowledge (cautiously, subtly, displaced on to a large number of characters who artfully combined the fictional with the real) to examine a historical period from the perspective of diverse social interests and classes. In our view, there is no reason to doubt that Pushkin in 1825 believed he had written an *accurate* historical drama – and what is more, one with many aesthetically pleasing elements that were later jettisoned when the manuscript was tailored for print. It is thus a sobering exercise to review the massive interpretive tradition that owes its existence to *narod bezmolvstvuet*. This critical tradition begins, as with so much else in the fading years of Russia's Golden Age, with Vissarion Belinsky.

Belinsky's hectoring, categorical opinion-pieces on Russian literature have not fared well in recent times, but they were authoritative in Russian circles for a hundred and fifty years. In his "Tenth Essay on Pushkin: *Boris Godunov*" (1845), Belinsky decreed that the composition in question was not a play at all but "an epic poem in conversational form."[5] Its hero could not succeed, he declared, because drama requires a struggle of ideas and the Russian seventeenth century, not knowing "personality," could not produce carriers of ideas. In his rambling appreciation, Belinsky inappropriately applied a great deal of German Romantic philosophy to Pushkin's aesthetics as well as to the sociopolitical reality of early modern Russia. He poorly construed the nature of Pushkin's debt to Karamzin, and only crudely addressed the formal aspects of the play. Not aware that Pushkin had written his play in 1825, he opened his essay with the pronouncement that "a completely new era in Pushkin's artistic activity began with *Poltava* [published in 1829] and *Boris Godunov*." Such lapses might be forgiven a civic critic like Belinsky from nonaristocratic circles writing in the 1840s; after all, he knew less about Pushkin than we know now, for manuscripts, archives, and memoirs are available only to posterity. But still, the "Tenth Essay" established some unfortunate priorities. After the sophisticated salon criticism of Pushkin's era, with its wit, insider epigrams, and album verse, its quasi-public "friendly letters" and verse epistles exchanged among practicing poets on arcane technical literary matters, startling critical precedent was set by Belinsky's peremptory tone. Belinsky made proclamations concerning historical events and a poet's creative process as if such matters had public answers. The "Tenth Essay" ends on a discussion of the ending, with suggestive ellipses. "*Narod bezmolvstvuet* ... This is the final word of the tragedy, containing in itself a profound feature worthy of Shakespeare... In this silence of the people can be heard the terrifying, tragic voice of a new Nemesis, proclaiming judgment over a new victim – over he who destroyed the clan of Godunovs ..."

Two enduring hypotheses are contained within this final paragraph of Belinsky's review. First, the refusal of the Russian people to respond to a command barked at them from above is seen as potent, majestic, a maturation of their collective wisdom, although the political significance of this delayed response is still undefined. And second, the target of their matured critical judgment is the Pretender Dmitry, from whom approval is withheld – both by history and, it is assumed, by Pushkin as well. Over the next century and a half, successive critics (assisted by the mandates of Church and State) will elaborate on this dual theme. Grishka Otrepiev/Dmitry, they will argue, might have appealed to Pushkin as a courtier, as a chameleon, as a warrior and lover in the Western style, as a surrogate for Romantic self-fashioning, and a symbol of poetic inspiration, but not as a serious contender for political power with a progressive agenda of reforms.

As shall be seen, the tendency to take Pushkin's Dmitry as a metaphor for ahistorical creativity, rather than as a historical agent, has been pursued at a high level of literary sophistication. In provocative essays by such eminent poet-critics and culturologists as Dmitry Merezhkovsky and (more recently) Yuri Lotman, Boris Uspensky, and Vladimir Turbin, "pretendership" is linked with the demonic, with the theatrical, with Gogol's pretender-hero Khlestakov from "The Inspector General," and with metaphysical freedom for the personality.[6] "Pretendership [*samozvanstvo*] is a caprice," Turbin writes. "A whim: what I want, I'll get. Pretenders cannot be produced by a society serially, the way tradesmen and monks, kings and beggars, clerks and peasants are produced. A pretender is extraordinary … a loner … an artist-improvisator, a discoverer of things: Otrepiev, Pugachev and Liza Muromskaia would get along with each other famously …" (79). This clustering of Grishka Otrepiev with Pugachev, and both these historical figures together with a wholly fictional heroine from the final story in Pushkin's *Tales of Belkin*, is characteristic of such speculative criticism. It is a liability assumed by all real historical personages touched by Pushkin's creative pen, the same order of risk that befell the historical Richard III in the wake of Shakespeare's history play and the historical Napoleon after Tolstoy's *War and Peace*. But the False Dmitry has been singularly disadvantaged by his "aestheticization." For Pushkin had to be cautious when writing publicly on a historical figure proscribed by Church, State, and Romanov dynasty – more cautious, arguably, than with the title role. Although Tsar Boris also changes shape significantly under pressure of Pushkin's genius, he retains his ambition, courage, a serious slate of complaints and reforms, desperate negotiations, and a death that was both disfiguring and ennobling. Much of Karamzin's complex psychological and political portrait of Boris remains in place, although shorn of Karamzin's moralizing conclusions. The Pretender, in contrast, is radically reconstructed. Very little of Karamzin's indistinct, rumor-ridden image survives. The False Dmitry becomes cleaner, more innocent and attractive – but on the surface, less serious as a historical force. Dmitry is both raised, and reduced, to art. In this transformation, too, there are important differences in detail between the 1825 and 1831 texts.

Here, then, is the received ideology of *Boris Godunov,* given its first authoritative statement in Belinsky's "Tenth Essay on Pushkin." Boris Godunov, the title character, is the sole historical agent. Perhaps he is even the sole consciousness worth our attention because all that matters in the play emanates from Boris's fears, memories, and practices. Grigory/Dmitry, in contrast, is an unknown entity, childhood personified, impulsive, "full of empty declamation," "not capable of anything great." To Belinsky, the people's horrified repudiation of him at the last minute made perfect sense. Unexpected or illicit silence (speechlessness) is a powerful tool. It passes judgment but does not participate; it speaks its mind without supplying the content of that mind. With that ending, Pushkin's play could mean almost anything.

During the 1899 Pushkin Centennial, the most durable aspects of Belinsky's interpretation were refined, revised, and supplied with less cavalier commentary on aspects of artistic form by a new generation of academic Pushkinists. The Centennial was a landmark in the domestication and sanctification of Alexander Pushkin by the Russian authorities. His move from dissident rebel poet (an aura that had clung to the poet for most of the century) to official spokesman for Russian culture was fixed in place. Pushkin was published in mass editions, his portrait displayed in schools and libraries. Exemplary of this new image is Andrei Filonov's 1899 *Pushkin's "Boris Godunov": An Attempt at Analysis from the Historical and Aesthetic Point of View.*[7] Its Part Two opens on the assertion (crucial to the tragic vision assumed to govern the play) that "at the base of every work of art there must lie a single main idea," which in this case is "the single stain on Boris's conscience" (63). Filonov sees all characters in the play as elaborations on good and evil sides of Boris's personality. Filonov insists that *Boris Godunov* is a stageable play with a single, highly dramatic hero. Thus he amends Belinsky by finding in the plot not only plenty of dramatic action, but also – what is arguably even more dramatic – a bold freezing of action at the end, a refusal to resolve the tension before the curtain goes down. To Filonov, the famous final stage direction meant that "the people are waiting for something *more:* perhaps everything is not yet over, another great drama will ensue" (88). This waiting has an upbeat, faintly optimistic hue. "Pushkin wished to portray the disasters not of the people, but of *Boris*" (89). Around Boris, reigning and then deceased, two parallel confrontations take place: one between tsar and people (*narod*), the other between fixed past and open future.

Despite renewed debate among Russian historians over the responsibility of Boris Godunov for the death of Tsarevich Dmitry in Uglich in 1591 – a contested issue fed by the revisionist work of Sergei Platonov in the early twentieth century – these critical parameters held firm from the twilight of the Romanovs through the flourishing of their Soviet successors. Pushkin's ideological intent was distributed among his dramatis personae as follows: The career of the gifted, ambitious, doomed Tsar Boris was confirmed as a disaster, but in a compellingly Romantic manner. The Pretender Dmitry was rendered trivially, as little more than an outgrowth of that career, a Nemesis controlled by the anxieties of the usurper-tsar and thus only a minor reality in his own right. Other historical personages carefully elaborated by Pushkin, and not always only in cameo roles (Pyotr Basmanov, Gavrila Pushkin, Vasily Shuisky, "Kurbsky's son," the mercenaries and cossacks in the battle scenes) were rarely discussed as carriers of political options. And the *narod*? It was cowed into silence but potentially heroic, inspired at the crucial moment by an intuitive collective discipline that prompted it *not* to obey, *not* to respond.

There was, of course, the nagging common knowledge that Pushkin himself did not share this optimistic view of the Russian people's collective virtue in times of crisis. The poet's own oft-expressed horror at popular rebellion, sure to be senseless, merciless, and bloody, was hardly a secret. But this sentiment was smoothed over and adapted to larger post-Centennial sociopolitical needs. According to the Soviet (and then émigré) scholar Ilya Serman, the idea of the *narod* as the hero of Pushkin's play appeared rather late in the critical canon.[8] Although present *in nuce* in Belinsky's essay and echoed throughout the nineteenth century, it gained wide currency only after 1905, among public intellectuals eager to find historical precedence for popular resistance within their ideal of a newly-conscious, progressive Russia. Such civic readings of this Time of Troubles play grew stronger during the years of war and revolution, even though anti-tsarist feeling among the *narod* was overwhelmingly a twentieth-century phenomenon.

End-driven readings in this populist spirit had to account, moreover, for the far-from-idealized image of the common people that the cumulative scenes of the play actually offered. One reassuring solution was offered by Boris Engelhardt, who drew a distinction between the mob (*tolpa*) that we see on stage and the authentic *narod*, a transcendental, idealized force behind the wings.[9] The first represents history as experienced in its own time; the second celebrates historical destiny. Engelhardt assures us that Pushkin could never have put his faith in the "senseless wild herd" that we actually see in the play – a force that is politically irrational, superstitious, ambivalent, and inconsistent. But he insists that the *narod* as such was a concept dear to the poet. Key to him, too, are the final moments of *Boris Godunov*, where this collective entity is elevated and dignified by its stunned silence.

It was not until the 1970s, with the explosion of interest in the "carnivalesque" among literary theorists, that the *narod*-as-hero in *Boris Godunov* received a wholly new rationale and lease on life. Refocusing on the naughty, witty Shakespearean resonances of the crowd scenes, carnival critics began to argue that it was neither silent potential nor high moral stance that made a positive hero, but (on the contrary) misbehavior, irreverence, and the raucous guffaw. Mikhail Bakhtin can be credited with the opening move of this transformation, in which the high genre of silence is trumped by its noisy low opposite. In the closing paragraphs of his 1965 monograph, *The Creative Work of François Rabelais and Popular Culture of the Middle Ages and Renaissance*, Bakhtin connects Pushkin's historical drama with the "drama of world history" – which, in the critic's view, is comedic. Refreshingly, a line other than the final stage direction is now made key for the text. Citing Grigory's nightmare in Pimen's cell (where the novice dreams he climbs a tower and is laughed down by the people on the public square), Bakhtin proclaimed that "all the acts of the drama of world history have taken place before a laughing popular chorus. If one fails to hear this chorus, it is impossible to understand the drama as a whole. Just try to imagine Pushkin's *Boris Godunov* without the *narod* scenes – such a conception of Pushkin's drama would not only be incomplete, but distorted as well."[10] Thus was Bakhtin's utopian program for laughter, a spin-off of the worldwide Bakhtin boom, applied to medieval Muscovy (however anachronistically and inappropriately). As elaborated by several eminent cultural historians, this model triggered a critical storm among Russian academics in the 1970s.[11] Attention was refocused from the *bezmolvstvuet* of the 1831 text to the loud, unruly behavior of commoners and folk heroes throughout the play. But, cautious skeptics pointed out, colorful metaconstructs such as a "world of laughter" do not necessarily explain real historical events. The role of the "carnivalized *narod*" in the Boris debates is admirably illustrated by Sergei Fomichev's contribution to this volume, which argues vigorously on behalf of a laughing substrate to the 1825 *Komediia*. This contested legacy will be discussed in chapter 5.

Here, too, we hope that the present volume can make a contribution. Pushkin, we argue, wrote his first full-length play with the intuitions of both dramatist and historian already well formed and highly disciplined. In it, sociohistorical issues were not mere ornament (as they were earlier, for example, in Sumarokov's eighteenth-century neoclassical tragedy *Dimitry the Pretender,* or as they would later be in Tchaikovsky's Ivan-the-Terrible opera *The Oprichnik*). Although presented in compact poetic form, these issues were meant to be grasped and taken seriously, even seditiously, by that generation of well-educated aristocrats who happened to be Pushkin's best friends. But later generations of readers had other priorities and were less well-informed. What is more, as a great work of art by a great poet, *Boris Godunov* has attracted throughout the years more serious attention among literary scholars than among professional historians. Understandably, when history *qua* history becomes central to an analysis – as it occasionally does – literary minds feel more at home in the aestheticized "semiotic models" of cultural history, with their manageable binary oppositions, than in the multivalent wilderness of archives or empirical data, where the best historians live. Literary professionals expect symmetrical structure and are adept at projecting it back from whatever end is provided. Historians, however, expect disorder; they try to remember that "ends" are arbitrary cut-off points, and they suspect that asymmetry rather than symmetry is the rule. Our task will be to demonstrate that Pushkin in 1825 achieved that rare aesthetic-historical amalgam: a symmetry that also, historically, "rang true." This version was later replaced by a revised text with another (arguably inferior) symmetry.

Our final sampling of twentieth-century interpretations was chosen with an eye to its relevance for our "rehabilitation" project. The overwhelming majority of twentieth-century critics worked solely with the 1831 text of *Boris Godunov*, confirmed as canonical by Grigory Vinokur's meticulous textological work for Volume VII ("Dramatic Works") of the Jubilee Edition of Pushkin, a product of the mid-1930s. It is one of the paradoxes of the present study that the mandated Leninist-Stalinist line on Pushkin and on the Time of Troubles – that the poet was a Decembrist-style radical, that "popular opinion" and "popular hatred toward the tsar" are all-decisive in the play, and that the *narod* was driven not only by legends but also by anger, poverty, and a quest for economic justice – turns out to be, in certain respects, more historically accurate than the romanticized, psychologized generalizations about the play that emerge from more liberal eras. Representative of an approved *Boris Godunov* for the 1930s is an anthology of essays by prominent Pushkinists published in 1936 under the auspices of the State Academic Drama Theater, intended as a guide to both the production and the reception of Pushkin's baffling play.[12]

B. P. Gorodetsky opens his essay for this 1936 anthology by echoing Belinsky's progressive reading: there was a "unified political line at the base of the tragedy," which was "elemental popular rebellion" (37–38). Given the portentous silence at the end, however, one must conclude that "the image of the *narod* is ambivalent"; it is a force in transition, "a general voice of the people, but not yet the opinion of the people" (39). In his contribution, A. L. Slonimsky explains the play's failure with its audience in similar fashion. Pushkin was determined to make the rebellious spirit of the people into the central hero, and thus withheld heroic status from both Tsar and Pretender (69). But how is a collective spirit transformed into a hero? One route, Slonimsky suggests, would be to replace traditional well-constructed dramatic acts and scenes (with their Shakespearean focus on individual eloquence and pathos) by a more diffuse, Karamzinian narrative model of "scene fragments" from history (62). Karamzin lent himself well to such adaptation because he was convinced of Boris's guilt while at the same time understanding well the role played by the people's fickle energy in bringing about the tsar's fall. Thus, Slonimsky assures us, in following the historian laureate's account of events, Pushkin had only to change the emphasis: "the moral motivation of Karamzin is replaced by the social" (66).

Chapters 2 and 3 of the present study will interrogate, yet again, this Karamzin connection, arguing that Pushkin in 1825 changed a great deal more than the "emphasis" of the scenes in his primary source, *The*

History of the Russian State. What we hope to show in addition, however, is that Pushkin's desire to be an alternative to Karamzin, not an echo of him, is far stronger in the original 1825 play. In both versions, the debt is profound. But debt is a complex matter. To quote reverently, to repeat faithfully but with an altered accent, to satirize, to react against, and to repudiate outright are very different gestures of indebtedness to one's mentor. A poet like Pushkin might code in several levels of appreciation simultaneously. But we will argue that Pushkin could have dedicated to Karamzin only the 1831 version of his play, not the 1825, if he wished to avoid intonations of disrespect or parodic intent.

Post-Stalinist readings of *Boris Godunov* were immeasurably more diverse and imaginative. The end-driven ideological interpretation, in which critics investigated Pushkin's "historicism" by pinning down the meaning Pushkin gave to events *in* history, began increasingly to be supplemented by speculation on the structure of the play as a statement *about* history. Such a "metahistorical" approach to the play, which continues to be very provocative, has been a mixed blessing. Crucially for many such readings, the poet's task is seen as competing with, not reinforcing, the task of the honest historian. In these instances, the carrier of the historical burden is Boris, and of the "poetic impulse" invariably the False Dmitry, the most curious, evasive character in both drama and history. We welcome the Pretender's return to the spotlight, but regret that this return has been largely in the role of the play's "internal muse." When Otrepiev/Dmitry stands in for poetic creativity, it comes at a price: Dmitry cannot stand for any historical option. It ceases to matter who he was or what he wished to accomplish.

An influential predecessor of these metareadings was the work of Ilya Serman. In a seminal essay from the late 1960s, Serman boldly broke out of politicized categories altogether by claiming for the Pretender a new, positive role.[13] According to his reading, Grishka Otrepiev, unlike Pimen or Tsar Boris, believes in *creating* miracles, not just recording them or warding them off with witchcraft. Grigory's "new word" begins when he understands Pimen's stories not as a pious novice or a future chronicler, but as a poet. Naturally Pimen cannot grasp what is going on; Pimen is a creature of the old, anonymous, chronicled, and foreordained world, a world that does not know free poetry or personal initiative. Grigory is of the new world, the world of fantasy and individual authorship. He is that responsive type of poet elsewhere so beloved by Pushkin – an improvisator. Pretendership shares with such poetry the talent to think up a solution on the spot and then to believe in one's own miracles, all the while retaining a certain outsideness and consciousness of artifice. Serman acknowledges that such an understanding of poetry was alien to the early seventeenth century. But he makes much of the line given to Gavrila Pushkin in the 1825 original (removed from the 1831 text), where the poet himself links this idea of the free poet with the *skomorokh,* or illicit Russian minstrel: a consummate actor, spontaneous wordsmith, and artist of the capricious deed.

Such were the "aestheticized" questions tackled by a new post-Stalinist generation of Pushkinists. What sort of historian *was* Pushkin? What was the relationship he envisaged between the "spirit" – or anarchic force, or destiny – of the people, and the proper, effective guidance of that spirit? Between structure and spontaneity? Specifically, how was this relationship reflected in the one character in *Boris Godunov* maximally free to move: Dmitry the Pretender? In what has become one of his most famous policy statements, from an unpublished draft for a review of Polevoi's *History of the Russian People,* Pushkin wrote: "Providence is not algebra. The human mind – as the folk expression goes – is not a prophet but a conjecturer; it sees the general course of things and can deduce from it profound suppositions, often justified by time, but it cannot foresee chance – that powerful, instantaneous tool of providence."[14] Part of Pushkin's remarkable accomplishment in his initial *Boris Godunov* was the creation of a character who represented free (and thus illicit) poetic energy, a buoyant disposition, a fiery imagination, fused with sociohistorical effectiveness documented in eyewitness accounts. Overwhelmingly, however, the "metaphorical poeticizations" of Dmitry have tended to downplay this politically effective side. Dmitry is presented as autonomous, a poet for himself alone, without larger care or cause. To enter poetry was to leave history behind. (As late as 1999, the inertia of this received portrait still made itself felt. In his *Pushkin. The Poet's Historical Thought,* V. D. Skvoznikov acknowledges that the great poet, after Karamzin the "most powerful, most substantial historian in Russia, who considered his investigations in this realm to be not the caprice of an artist but a professional occupation" [9], nevertheless embodies in his Dmitry no more than his beloved principle of Chance, an irresponsible figure incapable of historical agency [40].[15]) The present volume will suggest an alternative argument: that Pushkin intuited a level where real history and poetry were indeed compatible – in fact, where the free, open-ended, asymmetrical historical particular could best be understood as a particle of poetic energy.[16] One truth need not be sacrificed to the other. A proper reading of the play must examine every scene, the order of the scenes, even what is happening behind the scenes, relying for its persuasiveness not on a frozen moment or point, like *narod bezmolvztvuet,* but on a dynamic.

Two final interpretations of the play from the 1970s to the 1980s will serve as cautionary reminders, however, of the tenacity of end-driven readings. As Communism grew tired and its teleological zeal waned, it became less mandatory to turn Pushkin into an optimist as regards the historical mission of the Russian people – or as regards history in general. On occasion a cynical, even a nihilist, edge crept in. One reading of Pushkin's play in this newly somber spirit was provided by Valentin Nepomnyashchy in his 1983 book, *Poetry and Fate.*[17] Neoclassical aesthetics, so the critic argued, had made Man and human agency the center of the universe; Romanticism reversed the hierarchy, opposing Man to society and consigning him, in Byronic fashion, to futile protest or self-duplication. In Nepomnyashchy's view, as dramatic principles these two ideologies were equally unsatisfactory to Pushkin. Drama is dialogue – with others and with the environment – and it develops reciprocally; it is not merely unfolded or recited. At every moment in Pushkin's fast-paced, disjointed scenes, the limited, merely human perspective of the participants denies them the requisite historical and political vision to act with authority in their own time. "*Boris Godunov,*" Nepomnyashchy concludes, "is not a 'historical tragedy' in the usual sense of the term, but a tragedy about History" (245).

Thus did the Soviet intelligentsia make a decisive break with the messianic, populist tradition laid down by Belinsky. But the break with that old mandate did not prompt a return to comedic frameworks, for all the continuing faddish appeal of Bakhtin's carnival. The association with tragedy remained. It is not surprising that in February 2001, when Antony Wood, in Pskov for a performance of Declan Donnellan's new Russian production of *Boris Godunov,* raised the question of the 1825 original and Chester Dunning's advocacy of it, Nepomnyashchy (also in attendance) "rejected the preference outright, saying it would destroy Pushkin's idea of the play."[18] Pushkin's sense of history had been so aestheticized and "metahistoricized," and in such a tragedic direction, that the comedic element so prominently displayed in the 1825 original was no longer investigated as a source of historical wisdom.

Our final Soviet-era reading, already at the beginning of the end, is the scandalous production of *Boris Godunov* mounted by Yury Liubimov at the Taganka Theater in Moscow in 1984.[19] In keeping with Pushkin's well-known comments from 1830 about the origins of all drama in the public square, Liubimov devised a fast-paced "popular spectacle" (*narodnoe zrelishche*). Scenes were dominated by an omnipresent, all-purpose chorus that sometimes echoed, sometimes ironically commented upon, the actions and utterances of the heroes. The end was highly provocative. Mosalsky informs the onstage chorus of the royal family's "suicide by poisoning." Then the actor who had played Boris Godunov – already several scenes dead – enters in street clothes from the back of the theater and climbs without ceremony onto the stage, addressing the play's final words directly to the theater audience: "So why are you silent! Shout: Long live Dimitry Ivanovich!" The *narod bezmolvstvuet* had moved from a stage direction to a transcript of our own cowardice, our desire to slip away after the show was over, safely protected by footlights. Instead we discover that we can't even clap, because – as always in true carnival – we have become a full participant.

The fate of this production is now familiar history, one of the more colorful flickers before the Soviet light went out altogether a decade later. The production was banned, and Liubimov heard news of his dismissal from his post while in London as a guest director in 1984. He remained in the West. Invited back home in 1988, at the peak of perestroika, Liubimov resumed his interrupted Taganka production. But already the wheel had turned. Rehearsals were uneventful and the response of the public lukewarm. People were no longer silent, true; but they were preoccupied with other matters. In a strange contemporary echo of the play's reception history from 1825 to 1831, the illicit tension that had fueled the 1984 performance of *Boris Godunov* was losing its bite and grip.

Is this the natural end of the mass market for *Boris Godunov,* a play whose reception has been lubricated by external politics ever since its earliest public readings by Pushkin himself? As will be suggested in later chapters, an interpretation of the play as a purely politicized tragedy, framed by police officers barking simultaneously at the crowds on stage and the crowds in the theater, cannot be sustained when the work is experienced as it was originally conceived, as a *comedy.* The comedic is a mode of behavior and a philosophy of history as well as an aesthetics. Genres of comedy often make common cause with the nihilistic (for comedy can be black) – but unlike tragic genres, comedic forms avoid closure on that note and tend to be highly unsentimental about violence.

It is fully possible to be, as Pushkin was, comedic and Machiavellian at the same time. Comedy knows loss, ridicule, and collapse of hope. But its trademark is the recuperation of energy, not a one-way expenditure of energy in punitive acts. (Consider Petrushka the puppet-clown, constantly beaten, constantly beating others.) Comedy is spared that narrowing of poetry to political allusion that was the mainstay of such productions as Liubimov's *Boris* of 1984. When Pushkin wrote in the late 1820s that part of what kept him from publishing his tragedy were those passages that would be taken as "allegories, hints, allusions" and that this was distasteful to him, one hears the frustrations of an unfree author, trying to establish his credentials as an historian, shake off the Decembrist shadow, and pay the tribute expected of him to Tsar Nicholas, a monarch of whom Pushkin had suspicions and with whom he had reverent relations in almost equal part, up to the hour of his death.[20] But he also sensed that allusions and allegories are usually tragic and incompatible with a comedic view of history.

∿

We close this Introduction as we began it, in the shadow of the opera. The overwhelming success of Musorgsky's opera, similar to the stage revivals previously discussed, has brought mixed benefits to Pushkin's play. It certainly familiarized the world with an otherwise little-known work by a great poet. The libretto contains a wealth of lines almost unchanged from the original. But the familiarity has been selective. With its immense musical and dramatic authority, in all its redactions and orchestrations (Rimsky-Korsakov's, Shostakovich's, Musorgsky's own), the opera highlights precisely those scenes and personalities that can be dehistoricized and sentimentalized. In the opera-goer's mind, two categories of scene are remembered: the Romantic and "high-literary" (the Tsar's melodramatic hallucination, the heightened death scene, the glitter and rhythm of the Polish dance-and-courtship episodes), and the declamatory comic scenes (most perfectly in the Tavern at the Lithuanian Border but also in the *narod* scenes that open and close the 1874 version of the opera). What we know about Boris is most memorably what he knows and sings about *himself*, which is, after all, what an opera aria is. But in fact, as Pushkin's play slyly demonstrates, there is more to be learned about Boris – and, for that matter, about the Pretender – from what others say about them, and from the flexibility they display in responding to others' utterances and events. Grand opera, even of Musorgsky's radical sort, is not designed for such multifaceted character portrayal or flexible response. Scenes and dialogic exchanges that Musorgsky did not choose to set, which are crucial in their specific historical content (between Shuisky and Afanasy Pushkin, Boris and Basmanov, Basmanov and Gavrila Pushkin), have tended over the years to fall out of cultural memory.

Musorgsky, like Tchaikovsky after him, has been roundly censured for the liberties he took with Pushkin en route to creating his operatic masterpiece. We suggest that in the case of *Boris Godunov*, a thorough knowledge of the opera can support the argument for a return to the original 1825 text. In constructing his libretto, Musorgsky, who had dramatic intuitions of a very high order, was obliged to leave out a great deal of the 1831 story – it takes a lot of time to sing a line. But in his revisions, he returned to one scene from 1825, "Maryna's Dressing Room," sensing its importance and setting it as part of the new Polish cluster. What is more, he ended his revised *Boris* on a wholly new scene, "Near Kromy," not present at all in Pushkin nor in the first version of the opera. Scholarly consensus holds that Kromy was inspired by crowd scenes in the work of Musorgsky's friends, his house-mate Rimsky-Korsakov and the populist historian Nikolai Kostomarov. We suggest that the scene was inspired as well by Pushkin's 1825 ending.[21] "Near Kromy" is one mass, rhythmically diverse cheer by a panorama of social groups welcoming Dmitry Ivanovich, who eventually makes his stage entrance mounted on horseback to the wild and unanimous applause of all classes. Whether this final scene is historically progressive or deluded to the point of desperation (and much depends on how the scene is played), one fact is indisputable: this is not *narod bezmolvstvuet*. This is Russia's first civil war, whose sociopolitical components Pushkin also glimpsed with epic equanimity in 1825.

The purpose of the present study is to add this 1825 text, in the shape that its creator set it before its first public, to the canon of Pushkin's work. We do not seek to displace the later, more familiar version, but rather to make possible an informed choice between them. As with everything involving Russia's national poet, whose works have been internalized by carriers of Russian culture to a degree unfathomable to outsiders, an adjustment to the canon is not a trivial matter. When, in 1935, Grigory Vinokur provided his lengthy narrative commentary on *Boris Godunov*, his scholarly practice had been closely watched. Volume VII, "Dramatic Works," was the trial (*probnyi*) text in the series. As it turned out, Stalin was not pleased with the result. Caustic reviews appeared obediently throughout 1936, condemning that "caste of Pushkinists" who, driven by "mercantile-professorial" interests, provided inflated commentary several times longer than Pushkin's text.[22] Soon after the scandal with Volume VII, the editorial commission of the Jubilee Edition adopted an entirely different methodology: there would be fastidious textological work on all variants, literary chronology in outline form, but no interpretation. Narrative commentary was tacitly taken to be a dangerous enterprise, bound to reflect a scholar's subjective opinions.

The present volume will not avoid these sinister charges entirely. But we have learned some lessons from that venerable precedent. Among them are the pliability of Pushkin's writing, its resistance to definitive political explication, the power of posthumous editions to shape reception, and the tenacity of the canonical text. Our offer of two candidates for that slot in the case of *Boris Godunov* is made in hopes of redeeming, to some degree, Pushkin's initial confidence in his very great play.

Notes

1. For a properly complex reading of authorial intent under such circumstances, see G. G. Krasukhin, "Vzyskatel'naia liubov' [on *Mednyi vsadnik*]," in his *Pushkin – Boldino, 1833: Novoe prochtenie*: 8–53, esp. 18–27. "The Bronze Horseman" too fell afoul of imperial censorship and was tinkered with for three years before being abandoned; its "canonical version" remains a partial correction undertaken in response to the Emperor's objections.

2. The 1870 premiere of Pushkin's play was praised for the historical accuracy of its sets and costumes, but for little else. As Pyotr Gnedich wrote in his memoirs some thirty-five years after the event: "Pushkin's Godunov *failed* triumphantly and brutally, despite the sumptuous production ... the roles were not securely prepared, the performance was so-so ... The comedy with couplets *The Claws of St. Petersburg* by Messrs. Khudyakov and Zhulev had an incomparably greater success than [Pushkin's] *Boris Godunov*." See "A Tale of Two Productions – St. Petersburg (1874–1882), Paris (1908)," in Emerson and Oldani, *Modest Musorgsky and Boris Godunov: Myths, Realities, Reconsiderations*, 92–93.

3. For a brief survey of these two sides as they stood during the late Soviet period (represented by the eminent Pushkinists Alekseev and Vinokur), see Emerson, *Boris Godunov: Transpositions of a Russian Theme*, 134–35, and notes 118–20, pp. 242–43.

4. G. O. Vinokur, "'Boris Godunov' Pushkina" (originally published in *Literaturnyi sovremennik*, 1935, no. 6, pp. 200–16), repr. in Vinokur, *Stat'i o Pushkine*: 83–119, esp. 94.

5. Belinsky's "Tenth Essay" was published in *Otechestvennye zapiski*, kn. 11 (1845).

Quotations from "Stat'ia desiatia: Boris Godunov," in Belinskii, *Sochineniia Aleksandra Pushkina:* 379–412, esp. 379, 380, 412.

6. Implicitly or explicitly, the Pretender Dmitry (often associated with his brig-and-"brother" Pugachev from later in Pushkin's career as an historian, and even with the "changeling" Onegin) is the subtext for the best writing about "*samozvantsvo*" – self-naming – in the Russian Romantic period, and a common device for linking the very different geniuses of Pushkin and Gogol. See as exemplary Iurii M. Lotman, "Concerning Khlestakov" (1975), in A. D. and A. S. Nakhimovsky, eds., *The Semiotics of Russian Cultural History,* 150–87; and V. N. Turbin, "Kharaktery samozvantsev v tvorchestve Pushkina," 63–88. Further page references to Turbin in text.

7. Andrei Filonov, *Boris Godunov A. S. Pushkina. Opyt razbora so storony istoricheskoi i esteticheskoi.* Further page references in text.

8. I. Z. Serman, "Paradoxes of the Popular Mind in Pushkin's *Boris Godunov,*" 25–39. Further page references in text.

9. B. Engel'gardt, "Istorizm Pushkina," in Vengerov, ed., *Pushkinist: Istoriko-literaturnyi sbornik,* 2: 67.

10. M. M. Bakhtin, *Tvorchestvo Fransua Rable i narodnaia kul'tura srednevekov'ia i Renessansa,* 524–25; there is an English translation in Mikhail Bakhtin, *Rabelais and His World,* 474.

11. The "carnival debate" as it relates to medieval Russian culture involved major scholars on both sides of the divide: Likhachev and Panchenko (inspired by Bakhtin) against Lotman and Uspenskii. Of more general relevance to this study is the whole appetite among literary scholars for semiotic "history lite," which allows them to attend to complexities on the aesthetic side, fully within their competence, by relegating historical complexity (far less familiar) to these stunning binary distinctions. On the temptations and dangers of such readings from the perspective of a professional historian, see David A. Frick, "Misrepresentations, Misunderstandings, and Silences: Problems of Seventeenth-Century Ruthenian and Muscovite Cultural History," 149–68, esp. 151–54.

12. K. N. Derzhavin, ed., *"Boris Godunov" A. S. Pushkina* (1936). The anthology, intended partly as scholarly contribution and partly as practical aid to performances of the play, contains essays by B. P. Gorodetskii, A. L. Slonimskii, M. P. Alekseev, G. O. Vinokur, and A. N. Glumov. Further page references in text.

13. I. Z. Serman, "Pushkin i russkaia istoricheskaia drama 1830-kh godov," 118–49, esp. 120–25.

14. "O vtorom tome 'Istorii russkogo naroda' Polovogo," in Aleksandr Pushkin, *Polnoe sobranie sochinenii* (1937–59) [hereafter cited as PS]:11, 127. The draft is dated October–November 1830 (that is, around the time that Pushkin was working on, and rejecting, his prefaces for *Boris Godunov*). Inexplicably, this famous passage is omitted from the extract of the draft Polevoi review included in Wolff, *Pushkin on Literature,* 240–41.

15. See, for example, V. D. Skvoznikov, *Pushkin. Istoricheskaia mysl' poeta.* Further page references in text.

16. A related argument has been made by David M. Bethea in his work on Push-

kin's unfinished *History of Pugachev*, and in his *Realizing Metaphors: Alexander Pushkin and the Life of the Poet.*

17. V. Nepomniashchii, *Poeziia i sud'ba. Stat'i i zametki o Pushkine*, ch. 4 [on *Boris Godunov*], "Naimenee poniatyi zhanr," 212–50. Further page references in text. The essay was originally written in 1974, then revised in 1981.

18. Communication from Antony Wood from London to Caryl Emerson, 5 March 2001; see also Wood's brief report, "Pushkin in Pskov" (April 2001). Wood, who saw both the Liubimov and Donnellan productions, reported this in March 2001: "Donnellan at least brought the play thoroughly to life (for the first time ever, said the Russians!). Some things he did were unimaginably brilliant – the garden scene with Marina and Dimitry as a real love scene ... and Marina drawing back at the last possible moments; and each new scene chipping in just before the previous one ended, to keep up tempo and tension; putting everyone onstage in frozen stance for the last scene. But he cut drastically, paring down the conscience theme and focusing on the replacement of one power faction by the next.... As after seeing Lyubimov's production, I still felt no nearer an answer as to what Pushkin's drama could be like." Communication from Antony Wood to Caryl Emerson, 5 March 2001.

19. For two different but vibrant accounts of this production, see Paul Debreczeny, "*Boris Godunov* at the Taganka: A Note on a Non-Performance," 99–101; and Nicholas Rzhevsky, "Adapting Drama to the Stage: Liubimov's *Boris Godunov*," 171–76.

20. Among the many virtues of T. J. Binyon's massive biography of Pushkin, which examines the cult of "poet versus Tsar" from the bottom up, is its sober recounting of all these moments where Nicholas I (while never relinquishing his right to "gratitude" – that is, groveling – from the poet whom he had pardoned) stood up for Pushkin and tried to moderate the worst moves of his enemies. On the tsar's dislike of Bulgarin, disapproval of Benckendorff, and hostility toward Heeckeren and d'Anthès, see Binyon, *Pushkin*, 316–21 and 639.

21. In fact, much of the debate about Musorgsky's operatic intentions and his interpretation of the *narod* is a direct outgrowth of scholarly puzzlement about Pushkin's interpretation of the *narod* in his historical drama. See Emerson, *Boris Godunov*, 173, 180–81, 198–201; Emerson and Oldani, *Modest Musorgsky*, 210, 219–24, 281–83; and Bowersock, "Roman Emperor," 145.

22. For an overview of this reception history from a post-communist perspective, see S. O. Shmidt, "G. O. Vinokur i akademicheskoe izdanie pushkinskogo 'Borisa Godunova,'" 6–35, esp. 27–30.

1

The Problem of *Boris Godunov*

A Review of Interpretations and the So-Called Canonical Text

∿ CHESTER DUNNING

Alexander Sergeevich Pushkin (1799–1837) wrote *Boris Godunov* in 1824–25, while living in exile on his father's estate under constant surveillance by tsarist authorities. With plenty of time on his hands, the angry young poet – by then widely acclaimed as one of Russia's greatest writers – created an extremely ambitious and provocative historical drama set in early modern Russia's darkest hour, the Time of Troubles (1598–1613). Inspired by reading volumes ten and eleven of Nikolai Karamzin's semi-official *History of the Russian State,* Pushkin conducted serious historical research for the first time in his life, and the play he wrote was a remarkable achievement in many ways. The original version of *Boris Godunov,* titled *Komediia o tsare Borise i o Grishke Otrep'eve* (*Comedy about Tsar Boris and Grishka Otrepiev*), was definitely not intended to win Pushkin's release from exile or to curry favor at the court of Tsar Alexander I (r. 1801–25). Nor was Pushkin's *Comedy* intended to echo Historian Laureate Karamzin's safe, conservative interpretation of the Time of Troubles.[1] "Instead, the play was a boldly defiant and subversive work written by an unrepentant young genius who refused to humble himself and was well aware that he was tempting fate with his bold pen."[2] Pushkin was very pleased with his play. Immediately upon completing it, he wrote to his friend, Pyotr Viazemsky: "My tragedy is finished; I reread it aloud, alone, and I clapped my hands and shouted, 'at a boy, Pushkin, 'at a boy, you son of a bitch!'"[3] Pushkin's enthusiasm for his historical drama stayed with him for the rest of his life. Of all the superb poetry and prose that he wrote, *Boris Godunov* was always his favorite. Indeed, he considered it to be his magnum opus.[4]

Pushkin finished his *Comedy about Tsar Boris and Grishka Otrepiev* in November 1825, just before Tsar Alexander I's sudden death triggered the ill-fated Decembrist Rebellion. When the poet, newly returned from exile in 1826, read his *Comedy* to his friends (including many of Russia's leading writers and intellectuals), they were stunned by the beauty and naturalness of the play's language, its revolutionary form, and its daring political content. Suffice it to say, Pushkin's *Comedy* was an instant and spectacular success.[5] Unfortunately, nervous censors working for the new tsar, Nicholas I (r. 1825–55), refused to allow publication of the highly provocative play in its original form. For the next several years, Pushkin tried repeatedly to publish his *Comedy* without alteration, only to be told by tsarist officials that changes were required. When an altered, "politically correct" version of the much-anticipated play (one that did not stray from Karamzin's interpretation of history) was finally published in 1831, it was received coolly by many critics; and *Boris Godunov* has confused and disappointed readers ever since.[6]

A quick review of the huge bibliography of *Pushkiniana* reveals that *Boris Godunov* has been the single most studied of the great poet's many works (edging out even *Evgenii Onegin*). The play has correctly been called Pushkin's "most ambitiously planned" and "most carefully executed work," and it is generally regarded as "one of the masterpieces of Russian drama." Nevertheless, the play that was published in 1831 puzzled many of Pushkin's contemporaries and is still considered to be "problematic" if not downright "incomprehensible" by leading scholars and critics.[7] *Boris Godunov* has seldom been performed and is usually regarded as a dramatic flop owing to its "failure to convey an important idea" and its somewhat awkward structure.[8] Especially difficult to assess is the published play's final line: the famous "silence" of the *narod* (the common people) in response to the announcement that young Tsar Feodor Borisovich and his mother have committed suicide – a convenient lie intended to facilitate the Pretender Dmitry's seizure of the throne. That ending has been much debated. It is not even clear if the final line of the play ("Narod bezmolvstvuet.") is meant to be read or is merely a stage direction.[9] There are many disagreements and radically different ideas about the play's final scene, yet there is no resolution of several basic questions.[10] For example, what did the *narod*'s silence mean?[11] What did Pushkin intend to convey? How can the play be staged, or did

Pushkin even intend for it to be staged?[12] Another difficult question to answer is how the final scene of *Boris Godunov* relates to the opening of the play – in which the cynical *narod* is forced to cheer at the accession of Tsar Boris Godunov (himself guilty of murdering the real Tsarevich Dmitry – the youngest son of Ivan the Terrible – several years earlier)? Was Pushkin trying to imitate Shakespeare? Is *Boris Godunov* a naive attempt at a Shakespearean tragic drama with a poor ending?[13] Or was Pushkin trying to move beyond Shakespearean tragic drama?[14] Could *Boris Godunov* be a deliberate parody of Shakespeare's plays?[15] There are a host of other important but unanswered questions about the play. For example, who is the dramatic hero, or is there a hero?[16]

One of the main goals of the present volume – especially in light of continuing scholarly debate and bewilderment about *Boris Godunov* – is to try to explain why Pushkin himself was so strongly attached to his troublesome play. A closely related question is why – in sharp contrast to most reviews of the published version of *Boris Godunov* – Pushkin's *Comedy* was so well received in 1826. Did Pushkin and his friends discern something in his *Comedy* that others later missed in *Boris Godunov*? In order to answer these questions satisfactorily it will first be necessary to review current scholarship about the play and about what constitutes its canonical text.

The problem of evaluating *Boris Godunov* is greatly complicated by the fact that Pushkin's *Comedy* contains three scenes and a number of other lines of dialogue that were omitted from the version published in 1831. Most strikingly, the original play also ends differently – not with silence but with the *narod* shouting "Long live Tsar Dimitry Ivanovich!"[17] This fact is well known to specialists but is often ignored in evaluations of the play. Most scholars and critics have assumed – without careful examination of the issue – that Pushkin changed his original play for purely aesthetic reasons and that the published text is the one he intended to write. Unfortunately, that longstanding hypothesis has prevented Pushkin scholars from moving very far beyond the initial puzzlement and disappointment that greeted *Boris Godunov* in the 1830s. In fact, often without realizing it, many modern interpretations of the play merely echo Vissarion Belinsky's influential assessment (written in 1845) of *Boris Godunov* as a magnificent failure, as the great poet's "Waterloo."[18] During the second half of the nineteenth century, however, some scholars took an interest in Pushkin's long battle to publish the original version of his historical drama and concluded that Nicholas I's censors had forced Pushkin to make changes that harmed the play. They argued, in effect, that the 1831 version was not what Pushkin intended and that his 1825 *Comedy* was the real *Boris Godunov*.[19]

Reconstructing Pushkin's original *Comedy* in order to compare it to *Boris Godunov* was extremely difficult, if not impossible, while Nicholas I still ruled. Only one of the provocative scenes that had been omitted from the play ("Ograda monastyrskaia" or "Monastery Wall") was published during Pushkin's lifetime, and it stirred considerable interest.[20] After Pushkin's death, his close friend Vasily Zhukovsky published the first edition of the collected works of the great poet, *Sochineniia Aleksandra Pushkina* (1838–41). Laboring under the watchful eyes of tsarist censors, however, Zhukovsky did not restore any of the missing scenes to *Boris Godunov* or even mention them. In fact, he had to work hard to overcome the genuine desire of some officials (and Tsar Nicholas) to have all of Pushkin's previously published writings subjected to additional censorship to remove material the censors might have missed the first time around.[21] Zhukovsky's faithful reprint of the 1831 version of Pushkin's play appeared in 1838 in volume one of *Sochineniia Aleksandra Pushkina*.[22] Possibly in reaction to the republication of the "politically correct" version of *Boris Godunov*, and certainly as a tribute to the dead poet, the editors of *Sovremennik* (a journal founded by Pushkin) published the omitted scene "Zamok voevody Mnishka v Sanbore. Ubornaia Mariny" ("Maryna's Dressing Room") in 1838.[23] In 1841, after switching to a private press, Zhukovsky quietly published two of the scenes omitted from *Boris Godunov* ("Maryna's Dressing Room" and "Devich'e pole. Novodevichii monastyr" or "Maidens' Field") in volume nine of *Sochineniia Aleksandra Pushkina* (1838–41).[24] Finally, in 1854, the last year of Tsar Nicholas I's life, the editors of the journal *Moskvitianin* published the "Monastery Wall" scene.[25] Although it is often forgotten by modern scholars, the early publication record of Pushkin's play makes it clear that most critics of *Boris Godunov* – including Belinsky – were either completely unaware of the existence of Pushkin's *Comedy* or were hampered by lack of access to (or even knowledge of) some of the scenes and other lines omitted from the published play.

During the first year of the reign of Alexander II (r. 1855–81), who loosened official censorship considerably, Pavel Annenkov was permitted to publish an edition of *Boris Godunov* with two scenes ("Maidens' Field" and "Maryna's Dressing Room") restored to the text. In an appendix, Annenkov also provided his readers with the controversial original

"Monastery Wall" scene and some of the other lines of text that had been trimmed from the 1831 edition.[26] To justify his "restored" version of *Boris Godunov*, Annenkov called attention to the existence of a manuscript of Pushkin's *Comedy* in the poet's own handwriting and – significantly – the lack of any manuscript ending with the *narod's* silence. Annenkov was the first to openly suggest that in preparing his play for publication Pushkin acted under pressure or merely passively capitulated to the demands of tsarist censors. Annenkov briefly chronicled Pushkin's frustrated attempts to publish his *Comedy*, and he listed the differences between it and *Boris Godunov*. Annenkov's edition did much to rehabilitate Pushkin's reputation, and it enjoyed great success.[27] Soon, other editors also began restoring the missing scenes to *Boris Godunov*. In 1859, for example, Grigory N. Gennadi published an edition of the play that, like Annenkov's, restored the "Maidens' Field" and "Maryna's Dressing Room" scenes to the text and included the "Monastery Wall" scene and many other omitted lines in an appendix.[28] As we have seen, in 1872, Modest Musorgsky made use of the new "restored" text of Pushkin's *Boris Godunov* in composing the second version of his opera, *Boris Godunov*, incorporating material from the "Maidens' Field" scene and including a scene inspired by "Maryna's Dressing Room."

Pushkin's reputation as Russia's national poet underwent a dramatic change in the second half of the nineteenth century, thanks in part to the efforts of Annenkov and others to demonstrate that he had been a serious writer whose poetry and prose had "social content." Previously dismissed by Belinsky and many other critics as a brilliant but frivolous aristocrat, Pushkin came to be viewed as a fighter for freedom and greater rights for the Russian people and even as the "father of Russian liberalism."[29] The highly successful Pushkin Celebration of 1880 did much to help restore the poet's reputation and to stir interest in his writings. During these festivities, Fyodor Dostoevsky gave the famous Pushkin speech in support of the poet's kinship with the *narod* and read a passage from *Boris Godunov*. (In his youth, Dostoevsky planned to write a play called *Boris Godunov*, of which no trace can be found.)[30] Popular sympathy for Pushkin grew rapidly in response to the publication in the 1880s of documents revealing for the first time just how agonizing his struggle with imperial censors had been and just how much of his work had been withheld from publication during Pushkin's own lifetime.[31] Several popular new editions of Pushkin's collected works were published in the late nineteenth century, and some of them restored all three omitted scenes to *Boris Godunov* and included the *Comedy*'s alternate ending in a footnote.[32]

One of the most successful new versions of Pushkin's collected works was published by Pyotr Morozov; it went through many editions by 1916. Morozov pointed out to his readers that Pushkin's *Comedy* had been enthusiastically received in 1826, and he detailed the poet's unsuccessful struggle to publish his original play. At first, Morozov was content merely to restore the omitted scenes to the play; he still called it *Boris Godunov* and let it end with the *narod*'s silence.[33] In later editions, however, Morozov boldly listed the play in his table of contents as *Komediia o tsare Borise i o Grishke Otrep'eve* and even restored the *narod*'s final shout: "Long live Tsar Dimitry Ivanovich!" Although Morozov followed the then-customary practice of placing the controversial "Monastery Wall" scene in an appendix immediately following the final scene, he painstakingly restored to the text of the play a number of other lines that had been omitted from the 1831 edition.[34] Thus, about seventy-five years after Pushkin wrote his *Comedy*, it finally came into print more or less in the form in which he originally intended to publish it.

As the tsarist regime became increasingly reactionary toward the end of the nineteenth century, the emergence of Alexander Pushkin as a popular symbol of liberalism and as a champion of the rights of the Russian people began to alarm persons close to Tsar Nicholas II (r. 1894–1917). Some politically conservative scholars decided to launch an all-out campaign to rescue "their Pushkin" from the radicals and to turn him into Russia's conservative national poet. The result was an aggressively promoted, officially sanctioned portrayal of Pushkin as a "favorite son" of Nicholas I and a staunch supporter of autocracy. The one hundredth anniversary of the poet's birth was declared "Pushkin Year" by Nicholas II; and, in planning the carefully scripted Pushkin Jubilee of 1899, many bureaucrats and professors went to extraordinary lengths to shape the image of Pushkin and his writings to suit the imperial government's purposes. To accomplish that task, however, they were forced to downplay (or even deny) Pushkin's struggle with the censors and to temporarily exile V. Ya. Yakushin, a leading scholar who had drawn attention to Pushkin's close ties with the Decembrists. With the approval of the tsar, conservatives "politically sterilized Pushkin" and "mercilessly smoothed out and simplified" his biography.[35]

Not surprisingly, the new official Romanov interpretation of Pushkin required rejection of the playwright's 1825 *Comedy* in favor of the less provocative *Boris Godunov* published in 1831. It soon became an article of faith among conservative scholars that, in composing his play, Pushkin had scrupulously followed the conservative interpretation of the Time of Troubles put forward by Nikolai Karamzin in his *History of the Russian State*. Therefore, it was asserted that Pushkin himself must have trimmed from the first version of his play those embarrassing lines that highlighted the *narod*'s support for the Pretender Dmitry – who was thoroughly despised by both Karamzin and Nicholas I. It was even boldly asserted that the silence of the *narod* at the end of *Boris Godunov* came directly from Karamzin and represented the development of Pushkin's more mature (that is, conservative) views.[36] Conspicuously absent from such "politically correct" interpretations was any discussion of censorship or Pushkin's struggle to publish his *Comedy*. As noted in the Introduction, the conservative scholar Andrei Filonov, in a highly influential study of *Boris Godunov* published in 1899, dwelled on Pushkin's dependence on Karamzin's *History* and completely ignored Pushkin's *Comedy*, his struggle with the censors, and all the scenes and other lines omitted from the 1831 edition of the play. Unfortunately, thanks to the work of Filonov (and a few others), the simplistic idea that Pushkin always intended to closely adhere to Karamzin's *History* became something of a fixed idea in Pushkin studies, and it has only rarely been challenged.[37]

Efforts to turn Pushkin into a staunch supporter of the Romanovs met with only marginal success during the twilight of imperial Russia. Most honest prerevolutionary scholars and members of the literary intelligentsia firmly rejected the crude falsification of Pushkin that had been manufactured by the government.[38] Nevertheless, in the Empire's last years, Morozov and other publishers were subjected to intense criticism from reactionary scholars and government officials for daring to print such works as Pushkin's subversive *Comedy*. On the eve of the Revolution of 1917, Morozov found himself very much on the defensive – subjected to increasingly fierce attacks by conservatives for obscuring the meaning of Pushkin's writings, for committing errors of transcription and interpretation, and especially for being unable to prove that Pushkin had been forced by the censors to alter the ending of his play.[39]

After the Russian Revolution and Civil War, debate about *Boris Godunov* resumed and was significantly affected by Marxist views of the Time of Troubles. During the 1920s, Tsar Dmitry was championed by Soviet historians as a "people's tsar" and as the leader of a "peasant revolution" against serfdom.[40] At another time, political imperatives might have

made it possible for scholars and literary critics to explore Pushkin's daring portrayal of popular support for the Pretender Dmitry in his *Comedy,* but Pushkin's reputation as a reactionary aristocrat got in the way. In
fact, Pushkin was utterly detested by many early Soviet writers. Government censors demanded changes in his writings, and Lenin's widow
(Nadezhda Krupskaya) even participated in a campaign to purge the
great poet's works from library shelves in the Soviet Union.[41] Eventually,
Pushkin was selectively reconstituted, but it was easier simply to demo-
nize Dmitry and dispense with the poet. By the time Pushkin was
rehabilitated during the early Stalin era, the official Soviet view of Tsar
Dmitry had shifted back to the standard prerevolutionary, completely
negative interpretation. During the 1930s, historians were expected to
denounce Dmitry as a tool of Polish intervention in Russia. Failure to
follow the party line could lead to disgrace and exile. (That was, for
example, the fate of Russia's leading historian of the Time of Troubles,
Sergei Platonov.)[42] Stalin-era scholars and literary critics who studied
Pushkin's historical drama also quickly came to reflect party views.
Unfortunately, there has been very little discussion of this important
issue by scholars writing about *Boris Godunov.*

In the era of Socialist Realism, further shifts in official ideology and
the creation of a pre-Soviet pantheon of greats brought about "Pushkin's
full-scale rehabilitation and incorporation into the Soviet cultural
canon." Through noisy and elaborately staged Jubilees, Tolstoy (in 1928)
became *the* nineteenth-century prose writer, and Pushkin (in 1937)
became poet laureate. Stalin-era scholars actually "revived the tsarist tradition of venerating Pushkin" as Russia's national poet, but – unlike the
Romanovs – they described him as a "progressive" instead of a conservative supporter of autocracy. Pushkin was even hailed as a forerunner of
the Bolsheviks and as a model for "the new Soviet man."[43] In order to
transform him into the "people's poet" and the poet laureate of the
Soviet Union, however, Soviet scholars first had to rescue him from
"tsarist-era falsification." Taking their cue from an article published in
1910 by Nikolai Pavlov-Silvansky (who had been strongly affected by
the 1905 Revolution), they seized upon the notion that in *Boris Godunov*
Pushkin had intended to show the decisive role of the *narod* in Russian
history, especially in fighting against autocracy.[44] It soon became an
article of faith that Pushkin had intended to portray the *narod* in *Boris
Godunov* as "heroic."[45] The stridently negative image of Tsar Dmitry in
Stalinist historiography, however, presented a serious problem because

1. Pushkin's drawing of Grishka Otrepiev. Detail from the margin of a manuscript page of the scene "Noch'. Kel'ia v Chudovom monastyre" in the rough draft of *Komediia o tsare Borise i o Grishke Otrep'eve*. From Institut russkoi literatury (Pushkinskii Dom) RAN, Rukopisnyi otdel, fond 244, opis' 1, No. 835, list 50. Courtesy of the Russian Academy of Sciences.

Pushkin's *narod* championed the cause of Dmitry – especially in his original *Comedy*. Realizing that the 1831 version of *Boris Godunov* was now more in keeping with the party line, some quick-witted Soviet scholars came up with a satisfactory solution. They simply repeated the claim of the official apologists of the Romanov regime that Pushkin had revised his *Comedy* on his own and not under pressure, but now they insisted that Pushkin's intention had always been to show the *narod* heroically resisting autocracy. Eerily echoing conservative prerevolutionary views, Stalin-era critics began to express great satisfaction with Pushkin's "critical" portrayal of the Pretender Dmitry in *Boris Godunov* (including the final silence of the *narod*), and they adamantly denied that the tsar's censors had much impact on the play. After all, it was argued, there was no "smoking gun" document showing that Pushkin had been forced to make the changes found in the 1831 edition.[46]

According to the official Stalinist interpretation of *Boris Godunov*, at some point Pushkin – on his own – decided to change his play in order to underline the *narod*'s moral outrage against the evil Pretender Dmitry. That well known hypothesis has been analyzed and questioned by many writers since the 1930s, and there are still many different interpretations of Pushkin's portrayal of the *narod*;[47] but, curiously, ever since the Stalin era there has been general acceptance by scholars worldwide that the 1831 version of *Boris Godunov* was the one Pushkin intended to publish. Even so, the awkwardness of the 1831 version of the play – noted by early critics – and the strong desire to demonstrate the progressiveness of Pushkin's ideas prompted Soviet scholars to restore definitively the third scene ("Maidens' Field") to *Boris Godunov*. The reintegration of that scene simultaneously showcased the *narod*'s cynicism about autocracy and made the play more comprehensible and aesthetically satisfactory. At least in this one instance, Soviet scholars openly acknowledged that Pushkin's play had suffered at the hands of tsarist censors.[48] On the other hand, all other changes found in the 1831 edition of *Boris Godunov* were deemed intentional by the poet and not the result of external pressure. Thus modified, the hybridized version of the 1831 edition quickly became the play generally studied and commented upon; it is still our so-called canonical text.[49]

Many scholars were involved in the development of the Stalin-era interpretation of Pushkin's writings, but Grigory Vinokur did more than anyone else to lock the Stalinist viewpoint into literary criticism and scholarship about *Boris Godunov* and to champion the hybridized version of the play as the canonical text. As noted in the Introduction, Vinokur's extensive commentary on *Boris Godunov*, planned for inclusion in a new Soviet edition of the collected works of Pushkin, was initially denounced by the Stalinist establishment as excessive, "scholastic," and "pseudoscientific." As a result, it was quickly relegated to the sidelines, and further volumes appeared without narrative commentary. Nevertheless, Vinokur's work has been extremely influential ever since it first appeared in 1935.[50] In spite of his early difficulties, Vinokur continued to be one of the main participants in the preparation of the new edition of the collected works of Pushkin sponsored by the Academy of Sciences and published between 1937 and 1959 (the Jubilee Edition). Vinokur played a leading role in the preparation of the canonical text of *Boris Godunov* included in the Jubilee edition.[51]

Vinokur's influential interpretation of Pushkin's play is worth a closer look. Not surprisingly, he started out by asserting that Karamzin's *History* was almost the only source used by Pushkin in writing *Boris Godunov*. Nevertheless, like other Soviet scholars, Vinokur claimed that at some point Pushkin moved beyond Karamzin's monarchist sympathies to a more progressive focus on the *narod*'s powerful role in Russian history – especially its decisive rejection of the usurper Tsar Boris.[52] Also like other Soviet scholars, Vinokur downplayed the impact of censorship on Pushkin. In fact, according to him, Pushkin actually triumphed over the censors because he did not make all the changes that had been demanded in the initial censor's report prepared for Nicholas I in 1826. Vinokur firmly believed that Pushkin himself was responsible for the silent ending of the 1831 edition of *Boris Godunov* and boldly declared that the content of the play was, in any case, not changed in the least by the altered ending "because that content is determined by the entire text of the tragedy and not by this one line alone."[53] He failed to mention, however, that some of the other lines and at least one scene that had been omitted from the 1831 edition gave the original cheer at the end of the *Comedy* a completely different meaning.

Vinokur's most important contribution to Stalin-era scholarship about *Boris Godunov* was his unsubstantiated assertion that Pushkin had reluctantly agreed to omit the "Maidens' Field" scene from his play in order to avoid having it appear in a bowdlerized form with some controversial lines deleted.[54] This clever argument made it possible for Vinokur to win almost instant Communist Party approval for the inclusion of the "Maidens' Field" scene in the new canonical text of the play. Stalinists were very pleased by the addition of that scene because it showed the *narod*'s rebellious spirit and cynicism about autocracy. Since publication of the "authoritative" Jubilee edition of Pushkin's works, only a handful of scholars have ever criticized the new canonical text of *Boris Godunov* for such arbitrarily established procedures. However, none of them called for a new look at Pushkin's original *Comedy*. Instead, they argued in favor of returning to the 1831 version of the play without the "Maidens' Field" scene.[55]

Many long-held ideas about Dmitry and the *narod* proved to be difficult, if not impossible, to overcome. For example, some scholars argued that Pushkin's Dmitry was basically "insignificant" in the play.[56] Others were convinced that Pushkin must have shared their own hostility toward the Pretender. Meanwhile, several sophisticated scholars managed to distance themselves from earlier, entirely negative views of Dmitry by focusing on Pushkin's own fascination with him. They concluded that the Pretender was meant to be portrayed as a Romantic character, perhaps as a poet-adventurer.[57] Nevertheless, all those researchers with differing ideas agreed on one point – that Pushkin definitely intended to show Dmitry as unworthy of the *narod*'s support. For Soviet scholars, the Russian people's embarrassing attachment to the Pretender was something that had to be explained away. Partly as a result, Pushkin's *narod* has usually been represented as gullible, fickle, or revolutionary. Depending on which characterization one chose, it was then claimed either that Dmitry eventually disappointed the Russian people who had supported him in order to topple the usurper Boris Godunov, or that the Pretender somehow failed to satisfy the revolutionary masses that brought him to power.[58] Either way the *narod* always ended up rejecting Dmitry. But is that what Pushkin really meant to say?

The problem of trying to determine Pushkin's real intentions concerning Dmitry and his relationship to the *narod* is greatly complicated by the play's final scene. As we saw in the Introduction, the canonical silence at the end of *Boris Godunov* has been interpreted as condemnation of the evil Pretender ever since the appearance of Belinsky's influential "Tenth Essay" on Pushkin.[59] Curiously, however, the *narod*'s cheer at the end of the original *Comedy* has also been described as condemnation, confusion, or disgruntled resignation, often by scholars who claimed not to see any significant difference between the two endings.[60] In fact, the general hostility to Dmitry among scholars studying Pushkin's play has been so great that the *narod*'s cheer has almost never been interpreted in the most obvious way – as a show of genuinely enthusiastic support for the new tsar. Not surprisingly, Pushkin's fairly positive characterization of Dmitry in the *Comedy* has drawn criticism from several writers.[61] Perhaps inadvertently, their complaints helped to generate the remarkably strange but not uncommon view that the original ending of the play was greatly improved by the censors who were instrumental in changing the *narod's* shout to a more respectable silence.[62] When some scholars see no difference between dramatically different endings and others actually welcome the intervention of tsarist censors, we may conclude that there is considerable confusion in post-Stalin era interpretations of *Boris Godunov*.

During the last twenty years some very good studies of Pushkin and his play have been published. Nevertheless, most work continues (perhaps by inertia) under the shadow of preconceived ideas about the playwright's intentions and the canonical text. A few researchers have pushed well beyond Stalin-era interpretations, but a brief review of current scholarship on *Boris Godunov* quickly demonstrates that, until very recently, there still existed a consensus that Pushkin intentionally omitted at least two scenes and dozens of lines of dialogue from his play and that he voluntarily changed the ending strictly for artistic reasons.

In a study of Pushkin's works published in 1983, Anthony Briggs took issue with the long-held view that *Boris Godunov* lacks a coherent overall structure. As long as that faulty view persists, he wrote, "the chances of restoring the reputation of *Boris Godunov* remain poor."[63] While admitting that the play has some problems, Briggs argued that Pushkin actually wrote a fine, stageable historical drama – one intended to revolutionize the Russian theater. Where others saw only a series of often brilliant but unrelated scenes and no overall unity, Briggs detected a five-act tragedy based on a Shakespearean model. He criticized Pushkin for not formally arranging his scenes into acts and then attempted to correct that problem by dividing the scenes into five groups or "acts." Although the time between each of the acts is often substantial, Briggs demonstrated that there is unity of time within each act and that the scenes are closely interrelated.[64] He used the canonical text to make his intriguing case, but he argued in favor of reinserting one passage from Pushkin's *Comedy* that had been deleted from *Boris Godunov* – lines spoken by the nobleman Peter Khrushchov in the scene "Krakov. Dom Vishnevetskogo" ("Cracow: Wiśniowiecki's House").[65]

In his influential study of early Russian drama published in 1985,

Simon Karlinsky ignored Pushkin's original *Comedy* along with the issue
of censorship. He correctly detected neoclassical elements in *Boris Godunov*, which had generally been interpreted as being purely Romantic.
Karlinsky concluded that Pushkin's historical drama is "on many levels
an unsatisfactory play." He noted that the poet studied Shakespeare's historical dramas and that *Boris Godunov* in some ways resembles *Richard
III*. Nevertheless, Karlinsky claimed that, although "Pushkin copied many
of Shakespeare's techniques, he somehow failed to notice that in each
of the historic plays he imitated there is a dramatic arch that unites the
activities of the antagonists and allows for the development of their
characters and for a satisfactory final resolution of the play's action."[66] It
is unfortunate that Karlinsky did not analyze the play with the original
ending of Pushkin's *Comedy* in place.

Caryl Emerson has studied Pushkin's *Boris Godunov* for many years,
and in 1986 she published a major work on the subject: *Boris Godunov:
Transpositions of a Russian Theme*. In sharp contrast to Karlinsky, Emerson openly acknowledged Pushkin's struggle with the censors. She
reviewed the scholarship on whether the 1825 *Comedy* or the 1831 *Boris
Godunov* should be preferred and came down – somewhat reluctantly –
on the side of the currently accepted canonical text ending with the
narod's silence. She has since changed her mind. In 1998, Emerson published an article in which she called for more careful study of the impact
of censorship (as well as less direct pressures) on Pushkin and other
artists who worked in early nineteenth-century imperial Russia.[67]

In 1989, Stephanie Sandler published an important book on Pushkin's
writings from the period of his exile, which fully acknowledges that his
work was subject to censorship. Curiously, however, she chose to ignore
Pushkin's 1825 *Comedy* in her analysis of *Boris Godunov* even though that
was the version of the play the angry young poet wrote while living in
exile. Relying instead on the canonical text, Sandler declared that Pushkin's play is difficult and frustrating to read, hard to make sense of, and
in places incomprehensible. In fact, she charged Pushkin with deliberately trying to frustrate his audience.[68] According to Sandler, one
possible explanation for *Boris Godunov*'s "failure" was Pushkin's unwillingness to follow Aristotle's advice about tragic drama. She wrote that
Pushkin "ignores Aristotle's treatment of the relationship between actor
and audience, which depended on … catharsis. Aristotle argued that the
actors would arouse the emotions of pity and fear in the audience, who
would be purged of these intense feelings by the climactic conclusion of

the drama." Sandler claimed that *Boris Godunov* "does not produce the bonding rituals typical of drama." According to her, the final scene of the play offers no well-focused emotional release mandatory for tragedy. (The costs of assessing *Boris Godunov* by "tragic" and "comedic" criteria will be thoroughly discussed in later chapters.) Sandler stated that while the *narod's* silence amounts to a strong moral condemnation of the Pretender Dmitry, it is not dramatically successful. Instead, the silence is sad testimony to the powerlessness of the common people.[69] She claimed that *Boris Godunov* is, therefore, a "self-consciously modern play" which is "meant to resist critics' attempts to reduce it to any single historical, political, moral, or even literary lesson."[70]

One of the main reasons for Sandler's disenchantment with the play might have been her own frustration with Pushkin's obvious sympathy for the Pretender Dmitry. Sandler did not doubt the received image: that Dmitry was an evil man, a rapist, and a tool of Catholic Poland's intervention in Russia's Time of Troubles. She chided Pushkin for his lack of historical objectivity concerning the odious impostor.[71] On this score, however, Pushkin was a very good historian who understood the biases of propaganda-influenced sources concerning Dmitry, and his portrayal of the Pretender was far more objective than that of the historians on whom Sandler – and she is by no means alone – relied in her analysis. Furthermore, Sandler seems to have misread Pushkin's own musings about Dmitry. In her discussion of his comparison of the Pretender with "Henry IV," for example, she mistakenly assumed (and in this too she is not alone) that Pushkin was referring to Shakespeare's King Henry IV.[72] In fact, Pushkin compared Dmitry to the highly admirable French king, Henri IV (founder of the Bourbon dynasty). Such readings as Sandler's, so provocative from the literary angle, are hampered by the dismissal of Pushkin as a sophisticated historian competent to weigh and assess his sources.

Monika Greenleaf published a fascinating book in 1994 that places Pushkin's work within the context of European (especially German) Romanticism. In her exploration of *Boris Godunov* she used only the canonical text and, somewhat in Sandler's spirit, argued that its "disorienting effect" on early critics was part of Pushkin's conscious strategy in writing the play. According to Greenleaf, *Boris Godunov* consists of many scenes (or "fragments") that are only loosely connected. One of the purposes served by Pushkin's use of this "montage" (or series of individualized "shots") was to avoid giving the audience the predictable closure usually found in drama.[73] Greenleaf very ably demonstrated the impact on *Boris Godunov* of the writings of Renaissance authors Shakespeare and Machiavelli – especially the "realpolitik" of characters in historical dramas such as *Julius Caesar,* who use "Machiavellian" techniques for success and survival. According to Greenleaf, Pushkin's portrayal of clever, cynical men manipulating the *narod* and each other in *Boris Godunov* was probably intended – at least in part – to help demystify imperial Russian politics and the tsars.[74] Following the mainstream opinion, Greenleaf denied that Pushkin had much interest in looking for truth in historical documents. Instead, she saw his Pretender Dmitry essentially as a literary device for exploring the "rhetoric of imposture" associated with certain literary geniuses of the Renaissance and the Age of Romanticism.[75]

In a very interesting article published in *Slavic Review* in 1996, Alyssa W. Dinega acknowledged the existence of the two versions of *Boris Godunov* and also noted the well-planned symmetry of the play's opening and closing scenes. In fact, she regarded that symmetry as clear evidence that Pushkin had some definite intellectual and aesthetic ideas in mind when he wrote the play's ending. Nevertheless, instead of examining the closing scene of Pushkin's *Comedy* and comparing it to the canonical version, she chose simply "to disregard the problem of authorial intention" and based her reading of *Boris Godunov* on the 1831 edition.[76] Dinega acknowledged Shakespeare's great influence on Pushkin but insisted that Pushkin was not merely an imitator. On the surface at least, *Boris Godunov* is certainly reminiscent of *Richard III,* and Dinega noted that the English people's silent reaction to the usurper King Richard may well have been a partial inspiration for the *narod*'s silence at the end of *Boris Godunov.*[77] Not surprisingly, she regarded the Pretender Dmitry as an evil man who was completely unworthy of the *narod*'s support. Nevertheless, according to Dinega, the silence of Pushkin's *narod* is not meant to show the common people as a moral force but is instead a parody of Shakespearean, cathartic, reunifying endings. She regarded the *narod*'s silence as Pushkin's declaration that Shakespeare's model failed when applied to the Russian context. Thus, Dinega actually regarded *Boris Godunov* as "antithetical" to *Richard III.*[78]

In 1997, Irena Ronen published an ambitious and stimulating study of *Boris Godunov* that attempts to move beyond traditional aesthetic criticism of the play and ideological interpretations of the "heroic" *narod.* Building on the work of Dmitry Blagoi, she rejected the usual claim that

Boris Godunov is poorly structured and demonstrated its pyramidic symmetry in which the first and second half of the play mirror each other. Ronen used the canonical text to construct her pyramid, apparently agreeing with Blagoi that Pushkin had removed two scenes in order to enhance the play's overall symmetry.[79] At no point, however, did she offer any evidence that Pushkin's revisions were motivated by such a desire. Ronen called attention to the parallel between the opening and closing scenes in both versions of the play, and she even noted that there was no historical basis for the *narod*'s silence at the end of *Boris Godunov*. Nevertheless, she accepted without question the long-held notion that Pushkin changed the ending of his play for artistic reasons and not under pressure. Therefore, she was forced to conclude that the playwright's goal had been to focus attention on the Pretender Dmitry's crime (ordering the murder of young Tsar Feodor Borisovich and his mother) and the *narod*'s silent, horror-struck rejection of him as the culmination of the play. Ronen openly acknowledged the historical accuracy of the *narod*'s cheer at the end of Pushkin's *Comedy*, but she regarded the altered version's silence as somehow more profoundly ironic.[80]

In 1999, Svetlana Evdokimova published a valuable study of Pushkin's thoughts about history and historical processes. She does an excellent job of demonstrating Pushkin's fascination with history and his belief that chance (or historical contingency) played an extremely important role in the development of Russia. Curiously, however, she did not examine the serious historical research that Pushkin conducted before penning *Boris Godunov*. Instead, Evdokimova claimed that while writing his historical drama the young poet was "guided by artistic considerations" rather than actual historical data. In fact, she called attention to this slighting of history on behalf of art as strikingly different from Pushkin's unfinished *History of Peter the Great* with its "enormous amount of painstakingly collected facts."[81] Evdokimova interpreted *Boris Godunov* as a sustained meditation on the role of chance in history, and she regarded Pushkin's portrayal of the Pretender Dmitry as part of that meditation. Accordingly, the "peculiarly inept" Dmitry's victory over the Godunovs was due entirely to chance – especially his reliance on the fickle *narod* for support.[82] Evdokimova asserted that in *Boris Godunov* Pushkin definitely intended to show the *narod* as unreliable and extremely unstable. To back up that statement, she claimed that the silent ending of the 1831 edition reveals the *narod*'s behavior as confused and politically apathetic. Turning to Pushkin's *Comedy*, Evdokimova boldly asserted that the *narod*'s final cheer for Tsar Dmitry is somehow even "more unambiguously consistent" with Pushkin's representation of the common people's "servile compliance and political indifference." Although Evdokimova acknowledged that censorship might have played a role in the altered ending of *Boris Godunov,* she claimed that both endings are really the same: both show a disoriented and inert *narod.* Evdokimova saw no evidence whatsoever of the *narod*'s political consciousness in the play.[83] She did not address those passages that show the *narod* being motivated by a strong desire for a legitimate ruler and by the belief that Dmitry would liberate them from serfdom. Here we encounter another unfortunate convention in reading *Boris Godunov:* certain scenes (the operatized ones) receive most of the attention, whereas the historical and military discussions are often overlooked. For example, very little attention has been paid to Pushkin's brilliant (and historically accurate) portrayal of Peter Basmanov.

In 2004, Douglas Clayton published an ambitious book that offers a "new" interpretation of *Boris Godunov* that sharply challenges many current ideas about Pushkin's intentions.[84] Instead of viewing the play as the somewhat awkward product of an exiled and angry young poet who despised Tsar Alexander I, questioned autocracy, and flirted with atheism, Clayton boldly argued that *Boris Godunov* marks a sharp break with the Decembrists and Pushkin's own youthful liberalism. According to Clayton, the play reveals Pushkin's emergence as a conservative and is best understood as a defense of autocracy and Russian Orthodox Christianity. Clayton discerned important religious elements in *Boris Godunov* that have long been ignored due primarily to prejudices dating from the Stalin era. He insisted that in the play "we find incarnated those three elements that were to become the slogan of Nicholas's Russia in the 1830s – autocracy, Orthodoxy, and nationality."

Clayton's thesis is startling, but he did not make a convincing case for viewing *Boris Godunov* as a manifesto of either Pushkin's "subtle adherence" to Orthodox Christianity or his movement toward political conservatism. For one thing, he ignored the context in which Pushkin wrote his *Comedy* and repeated the error of several of Pushkin's friends in claiming that the play was intended to please the tsar. He also simplified and deformed Pushkin's political views – for example, by regarding Pushkin's support of monarchy as an endorsement of autocracy. All evidence suggests that the poet was a liberal aristocrat who was deeply suspicious of autocracy. In fact, Pushkin and his contemporaries (including the conservative Karamzin) held rather sophisticated views concerning the differences between monarchy and autocracy. Clayton also misread Pushkin's attitude toward serfdom and failed to comprehend how that controversial issue was dealt with in the play. His attempt to find religious elements in *Boris Godunov* also suggests a lack of sophistication about early modern Russian culture and the Time of Troubles. Clayton failed to grapple with Pushkin's consideration of atheism at the time he wrote *Boris Godunov,* and (another side of the same problem) his discussion of Pushkin's handling of "miracles" associated with "St. Dmitry" is unpersuasive. Unsurprisingly, Clayton joins the chorus of critics who diminish the Pretender Dmitry, assuming that the poet shared his own disdain for the "despot." Clayton focuses almost exclusively on Pushkin's literary effort to compare Dmitry to Napoleon.

It is tempting to see Clayton's book as a throwback to tendentious tsarist interpretations or as an overreaction to Marxist scholarship. But it is in fact more significant and up-to-date: an accurate reflection of the new wave of Russian scholarship that attempts to portray Pushkin throughout his life as a devout Orthodox Christian and strong supporter of autocracy. It is, of course, natural that long-repressed aspects of any great creative figure will be disproportionately highlighted when repression is lifted. But we must be alert to the dynamics. Since the breakup of the Soviet Union, Valentin Nepomniashchy and other prominent Pushkinists have systematically reshaped – and at times distorted – Pushkin's biography and writings in order to turn him into a social conservative and a profoundly religious figure. The wheel turns, and Pushkin is strapped to it: Russia's national poet is once again being adjusted to suit the needs of "patriots."[85] As Stephanie Sandler wisely noted, even two hundred years after the great poet's birth it continues to be difficult to separate Pushkin "from the fantasies and desires projected onto him."[86]

Nevertheless, fathoming Pushkin's own intentions has remained the goal of many experienced researchers, even in this unprecedentedly free and sensation-seeking era. Two such veteran researchers, Sergei Fomichev and Lidiia Lotman, published an important annotated edition of Pushkin's play in 1996 in which they pointed out that the Stalin-era hybrid text of *Boris Godunov* was definitely not what Pushkin had in mind, either in 1825 or in 1831.[87] Their edition of the play is true to the version published in 1831. Fomichev also published a limited edition of Pushkin's original *Comedy* in 1993, thereby bringing it back into print for the first time since the Revolution of 1917.[88] Fomichev has, in fact, long been interested in the *Comedy*'s comedic elements that were muted in the version of the play published in 1831.[89] After long and careful study, both Fomichev and Lotman now agree that the *Comedy about Tsar Boris and Grishka Otrepiev* is just as important and interesting as the canonical text of *Boris Godunov.* They join with the other contributors to this volume in calling for the inclusion of Pushkin's *Comedy* in the canon of his works.

It is obvious from this brief review of recent scholarship and literary criticism about Pushkin's *Boris Godunov* that much sophisticated analysis of the play has been written during the last generation. Nevertheless, there are still a number of significant issues that have not yet been adequately addressed. Perhaps most important, very little attention has been paid to the content or significance of Pushkin's original *Comedy.* In fact, with the exception of the final line of the play, no systematic study of the differences between the 1825 and the 1831 versions of *Boris Godunov* has ever been conducted. Moreover, altogether too little attention has been paid to the radically different contexts in which the two versions were produced. In many studies of the play there is no mention whatsoever of coercion or state-sponsored censorship. Curiously, also missing from most studies of *Boris Godunov* is careful consideration of Pushkin's own historical perspective on the events and characters of the Time of Troubles and how that helped shape his play. Focus on these crucial issues – the task of the next two chapters – will shed valuable light on Pushkin's troublesome historical drama and why he valued it so highly.

Readers are, of course, free to choose whichever version of *Boris Godunov* they wish to regard as the one Pushkin intended. But there are very good reasons to pay more attention to the understudied and undervalued *Comedy.* Unfortunately, the *Comedy* has been extremely difficult to obtain, reconstruct, or study.[90] It deserves a better fate than to be simply ignored or relegated to notes accompanying the canonical text. Indeed, one can make a reasonable case for setting aside altogether the wellknown version of *Boris Godunov* in favor of Pushkin's *Comedy.* Unlike the 1831 edition (or the canonical version that coalesced a century later), the *Comedy* was – on one level at least – clearly intended to be Shakespearean in form, complete with a cathartic resolution in the final scene. (In fact, it is more than a little reminiscent of *Richard III.*) The play published in 1831, on the other hand, was the product of many different pressures on Pushkin – few of them artistic.

Notes

1. Dunning, "Rethinking," 569–91.
2. Cooke and Dunning, "Tempting Fate," 44.
3. Pushkin, *The Letters of Alexander Pushkin* [hereafter cited as *Letters*], 261; idem, *Polnoe sobranie sochinenii* (1937–59) [hereafter cited as PS], 13: 239.
4. PS, 14: 56, 118, 139, 150; *Letters*, 371, 398, 434, 449, 458; Tsiavlovskii and Tarkhova, *Letopis' zhizni i tvorchestva Aleksandra Pushkina* [hereafter cited as TL], 2: 89; 3: 253, 284; Vinokur, *Stat'i*, 83; Simmons, *Pushkin*, 233; Zagorskii, *Pushkin*, 91; Mirsky, *Pushkin*, 153; Vickery, *Alexander Pushkin* (1970), 65; Briggs, *Alexander Pushkin*, 158; Emerson, *Boris Godunov*, 1; idem, "Pretenders," 257.
5. On the enthusiastic initial response to Pushkin's play see Binyon, *Pushkin*, 246–47; Simmons, *Pushkin*, 259–62, 272; Mirsky, *Pushkin*, 106, 159–60; Briggs, "Hidden Forces," 43; Ashukin, *Pushkinskaia Moskva*, 119–29.
6. For disappointment and confusion about *Boris Godunov* since 1831 see Pushkin, *Boris Godunov: Tragediia* [hereafter cited as BG], 490–525; Kireevskii, *Polnoe sobranie*, 2: 46; Belinskii, *Stat'i*, 250–95; Pushkin, *Sochineniia i pis'ma* (1903–6), 3: 257–58; Vinokur, "Kommentarii," 436–59; idem, *Stat'i*, 90–92; Serman, "Pushkin," 118–20; Alekseev, "A. S. Pushkin," 174–76; Zel'dovich and Livshits, *Russkaia literatura*, 167–69; Brown, *History*, 3: 105–11; Terras, *Belinskij*, 132–33, 174; Fomichev, *Prazdnik*, 90; Emerson, "Pretenders," 257–58; Greenleaf, *Pushkin*, 157–59; and Ronen, *Smyslovoi stroi*, 5, 9–14.
7. For examples of scholarly puzzlement about Pushkin's play see Gifford, "Shakespearean Elements," 158; Bayley, *Pushkin*, 165–66, 173; Sandler, *Distant Pleasures*, 9, 11–12, 77–79, 108–9, 136–37; Mirsky, *Pushkin*, 95, 153–54, 158–60; Karlinsky, *Russian Drama*, 321–23; and Emerson, "Pretenders," 257–58, 260.
8. For examples of critical assessments of the play see Kireevskii, *Polnoe sobranie*, 2: 42–47; Belinskii, *Stat'i*, 250–95; Rassadin, *Dramaturg*, 5–8; Terras, *History*, 281; Fennell, "Pushkin," 109; Gozenpud, "O stsenichnosti," 346–48; Briggs, "Hidden Forces," 43–44; idem, *Alexander Pushkin*, 157–64; Simmons, *Pushkin*, 234–35; Bayley, *Pushkin*, 173, 176–77; Sandler, "Solitude," 171; Leach and Borovsky, *History*, 97–99; and Vickery, *Alexander Pushkin* (1970), 59, 65–70.
9. See, for example, BG 348–49; Blagoi, *Tvorcheskii put'* (1813–1826), 472; and Shervinsky, "Stage Directions," 141–58.
10. For attempts to interpret the final scene of *Boris Godunov* see Vinokur, "Kommentarii," 430–31; Rassadin, *Dramaturg*, 50–58; Balashov, "Boris Godunov," 212–13; Alekseev, "Remarka," 36–58; Listov and Tarkhova, "K istorii," 126–29; Mikhailova, "K istochnikam," 150–53; Stroganov, "Eshche raz," 126–29; Mikkelson, "Narod," 273–82; Vickery, *Alexander Pushkin* (1970), 69–70; Lotman, "Eshche raz," 160–70; idem, "Sud'by," 101–08; and Fomichev, *Prazdnik*, 93–99, 104.
11. For works exploring Pushkin's intention in using silence to end the play see Belinskii, *O drame*, 2: 357; Filonov, *Boris Godunov*, 145; Vinokur, *Stat'i*, 103–4; Gorodetskii, *Tragediia*, 161–62; idem, "Boris Godunov," 37–40; Balashov, "Boris Godunov," 212–13; Rassadin, *Dramaturg*, 55–56; Moss, "Last Word," 195–96; Levin,

Shekspir, 41; Fel'dman, *Sud'ba*, 66; Brown, *History*, 3: 109–11; Emerson, *Boris Godunov*, 72–73, 131–39; Ronen, *Smyslovoi stroi*, 7–8, 14–16; Dinega, "Ambiguity," 549–51; Vickery, *Alexander Pushkin* (1970), 65–69; BG 348–49, 352–57; Lotman, "Eshche raz," 168; Pomar, "Russian Historical Drama," 264, 285; and Evdokimova, *Pushkin's Historical Imagination*, 60–65.

12. For discussion of the stageability of *Boris Godunov* see Arkhangel'skii, "Problema," 5–16; Bayley, *Pushkin*, 165–85; Bondi, *O Pushkine*, 169–241; Wolff, "Shakespeare's Influence," 93–105; Zagorskii, *Pushkin*, 94–96; Rassadin, *Dramaturg*, 57–58; Briggs, "Hidden Forces," 43–44; idem, *Alexander Pushkin*, 157–77; Gozenpud, "O stsenochnosti," 339–56; Alekseev, "A. S. Pushkin," 174–75; Leach and Borovsky, *History*, 97–99; Brown, *History*, 3: 105–13; Shcherbakova, *Pushkin*, 4–8, 164–65; Emerson, *Boris Godunov*, 105–7, 133–34, 235 nn. 47–48; and idem, "Pretenders," 258–60.

13. On the relationship between *Boris Godunov* and Shakespearean drama see *Letters*, 365; Kireevskii, *Polnoe sobranie*, 2: 45–47; Pushkin, *Sochineniia i pis'ma*, 3: 239, 242, 252–53, 260, 639–40; Verkhovskii, "Zapadnoevropeiskaia drama," 187–226; Vinokur, *Stat'i*, 114–19; Gifford, "Shakespearean Elements," 152–60; Mirsky, *Pushkin*, 156–59; Wolff, "Shakespeare's Influence," 93–98; Alekseev, "A.S. Pushkin," 162–200; Karlinsky, *Russian Drama*, 322; Fennell, "Pushkin," 109–10; Simmons, *Pushkin*, 233–34, 272; Balashov, "Boris Godunov," 253–92; Bethea, "Pushkin," 83–86; Emerson, "Pretenders," 259–60; and Levin, *Shekspir*, 38–41, 55.

14. See, for example, Levin, "Nekotorye voprosy," 62; Alekseev, "A. S. Pushkin," 177–78; and Sandler, "Problem," 133–34.

15. On *Boris Godunov* as a possible parody of Shakespearean drama see Emerson, "Queen," 112–13, 137–41; and Dinega, "Ambiguity," 525–27, 549–51.

16. For discussion of the dramatic hero in *Boris Godunov* see Serman, "Paradoxes," 25–39; idem, "Pushkin," 120–25; Tomashevskii, *Pushkin*, 2: 174; Vinokur, *Stat'i*, 104; Rassadin, *Dramaturg*, 27; Litvinenko, *Pushkin*, 210–11; Slonimskii, "Boris Godunov," 68–71; Mikkelson, "Narod," 273–82; Mal'tsev, *Tema*, 67; Meilakh, *A. S. Pushkin*, 174; Nepomniashchii, *Poeziia*, 225–26, 245; Brody, *Demetrius Legend*, 242–43; Brown, *History*, 3: 108–11; Emerson, *Boris Godunov*, 135–37; idem, "Pretenders," 263; and Gurevich, "Istoriia," 204–14.

17. See Pushkin, *Komediia*, 227, 246–49; and Fomichev, *Prazdnik*, 80–107.

18. Belinskii, *Stat'i*, 251.

19. See, for example, Pushkin, *Sochineniia Pushkina* (1855–57), 4: 457; BG, 350–52; Mirsky, *Pushkin*, 161–62; Emerson, *Boris Godunov*, 134; Alekseev, "Remarka," 41–42, 46; and Vinokur, "Kommentarii," 425.

20. The scene "Ograda monastyrskaia" was first published (in German) as a note to Egor Rozen's German review of Pushkin's *Boris Godunov* in *Dorpater Jahrbücher für Litteratur, Statistik und Kunst, besonders Russlands*, 1833, no. 1: 56–58. A Russian translation of Rozen's German version of the scene was published in *Literaturnye Pribavleniia k Russkomu Invalidu*, 1834, no. 3: 23. See Gennadi, *Prilozheniia*, 73; Annenkov, *Vospominaniia*, 3: 453–54; Rosen, "Boris Godunov," 249–59.

21. Nikitenko, *Diary*, 71–72; Binyon, *Pushkin*, 644–45; Levitt, "Pushkin," 187–88; Shchegolev, *Duel*, 208.

22. See Pushkin, *Sochineniia Aleksandra Pushkina* (1838–41), 1: 257–373; Kahn, "New Academy Pushkin," 428.

23. *Sovremennik*, 10 (1838), no. 2: 152.

24. See Pushkin, *Sochineniia Aleksandra Pushkina* (1838–41), 9: 193–99; idem, *Sochineniia i pis'ma* (1903–6), 3: 631, 637.

25. *Moskvitianin*, 1854, no. 5, otdel iv. This scene was published in anticipation of Pavel Annenkov's "radical" new edition of Pushkin's works.

26. Pushkin, *Sochineniia Pushkina* (1855–57), 4: 245–47, 455–58; 7: 76.

27. Annenkov, *Vospominaniia*, 3: 226–30, 453–58; Levitt, *Russian Literary Politics*, 22–27.

28. Pushkin, *Sochineniia A. S. Pushkina* (1859), 3: 243–45, 288–91, 336–38.

29. Levitt, *Russian Literary Politics*, 4–8, 21–23, 26–29; Annenkov, *Vospominaniia*, 3: 266–67; Modzalevskii, *Pushkin*, 275–396.

30. Brody, "Schiller's Demetrius," 291–94; Levitt, *Russian Literary Politics*, 59–146; Grossman, *Dostoevskii*, 36; Jackson, *Dostoevsky's Quest*, 18, 119; Slater, "Patriots' Pushkin," 412–13. See also Blake, "Dostoevskii's Dialogue."

31. See, for example, Sukhomlinov, *Izsledovaniia*, 2: 219–22; Levitt, *Russian Literary Politics*, 22; idem, "Pushkin," 183.

32. See, for example, Pushkin, *Sochineniia; polnoe sobranie* (1891, Skabichevskii), 3: 77–156. This particular edition actually restored the "Monastery Wall" scene directly to the main text of the play (pages 92–93) instead of relegating it to an appendix, as was customary in late tsarist Russia. See, for example, Pushkin, *Sochineniia A. S. Pushkina* (1887, Suvorin), 2: 1–117; and idem, *Sochineniia A. S. Pushkina: Polnoe sobranie v odnom tome* (1909), cols. 607–68.

33. See Pushkin, *Sochineniia A. S. Pushkina* (1887, Morozov), 3: 1–84.

34. See Pushkin, *Sochineniia i pis'ma* (1903–6), 3: v, 239–61, 264–354, 629–40.

35. Levitt, "Russian Literary Politics," 158–59; idem, "Pushkin," 183–92; Gorodetskii, Izmailov, and Meilakh, *Pushkin*, 274; Slater, "Patriots' Pushkin," 413.

36. See, for example, Filonov, *Boris Godunov*, 1, 54–58, 88–89, 145.

37. On the question of Pushkin's reliance on Karamzin's *History* see Rybinskii, *Sbornik*, 133–47; Shmurlo, "Etiudy," 5–40; Rabinovich, "Boris Godunov," 307–17; Orlov, "Tragediia," 3–10; Vinokur, *Stat'i*, 93–9; Toibin, "Istoriia," 37–48; Gorodetskii, *Tragediia*, 138–40; Bochkarev, *Russkaia istoricheskaia dramaturgiia*, 347–55; Luzianina, "Istoriia," 45–57; Serman, "Pushkin," 23; Pomar, "Russian Historical Drama," 197–201; and Emerson, *Boris Godunov*, 119–31.

38. Levitt, "Pushkin," 192–96.

39. See Levitt, "Pushkin," 188; idem, *Russian Literary Politics*, 158–59; Emerson, *Boris Godunov*, 134–35.

40. See, for example, Pokrovsky, *Brief History*, 1: 73–76; and Mavrodin, "Soviet Historical Literature," 44.

41. Richmond, "Conditions," 15, 24, 31–32, 35, 38; Brandenberger, "People's Poet," 68.

42. Mavrodin, "Soviet Historical Literature," 50–51; Dunning, *Russia's First Civil War* [hereafter cited as RFCW], 7–8; Platonov, *Boris Godunov*, xxxiv–xxxv.

43. Levitt, *Russian Literary Politics*, 162–65; Brandenberger, "People's Poet," 68, 72–73; Slater, "Patriots' Pushkin," 414–15, 427; Virolainen, *Legendy*, 123–26; Chukovskii, *Dnevnik*, 2: 116–17; Emerson, "Pushkin," 658–59. Early examples of the rehabilitation of Pushkin include Blagoi, *Sotsiologiia* (1929) and Grushkin, *K voprosu* (1931).

44. Pavlov-Sil'vanskii, "Narod," 289–303; Bazilevich, "Boris Godunov," 35, 40; Serman, "Paradoxes," 26; Briggs, *Alexander Pushkin*, 160. See also Engel'gardt, "Istorizm," 58–75; Raskol'nikov, "Boris Godunov," 157.

45. For Soviet scholarly views of the heroic *narod* in *Boris Godunov* see Grekov, "Istoricheskie vozzreniia," 3–28; Kotliarevskii, *Literaturnye napravleniia*, 213–14; Bondi, "Dramaticheskie proizvedeniia," 491–92; Gukovskii, *Pushkin*, 25; Rabinovich, "Boris Godunov," 308–17; Rassadin, *Dramaturg*, 50–58; Bochkarev, *Russkaia istoricheskaia dramaturgiia*, 455–65; Gorodetskii, *Tragediia*, 195; Gorodetskii, Izmailov, and Meilakh, *Pushkin*, 446–53; Serman, "Paradoxes," 25–39; Listov and Tarkhova, "K istorii," 96–101; Mal'tsev, *Tema*, 67; BG, 349–53; Alekseev, "Remarka," 36–58; Shervinsky, "Stage Directions," 154–55; Meilakh, *A. S. Pushkin*, 174; Tomashevskii, *Pushkin*, 2: 174; Litvinenko, *Pushkin*, 210–11; Mikkelson, "Narod," 273; Vorob'eva, *Printsip*, 63; Lotman, "Eshche raz," 160–70; and Slater, "Patriots' Pushkin," 414–15. See also Brody, *Demetrius Legend*, 242–43; and Arkhangel'skii, "Poet," 123–37.

46. On the denial of any significant impact on Pushkin's play by tsarist censors see Vinokur, "Kommentarii," 430–31; Alekseev, "Remarka," 36–40, 51–53; Balashov, "Boris Godunov," 212–18; Levitt, *Russian Literary Politics*, 159, 162–65; BG, 348–49, 352–57; Gorodetskii, *Tragediia*, 161–62; Emerson, *Boris Godunov*, 135–36; Ronen, *Smyslovoi stroi*, 14–15, 132; Evdokimova, *Pushkin's Historical Imagination*, 25, 61; and Slater, "Patriots' Pushkin," 414.

47. For works questioning the *narod*'s heroism in *Boris Godunov* see Gozenpud, "Iz istorii," 264–66; Serman, "Paradoxes," 25–27, 34–37; Moss, "Last Word," 195–96; Bayley, *Pushkin*, 175–76; Vickery, *Alexander Pushkin* (1970), 59–60, 65–70; Pomar, "Russian Historical Drama," 241–64; Mikkelson, "Narod," 273–76, 281–82; Brown, *History*, 3: 110–11; Emerson, *Boris Godunov*, 131–41; Sandler, "Problem," 59–63; idem, *Distant Pleasures*, 88, 128–30, 137–39; Ronen, *Smyslovoi stroi*, 16; Fomichev, *Prazdnik*, 94–97; Dinega, "Ambiguity," 549–51; Raskol'nikov, "Boris Godunov," 159–62; and Evdokimova, *Pushkin's Historical Imagination*, 59–62.

48. Vinokur, *Kommentarii*, 242; Gorodetskii, *Tragediia*, 82–83; Tomashevskii, "Primechaniia," 509.

49. See PS, 7: 1–98.

50. Brandenberger, "People's Poet," 69–70; Chukovskii, *Dnevnik*, 2: 139. Vinokur's "Kommentarii" was first published in *Polnoe sobranie sochinenii A. S. Pushkina*, vol. 7 (*Dramaticheskie proizvedeniia*) (Moscow: Izdatel'stvo Akademii nauk SSSR, 1935), 385–505. It was reprinted in 1999 in Vinokur, *Kommentarii*, 171–349.

51. Kahn, "New Academy Pushkin," 428–33; Lotman, *Pushkin*, 372.

52. Vinokur, *Stat'i*, 93–96, 98–105. See also Slonimskii, "Boris Godunov," 66.

53. Vinokur, "Kommentarii," 430–31; idem, *Kommentarii*, 239–40. See also Raskol'nikov, "Boris Godunov," 157.

54. Vinokur, *Stat'i*, 89–90.

55. See BG, 127–28; Fomichev, "Zvezda," 3–7; Lotman, *Pushkin*, 369–73; Kahn, "New Academy Pushkin," 428; Brandenberger, "People's Poet," 66–69.

56. Bazilevich, "Boris Godunov," 35, 40; Serman, "Paradoxes," 27–28; Gorodetskii, Izmailov, and Meilakh, *Pushkin*, 451–52; Rassadin, *Dramaturg*, 27; Sandler, "Problem," 64.

57. Serman, "Pushkin," 118–25; idem, "Paradoxes," 28–29, 31–33; Bondi, "Dramaticheskie proizvedeniia," 494–95; Turbin, "Kharaktery," 74–75. See also Kireevskii, *Polnoe sobranie*, 2: 45; Bethea, "Pushkin's Pretenders," 61–65; Raskol'nikov, "Boris Godunov," 163–64; Dinega, "Ambiguity," 546–47.

58. Serman, "Paradoxes," 34–39; Balashov, "Boris Godunov," 218; Bondi, "Dramaticheskie proizvedeniia," 491–92; Blagoi, *Ot Kantemira*, 2: 108–10; Lotman, "Eshche raz," 161–64, 168. See also Vinokur, "Kommentarii," 486; Raskol'nikov, "Boris Godunov," 157, 162.

59. Belinskii, *Stat'i*, 270–71.

60. See, for example, Gozenpud, "Iz istorii," 264; Bayley, *Pushkin*, 176; Brown, *History*, 3: 110–11. See also Evdokimova, *Pushkin's Historical Imagination*, 59–62.

61. See, for example, Vinokur, "Kommentarii," 436–59; and Serman, "Pushkin," 118–19. See also Raskol'nikov, "Boris Godunov," 163.

62. See, for example, Bayley, *Pushkin*, 176; Wolff, "Shakespeare's Influence," 97, 105; Edmonds, *Pushkin*, 172; Mirsky, *Pushkin*, 161–62; Vickery, *Alexander Pushkin* (1970), 196 n. 19; and Brody, "Pushkin's 'Boris Godunov,'" 873.

63. Briggs, *Alexander Pushkin*, 164.

64. Ibid., 164–73. See also Fennell, "Pushkin," 109; and Leach and Borovsky, *History*, 97–98.

65. Briggs, *Alexander Pushkin*, 172, 244 n. 14. See also PS, 7: 268–69.

66. Karlinsky, *Russian Drama*, 312–13, 316–23. See also Bethea, "Pushkin," 84–85.

67. Emerson, "Pushkin," 653–72.

68. Sandler, *Distant Pleasures*, 9, 11–12, 77–79, 108–9, 129, 136–37; idem, "Solitude," 171.

69. Sandler, "Problem," 60–63; idem, *Distant Pleasures*, 79, 88, 129–30, 137–39. See also Wolff, "Shakespeare's Influence," 98; and Vickery, *Alexander Pushkin* (1970), 69.

70. Sandler, "Problem," 133–34; idem, *Distant Pleasures*, 136.

71. Sandler, *Distant Pleasures*, 127–28; idem, "Problem," 80, 102–3.

72. Sandler, *Distant Pleasures*, 127. See also Levin, *Shekspir*, 39–40; and Emerson and Oldani, *Modest Musorgsky*, 32.

73. Greenleaf, *Pushkin*, 157–62; idem, "Tynianov," 283–84. See also Tynianov, *Pushkin*, 148; Moss, "Last Word," 187–97; and Emerson, *Boris Godunov*, 131–41.

74. Greenleaf, *Pushkin*, 172–80, 196.

75. Ibid., 158, 179, 204. Cf. Bethea, "Pushkin," 85–86.

76. Dinega, "Ambiguity," 539–40, 540 n. 28.

77. Ibid., 525–27, 540 n. 28.

78. Ibid., 549–51.

79. Ronen, *Smyslovoi stroi*, 7–8, 121–29. See also Blagoi, *Masterstvo*, 116–42; idem, *Ot Kantemira*, 2: 102–24.

80. Ronen, *Smyslovoi stroi*, 14–16, 117–19, 131–32.

81. Evdokimova, *Pushkin's Historical Imagination*, 25.

82. Ibid., 56, 62, 65.

83. Ibid., 59–62. Cf. Pomar, "Russian Historical Drama," 264, 285; Moss, "Last Word," 195–96; Brown, *History*, 3: 110–11.

84. Clayton, *Dimitry's Shade*.

85. Slater, "Patriots' Pushkin," 420–27; Horowitz, "Thus Spoke," 434–39.

86. Sandler, "Introduction," 283. See also Emerson, "Pretenders," 257; idem, "Pushkin," 659.

87. BG, 127–28.

88. Pushkin, *Komediia*.

89. Ibid., 236–48; Fomichev, *Prazdnik*, 82–107.

90. An imperfect version of Pushkin's *Komediia* can, with difficulty, be reconstructed by using the appendix to volume seven of the Jubilee edition. (See PS, 7: 263–302.) Sergei Fomichev's handsome, limited edition of *Komediia* is more accurate, but it still contains some errors and is extremely hard to obtain. There are also copies of Peter Morozov's various prerevolutionary editions of Pushkin's works (containing an imperfect version of *Komediia*) still collecting dust on library shelves. Until now, *Komediia* has never been translated into English or any other language.

2

The Exiled Poet-Historian and the Creation of His *Comedy*

∾ CHESTER DUNNING

Apropos of Pushkin's *Boris Godunov*, Stephanie Sandler once commented that "no one who has written about this play has been able to read it with the kind of sustained attention it demands."[1] Perhaps that is because so few studies of Pushkin's troublesome drama have taken an historical approach to the task of understanding it. Only by studying the context in which the young genius wrote his *Comedy*, and by carefully examining the sources he used to create it and the interpretation of Russian history he intended to convey through it, will we be able to appreciate why the "poet-historian" was so fond of his play.

It is, of course, well known that Pushkin wrote the original version of *Boris Godunov* while living in "rustic captivity," and the impact of his isolation and punishment on the content of the play has received considerable scholarly attention.[2] All too often, however, Pushkin's misbehavior and rebelliousness are attributed to the vague restlessness of youth or to the Byronic Romantic model; the precise political reasons why Tsar Alexander I (r. 1801–25) exiled the twenty-one-year-old aristocrat (his "dangerous" liberal ideas and his religious skepticism) are underplayed, even though they are highly relevant to understanding his *Comedy*. It is also well known that Pushkin was inspired to write his play by reading volumes ten and eleven of Nikolai Karamzin's *History of the Russian State*. In fact, the impact of Karamzin's *History* on *Boris Godunov* has long been one of the favorite topics of scholars and literary critics.[3] Nevertheless, a very significant weakness in current scholarship about the play is the widespread assumption that Pushkin adhered closely to Karamzin's interpretation of the Time of Troubles (1598–1613). Careful analysis reveals that Pushkin's original *Comedy* does not "slavishly" follow Karamzin. Instead, it amounts to a dialogue with Karamzin's *History*, one written by an independent-minded poet-historian who, while grateful to Karamzin's pioneering efforts, conducted his own research and drew his own conclusions.

Most studies of *Boris Godunov* have paid little, if any, attention to Pushkin's intense interest in the history of his country. They have fallen short in their interpretations of that history and the angry young poet's sophisticated use of historical sources *other* than Karamzin's *History*. Those oversights are regrettable because Pushkin was actually an historian of considerable ability.[4] Indeed, in 1831, Tsar Nicholas I appointed him Russia's official historian laureate (*istoriograf* or "historiographer") – the second one ever, following Karamzin.[5] It is important to remember that, at that time, history and literature were not regarded as separate disciplines. Pushkin basked in the glory of his special position (the leading literary figure of his country), which was the same as Karamzin's before him and the same honor Louis XV had bestowed on Voltaire. That was well known to Pushkin, who greatly admired both of those famous professional writers.[6]

One of the main reasons studies of *Boris Godunov* have not devoted more attention to the historical content of the play is the simple fact that scholars interested in Pushkin as an historian have focused almost exclusively on his writings during the 1830s – that is to say, *after* he became Russia's historian laureate.[7] But Pushkin's interest in and talent for history actually showed up much earlier in his life. As a youth, he displayed a real passion for reading and thinking about history;[8] and throughout his life the highly original poet-historian, keeping pace with debates about historical scholarship in Western Europe, was deeply concerned about the relationship between history and literature.[9] Among other endeavors, Pushkin actively strove for a high degree of historical accuracy, not just in his nonfiction writing but in his poetry and prose fiction as well, and this was certainly true in the case of his *Comedy*.[10] In fact, Pushkin saw no real conflict between his task as an historian and his task as a dramatist. Like several other great writers in the Age of Romanticism (such as Friedrich von Schiller), Pushkin wished to be – and was – a poet and an historian at the same time.[11]

Pushkin received his formal education (1811–17) at Tsar Alexander I's new Lycée in Tsarskoe Selo, where he studied with other bright young aristocrats destined for high-ranking positions in government service.[12] While attending the Lycée, young Pushkin heard lectures that stirred his interest in Russian history, especially in the horrifying period known as the Time of Troubles – the decade and a half of political turmoil, famine, regicide, civil war, and foreign military intervention that preceded the founding of the Romanov dynasty. The Time of Troubles (when Polish-, German-, and French-speaking soldiers marched all over Russia and fought battles near Moscow) must have seemed eerily familiar to Russians who endured Napoleon's invasion in 1812. Tsar Alexander's glorious "victory" over Napoleon and the closely-related bicentennial celebration of the election of Tsar Mikhail Romanov in 1613 produced a flood of patriotic literature and much public discussion about the similarities between Russia's heroic struggles for survival at the dawn of the seventeenth and the dawn of the nineteenth centuries. As a result, at the Lycée (and elsewhere) young Pushkin became quite familiar with the careers of two of the major figures of the Time of Troubles, Boris Godunov and the Pretender Dmitry.[13] Pushkin's interest in those larger-than-life individuals stayed with him for the rest of his life.

While attending the Lycée, Pushkin established lifelong friendships with several fellow students, including Anton A. Delvig and the future Decembrist, Ivan I. Pushchin, who shared his growing love of freedom and hostility to tyranny. Influenced by such teachers as V. F. Malinovsky and A. P. Kunitsyn, these privileged teenagers developed liberal values and a patriotic but progressive "spirit of the Lycée" that initially placed great hope in the reformist potential of Tsar Alexander, the "Liberator of Europe." Eventually, however, Pushkin and his friends grew disenchanted with the reactionary policies pursued by Tsar Alexander in the years following Napoleon's defeat. By the time these elite liberal-minded students graduated from the Lycée, they were strongly opposed to autocracy, asked hard questions about the morality of serfdom, and increasingly questioned the direction their country was taking.[14]

While Pushkin was attending the Lycée, he also met Russia's most renowned historian, Nikolai Karamzin, who was very impressed by the young poet. Karamzin invited him into his home and introduced him to many leading Russian literary figures, including the poet Vasily Zhukovsky. Pushkin – who was something of a stranger in his own home – visited Karamzin's home almost every day after classes, and he actually lived there for a few months in 1816.[15] He greatly admired Karamzin as a writer and thinker and enjoyed debating about history with the historian laureate. Not surprisingly, Karamzin became Pushkin's first patron and adviser.[16] In addition to Karamzin's interest in Russian history, it is quite possible that his love of Shakespeare had some influence on Pushkin. (In his youth, Karamzin had published, anonymously, the first Russian translation of *Julius Caesar*.)[17] Although a devoted monarchist, Karamzin held political views strongly influenced by the Enlightenment. Far from accepting autocracy without question, he shared Montesquieu's opposition to despotism and tyranny, firm commitment to the rule of law, and support of basic civil rights for ordinary subjects.[18] Young Pushkin was certainly more liberal than Karamzin, but he deeply respected his mentor's ideas. It is even possible that Karamzin's condemnation of the assassination of Tsar Paul I (Alexander I's father) influenced Pushkin's growing dissatisfaction with the Liberator of Europe.[19]

Pushkin's lifelong friendship with Vasily Zhukovsky began with lively, wide-ranging discussions in Karamzin's home, and Russia's leading Romantic poet came to have a strong influence on young Pushkin. Although he was a political moderate, Zhukovsky's enlightened, humane ideas included an acute sensitivity to political tyranny. In addition to writing poetry, Zhukovsky became a renowned translator of the works of Friedrich von Schiller (1759–1805), and he actively encouraged Pushkin to acquaint himself with the great German poet-historian's poems and historical dramas. Although Pushkin had already been introduced to Schiller's writings at the Lycée, it was undoubtedly Zhukovsky's enthusiasm for the plays, poetry, ideas, and idealism of Schiller that stirred Pushkin's interest in that Romantic genius. For young Pushkin and many of his patriotic friends, Romanticism itself became something of a badge signifying progressive ideas and a questioning of autocracy and serfdom. Russian Romanticism had not yet settled into its distinctly conservative (even reactionary) form.[20]

In 1816, while still attending the Lycée, Pushkin met and became a friend and admirer of Pyotr Chaadaev, his senior by several years and one of the leading intellectuals of early nineteenth-century Russia. Chaadaev, whose idealism was influenced by many writers (including Schiller), quickly became one of Pushkin's mentors. In 1818, Pushkin wrote a politically risky poem, "To Chaadaev," in which he expressed very progressive ideas. Although it has been exaggerated by some scholars, the increasingly liberal Pushkin doubtless even exerted some influence on his new mentor, Chaadaev.[21] In this period, Pushkin also became fascinated by the ideas and life experience of the famous Russian radical, Alexander Radishchev, "the inspirer of liberal thought in Russia." (Radishchev was sentenced to death by Catherine the Great for writing the first Russian book challenging serfdom, *Journey from St. Petersburg to Moscow* [1790]. Catherine subsequently commuted his sentence to exile in Siberia, where he lived until Tsar Paul I released him. Although Radishchev's book was banned, it was eagerly read by every subsequent generation of Russian intellectuals.) Pushkin borrowed the title of his "Ode to Freedom" (1817) directly from Radishchev, and in that poem Pushkin expressed strong opposition to both autocracy and serfdom and even dared to condemn Tsar Paul's assassination (in which Alexander I was implicated). Widely circulated in unpublished copies, Pushkin's politically provocative "Ode to Freedom" was cherished by several future Decembrists and eventually helped convince Tsar Alexander to send the young troublemaker into exile.[22] Pushkin is usually studied as a great poet, not as a political writer or thinker. But as a young man, he played a very important part in the formation of the Russian intelligentsia. Although some scholars object to applying the term "intelligentsia" to Pushkin's generation (arguing that the intelligentsia proper only emerged in the mid-nineteenth century), the roots of the Russian intelligentsia can easily be traced back to aristocratic intellectual alienation from autocracy and serfdom in the late-eighteenth century (e.g., Radishchev). Pushkin's transitional generation played a vital role in setting the agenda for later decades. In fact, Pushkin and his circle, including Chaadaev, laid much of the foundation for the emergence of the Slavophiles and Westernizers, whose debate largely shaped the emergence of a mature Russian intelligentsia.[23]

In 1817, Pushkin was inducted into the "Arzamas Society of Obscure People," an intellectually playful literary circle (or "mock-masonic society") that was dedicated to promoting the literary reputation of Nikolai Karamzin. The Arzamas Society was composed primarily of progressive nationalists, including Vasily Zhukovsky, Pyotr Viazemsky, Sergei Uvarov, Denis Davydov, Nikita Muraviev, Mikhail Orlov, Dmitry Dashkov, the brothers Alexander and Nikolai Turgenev, and Pushkin's uncle, Vasily L. Pushkin.[24] Young Pushkin enjoyed many scintillating and ribald conversations with his fellow Arzamassians. He quickly became close friends with several of them, especially the Turgenevs. The liberal-minded Alexander Turgenev (who had helped Pushkin gain admittance to the Lycée) became one of the young poet-historian's mentors. Described as

"one of the most enlightened members of the Russian intelligentsia,"
Turgenev was a gifted historian who helped found the scientific study of
sources for reconstructing early modern Russian history. Not surprisingly, his fascination with historical sources was of considerable interest
to Pushkin. Turgenev eventually published a valuable collection of early
modern sources gleaned from Western archives, and for many years he
tirelessly provided historical documents to Russia's first two historian
laureates, Karamzin and Pushkin.[25] Alexander Turgenev strongly opposed serfdom and autocracy, but his views were moderate compared
to those of his brother, the future Decembrist, Nikolai Turgenev, who
also became one of Pushkin's mentors. Nikolai Turgenev worked actively
to promote the emancipation of the serfs and even tried (unsuccessfully)
to involve the Arzamas Society in that controversial cause. He strongly
influenced Pushkin's ideas about serfdom as well as the young poet-
historian's growing unhappiness with Tsar Alexander.[26] Other Arzamassians – including Pushkin's lifelong friend, Pyotr Viazemsky – also
advocated liberating the serfs.[27]

Arzamassians tended to lionize Nikolai Karamzin's literary skill, but
not all of them were in agreement with the safe, official Romanov interpretation of Russian history found in the historian laureate's writings.
When Karamzin published the first volume of his *History of the Russian
State* (which was dedicated to Tsar Alexander I) in 1816, it became a bestseller and stirred much praise and discussion about his "scientific" use of
sources.[28] Nevertheless, when the next seven volumes of his *History* were
published in 1818, Pushkin quickly joined fellow Arazamassians Alexander and Nikolai Turgenev (and other liberals) in strongly criticizing
Karamzin for his politically correct defense of autocracy and serfdom.[29]
Stung by Pushkin's criticism, Karamzin apparently stopped speaking to
him. Pushkin, in turn, was deeply hurt by his respected mentor's
reaction.[30] In 1819, the young poet struck back with a sharply pointed
epigram: "With elegance and simplicity his *History* / Proves to us, utterly
impartially, / The necessity of despotism / And the charm of the knout."[31]
The twenty-year-old liberal had taken an independent stand against the
venerable first historian of the Russian land. Pushkin and Karamzin,
who still cared deeply about each other, remained somewhat estranged
for many years.[32]

To the surprise of many, Karamzin proved to be more courageous in
volume nine of his *History*, which he published in 1821. There, in discussing the reign of Tsar Ivan IV (the Terrible), Karamzin launched an

unprecedented assault on Tsar Ivan's abuse of power and mistreatment of his subjects. Still firmly committed to autocracy (and, more reluctantly, to serfdom), Karamzin nonetheless forcefully condemned Ivan's despotism. Such a startling departure from the tone of earlier volumes of his *History* did not please Tsar Alexander and actually prompted some reactionary supporters of the tsar to condemn the historian laureate's views as unpatriotic. At the same time, however, volume nine prompted some former critics of Karamzin to applaud him.[33] As pleased as Pushkin undoubtedly was by Karamzin's denunciation of tyranny, the young poet (by then quite emancipated, already in trouble with the authorities, and exiled to the southern provinces) still disapproved of his old mentor's support of serfdom and continued to criticize other aspects of his work. Pushkin would undoubtedly have agreed with contemporary writers who complained that Karamzin's *History* focused only on the Russian state and basically ignored the Russian people.[34]

By 1820, Pushkin's "Ode to Freedom" and his radical ideas (including opposition to serfdom and autocracy) had gotten him into serious trouble with Tsar Alexander, who persecuted the young aristocrat along with several other progressive former Arzamassians – including the Turgenev brothers, Pyotr Viazemsky, Denis Davydov, Nikita Muraviev, and Mikhail Orlov. In exasperation, some of those harassed men eventually joined secret societies and participated in the ill-fated Decembrist Rebellion of 1825. In light of the highly-publicized and later romanticized martyrdom or exile of those heroic individuals, it is often forgotten that Pushkin was actually the first former Arzamassian to suffer punishment for politically incorrect ideas.[35] Already in exile at the time of the Decembrist Rebellion, Pushkin was not among those recklessly brave souls (who included many of his friends), but he greatly admired them for challenging autocracy and serfdom.[36] Pushkin would have agreed wholeheartedly with Peter Viazemsky's perceptive comment that the Decembrists had rebelled against the views contained in Karamzin's *History.*[37]

Pushkin remained in some form of internal exile under close surveillance by tsarist authorities from 1820 to 1826. In fact, it was only the intervention of his mentors (Karamzin, Zhukovsky, Chaadaev, and Alexander Turgenev) that prevented Tsar Alexander from sending the young liberal to Siberia. In return, Pushkin promised Karamzin that he would write nothing against the government for at least two years.[38] Nevertheless, Pushkin was sent far away from St. Petersburg and Moscow because the tsar really did fear Pushkin's pen and his ability to influence others with his dangerous ideas.[39] At first, Pushkin was sent to the southern provinces where he had considerable freedom of movement. Then, suddenly, in 1824, he was rearrested on a pretext – an intercepted private letter in which he announced that he was flirting with atheism – but he was not officially informed of the charges leveled against him. Instead, he was hastily shipped off to his family's estate in Mikhailovskoe (near Pskov), where he was placed under house arrest. Thus began his "northern exile." For the next two years, Pushkin was isolated from his friends and constantly spied upon.[40] Tsarist authorities continued to regard him with deep suspicion as a radical atheist and, at one point, even dispatched a secret agent to find out if he was "inciting the peasants to revolt."[41] He was doing no such thing, of course. Instead, the restless young man, miserable but defiant, worried about the cause of his arrest and wondered how long he would be forced to remain in exile.[42] He grew bored and increasingly frustrated with his open-ended house arrest, at times even contemplating a request for transfer to prison or to Siberia.[43] In the meantime, he read widely and continued to nurse a grudge against Tsar Alexander.[44]

Pushkin's friends urged him to use his forced isolation to attempt a large, serious work, and the idea appealed to him.[45] He had already been encouraged to throw his energy into reading and thinking about Russian history while in his southern exile.[46] Like other poet-historians of the Romantic era (and some future Decembrists), Pushkin was strongly drawn to and sympathized with historical examples of resistance to tyranny and the struggle of ordinary people for freedom.[47] In fact, in this period he often expressed interest in writing about the "heroes" of Russia's past, and he focused his reading increasingly on great crises, rebellions, and historical turning points.[48] Pushkin grew impatient with distorted accounts of such phenomena found in patriotic histories, and he came to believe that real-life characters and popular uprisings could be more accurately and powerfully portrayed in drama than in a sentimental narrative. While still in his southern exile (and reflecting his hostility to autocracy), Pushkin toyed with the idea of writing historical dramas based on old Russian chronicle accounts of the resistance to Prince Riurik's "autocratic" rule in the ninth century and the development of "republican" consciousness in medieval Novgorod.[49] Pushkin was well aware that this subject had already been famously dealt with in Yakov Kniazhnin's tragic drama, *Vadim of Novgorod* (1789) – a mildly provocative play that had been harshly denounced as "dangerously republican" by Catherine the Great, who not only banned it but also ordered the search of private homes in order to confiscate all known copies. Nevertheless, like Radischchev's *Journey from St. Petersburg to Moscow*, Kniazhnin's banned play was avidly read and discussed by the next two generations of Russia's proto-intelligentsia.[50] Although Pushkin soon abandoned these early projects, he continued to contemplate the use of historical material in the form of a play as a way to bring past heroes to life and to indirectly discuss contemporary problems. Among the works that influenced the exiled young poet were early nineteenth-century "civic comedies" (including plays by Nikolai Khmelnitsky and Alexander Griboedov) and the future Decembrist Kondraty Ryleev's *Bogdan Khmelnitsky* (1822), an historical drama about the famous leader of the "Ukrainian revolution" of 1648.[51] Once ensconced in Mikhailovskoe, the poet-historian eventually settled down to write his *Comedy about Tsar Boris and Grishka Otrepiev*. As Stephanie Sandler correctly claims, it "bears the mark of his exile."[52]

There are many reasons why Pushkin ended up writing a play about the Time of Troubles. While in his southern exile, he had access to early accounts of the Pretender Dmitry and to the first book ever written about "revolutions" in Russian history – Jacques Lacombe's *Histoire des revolutions de l'empire de Russie* (1760), which included a section on the Time of Troubles.[53] In fact, Pushkin made a concerted effort to gain information about all three great popular uprisings against the tsars – the rebellions led by Stepan Razin in the 1670s and Emilian Pugachev in the 1770s as well as the poorly understood uprisings associated with the Pretender Dmitry during the Time of Troubles. Pushkin was particularly intrigued by Razin, regarding him as "the only poetic figure in Russian history."[54] He also greatly admired the cossacks who participated in all early modern Russian rebellions, attending especially to Pugachev, Russia's most famous rebel pretender (about whom he would eventually write the first scholarly book-length historical study).[55] Once transferred to Mikhailovskoe, Pushkin continued to read about and to request material on Razin, Pugachev, and cossack rebels.[56]

With plenty of time on his hands, the poet-historian also began to study the Pushkin family papers. He was, of course, already proud of his family's ancient lineage and high status.[57] But he soon discovered, to his delight, that many of his illustrious ancestors had themselves been rebels and troublemakers. Pushkin read with fascination about family members who had been exiled to Siberia by Boris Godunov and Peter the

Great and about other Pushkins who had opposed Catherine the Great's coup d'état against Peter III or were associated with the "radical" Alexander Radishchev.[58] The poet-historian also discovered that many of his ancestors had been prominent during Russia's Time of Troubles. Several Pushkins served as military commanders under Tsar Boris Godunov and his successors, and at least five Pushkins were on hand to sign the official proclamation affirming the election of Mikhail Romanov as tsar in 1613.[59] Of particular interest to young Alexander was the remarkable career of his ancestor, Gavrila Pushkin, who became a very important supporter of the Pretender Dmitry and was the person most responsible for inciting the common people of Moscow to overthrow the Godunov dynasty on June 1, 1605.[60]

Pushkin made up his mind to write an ambitious historical drama about the Time of Troubles immediately after reading the newly published volumes ten and eleven of Karamzin's *History,* which appeared in 1824. Karamzin's gripping tale of the rise to power of Boris Godunov, the murder of Tsarevich Dmitry in Uglich, Tsar Boris's election and reign, the great famine of 1601–3, the remarkable career of the Pretender Dmitry, and the popular uprisings that helped overthrow the Godunovs convinced Pushkin that the Time of Troubles would make an excellent subject for historical drama. No doubt the chance to showcase one of his own "rebellious" ancestors also appealed to the young exile. Partly inspired by the works of Shakespeare and Schiller, the poet-historian channeled his anger and frustration into writing a boldly defiant and subversive play that made provocative use of historical sources to express his own proud, rebellious spirit and his politically incorrect views of Russian history, autocracy, and serfdom. Pushkin also undertook radical innovations in dramatic form, language, and versification in composing his *Comedy.* The result was a remarkable tour de force and a major but decidedly risky achievement in the history of Russian drama. According to Brett Cooke, "the potential danger of his undertaking may explain why Pushkin cited *Boris Godunov* as his favorite work."[61]

In writing his play, Pushkin really did plan to revolutionize Russian drama.[62] It is important to remember that he belonged to a generation of artists and intellectuals who deplored the poor quality of early nineteenth-century Russian historical drama and who openly called for a new type of history play. Pushkin shared the annoyance of his friend Pyotr Viazemsky (and many others) with Russian historical dramas that were heavy-handedly patriotic, historically inaccurate, and prone to portray tyrants as benevolent rulers.[63] In the Age of Romanticism, in Russia as elsewhere in Europe, Shakespeare's plays were being "rediscovered" and were frequently held up as a model of realistic and vigorous historical drama. It is certainly no surprise that Pushkin turned to Shakespeare for some inspiration in writing his own "revolutionary" play.[64] Shakespeare's concerns with such issues as the nature of kingship, legitimacy, the relationship between rulers and subjects, and the personality and psychology of monarchs were of great interest to Pushkin. Also of interest to Pushkin were Shakespeare's use of true-to-life characters from all walks of life, the naturalness of his characters' language, and his attention to historical detail.[65] It is also worth noting that Pushkin had been surrounded by Shakespeare enthusiasts for most of his life; Karamzin loved Shakespeare, and Viazemsky and many other friends (including future Decembrists) adored the English bard.[66] Scholars who have carefully studied Pushkin's *Boris Godunov* have found many Shakespearean elements in it.[67] Not surprisingly, the first Shakespeare play completely translated into Russian (in 1783), *Richard III*, has been frequently cited as an important source of inspiration for Pushkin's historical drama.[68] One of the principal attractions of Shakespeare's plays to Pushkin was their brilliant mixture of serious and comedic elements. As mentioned earlier, the poet-historian had already studied Russian "civic comedy" and had even briefly experimented with the use of comedy in historical drama while in his southern exile; once in Mikhailovskoe, he carefully studied Shakespeare's masterful way of using comedy to enhance the serious content of a play.[69] Here it should be noted that, in addition to Shakespeare, Pushkin's *Comedy* was modestly influenced by at least two Russian comedies – Griboedov's *Woe from Wit* (1824) and Khmelnitsky's *Castles in the Air* (1818).[70]

Karamzin's *History* was, of course, the most important source for *Boris Godunov*, which has led many scholars to assume that Pushkin adhered closely to Karamzin's interpretation of the Time of Troubles.[71] But Pushkin's play actually departs from Karamzin's interpretation of Russian history in important ways.[72] Among other differences, Pushkin continued to reject Karamzin's essentially positive portrayal of autocracy and serfdom, but this time he did so by heeding the sage advice of the poet Ivan Dmitriev: "It's necessary to beat Karamzin not with epigrams, but with chronicles."[73]

In composing his *Comedy*, Pushkin carefully studied Karamzin's *History* – especially his voluminous notes (*Primechaniia*), which systematically explored sources and frequently pointed to conclusions that differed from those found in the politically safe main text. Controversial topics tended to be handled fairly objectively in the *Primechaniia*, which stood as a model of academic rigor in the early nineteenth century.[74] According to Pushkin, "Karamzin is the first of our historians and the last of our chroniclers ... wherever his tale is unsatisfactory, one can turn to his sources; he does not make guesses in them."[75] Pushkin was fascinated by Karamzin's sources and energetically sought direct access to them as well as to histories of Russia *other* than Karamzin's. According to David Bethea, the play Pushkin wrote amounted to a "spirited dialogue" with Karamzin's sources.[76] In fact, Pushkin's interest in the Time of Troubles had been so stimulated by reading Karamzin's *Primechaniia* that he settled down to carefully study Russian chronicles and foreign accounts – conducting serious historical research for the first time in his life.[77] Pushkin developed into an excellent scholar with a deep understanding of Russian history.

Russian chronicle accounts of the Time of Troubles proved to be very important sources for Pushkin's play.[78] The poet-historian praised the chronicles highly, and he was as much interested in capturing their unique historical perspective and archaic language as he was in using the specific information in them concerning Boris Godunov and the Pretender Dmitry.[79] The chronicle that most influenced Pushkin's play was undoubtedly the *Letopis' o mnogikh miatezhakh* (1788) [*Chronicle of Many Rebellions*], a colorful, semi-official Romanov interpretation of the Troubles that Pushkin used with caution. One version of that chronicle was actually titled *Concerning a True Calamity that Befell the State of Muscovy and Grishka Otrepiev*.[80] Another chronicle that Pushkin made use of – one written by a monk who lived in the Trinity Monastery during the Time of Troubles – was Avraamy Palitsyn's *Skazanie ob osade Troitsko-Sergieva monastyria ot Poliakov i Litvy, i o byvshikh potom v Rossii miatezhakh* (1784) [*Tale of the Siege of the Trinity Monastery by the Poles and Lithuanians and of the Rebellions which have since occurred in Russia*].[81] Pushkin even toyed with the idea of using an archaic-sounding, long chronicle title as the title of his play; and at one point he came up with the *Comedy about a True Calamity that Befell the State of Muscovy, about Tsar Boris and Grishka Otrepiev; Written by God's Servant Alexander Son of Sergei Pushkin in the Year 7333* [1825], *on the site of the*

2. Pushkin's drawing of Historian Laureate Nikolai Karamzin and some devils. Detail from the margin of a manuscript page of the scene "Noch'. Kel'ia v Chudovom monastyre" in the rough draft of *Komediia o tsare Borise i o Grishke Otrep'eve*. From Institut russkoi literatury (Pushkinskii Dom) RAN, Rukopisnyi otdel, fond 244, opis' 1, No. 835, list 56. Courtesy of the Russian Academy of Sciences.

Ancient Town of Voronich.[82] According to John Bayley, Pushkin got the idea of giving his *Comedy* an "affectedly antiquarian" title from his future enemy Faddei Bulgarin, who had praised Russian chronicles highly in a publication Pushkin read while in Mikhailovskoe – *Ruskaia Taliia.*[83] In fact, Bulgarin also discussed the finer points of Russian "comedy" in the same book.[84] It is just as likely, however, that Pushkin was influenced by Nikolai Grech's essay on the development of the Russian theater, which was also included in *Ruskaia Taliia.* Grech's essay contained the long and archaic names of several old Russian "comedies."[85]

Whatever the source of his inspiration, Pushkin playfully imagined himself as a chronicler and his play as a chronicle of the first phase of the Time of Troubles. He organized scenes as if they were chronicle entries, with dates preceding titles of scenes, and ended his *Comedy* with a mock-serious chronicler's prayer: "Glory be to the Father, and the Son, and to the Holy Ghost, Amen." Pushkin took his responsibilities as a chronicler seriously. Not only does his *Comedy* stick closely to the known facts about the Time of Troubles, but Pushkin also imitated the archaic language used in the chronicles.[86] He was also careful to use precise seventeenth-century Russian terms for decrees, institutions, officials, aristocrats, and various groups of gentry and common people. (This remarkable historical accuracy is noted in particular cases in the annotation to the *Comedy* contained in this book.) In addition, Pushkin actively sought material to enhance the historical accuracy of his play and to add depth to his characters. Scholars have discovered that in some places he clearly preferred chronicle accounts to what he read in Karamzin's *History* and that in other places Pushkin used information from chronicles that had not been included in Karamzin's text or in his *Primechaniia.*[87] In fact, gaps in Karamzin's narrative and character sketches provided opportunities for the poet-historian to dig deeper than Karamzin in order to better understand many personalities.[88] For example, Pushkin included material in his *Comedy* that was not derived from Karamzin concerning the Pretender Dmitry's strong attachment to his wounded horse ("Forest" scene); the *narod*'s lack of enthusiasm for the new tsar, including the idea of generating fake tears of joy ("Maiden's Field. Novodevichy Convent" scene); and Prince Vasily Shuisky's behind-the-scenes opposition to the election of Boris Godunov ("Kremlin Palace: February 20, 1598" scene) – all of which he found in Russian chronicles or in the published works of the eighteenth-century historian Mikhail Shcherbatov.[89]

Pushkin's brilliant characterization of Prince Shuisky as a clever, hypocritical intriguer was not only much more sophisticated and historically accurate than Karamzin's portrayal, but the poet-historian actually included information about Shuisky in his *Comedy* that is more reliable than that found in several highly reputable twentieth-century scholarly studies of the Time of Troubles.[90] Pushkin also made Shuisky the subject of one of the *Comedy*'s "good jokes." In the scene "Tsarskaia duma" ("The Tsar's Council"), Prince Shuisky objects to the Patriarch's idea of bringing the remains of the child-martyr, "St. Dmitry," from Uglich to Moscow in order to prove to the Russian people that the Pretender Dmitry was an impostor. Shuisky says, "It will be said that we crudely turn a shrine into a tool for secular affairs." Pushkin and his intended audience were well aware that it was actually Shuisky himself (after orchestrating the assassination of Tsar Dmitry) who devised the bizarre and cynical spectacle of the transfer of St. Dmitry's miraculously preserved and "miracle-working" relics to a Kremlin cathedral – an almost comical episode except for the fact that a "fresh" innocent child had to be murdered in order to perpetrate the hoax.[91]

Another example of Pushkin's careful research and highly developed historical imagination is his remarkable characterization of Pyotr Basmanov, one of Tsar Boris's best generals. Not only is the psychological portrait of Basmanov in the *Comedy* far more sophisticated than Karamzin's, but the poet-historian's exploration of Basmanov's struggle for status and advancement within the confines of a rigid hierarchy based on birth instead of merit is highly accurate and thought provoking. Pushkin's audience could not have failed to smile at Basmanov's discussion with Tsar Boris of the evils of appointing generals based on family background instead of talent (in the scene "Moscow: The Tsar's Chambers").[92] In fact, so accurate and successful was Pushkin's portrayal of Basmanov that his literary rival, Faddei Bulgarin, could not resist plagiarizing it a few years later – a topic to be discussed in chapter 3.

One more example of the poet-historian's independent research and judgment is worth mentioning here. While writing his play, Pushkin had access to two unusually positive, *source-based* characterizations of the bright and energetic Maryna Mniszech that were published in the journal *Severnyi arkhiv:* Faddei Bulgarin's "Marina Mniszekh, supruga Dimitriia Samozvantsa" (1824) and an eyewitness account of the Time of Troubles, "Dnevnik Samuila Maskevicha" (1825). These two works may very well have influenced Pushkin's portrayal of Maryna. By contrast, no

Russian sources available to Pushkin spoke positively of her, and none of the Polish sources for the *Severnyi arkhiv* material concerning Maryna had been included in Karamzin's text or notes.[93]

Of particular interest to the poet-historian Pushkin (as it had been to Alexander Turgenev) in Karamzin's *Primechaniia* was his groundbreaking use of early modern West European sources that frequently contradicted more familiar native Russian sources.[94] In fact, it was Karamzin's keen interest in foreign sources that led directly to the systematic gathering and copying of manuscripts, the republication of many rare books, and the production of Russian translations of West European accounts of the Time of Troubles. Thanks to Karamzin, the study of foreign accounts of early modern Russia quickly blossomed into a vigorous branch of Russian historiography.[95] Significantly, Karamzin's own portrayal of Boris Godunov and his *History*'s influential discussion of the parallel fates of Tsarevich Dmitry in 1591 and Tsar Boris's son, Fedor, in 1605 depended heavily upon seventeenth-century West European sources – especially the Saxon mercenary Conrad Bussow's account of the Time of Troubles.[96]

Pushkin quickly discovered that foreign accounts (unlike censored native sources) made it abundantly clear that in 1598 the Russia people had been forced to cheer for the new tsar, Boris Godunov, even though many of them actually regarded him as a regicide and usurper. Furthermore, those same foreign sources clearly showed that the Russian people (including Pushkin's ancestor, Gavrila Pushkin) welcomed the Pretender Dmitry with joy and helped put him on the throne. Pushkin was struck by the historically and dramatically valuable insights contained in those foreign accounts – insights not found in Karamzin's main text.[97]

One of the most important foreign accounts used by Karamzin and studied by Pushkin was written and published in 1607 by Captain Jacques Margeret (co-commander of foreign troops under Tsar Boris and captain of Tsar Dmitry's bodyguard). Although quite rare, Margeret's excellent book, *Estat de l'Empire de Russie et Grand Duché de Moscovie* – written by command of King Henri IV of France – had been extremely influential in the West and was used extensively by French historians during the eighteenth century. Margeret's account was vaguely known by Russia's first serious historians, Vasily Tatishchev and Mikhail Shcherbatov, but it was actually Karamzin's strong interest in Margeret's book that led to its republication and widespread use by Russian historians in the nineteenth century.[98] So rare was Margeret's book by the time

Karamzin wished to make use of it, however, that he was obliged to request that a new edition be printed in Paris in 1821.[99] Karamzin had a particularly high regard for the Frenchman's remarkably objective and accurate account, in part at least because Margeret shared his belief that absolute monarchy was the best form of government for Russia.[100] Karamzin made extensive use of Margeret's account in composing volume eleven of his *History*.

Pushkin managed to obtain a copy of the new edition of Margeret's book.[101] He too was captivated by the Frenchman's accurate first-hand account and made extensive use of it. He even went so far as to make Captain Margeret a minor character in his play and to have him speak some colorful lines from his own book.[102] Margeret's appearance in Pushkin's play was not merely intended as a joke, however. Margeret's famous account was the most important source claiming that the Pretender Dmitry was not a bloodthirsty defrocked monk intent upon destroying the Russian Orthodox Church (the view of most Russian chronicles and of Karamzin) but was instead a brave warrior-prince with a good education and an aversion to bloodshed – a heroic figure who was very popular with the Russian people.[103] Pushkin was intrigued with Margeret's extremely positive assessment of Dmitry and by the evidence he found in several foreign accounts that Dmitry managed to come to power by means of popular uprisings in support of his claim to the throne. Pushkin was particularly struck by the fact that, in support of Dmitry, the Russian people had for the very first time dared to rebel against a reigning tsar.[104]

At the time Pushkin was writing his play, the traditional Russian view of the Pretender Dmitry was entirely negative; he was regarded by Karamzin and many others as an evil impostor and a tool of Catholic Poland and the Jesuits.[105] Based upon a careful reading of historical sources, Pushkin moved sharply away from the standard interpretation of Dmitry as an obvious fraud who had been quickly rejected by the Russian people and toward a more historically accurate view. Many Russians, it turned out, really did believe that the Pretender Dmitry truly was the son of Ivan the Terrible, and they were willing to fight for him against the "usurper" Boris Godunov.[106] That historical insight made Dmitry's victory over the Godunovs more complex and far more interesting than Karamzin's chronicle-based version of the story. Pushkin saw immediately that the Pretender Dmitry had real positive theatrical value and that he had been an admirable, romantic character – a view remarkably similar to that found in Schiller's *Demetrius* (to be discussed below).[107] Pushkin became quite sympathetic to Tsar Dmitry, a "liberal" ruler who really did believe that he was the true Dmitry and who wished to govern in the interests of his subjects rather than as a tyrant.[108] Pushkin actually compared Tsar Dmitry to the heroic and highly respected King Henri IV of France. (He took that idea directly from Margeret and Karamzin.) He also compared Tsar Dmitry to Peter the Great.[109]

Until very recently, most historical accounts of the Time of Troubles contained very negative views of Tsar Dmitry, essentially the same as those found in Russian chronicles and in Karamzin's *History*.[110] Therefore, scholars and literary critics quite naturally assumed that Pushkin must have shared their own outrage at the evil Grishka Otrepiev's allegedly lewd and violent behavior. This accounts for all the misguided attempts to portray Pushkin's interpretation of the Pretender Dmitry as a negative one. This problem was compounded by the use of the so-called canonical text of *Boris Godunov*, which omitted a number of Pushkin's provocative statements about Dmitry. For example, the 1831 published version of Pushkin's play deleted a key scene ("Maryna's Dressing Room") in which it is revealed that a great many people, including Dmitry's future bride, believed that the Pretender was indeed the son of Ivan the Terrible. The veracity of the scene in terms of ideology and psychology is often overlooked because of its comic, "gossipy" tone; indeed, as shall be discussed in chapter 6, for Pushkin, the truth of a situation came out as often (or more often) in comedy as in tragedy. The canonical text also omitted the speech of Pyotr Khrushchov in the scene "Krakov. Dom Vishnevetskogo" ("Cracow. Wiśniowiecki's House") in which he reveals that the Russian *narod*, and even some boyars, firmly believed in Dmitry and joyfully awaited his return to Russia in order to claim his throne.[111] Having read his sources carefully, Pushkin confidently moved beyond Karamzin's politically safe interpretation of Tsar Dmitry. Pushkin was also well aware of the great debates among historians of his own generation concerning Dmitry's true identity and intentions.[112] His own sympathetic and historically accurate portrayal of the Pretender Dmitry was consciously intended to shock his audience. But it was not intended just for effect. Pushkin's research had led him to a serious (and "dangerous") conclusion about Dmitry and the rebellions that brought him to power.

Astonishingly enough, based upon the books available to him while in exile, Pushkin came up with the original idea that the Pretender Dmitry's successful military campaign against Boris Godunov was tremendously aided by the *narod*'s expectation that Dmitry would abolish nascent serfdom (first fixed in place by Boris Godunov when he was Regent) by restoring the St. George's Day right of peasant movement.[113] This is clearly reflected in the play, especially in the conversation between Afanasy Pushkin and Vasily Shuisky in the scene "Moskva. Dom Shuiskogo" ("Moscow. Shuiskii's House").[114] In startling contrast to Karamzin's *History*, Pushkin's play contains the first written claim that Dmitry's positive relationship with the Russian masses was, at least in part, dependent upon the promise to abolish serfdom.[115] No wonder the *narod* shouts "Long live Tsar Dmitry Ivanovich!" at the end of Pushkin's *Comedy*. The poet-historian did not make this up; his observation was historically accurate.[116] And by ending his *Comedy* with the standard cheer found at the end of many patriotic Russian historical dramas, Pushkin certainly meant to put new life and a new twist into that well-worn cliché.[117] Pushkin's understanding of the *narod*'s strong attraction to Dmitry was far deeper than Karamzin's.[118] It was also far more controversial, and it deeply shocked tsarist censors when they finally saw the finished play.[119] They suspected, rightly, that the dangerous young liberal aristocrat was using his play to comment on sensitive contemporary issues.[120]

At this point, it will be useful to consider another important but generally overlooked influence on Pushkin's *Comedy* – the work of the great German Romantic poet-historian, Friedrich von Schiller. Schiller's reputation loomed large throughout Europe in the early nineteenth century, and serious discussions about reforming Russian drama – in which Pushkin actively participated – invariably drew on his ideas and practice.[121] Revolutions and the struggle of ordinary people against oppression were the substance of Schiller's plays.[122] His realistic historical dramas about freedom fighters were very popular among Pushkin's friends, including some future Decembrists.[123] As noted earlier, in his youth Pushkin had become familiar with some of Schiller's works and discussed them with Vasily Zhukovsky, Russia's foremost translator of Schiller. Even in exile, the poet-historian closely monitored the St. Petersburg staging of Zhukovsky's translation of Schiller's play *Maid of Orleans*. Pushkin was attracted to Schiller's historical dramas not only because of the liberal values contained in them but also because Schiller conducted extensive historical research before writing his plays, and the high degree of historical accuracy in his dramas made them look and feel far more realistic than anything seen on stage before. That historical realism definitely influenced Pushkin's historical drama, a point made by several of his contemporaries.[124] In fact, while Pushkin was working on his *Comedy,* one of his friends – Nikolai Raevsky – exhorted him to emulate Schiller's careful study of historical sources before writing a play intended to reform the Russian theater.[125] And when Pushkin finally read his newly completed *Comedy* to his friends and fellow poets in 1826, they were enthralled by it and compared Pushkin to Shakespeare and Schiller.[126]

Assessing the extent of Schiller's influence on Pushkin's historical drama is both complicated and enriched by the fact that Schiller was writing a play about Russia's Time of Troubles when he died in 1805. His unfinished masterpiece, *Demetrius,* had been very carefully researched, and it presented a highly accurate and decidedly sympathetic portrait of the Pretender Dmitry – one strikingly similar to that found in Pushkin's *Comedy.* Did Pushkin read Schiller's *Demetrius* while working on his *Comedy?* Scholars investigating this question have not yet reached a consensus.[127] Although there are some remarkable similarities between the two plays, there are also important differences. For example, unlike Pushkin's conscious pretender, Grishka Otrepiev, Schiller's Dmitry grew up in a monastery believing that he was the true son of Ivan the Terrible – only to learn late in the play that he was not the true Dmitry but had instead been duped from childhood by a cynical old monk who planned to use him to topple Boris Godunov. Despite such differences, however, Pushkin was certainly aware of the existence of Schiller's unfinished play. It is worth noting that Zhukovsky had planned to translate *Demetrius* before Pushkin's exile (but then changed his mind); and Pushkin, while writing his *Comedy,* specifically requested a new French translation of the collected works of Schiller, *Oeuvres dramatiques de F. Schiller, traduite de l'allemand* (1821), which included his unfinished *Demetrius.*[128] (Pushkin did not read German.)

Especially intriguing is the possible influence of Schiller's play on the highly original assertion contained in Pushkin's *Comedy* of a direct link between popular support for Dmitry and his alleged willingness to abolish serfdom. Consider this: Twenty years before Pushkin wrote his play, Schiller presented Dmitry as "the people's friend" who planned to abolish serfdom and who was enthusiastically supported by armed peasants and cossacks (act 2, scene 3). In fact, one of Dmitry's supporters is appropriately named "Razin" (act 2, scene 2). Early in the play, Schiller had Dmitry declare: "The glorious freedom [of Poland] I will transplant within my native land. The bondman shall be made a happy man. I would not lord it over slavish souls" (act 1, scene 1). Although Schiller had the king of Poland immediately try to talk Dmitry out of taking such a radical step, later in the play Dmitry's triumph over the Godunovs is referred to as a "revolution" (act 3).[129] It is quite possible that Schiller's provocative interpretation of a radical, even revolutionary, Dmitry may have influenced Pushkin's daring *Comedy*. On the other hand, it is also possible that some of the similarities between the two plays may simply be the result of the careful historical research conducted by the two brilliant poet-historians.[130] In fact, it turns out that Schiller studied some of the very same sources that Pushkin later consulted, and – further complicating the issue – the great German writer actually sought the advice of Russia's first historian laureate, Nicholas Karamzin, about which sources to read concerning Russia's horrific Time of Troubles.[131]

Among the more important sources used by both Schiller and Pushkin in writing their plays were Mikhail Shcherbatov's *Kratkaia povest' o byvshikh v Rossii samozvantsakh* [*Brief Tale of Former Pretenders in Russia*] (2nd ed., 1778) and a very popular history of Russia, *Histoire de Russie,* written by Pierre Charles Levesque that was first published in 1782.[132] Significantly (as noted earlier), Shcherbatov had been one of the very first scholars to suggest that rebellions in the Time of Troubles were related to the enserfment of the Russian peasants in the 1590s. It is possible, therefore, that both poet-historians merely connected the dots between Shcherbatov's observations and Dmitry's campaign for the throne. And careful study of Levesque's famous history, which painted a very sympathetic image of Tsar Dmitry, reveals that it was based primarily on Captain Margeret's influential little book.[133] Thus, Margeret's account seems to have powerfully influenced the image of Dmitry found in the writings of Pushkin *and* Schiller.

Nevertheless, it will take more than Margeret's book to explain the remarkable similarities between Schiller's *Demetrius* and Pushkin's *Comedy*. In sharp contrast to Karamzin, both Schiller and Pushkin portrayed Tsar Dmitry as a romantic hero who espoused values closer to those of the French Revolution than to medieval Muscovy. That requires explanation, but – so far, at least – scholars have not done a very good job of accounting for the two poet-historians' fascination with the reform-minded Tsar Dmitry. In the case of Pushkin, as might be expected, the problem is directly related to most scholars' and critics' assumption that Pushkin shared their own aversion to Dmitry – an error compounded by their reliance upon the canonical text of *Boris Godunov*. In the case of Schiller, there is a different issue involved. Most studies of *Demetrius* have criticized Schiller for being more interested in using Dmitry as a symbol of liberal values than in trying to understand the real historical Tsar Dmitry. But the passages in *Demetrius* invariably cited to demonstrate this "problem" actually reveal the critics' own profound ignorance of the historical sources studied by the great German Romantic. For example, Schiller is frequently criticized for an "ahistorical" and "unbelievable" scene in which Dmitry is rejected as an impostor by his putative mother, the nun Marfa.[134] In fact, Schiller was merely making use of a well-known early seventeenth-century Russian chronicle account of the assassination of Tsar Dmitry.[135] Schiller really did try to understand the historical character he was writing about. And, of course, so did Pushkin. Both writers were tireless researchers and excellent historians. But, beyond a general interest in popular rebellions, why were they so interested in Dmitry?

It is well known that Schiller and Pushkin were both fascinated by pretenders and usurpers in Russian history. Schiller was actually writing a play about the English pretender Perkin Warbeck, who claimed to be King Henry VII, when he suddenly dropped that project in order to write *Demetrius;* and Pushkin went on to write the first historical monograph about Emilian Pugachev, the man who pretended to be Catherine the Great's dead husband (Tsar Peter III) in order to topple her from power.[136] In fact, it seems likely that Schiller and Pushkin were both influenced in their choice of subject matter by the spectacle of the powerful and bloody Pugachev Rebellion (1773–74) that challenged serfdom from below and terrified Catherine II and most Russian lords. In this context, it is interesting to note that both Schiller and Pushkin were well aware that the nervous usurper, Catherine the Great, had been greatly displeased by the German playwright Johann August von Kotzebue (1761–1819) for his mediocre historical drama, *Demetrius Iwanowitsch. Zaar von Moscau,* which was performed in 1782, less than a decade after the suppression of the Pugachev Rebellion. Kotzebue actually had the temerity to portray Tsar Dmitry as the real son of Ivan the Terrible and not as an odious impostor. Catherine's officials were shocked by that and suspected that Kotzebue's play might be a thinly veiled commentary on the empress' seizure of power. As a result, the Russian government forced Kotzebue to change the title of his play (removing the word "Zaar") and to publicly acknowledge that Dmitry had really been the impostor Grishka Otrepiev. Kotzebue was also not allowed to put his play on stage again or to publish a Russian translation of it.[137] (For students of the fate of Pushkin's *Comedy*, this seems hauntingly familiar.) It is possible that Schiller and Pushkin were both influenced by the novelty and fate of Kotzebue's play. It is worth noting that before Pushkin was sent into exile, the young poet attended performances of Kotzebue's less controversial plays in St. Petersburg; and, in 1819, Pushkin (like many of his friends) was shocked to learn of Kotzebue's assassination at the hands of a radical student – an infamous event that triggered Prince Metternich's reactionary crackdown on German universities and the press.[138]

What else may have motivated both poet-historians to study and write about Dmitry? Consider this: It has long been known that the portrayal of Boris Godunov as a regicide in Pushkin's play was intended, on one level at least, to criticize the exile's tormentor, Tsar Alexander I, who was despised by Pushkin for (among other things) complicity in the murder of Alexander's father, Tsar Paul, in 1801.[139] Strangely enough, close examination of Schiller's decision to write *Demetrius* reveals that one of his primary motivations was his shock at the assassination of Tsar Paul.[140] Clearly, more work needs to be done on the subject of Schiller's influence on Pushkin, and it seems likely that future research will uncover additional connections and parallels between Schiller's *Demetrius* and Pushkin's *Comedy*.

As might be expected, in addition to subversive commentary on serfdom and regicide, Pushkin used his historical drama to playfully express his own religious skepticism and to make fun of the Russian Orthodox Church.[141] More important, in his *Comedy* Pushkin took aim at autocracy and – indirectly – at Tsar Alexander I. Among other concerns, the poet-historian was interested in the "metamorphosis of a humane and educated monarch into a cruel and suspicious ruler."[142] In some ways, Pushkin's play amounts to an aristocratic meditation on the problems of unrestricted autocracy.[143] His historically accurate portrayal of Boris Godunov as a tyrant (à la Tiberius) is quite effective and differs in significant ways from Karamzin's softer interpretation – a point easily overlooked by scholars using the canonical text of Pushkin's play and by the general public who recall primarily the sentimentally reworked scenes in Musorgsky's opera rather than the hard-hitting second half of Pushkin's play.[144] Pushkin's portrayal of Boris Godunov as a regicide and tyrant really did amount to a thinly veiled denunciation of Tsar Alexander's complicity in the murder of his father as well as his increasingly reactionary policies in the years following the defeat of Napoleon.[145]

One of the ways Pushkin accomplished his subversive goals was by inventing the character Prince Kurbsky, the imaginary son of the real Prince Andrei Kurbsky who became a bitter foe of Ivan the Terrible. Andrei Kurbsky's polemic with Tsar Ivan about the problems of autocracy (with Kurbsky taking the aristocratic point of view against despotism) was extremely famous and controversial by the early nineteenth century. In fact, while in Mikhailovskoe, Pushkin read Boris M. Fedorov's novel about Andrei Kurbsky, *Kniaz' Kurbskii*, which was first published in installments in 1825. (Interestingly enough, the novel included a holy fool as one of the characters.)[146] It is also possible that Pushkin read an article about Kurbsky written by K. F. Kalaidovich that was published in *Severnyi Arkhiv* in 1824.[147] More important, Karamzin had used Kurbsky's provocative writings extensively in describing Tsar Ivan's excesses, but he had always been careful to denounce Andrei Kurbsky as a "traitor." Pushkin, on the other hand, was quite sympathetic to Andrei Kurbsky and his powerful aristocratic critique of autocracy.[148] As a result, Pushkin made his own fictional Prince Kurbsky an extremely attractive and heroic character – the effect of which is to bolster the image of Boris Godunov as tyrant.[149] There are also echoes of Andrei Kurbsky's eloquent challenge to Tsar Ivan embedded in Pushkin's play. For example, at the end of the scene "Noch'. Kel'ia v Chudovom monastyre" ("Night. A Cell in the Chudov Monastery"), Grigory Otrepiev says of Tsar Boris: "You'll not escape the judgement of the world, / You'll not escape the judgement too of God." That statement is very similar to several passages contained in Kurbsky's letters to Ivan the Terrible.[150] (Equally interesting, in the *Comedy*'s scene "Granitsa Litovskaia" ["The Lithuanian Border"], Pushkin has Kurbsky's son refer to Russia as "Holy Rus" – a memorable term that originated in writings attributed to Prince Andrei Kurbsky and that was much discussed in the early nineteenth century.)[151] When describing the excesses of Boris Godunov in his *Comedy*, Pushkin probably had contemporary tsarist tyranny in mind. Later, in 1827, Pushkin boldly declared that he would write about Tsar Alexander "with the pen of Kurbsky."[152]

Pushkin was understandably proud of his "revolutionary" historical drama, and his *Comedy* was received with great enthusiasm by Russia's leading intellectuals and poets in 1826.[153] In Pushkin's play as originally written, the opening and closing scenes are paralleled (on the surface at least) to good, Shakespearean effect. Pushkin contrasted the cynical *narod*'s unenthusiastic response to the accession of Boris Godunov in the third scene of the play, "Maidens' Field" (which was omitted from the 1831 published edition), with the *narod*'s enthusiastic cheer for Tsar Dmitry in the final scene. Thus, the original ending of the play is dramatically powerful in its cathartic, reunifying structure. Pushkin's *Comedy* is a highly original, source-based work in many ways reminiscent of *Richard III*. For instance, the 1825 version of *Boris Godunov* contained a sophisticated but decidedly unofficial meditation on the Time of Troubles which challenged a number of Karamzin's assumptions about Tsar Dmitry, popular consciousness, and the meaning and nature of rebellions in early modern Russia. As such, it was certainly not calculated to please Pushkin's old mentor or to curry favor at court. In fact, just before Pushkin finished writing his *Comedy*, he wrote to his friend Pyotr Viazemsky: "Zhukovsky says that the Tsar will forgive me because of my tragedy – hardly, my dear fellow. Although it is written in a good spirit, there's no way I could hide my ears completely under the pointed cap of the holy fool. They stick out!"[154] Nevertheless, it should be remembered that Pushkin himself distrusted popular violence and was somewhat fearful of Russian peasants rising against serfdom, so the *narod*'s cheer for Tsar Dmitry – which seems to end the play on a "happy" or "comic" note – may actually have been Pushkin's clever but shocking reminder to his audience of the possible consequences of an uprising by the Russian people.[155] Pushkin's contemporaries were well aware that Tsar Dmitry's victory was followed within the year by his assassination, a long and bloody civil war, and foreign intervention that nearly destroyed Russia before Mikhail Romanov's election finally put an end to the Time of Troubles.

Pushkin's take on autocracy and serfdom in his *Comedy* – in turn playful, provocative, and seditious – accurately reflected the general concerns of many members of Russia's young proto-intelligentsia. But his challenge to the official Romanov interpretation of the Time of Troubles and his discussion of the taboo subject of rebellion against serfdom made his play stand out sharply from most other historical and literary works produced in early nineteenth-century Russia. Pushkin scholars have been slow to acknowledge that not until 1849 was any other Russian writer allowed to publish anything remotely similar concerning popular uprisings using Dmitry's name, and even then some tsarist censors considered the topic too dangerous to publish.[156] Obviously, Pushkin hoped that his play would demonstrate his strong (but not naive) commitment to liberal values and that it would put an end to rumors that, while in exile, he had somehow "sold out."[157] Several scholars have even noticed a distinctly "Decembrist spirit" in Pushkin's historical drama.[158]

One of Pushkin's main goals in writing his *Comedy* was to playfully challenge Karamzin's conservative view of history.[159] In fact, over the course of many years, Pushkin wrote several "ironic rejoinders" to Karamzin's works – including *Istoriia sela Goriukhina* [*History of the Village of Goriukhino*] (1830), *Puteshestvie v Arzrum* [*A Journey to Erzurum*] (1835), and his review of Nikolai Polevoi's *Istoriia russkogo naroda* [*History of the Russian People*] which appeared in *Literaturnaia gazeta* (1830).[160] But the desire on the poet's part to correct the historical record, to make it a more precise reflection of past realities and less conditioned by inherited myths or aesthetic convention, has been underappreciated. Critics have tended to see Pushkin's dramatic innovations moving history more in the direction of anarchy than of calculated political consequences. As we saw in chapter 1, critics have claimed that one of Pushkin's goals in writing his play was to demonstrate the powerful impact of chance in history; others have specifically suggested that Pushkin used the fickle *narod* as the personification of chance.[161] No doubt Pushkin was interested in the impact of historical contingency in Russian history, but his interest in chance was probably not his main concern in his *Comedy*. It seems more likely that Pushkin's primary intent was to make sense out of early modern Russian history and to understand (and fairly represent) the *narod*'s true role as a potentially powerful historical force.[162] There is every reason to believe that Pushkin, as a Romantic poet-historian, intended his play to be a bold experiment in drama in which the historical struggle of ordinary people for freedom was to be represented as accurately as possible.[163] Pushkin also intended his play to encourage his audience to think about important contemporary issues – including the problems of autocracy and serfdom.[164] He certainly had a sophisticated audience in mind for his subversive *Comedy* – "historically conscious" theatergoers who had read Karamzin, who fully expected Pushkin's play to help them "decode the zigzags of history," and who could appreciate the playwright's "good jokes and delicate allusions to the history of the time."[165]

As noted in chapter 1, many scholars and literary critics doubted that Pushkin ever intended for his play to be performed, and some have suggested that – in any case – it was not really stageable. Proponents of those theories, however, have focused exclusively on the canonical text of *Boris Godunov*, which does have its problems. They have also been overly influenced by comments made by one of Pushkin's most bitter enemies, the infamous Faddei Bulgarin, who actively worked to suppress Pushkin's *Comedy*.[166] In fact, Pushkin really did intend for his provocative play to be performed on stage and, he hoped, to revolutionize Russian drama.[167] He even gave some thought to who might be cast in his play if he did manage to stage it.[168] The fact that his *Comedy* was too controversial to be passed by tsarist censors does not justify the conclusion that Pushkin intended it to be a closet drama – a case that could be made, for example, for Pushkin's "Little Tragedies" of 1830.[169]

If Pushkin had not had so much difficulty getting his play into print, there are convincing reasons to believe that he would have written two more historical dramas about the Time of Troubles. Pushkin's plan to write these sequels to his *Comedy* was probably influenced by his interest in ancient Greek tragic drama, in which injustices were never resolved in the first play of a trilogy. Several scholars have actually detected the possible influence of ancient Greek tragedies on *Boris Godunov* – seeing strong parallels, for example, between Pushkin's portrayal of Tsar Boris (guilty of the murder of Tsarevich Dmitry) and Sophocles' study of King Oedipus; between Pushkin's treatment of the murder of Boris's son and Aeschylus's trilogy, the *Oresteia*, in which punishment for Agamemnon's guilt (sacrificing his daughter, Iphigenia) is visited on his son, Orestes; and between Pushkin's concern for the fate of Russia and Euripides' fascination with the suffering of innocent people as well as the guilty.[170] Other scholars have focused attention on Pushkin's use of the *narod* as an instrument of fate, echoing one of the favorite themes of Athenian playwrights.[171]

Pushkin definitely planned to produce a trilogy dramatizing the Time of Troubles from beginning to end – that is, from the election of Boris Godunov in 1598 to the election of Mikhail Romanov in 1613.[172] The *Comedy about Tsar Boris and Grishka Otrepiev* was to be followed by a tragedy tentatively titled *Dmitrii Samozvanets* [*Dmitry the Pretender*].[173] We even have information on how that play was to be structured. Pushkin planned to open it with a historically accurate scene in which the newly-installed Tsar Dmitry presides over the planned execution of Prince Vasily Shuisky – who had been arrested at the outset of Dmitry's reign for denouncing the tsar as an impostor and plotting to overthrow him. The opening scene would have taken place on Red Square with Shuisky about to be beheaded but then saved at the very last minute by what Pushkin referred to as Tsar Dmitry's "hare-brained generosity."[174] It is not difficult to imagine *Dmitry the Pretender* ending with a historically accurate, mirror-image scene that played out on Red Square about a year later – on the day of Tsar Dmitry's assassination. To provide cover for the assassins, Vasily Shuisky cleverly incited a riot by falsely proclaiming that the Poles who had come to Moscow to celebrate Dmitry's wedding were trying to kill the tsar. In the chaos that ensued, hundreds of people were killed. Just as the bloodshed began to subside, the rioters were stunned by the spectacle of the dead and naked Dmitry being dragged onto Red Square by his genitals. Shuisky's henchmen accompanied the corpse, shouting that the false tsar had admitted he was Grishka Otrepiev before being hacked to death. Within a few days, Shuisky managed to have himself proclaimed tsar, but he was never able to put Dmitry's ghost to rest.[175]

We do not have any information about what Pushkin planned to include in *Dmitry the Pretender*, apart from the first scene, a demonstration of Tsar Dmitry's enlightened rule, and his marriage to Maryna Mniszech. Scholars have speculated that Pushkin intended to portray Dmitry as secretly regretting the murder of Boris Godunov's son, Tsar Fedor – thereby setting the audience up for the wheel of justice to turn inexorably against the false tsar.

Would Pushkin's Tsar Dmitry have been tortured with self-doubt because he was an impostor? Perhaps. Or would the poet-historian have made use of the newly published research of Metropolitan Platon contending that, whoever Tsar Dmitry really was, he was certainly *not* the monk Otrepiev?[176] If Pushkin wished to follow that line of research, he might have written a scene in which it is dramatically revealed to Tsar Dmitry that he had been saved from Godunov's assassins as a small child and given a false identity as Grishka Otrepiev in order to protect him. Such a plot line would have been the exact reverse of Schiller's *Demetrius*. In any case, Pushkin's careful reading of foreign accounts of the Time of Troubles would undoubtedly have prevented him from presenting Tsar Dmitry as described in Romanov-influenced chronicles and by Karamzin – that is, as an evil impostor who was despised by the Russian people and toppled by a popular hero, Vasily Shuisky. Instead, Pushkin would have insisted on what he had come to believe was historically accurate, which would have involved the *narod*'s love for Tsar Dmitry and the shock felt by most Russians at the news of his assassination by a small group of Shuisky's henchmen.[177]

The third play in Pushkin's planned trilogy was to have been called *Tsar Vasily Ivanovich Shuisky;*[178] however, there are good reasons to believe that, if it had been written, the title might have been changed to something like *Tsar Vasily Shuisky and Maryna Mniszech.* Pushkin had a strong interest in the character of the crafty Prince Shuisky, so brilliantly portrayed in his *Comedy about Tsar Boris and Grishka Otrepiev.* The lethal Shuisky and his checkered career as tsar had to be brought on stage.[179] But Pushkin was also utterly fascinated by the ambitious Princess Maryna Mniszech, who, with courage and resilience approaching insane levels, fought for years against Shuisky by teaming up with an unsavory impostor known to history as the "second false Dmitry."[180] No doubt Pushkin would have enjoyed the comedic possibilities of Maryna Mniszech's wild career wandering around southern Russia with her band of cossack supporters. Historians who have carefully studied the Time of Troubles would have an easy time imagining the closely paralleled opening and closing scenes of the third play in Pushkin's planned trilogy. A few days after Tsar Dmitry's assassination, a small crowd of carefully chosen (and bribed) onlookers – including merchants, pie sellers, and cobblers – appeared on Red Square to cheer on cue for the self-proclaimed new tsar, Vasily Shuisky, while many confused and angry Russians withheld their support from the assassin-tsar.[181] Russia was almost immediately engulfed in civil war and foreign intervention, which resulted in the toppling of Tsar Vasily and the temporary occupation of Moscow by Polish troops. No doubt the play (and the trilogy) would have ended with the historically accurate cheer of the *narod* in response to the election of Tsar Mikhail Romanov in 1613 – not on Red Square this time but in the nearby suburbs of the burned capital, newly liberated from Polish captivity. It is also easy to imagine the playful Pushkin including in the final scene of his play the historically accurate (and possibly comedic) appearance of several Pushkins eager to sign the charter affirming Tsar Mikhail's election.[182] In any case, the *narod*'s final cheer would surely have been a celebration of Russia's survival, the end of the horrific Time of Troubles, and the restoration after many years of the frayed bond between the Russian people and their ruler.[183] Thus the *Comedy* (itself ending something like *Richard III*) might have ultimately fused with *Henry VIII* and patriotic pageant history plays.

Pushkin had deftly included the Romanovs in his *Comedy* as victims and opponents of Boris Godunov, a portrayal that was historically accurate.[184] It is easy to imagine the poet-historian choosing to accurately portray the Romanovs in his sequels as strong supporters of Tsar Dmitry and then as court favorites of the "second false Dmitry" – information terribly embarrassing to the ruling family that was openly discussed in those troublesome foreign accounts but that had not been included in Karamzin's *History* or in Romanov-influenced chronicles.[185] Perhaps less obviously provocative but certainly no less important, by ending his trilogy with the celebration of the founding of the Romanov dynasty and Russia's survival from foreign invasion, Pushkin would have been inviting his audience to meditate simultaneously on Russia's recent triumph over Napoleon, the two hundredth anniversary of the election of Tsar Mikhail, and the great hopes the *narod* had for the Romanovs at the beginning of the seventeenth and the nineteenth centuries.

Sadly, Pushkin did not write any sequels to his *Comedy*. Instead, as will be discussed in chapter 3, he grew increasingly frustrated by the refusal of tsarist censors to allow him to publish his first play in its original form. As a result, he gave up the idea of writing any more plays about the Time of Troubles. Fortunately, amid all these half-realized shadows, we still have his *Comedy* – a remarkable and daring historical drama in which Pushkin demonstrated great skill as a poet and as an historian.

Notes

1. Sandler, *Distant Pleasures*, 77.

2. See, for example, Sandler, *Distant Pleasures;* Greenleaf, *Pushkin*, 156–204; and Cooke and Dunning, "Tempting Fate."

3. See, for example, Rabinovich, "Boris Godunov"; Shmurlo, "Etiudy"; Orlov, "Tragediia"; Toibin, "Istoriia"; Luzianina, "Istoriia"; and Emerson, *Boris Godunov*, 119–31.

4. On Pushkin as an historian see Grekov, "Istoricheskie vozzreniia," 3–28; Blok, *Pushkin;* Dymshits, *Pushkin*, 108; Bazilevich, "Boris Godunov," 53–54; Cherepnin, "Istoriia," 25–44; Tarle, "Pushkin," 211–20; Meilakh, *Pushkin i ego epokha*, 297–98; Chkheidze, *Istoriia*, 45; Lavrin, *Panorama*, 57; Ovchinnikov, *Pushkin;* Vernadsky, *Russian Historiography*, 53–54; Riasanovsky, *Image*, 87–90; Eidel'man, *Pushkin*, 361–62; Schapiro, *Rationalism*, 54; *The Modern Encyclopedia of Russian and Soviet History* [hereafter MERSH], 30: 96; Emerson, "Pushkin," 653; Lotman, *Pushkin*, 106; and Dolinin, "Historicism," 291–308.

5. On Pushkin's appointment as historian laureate see Annenkov, *Pushkin*, 255–

56; Riasanovsky, *Image*, 7–8, 90; Chkheidze, *Istoriia*, 45–46; Kochetkova, *Nikolay Karamzin*, 119; *Letters*, 68, 515; and Debreczeny, *The Other Pushkin*, 220.

6. On Pushkin as Karamzin's successor see Sandler, "Problem," 136, 301; Black, *Essays*, 16; Kochetkova, *Nikolay Karamzin*, 129–30; Brun-Zejmis, "Chaadaev," 284–88; Simmons, *Pushkin*, 258; Emerson, *Boris Godunov*, 34, 85; Todd, *Fiction*, 85–86; Vatsuro, "Podvig," 8–51; and Pogodin, *Nikolai Karamzin*, 2: 204, 329–31. On Pushkin's admiration of Voltaire see TL, 1: 414; 2: 73–74, 112, 251, 418; Karlinsky, *Russian Drama*, 313; Simmons, *Pushkin*, 250; and Baer, "Between Public and Private," 40.

7. See, for example, Pomar, "Russian Historical Drama," 267–69; and Sandler, "Problem," 86.

8. Meilakh, *Pushkin i ego epokha*, 92; Edmonds, *Pushkin*, 46–47; Vernadsky, *Russian Historiography*, 53–54; Karlinsky, *Russian Drama*, 313.

9. Evdokimova, *Pushkin's Historical Imagination*, 3, 19, 21–22, 129.

10. Maikov, *Pamiati*, li–liv, 327; Lotman, *Pushkin*, 106. See, for example, Grekov, "Istoricheskie vozzreniia," 18–21; Bazilevich, "Boris Godunov," 51–54; Meilakh, *Pushkin i ego epokha*, 297–303; and Cherepnin, "Istoriia," 36.

11. See Evdokimova, *Pushkin's Historical Imagination*, 1–2, 5, 21, 24, 31, 33–34, 171–72, 242–43 n. 6.

12. Vickery, *Alexander Pushkin* (1992), 1–2; MERSH, 9: 40.

13. See Rybinskii, *Sbornik*, 143–44; Billington, *Icon*, 314; Meilakh, *Pushkin i ego epokha*, 92; Shevyrev, "Rasskazy," 38; and Institut russkoi literatury (Pushkinskii Dom) RAN, Rukopisnyi otdel [hereafter cited as PD], fond 244, opis' 25, No. 368 (A. M. Gorchakov's summary of lectures on Russian history), listy 350b-37. See also Zorin, *Kormia dvuglavogo Orla*, 159–86.

14. Schapiro, *Rationalism*, 31, 48–54; Evdokimova, *Pushkin's Historical Imagination*, 243 n. 2; MERSH, 9: 40–41; 30: 92, 95; Palmer, *Alexander I*, 343.

15. Black, *Nicholas Karamzin*, 68.

16. Pogodin, *Karamzin*, 2: 204; 329–31; Vatsuro, *Pushkinskaia pora*, 97–98; Shmurlo, "Etiudy," 28–30.

17. See Zaborov, "Shekspir," 72; MERSH, 16: 9; Lavrin, *Pushkin*, 142.

18. Pipes, "Karamzin's Conception," 112–13, 116–17; Sanders, *Historiography*, 51; Kochetkova, *Nikolay Karamzin*, 120–21.

19. See Pipes, *Karamzin's Memoir*, 136–37. See also Raskol'nikov, "Boris Godunov," 161; and Vinokur, *Stat'i*, 97.

20. MERSH, 46: 67–70; Bayley, *Pushkin*, 170; Fischer, "Schiller," 603–11; Lincoln, *Between Heaven and Hell*, 128–30; Mordovchenko, *Russkaia kritika*, 143; Donchin, "Pushkin," 20; Levin, "Literatura," 129, 134–36; Schapiro, *Rationalism*, 23–25, 47–54; Terras, *History*, 182–83; Malia, *Alexander Herzen*, 40–44, 434 n. 6.

21. McNally, *Chaadaev*, 11–12; Fischer, "Schiller," 605; Schapiro, *Rationalism*, 45–48; Lemke, *Nikolaevskie zhandarmy*, 367; Vickery, *Alexander Pushkin* (1992), 3, 20; Feinstein, *Pushkin*, 44; MERSH, 6: 185–90; 30: 95; Donchin, "Pushkin," 19–20; Brun-Zejmis, "Chaadaev," 7–8, 11–12; Binyon, *Pushkin*, 60–61.

22. Vickery, *Alexander Pushkin* (1992), 3–4; Lotman, *Pushkin*, 765–85; Sakulin, *Pushkin*; Donchin, "Pushkin," 19–20; Feinstein, *Pushkin*, 44, 140; Tsiavlovskii,

Letopis', 579; Simmons, *Pushkin,* 250; Sandler, *Distant Pleasures,* 2; Wolff, *Pushkin,* 11, 111 n. 1.

23. Levitt, *Russian Literary Politics,* 4–6; Simmons, *Pushkin,* 250; Brody, "Schiller's 'Demetrius,'" 276; Evdokimova, *Pushkin's Historical Imagination,* x–xi; Gillel'son, *Ot arzamasskogo bratstva,* 7–8, 12–15, 198; Mirsky, *Pushkin,* 201; Schapiro, *Rationalism,* 45; Brun-Zejmis, "Chaadaev," 7–8. See also McNally, *Chaadayev,* 13; and Riasanovsky, *Image,* 86–87, 98.

24. On Arzamas see Vatsuro and Ospovata, *Arzamas,* 1: 28; MERSH, 46: 68; 54: 99; Black, *Nicholas Karamzin,* 68–70; Hollingsworth, "Arzamas," 306–26; Whittaker, *Origins,* 29–30; Martin, *Romantics,* 187–88; Gillel'son, *Ot arzamasskogo bratstva,* 6–7; and idem, *Molodoi Pushkin,* 141–59.

25. Pogodin, *Nikolai Karamzin,* 2: 319; Sandler, "Problem," 85; Gillel'son, *Molodoi Pushkin,* 159–73; MERSH, 54: 98–103; Vernadsky, *Russian Historiography,* 57–58. See also Turgenev, ed., *Historica Russiae monumenta.*

26. MERSH, 40: 89–93; Vatsuro, *Pushkinskaia pora,* 103–4; Black, *Nicholas Karamzin,* 63, 68; Vickery, *Alexander Pushkin* (1992), 3; Simmons, *Pushkin,* 91; Brun-Zejmis, "Chaadaev," 37; McNally, *Chaadayev,* 12–13; Sandler, "Problem," 85.

27. MERSH, 42: 79; 54: 99, 101–2.

28. See Karamzin, *Istoriia,* 1st ed. (1816–29). See also Black, *Essays,* 18–21.

29. Karamzin's *History* was so popular that, at the same time volumes 2–8 were published in 1818, a second (corrected) edition of the entire *History,* vols. 1–8, was also launched. See Karamzin, *Istoriia,* 2nd ed. (1818–29). On the reaction of Pushkin and other liberals to Karamzin's *History* see Meilakh, *Pushkin i ego epokha,* 295–96; Vatsuro, "Podvig," 17–28, 81; idem, *Pushkinskaia pora,* 103–6; Vickery, *Alexander Pushkin* (1992), 3–4, 20; Whittaker, *Origins,* 32–33, 105; Sandler, "Problem," 84–85, 171–72; Kochetkova, *Nikolay Karamzin,* 122–23; Emerson, *Boris Godunov,* 30–34; Sanders, *Historiography,* 4, 50; Gillel'son, *Molodoi Pushkin,* 159–61; Mocha, "Polish and Russian Sources," 46–47; MERSH, 16: 10; 40: 89–92; 54: 99; Schönle, *Authenticity,* 193; Brun-Zejmis, "Chaadaev," 37; and Ziolkowski, *Hagiography,* 37.

30. *Letters,* 313.

31. See PS, 17: 16. The translation is by Caryl Emerson (*Boris Godunov,* 34).

32. Pogodin, *Karamzin,* 204; Meilakh, *Pushkin i ego epokha,* 297; Vatsuro, *Pushkinskaia pora,* 92–98; Eidel'man, *Stat'i,* 105–24; Schönle, *Authenticity,* 193. See also *Letters,* 240, 313; Binyon, *Pushkin,* 39–40, 83–84; Sandler, "Problem," 85–86.

33. On contemporary reactions to volume nine of Karamzin's *History* see Barsukov, *Zhizn' Pogodina,* 3: 188, 206; Pypin, *Religioznye dvizheniia,* 158; Vatsuro, "Podvig," 81; Sakharov, *Aleksandr I,* 143; Kochetkova, *Karamzin,* 120–28; Eidel'man, *Stat'i,* 122–24; Sanders, *Historiography,* 51; Emerson, *Boris Godunov,* 34; Kozlov, "Polemika," 94–95; Martin, *Romantics,* 187–88; Sandler, "Problem," 171–72; Pipes, "Karamzin's Conception," 116; Black, "*Primechaniia,*" 135, 143–44; idem, *Essays,* 11, 19; Rothe, "Karamzin," 176; and Lotman, *Pushkin,* 197.

34. See Vatsuro, "Podvig," 17–28, 81; Kochetkova, *Nikolay Karamzin,* 123; MERSH 16: 10–11; Sanders, *Historiography,* 51; and Sandler, "Problem," 85–86.

35. Simmons, *Pushkin,* 250–51; Vickery, *Alexander Pushkin* (1992), 3–4; Schapiro,

Rationalism, 53; Donchin, "Pushkin," 19–20; Lincoln, *Between Heaven and Hell,* 133–34; Sandler, *Distant Pleasures,* 2; MERSH, 9: 40–42; Gillel'son, *Molodoi Pushkin,* 192–213.

36. On Pushkin and the Decembrists see *Letters,* 302; Rabinovich, "Boris Godunov," 309; Gillel'son, *Ot arzamasskogo bratstva,* 6–7; Simmons, *Pushkin,* 242–44, 250–53; Driver, *Pushkin,* 2, 37–38; Sandler, *Distant Pleasures,* 6; MERSH, 30: 95–97; 40: 91–93; 42: 79; 54: 99–100; and Palmer, *Alexander I,* 343, 385, 411 n.

37. See Barsukov, *Zhizn' Pogodina,* 1: 79; Rothe, "Karamzin," 150–51; MERSH, 16: 10; and Sanders, *Historiography,* 4.

38. Vickery, *Alexander Pushkin* (1992), 4; MERSH, 54: 102; Schönle, *Authenticity,* 193; Lincoln, *Between Heaven and Hell,* 133–34.

39. Tsiavlovskii, *Letopis',* 473, 492, 537; Sandler, *Distant Pleasures,* 6.

40. Tsiavlovskii, *Letopis',* 307, 456, 482; *Letters,* 186, 190, 307; PS, 13: 124, 142, 256, 259; Arinshtein, "K istorii," 286–91, 296, 303–4; Veresaev, *Pushkin,* 1: 238, 260, 262, 263; Vol'pert, "Druzheskaia perepiska,"50, 54–55; Cooke and Dunning, "Tempting Fate," 43–48.

41. TL, 2: 128–29; Modzalevskii, *Pushkin,* 19–20; Monas, *The Third Section,* 201. See also Veresaev, *Pushkin,* 1: 290, 300.

42. Cooke and Dunning, "Tempting Fate," 43–52. See also Greenleaf, *Pushkin,* 156–204.

43. *Letters,* 182, 185, 186, 256; Wolff, *Pushkin,* 110–11; Gordin, *Pushkin,* 112, 116; Cooke and Dunning, "Tempting Fate," 47–49.

44. *Letters,* 186, 188, 253, 256, 303; PS, 11: 23–24; Tsiavlovskii, *Letopis',* 473, 492; Gillel'son, *Molodoi Pushkin,* 213–22; Varneke, "Istochniki," 17–19; Brody, "Schiller's 'Demetrius,'" 276; Bayley, *Pushkin,* 178; Bowersock, "Roman Emperor," 136; Baer, "Between Public and Private," 36; Greenleaf, *Pushkin,* 211, 387 n. 15; Rabinovich, "Boris Godunov," 309; Filippova, *Narodnaia drama,* 15. See also Raskol'nikov, "Boris Godunov," 161.

45. PS, 13: 230, 271; Tsiavlovskii, *Letopis',* 473, 564, 567, 615.

46. Meilakh, *Pushkin i ego epokha,* 300–301.

47. Bochkarev, *Russkaia istoricheskaia dramaturgiia,* 461; Bazilevich, "Boris Godunov," 35, 40; Vinokur, *Stat'i,* 107; MERSH, 30: 97; Levin, "Nekotorye voprosy," 160; Evdokimova, *Pushkin's Historical Imagination,* 42–43; Sandler, *Distant Pleasures,* 128; Brody, "Schiller's 'Demetrius,'" 269–70, 275–77; idem, *Demetrius Legend,* 249–50; Slonimskii, "Boris Godunov," 75–76; Lotman, *Pushkin,* 102.

48. Brody, "Schiller's 'Demetrius,'" 275; idem, "Pushkin's 'Boris Godunov,'" 859; *Letters,* 37; Binyon, *Pushkin,* 296.

49. Karlinsky, *Russian Drama,* 317; Baer, "Between Public and Private," 26, 28, 36; Rabinovich, "Boris Godunov," 309–10. See also Emerson, *Boris Godunov,* 95–96.

50. Karlinsky, *Russian Drama,* 134–41.

51. Gorodetskii, *Tragediia,* 72; Pomar, "Russian Historical Drama," 179; TL, 1: 146, 159, 300, 322; 492, 502; Karlinsky, *Russian Drama,* 250, 252, 254–55, 257, 286–87, 289, 302, 303, 312–21, 324–27, 330–31. See also Pushkin, *Sochineniia Pushkina* (1855–57), 1: 128–29, 240; and *Letters,* 100–101, 113, 130, 220, 285.

52. Sandler, *Distant Pleasures*, 76–139; idem, "Solitude," 171, 183; Greenleaf, *Pushkin*, 156.

53. See Pushkin, *Boris Godunov* (1965), 7; and Lacombe, *Histoire*, 77.

54. Kornblatt, *Cossack Hero*, 22; Bochkarev, *Russkaia istoricheskaia dramaturgiia*, 461; MERSH, 30: 97; Vinokur, *Stat'i*, 97; Rybinskii, *Sbornik*, 151. Pushkin also became very interested in the Ukrainian cossack rebel leader, Ivan Mazepa, who fought against Peter the Great; see Binyon, *Pushkin*, 167, 168, 297.

55. Kornblatt, *Cossack Hero*, 5, 15–22, 37; Tsvetaeva, *Captive Spirit*, 372–403; Debreczeny, *The Other Pushkin*, 239; Tarle, "Pushkin," 216; Sandler, *Distant Pleasures*, 128; Bethea, "Pushkin's Pretenders," 61. See also Pushkin, *History of Pugachev*; Vernadsky, *Russian Historiography*, 53.

56. Pushkin, *Sochineniia Pushkina* (1855–57), 1: 240; PS, 13: 119; *Letters*, 187; Lobanova, *Mikhailovskaia biblioteka*, 27, 35, 37–38. See also Modzalevskii, *Biblioteka*, 59–60, 82, 319. Pushkin may have read an article about Stenka Razin that was written by the future Decembrist, A. O. Kornilovich, and published in *Severnyi Arkhiv*, 1824, No. 7, 27–32; see Bochkarev, *Russkaia istoricheskaia dramaturgiia*, 461.

57. Veselovskii, *Issledovaniia*, 39–139; Vinokur, *Stat'i*, 101; Stark, "Pushkin," 65–83; Feinstein, *Pushkin*, 19; Tarle, "Pushkin," 211–14.

58. Mirsky, *Pushkin*, 2–3; Veselovskii, *Issledovaniia*, 135; Gurevich, "Istoriia," 205–7; Skrynnikov, "Boris Godunov," 131–33; Stark, "Pushkin," 67–68, 71–75; Vinokur, *Stat'i*, 104–5; Emerson, "Pushkin," 656–57; Khokhlenko, *Skazaniia*, 92–98, 155–77.

59. Mirsky, *Pushkin*, 2; Vinokur, *Stat'i*, 101; RFCW, 303, 307, 322, 342, 385, 479, 522 n. 129.

60. *Letters*, 365–67; TL, 3: 68; Pushkin, *Sochineniia* (1887), 3: 82–83; Gurevich, "Istoriia," 208–9; Skrynnikov, "Boris Godunov," 131–33; Rabinovich, "Boris Goduniv," 309; Grekov, "Istoricheskie vozzreniia," 20–21; RFCW, 194.

61. Cooke and Dunning, "Tempting Fate," 43.

62. Pushkin, *Sochineniia i pis'ma* (1903–6), 3: 239–40; Vinokur, *Stat'i*, 110–12; Briggs, *Alexander Pushkin*, 158; Sandler, *Distant Pleasures*, 213; Feinstein, *Pushkin*, 122; Pomar, "Russian Historical Drama," 178, 186, 188–90.

63. Viazemskii, *Polnoe sobranie sochinenii*, 1: 171–72; Karlinsky, *Russian Drama*, 316–17; Pomar, "Russian Historical Drama," 160–69; Bochkarev, *Russkaia istoricheskaia dramaturgiia*, 136.

64. PS, 11: 140; TL, 2: 203; *Letters*, 365–67; Vinokur, *Stat'i*, 114–19; Blagoi, *Tvorcheskii put'* (*1826–1830*), 565; Levin, *Shekspir*, 32–63; Alekseev, "A. S. Pushkin," 163–74; Karlinsky, *Russian Drama*, 321–22, 337; Greenleaf, *Pushkin*, 159–62; Brown, *History*, 3: 106–9; Wolff, "Shakespeare's Influence," 94–97; Pomar, "Russian Historical Drama," 186–88; Mirsky, *Pushkin*, 154–56; Vickery, *Alexander Pushkin* (1970), 58–60, 66; Emerson, *Boris Godunov*, 110–11, 237 n. 67, 238 n. 69.

65. Bethea, "Pushkin," 84; Brody, "Pushkin's 'Boris Godunov,'" 862–63; Alekseev, "A. S. Pushkin," 173; Bochkarev, *Russkaia istoricheskaia dramaturgiia*, 21; Briggs, *Alexander Pushkin*, 160–61; Pomar, "Russian Historical Drama," 182–84.

66. Lavrin, *Pushkin*, 142; Levin, "Literatura," 129–36; idem, "Nekotorye voprosy," 62.

67. Wolff, "Shakespeare's Influence," 94; Gifford, "Shakespearean Elements," 152–60; Levin, *Shekspir*, 32–63; Greenleaf, *Pushkin*, 176–77, 189–96, 381 n. 33; Shaw, "Romeo," 1–35.

68. Lavrin, *Pushkin*, 142 n. 1; Wolff, "Shakespeare's Influence," 95–97; Gifford, "Shakespearean Elements," 154–56; Karlinsky, *Russian Drama*, 322–23; Verkhovskii, "Zapadnoevropeiskaia istoricheskaia drama," 216, 220, 223; Levin, *Shekspir*, 41; Briggs, *Alexander Pushkin*, 160–61; Vickery, *Alexander Pushkin* (1970), 69; Brody, *Demetrius Legend*, 244; Bayley, *Pushkin*, 175.

69. Pomar, "Russian Historical Drama," 179–84; Karlinsky, *Russian Drama*, 316–21. It is possible that Pushkin may also have been influenced by progressive ideas contained in some eighteenth-century Russian dramas, including the first Russian play about the Pretender Dmitry – Alexander Sumarokov's *Dimitrii Samozvanets*, written in 1771. On the commitment to Enlightenment principles contained in eighteenth-century Russian plays, see Sumarokov, *Selected Tragedies*, 19; and Wirtschafter, *Play of Ideas*.

70. See Karlinsky, *Russian Drama*, 286–87, 324; and Gorodetskii, *Dramaturgiia*, 72. Excerpts from Griboedov's play were first published in *Ruskaia Taliia* in 1825, and Pushkin had access to that book; see Bayley, *Pushkin*, 177; Bochkarev, *Russkaia istoricheskaia dramaturgiia*, 463, 467.

71. For scholars believing that Pushkin adhered closely to Karamzin's *History* see Barsukov, *Zhizn' Pogodina*, 3: 244; Vinokur, *Stat'i*, 93–94; Filonov, *Boris Godunov*; Toibin, "*Istoriia*," 37–48; Rothe, "Karamzin," 176; Greenleaf, *Pushkin*, 171; and Luzianina, "Istoriia," 45–57.

72. On Pushkin's departures from Karamzin's text see Gorodetskii, *Tragediia*, 28–44; Serman, "Pushkin," 118–49; Rabinovich, "Boris Godunov," 310–17; Vinokur, *Stat'i*, 99; Rybinskii, *Sbornik*, 144–47; Raskol'nikov, "Boris Godunov," 163; Bochkarev, *Russkaia istoricheskaia dramaturgiia*, 401–28, 455–56; Kochetkova, *Nikolay Karamzin*, 129–30; Brody, *Demetrius Legend*, 240; Pomar, "Russian Historical Drama," 200–201; Brun-Zejmis, "Chaadaev," 287–88; Sandler, "Problem," 87–88; Mocha, "Polish and Russian Sources," 45–51; Ronen, *Smyslovoi stroi*, 17–18; Orlov, "Tragediia," 3–10; Emerson, "Pretenders," 259, 264; Evdokimova, *Pushkin's Historical Imagination*, 42–43; and Emerson and Oldani, *Modest Musorgsky*, 12, 23.

73. Quoted in Volk, *Istoricheskie vzgliady*, 291; and Ziolkowski, *Hagiography*, 39.

74. See Black, "*Primechanija*," 127–47; Vernadsky, *Russian Historiography*, 51–52; and Emerson, *Boris Godunov*, 32–35.

75. PS, 11: 120; Todd, *Fiction*, 86; Mocha, "Polish and Russian Sources," 48; Luzianina, "Istoriia," 46.

76. Bethea, "Pushkin: From Byron to Shakespeare," 84.

77. On Pushkin's interest in early modern sources and his growth as an historian see Tsiavlovskii, *Letopis'*, 558; Gorodetskii, *Tragediia*, 36–43; Vernadsky, *Russian Historiography*, 53; Brody, *Demetrius Legend*, 240; Toibin, "Istoriia," 10–23; Balashov, "Boris Godunov," 214; Mocha, "Polish and Russian Sources," 45–51; Pushkin, *Sochineniia i pis'ma A. S. Pushkina* (1903–6), 3: 253; Brun-Zejmis, "Chaadaev," 287–88; Vinokur, "Kommentarii," 466–67; Sandler, "Problem," 87–88; and Emerson, *Boris Godunov*, 85.

78. *Letters,* 247; Rabinovich, "Boris Godunov," 310–12, 316–17; Bochkarev, *Russkaia istoricheskaia dramaturgiia,* 457–60; Mocha, "Polish and Russian Sources," 47; Pomar, "Russian Historical Drama," 198–200; Modzalevskii, *Biblioteka,* 60, 86; Lobanova, *Mikhailovskaia biblioteka,* 27, 35; Sandler, *Distant Pleasures,* 87–88; Greenleaf, *Pushkin,* 180; Shmurlo, "Etiudy," 12–13, 21–22.

79. Pushkin, *Sochineniia i pis'ma* (1903–6), 3: 253; Blagoi, *Tvorcheskii put' (1813–26),* 436; Bochkarev, *Russkaia istoricheskaia dramaturgiia,* 470; Pomar, "Russian Historical Drama," 222–23, 231; Dolinin, "Historicism," 297; Brown, *History,* 3: 106–7; Brody, *Demetrius Legend,* 240; Rybinskii, *Sbornik,* 144–46.

80. See *Letopis' o mnogikh miatezhakh* (1788). In Mikhailovskoe, Pushkin had access to the version of this chronicle published in *Russkaia letopis' po Nikonovu spisku,* volume 8. See Lobanova, *Mikhailovskaia biblioteka,* 27; Modzalevskii, *Biblioteka,* 60; Pogodin, *Nikolai Karamzin,* 2: 293–94; Shmurlo, "Etiudy," 22; Vinokur, *Stat'i,* 93; Gorodetskii, *Tragediia,* 36–41; Rabinovich, "Boris Godunov," 312–13, 316–17; Onegin, *Neizdannyi Pushkin,* 37; Bazilevich, "Boris Godunov," 32; and Billington, *Icon,* 124.

81. See Palitsyn, *Skazanie ob osade Troitsko-Sergieva monastyria … (*1784). Pushkin had access to this chronicle in Mikhailovskoe; see Lobanova, *Mikhailovskaia biblioteka,* 35; Onegin, *Neizdannyi Pushkin,* 37; and Pomar, "Russian Historical Drama," 200.

82. *Letters,* 230.

83. Bulgarin, *Ruskaia Taliia,* 350; See Bayley, *Pushkin,* 177; and *Letters,* 219, 285. See also Onegin, *Neizdannyi Pushkin,* 37–38; Bochkarev, *Russkaia istoricheskaia dramaturgiia,* 463–65; Pomar, "Russian Historical Drama," 239; and BG, 120–21.

84. Bulgarin, *Ruskaia Taliia,* 352–53.

85. Ibid., 1–36. Grech cited as one of his sources a book published in the late-eighteenth century which contained the texts of three old Russian "comedies," including Simeon Polotsky's *Komidiia pritchi o bludnom syne (Comedy on the Parable of the Prodigal Son);* see *Drevniaia Rossiiskaia Vivliofika,* vol. 8. It is possible that Pushkin himself consulted that volume of *Drevniaia Rossiiskaia Vivliofika* while writing his play. At some point, the poet acquired that work for his own library; see Modzalevskii, *Biblioteka,* 38.

86. Annenkov, *Vospominaniia,* 458; Gorodetskii, *Dramaturgiia,* 186–95; Blagoi, *Tvorcheskii put' (1813–1826),* 436; Gukovskii, *Pushkin,* 56; Bochkarev, *Russkaia istoricheskaia dramaturgiia,* 470; and Pomar, "Russian Historical Drama," 221–32.

87. Rabinovich, "Boris Godunov," 312–13, 316–17; Bochkarev, *Russkaia istoricheskaia dramaturgiia,* 455–57; Mocha, "Polish and Russian Sources," 45–47; Pomar, "Russian Historical Drama," 200–201.

88. See, for example, Bochkarev, *Russkaia istoricheskaia dramaturgiia,* 401.

89. See Shcherbatov, *Kratkaia povest';* idem, *Istoriia,* volume 6–7, 12; Lobanova, *Mikhailovskaia biblioteka,* 38; Vinokur, *Stat'i,* 92–93; Shmurlo, "Etiudy," 10–12; Gorodetskii, *Tragediia,* 33–35, 153; Bochkarev, *Russkaia istoricheskaia dramaturgiia,* 407–10, 455–57; Pomar, "Russian Historical Drama," 200–201; Mocha, "Polish and

Russian Sources," 47–48; Brody, *Demetrius Legend*, 241–42; and Rabinovich, "Boris Godunov," 309, 312–17.

90. For example, Pushkin accurately refers to Vasily Shuisky's *uncle* (Ivan Petrovich Shuisky) as a victim of Boris Godunov's ambition (in the scene "Chambers in the Kremlin: 20th February 1598"), whereas several modern studies of the Time of Troubles mistakenly refer to him as Prince Vasily's *father* (e.g., Skrynnikov, *Boris Godunov*, 24; Vernadsky, *Tsardom*, 1: 189; Abramovich, *Kniaz'ia Shuiskie*, 111).

91. See RFCW, 245–48.

92. See Brody, "Pushkin's 'Boris Godunov,'" 871–72; Rabinovich, "Boris Godunov," 314–15.

93. See Bulgarin, "Marina Mnishek"; "Dnevnik Samuila Maskevicha"; Mocha, "Polish and Russian Sources," 47–51; and Modzalevskii, *Biblioteka*, 134.

94. Black, *Essays*, 11; idem, "*Primechanija*," 133–35, 143–47; idem, *Nicholas Karamzin*, 45. See also Turgenev, *Historica Russiae monumenta*; Mocha, "Polish and Russian Sources," 48; Luzianina, "Istoriia," 46; and Vernadsky, *Russian Historiography*, 57.

95. On the use of early modern foreign sources by early nineteenth-century Russian historians see Pogodin, *Nikolai Karamzin*, 2: 266–308; Margeret, *Sostoianie*, iii–xxii; Ustrialov, *Skazaniia*; Dunning, "Use and Abuse," 359–60; and Black, "*Primechanija*," 135.

96. Conrad Bussow's important contemporaneous account of Russia's Time of Troubles was misidentified by early nineteenth-century scholars as the work of the Lutheran pastor, Martin Beer. See Pogodin, *Nikolai Karamzin*, 2: 266–71, 285–87; and Bussow, *Disturbed State*, xxxiv–xxxv. See also Brody, "Pushkin's 'Boris Godunov,'" 874.

97. On foreign accounts of Boris Godunov and Tsar Dmitry which differ from Karamzin's interpretation see Bussow, *Disturbed State*, 9–12; Margeret, *Russian Empire*, 16–18, 60–64, 66–68; and Massa, *Short History*, 25–26, 30–43, 72–110. See also Brody, *Demetrius Legend*, 241–42.

98. On the use of Margeret's book by historians see Dunning, "Use and Abuse," 359–69. Margeret's book was used extensively by Pierre Charles Levesque in volume 3 of his *Histoire de Russie* (1782). Levesque's influential *Histoire* was translated into Russian by 1787 and went through four French editions by 1812. On early Russian historians' awareness of Margeret's book see Tatishchev, *Istoriia*, 7: 449.

99. Dunning, "Use and Abuse," 359–60; Cooke and Dunning, "Tempting Fate," 54–55.

100. See Karamzin, *Pis'ma*, 378–80; Black, "*Primechanija*," 134–35; and idem, *Nicholas Karamzin*, 45.

101. Modzalevskii, *Biblioteka*, 281. Pushkin also had access to the 1669 edition of Margeret's book while in his southern exile; see Pushkin, *Boris Godunov* (1965), 7.

102. See PS, 7: 73; and Margeret, *Russian Empire*, 62, 155 n. 203;

103. See Margeret, *Russian Empire*, xxxiii–xxxv; idem, *Sostoianie*, xxi–xxii; and Ustrialov, *Skazaniia*, 1: 241.

104. *Letters,* 365–66; Brody, *Demetrius Legend,* 242–44; Fennell, "Pushkin," 110–11, 115; Emerson, *Boris Godunov,* 125; Vickery, *Alexander Pushkin* (1992), 56; BG, 346–47.

105. Brody, "Pushkin's 'Boris Godunov,'" 866; Bochkarev, *Russkaia istoricheskaia dramaturgiia,* 416.

106. See Margeret, *Russian Empire,* 69, 75, 80, 90–91; Dunning, "Who Was Tsar Dmitrii?" 705–29; and Crummey, *Formation,* 217–18. See also Vinokur, *Stat'i,* 103–5; Rabinovich, "Boris Godunov," 313, 316–17; Meilakh, *Pushkin i ego epokha,* 303; Brody, *Demetrius Legend,* 241–42; Serman, "Paradoxes," 34–37.

107. Emerson and Oldani, *Modest Musorgsky,* 31; Emerson, *Boris Godunov,* 14; Bayley, *Pushkin,* 172; Dyck, "Deceit," 103; Wiese, *Friedrich Schiller,* 793.

108. *Letters,* 365–67; Emerson, *Boris Godunov,* 14, 125; Dinega, "Ambiguity," 546–47; Sandler, *Distant Pleasures,* 128, 135; Brody, "Schiller's 'Demetrius,'" 250, 261, 263, 266–67, 274, 282–83; Bochkarev, *Russkaia istoricheskaia dramaturgiia,* 416–20; Raskol'nikov, "Boris Godunov," 163–64; Gurevich, "Istoriia," 211; Mocha, "Polish and Russian Sources," 50–51; Lavrin, *Panorama,* 57; Bethea, "Pushkin," 85–86.

109. *Letters,* 366, 396 n. 10; Margeret, *Russian Empire,* xxviii–xxix, 75; Karamzin, *Istoriia* (1892), 11: 130–31; Vinokur, "Kommentarii," 486; Serman, "Paradoxes," 28–29; Bayley, *Pushkin,* 179.

110. See Dunning, "Who Was Tsar Dmitrii?"

111. See PS, 7: 265–69.

112. See, for example, PS, 13: 235; Pushkin, *Sochineniia* (1887), 3: 84; idem, *Sochineniia i pis'ma* (1903–6), 3: 255.

113. During the 1590s, Boris Godunov (acting as regent for Tsar Fedor Ivanovich) informally enserfed the Russian peasants by "temporarily" suspending their long-held right to leave a lord's service after the fall harvest – during the two weeks surrounding St. George's Day in late November. The Russian people were well aware at the time that Godunov was responsible for their bondage, and many of them hated him for it. The resulting "forbidden years" effectively tied the peasants to the land until serfdom was formally codified in the *Ulozhenie* of 1649. See Skrynnikov, *Boris Godunov,* 75–80; and Hellie, *Enserfment,* 1–18, 97–98, 103.

114. PS, 7: 40–41. See also Gorodetskii, *Tragediia,* 131–34; Rabinovich, "Boris Godunov," 309.

115. Pushkin's strikingly original conclusion may have been influenced by reading histories of Russia written in the generation before Karamzin. The first historian to suggest a connection between the establishment of serfdom in the 1590s and popular unrest in the Time of Troubles was V. N. Tatishchev; similar ideas were expressed by M. M. Shcherbatov. See Tatishchev, *Istoriia,* 7: 367; Shcherbatov, *Istoriia,* 7(2): 147–48, 181–82; Rabinovich, "Boris Godunov," 308–9; Blagoi, *Ot Kantemira,* 2: 108–10; Gurevich, "Istoriia," 205; Lobanova, *Mikhailovskaia biblioteka,* 38; Pomar, "Russian Historical Drama," 260; Gorodetskii, *Tragediia,* 33–43, 69–70; Shmurlo, "Etiudy," 10–11; and Raskol'nikov, "Boris Godunov," 157, 162–63.

116. Even Karamzin had been forced to admit that the triumphant Dmitry was cheered by many ordinary Russians. (See Karamzin, *Istoriia* [1892], 11: 120, 127; Bus-

sow, *Disturbed State,* 50- 51; and Rabinovich, "Boris Godunov," 316–17.) The assumption by some scholars and literary critics that the *narod*'s shout at the end of Pushkin's *Comedy* was not meant to be a show of enthusiastic support is based upon a poor understanding of Pushkin's view of Dmitry and the popular support he generated. For examples of that conventional interpretation see Mirsky, *Pushkin,* 162; Bayley, *Pushkin,* 175–76; Sandler, "Problem," 60–63; Brody, "Pushkin's 'Boris Godunov,'" 873; Raskol'nikov, "Boris Godunov," 160–63; Pomar, "Russian Historical Drama," 260–61; Brown, *History,* 3: 109; and Evdokimova, *Pushkin's Historical Imagination,* 59–61.

117. On the standard patriotic ending and "puerile emotionalism" of early nineteenth-century Russian historical dramas see Bochkarev, *Russkaia istoricheskaia dramaturgiia,* 277–78, 337; and Pomar, "Russian Historical Drama," 160–65, 264.

118. Grekov, "Istoricheskie vozzreniia," 20–21; Brown, *History,* 3: 110; Rybinskii, *Sbornik,* 147; Gorodetskii, *Tragediia,* 33–34; Lysenkova, "O probleme," 63–64, 68; Lavrin, *Pushkin,* 152–53; Alekseev, "A. S. Pushkin," 177–78; Brown, *History,* 3: 110; Rabinovich, "Boris Godunov," 315–17; Verkhovskii, "Zapadnoevropeiskaia istoricheskaia drama," 224–26; Raskol'nikov, "Boris Godunov," 162.

119. Bazilevich, "Boris Godunov," 53; Rabinovich, "Boris Godunov," 309.

120. See Slonimskii, "Boris Godunov," 75–76; Vol'pert, "Druzheskaia perepiska," 59; and Brody, *Demetrius Legend,* 249–50.

121. Pushkin, *Sochineniia Pushkina* (1855–57), 1: 109; Vatsuro, "Istoricheskaia tragediia," 327–29; Pomar, "Russian Historical Drama," 166, 171–72, 288; Karlinsky, *Russian Drama,* 313, 337.

122. Fischer, "Schiller," 609–11; Maikov, *Pamiati,* li–lii, 330, 337; Meilakh, *Pushkin i ego epokha,* 560; Alekseev, "A. S. Pushkin," 106; Brody, *Demetrius Legend,* 222; idem, "Schiller's 'Demetrius,'" 246–50; Pomar, "Russian Historical Drama," 204; Lysenkova, "O probleme," 59–61.

123. TL, 2: 345; Kostka, *Schiller,* 17–18, 216 n 5; Fischer, "Schiller," 604; *Istoriia russkogo dramaticheskogo teatra,* 2: 130–34; Levin, "Literatura," 159; Zagorskii, *Pushkin,* 110; Brody, "Schiller's 'Demetrius,'" 244, 269–77; Nechkina, *A. S. Griboedov,* 98–99; Lincoln, *Between Heaven and Hell,* 130–32.

124. Zagorskii, *Pushkin,* 95, 127–29; Kostka, *Schiller,* 18, 216 n 5; Maikov, *Pamiati,* 330; Modzalevskii, *Pushkin i ego sovremenniki,* 103; Peterson, *Schiller,* 184–85; Bayley, *Pushkin,* 170.

125. Pushkin, *Sochineniia i pis'ma* (1903–6), 3: 240; Maikov, *Pamiati,* 143.

126. TL, 2: 135, 181; Modzalevskii, *Pushkin i ego sovremenniki,* 103, 277; Vatsuro, *A. S. Pushkin,* 2: 21.

127. See Brody, "Schiller's 'Demetrius,'" 258–59; Dyck, "Deceit," 96–110; Lysenkova, "O probleme," 59–69; Fischer, "Schiller," 603–11; Osterwald, *Das Demetrius-Thema,* 261–62.

128. *Letters,* 215; Bayley, *Pushkin,* 170; Brody, *Demetrius Legend,* 221, 246; Osterwald, *Das Demetrius-Thema,* 261–62; Kostka, *Schiller,* 18, 216. Schiller's *Demetrius* was first published in 1815. The second edition was published in 1818; see Schiller, *Sämmtliche Werke,* 12: 293–368. The first French translation of Schiller's *Demetrius*

was contained in the 1821 edition of his works that Pushkin requested while writing his *Comedy*; see Schiller, *Oeuvres*, volume 6.

129. Translations of passages from Schiller's *Demetrius* cited here are taken from the first English translation of his unfinished play; see Schiller, *Early Dramas and Romances* (1833). See also Brody, "Schiller's 'Demetrius,'" 269–73; idem, *Demetrius Legend*, 218–19.

130. See Lysenkova, "O probleme," 60–63; Dyck, "Deceit," 96–110; Brody, *Demetrius Legend*, 218–19, 222; and idem, "Schiller's 'Demetrius,'" 249, 258–59, 269–70.

131. Brody, *Demetrius Legend*, 222; idem, "Schiller's 'Demetrius,'" 247–50; Alekseev, "Boris Godunov," 106–8; Wiese, *Friedrich Schiller*, 793.

132. Osterwald, *Das Demetrius-Thema*, 143–44; Dyck, "Deceit and Conviction," 103; Bochkarev, *Russkaia istoricheskaia dramaturgiia*, 408–9; Alekseev, "Boris Godunov,"106–8; Brody, "Schiller's 'Demetrius,'" 247; idem, *Demetrius Legend*, 222.

133. See Levesques, *Histoire*, vol. 3, passim; and Dunning, "Use and Abuse," 359.

134. See, for example, Bayley, *Pushkin*, 176; Brody, "Schiller's 'Demetrius,'" 246, 249–63; Pomar, "Russian Historical Drama," 204.

135. See *Polnoe sobranie russkikh letopisei* [hereafter cited as PSRL], 14: 69; Skrynnikov, *Time of Troubles*, 40.

136. See Weise, *Friedrich Schiller*, 697; Brody, "Schiller's 'Demetrius,'" 249; Dyck, "Deceit and Conviction," 96–97; Alekseev, "Boris Godunov," 104–5; and Pushkin, *History of Pugachev*.

137. Brody, *Demetrius Legend*, 220, 237; Bayley, *Pushkin*, 172. Cf. *Istoriia russkogo dramaticheskogo teatra*, 1: 237, 249–50, 256–60; 2: 134–37.

138. TL, 1: 114, 119, 489; Holborn, *History*, 465–68. In 1823 (during his "southern exile"), Pushkin drew a portrait of Kotzebue; see Pushkin, *Complete Collection of Drawings*, 80.

139. See, for example, Vinokur, *Stati*, 96–97; Bayley, *Pushkin*, 178; Bowersock, "Roman Emperor," 136; Gurevich, "Istoriia," 212–13; and Raskol'nikov, "Boris Godunov," 161.

140. Alekseev, "Boris Godunov," 105–6; Brody, *Demetrius Legend*, 228.

141. Cooke and Dunning, "Tempting Fate," 58–62; Teplov, "Ateisticheskaia tema," 21; Emerson, *Boris Godunov*, 192–97; Sandler, "Problem," 89–90; Greenleaf, *Pushkin*, 383 n. 43; *Letters*, 367; BG, 488; Thompson, *Understanding Russia*, 128–30. See also Davydov, "Pushkin's Easter Triptych," 44–45.

142. Ronen, *Smyslovoi stroi*, 80.

143. Black, *Nicholas Karamzin*, 68; Baer, "Between Public and Private," 33–34, 44; Mocha, "Polish and Russian Sources," 46; Greenleaf, *Pushkin*, 175–77. On Pushkin's aristocratic perspective see Rabinovich, "Boris Godunov," 317; and Evdokimova, *Pushkin's Historical Imagination*, 39–41.

144. Bazilevich, "Boris Godunov," 37; Brody, *Demetrius Legend*, 242–43; Evdokimova, *Pushkin's Historical Imagination*, 43. See also BG, 140–42; Bowersock, "Roman Emperor," 130–47; Pokrovskii, "Pushkin," 478–86; and Reizov, "Pushkin," 66–82.

145. Tarle, "Pushkin," 211–15; Gurevich, "Istoriia," 212–13; Varneke, "Istochniki,"

17–19; Zagorskii, *Pushkin*, 117; Rassadin, *Dramaturg Pushkin*, 38; Bazilevich, "Boris Godunov," 53; Baer, "Between Public and Private," 44; Lotman, *Pushkin*, 197–98; Greenleaf, *Pushkin*, 175–77; Ronen, *Smyslovoi stroi*, 80; Evdokimova, *Pushkin's Historical Imagination*, 39–41.

146. See *Letters*, 267, 297; TL, 2: 100–101; Meilakh, *Pushkin i ego epokha*, 560; and Fedorov, *Kniaz' Kurbskii*, passim.

147. See Meilakh, *Pushkin i ego epokha*, 560; BG, 314–15.

148. To examine the differences between Karamzin's and Pushkin's views of Kurbsky see Karamzin, *Istoriia* (1892), 9: 37–38; 11: 76; Pipes, "Karamzin's Conception," 112–13; BG, 314–15; Black, "*Primechanija*," 143–44; Brody, *Demetrius Legend*, 240; idem, "Pushkin's 'Boris Godunov,'" 870–71; and Greenleaf, *Pushkin*, 177, 180, 195.

149. Baer, "Between Public and Private," 33–36; Blagoi, *Tvorcheskii put'* (1813–1826), 565–66; Bochkarev, *Russkaia istoricheskaia dramaturgiia*, 418–19; Brody, "Pushkin's 'Boris Godunov,'" 863, 870–71; idem, *Demetrius Legend*, 243.

150. See Fennell, *Correspondence*, 5, 9, 183, 185, 217, 229, 239. Cf. Emerson and Oldani, *Modest Musorgsky*, 32.

151. See RFCW, 474–76, 590 n. 87.

152. TL, 2: 302; Vatsuro, *A. S. Pushkin*, 1: 449–50; Greenleaf, *Pushkin*, 211; Baer, "Between Public and Private," 36.

153. On the enthusiastic initial response to Pushkin's *Comedy* see Barsukov, *Zhizn' Pogodina*, 2: 43–45; Simmons, *Pushkin*, 259–62, 272; Mirsky, *Pushkin*, 106, 153–56, 159–60; Briggs, "Hidden Forces," 43; Edmonds, *Pushkin*, 114–15; Emerson, "Pretenders," 259; Sandler, *Distant Pleasures*, 104–5, 213; Ashukin, *Pushkinskaia Moskva*, 119–29.

154. *Letters*, 261.

155. See *Letters*, 313; Pushkin, *History*, 36–37, 105; Avrich, *Russian Rebels*, 1, 258, 270; Brody, "Pushkin's 'Boris Godunov,'" 874; idem, "Schiller's 'Demetrius,'" 269–70, 275–77; Dolinin, "Historicism," 298–300.

156. See Solov'ev, "Obzor sobytii," 11; Rossiiskii gosudarstvennyi istoricheskii arkhiv, fond 772, opis' 1, delo No. 2209, list 2; and Lincoln, *Nicholas I*, 320–21.

157. On rumors that Pushkin had "sold out" to tsarist authorities see Tsiavlovskii, *Letopis'*, 520; *Letters*, 218; Vinokur, *Stat'i*, 86; and Simmons, *Pushkin*, 250–51.

158. On the "Decembrist spirit" of Pushkin's play see Levin, "Literatura," 129; Slonimskii, "Boris Godunov," 75–76; Brody, "Schiller's 'Demetrius,'" 269–70, 275–77; idem, *Demetrius Legend*, 249–50; idem, "Pushkin's 'Boris Godunov,'" 874; and Mocha, "Polish and Russian Sources," 46.

159. Brown, *History*, 3: 106; Rabinovich, "Boris Godunov," 317; Emerson, "Pretenders," 259; Evdokimova, *Pushkin's Historical Imagination*, 42–43.

160. See *Literaturnaia gazeta*, 1830, no. 4 (10 January), otd. "Bibliografiia," 31–32; no. 12 (25 February), otd. "Bibliografiia," 96–98; PS, 8/1: 125–40, 441–90; 11: 119–24; Strakhov, "Glavnoe sokrovishche," 17–34; Brody, "Pushkin's 'Boris Godunov,'" 862; Schönle, *Authenticity*, 181–202; Kropf, *Authorship*, 99–100; Debreczeny, *The Other Pushkin*, 71. David Bethea has a somewhat different interpretation of Pushkin's view

of Karamzin's *History of the Russian State*, but his argument ignores Pushkin's original *Comedy* and depends on the 1831 version of *Boris Godunov;* see Bethea, "The [Hi]story of the Village," 291–309.

161. Bayley, *Pushkin*, 166, 175; Karlinsky, *Russian Drama*, 323; Leach and Borovsky, *History*, 97; Raskol'nikov, "Boris Godunov," 161–63; Evdokimova, *Pushkin's Historical Imagination*, 42–43, 56, 60–62, 65.

162. Brown, *History*, 3: 109–10.

163. Brown, *History*, 3: 106; Pomar, "Russian Historical Drama," 184; Wolff, *Pushkin*, 264. See also Blagoi, *Tvorcheskii put' (1813–1826)*, 416; Fischer, "Schiller," 609–11; and Brody, "Pushkin's 'Boris Godunov,'" 862–63.

164. Gorodetskii, *Tragediia*, 72; Pomar, "Russian Historical Drama," 179; Gurevich, "Istoriia," 213; Lotman, *Pushkin*, 106. See also *Letters*, 267.

165. *Letters*, 365; Brody, "Schiller's 'Demetrius,'" 280; Sandler, *Distant Pleasures*, 105; Debreczeny, *Social Function*, 139–40. According to J. Thomas Shaw, Pushkin's reference to "allusions" would have had special significance to former members of certain secret societies that had been active during the early 1820s; see *Letters*, 395 n. 3.

166. See Alekseev, "A. S. Pushkin," 174–76; "O 'Borise Godunove,'" 445–55; Dinega, "Ambiguity," 526 n. 7; and Pushkin, *Critical Prose*, 122. See Chapter 3 for a discussion of Bulgarin as the author of the 1826 censor's report concerning Pushkin's *Comedy* and as the probable author of later reviews of *Boris Godunov* that echoed that censor's report.

167. TL, 3: 244; Abramkin, "Pushkin," 231; Emerson, *Boris Godunov*, 105–7, 235 nn. 47–48; Arkhangel'skii, "Problema," 5–16; Briggs, "Hidden Forces," 43–44; idem, *Alexander Pushkin*, 168, 176; Karlinsky, *Russian Drama*, 316; Leach and Borovsky, *History*, 98–99; Brown, *History*, 3: 105; Sandler, "Problem," 128–29; Wolff, "Shakespeare's Influence," 99–100; and Zagorskii, *Pushkin i teatr*, 94–96. See also Briggs, *Alexander Pushkin*, 168, 176.

168. PS, 13: 282; TL, 2: 151; Vinokur, *Stat'i*, 110.

169. See Bondi, *O Pushkine*, 169–241; and Brown, *History*, 3: 107.

170. On the possible influence of ancient Greek drama on Pushkin's play see Varneke, "Istochniki," 14; Mirsky, *Pushkin*, 157–58; Aronovskaia, "O vine Borisa Godunova," 128–56; Brown, *History*, 3: 109; and Ronen, *Smyslovoi stroi*, 6, 116–18; Emerson, *Boris Godunov*, 19.

171. Vatsuro, "Istoricheskaia tragediia," 331; Rassadin, *Dramaturg Pushkin*, 55; Verkhovskii, "Zapadnoevropeiskaia istoricheskaia drama," 224–26; Raskol'nikov, "Boris Godunov," 162; Emerson, *Boris Godunov*, 155; Ronen, *Smyslovoi stroi*, 114.

172. TL, 2: 204–5; Vinokur, "Kommentarii," 504–5; Blagoi, *Tvorcheskii put' (1826–1830)*, 565; Brody, "Pushkin's 'Boris Godunov,'" 860; Emerson and Oldani, *Modest Musorgsky*, 15; Greenleaf, *Pushkin*, 162.

173. TL, 2: 171, 204–5; Barsukov, *Zhizn' Pogodina*, 2: 9; Maikov, *Pushkin*, 330; Meilakh, *Pushkin i ego epokha*, 560; Rybinskii, *Sbornik*, 150; Vinokur, "Kommentarii," 504; Mocha, "Polish and Russian Sources," 48–49.

174. TL, 2: 171, 190–91; *Letters*, 365–67; Zagorskii, *Pushkin*, 108. See also RFCW, 206–8.

175. See RFCW, 234–38; and Dunning, "Who Was Tsar Dmitrii?" 723–24.

176. See PS, 13: 235; Platon, *Kratkaia Tserkovnaia Rossiiskaia istoriia,* 2: 167–79; Pushkin, *Sochineniia* (1887), 3: 84; idem, *Sochineniia i pis'ma* (1903–6), 3: 255; Solov'ev, *Sobranie sochinenii,* col. 1388.

177. On the reaction of the Russian people to the assassination of Tsar Dmitry see RFCW, chapters 13–14.

178. TL, 2: 204–5.

179. TL, 3: 68; *Letters,* 365–67; Maikov, *Pushkin,* 330; Rybinskii, *Sbornik,* 150–51; Blagoi, *Tvorcheskii put' (1826–1830),* 565; and Brody, "Pushkin's 'Boris Godunov,'" 867–68.

180. *Letters,* 365–67; Annenkov, *P. V. Annenkov,* 484–85; Vinokur, *Kommentarii,* 347–48; Rybinskii, *Sbornik,* 151; Maikov, *Pushkin,* 330; Blagoi, *Tvorcheskii put',* 565–66; Pomar, "Russian Historical Drama," 195; Mocha, "Russian and Polish Sources," 49; and Mucha, "Samozwańcza," 529–36.

181. See RFCW, 242–44.

182. See *Letters,* 225, 366; Vinokur, *Stat'i,* 100; Gurevich, "Istoriia," 211–13; Mirsky, *Pushkin,* 2; and Brody, "Pushkin's 'Boris Godunov,'" 860.

183. See TL, 2: 204–5; Vinokur, "Kommentarii," 504–5; Maikov, *Pushkin,* 330; Pavlov-Sil'vanskii, "Narod," 289–90; Gurevich, "Istoriia," 211–13; Emerson and Oldani, *Modest Musorgsky,* 15; and Greenleaf, *Pushkin,* 162.

184. See Rassadin, *Dramaturg Pushkin,* 39; Gurevich, "Istoriia," 206, 211–12; RFCW, 95–96, 124; Margeret, *Russian Empire,* 81; and Bussow, *Disturbed State,* 27.

185. On the Romanovs as supporters of Tsar Dmitry and as courtiers of the "second false Dmitry" see RFCW, 209–10, 394; and Bussow, *Disturbed State,* 115.

3

The Tragic Fate of Pushkin's *Comedy*

∽ CHESTER DUNNING

Pushkin finished writing his *Comedy* on November 7, 1825, and was extremely proud of it. The exiled poet-historian sincerely hoped that his play would revolutionize Russian drama and demonstrate his continuing commitment to enlightened values. He was especially anxious to put an end to lingering rumors that he had somehow "sold out" to tsarist authorities while living in exile.[1] Unfortunately, Pushkin was "unlucky in his timing."[2] Less than two weeks after he had completed his masterpiece, the childless Tsar Alexander I died unexpectedly, triggering the ill-fated Decembrist Rebellion. Alexander's younger brother, Nicholas, quickly crushed the rebellion and took the throne; and within a few months he ushered in a new era of suspicion, much tighter censorship, and dramatically increased police surveillance over Russian society. Among other things, Nicholas I established the notorious Third Section of His Majesty's Own Imperial Chancery, which soon came to symbolize his reign. Presided over by General Count Alexander Benckendorff, the Third Section supervised and coordinated the regular and political police, gathered intelligence, spied on suspected troublemakers, arrested and exiled dissidents, ran the prison system, and handled the censorship of all Russian books and periodicals.[3]

Preliminary investigation of the Decembrist Rebellion led some officials to suspect that, even in exile, Pushkin had played a part in the quixotic uprising of liberals and radicals. Several of Pushkin's friends had been arrested for participating in the rebellion, and copies of his politically incorrect poems were found among their papers. Under interrogation, some Decembrists openly admitted that Pushkin's poetry had helped inspire them to rebel.[4] In fact, one of the Decembrists – Pushkin's old friend, Ivan Pushchin – had summoned Pushkin to St. Petersburg on the eve of the rebellion. Pushkin secretly started out for the capital in early December, 1825, but quickly returned to Mikhailovskoe due to "ill omens." Had he reached St. Petersburg, there is no doubt that he would have participated in the Decembrist Rebellion.[5]

Following the collapse of the rebellion, Pushkin feared that he would be arrested; and he burned potentially incriminating papers before tsarist officials could seize them.[6] A few of Pushkin's friends were interrogated solely because of their connection to him, while others destroyed copies of his dangerous poems as a precaution.[7] Although some Russians called for the poet's release from exile as a way to show the new tsar's mercy and to gain public favor for his regime, Nicholas I and Benckendorff did not trust Pushkin. They feared that the popular young poet might become a magnet for malcontents. Therefore, Nicholas was in no hurry to end Pushkin's exile. Instead, more spies were enlisted to investigate the "dangerous" young man. One of the reasons for continuing suspicion about him was that Pushkin, who had been under constant surveillance since 1820, reportedly denounced Tsar Alexander as a "tyrant" upon hearing of his death.[8] Benckendorff also received an alarming report that Pushkin was continuing his "rebellious, disgraceful behavior" and even inciting local peasants to revolt. Officials sent to look into that matter carried with them an open warrant for Pushkin's arrest just in case the report was confirmed. Fortunately, the poet's neighbors spoke kindly of him and assured the investigators that he was behaving modestly and not stirring up a peasant rebellion.[9]

Astonishingly enough, in spite of the Decembrist Rebellion, by the end of 1825 several literary journals gleefully announced that Pushkin had completed his historical drama, and – without seeing it – they pronounced it a monumental contribution to Russian literature.[10] Expectations for Pushkin's long-awaited *Comedy* were extraordinarily high. In fact, in Western Europe as well as in Russia, it was probably the most anticipated of Pushkin's works.[11] During the first half of 1826, the restless young exile received a constant stream of letters from friends and colleagues requesting to see his new play.[12] Pushkin responded to this intense interest by withholding his *Comedy* from eager publishers and by refusing to send copies to his friends. Instead, he claimed to be looking forward to reading his play to them in person – hoping thereby to convince them to exert pressure on the authorities to release him from exile.[13] To his friend Pyotr Pletnev, he wrote, "There will be no *Boris* for you until you summon me to Petersburg."[14]

Pushkin's repeated requests for help in securing his release from exile prompted his friends Pletnev, Vasily Zhukovsky, and even Nicholas Karamzin to plead his case to tsarist officials.[15] But Zhukovsky also warned Pushkin that the discovery of his poems among the papers of the Decembrists had not made him many friends at court, and, as a result, the time was not yet ripe for him to come to the capital.[16] It should be noted that Zhukovsky and others had previously encouraged Pushkin to think that his play might "open the doors of freedom" to him – especially if he behaved himself;[17] and Pushkin himself occasionally seemed to believe that his *Comedy* really could help him escape from exile.[18] But he was also well aware that his provocative play, as originally written, would not be approved by tsarist censors.[19] A few of Pushkin's contemporaries actually predicted trouble with the censors over the content of his new play.[20]

Since his *Comedy* challenged Karamzin's conservative views, Pushkin wisely hesitated to let his mentor read it (and possibly take offense) while Karamzin was trying to help him escape from exile. The two old friends had cautiously reestablished indirect contact with each other while Pushkin was writing his historical drama, and during the early months of 1826 Karamzin attempted to obtain a copy of Pushkin's much-discussed play.[21] Karamzin had a strong interest in Pushkin's *Comedy* and even tried to help him improve it – especially the characterization of Tsar Boris.[22] Although Pushkin was very fond of Karamzin and grateful for his help, he still recalled with anguish their falling out years earlier and never shared his *Comedy* with the historian laureate, who died in May 1826.[23] It is, of course, well known that Pushkin eventually dedicated the published version of *Boris Godunov* to Karamzin, but there is no truth to the claim that he made up his mind to dedicate it to his old friend while the latter was still alive.[24]

In the months before Karamzin's death, Tsar Nicholas sought the historian laureate's advice on several new government appointments, including those of former Arzamassians Dmitry Dashkov and Sergei Uvarov.[25] In quiet discussions with the tsar, Karamzin also interceded on behalf of another former Arzamassian, Alexander Pushkin. Karamzin probably told Nicholas that Russia's most famous young man-of-letters was no longer dangerous and could be very useful to the tsar – both as a world-renowned symbol of his reign (in the way Karamzin had been a symbol of Alexander's reign) and as a writer who could help stir interest and pride in Russian history, something dear to the heart of Nicholas I.[26]

Once the tsar became convinced that Pushkin was not stirring up trouble, he decided to release him from exile but to keep him under surveillance. Nicholas hoped that this display of generosity would help counter-balance his image as the crusher of the Decembrist Rebellion. He also hoped that Pushkin might somehow be persuaded to use his powerful pen in support of the new regime.[27] Shortly after his coronation in late August 1826, Nicholas ordered a military escort to bring Pushkin directly from Mikhailovskoe to Moscow for a face-to-face meeting. At first, Pushkin thought the soldiers had come to take him away to Siberia.[28] After so many years in exile, he found it hard to believe that the tsar intended to release him. But, to Pushkin's great surprise, in a famous encounter in the Kremlin's Chudov Monastery on September 8, the road-weary and disheveled poet was received graciously by Nicholas, who tried to convince him that he was not a tyrant and actually intended to introduce some reforms "from above."[29] Both men wanted the meeting to go well, and Pushkin was more than willing to give Nicholas a chance to prove that he could become a new Peter the Great – a ruler greatly admired by Pushkin. The young poet was not only extremely grateful to be released from exile but even dared to hope that he might have the opportunity to give the new tsar his own views on how to transform Russia – just as Karamzin had done during the reign of Alexander I.[30]

Pushkin forthrightly told Nicholas that some of his close friends had been Decembrists and that he would have joined their rebellion if he had been in St. Petersburg. He then promised that he would not become a troublemaker again. The tsar responded enthusiastically to the poet's honesty and willingness to turn a new leaf. To Pushkin's astonishment and delight, Nicholas informed him that he, Nicholas, would be the poet's censor from that point forward.[31] The newly-freed poet was – at first – completely won over by Nicholas' kindness and generosity, and to his friends he spoke with gratitude and devotion about the new tsar.[32] Soon after his meeting with Nicholas, Pushkin was contacted by Benckendorff, who told him that the tsar wanted to employ the poet's talents for Russia and requested that he write a report about his ideas concerning the education of young people. Pushkin took the assignment seriously and tried to do a good job, but he also strove to maintain his integrity. His report clearly demonstrated that he was not going to become an apologist for autocracy.[33] That must have disappointed Nicholas, who regarded Pushkin as one of the most intelligent men in Russia and desired to bind him "with silken chains" in order to turn the brilliant poet into "an adornment to his reign."[34]

In the weeks immediately following his meeting with Nicholas, Pushkin remained completely unaware of just how much of a sham his pardon had been and how illusory his new freedom really was. He had no idea that Benckendorff's agents continued to spy on him or that the tsar had no intention of keeping his promise to be Pushkin's personal censor.[35] In his naive initial enthusiasm about being freed from exile and being favored by Nicholas, Pushkin wrote to a friend: "The tsar has freed me from censorship. He himself is my censor. The advantage is, of course, enormous. Thus we shall print Godunov."[36] Pushkin completely misinterpreted his situation and was certainly wrong about the immediate prospects for publishing his play.[37] Only two days after meeting with Nicholas, the proud poet began exercising his new freedom by giving a series of high-profile readings of his Comedy to many distinguished friends and colleagues in Moscow – for which he received "the greatest public acclaim he ever experienced."[38]

Pushkin's audience during those famous readings in September and October 1826 made up a significant portion of Russia's proto-intelligentsia – including Pyotr Chaadaev, Aleksei Khomiakov, the brothers Ivan and Pyotr Kireevsky, and many others who were particularly interested in importing German Romantic drama to Russia.[39] Most of them listened to Pushkin's Comedy with "stunned admiration."[40] Pushkin was described by many of them later as a genius who had written an excellent and beautiful play – one that could indeed usher in a new era for Russian theater and literature.[41] Indeed, he was compared favorably to Shakespeare and Schiller.[42] It is important to remember that Pushkin's audience was expressing enthusiasm for his Comedy, not for the compromised version of Boris Godunov, which was published several years later.[43] They fully understood his original play to be Shakespearean, revolutionary in form, anti-autocratic, and opposed to serfdom.[44] They also knew that Pushkin had just been released from exile, that he was apparently permitted to read his radical play to them, and that he was optimistic about publishing his provocative Comedy. That must have at least temporarily lowered their post-Decembrist anxiety and may even have stirred some hope for the new regime of Nicholas I.[45]

Mikhail Pogodin, who became a famous conservative historian, recorded the reaction of Pushkin's high-powered audience to the newly liberated poet's dramatic reading of his play, which Pogodin still recalled vividly forty years later:[46]

> What effect that reading had on all of us is impossible to convey.... Instead of the high-flown language of the gods, we heard speech that was simple, clear, ordinary, but at the same time poetically captivating!... The scene with the chronicler and Grigory overwhelmed us. It seemed to me that my dear old Nestor had arisen from the grave and had begun to speak. I heard the living voice of the ancient Russian chronicler. When Pushkin came to the part where Pimen describes [Tsar] Ivan's visit to the Kirillov monastery and the prayer of the monks, we simply began to lose our minds. Some were thrown into a sweat, others shivered. One's hair stood on end. It was impossible to restrain oneself. Now someone would suddenly leap to his feet, now another would cry out. One minute there was silence, then an outburst of exclamations.... The reading ended. For a long time we looked at each other and then threw ourselves at Pushkin. Embraces began, a din arose, laughter broke out, and tears flowed amid the congratulations.... Then the champagne appeared, and Pushkin grew animated, seeing the effect he had produced on this select company of young men. Our excitement pleased him. With mounting passion he began to read us songs about Stenka Razin.

Pushkin went on that same evening to describe plans for a sequel to his *Comedy* to be called *Dmitry the Pretender*.[47] Upon reflection, it is somewhat puzzling that Pogodin's famous description of the audience's reaction to the original version of Pushkin's play did not – long ago – stir more interest in the *Comedy* among scholars and critics disappointed in or confused by *Boris Godunov*.

Pushkin was understandably thrilled by the acclaim his *Comedy* received, and he immediately made arrangements for the publication of one scene from his play ("Night. A Cell in the Chudov Monastery") in a new journal to be edited by Pogodin – *Moskovskii Vestnik*. That involved submitting the scene to tsarist censors operating under Nicholas I's tough new censorship statute. But after a few bureaucratic delays, official permission was granted and the scene appeared in print in early January 1827.[48] Pushkin also began making plans to publish the entire text of the *Comedy*, but gendarmes of the Third Section found out about his readings of the play and reported them to their boss.[49] Benckendorff then sent Pushkin a letter scolding him for reading his play without the tsar's permission. The letter also made it clear to the poet that he was still under constant police surveillance and had apparently misunderstood the terms of his "parole" as well as the censorship rules that applied to him. The chief of gendarmes reiterated that all work written by Pushkin had to be approved by Nicholas before being published or read in public.[50]

Pushkin was quickly sobered by Benckendorff's letter and immediately sent him a letter of apology in which he claimed that he had intended to send Nicholas his play after removing a few "indelicate expressions" from it and making a second copy for himself. Those plans were now dropped, and he quickly forwarded to Benckendorff his only copy of the *Comedy* "in the same form" as it was when he read it to his friends.[51] Pushkin assumed, of course, that Benckendorff would give his play to Nicholas – his personal censor – to read; and, indeed, the tsar did want to see Pushkin's *Comedy*.[52] But instead of immediately giving the play to the tsar, Benckendorff commissioned a censor's report on it. That secret report was completed in early December and was overall negative. The author of the report urged that Pushkin's *Comedy* not be published or performed on stage because it violated Nicholas' new censorship rules.[53] As Pushkin had anticipated, the censor objected to the presence of vulgar language in the play (lines spoken by Captain Margeret in the scene "A Plain near Novgorod-Seversky").[54] The censor's report also objected to the portrayal of vagrant monks and to the presence in the play of the patriarch of the Russian Orthodox Church – a very sensitive topic ever since Peter the Great had abolished that holy office in the early eighteenth century.[55] The censor, who was influenced by an essay on the history of the Russian theater that Nikolai Grech had published in *Ruskaia Taliia,* also criticized the radical form of Pushkin's play – likening it to the then-popular novels of Walter Scott.[56]

Far more devastating, the censor expressed alarm about Pushkin's negative portrayal of "tsarist power" and especially about the play's discussion of the Pretender Dmitry's promise of freedom to Russian serfs in return for supporting his campaign for the throne – a completely taboo subject during Nicholas' reign.[57] When Benckendorff showed the report to the tsar and declared that Pushkin's *Comedy* violated Nicholas' own censorship rules, he drew particular attention to the play's inclusion of a rebellion by the *narod* against a legitimate ruler.[58] The tsar then (by way of Benckendorff) informed Pushkin that his play could not be published, in part because of passages that might be interpreted as references to recent "circumstances" – meaning the Decembrist Rebellion.[59] Benckendorff told Pushkin that the tsar had read his play and that Nicholas had written "in his own handwriting" this message for the poet: "I think that Mr. Pushkin's goal would be achieved if, after cleansing it as needed, he turned his *Comedy* into an historical tale or novel in the manner of Walter Scott."[60] Many scholars have questioned Benckendorff's claim about the authorship of the "tsar's" message to Pushkin, regarding it instead as the product of the censor or of Benckendorff himself.[61]

Pushkin was stunned by Nicholas' refusal to allow him to publish his *Comedy*. On January 3, 1827, he wrote a letter to Benckendorff in which he tartly rejected the idea of converting his play into a novel: "I regret that I have not the power to re-do what I have once written."[62] But the tsar's decision was a "cruel blow" to Pushkin and his plans for reforming Russian drama.[63] In spite of the setback, however, general enthusiasm for Pushkin's unpublished play continued to grow.[64] For example, the publication of the scene "Night. A Cell in the Chudov Monastery" in *Moskovskii Vestnik* in early 1827 provoked extremely positive comments from many people, including Alexander Griboedov, who "loved" the monastery scene and longed to see the entire play,[65] and the great Polish poet Adam Mickiewicz, who compared the author of the *Comedy* to Shakespeare.[66]

Well aware that he was still under police surveillance, Pushkin continued to hold somewhat risky readings of his play. In fact, at a reading of *Comedy* at the Karamzin family home he met one of Benckendorff's censors, who seemed friendly enough at the time.[67] Pushkin also continued to make plans for the publication of another scene from his play ("The Lithuanian Border") in the journal *Severnye tsvety*.[68] In this period, his historical drama was frequently called a "superior work" or his "best work" – one that would certainly "secure his fame."[69] Fragments of the *Comedy* kept appearing in print (sometimes without Pushkin's knowledge or permission), and critical acclaim for the play continued throughout 1827 and 1828.[70] Requests to publish other scenes from the *Comedy* poured in, and Pushkin continued to read his play to selected audiences – including Griboedov, Mickiewicz, Nikolai Karamzin's sons, and Pushkin's friend Peter Viazemsky.[71] Not surprisingly, those readings generated extraordinary praise for Pushkin's play, as well as demands for the publication of the *Comedy* as a "drama to make Russia proud," and calls for its translation to show off Russia's "national spirit."[72] Remarkably enough, Pushkin's play also received considerable positive attention in West European journals, including *Revue Encyclopédique* (published in Paris). In fact, the January 1829 issue of *The Foreign Quarterly Review* (published in London) hailed Pushkin's *Comedy* as the beginning of a "new era in Russian dramatic literature."[73]

While Pushkin's *Comedy* was receiving all this acclaim, Pushkin himself was growing increasingly frustrated by his own circumstances – including being denied the opportunity for "meaningful service" to his country, being spied upon constantly, having his mail opened by the authorities, and being denied permission to publish his play. Benckendorff, who despised Pushkin, went out of his way to harass the poet, to stymie his career, and to encourage the tsar's doubts about the poet's loyalty.[74] Choosing his moment carefully, in June 1828, Benckendorff informed Nicholas that Pushkin was still reading his *Comedy* to select audiences. The tsar responded by ordering Pushkin not to read his play to others and sternly reminding him that he, Nicholas, was the poet's censor and that Pushkin was already well aware of that.[75] The tsar's message had an immediate impact: readings of the *Comedy* quickly dwindled. But Pushkin and his friends continued to discuss ways to see his play into print. More lenient censorship rules imposed in 1828 may have encouraged them, but Pushkin's problems – especially with the Third Section – kept interfering with his plans.[76]

By 1829, Pushkin began to have misgivings about publishing his *Comedy*. He recognized by then that, as Nicholas' regime grew increasingly conservative, the timing was not right for his radical plan to revolutionize Russian drama. In fact, he began to suspect that his *Comedy* had become an anachronism.[77] He had also grown weary of people thinking that his play was some kind of commentary on the Decembrist Rebellion. Nevertheless, the combination of his marriage plans, the decline of the poetry market, and his sense of growing older pushed him to seek increased security, status, and income. It is not surprising, therefore, that he still wanted to publish his play;[78] and he eventually came up with an ingenious plan to get it past Benckendorff's censors. The beleaguered poet asked his dear friend Vasily Zhukovsky – whom Nicholas trusted completely – to take responsibility for making a few cosmetic changes in the play in order to satisfy the tsar. In a draft letter to his friend Nikolai Raevsky (probably written on June 30, 1829), Pushkin claimed that the play's "gross indecencies" would be removed in preparation for publication, and he expressed optimism about writing sequels to his *Comedy*.[79] On July 20, 1829, Pushkin's friend Pyotr Pletnev formally submitted a "revised" version of the *Comedy* to the Third Section. Pletnev informed the authorities that Zhukovsky had "corrected and improved" Pushkin's play in response to the tsar's concerns expressed back in 1826.[80]

Unfortunately, this bold strategy did not succeed. Once again, Benckendorff recommended that Nicholas refuse permission to publish the play. He pointed out that Pushkin had failed to heed the tsar's request to convert his *Comedy* into a novel, and he emphasized that the changes made by Zhukovsky were insignificant. Nicholas agreed with Benckendorff's analysis and on October 10, 1829, he officially denied Pushkin's request. But the chief of gendarmes was in no hurry to inform Pushkin of the decision. Pushkin eventually sent him a letter requesting information about the fate of his play. Finally, on January 21, 1830, Benckendorff wrote Pushkin a letter stating that his play could not be published without further revisions because the changes made in "your *Comedy*" were "too trivial."[81] To be honest, the changes were trivial. To illustrate, it is easy to imagine the exasperation of Benckendorff's censors when they came across the proposed change in Captain Margeret's lines in "A Plain Near Novgorod-Seversky." Pushkin had acknowledged as far back as 1825 that the Frenchman's swearing would not get past the censors.[82] Margeret's original comment about the Pretender Dmitry's energetic military campaign was obscene, but at least it did not praise Dmitry – whom Nicholas truly hated:[83]

> Tudieu! Il y fait chaud! Ce diable de Pre-tend-er, comme ils
>   l'appellent, est un bougre qui a du poil au cul.

The "improved and corrected" lines (handed off to Margeret's co-commander, W. Rosen), on the other hand, praised the Pretender:[84]

> Diable, il y fait chaud! Ce diable de Samozvanets,
>   Comme il s'appelle, est un brave à trois poils.

Under the circumstances, it is no surprise that Nicholas continued to refuse to let Pushkin's *Comedy* be published. Ironically, even as Benckendorff penned his letter of rejection, scenes from Pushkin's play continued to appear in print and draw considerable praise.[85]

Sometime toward the end of 1829, while waiting anxiously to hear about the fate of his play, Pushkin found out that Benckendorff had been working actively against him on behalf of Pushkin's main literary rival, Faddei Bulgarin – an unscrupulous informer who would take any measure to destroy Pushkin. Pushkin learned that Benckendorff wanted to make sure that Bulgarin's new novel about the Pretender Dmitry, *Dimitrii Samozvanets,* was published before Pushkin's play ever saw the light of day.[86] That was not the only shocking news. Pushkin also learned that Bulgarin had not only been working closely with Benckendorff to frustrate Pushkin's career but had actually helped tsarist censors develop their arguments against his "dangerous" play.[87]

Faddei Bulgarin was the son of a fanatically patriotic Polish Catholic who, in 1794, had supported Tadeusz Kosciuszko's failed uprising against Russian domination of Poland. Faddei himself had a checkered career before he became a leading apologist for Russian autocracy. At one time a soldier in Napoleon's army and later a friend of some future Decembrists, the politically vulnerable Bulgarin went out of his way in 1826 to prove his loyalty to Tsar Nicholas and the Russian empire.[88] He wrote approvingly of censorship and encouraged the government to support patriotic writers.[89] Along with his business partner, Nikolai Grech, Bulgarin published newspapers and journals that promoted the policies of Nicholas I and ruthlessly attacked Bulgarin's literary rivals, including Pushkin.[90] Bulgarin also wrote periodic intelligence reports for the Third Section in which he identified persons and publications he regarded as subversive or disloyal to the tsar.[91] Bulgarin was a very popular writer, but he was despised by most Russian intellectuals as a dishonest hack, police spy, and immoral opportunist.[92] Benckendorff, however, found the odious Bulgarin to be extremely useful; he often praised Bulgarin's patriotic newspaper, *The Northern Bee* – in which agents of the Third Section were permitted to publish politically correct articles anonymously.[93] Benckendorff carefully protected Bulgarin's business activities, helped him become rich, and tirelessly promoted him to Nicholas as the "conscience" of Russian writers and as the country's leading man of letters.[94] The chief of gendarmes also helped Bulgarin in his struggle against Pushkin, which – contrary to the conclusions of some scholars – began long before 1829.[95]

At about the same time that Nicholas released Pushkin from exile, Benckendorff recommended to the tsar that Bulgarin be appointed as a salaried "special agent" in the Ministry of Education, which was directly involved in the censorship of Russian books and periodicals. Nicholas agreed, and Bulgarin began his secret career as a censor and spy in November 1826.[96] One of the very first assignments he received from Benckendorff was to write a report about Pushkin's *Comedy*. Most scholars who have studied the subject agree that Bulgarin was the author of the secret censor's report that condemned Pushkin's play and recommended against its publication.[97] Interestingly enough, those few scholars who dispute this conclusion have suggested instead that it was Bulgarin's business partner, Nikolai Grech, who wrote the report.[98] There are, however, very convincing reasons to believe that Bulgarin was the author. For example, whoever wrote the report mixed "Polonisms" with his Russian and was, therefore, almost certainly a native Polish speaker – which disqualifies Grech and points to Bulgarin. Bulgarin was also extremely well informed before anyone else – including Pushkin – about the changes that were required in order to get Pushkin's play past the censors. In addition, starting as early as 1827, Bulgarin's friend Alexander Griboedov kept pestering Bulgarin for a chance to see the complete text of Pushkin's unpublished play. [99]

When excerpts from Bulgarin's soon-to-be-published novel *Dimitrii Samozvanets* first appeared in print in November 1829, Pushkin immediately realized that Benckendorff must have given Bulgarin access to the manuscript of his *Comedy* because Bulgarin's novel contained material that had clearly been stolen from Pushkin's unpublished play.[100] At about the same time, Pushkin's fellow former Arzamassian, Dmitry Dashkov – whose official duties gave him routine access to the files of the Third Section – came across the 1826 censor's report on the *Comedy* and informed Pushkin's friends Viazemsky and Zhukovsky about it. Dashkov also told them that Bulgarin was, indeed, a police spy – just as they had suspected.[101] Pushkin was understandably outraged by the combination of Bulgarin's activities, the delay in getting his play into print, and especially Bulgarin's shameless plagiarism of his *Comedy*. He contemplated demanding an immediate public apology from his hated rival.[102] At about the same time (November 1829), Bulgarin – sensing that Pushkin's reputation was not as strong as it had been earlier and knowing all about the poet's ongoing difficulties with the Third Section – redoubled his own efforts to destroy Pushkin's reputation in the eyes of the tsar and the Russian reading public.[103] Bulgarin had recently made a considerable sum of money from his first novel, *Ivan Vyzhigin*, and now fancied himself Russia's leading writer. He regarded Pushkin as his only significant rival and actively plotted to discredit him in order to elevate himself. The result was a long and bitter struggle for dominance in the Russian literary world.[104]

Pushkin certainly had Bulgarin in mind when he joined forces with his friends Viazemsky, Zhukovsky, and Anton Delvig in December 1829 to create the new weekly journal *Literary Gazette,* which simultaneously promoted Pushkin's literary career and waged war against Bulgarin, Grech, and the *Northern Bee.*[105] With Delvig serving as editor, *Literary Gazette* began publication in January 1830; and, from the very beginning, it took aim at Bulgarin.[106] Unfortunately for Pushkin and Delvig, the Third Section actively helped Bulgarin during their highly public struggle.[107]

At the center of the initial clash between Pushkin and Bulgarin was the latter's new novel *Dimitrii Samozvanets.* Pushkin had, of course, rejected Nicholas's suggestion that he convert his *Comedy* into a novel, but Bulgarin – who had access to Pushkin's play and was well aware of the "tsar's" comments about it – seized the opportunity to write a novel about the Time of Troubles that Nicholas would enjoy. *Dimitrii Samozvanets* was published in late 1829 and went on sale to the public in February 1830. It was a big success; the first edition sold out almost immediately, and a second edition was published in March 1830.[108] Bulgarin made a small fortune from the novel, and Benckendorff effusively praised it to the tsar.[109] The chief of gendarmes managed to persuade Nicholas to award Bulgarin a gold and jewel ring for *Dimitrii Samozvanets,* and Bulgarin openly gloated over his success at Pushkin's expense.[110]

Bulgarin's novel – as dull as it is – is important. *Dimitrii Samozvanets* contains dozens of passages stolen directly from Pushkin's *Comedy* – including Boris Godunov's conversation with Basmanov about the abolition of *mestnichestvo,* his conversation with his son Fyodor about the young man's newly drawn map of Russia, and Vasily Shuisky informing the tsar of the existence of the Pretender Dmitry.[111] But Bulgarin's novel was not just a plagiarized imitation of Pushkin's play. Instead, it was cleverly designed to discredit the dangerous ideas about the Time of Troubles found in Pushkin's *Comedy.* In *Dimitrii Samozvanets,* Bulgarin carried on a polemic with Pushkin's still-unpublished ideas and, in the process, played directly to Benckendorff and the censors. Bulgarin offered a more patriotic interpretation of the period than Pushkin did, including a far more negative portrayal of the Pretender Dmitry. By citing the most recent politically safe scholarship on the Time of Troubles, Bulgarin also attempted to make Pushkin's interpretation of Dmitry obsolete. The Pretender's success, according to Bulgarin, was the result of a Polish Catholic plot and not – as Pushkin had suggested – the result of the unhappy Russian masses.[112] In *Dimitrii Samozvanets*, Bulgarin also went out of his way to vilify Pushkin's ancestor Gavrila Pushkin (an important character in the *Comedy*) as well as to attack the experimental and controversial aspects of Pushkin's daring play – including his characterization of Prince Kurbsky. In his novel and elsewhere Bulgarin also slyly associated Pushkin with the hated Jesuits.[113] At the same time, Pushkin's unscrupulous rival cleverly linked his own work to that of Karamzin and dreamed of succeeding the great man as Russia's foremost writer.[114]

Interestingly enough, Bulgarin's novel is heavily annotated, with extremely good historical commentary on the many original sources used by the author. These notes were almost certainly written by Bulgarin's protégé, a young St. Petersburg University instructor named Nikolai Ustrialov.[115] Significantly, Ustrialov himself was allowed by tsarist censors to publish a Russian translation of Margeret's important but controversial account of the Time of Troubles in 1830 – before Pushkin was allowed to publish his *Comedy*. In the introduction to that translation, Ustrialov discredited the Frenchman's (and, by implication, Pushkin's) interpretation of Dmitry while at the same time extravagantly praising Karamzin's views. In fact, so eager was Ustrialov to be associated with Karamzin that he actually mistranslated some passages in Margeret's book in order to make it conform to the historian laureate's interpretation of Boris Godunov and the Time of Troubles.[116]

The efforts of Bulgarin and Ustrialov to associate themselves with Karamzin had a serious purpose related to Bulgarin's struggle with Pushkin. During the years following the death of Karamzin and the publication of the final, posthumous volume of his *History of the Russian State*, Karamin's work became the subject of a heated scholarly debate. By 1830, with the active support of the government, Count Sergei Uvarov (president of the Russian Academy) and several other former Arzamassians succeeded in imposing Karamzin's views of Russian history as canonical. As Nicholas I's regime became increasingly conservative, sharp criticism and official displeasure awaited writers who dared to challenge Karamzin's work.[117] Mikhail Pogodin, for example, came under such ferocious attack for criticizing Karamzin's *History* that, in order to salvage his own reputation, he felt compelled to transform himself into an unquestioning cheerleader of Karamzin's works.[118] Prodded by his fellow former Arzamassians Zhukovsky and Viazemsky, Pushkin eventually joined in the public defense of Karamzin and his *History*.[119] Nevertheless, he

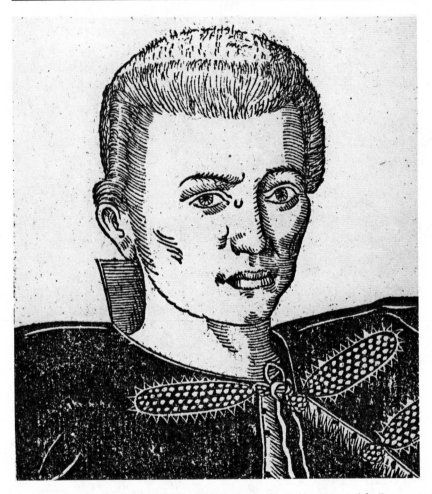

3. Early-seventeenth-century woodcut of the Pretender Dmitry Ivanovich. From
D. A. Rovinskii, *Materialy dlia Russkoi Ikonografii,* part 2 (St. Petersburg, 1884).
Courtesy of Houghton Library, Harvard University.

resisted the temptation to revise his *Comedy* to conform to Karamzin's
interpretation of the Time of Troubles. In fact, Pushkin's praise of
Karamzin in this period has been aptly described as "suspiciously strong"
(if sincere) and directly related to his "ferocious struggle" with Bulgarin
to inherit Karamzin's position as Russia's leading writer. When Pushkin
observed Bulgarin maneuvering to link himself to Karamzin, Pushkin
openly accused him of plagiarism and set out to challenge Bulgarin's

bold effort to promote himself as Karamzin's successor. It is no exaggeration to say that it was his competition with Bulgarin, more than anything else, that compelled Pushkin "to pursue seriously his claim that Karamzin's mantle of greatness should rightfully fall on his shoulders."[120]

During his conflict with Pushkin, Bulgarin continued to help his young protégé Ustrialov establish his own reputation as a highly productive historian totally loyal to Karamzin's ideas. In addition to encouraging him to translate Margeret's book, Bulgarin urged Ustrialov to publish Russian translations of Polish sources on the Time of Troubles. He even provided him with two important Polish sources already translated (and previously published) by Bulgarin himself that Ustrialov subsequently reworked slightly and put into print under his own name – thereby adding two more books to his fast-growing résumé.[121] It was certainly no coincidence that the powerful Count Uvarov also took an interest in promoting Ustrialov's career at this time and began grooming him as a potential successor to Karamzin as historian laureate of Russia. As one of Uvarov's "discoveries," Ustrialov enjoyed many of the benefits of his patronage – for example, a promotion at the university, swift publication of his books at presses associated with or controlled by Uvarov, and friendly censors (including one of Bulgarin's close friends, Osip Senkovsky, who was despised by Pushkin).[122] Ustrialov thrived under the care of Bulgarin and Uvarov and aggressively promoted the conservative ideas put forward in Karamzin's *History* and Tsar Nicholas I's doctrine of "Official Nationality."[123] Despite Uvarov's strenuous efforts to simultaneously hinder Pushkin's career and promote the patriotic Ustrialov as the logical successor to Karamzin, Uvarov's "discovery" did not manage to become historian laureate of Russia until several years after Pushkin's death.

Uvarov's relationship with Pushkin needs clarification. It has generally been assumed that he became Pushkin's enemy only after becoming Minister of Education in 1834. But Pushkin, along with several other former Arzamassians, actually broke with Uvarov in 1822 over his unethical business practices. Pushkin even satirized Uvarov's corruption, and the latter never forgave him for it.[124] Although professing friendship with Pushkin, Uvarov "secretly disliked him."[125] Uvarov, for instance, harbored "jealous resentment" of Pushkin dating from the very beginning of Nicholas' reign when the new tsar asked Pushkin – and not Uvarov – to draw up a plan for education reform in Russia. As a newly appointed official in the ministry of education, Uvarov probably felt that he should have received that assignment and the imperial favor it implied. Uvarov has sometimes been described as having been a "liberal" during the 1820s, but James Flynn has demonstrated that he was actually an ardent supporter of heavy censorship and served as a supervisor of imperial censors starting in 1828. Uvarov also unflinchingly sacrificed others in pursuit of his own career, including Pushkin. Not only did he gladly participate in censoring Pushkin's works for publication, but – like Benckendorff – he intrigued to impose heavier censorship on Pushkin than Tsar Nicholas ever intended.[126] Uvarov maintained a reasonably good relationship with Bulgarin and Grech and shared their hostility toward Pushkin. During the literary war between Pushkin and Bulgarin, Uvarov gladly provided sensitive information about Pushkin's family to aid Bulgarin's shrill campaign to destroy the poet's reputation.[127]

By 1830, Pushkin found his career as a writer being actively frustrated by the powerful combination of Benckendorff, Bulgarin, and Uvarov. During the struggle between Pushkin and Bulgarin, the chief of gendarmes tirelessly promoted Bulgarin as Russia's new literary giant and urged Nicholas to reward the man's steadfast loyalty. To illustrate, Bulgarin became the tsar's adviser on Polish affairs, and Bulgarin's partner (Nikolai Grech) was awarded the lucrative contract to publish a new edition of Karamzin's *History*.[128] Under the circumstances, it should be no surprise that throughout 1830 Bulgarin felt free to attack Pushkin relentlessly in print and even assumed that he would be rewarded for his efforts. Indeed, with Benckendorff's approval, Bulgarin aimed at nothing less than establishing a complete "monopoly" in the Russian literary scene. He arrogantly divided all Russian writers into two groups – those patriots who stood with him and those of questionable loyalty who opposed him.[129]

When Bulgarin first learned that Pushkin had denounced him as a plagiarist, he wrote him a letter (February 18, 1830) denying the charge and asserting that Pushkin's unpublished *Comedy* and his own *Dimitrii Samozvanets* were actually "complete opposites."[130] As soon as Bulgarin's novel went on sale in February 1830, Pushkin and Delvig pounced on it in *Literary Gazette*. Delvig published a scathing review of *Dimitrii Samozvanets* in which he accused Bulgarin of being too pro-Polish – a charge that actually frightened Bulgarin. Other critics (for example, in *Moskovskii Vestnik*, *Galateia*, and *Ateneia*) also dismissed *Dimitrii Samozvanets* as a second-rate novel and alluded to the existence of a vastly superior (but still unpublished) literary work with a much better interpretation of the Time of Troubles.[131] That criticism infuriated Bulgarin, who hastily denied in print that his novel was pro-Polish and struck back at Pushkin with crude attacks on his character – accusing him, in particular, of being a dangerous atheist and a mulatto who cheated at cards.[132] Incredibly, Bulgarin even brazenly accused Pushkin of plagiarizing *his* novel. Pushkin's responses ridiculed the charges leveled against him and pointed out that Bulgarin, not he, was the real plagiarist.[133] Pushkin also went public with the accusation that Bulgarin was a police spy.[134]

Throughout 1830, the *Literary Gazette* and the *Northern Bee* traded barbs and insults back and forth, with Bulgarin using the most dishonorable means to destroy the reputation of his rival (as well as the entire Pushkin family) and Pushkin and Delvig doggedly and cleverly fighting back.[135] In those exchanges, Pushkin and Delvig managed to seriously undermine Bulgarin's reputation – both literary and personal.[136] But Bulgarin could still count on the powerful support of Benckendorff. As a result, Pushkin continued to have trouble with the Third Section; and Benckendorff personally harassed and generally tormented Delvig – eventually removing him as editor of the *Literary Gazette* and temporarily shutting down the "dangerously liberal" journal.[137] When the harassed Delvig died soon thereafter, many Russians blamed the chief of gendarmes for his untimely death.[138] Pushkin himself seemed to admit defeat at the hands of his enemies when, in December 1830, he sadly observed that "Russian literature has been delivered up – head, neck, and ears – to Bulgarin and Grech!"[139]

The viciousness of Bulgarin's attacks on his rivals did not go unnoticed by Nicholas I. Although Bulgarin claimed to have the tsar's personal patronage, it was really Benckendorff – not Nicholas – who promoted his career. In fact, the tsar had never really liked or trusted Bulgarin and only grudgingly tolerated him due to Benckendorff's attachment to the odious man.[140] In late January 1830, Nicholas actually forced his reluctant chief of gendarmes to arrest and briefly jail Bulgarin and Grech for overzealously attacking their rivals after having been warned by the government to back off. Bulgarin's embarrassing arrest provoked joy in much of St. Petersburg society, but the wily Benckendorff managed to persuade the tsar that the arrest had made a bad impression. Released with just a slap on the wrist, Bulgarin resumed his attacks, increasingly focusing the *Northern Bee*'s negative attention on Pushkin and his friends – something Bulgarin knew would please the chief of gendarmes, if not the tsar.[141] Pushkin was by then well aware of Benckendorff's hostile attitude toward him. Nevertheless, without any real hope for official action to stop the character assassination of himself and his friends by the *Northern Bee* (including references to Pushkin as a "debauched and fawning" French poet, an atheistic card shark, and a politically unreliable "Negro prince"), Pushkin wrote a letter to Benckendorff on March 24, 1830, in which he complained about Bulgarin's unfair attacks and referred to him as "one of my most rabid enemies" who was capable of doing "me infinite harm."[142] In fact, Nicholas was also upset by Bulgarin's crude attacks on Pushkin, but Benckendorff managed to protect his ally from the wrath of the tsar and, in the process, continued trying to undermine Pushkin's reputation at court.[143]

Pushkin on his own might have been totally defeated at this time, but Bulgarin went too far when he began attacking Vasily Zhukovsky, Pushkin's close friend and the tsarevich's tutor.[144] That attack greatly angered the tsar – in part because Nicholas trusted Zhukovsky completely and greatly admired his poetry. When the tsar gave gifts, he often gave copies of the works of Zhukovsky and Pushkin – never the mediocre works of Bulgarin.[145] In fact, Nicholas still dreamed of having the internationally renowned Pushkin as "an adornment to his reign" instead of the self-promoting Bulgarin, and Zhukovsky actively encouraged the tsar to believe this was still possible. Nicholas was, of course, well aware of the credible charge of plagiarism leveled against Bulgarin as well as the fact that before he tried to claim the mantle of Karamzin Bulgarin had actually been highly critical of the historian laureate's *History*. The tsar was also well aware of Pushkin's desire to marry and the poet's unsuccessful attempts since 1826 to see his play into print.[146] For all these reasons, by April 1830, Nicholas signaled a new willingness to assist the beleaguered Pushkin. Zhukovsky (via Viazemsky) was delighted to inform Pushkin – "our romantic poet" – that it was now a good time to ask the tsar for permission to publish his *Comedy*.[147]

Pushkin wasted no time. He wrote a letter to Benckendorff on April 16, 1830, informing him of his marriage plans, his need for money, and his continuing desire to publish his play.[148] By this time, Pushkin was very deep in debt – mostly from gambling.[149] He was planning to wed Natalia Goncharova, a young woman with very expensive tastes and a mother who was deeply skeptical about Pushkin's ability to provide for her daughter.[150] Pushkin hoped to earn up to fifteen thousand rubles by publishing his play, and he was well aware of the concerns about his *Comedy* expressed in the censor's report written back in 1826. In fact, thanks to Dashkov, Pushkin may actually have seen the censor's report or at least heard details of its contents.[151] In any case, he chose his words carefully in seeking Benckendorff's (and the tsar's) approval. Because Benckendorff's most recent rejection letter had left open the possibility of resubmitting a *revised* version of his play, Pushkin delicately and diplomatically touched on that subject in his letter to the chief of gendarmes: "The Emperor, having deigned to read [my play], criticized some passages that are too free, and I must confess that His Majesty is only too right."[152] The brave poet-historian went on, however, to reject the tsar's notion that a few passages in his play "seemed to present allusions to circumstances that were then recent" – meaning, of course, the Decembrist Rebellion. He wrote that in "rereading them at present, I doubt that one could find such meaning in them." He defended an author's right to represent historical characters accurately and urged that his work be judged in the *spirit in which the entire work is conceived*." Pushkin ended his plea with these words:

> My tragedy is a work of good faith, and I cannot in good conscience suppress what appears to me to be essential. I beseech His Majesty to pardon me the liberty which I am taking to contradict him; I well know that this opposition by a poet may evoke laughter, but up to now I have always steadfastly refused all proposals of the booksellers; I have been happy to make in silence this sacrifice to His Majesty's will. Present circumstances are pressing me, and I now beseech His Majesty to unbind my hands and to permit me to publish my tragedy as I think proper.[153]

Whether influenced by his anger at Bulgarin or his approval of Pushkin's marriage, Nicholas finally agreed to let Pushkin publish his play "on his own responsibility." Benckendorff informed the surprised and greatly relieved Pushkin of the tsar's decision and of Nicholas' continuing "paternal solicitude" for him in a letter dated April 28, 1830. In that same letter Benckendorff falsely told Pushkin that he was not – and never had been – under police surveillance.[154] Within a few days, Pushkin wrote to his family with the good news that the tsar had approved of his marriage plans and "has permitted me to publish my tragedy as I felt proper."[155] He also wrote exuberantly to his friend Pyotr Pletnev: "Dear Fellow! Victory! The Tsar is permitting me to publish *Godunov* in its pristine beauty."[156] Soon thereafter, an excited Mikhail Pogodin wrote to

Pushkin to say that he had just learned that Nicholas had given Pushkin permission to publish his play "without changes."[157]

Being permitted to publish his *Comedy* "on his own responsibility" supposedly meant that Pushkin would only have to submit his play for regular censorship instead of first giving it to Benckendorff and Nicholas to read. As he contemplated what lines he might be willing to remove and which passages he definitely wanted to leave in, Pushkin worked on a draft foreword to the play and thought seriously about aiming it directly against his antagonist. To Pletnev he wrote: "My hands are itching to crush Bulgarin."[158] But Pletnev advised him against descending to Bulgarin's level in the preface to his important play, and Pushkin quickly abandoned the idea.[159] After all, Pushkin hoped that publication of his historical drama would confirm his reputation as a great writer – not merely as Bulgarin's clever foe.[160] By this time, of course, Pushkin was no longer operating under any illusion that his attempt to reform the Russian theater by means of his innovative *Comedy* would succeed; and he fully expected harsh reviews of his "anachronism." Nevertheless, he confessed that "the failure of my play would grieve me."[161]

In July 1830, Pushkin went to St. Petersburg to work out final details for the publication of his play. By early August he departed from the capital, leaving behind a "corrected" copy of his historical drama for his close friends Pletnev and Zhukovsky to guide through the regular censorship process and into print. Pushkin himself was not directly involved in the final stages of publishing his play.[162] Despite several generations of scholarly speculation, it is still very difficult to determine what factors played a role in the revision of Pushkin's *Comedy* or who was responsible for each specific change.[163] While Pushkin was still in St. Petersburg, he expressed great anger over Bulgarin's latest barrage against him and learned of the July Revolution in France.[164] Both of those developments probably affected his decisions about revising his beloved play.

The shockwave of the July Revolution, which swept across Europe and touched off the Warsaw uprising against Russian control in November 1830, provoked increased vigilance by the Third Section and greatly reduced the chances for anything even remotely "radical" to be published in the Russian empire. Even before the July Revolution, Nicholas and Benckendorff had been increasingly fearful of a possible rebellion against serfdom.[165] Under the circumstances, as Pushkin thought about putting his play into print, he was undoubtedly aware that anything disagreeing with the official Karamzinian view of the Pretender Dmitry and the role of the evil Catholic Poles in stirring up a rebellion of the *narod* during the Time of Troubles had little chance for approval – even by ordinary, low-level tsarist censors. Nicholas also personally hated the "False Dmitry" as a tool of Polish intervention in Russia. The tsar was a good student of Russian history who had been raised to believe that the Pretender was an odious defrocked monk. Nicholas was also well aware of the somewhat embarrassing connection between Dmitry and the *narod,* and he would therefore certainly look with disfavor upon any nuanced interpretation of Dmitry or his campaign for the throne that deviated from Karamzin's stern judgment.[166] Probably out of desperation, therefore, Pushkin came up with a brilliant strategy to outmaneuver his enemies and publish his play; he would directly challenge Bulgarin's self-promotion as the successor to Karamzin. Since, after the July Revolution, the original version of his provocative *Comedy* was altogether a non-starter, the astute and practical Pushkin decided to publish a more politically palatable – that is, Karamzinian – version of his play. As Pushkin was about to embark on his new life with Natalia Goncharova and was beginning to plan his career as a professional historian, all he really needed to do to please Nicholas, secure his own future, and defeat Bulgarin (at least temporarily) was to tuck his holy fool's ears back under his cap. By August 1830, he made just such a decision.

Based on Pushkin's correspondence in this period, it is possible to conclude that his eminently practical decision was influenced primarily by his staggering debt.[167] But Pushkin may also have been influenced by the fate of Griboedov's *Woe from Wit.* Only after agreeing to heavy-handed censorship had Griboedov been allowed to publish part of his play – in Bulgarin's *Ruskaia Taliia.* Having bowed to the censors, however, Griboedov's friend Bulgarin was eventually permitted to put *Woe from Wit* on stage.[168] It premiered in January 1831, and Pushkin was probably aware of the preparations for that production at the time he decided to publish a revised version of his own play. Thus, Pushkin may have hoped – even without the benefit of Bulgarin's friendship and connections – that he would be permitted to put his historical drama on stage if he were willing to make compromises with the censors.

While Zhukovsky and Pletnev presided over publication of his play, Pushkin initially contemplated dedicating it to Zhukovsky – without whose help *Boris Godunov* would never have been allowed into print. Soon, however, the poet-historian came up with an even better idea. By October 1830, he managed to secure the permission of the late historian laureate's daughters to dedicate his play to their father. Pushkin then asked Pletnev to print his dedication to Karamzin on the title page of his play – if it was not too late to do that. In fact, it was too late; so Pletnev hastily arranged for the dedication to be printed on separate sheets of paper that were then tipped into the already bound volumes. The dedication read: "To the memory precious to Russians of Nikolai Mikhailovich Karamzin this work, inspired by his genius, is dedicated with veneration and gratitude by Alexander Pushkin."[169]

At the end of December 1830, just as Russian troops were poised to invade rebellious Poland, Pushkin's play (which bears a January 1831 publication date) finally made its way into print.[170] Much to the delight of Nicholas, the 1831 version of Boris Godunov clearly dissociated Pushkin from the Jesuits, the Poles, and "False Dmitry." The new final scene also showed that Dmitry was not supported by the narod. Almost overnight Pushkin's Comedy had been transformed into a tragedy more or less in line with Karamzin's interpretation of the Time of Troubles.[171] To the surprise of many people, Pushkin also began to speak and write in favor of suppressing the Polish rebellion.[172] Some apologists for Pushkin have claimed that this illiberal sentiment was just part of his naive strategy to save "reform" in Russia as the increasingly reactionary Nicholas prepared to crack down on the Poles; and it is true that the poet still harbored some hope that Nicholas might eventually forgive the Decembrists.[173] But it is far more likely that Pushkin's patriotic outburst at this time was primarily intended to counter Bulgarin's highly public efforts to support the Russian invasion of Poland. In fact, when Pushkin wrote in a letter approvingly of exterminating some Poles, it is easy to imagine that he had Bulgarin in mind.[174]

Pushkin's reward for good behavior and for publishing a politically correct version of his play was far more than the ten thousand rubles in royalties that he earned. In 1831, a grateful tsar – who read Boris Godunov "with great pleasure" – appointed him historian laureate of Russia at twice the salary Karamzin had received.[175] Pushkin was then given almost unlimited access to imperial archives in order to pursue various historical projects – especially a planned History of Peter the Great which Pushkin hoped would earn him a lot of money.[176] In fact, Pushkin remained the only scholar with access to sensitive historical archives for the rest of his life. Much to their annoyance and frustration, none of the other historians (even more politically trustworthy ones such as Ustrialov) was allowed to conduct archival research until several years after

Historian Laureate Pushkin's death.[177] Nevertheless, in spite of Nicholas' willingness to appoint Pushkin as Karamzin's successor, the new historian laureate was never permitted to put *Boris Godunov* on stage – even though he and his friends made several requests to do so.[178]

As noted in chapter 1, the published version of *Boris Godunov* was received coolly by many critics. They accused Pushkin of "slavishly" following Karamzin's official interpretation of the Time of Troubles, of producing a poor imitation of a Shakespearean drama, and of writing a disjointed and incoherent play devoid of any real meaning.[179] At least two of those negative reviews (one published in the *Northern Bee* and another published as a pamphlet) were strikingly similar to the 1826 censor's report (especially in dismissing the play as an unstageable collection of "fragments") and were almost certainly the work of Bulgarin. By this time, however, Bulgarin had grown more cautious in his attacks on the now-favored Pushkin and wisely published his critical reviews anonymously.[180] Although often ignored by scholars today, the main reason for the critics' disappointment in Pushkin's play was simply that *Boris Godunov* had been seriously compromised by the censors and editors while being prepared for publication. It has frequently been claimed that Zhukovsky, rather than the censors, was responsible for most of the changes in the published version of Pushkin's play.[181] No doubt Zhukovsky did help convert Pushkin's *Comedy* into something more Karamzinian, but he also greatly admired Pushkin's work. It is an insult to a fine poet to claim that Zhukovsky was single-handedly responsible for the clumsy "cleansing" of *Boris Godunov*.

It is often forgotten that, after editing Pushkin's play, Zhukovsky was forced to submit the revised version to the censors.[182] In fact, close examination of this subject reveals that, in addition to low level tsarist officials, both Nicholas and Benckendorff were directly involved in censoring and publishing *Boris Godunov*. Although that may not have been planned originally, the atmosphere at court after the July Revolution produced sharply increased vigilance and more rigorous censorship. Under the circumstances, we should not be surprised to learn that the chief of gendarmes personally arranged for Pushkin's play, once it had been "cleansed," to be published by a politically reliable press – none other than the press of the Ministry of Education, the very same organization that handled censorship.[183] That choice of presses – which informally put Nicholas' stamp of approval on Pushkin's play – was a surprise to some people at the time, but it has attracted virtually no attention from scholars since the nineteenth century. The 1831 edition of *Boris Godunov* also lacked the usual name of the censor who had approved it; instead, the book contains the somewhat unusual phrase: "published with the approval of the Government."[184]

According to reliable sources – Zhukovsky and Pletnev – many of the changes in the published version of Pushkin's play were the direct result of pressure from Nicholas and the censors. Zhukovsky actually kept the marked up manuscript of *Boris Godunov* with the tsar's personal suggestions for cuts written on it in red pencil.[185] A professor of literature who later served as the principal censor of Pushkin's works, Alexander Nikitenko, also saw Zhukovsky's marked-up manuscript of the play and confirmed that Nicholas was personally responsible for deleting some passages. On March 22, 1837, Nikitenko wrote the following in his diary:[186]

> I visited Zhukovsky. He showed me Pushkin's manuscript of *Boris Godunov* with the passages censored by the emperor. He had cut out a great deal. That's why the published version of *Godunov* appears incomplete and why there appear to be so many gaps, causing some critics to say that this play is only a collection of fragments.

It is worth noting here that careful study of this issue led the famous Soviet scholar Mikhail Alekseev (whose notion of the origins of Pushkin's use of silence to end the play is currently regarded as authoritative) to suspect that the 1831 ending was not Pushkin's – that it did not "organically conclude the author's text of the play."[187]

During the editing and "cleansing" of Pushkin's play for publication, substantial changes were made; three scenes and many other lines were deleted. Unfortunately, that introduced some confusion and discontinuity. In subsequent chapters Sergei Fomichev and Caryl Emerson will examine the impact of those cuts in reducing the comedic element in Pushkin's play. But there are several other issues related to editing and censorship that also deserve some attention. For example, the motivation to purge the scene "Monastery Wall" was probably primarily to expunge "atheistic" elements from the play. That omission, however, makes it virtually impossible for the audience to understand how, why, and under whose influence the monk Grigory Otrepiev decided to assume the identity of Tsarevich Dmitry.[188] Several scholars have argued that Pushkin himself may have cut this scene in order to make the old monk-chronicler Pimen the primary influence on Otrepiev's decision.[189]

But Pushkin was reportedly unhappy about the omission of this scene and talked of restoring it to a planned second edition of *Boris Godunov* that he never published.[190]

Far more serious, due to "cleansing," the dramatically powerful paralleling of the opening and closing of the play was completely lost by the deletion of the third scene ("Maiden's Field. Novodevichy Monastery") and by the altered ending.[191] The deletion of the third scene (with its depiction of the cynical *narod* being forced to cheer for Tsar Boris) brought the play more or less into line with Karamzin's *History*, but – as noted in chapter 1 – Soviet scholars long ago declared that it was cut by tsarist censors and restored it to the canonical text of the play. Without providing any evidence, Vinokur and others claimed that Pushkin preferred to cut the scene entirely rather than have a censored and mutilated version of it appear in print.[192] The deletion of yet another scene ("Maryna's Dressing Room") also had a significant impact on the play; it simultaneously eliminated some pro-Polish sentiment that was unpopular at the court of Nicholas I, distorted and darkened the character and motivation of Tsar Dmitry's future bride, and expunged an embarrassing reference to the positive response of the *narod* to the appearance of the Pretender.[193] Similarly, omission of Khrushchov's longest speech from scene 12 ("Cracow. Wiśniowiecki's House") eliminated the revelation that the *narod* (and some boyars) supported the Pretender's cause and truly believed that he was Dmitry. Perhaps inadvertently, that deletion also eliminated Khrushchov's reference to Tsar Boris' grave illness, making his death later in the play sudden and unexpected. Anthony Briggs has argued persuasively that Khrushchov's lines must be restored to the play in order to make it more intelligible.[194]

Although there are serious problems with the interpretation that Pushkin altered his *Comedy* for purely aesthetic reasons, a plausible argument can be made in favor of an artistic motivation for at least a few of the changes found in the printed version of the play. Take, for example, the title change. Fomichev and Emerson will discuss the significance of dropping "Comedy" from the title in subsequent chapters, but two changes should be highlighted here. First, the title change took the spotlight off the hated Pretender – which was in line with Nicholas' preferences and the general downplaying of Dmitry that other deletions produced.[195] Secondly, the new title may have been intended to remind people of Shakespeare's history plays. It is also remotely possible that the deletion of Ksenia's lines at the very beginning of scene 11 ("The Tsar's

Palace") may have been done for aesthetic reasons, although the omitted lament for her dead fiancé brilliantly demonstrated the forced seclusion of elite women in pre-Petrine Russia – a delicate and somewhat controversial subject in the early nineteenth century. Finally, Antony Wood calls our attention to the fact that Ksenia's lament and two entire scenes omitted from *Boris Godunov* were written in meters other than blank verse, noting that it was almost as if neoclassical taste was being exercised here on behalf of stylistic unity. That observation is particularly interesting because Zhukovsky was, of course, a renowned *Romantic* poet. The person directly involved in "cleansing" Pushkin's play who did have neoclassical taste was Tsar Nicholas.

Great care was taken to delete "dangerous" and controversial elements from *Boris Godunov,* but in a few places Pushkin's ears still stuck out. For example, despite strong protests in the censor's report against Afanasy Pushkin's speech that alluded to Dmitry's promise to abolish serfdom (in the scene "Moscow. Shuisky's House"), those provocative lines somehow made it into print. Vinokur and others rightly declared this to be one of Pushkin's "victories" over the censors.[196] The survival of Afanasy Pushkin's speech was noted at the time by at least one reviewer, Ivan Kireevsky, who had listened to Pushkin read his *Comedy* back in 1826. Kireevsky was well aware that the playwright had intended to draw attention to the importance (to Dmitry's success) of a taboo phenomenon – a rebellion of the *narod*.[197]

A few other controversial comments about the Pretender Dmitry's peaceful conquest of much of Russia and about the voluntary surrender of many towns to him (in the scene "Field Headquarters") also made it past the censors. Curiously enough, also surviving the cleansing of the play was a statement showing that the *narod* rejected the official identification of the Pretender as the monk Otrepiev (in scene 18, "Square in front of the Cathedral").[198] In fact, the printed *Boris Godunov*'s arbitrary reversal of the order of the original *Comedy*'s scenes 18 and 19 ("A Plain near Novgorod-Seversky") is confusing and makes no sense at all – especially for staging the play; but it does mask somewhat the powerful, combined impact of the Patriarch's comments that revealed Tsar Boris' complicity in the Uglich tragedy found in scene 17 ("The Tsar's Council") and the holy fool's indictment of Boris as King Herod in what was originally the very next scene. It is not clear, however, whether the artificial separation of those two scenes in the printed version of the play was intended to soften their impact or was intended to sneak controversial elements in the scene "Square in front of the Cathedral" past the censors. Finally, after all the fuss over Captain Margeret's swearing, his salty line managed to survive in *Boris Godunov*. No wonder Tsar Nicholas later encouraged Zhukovsky to reedit Pushkin's play before republishing it in order to remove "everything indecent" that the censors had missed the first time around.[199]

What about the silent ending of *Boris Godunov*? As noted in chapter 1, the *narod*'s famous silence replaced the original cheer for Tsar Dmitry found at the end of Pushkin's *Comedy*, and that silence has been variously interpreted ever since 1831. Several scholars have argued that the cheer for Dmitry seemed too "immoral" to Nicholas and the censors, so it had to be changed to a more respectable silence.[200] Other scholars have argued that Pushkin himself changed the ending of his play for artistic reasons.[201] The problem is compounded by the fact that there exists no manuscript of the play containing the silent ending that mysteriously appeared in *Boris Godunov*, causing some scholars to conclude that the silent ending must have been the result of censorship.[202] Some have plausibly claimed that the silent ending was derived from Karamzin, who used "silence" frequently and effectively in his *History*.[203] Others have suggested with reason that Shakespeare (especially *Richard III*) may have been the source.[204] There are several other less plausible theories.[205]

Mikhail Alekseev's widely accepted explanation is that the silence was derived from the 1828 edition of Adolphe Thiers' *Histoire de la révolution française* (which Pushkin *may* have had the opportunity to read) in which Mirabeau is quoted as saying that in 1789 Louis XVI was greeted with silence by the French people.[206] Alekseev's imaginative hypothesis should, however, be viewed with extreme skepticism. It is far more likely that the closing line of *Boris Godunov* did come from Karamzin. Caryl Emerson saw it as a possible parody of Karamzin's "overdetermined story" in his *History*.[207] It is also quite possible that the silence actually came from Bulgarin's novel. Bulgarin ended *Dimitrii Samozvanets* with the *narod*'s unenthusiastic silence in response to the accession of the new tsar, Vasily Shuisky – the regicide and usurper who followed Tsar Dmitry to the throne. In fact, in 1831, Bulgarin boldly accused Pushkin of plagiarism for this borrowing.[208] It seems highly likely that Pushkin finally got one up on the notorious Bulgarin by stealing the best line from an otherwise dull novel – in effect, tormenting his tormentor by plagiarizing the plagiarist. That sounds more like Pushkin than the traditional interpretation of the origin of the play's silent ending.[209]

But if Pushkin was responsible for the silence at the end of *Boris Godunov*, what did he mean by it? Was he merely surrendering to tsarist pressure, or was the revised ending actually a Trojan horse? Consider this: West European visitors to Nicholas' Russian empire often commented on the pervasive "silence" of the Russian people; the Marquis de Custine actually referred to it as "indispensable for oppression."[210] Moreover, Pushkin himself wrote of his own *silent* acceptance of the tsar's refusal to allow him to publish his *Comedy*.[211] It should also be remembered that Pushkin was a careful student of old chronicles and tales about the Time of Troubles. In several of those sources that he knew very well (including Avraamy Palitsyn's *Skazanie*), the "silence" of the Russian people concerning the immoral and tyrannical behavior of Ivan the Terrible and Boris Godunov was harshly condemned as impious, guilty silence – as complicity.[212] The poet-historian, a highly responsible artist, may have been implying in the published ending of *Boris Godunov* that the silence of the *narod* is Pushkin's own stilled voice – now tamed, now safe for the likes of Nicholas and the censors but still (obscurely) speaking to his audience and saying: This is not right, and we should not all be silent.[213]

Pushkin paid a steep price to rescue Karamzin's mantle from Bulgarin, but he could console himself that – even compromised in his own eyes and in the eyes of some of his friends – he was still a morally and aesthetically superior symbol and champion of Russian literature than his amoral and mediocre antagonist would have been. It took some time, however, for Pushkin to adjust to his new role and to accept the irreversibility and inevitable consequences of his decision to publicly tuck his holy fool's ears under his cap. His equivocation about his choice is clearly evident in a letter he sent to Pletnev on January 7, 1831. In it, Pushkin expressed great surprise that *Boris Godunov* was off to a good start; in fact, four hundred copies had been sold on the first day it was available for purchase, and some people (especially in St. Petersburg) actually said and wrote nice comments about it. Having already steeled himself for harsh reviews of his compromised "anachronism," Pushkin openly wondered what could explain his play's "strange" and "incomprehensible" early success. Not surprisingly, he suspected that Tsar Nicholas' positive opinion of the politically correct version of his play might be the cause of the unexpected good news.[214]

In his letter to Pletnev, Pushkin expressed confidence that the French would eagerly mine *Boris Godunov* for its possible "political applications to the Warsaw uprising." But he knew perfectly well that many Russians –

especially those who had been inspired by his public readings of *Comedy* – would be greatly disappointed with his denatured *Boris Godunov* and would conclude that he had gone "completely downhill." Nevertheless, Pushkin still loved his play and half-heartedly expressed disillusionment with the anticipated criticism of it – especially by persons such as Pavel Katenin whose judgment he trusted.[215] In fact, Katenin had been highly critical of Karamzin's *History* in the past and was still strongly committed to rescuing "Russian drama from the themes of patriotism and reactionary politics." He and many others were therefore understandably horrified by the combination of Nicholas' crackdown on Poland and the simultaneous publication of a Karamzinian version of Pushkin's once-radical play.[216] In his heart of hearts, Pushkin may have been pained by the thought of Katenin's reaction to *Boris Godunov*, but he could not have been surprised by it. The disillusionment of his friends concerning the tragic fate of his *Comedy* left a bitter aftertaste in the poet-historian's mouth.

Less than a fortnight after writing to Pletnev, the somewhat sad poet-historian found himself already struggling (uncomfortably) to become "a tsar's favorite." In a letter to Benckendorff acknowledging receipt of the news that Nicholas had read *Boris Godunov* with "great pleasure," Pushkin expressed the obligatory "profound gratitude" for the tsar's "favorable opinion" of his historical drama. He then penned what must have been some of the most painful and ironic lines he ever wrote to his powerful enemy, the chief of gendarmes:[217]

> Written during the last reign, *Boris Godunov* owes its appearance not only to the private protection with which the Sovereign has honored me, but also to the freedom boldly granted by the Monarch to Russian writers at such a time and in such circumstances when any other government would have endeavored to repress and fetter the publishing of books.

Interestingly enough, in the decade following the publication of *Boris Godunov*, many dramas about the Time of Troubles and Tsar Dmitry were produced by Russian writers who had been strongly influenced by Pushkin's play.[218] Each one of those dramas "entered into its own eerie dialogue with Pushkin."[219] Although usually ignored by scholars, many of those plays were actually responding to Pushkin's *Comedy* instead of to *Boris Godunov*. For example, Aleksei Khomiakov's *Dmitrii Samozvanets* was deliberately intended as a sequel to Pushkin's play, but Khomiakov had never been able to forget the original version he heard Pushkin read in 1826. As a result, his *Dmitrii Samozvanets* opens with the *narod* enthusiastically hailing Tsar Dmitry instead of greeting him in silence – in effect, restoring the original ending of Pushkin's *Comedy*. Not surprisingly, tsarist censors also forced changes in the final lines of Khomiakov's play.[220]

Mikhail Pogodin (the young intellectual who had been greatly moved by Pushkin's dramatic reading of the *Comedy* in 1826) was also unable to forget the original ending of the play. In the 1830s, he produced a drama about Tsar Boris which ended with the *narod* shouting "Long live Tsar Dmitry!" Pogodin was convinced that this cheer was what Pushkin had intended and what had so excited his contemporaries; it also happened to be historically accurate. Pogodin also published a fairly sympathetic drama about Tsar Dmitry that was strongly influenced by Pushkin's *Comedy,* and he formally dedicated it to Russia's new historian laureate Alexander Pushkin.[221] Pogodin (whose father had been a serf) was particularly struck by Pushkin's insight into why the Russian people had been attracted to the Pretender Dmitry's cause; in fact, he later undertook his own scholarly study of the origins of serfdom and the Time of Troubles.[222] Pogodin also encouraged his most famous pupil, the eminent historian Sergei Soloviev, to write on the subject. Soloviev's controversial findings were then intentionally published in 1849 in Pushkin's journal, *Sovremennik,* which just then happened to be presided over by the sympathetic Alexander Nikitenko – himself a former serf.[223] Soloviev's article was the very first historical account of the Time of Troubles to directly associate the "peasant war" with Dmitry's campaign for the throne – just as Pushkin's play had done. Needless to say, tsarist censors were extremely unhappy about the potential impact of Soloviev's "dangerous" ideas on a large, nonacademic reading public.[224]

During the 1830s, Egor Rozen, who greatly admired Pushkin's historical drama, wrote plays focusing on Pyotr Basmanov and Prince Kurbsky. Rozen also began the task of trying to rescue scenes deleted from *Boris Godunov,* and he cleverly managed to publish the controversial "Monastery Wall" scene in 1833.[225] As noted in chapter 1, after Pushkin's death, interest in his original *Comedy* remained strong. In 1841, Zhukovsky managed to quietly publish two of the scenes omitted from *Boris Godunov.* The editors of Pushkin's journal, *Sovremennik,* also managed to work around the censors to put an omitted scene into print while Nicholas was still on the throne, as did Mikhail Pogodin (as editor of

Moskvitianin) in 1854. Of course, after Nicholas died, scholars such as Pavel Annenkov and Peter Morozov made Pushkin's *Comedy* widely available – inspiring Modest Musorgsky among others. It was only after the Russian Revolution of 1917 that Pushkin's *Comedy* fell into obscurity.

Notes

1. PS, 13: 166–67; *Letters,* 218; Tsiavlovskii, *Letopis',* 520; Vinokur, *Stat'i,* 86; Simmons, *Pushkin,* 250–51.
2. Briggs, *Alexander Pushkin,* 158.
3. TL, 2: 134; Brown, *History,* 3: 107.
4. Lincoln, *Between Heaven and Hell,* 132, 135; Wolff, *Pushkin,* 108; Simmons, *Pushkin,* 244. See also Tsiavlovskii, *Letopis',* 579.
5. Barsukov, *Zhizn',* 2: 71; Tsiavlovskii, *Letopis',* 577; Simmons, *Pushkin,* 242–43, 250. See also *Letters,* 313.
6. Lincoln, *Between Heaven and Hell,* 135; Tsiavlovskii, *Letopis',* 615–16; Veresaev, *Pushkin,* 1: 295; Gordin, *Pushkin,* 141; Simmons, *Pushkin,* 244; Cooke and Dunning, "Tempting Fate," 51.
7. Simmons, *Pushkin,* 247, 257; Tsiavlovskii, *Letopis',* 579, 617, 622.
8. TL, 2: 128–29. See also PS, 13: 259; *Letters,* 303.
9. Tsiavlovskii, *Letopis',* 604; Modzalevskii, *Pushkin pod tainym nazdorom,* 13–16; Binyon, *Pushkin,* 238–40.
10. TL, 2: 102–3.
11. TL, 2: 84, 113, 122, 125, 135, 137, 155; Ershoff, "Prizhiznennaia izvestnost'," 68–78.
12. TL, 2: 86, 118, 123, 131; Tsiavlovskii, *Letopis',* 606; *Letters,* 307–8.
13. TL, 2: 142; Tsiavlovskii, *Letopis',* 615–16, 620; Cooke and Dunning, "Tempting Fate," 62–63.
14. PS, 13: 248–49, 264–65; *Letters,* 267, 306; Binyon, *Pushkin,* 235–36; Veresaev, *Pushkin,* 1: 380, 387.
15. Tsiavlovskii, *Letopis',* 594; Simmons, *Pushkin,* 244–45, 255–56.
16. Lincoln, *Between Heaven and Hell,* 135; Binyon, *Pushkin,* 224–25.
17. Tsiavlovskii, *Letopis',* 564; PS, 13: 171–72, 271; Vinokur, *Stat'i,* 86; Cooke and Dunning, "Tempting Fate," 49. See also TL, 2: 95.
18. PS, 13: 237; Sandler, "Problem," 57.
19. *Letters,* 261, 334; TL, 2: 95, 131; PS, 13: 239–40; Pushkin, *Sochineniia i pis'ma,* 3: 244; Vinokur, *Stat'i,* 86–88; Sandler, *Distant Pleasures,* 105; idem, "Solitude," 183.
20. See, for example, TL, 2: 132, 134; and PS, 13: 282.
21. TL, 2: 118; PS, 13: 225–27; *Letters,* 254–55, 294 n. 10.
22. TL, 2: 81; Tsiavlovskii, *Letopis',* 559–60; *Letters,* 254–55.
23. See *Letters,* 240, 313; Emerson, *Boris Godunov,* 83.
24. For a claim that Pushkin dedicated his play to Karamzin as early as July 1825, see TL, 2: 74.

25. Whittaker, *Origins*, 88; Lincoln, *Nicholas I*, 87.

26. Tsiavlovskii, *Letopis'*, 594; Monas, *Third Section*, 59–60, 71–72; Billington, *Icon and Axe*, 314–15; Simmons, *Pushkin*, 244–45, 255–56; Bitsilli, "Pushkin," 320.

27. Vickery, *Alexander Pushkin* (1992), 9; Binyon, *Pushkin*, 244. See also Monas, *Third Section*, 59–60, 71.

28. Veresaev, *Pushkin*, 1: 307.

29. Lotman, *Pushkin*, 137–42; Binyon, *Pushkin*, 240–42; Vickery, *Alexander Pushkin* (1992), 10; Listov, "Pushkin," 285.

30. Simmons, *Pushkin*, 269; Schönle, *Authenticity*, 193–94.

31. Tsiavlovskii, *Letopis'*, 50; Mazur and Malov, "Novye materialy," 237–38; Binyon, *Pushkin*, 242–43; Simmons, *Pushkin*, 253; Driver, *Pushkin*, 237–38; Vickery, *Alexander Pushkin* (1992), 8–10. See also *Letters*, 313.

32. Binyon, *Pushkin*, 256; Vyskochkov, *Imperator*, 542.

33. PS, 11: 43–47; Schönle, *Authenticity*, 194; Simmons, *Pushkin*, 269–70; Bitsilli, "Pushkin," 320; Mirsky, *Pushkin*, 103; Binyon, *Pushkin*, 253–54.

34. Simmons, *Pushkin*, 255–57; Binyon, *Pushkin*, 242–44; Vickery, *Alexander Pushkin* (1992), 10.

35. Donchin, "Pushkin," 23; Simmons, *Pushkin*, 257; Vickery, *Alexander Pushkin* (1992), 10; Yefimov, "Duel," 580.

36. *Letters*, 333; PS, 13: 305.

37. Binyon, *Pushkin*, 243–44.

38. Cooke and Dunning, "Tempting Fate," 63; Binyon, *Pushkin*, 246–47; Briggs, "Hidden Forces," 43; Mirsky, *Pushkin*, 106, 159–60; Bogaevskaia, "Pervye chteniia," 46–47.

39. TL, 2: 171, 183, 190–91, 462 n. 102, 463 n. 110; Barsukov, *Zhizn'*, 2: 43–45; Ashukin, *Pushkinskaia Moskva*, 119–25; Rybinskii, *Sbornik statei*, 150; Simmons, *Pushkin*, 259–62; Vatsuro, "Istoricheskaia tragediia," 327–29.

40. TL, 2: 198; Briggs, *Alexander Pushkin*, 158. See also Ashukin, *Pushkinskaia Moskva*, 125.

41. TL, 2: 135, 176, 182, 190, 192, 195, 198–99, 203, 204–5, 221; Bartenev, "Iz pisem," 93; Simmons, *Pushkin*, 234, 262; Pushkin, *Sochineniia i pis'ma*, 3: 239–40, 242; Mirsky, *Pushkin*, 106, 153–56; Mazur and Malov, "Novye materialy," 237–40; Vickery, *Alexander Pushkin* (1992), 52–53, 58–59; Sandler, *Distant Pleasures*, 104–5, 213.

42. TL, 2: 135, 181, 183; Pushkin, *Sochineniia i pis'ma*, 3: 242; Doldobanov and Makarov, *Khronika*, 1: 50; Ashukin, *Pushkinskaia Moskva*, 120; Vatsuro, *A. S. Pushkin*, 2: 21.

43. Fomichev, "Neizvestnaia p'esa," 249.

44. See, for example, Kireevskii, *Polnoe sobranie sochinenii*, 2: 46; Alekseev, "A. S. Pushkin," 174; and Monas, *Third Section*, 207–8.

45. See Viazemskii, *Polnoe sobranie sochinenii*, 10: 266; and TL, 2: 184, 188, 199, 201.

46. Barsukov, *Zhizn'*, 2: 43–45; Binyon, *Pushkin*, 247; Simmons, *Pushkin*, 261–62; Ashukin, *Pushkinskaia Moskva*, 124–26; Veresaev, *Pushkin*, 1: 326; Wolff, *Pushkin*, 180–81; Edmonds, *Pushkin*, 114–15.

47. TL, 2: 170, 190–91; Ashukin, *Pushkinskaia Moskva*, 126.

48. TL, 2: 196–97, 198, 199–200, 202, 203, 210–11, 220, 222; Ashukin, *Pushkinskaia Moskva*, 130–31; Ruud, *Fighting Words*, 52; Lemke, *Ocherki*, 382.

49. TL, 2: 188, 199, 221; Modzalevskii, *Pushkin*, 61–62.

50. TL, 2: 464; Barsukov, *Zhizn'*, 2: 58; Binyon, *Pushkin*, 253; Simmons, *Pushkin*, 271.

51. PS, 13: 308; *Letters*, 334; TL, 2: 207, 211; Binyon, *Pushkin*, 253–54.

52. TL, 2: 210; Lemke, *Nikolaevskie zhandarmy*, 474.

53. For the censor's report ("Zamechaniia na 'Komediiu o Tsare Borise i Grishke Otrep'eve'") see PD, 244, opis' 16, No. 10, listy 10–17; Sukhomlinov, *Izsledovaniia*, 2: 219–22; Lemke, *Nikolaevskie zhandarmy*, 607–14; Kunin, *Zhizn'*, 2: 65–68; Reitblat, *Vidok Figliarin*, 91–99. See also TL, 2: 211–12; Gozenpud, "Iz istorii," 253–54; Simmons, *Pushkin*, 272.

54. Lemke, *Nikolaevskie zhandarmy*, 608; Reitblat, *Vidok Figliarin*, 94; Gozenpud, "Iz istorii," 255; *Letters*, 261; Vinokur, *Stat'i*, 87.

55. Lemke, *Nikolaevskie zhandarmy*, 609; Reitblat, *Vidok Figliarin*, 93; Gozenpud, "O stsenichnosti," 343–44. See also TL, 2: 424.

56. Reitblat, *Vidok Figliarin*, 98; Lemke, *Nikolaevskie zhandarmy*, 608; Alekseev, "A. S. Pushkin," 175; Fomichev, "Neizvestnaia p'esa," 244–45.

57. Lemke, *Nikolaevskie zhandarmy*, 609; Reitblat, *Vidok Figliarin*, 92; TL, 2: 213; Bazilevich, "Boris Godunov," 53; Rabinovich, "Boris Godunov," 309; Vinokur, *Stat'i*, 89; Gorodetskii, *Tragediia*, 69–70.

58. TL, 2: 213; Gozenpud, "Iz istorii," 254.

59. PS, 14: 78; *Letters*, 408.

60. PS, 13: 313; Binyon, *Pushkin*, 254.

61. Vinokur, "Kto byl tsenzorom," 203; Monas, *Third Section*, 206; Gorodetskii, *Tragediia*, 66.

62. PS, 13: 317; *Letters*, 338; TL, 2: 223; Binyon, *Pushkin*, 255.

63. Simmons, *Pushkin*, 272; Monas, *Third Section*, 206.

64. TL, 2: 262, 289, 311, 472 n. 229; Wolff, *Pushkin*, 223 n. 2.

65. TL, 2: 259; TL, 3: 130.

66. TL, 2: 187; Binyon, *Pushkin*, 250; Ashukin, *Pushkinskaia Moskva*, 120.

67. TL, 2: 269, 274; Modzalevskii, *Pushkin*, 207–8.

68. TL, 2: 270, 271–72, 285, 310, 329, 331.

69. TL, 2: 311, 320, 332.

70. TL, 2: 320, 332, 333, 337, 339, 340, 341, 345, 347.

71. PS, 14: 9, 16; TL, 2: 366, 385; TL, 3: 67.

72. TL, 2: 385, 387; Koliupanov, *Biografiia*, vol.1, book 2: 202.

73. TL, 2: 414; TL, 3: 17.

74. Monas, *Third Section*, 209–10; Mirsky, *Pushkin*, 105; Vickery, *Alexander Pushkin* (1992), 10–11; Edmonds, *Pushkin*, 115; Emerson, "Pushkin," 659–60; Yefimov, "Duel," 580–81.

75. TL, 2: 396; Lemke, *Nikolaevskie zhandarmy*, 473; Modzalevskii, *Pushkin pod tainym nazdorom*, 88–92.

76. Pushkin, *Critical Prose*, 65–67; Lincoln, *Nicholas I*, 237–38.

77. Wolff, *Pushkin*, 222–23; Levkovich, "Kavkazskii dnevnik," 12.

78. TL, 3: 79; Pushkin, *Critical Prose*, 98–99.

79. PD, fond 244, opis' 1, No. 302, listy 1–4; Pushkin, *Sochineniia Pushkina* (1855–57), 1: 133–35, 442–45; PS, 14: 46–48; *Letters*, 365–67. See also TL, 3: 79; Vinokur, "Kommentarii," 409; and Pomar, "Russian Historical Drama," 236. This letter was probably written in June 1829 (or, according to Sergei Fomichev, possibly July 1829) – but definitely *not* January 1829, as some scholars incorrectly concluded; see TL, 3: 535 n. 51; PS 14: 46.

80. *Dela III-go otdeleniia*, 90; Pushkin, *Sochineniia i pis'ma*, 3: 256; TL, 3: 26, 79; Gorodetskii, *Tragediia*, 77–79; Wolff, "Shakespeare's Influence," 99.

81. *Dela III-go otdeleniia*, 92–93, 99; Lemke, *Nikolaevskie zhandarmy*, 494; TL, 3: 89, 101, 132–33, 142; Gozenpud, "Iz istorii," 267, 270; Wolff, "Shakespeare's Influence," 99; PS, 14: 56, 58–59; *Letters*, 371–72; Gorodetskii, *Tragediia*, 77–79; Binyon, *Pushkin*, 313.

82. PS, 13: 239; *Letters*, 261.

83. PS, 7: 74; Balashov, "Boris Godunov," 213.

84. PS, 7: 297.

85. TL, 3: 121–22, 134, 152.

86. TL, 3: 123, 155; Barsukov, *Zhizn'*, 3: 15; Gozenpud, "Iz istorii," 268; Gorodetskii, *Tragediia*, 77–79; Ruud, *Fighting Words*, 65.

87. Reitblat, *Vidok Figliarin*, 678–79.

88. Modzalevskii, *Pushkin pod tainym nazdorom*, 20–27; Riasanovsky, *Nicholas I*, 60–64, 103; Gozenpud, "Iz istorii," 253; Koepnick, "Journalistic Careers," 10–15, 95; Binyon, *Pushkin*, 311–12.

89. Monas, "Šiškov," 134–35; Ruud, *Fighting Words*, 63–64; MERSH, 6: 18–19.

90. Grech, *Zapiski*, 340–42, 352–53; Del'vig, *Polveka*, 1: 128; Gozenpud, "Iz istorii," 252–53, 260; Todd, "Periodicals," 42; Koepnick, "Journalistic Careers," 16–18, 48, 69–70, 72–74, 88–90; Binyon, *Pushkin*, 311–12.

91. Lemke, *Ocherki*, 382–87; idem, *Nikolaevskie zhandarmy*, 232–43; Modzalevskii, *Pushkin pod tainym nazdorom*, 20–27; Mirsky, *Pushkin*, 121–22; Koepnick, "Journalistic Careers," 95–98.

92. Riasanovsky, *Nicholas I*, 64–65; Koepnick, "Journalistic Careers," 23–24, 95.

93. Koepnick, "Journalistic Careers," 49–50, 106; Ruud, *Fighting Words*, 63–64.

94. Lemke, *Nikolaevskie zhandarmy*, 246–52, 260–61, 286, 499; Gozenpud, "Iz istorii," 253; Todd, *Fiction*, 75; Koepnick, "Journalistic Careers," 108–9; Kropf, *Authorship*, 97; MERSH, 6: 17–18.

95. Monas, *Third Section*, 209–10; Gozenpud, "Iz istorii," 252–53, 259–61.

96. Monas, "Šiškov," 134–35; *Ocherki po istorii russkoi zhurnalistiki*, 1: 244; Ruud, *Fighting Words*, 64–65; Koepnick, "Journalistic Careers," 95. See also Foote, "St. Petersburg Censorship Committee," 61–62; Grinchenko, "Istoriia," 48.

97. See Vinokur, "Kto," 203–14; idem, *Stat'i*, 88–89; Gippius, "Pushkin," 235; Gozenpud, "Iz istorii," 252–59, 273–74; Alekseev, "A. S. Pushkin," 174–75; Monas, *Third Section*, 117–20, 205–11; Simmons, *Pushkin*, 272; and BG, 212–16.

98. See Gorodetskii, "Kto zhe byl tsenzorom," 117–18; and Gozenpud, "Iz istorii," 254–56, 259–60, 270. It is true that Grech had been a tsarist censor himself a decade earlier (Foote, "St. Petersburg Censorship Committee," 61 n. 2; Koepnick, "Journalistic Careers," 21–22; Grinchenko, "Istoriia," 63) and that, whoever the censor of Pushkin's play was, he was definitely influenced by an article Grech had published a year earlier (Reitblat, *Vidok Figliarin,* 98 n. 2).

99. Vinokur, *Kommentarii,* 388–403; Gozenpud, "Iz istorii," 256; TL, 2: 276; TL, 3: 130.

100. Binyon, *Pushkin,* 313–14; TL, 3: 108; Gozenpud, "Iz istorii," 260, 268–70; Gorodteskii, *Tragediia,* 77–79; Monas, *Third Section,* 214; Binyon, *Pushkin,* 313–14. See also Simmons, *Pushkin,* 272; and Lotman, *Aleksandr Sergeevich Pushkin* (1983), 168–69.

101. Binyon, *Pushkin,* 312; Gozenpud, "Iz istorii," 260.

102. TL, 3: 121–22, 123; Barsukov, *Zhizn',* 3: 15; Reitblat, *Vidok Figliarin,* 678–79; Gozenpud, "Iz istorii," 267–68; Gorodetskii, *Dramaturgiia,* 221.

103. Monas, *Third Section,* 210; Gozenpud, "Iz istorii," 267.

104. Gozenpud, "Iz istorii," 259, 266, 270.

105. Del'vig, *Polveka,* 1: 128; MERSH, 9: 40–42; Mirsky, *Pushkin,* 122; Monas, *Third Section,* 209; Reitblat, *Vidok Figliarin,* 678–79; Koepnick, "Journalistic Careers," 74; Binyon, *Pushkin,* 312–13.

106. Annenkov, *Vospominaniia,* 3: 227–30; Gippius, "Pushkin," 235–55; Gozenpud, "Iz istorii," 253, 273–74; Todd, *Fiction,* 79, 85; Simmons, *Pushkin,* 314–15; Koepnick, "Journalistic Careers," 71–73.

107. Todd, "Periodicals," 42; Driver, *Pushkin,* 17–18; Monas, *Third Section,* 210.

108. TL, 3: 155–56; Gozenpud, "Iz istorii," 271.

109. Lemke, *Nikolaevskie zhandarmy,* 499; Serman, "Pushkin," 137.

110. Monas, *Third Section,* 206; Gorodetskii, *Tragediia,* 77–79; Gozenpud, "Iz istorii," 266–67, 272.

111. Pushkin, *Sochineniia A. S. Pushkina* (Morozov, 1887), 3: 84; TL, 3: 108; Gozenpud, "Iz istorii," 268; Simmons, *Pushkin,* 272; Binyon, *Pushkin,* 314; BG, 335–36.

112. Bulgarin, *Dimitrii Samozvanets,* 1: iii–vi; Gozenpud, "Iz istorii," 260–66; Serman, "Pushkin," 136–37. See also Platon, *Kratkaia Tserkovnaia Rossiiskaia istoriia,* 2: chapter 67.

113. Bulgarin, *Dimitrii Samozvanets,* 1: ix–xxvii, xxxi–lvi, 3: 327–28, 4: 304–17, 483; Serman, "Pushkin," 135–36; Gozenpud, "Iz istorii," 252–53, 259–61, 264–70, 275; Brody, *Demetrius Legend,* 40.

114. Gozenpud, "Iz istorii," 260–63; Serman, "Pushkin," 136; Todd, "Periodicals," 50–52; idem, *Fiction,* 88–89, 97; Riasanovsky, *Nicholas I,* 52, 162. See also Bulgarin, *Dimitrii Samozvanets,* 1: xviii–xix, xxxi–xxxix, xliii–lix.

115. See MERSH, 41: 141; Riasanovsky, *Nicholas I,* 102; Bulgarin, *Dimitrii Samozvanets,* 2: 284–89, 3: 338–45, and 4: 484–504. Bulgarin's notes bear a striking similarity to those published elsewhere by Ustrialov; see, for example, Margeret, *Sostoianie;* and Ustrialov, *Skazaniia sovremennikov.*

116. See Margeret, *Sostoianie,* xiii–xxii; Ustrialov, *Skazaniia sovremennikov,* 1:

242; Dunning, "Use and Abuse," 360–62; Margeret, *Russian Empire*, xxxv–xxxvi, 95 n. 3, 105 n. 98, 118 n. 47, 179 n. 302; and MERSH, 41: 141.

117. On the semi-official exaltation of Karamzin see MERSH, 16:10–11; and 28:178–80; Black, *Nicholas Karamzin*, 144–54; Rothe, "Karamzin," 148–58, 176; Barsukov, *Zhizn'*, 2: 403, and 3: 40, 188, 206; Serman, "Pushkin," 118; Vernadsky, *Russian Historiography*, 64–65; Koepnick, "Journalistic Careers," 152; Todd, "Periodicals," 49–52, 64, 73–74; and idem, *Fiction*, 85–86.

118. Viazemskii, *Polnoe sobranie sochinenii*, 2: 83; MERSH, 28: 154; Umbrashko, *M. P. Pogodin*, 74–75, 77–78; Rothe, "Karamzin," 154–55.

119. Tatarinova, *Zhurnal*, 14–16; Umbrashko, *M. P. Pogodin*, 75–76; Rzadkiewicz, "N. A. Polevoi's 'Moscow Telegraph,'" 79–81; MERSH, 42: 79–80; Vernadsky, *Russian Historiography*, 65; Dolinin, "Historicism," 296–97; Todd, *Fiction*, 87; Sandler, "Problem," 86; Bethea, "[Hi]story," 294–95.

120. Vatsuro, "Podvig," 23–26; Todd, *Fiction*, 88–89; idem, "Periodicals," 51–52; Sandler, "Problem," 136.

121. See Bulgarin, "Marina Mnishek"; "Dnevnik Samuila Maskevicha"; Mocha, "Polish and Russian Sources," 49–51; and Ustrialov, *Skazaniia sovremennikov*, vol. 4 (*Dnevnik Mariny Mnishek i poslov Pol'skikh*) and vol. 5 (*Zapiski Maskievicha*).

122. Whittaker, *Origins*, 163; MERSH, 41: 141; *Great Soviet Encyclopedia*, 27: 702; *Entsiklopedicheskii slovar'*, 35: 50; Monas, "Šiškov," 129; Koepnick, "Journalistic Careers," 65. Ustrialov published his five-volume *Skazaniia sovremennikov* with Uvarov's Russian Academy Press, and the edition of Ustrialov's translation of Margeret that appeared in Moscow in 1830 (Margeret, *Istoricheskiia zapiski ...*) was published by a press closely associated with Uvarov – Tipografiia Lazarevykh vostochnykh iazykov.

123. Vernadsky, *Russian Historiography*, 67; Riasanovsky, *Nicholas I*, 102; Black, *Essays*, 20.

124. Whittaker, *Origins*, 124–25; Binyon, *Pushkin*, 481–82.

125. Binyon, *Pushkin*, 320.

126. Monas, "Šiškov," 139; Foote, "St. Petersburg Censorship Committee," 61–62, 87; Binyon, *Pushkin*, 481; MERSH, 41: 150; Ruud, *Fighting Words*, 52, 63; Whittaker, *Origins*, 88, 114–15.

127. Flynn, "Uvarov's 'Liberal' Years," 481–91; Reitblat, *Vidok Figliarin*, 692; Riasanovsky, *Nicholas I*, 52; Koepnick, "Journalistic Careers," 8; Grech, *Zapiski*, 340–42; Binyon, *Pushkin*, 320.

128. On official opposition to Pushkin and Benckendorff's efforts to promote Bulgarin's career see Todd, "Periodicals," 42; Ruud, *Fighting Words*, 63–65; MERSH, 6: 19, and 9: 42; Gozenpud, "Iz istorii," 260, 263, 266–67; Serman, "Pushkin," 137; Lemke, *Nikolaevskie zhandarmy*, 499; Monas, *Third Section*, 210–12; Simmons, *Pushkin*, 314–15, 319; and Driver, *Pushkin*, 17–18.

129. Annenkov, *Vospominaniia*, 3: 227–30; Monas, "Šiškov," 129; Todd, *Fiction*, 79, 85; Del'vig, *Polveka*, 1: 128; Koepnick, "Journalistic Careers," 65, 70, 74.

130. PS, 14: 67; TL, 3: 156; Gozenpud, "Iz istorii," 268, 270–71; Binyon, *Pushkin*, 314.

131. TL, 3: 161; Binyon, *Pushkin*, 314–15; Gozenpud, "Iz istorii," 272–73.

132. Binyon, *Pushkin*, 315–16, 319–20; TL, 3: 161–62, 195, 224; Koepnick, "Journalistic Careers," 74–75, 90.

133. Bulgarin, *Dimitrii Samozvanets*, 1: xxviii–lvi; Vinokur, "Kommentarii," 205; Gozenpud, "Iz istorii," 270–72; Monas, *Third Section*, 213–14; PS, 11: 396; Reiblat, *Vidok Figliarin*, 678–79; Ruud, *Fighting Words*, 45, 65.

134. Koepnick, "Journalistic Careers," 75; Gozenpud, "Iz istorii," 273; Driver, *Pushkin*, 18.

135. MERSH, 9: 42; Monas, *Third Section*, 211; TL, 3: 224; Binyon, *Pushkin*, 317–20; Reitblat, *Vidok Figliarin*, 679.

136. Annenkov, *Vospominaniia*, 3: 229–30; Mirsky, *Pushkin*, 122.

137. MERSH, 9: 42; TL, 3: 184–85, 229–30; *Letters*, 434; Binyon, *Pushkin*, 351–52; Driver, *Pushkin*, 18.

138. Ruud, *Fighting Words*, 61–62.

139. PS, 14: 133; *Letters*, 446. See also Ruud, *Fighting Words*, 76–77.

140. Ruud, *Fighting Words*, 64–65; Koepnick, "Journalistic Careers," 110; Binyon, *Pushkin*, 316–17.

141. Monas, *Third Section*, 211–12; Koepnick, "Journalistic Careers," 70–71.

142. *Letters*, 381; PS, 14: 73. For Bulgarin's attacks on Pushkin that were printed in the *Northern Bee* see TL, 3: 161–62, 184, 195, 224; Binyon, *Pushkin*, 315–16, 319–20; and Koepnick, "Journalistic Careers," 74–75, 90.

143. Driver, *Pushkin*, 18; Koepnick, "Journalistic Careers," 71, 110; Binyon, *Pushkin*, 315–16.

144. TL, 3: 187.

145. Vyskochkov, *Imperator*, 543.

146. See, for example, TL, 3: 175–76; Koepnick, "Journalistic Careers," 47–48; Serman, "Pushkin," 136.

147. TL, 3: 186–87; PS, 14: 80.

148. *Letters*, 407–8; PS, 14: 77–78; Simmons, *Pushkin*, 319; Donchin, "Pushkin," 24; Fomichev, *Prazdnik*, 88–89.

149. See *Letters*, 414, 415, 417–20; Driver, *Pushkin*, 19; Kropf, *Authorship*, 97; and Helfant, "Pushkin's Ironic Performance," 379.

150. Schönle, *Authenticity*, 195; Monas, *Third Section*, 212.

151. See Binyon, *Pushkin*, 313 n; *Letters*, 371, 398 n. 3; PS, 14: 268–69.

152. PS, 14: 78; *Letters*, 408.

153. *Letters*, 408.

154. PS, 14: 81–82; TL, 3: 183–84; BG, 127; Mirsky, *Pushkin*, 128.

155. *Letters*, 411–12; PS, 14: 88.

156. *Letters*, 413; PS, 14: 89.

157. TL, 3: 195; Vatsuro, *A. S. Pushkin*, 2: 29.

158. *Letters*, 413; PS, 14: 89.

159. Binyon, *Pushkin*, 350; TL, 3: 194, 199, 218, 544 n. 172; PS, 14: 93.

160. See, for example, TL, 3: 265.

161. PS, 11: 141; Mirsky, *Pushkin*, 154.

162. TL, 3: 219, 225; Chereiskii, *Pushkin*, 520; Pushkin, *Sochineniia i pis'ma*, 3: 256, 260–61; Gorodetskii, *Tragediia*, 77–79, 82; Binyon, *Pushkin*, 333.

163. See, for example, Pushkin, *Sochineniia i pis'ma*, 3: 639–40.

164. TL, 3: 219, 222–23; Gillel'son, *Ot arzamasskogo bratstva*, 37.

165. Serman, "Pushkin," 135; Blok, *Pushkin*, 1.

166. Balashov, "Boris Godunov," 213.

167. See, for example, *Letters*, 427, 430, 437, 446, and 449. On at least one previous occasion, Pushkin actually threatened to let finances rather than aesthetics govern the editing of his work for publication; see *Letters*, 196–97.

168. See Bulgarin, *Ruskaia Taliia*, 257–316; Karlinsky, *Russian Drama*, 305.

169. *Letters*, 430, 433–34; PS, 14: 117–18; Izmailov, "Pushkin," 13–14; Gorodetskii, *Tragediia*, 82, 109; Binyon, *Pushkin*, 350–51.

170. *Dela III-go otdeleniia*, 117; Ovchinnikova, *Pushkin*, 60.

171. See TL, 3: 275, 283; Pushkin, *Sochineniia i pis'ma*, 3: 257; Balashov, "Boris Godunov," 213; Edmonds, *Pushkin*, 172–73; Gorodetskii, *Tragediia*, 161–62; and Kochetkova, *Karamzin*, 129–30.

172. See *Letters*, 446–47; Binyon, *Pushkin*, 347–50, 377–80; Serman, "Pushkin," 135; Listov, "Pushkin," 289–90; Budgen, "Pushkin," 27–28; Balashov, "Boris Godunov," 179; and Lednicki, *Pouchkine*, 5–9, 146.

173. Listov, "Pushkin," 287–89; *Letters*, 437–38.

174. Koepnick, "Journalistic Careers," 129–31; *Letters*, 447.

175. See Annenkov, *Pushkin*, 255–57; Riasanovsky, *Image*, 90; and Chkheidze, *Istoriia Pugacheva*, 45–46. In 1835, Mikhail Pogodin dedicated his *Istoriia v litsakh o Dimitrie Samozvantse* to "historian laureate" Alexander Pushkin. Recently, Binyon (*Pushkin*, 351, 367–68, 390) incorrectly wrote that Pushkin did not actually receive Karamzin's title "istoriograf," probably basing his claim on Pushkin's own statement that he did not want the burden it implied; see PS, 14: 256. In fact, Pushkin was historian laureate of Russia from 1831 until his death.

176. Pushkin, *Sochineniia i pis'ma*, 3: 257; *Letters*, 285 n. 7; 515, 570; Monas, *Third Section*, 212; Bayley, *Pushkin*, 345; Debreczeny, *Other Pushkin*, 240; Binyon, *Pushkin*, 351, 367–68, 390; Feinberg, *Chitaia tetradi*, 40.

177. Riasanovsky, *Image*, 90, 109–15; Vernadsky, *Russian Historiography*, 67; Whittaker, *Origins*, 163.

178. TL, 3: 224; Abramkin, "Pushkin," 231; Wolff, "Shakespeare's Influence," 99–100; Emerson and Oldani, *Modest Musorgsky*, 129.

179. Pushkin, *Sochineniia i pis'ma*, 3: 257–60; Filonov, *Boris Godunov*, 57–58; Maikov, *Pamiati*, 331–32; Tynianov, *Pushkin*, 147; Kireevskii, *Polnoe sobranie sochinenii*, 2: 42–45; Zagorskii, *Pushkin*, 96–97; Barsukov, *Zhizn'*, 3: 244; Terras, *Belinskij*, 132–33, 174; idem, "Pushkin," 53; Brown, *History*, 3: 108; Gorodetskii, *Tragediia*, 84–108; Emerson, "Pretenders," 257–60; BG, 348–51; Bayley, *Pushkin*, 173, 176–77, 180; Alekseev, "A. S. Pushkin," 175; Serman, "Pushkin," 118–19; Zel'dovich and Livshits, *Russkaia literatura*, 167–69; Bochkarev, *Russkaia istoricheskaia dramaturgiia*, 428–32; Pomar, "Russian Historical Drama," 173; Greenleaf, *Pushkin*, 159.

180. See the review of *Boris Godunov* in the June 28, 1831 issue of *Severnaia pchela*

(no. 167, pages 2–3). Cf. "O 'Borise Godunove,'" 445–55. See also *Pushkin i ego sovre-menniki,* 175–76; and Alekseev, "A. S. Pushkin," 174–75. Mikhail Gronas also identi-fied Bulgarin as the probable author of the anonymous pamphlet (*O "Borise Godunove"*) in a paper presented at the December 2000 meeting of AATSEEL.

181. Pushkin, *Sochineniia i pis'ma,* 3: 256–57, 260–61; Bayley, *Pushkin,* 173; Mikkelson, "Narod," 277–78; Alekseev, "A. S. Pushkin," 174; Gorodetskii, *Tragediia,* 69–71, 77–83; Emerson, *Boris Godunov,* 23; Wolff, "Shakespeare's Influence," 99.

182. Tomashevskii, "Primechaniia," 509; Abramkin, "Pushkin," 230.

183. TL, 3: 251; *Dela III-go otdeleniia,* 96; Sukhomlinov, *Izsledovaniia,* 2: 232; Lemke, *Nikolaevskie zhandarmy,* 503.

184. Pushkin, *Sochineniia A. S. Pushkina* (Morozov, 1887), 3: 80; Annenkov, *Vospominaniia,* 453.

185. Pushkin, *Sochineniia i pis'ma,* 3: 260–61; BG, 349–51; Vinokur, "Komentarii," 425; Vinogradov, *Merime,* 175; Gorodetskii, *Tragediia,* 82; Abramkin, "Pushkin," 230.

186. Nikitenko, *Diary,* 71; idem, *Dnevnik,* 1: 198.

187. Alekseev, "Remarka," 49; Bayley, *Pushkin,* 176, 180.

188. Tomashevskii, "Primechaniia," 509; Bayley, *Pushkin,* 173. For other concerns about the play's irreligious elements see TL, 2: 424; Cooke and Dunning, "Tempting Fate," 62.

189. Rassadin, *Dramaturg Pushkin,* 21–23; Lysenkova, "O probleme," 63–64; Emerson, *Boris Godunov,* 122–23; Baer, "Between Public and Private," 33; Greenleaf, *Pushkin,* 383 n. 43.

190. Vinokur, *Kommentarii,* 243; Tomashevskii, "Primechaniia," 510.

191. Tomashevskii, "Primechaniia," 509; Bayley, *Pushkin,* 176, 180.

192. Vinokur, *Stat'i,* 90; Wolff, "Shakespeare's Influence," 99.

193. Brown, *History,* 3: 113; Mocha, "Polish and Russian Sources," 49.

194. See Pushkin, *Sochineniia i pis'ma,* 3: 309; Briggs, *Alexander Pushkin,* 244 n. 14.

195. Gurevich, "Istoriia," 213; Serman, "Paradoxes," 27–28.

196. Vinokur, *Stat'i,* 90; Gorodetskii, *Tragediia,* 83.

197. Kireevskii, *Polnoe sobranie sochinenii,* 2: 45–46; Alekseev, "A. S. Pushkin," 174; Serman, "Paradoxes," 27–28.

198. Serman, "Paradoxes," 35–37.

199. Pushkin, *Sochineniia A. S. Pushkina* (Morozov, 1887), 3: 80; Binyon, *Pushkin,* 644–45; Nikitenko, *Diary,* 71–72; Shchegolev, *Duel,* 208; Levitt, "Pushkin," 187–88.

200. Pushkin, *Sochineniia A. S. Pushkina* (Morozov, 1887), 3: 76–77; Gurevich, "Istoriia," 213; Mirsky, *Pushkin,* 161–62; Balashov, "Boris Godunov," 213; Edmonds, *Pushkin,* 172; Wolff, *Pushkin,* 105–6; Gorodetskii, *Tragediia,* 82, 161–62; Brody, "Pushkin's 'Boris Godunov,'" 873; Brown, *History,* 3: 111; Alekseev, "Remarka," 46.

201. TL, 3: 225; Alekseev, "Remarka," 49, 51; Lotman, "Eshche raz," 168; Wolff, "Shakespeare's Influence," 97, 105; Stroganov, "Eshche raz," 127; Shervinsky, "Stage Directions," 154; Evdokimova, *Pushkin's Historical Imagination,* 25; Ronen, *Smyslovoi stroi,* 131–32.

202. See Pushkin, *Sochineniia A. S. Pushkina* (Morozov, 1887), 3: 76; Alekseeva, "Remarka," 46; Emerson, *Boris Godunov,* 243 n. 120.

203. See Filonov, *Boris Godunov*, 54–55, 145; BG, 354–57, 448–49; Vinokur, *Kommentarii*, 307; Listov and Tarkhova, "K istorii," 96–102; Luzianina, "Istoriia," 45–47; Kochetkova, *Nikolay Karamzin*, 124–25; Gorodetskii, "Boris Godunov," 39–40; idem, *Tragediia*, 162; Rabinovich, "Boris Godunov," 314–16; Emerson, *Boris Godunov*, 72–73.

204. Belinskii, *Stat'i*, 270–71; Gifford, "Shakespearean Elements," 156; Levin, *Shekspir*, 41; Wolff, "Shakespeare's Influence," 97; Vickery, *Alexander Pushkin* (1970), 69; Dinega, "Ambiguity," 540 n. 28; Sandler, *Distant Pleasures*, 88, 137.

205. For example, it has been suggested that Pushkin was influenced by Plutarch's use of silence (Mikhailova, "K istochnikam," 151), by the crowd's silent reaction to the failure of the Decembrist Rebellion (Gorodetskii, *Dramaturgiia Pushkin*, 237), and by Pushkin's own use of silence in his "Ode to Liberty" (Stroganov, "Eshche raz," 127).

206. See Alekseev, "Remarka," 54–58; Gillel'son, *Molodoi Pushkin*, 169; Mikhailova, "K istochnikam," 150–53; Rabinovich, "Boris Godunov," 308; Stroganov, "Eshche raz," 126–28; Brown, *History*, 3: 111; and BG, 352–53, 356–57.

207. Emerson, "Queen," 33; idem, *Boris Godunov*, 137–41.

208. See Bulgarin, *Dimitrii Samozvanets*, 4: 482–83; Monas, *Third Section*, 213–14; BG, 353–54; Gozenpud, "Iz istorii," 264; and Mocha, "Polish and Russian Sources," 49–51.

209. Some scholars have claimed that Pushkin changed the end of his play from a cheer to silence in order to distinguish it from the *narod*'s shout of approval for Tsar Dmitry in Bulgarin's novel, *Dimitrii Samozvanets*; see Stroganov, "Eshche raz," 129; Listov and Tarkhova, "K istorii," 97.

210. Custine, *Letters*, 58, 104, 129.

211. *Letters*, 408. See also Greenleaf, *Pushkin*, 177–78.

212. See Iakovlev, "Bezumnoe molchanie," 651–78; Soloviev, *Holy Russia*, 28–29; Rowland, "Problem," 260, 274–75; Filonov, *Boris Godunov*, 145; and Billington, *Icon and Axe*, 124.

213. See Brody, "Schiller's 'Demetrius,'" 275–76.

214. PS, 14: 141–42; *Letters*, 452. See also TL, 3: 287, 294; *Letters*, 458; Debreczeny, *Other Pushkin*, 140.

215. *Letters*, 449, 452; TL, 3: 284; Binyon, *Pushkin*, 351.

216. Katenin, "'Neustanovlennomu litsu," 101–2; Dolinin, *Russkie pisateli*, 49; Brown, *History*, 3: 105; Rothe, "Karamzin," 148–49.

217. PS, 14: 146; *Letters*, 454; Binyon, *Pushkin*, 351.

218. Meilakh, *Pushkin i ego epokha*, 569–70; Emerson, "Pushkin," 264.

219. Emerson, *Boris Godunov*, 21; idem, "Pretenders," 263–68; Serman, "Pushkin," 129–49; Rothe, "Karamzin," 176.

220. Khomiakov, *Stikhotvoreniia*, 12, 19, 578 n. 103; MERSH, 16: 169; Brody, *Demetrius Legend*, 250–53; Zagorskii, *Pushkin*, 108, 113–14; Gukovskii, *Pushkin*, 68–69; Levin, "Literatura," 141, 159–61; Pomar, "Russian Historical Drama," 289–91; Emerson, "Pretenders," 265–67; Serman, "Paradoxes," 27–28; idem, "Pushkin," 129–30.

221. Pogodin, "Smert'," 247–78; idem, *Istoriia v litsakh o tsare Borise*, 144; idem, *Istoriia v litsakh o Dimitrie Samozvantse;* Zagorskii, *Pushkin*, 111–13; Serman, "Pushkin," 132–33, 148; Pomar, "Russian Historical Drama," 287.

222. MERSH, 28: 153–55.

223. MERSH, 24: 222–25; Annenkov, *Extraordinary Decade*, 163; Koepnick, "Journalistic Careers," 53–54, 249–50. See also Monas, "Šiškov," 146; Nikitenko, *Diary*, 376 n. 2.

224. See Rossiiskii gosudarstvennyi istoricheskii arkhiv, fond 722, opis' 1, delo No. 2209 (Buturlin Committee's secret report to Count S. S. Uvarov, 29 January 1849), listy 1–3; Solov'ev, "Obzor sobytii," 11; Lincoln, *Nicholas I*, 320–21; and Sanders, *Historiography*, 218.

225. Serman, "Pushkin," 129, 138–40; Annenkov, *Vospominaniia*, 3: 453–54; Rosen, "Boris Godunov," 249–59; Gennadi, *Prilozheniia*, 73; Bayley, *Pushkin*, 173. The Romantic writer Vilgelm Kiukhelbeker, who was strongly influenced by both Schiller and Pushkin, also wrote several dramas about the Time of Troubles – including one about Grishka Otrepiev and one about Vasily Shuisky. See Levin, "Literatura," 141, 159–62.

4

The World of Laughter in Pushkin's *Comedy*

∾ SERGEI FOMICHEV

Pushkin was inspired to begin work on his *Comedy about Tsar Boris and Grishka Otrepiev* by reading volumes 10 and 11 of Nicholas Karamzin's *History of the Russian State*. In one of Pushkin's working notebooks (the "Second Masonic Notebook"), in an entry dated November 1824, is a synopsis of events taken from Karamzin's *History*, concerned primarily with "The murder of S[aint] Dmitry" in 1591. After this event the synopsis moves straight to the year 1598: "The State Secretary and *pechatnik* Vasily Shchelkalov asks for an oath in the name of the Boyar Duma. Elect[ion] of Godunov." Following the synopsis, however, is a list of "banishments and executions 1584–1587" as well as a list of the members of the boyar council in 1584, the last-mentioned of whom is "Godunov, son-in-law of Maliuta Skuratov."[1] This supplementary information was no doubt important to Pushkin as evidence of Boris Godunov's long-standing, systematic, and treacherous preparations for clearing a path to the throne for himself – dating back to the beginning of the reign of Ivan the Terrible's power-shy successor Tsar Feodor. On the next page of Pushkin's "Second Masonic Notebook" is a synopsis of the play:[2]

God[unov] in monastery. Princes' conversation – news – square, news of election.
God[unov] holy fool – Chronicler. Otrepiev – flight of Otrepiev.
God[unov] in monastery. His repentance – fugitive monks. God[unov] with his family –

God[unov] in Council. Talk on the square. – News of betrayals, death of
   Irina. God[unov] and sorcerers.
Pretender [in the midst of] battle –
Death of Godunov (– news of first victory, feasting, appearance of the
   Pretender) boyars' oath, betrayal.
Pushkin and Pleshcheev on the square – Dmitry's letter – veche – mur-
   der of the tsar – Pretender enters Moscow.

In the course of the play's composition this plan was radically altered in
the following respects: 1) The Polish scenes are added. 2) The death of
Irina and the tsar's consultation with sorcerers are barely mentioned;
there are no individual scenes relating to these subjects or to "Godunov
in monastery." 3) The Pretender appears in a greater number of scenes
(but not his entry into Moscow) and acquires parity with Godunov in
the plot.

Especially noteworthy in this synopsis (and also in Karamzin's *History*) is the absence of comic scenes, with the possible exception of
"Godunov holy fool [*iurodivyi*]" – but even that is deleted from the first
manuscript of the *Comedy*. Pushkin's note regarding "Godunov holy
fool" is usually taken as a reference to scene 18 ("Square in front of the
Cathedral, Moscow"), even though that scene is surely being referred to
in the synopsis two paragraphs below by the words: "Talk on the square."
In fact, another interpretation of Pushkin's intentions here is possible –
that Boris, after agreeing to accept the throne, did not immediately leave
the monastery, but instead spent more time there and indeed began his
reign there. Following the course of events surrounding Boris Godunov's
election expounded in volume 11 of the *History of the Russian State*,
Pushkin might, at this early stage, have been fixing his attention on the
following observation of Karamzin's:[3]

> Both prelates and great lords attempted in vain to persuade the tsar to
> leave a dwelling-place that was sad for him, to settle with his wife and chil-
> dren in the Kremlin palace and show himself to the people crowned and
> enthroned; Boris replied: "I cannot part from the great queen [Tsar
> Feodor's widow], my ill-fated sister," and once again, *indefatigable in his
> hypocrisy* [italics – S. F.], declared that he had no wish to be tsar.

This episode in the enthronement of a Boris who was a hypocrite (or
who played the "holy fool") might have served as the content of the scene

noted in the synopsis and then dropped. However, among variant drafts for the beginning of the first scene, which was written immediately after the synopsis, the following exchange takes place between Vorotynsky and Shuisky about Boris's behaviour before his accession:

> – What do you think? How will this business end?
> – How will it end? Not difficult to guess –
>   The people will still groan upon their knees,
>   Boris will show a little more impatience,
>   And then at last, from generosity,
>   Most humbly, he will take the crown at last,
>   And then – once more he will proceed to rule us
>   Exactly as before.
> – *The cunning clown* [*skomorokh*]!
>
> [italics – S. F.]

Compare that with the final version of the text:

> *Vorotynsky*
> […] How will this business end?
>   What do you think?
>
> *Shuisky*
> Not difficult to guess:
>   The people will weep and wail a little more,
>   Boris will wear his frown a little more,
>   Just like a drunkard peering at his cup;
>   And out of boundless generosity,
>   Most humbly, he will take the crown at last;
>   And then – why then, he will proceed to rule us
>   Exactly as before.

The *skomorokh* (wandering minstrel and actor) and the holy fool were the two stock-in-trades of the medieval Russian comic world.[4] As we shall see, in the course of working on the play Pushkin was to give these figures their genuine value, and not merely use them as assumed masks. At first, in accordance with the synopsis of November 1824, they were clearly subordinated to the central figure of the drama, who, as the composition progressed, was increasingly surrounded by a host of additional characters (there are more than eighty speaking parts in the play). The action increasingly shifts to the public square, with the people taking the main role and becoming as important – in terms of the number of scenes in which they appear – as the two central historical characters, Boris and Grishka Otrepiev. Furthermore, the struggle between the two protagonists comes to be played out primarily through echoes in "the esteem of the people."

Pushkin observed in 1830 that

> Drama was born on the public square and was a form of popular entertainment. The people, just as children do, demand diversion and action. Drama appears to them an extraordinary and strange phenomenon. The people demand strong sensations; for them even executions are spectacles. Laughter, pity and fear are the three strings of our imagination which are touched by the magic of drama. But laughter soon grows weak, and it is impossible to base a complete dramatic action on it alone…. Let us note that high comedy is not based solely on laughter, but on the development of characters, and that it not infrequently approaches tragedy.[5]

Pushkin, of course, plays on all three "strings of the imagination" in his drama. The concern of this chapter, however, is to investigate the comic element in the play, and not to consider the action in its entirety, so infinitely diverse and topical. It should be noted here that the rough draft of the first scene in Pushkin's working notebook is interrupted by an extraneous prose fragment relating, it would appear, to some autobiographical notes Pushkin was writing simultaneously with his work on the play:[6]

> If I were the Tsar I would summon Alexander Pushkin and say to him: "Alexander Sergeevich, you write excellent poetry." Alexander Pushkin would bow to me with a touch of embarrassed modesty, and I would continue: "I've read your *Ode to Freedom*. It is written in a somewhat rambling style and is not thought out deeply enough, but there are three stanzas here which are very good. Although you have behaved very irresponsibly, you have nevertheless not tried to blacken me in the people's eyes by the spreading of a foolish slander …

Pushkin imagines that the interview would very likely have ended on a serious note:

> But here Pushkin would have flared up and would have blurted out a whole lot of unnecessary remarks, and I would have grown angry and would have banished him to Siberia, where he would have written a narrative poem *Yermak* or *Kuchum* in various rhyming measures.

Pushkin's train of thought is clear. Alexander I owed his throne to a crime, the murder of his father, Paul I. The "official" cause of Paul's death was an apoplectic stroke, so the three stanzas in Pushkin's ode reconstructing the actual events of 1 March 1801 were indeed "irresponsible." But from Alexander I's point of view (as imagined by Pushkin), they were "good" because at least he wasn't accused of the crime in the manner of Boris Godunov – although rumours of the heir to the throne's links with the conspirators had circulated. This associative link clears up, in the present author's view, a later comment of Pushkin's in a letter to Pyotr Viazemsky written just after he had completed his play: "Zhukovsky says that the Tsar will pardon me because of my tragedy – hardly, my dear fellow. Although it is written in a well-meaning spirit, I couldn't hide my ears completely beneath the holy fool's pointed cap. They stick out!"[7]

Pushkin's humorous tone – which, as stated above, is not present in the synopsis – soon appears in the play itself, in scene 3 ("Maiden's Field. Novodevichy Convent"). It is instructive to trace the strengthening of the comic element in this scene through the process of its composition. In Pushkin's first draft, the scene lacked the woman who threatens her child with "the bogeyman" to keep him quiet, and then later, when the child stays quiet at a time when everyone is supposed to be weeping, throws him to the ground to make him cry again.[8] While working on his *Comedy*, Pushkin read the abundant documentary material contained in Karamzin's notes to his *History* with close attention, and it was here that he picked up the detail of fabricated tears: "One Chronicle describes how some in the crowd, fearful because they were not weeping, and being unable to weep, smeared their eyes with saliva."[9] Having completed the first draft of the scene, Pushkin worked up this passage: "But I can't – I'll pinch you / Or tear out a piece of your beard – be quiet. / This is no time to make jokes – has anyone got an onion?"

Pushkin also added the two passages with the woman and child. In the first passage, near the beginning of the scene, the woman quiets her child with a threat: "Don't cry! Don't cry! Now then! Here's the bogeyman! I'll give you / To the bogeyman – now then! Don't cry, don't cry." And before the final acclamation for Boris, the woman replies to the line, "The people were wailing – what are you weeping for, woman?" with the following: "How do I know, it's the boyars that know that, / It's none of our business! – Just when you're supposed to weep, / Then you go all quiet! The bogeyman is coming to eat you. / Cry, you brat!" This time the detail comes not from Karamzin's *History* but from Pushkin's own *Skazki: Noël* or "Fairy Tales: Noel" (1818), deriding the "wandering despot" Alexander I with his promises of political reform.[10] There too a woman frightens her child: "Don't cry, my child, don't cry, sire: / Here comes the bogeyman, the bogeyman – the Tsar of Russia!"

This threat, V. V. Golovin has noted, "rests both on the nursery figure well-known to everyone and on the fear of the tsar deep in the mind of every Russian. The bogeyman is a demonological figure, an inhabitant of foreign space, in the popular mind an 'alien' who brings danger. In the folklore of the nursery the bogeyman makes his appearance on the border between his own world and the familiar everyday world, and so he is assiduously chased away, as for example in the words: 'Hush-a-bye, hush-a-bye / Bogeyman, stay on the boundary.'"[11] Boundary space is sharply impressed on the "Maiden's Field" scene: the crowd is seen from behind – and an historic event, the offer of the throne, takes place somewhere in the distance, beyond the bounds of the scene.

Pushkin's final revision of the "Maiden's Field" scene "relied" once more on *The History of the Russian State* (in fact, making alterations to the historian's account). Of the crowd's appeal to Boris to take the crown, Karamzin wrote: "Mothers threw their suckling babes to the ground, deaf to their wailing. Sincerity conquered sham, inspiration affected both the indifferent and the most dissembling."[12] In the final revision of the "Maiden's Field" scene, the woman's second speech ends: "Now cry, you brat! / *(Throws the infant to the ground; he yells.)* / That's it." It was during work on this scene that Pushkin found the tone that was to characterize most of the crowd scenes in his *Comedy*.

"Everything truly great," observed Mikhail Bakhtin, "must include the element of laughter. Without this, it is menacing, terrible or stilted; in any case, limited. Humour lifts the barriers and frees the way ahead."[13] Defining the nature of humour in popular culture, Dmitry Likhachev wrote: "Laughter destroys existing links and meanings in life. Laughter points to the senselessness and inanity of the relations obtaining in the social world: relations of cause and effect, relations that give existing phenomena their meaning, the conventions of human behaviour in social life. Laughter 'distorts,' 'reveals,' 'unmasks,' 'lays bare.' It, as it were, returns the world to its primordial chaotic state."[14] Now this "chaos," sedition, instinctive resistance to the system, is embodied by the people, who, when required to subordinate themselves to the system, direct their laughter at themselves. "One of the chief characteristics of medieval laughter is that it is directed at the one who laughs.... The 'antics of the fool' contain, in secret or openly, criticism of the existing world, and expose social relations, conditions of social justice. The 'fool' is therefore, to some degree, clever: he knows more about the world than those around him."[15]

Pushkin repeatedly stressed that the course of events in his drama followed Karamzin's *History* precisely, in chronology and in detail. It is in this sense that his famous comment to Vasily Zhukovsky should be understood: "What a marvel these last 2 volumes of Karamzin are! What vigour! *C'est palpitant comme la gazette d'hier,* as I wrote to Raevsky."[16] The French phrase is sometimes translated into Russian as: "This is as topical as the latest newspaper."[17] In studies of *Boris Godunov,* Pushkin's words have usually been quoted in that way as proof of the work's political allusiveness. The real meaning of the word *palpitant,* however, is quite different: "This is as *lively* as the latest newspaper." Pushkin's phrase refers to the graphic precision of Karamzin's account of events – in other words, his *History*'s effect on the reader as almost journalistic reportage.

But what fired the imagination of Karamzin – his interpretation of historical vicissitudes, the inscrutability of fate, the will of providence – was alien to Pushkin, who was at times not far from making fun of Karamzin, dismissing his account of events and at the same time substantially revising it to fit his artistic ideas. It is in light of this approach to Karamzin that Pushkin's comment in the draft preface to his tragedy (written in 1830 in the form of a letter to Nikolai Raevsky) should be read:[18]

> Here is my tragedy since you want it so much, but before you read it I demand that you look through Karamzin's latest volume. It is full of good jokes and subtle references to the history of that time, like our talks at Kiev and Kamenka.[19] It is necessary to understand them – a *sine qua non.*

Thus in scene 7 ("The Patriarch's Palace") Pushkin used Karamzin's comment that when Otrepiev's bold claims "reached the hearing of Iona, metropolitan of Rostov, who reported to the Patriarch and to the Tsar himself that 'the unworthy monk Grigory wishes to be an instrument of the Devil,' the good-natured Patriarch did not accept the metropolitan's denunciation."[20] In one of his draft prefaces Pushkin jokingly commented: "Griboedov has criticized the character of Iov. The Patriarch, it is true, was a man of great intellect; I've thoughtlessly made him a fool."[21] "Thoughtlessly" is, of course, Pushkin's joke. For Karamzin, Patriarch Iov was a wise associate of the tsar, a guarantor of social stability. The open-hearted ingenuousness of Pushkin's Patriarch allies him with the fools of fairy tales.

One particular detail is worth noting. In Karamzin's *History*, Otrepiev's flight is reported to the Patriarch and to the Tsar simultaneously, but in Pushkin's drama, to the former only, who in his naivety gives the order not "to report any of this to the Tsar – mustn't trouble the Sovereign-Father." This heightens the comic effect of the moment in scene 9 ("A Tavern on the Lithuanian Border"), when the frontier guards frighten the company by producing a *Tsar's decree* for the capture of the runaway monk who, "instructed by the Devil, has had the audacity to distress the holy brotherhood by all manner of incitements and iniquities." But news of the Pretender's appearance is not actually shown reaching the Tsar until later in the drama – like a sudden thunderclap, a terrible foreboding. Preparing for this most powerful dramatic effect, Pushkin boldly departs from Karamzin's course of events for artistic purposes, telescoping the time between Otrepiev's flight and his appearance as the Pretender. In historical fact, Otrepiev ran away from the monastery in February 1602, a year *before* the date at which Pushkin depicts him with Pimen at the Chudov Monastery (scene 5); and news of the Pretender had reached the Tsar from various sources by the beginning of 1604, even before the former's appearance at Wiśniowiecki's house.[22]

In the Tavern scene, although Pushkin borrowed the names of Grigory's companions from Karamzin, he gave these runaway monks characteristics that he may have observed in real monks at the Uspensky monastery (near Mikhailovskoe), whose conduct left a good deal to be desired. "This monastery was mentioned on some special lists as a reformatory, for priests who had committed offences. All its inmates had been exiled there – some for corruption of mind or heart, some for adultery, some for theft or other major transgressions."[23] Pushkin's friend Aleksei Vulf pointed out that a favourite saying of the father superior of the Uspensky monastery was: "Our Foma / Drinks to the bottom, / Drinks it all and turns it over, / Then drubs it on the bottom."[24] This is clearly reflected in Varlaam's rhyming utterance in scene 9 ("A Tavern on the Lithuanian Border"): "drink up, and drink to the bottom o' the tankar'; turn 'er upside-down and spank 'er."

The place of the Tavern scene in Pushkin's play conforms to the culture of the *skomorokh*, the wandering minstrel-cum-clown. "The tradition of playing and singing in taverns," writes one modern scholar of the subject Z. I. Vlasova, "arose almost from the time taverns were first introduced into Russia during the reign of Ivan IV." Vlasova correctly contends that the central figure in this scene, Varlaam, is primarily a *skomorokh* by nature: "In one example of popular buffoonery that has come down to us, 'Buffoonery about monks,' the figure of the happy wandering monk is reminiscent of Pushkin's Varlaam."[25] This particular type of text consists of a sequence of parallel passages, in which the first line names the alms and the second explains what the monk gets. His demands become more and more audacious, until a girl is brought to him: "He embraces her beneath his hair shirt," and, satisfied, says: "There's a fine nun. There's a fine sister, and a wife for alms."[26]

The ageing Varlaam and his companion Misail do not chase women, but Varlaam wholeheartedly spurs Grigory on: "Oho, my friend! Sweetening up our hostess, eh? You won't have wine and you won't have song, it's women for you, all the way. At 'er boy!" And one of the songs, here in its entirety, he begins to sing earlier in the scene completely matches the mood:[27]

> You walk past my cell, my dear one,
> By the cell where a poor monk grieves,
> Where a fine young man takes his vows against his will,
> Tell me, beautiful girl, the whole truth,
> Or have people gone quite blind,
> Why does everyone call me an old man?
> Take from me, my dear one, my kamelaukion,[28]
> And take from me, my darling, my black cassock,
> Put your white hand on my breast,
> And feel how my heart trembles,
> Flushed with blood because of my rapid sighs …

In true *skomorokh* style, Varlaam constantly scatters sayings and catchphrases, sometimes of a fairly risqué nature. The tsarist censor made a special note in his official report on the play: "The saying is: 'Freedom for the free, and paradise for the *saved*,' and it has been altered to: 'Freedom for the free, and Paradise for the *drinker*.'"[29] But Pushkin must have been well aware that *skomorokhi* would make up such catchphrases "to give well-known humorous sayings greater sharpness: 'Glory to God, glory be: Lord the Saviour and lucky we!'; ... 'The priest to the bell, and we to the [drinking] bowl'; ... 'The bold ones are on the Volga or in jail, the clever ones are in the monastery or the tavern, the fools have become priests.'"[30]

In Pushkin's original synopsis, the action in the tavern completed the first part of the play. One third of the scenes in this part are in markedly comic mode, and this determined the original title of the play. On 13 July 1825, Pushkin wrote to Pyotr Viazemsky: "Before me lies my tragedy. I cannot help copying out its title: *Comedy about a True Calamity that Befell the State of Muscovy, about Ts[ar] Boris and Grishka Otr[epiev]; Written by God's Servant Aleks[andr] Son of Sergei Pushkin in the Year 7333 [1825] on the Site of the Ancient Town of Voronich.* What do you think?"[31] This draft title is also recorded elsewhere in Pushkin's manuscripts.[32] But the line concerning authorship was revised in successive stages. At first it read: "composed by [A.] Valerian Palitsyn." This revealed Pushkin's familiarity with Palitsyn's *Skazanie Avraamiia Palitsyna ob osade Troitse-Sergieva monastyria* [*Avraamy Palitsyn's Tale about the Siege of the Trinity-St. Sergius Monastery*], an outstanding eyewitness account of the events of the Time of Troubles.[33] The substitution of the name "Avraamii" (Pushkin first wrote "A...") was certainly no error but the germ of a conscious piece of mystification. However, in the manuscript containing the draft title, details of the author are corrected: "written by Aleksashka Pushkin." In this self-denigratory naming of himself, the same humorous note is struck as we have observed emerging in the text of Pushkin's *Comedy*.

The first tentative title of Pushkin's play also echoed the style of the earliest works of the Russian theater (1672–76), performed during the reign of Aleksei Mikhailovich – in particular the *Comedy of Adam and Eve*, the *Comedy of David and Goliath*, and the *Comedy of Bacchus and Venus*. But Pushkin took his most prolix formula from a chronicle account of the Troubles entitled *Letopis' o mnogikh miatezhakh* [*Chronicle of Many Rebellions*]. One of the titles of this composite work, compiled during the reign of Aleksei Mikhailovich and published in 1772, was "Concerning a True Calamity that Befell the State of Muscovy and Grishka Otrepiev."[34]

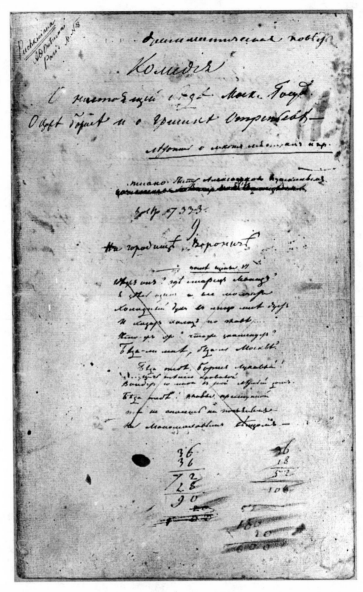

4. Preliminary title of Pushkin's play: *Comedy about a True Calamity that Befell the State of Muscovy, about Tsar Boris and Grishka Otrepiev; Written by God's Servant Alexander Son of Sergei Pushkin in the Year 7333 [1825], on the site of the Ancient Town of Voronich,* dated approximately July 13, 1825. From Institut russkoi literatury (Pushkinskii Dom) RAN, Rukopisnyi otdel, fond 244, opis' 1, No. 73, list 1. Courtesy of the Russian Academy of Sciences.

In seventeenth-century usage the word "comedy" generally meant "play." But Pushkin's imitation of period style certainly also contains, to some degree, the sense of the word that belonged to his own time, and this at once produced an inevitable contrast: "Comedy ... about a disaster," defining the complex stylistics of his tragedy. Pushkin may possibly have had in mind the popular play *The Comedy of Tsar Maximilian and his son Adolf,* in which the tsar unsuccessfully tries to make his son renounce his Christian beliefs and executes him, though this is not how the play ends. As Anatoly Belkin wrote:[35]

> The dénouements of *Tsar Maximilian* ... are original. Each variant is different, but what they have in common is that by the end of the play the image of the tsar has somehow been tarnished.... In some variants the tsar is overthrown or is overtaken by Death. But the most interesting endings are those where the tsar succumbs to a carnivalesque dethronement in something like "a game of being tsar." The essence of such a game was that the players first chose a tsar and "submitted" to his rule, carrying out all his whims and commands – and then, at the end of the game, they would mock him, sometimes even beat him up – i.e., they unmasked him, deposed him.

The very plot of Pushkin's play has the flavour of this sort of public game. Even if it turned out to be a merely typological similarity, this is still worth noting.

S. B. Rassadin, noting the "tragi-farcical" stylistic pattern of the first part of Pushkin's *Comedy,* suggested that the ironic (it would be better to say "humorous") tone of this beginning contrasts with the tragic ending, producing "that strangeness which is due to an unusually bold clash of tragic and farcical (or rather, to their joint perspective – we should recall the beginning of the play), and to the striking tendency towards contrasts manifested not only in the combination of high and low, humorous and terrible, but even in the transitions and breaks between scenes, and in the distinctive contributions that each of the chief characters makes to the plot."[36] Switches from comedy to tragedy occur, of course, throughout the play. Pushkin's pen in no way loses its humorous impulses after the first part of the play.

"He is not afraid to resort to humor," noted O. M. Feldman, "in the most crucial scenes. The most seditious moment of the play, a fervent anti-Godunov speech, is given to an inebriated Afanasy Pushkin" (in

scene 10, "Moscow. Shuisky's House").[37] A comic impression is maintained even in scene 11 ("The Tsar's Palace"), where Godunov plays with
Shuisky in order to worm out what he can about the appearance of the
Pretender, and where even the criminal tsar's mortal fear, heavy with a
terrible significance, is still couched in terms of comic absurdity:

> Whoever heard of corpses leaving graves
> To question tsars, rightful and lawful tsars,
> Named and chosen by the assembled people,
> Crowned by the holy Patriarch himself?
> Laughable, is it not? Why aren't you laughing?

There follows a scene with a different tone, scene 12 ("Cracow.
Wiśniowiecki's House"), in which the Pretender charms, one after the
other, the Jesuit priest, the young Kurbsky, the Polish nobleman
Sobański, the Moscow courtier Khrushchov, and the panegyric poet; he
is unconcerned that his promises to so many different persons are mutu-
ally incompatible. He would seem to have won over everyone; even the
Polish ladies at the ball (in scene 14, "Suite of Illuminated Rooms.
Music") are prepared to concede that "One clearly sees the royal line in
him." However, the Pretender has in fact deceived everyone and turned
himself into a phantom, which is emphasized in scene 15 ("Night. Garden. Fountain") in his audacious words: "I will not share my loved one
with a corpse." He indeed belongs to some antiworld, a world of the
topsy-turvy, of outer darkness, hovering on the border between comedy
and tragedy – the world of laughter. He is Boris Godunov's shadow, a
masker, a Pretender.

In Pushkin's original *Comedy* the Polish scenes form a richer sequence
than in the cut-down text published in 1831. The freely rhyming iambics
of scene 13 ("Maryna's Dressing Room") take the play in another direction, replacing the note of grand political intrigue just sounded by the
Pretender with light comedy in the conversation between Maryna and
her maidservant – who, appropriately in this world of laughter, is certainly as intelligent as her mistress. Of still more significance is the
exchange in scene 12 ("Cracow. Wiśniowiecki's House") between Gavrila
Pushkin and Khrushchov during the Pretender's conversation with the
Latinist poet. Except for the last five words, this passage was omitted
from the 1831 text:

> *Khrushchov*
> *(in a low voice to Pushkin)*
> Who's that?

> *Pushkin*
> A bard.

> *Khrushchov*
> What's that?

> *Pushkin*
> How shall I say?
> In Russian – scribbler of verses, or a minstrel.

> *Pretender*
> Excellent verses! I believe in bards'
> Prophecies.

Bards' prophecies, it is plain, are bought, and to be valued accordingly. But a wandering minstrel is not only a scribbler, he is first and foremost a dissembler, and the underlying reference here is to the Pretender; see scene 7 ("The Patriarch's Palace"), where Grishka too is a scribbler: "he composed hymns to the saints, but such education could not have come to him from the Lord God."

The comic element functions just as significantly in the ten short last scenes of Pushkin's play. In the version of 1825, scene 17 ("The Tsar's Council") is immediately followed by the scene with the Holy Fool (scene 18, "Square in front of the Cathedral, Moscow"), which carries just as strong a tragic charge. In both scenes the shade of the murdered young Dmitry appears – in the first, in the simple-minded Patriarch's story of the healing remains of the Tsarevich, and in the second, in the holy fool's direct indictment of the murderer-tsar. In the tsar's council, the Patriarch suggests that the Pretender can be destroyed by the display of the holy relics in public in Moscow. But the boy has found sanctity as an innocent child murdered by order of a court favourite, and the quick-witted Shuisky smothers the dangerous project: "The people's mood swings wildly as it is, / There's quite enough unruly talk already...."

The next stage of the action takes place on the square in front of the cathedral (scene 18), and again, as in scene 3 ("Maiden's Field"), an official ceremony takes place offstage (inside the cathedral) and is interpreted in the comments of the people:

First
What's that? 'ave they pronounced the curse on '*im* yet?

Second
I was standing on the porch and I heard the Deacon shout: "Grishka Otrepiev – he shall be Anathema!"

First
They can curse 'im 's much as they like – the Tsarevich ain't got nothin' to do with Otrepiev.

Second
Now they're chanting eternal remembrance for the Tsarevich.

First
Eternal remembrance for the living! They'll catch it for that, the godless scoundrels.

Such comments, rejecting the official view of events, would seem perfectly logical. But it turns out that the people's real opinion is quite different. It is precisely expressed by the simpleton, the holy fool, Nikolka who has just been insulted by the children:

Tsar
Give him alms. Why is he weeping?

Holy Fool
The little children have insulted Nikolka.... Have their throats cut, as you cut the young Tsarevich's.

Boyars
Away with you, old fool! Seize the fool!

Tsar
Leave him alone. Pray for me, blessed fool.

(Exit.)

Holy Fool
(after him)
No, no! No-one must pray for King Herod – The Mother of
God forbids it.

It turns out that in the chaotic consciousness of the people, there is overall no such thing as logic. If the Tsar is a murderer, then there is no Dmitry
in this world. How then is it possible to sympathize with the purloiner of
Dmitry's name – for him to be supported by "popular esteem"?[38] There is
no logic here. However, a higher truth may be dimly (chaotically) sensed.
"In Pushkin," A. M. Panchenko emphasized while analyzing the Russian
national phenomenon of *iurodstvo* (holy foolishness) as a manifestation of
the world of laughter, "a holy fool insulted by children is the audacious and
unpunished denouncer of the child murderer Boris Godunov.... the holy
fool speaks for [the people] – and speaks fearlessly."[39] In this scene Pushkin
deftly catches the paradoxical quality of Russian popular comic tradition,
in which the comic often tipped over into horror. This is why he writes of
the *mingling* of comic and tragic – not only the alternation of the two – and
notes: "The ghost scene in *Hamlet* is all written in jocular language, but
one's hair stands on end at Hamlet's jokes."[40]

Following this shattering scene in Pushkin's original *Comedy* is an
unabashedly farcical scene (scene 19, "A Plain Near Novgorod-Seversky")
that would seem to be an impossible way to depict bloody battle. But the
confusion of battle is effectively communicated here by purely linguistic
means – by cacophonic dissonance:

Margeret
Quoi? Quoi?

Another Soldier
Kwa! Kwa! All very well for a foreign crow like you to croak
at the Russian Tsarevich. We're Orthodox, we are.

Margeret
Qu'est-ce à dire "*Orthodoxe*"?

The prose medium of this scene and scenes 7 ("The Patriarch's Palace"), 9 ("A Tavern on the Lithuanian Border"), and 18 ("Square in front of the Cathedral, Moscow") stands in sharp contrast to the measured, rather solemn language of the main body of the play, which is in verse. The element of comedy enters these scenes for just this reason. The Patriarch, the vagrant monks Varlaam and Misail, the captains Margeret and Rosen, Nikolka the Holy Fool – all these are figures from the comic world. But if such is indeed the pattern of Pushkin's prose scenes, then we must look at the last scene in the same light. In the original *Comedy* nothing contradicts this. The gruesome treatment of Boris's widow and heir, the young Feodor, by the Pretender's supporters is carried out, once more, behind the scene at the end of which the people obediently shout: "Long live Tsar Dimitry Ivanovich!" This makes a striking parallel to scene 3 ("Maiden's Field"), at the end of which the people shout: "We have a tsar! Tsar Boris! Long live Boris!"

As discussed in chapter 1, the "Maiden's Field" scene (omitted from the 1831 text of *Boris Godunov*) was restored in many subsequent editions, although at the end of that reconstructed version of the play the people are still made to "remain silent." As S. G. Bocharov noted:

> The restoration of the "Maiden's Field" scene was based on the argument that its omission from the 1831 edition was due to censorship, if we may judge from Pushkin's letter to Viazemsky of 2 January 1831, regretting the omission of "scenes with the people" (including, for example, "the foul language in French and Russian"); but the censor did not prevent publication of this scene in a posthumous edition of Pushkin's works that appeared ten years later. This scene and the original ending of 1825 have a kinship in that the depiction of the people and their behaviour at the accession of a new tsar is clearly similar in both. The kinship is further shared in the omission of the "Maiden's Field" scene and the amended ending in the 1831 edition. Of course, it would now be impossible to produce *Godunov* without this scene. But it is necessary to be aware that the canonical text of Volume 7 of the Academy Edition contains a contaminated text *which is not Pushkin's*.[41]

The "contamination" found in the canonical text of *Boris Godunov* cannot be correct in principle. By contrast, Pushkin himself was directly involved in the composition of both his 1825 *Comedy* and his 1831 tragedy. Of course, aside from a relatively small number of what would appear to be very minor amendments, there are significant material differences between the text published in 1831 and Pushkin's manuscript of the play completed in 1825. In the original *Comedy:*

1. There is a different title, *Komediia o tsare Borise i o Grishke Otrep'eve.*
2. There is no dedication to Nikolai Karamzin.
3. There are three scenes that were omitted from the 1831 edition: scene 3 ("Maiden's Field. Novodevichy Convent"), scene 6 ("Monastery Wall"), and scene 13 ("Maryna's Dressing Room").
4. Scene 11 ("The Tsar's Palace") is slightly longer, and scene 12 ("Cracow. Wiśniowiecki's House") is significantly longer.
5. In scene 9 ("A Tavern on the Lithuanian Border"), Varlaam begins to sing the song "You walk past my cell, my dear one...."
6. Scene 18 ("Square in front of the Cathedral, Moscow") precedes scene 19 ("A Plain near Novgorod-Seversky").
7. The play ends as follows:

People
Long live Tsar Dimitry Ivanovich!
End of the comedy in which
the leading person is Tsar Boris Godunov.
Glory be to the father, and to the Son, and to the Holy Ghost,
AMEN.

As is well known, when Pushkin, newly released from exile, read his *Comedy* out loud to his Moscow and St Petersburg friends – the literary elite of his time – it was received with a furor of admiration. But, as discussed in chapter 3, Benkendorf was displeased and forbade further public readings, and Nicholas I rendered his famous opinion that "Mr. Pushkin's goal would be achieved" if he were to recast his comedy into a narrative in the style of Walter Scott. For several years, of course, Pushkin refused to alter his beloved *Comedy*. However, in 1830, when Pushkin – on the advice of his friends – applied for permission to publish the play with the idea of improving his financial situation on the eve of his marriage, it was granted "on his own [Pushkin's] responsibility."[42] Pushkin's forthcoming marriage to Natalia Goncharova evidently inspired the government with confidence that from now on he would be well-behaved and wholly loyal.

The tragedy *Boris Godunov* was published at the end of December 1830 with the amendments indicated above. But not all of these revisions had to do with censorship. It should be remembered that Pushkin's *Comedy* had originally been intended to help reform the Russian theater.[43] By 1830, however, it became clear to Pushkin that his play would not be performed on the stage during his lifetime. In publishing it, he therefore did everything possible to accommodate his play to the needs of the reader. That may be the reason why *Boris Godunov* frequently tones down the comic element that has such free rein in the earlier, fully independent *Comedy about Tsar Boris and Grishka Otrepiev.*

In stage performance, *Boris Godunov,* despite a number of magnificent actors' contributions and some interesting directorial ideas, has not met with great success. In fact, only two productions have been truly revelatory: Yury Liubimov's at the Tanganka Theatre in Moscow in the 1980s and Declan Donnellan's Moscow production of 2001. Comment on these productions is not called for here. It is important only to note that each in its own way reconstituted the *comic element* of the play to the fullest – skillfully updating it without weakening the tragic force of Pushkin's historical drama about a guilt-ridden ruler and the sufferings of an – alas – long-suffering people. In this context, it would be very interesting to see how a modern (or postmodern) director might stage Pushkin's original *Comedy* – which, of course, has *never* been performed.

In literature at large, the two intonations of tragedy and comedy, death and survival, have a long history of cohabitation. A fresh look at the original 1825 version of *Boris Godunov* confirms just how creative and cunning their interaction can be. Without doubt, Pushkin's *Comedy* merits greater attention and appreciation than it has so far received. Considering all the problems with the compromised canonical text of the play, Pushkin's *Comedy about Tsar Boris and Grishka Otrepiev* also deserves to be placed in the canon of the great poet's work.

Notes

1. PD, fond 244, opis' 1, No. 835, listy 44–44ob; Pushkin, *Rabochie tetradi,* 4: 44–44ob.
2. Pushkin, *Rabochie tetradi,* 4: 45.
3. Karamzin, *Istoriia* (1892), 11: 5–6.
4. See Likhachev, Panchenko, and Ponyrko, *Smekh v drevnei Rusi.*
5. PS, 11: 178; Wolff, *Pushkin,* 265.

6. Pushkin's imaginary conversation with Alexander I was written sometime between 29 December 1824 and 15 February 1825; see PS, 11: 23–24; Wolff, *Pushkin,* 110–11.

7. *Letters,* 261; Binyon, *Pushkin,* 225.

8. See PD, fond 244, opis' 1, No. 835, list 48; Pushkin, *Rabochie tetradi,* 4: 48.

9. Karamzin, *Istoriia,* 10: note 397.

10. See PS, 2: 69; Blagoi, *Sotsiologiia,* 72–73; Arkhangel'skii, "Poet – Istoriia – Vlast'," 127–28.

11. Golovin, *Russkaia kolybel'naia pesnia,* 313.

12. Karamzin, *Istoriia* (1892), 10: 139–40.

13. Bakhtin, *Estetika,* 339; idem, *Speech Genres,* 135.

14. Likhachev, Panchenko, and Ponyrko, *Smekh,* 3.

15. Ibid., 4.

16. *Letters,* 247; PS, 13: 211; Wolff, *Pushkin,* 158.

17. See, for example, PS, 13: 545.

18. PS, 11: 140; Wolff, *Pushkin,* 245.

19. During his exile in Kishinev, Pushkin paid a visit to the future Decembrist V. V. Davydov's estate at Kamenka and to Kiev, where he met many other liberals. Of this moment in Pushkin's life his first biographer, P. V. Annenkov, wrote: "Before no one so much as the friends left behind in Kamenka did Pushkin so love to dazzle with his liberal views, freedom *from prejudice,* boldness of expression and judgement." (See Pushkin, *Sochineniia Pushkina* [1855–57], 1: 181). But the mockery of Karamzin's *History* began as soon as the first volumes appeared. Pushkin recalled this in some autobiographical notes probably written in Mikhailovskoe in 1825: "At supper some wits translated the first chapters of Titus Livius into the style of Karamzin. The Romans of the Tarquinian period unable to understand *the salutary benefits of autocracy,* Brutus condemning his sons to death *because the founders of republics are seldom renowned for their finer feelings,* all this of course was very funny." (See PS, 12: 306.)

20. Karamzin, *Istoriia* (1892), 11: 75.

21. PS, 11: 141; Wolff, *Pushkin,* 246. In referring to his characterization of Patriarch Iov, Pushkin used the French term "un sot," which may be translated as "fool" but has somewhat different connotations than the Russian terms "iurodivyi" or "durak."

22. See Karamzin, *Istoriia* (1892), 11: 84–85.

23. Geichenko, *U lukomor'ia,* 36.

24. Vatsuro, *A. S. Pushkin,* 1: 414.

25. Vlasova, *Skomorokhi,* 418.

26. Ibid., 343.

27. See BG, 299–301.

28. A kamelaukion is a bonnet-like, miter-shaped headdress, apparently of Byzantine origin. It was sometimes made of precious metal and richly adorned with jewels. Although there is no textual evidence behind this speculation, it is remotely possible that it reminded Pushkin of the iron hat of the holy fool Nikolka.

29. Vinokur, "Kommentarii," 414.

30. Vlasova, *Skomorokhi*, 342.

31. *Letters*, 230.

32. PD, fond 244, opis' 1, No. 73, list 1. This draft title was probably originally intended as a title page for the drama, of which by that point rough drafts had very likely been made of only the first part (i.e., up to the Tavern scene). This supposition is supported by the "List of characters in the first part," written on PD, fond 244, opis' 1, No. 73, list 1ob, which, furthermore, proves that one of the most important scenes of the play, scene 8 ("The Tsar's Palace"), had not yet been written. If it had already been written, the two courtiers whose conversation opens this scene would have been included. It is most likely that this scene was not written until after 13 September 1825, when Pushkin wrote to Viazemsky: "I finished the second part of my tragedy today – I think there will be four altogether. My Marina is a wonderful woman: a real Katerina Orlova! Do you know her? But don't tell anybody about this. Thank you for sending Karamzin's comment on the character of Boris. It has been very useful to me. I had been looking at Boris from a political point of view, not noticing his poetic side. I'll sit him down with the Gospels, I'll make him read the story of Herod and things like that." (See PD, 13: 226–27; *Letters*, 254–55.) If scene 8 had been written by July 1825, Pushkin would not have criticized himself for not noticing Boris's "poetic side." And the exclamation, "And blood-bathed boys appear before the eyes" – not just a single murdered "boy" – would appear to be an indirect reference to "the story of Herod."

33. See BG, 120–21; Bayley, *Pushkin*, 177; Bochkarev, *Russkaia istoricheskaia dramaturgiia*, 463–65; Pomar, "Russian Historical Drama," 239.

34. See Gorodetskii, *Dramaturgiia*, 181; Lobanova, *Mikhailovskaia biblioteka*, 27; Vinokur, *Stat'i*, 93; Rabinovich, "Boris Godunov," 312–13, 316–17.

35. Belkin, *Russkii dramaticheskii teatr*, 13, 15.

36. See Rassadin, *Dramaturg Pushkin*. Rassadin sees Pushkin's play as a consistent combination of three smaller tragedies of different kinds: a drama with comic elements, a tragedy in pure form, and a dramatic chronicle.

37. Fel'dman, *Sud'ba*, 65. On the comic element in Pushkin's drama see also Bochkarev, *Tragediia*, 13–16.

38. This contradiction has been noted before; see Gorodetskii, *Dramaturgiia*, 133; Serman, "Pushkin," 122–26.

39. See Likhachev, Panchenko, and Ponyrko, *Smekh*, 116.

40. PS, 11: 73; Wolff, *Pushkin*, 226.

41. Bocharov, *Siuzhety*, 50.

42. PS, 14: 81–82; Vinokur, "Kommentarii," 413–15, 427.

43. See Vinokur, *Stat'i*, 110–12; and Wolff, *Pushkin*, 249.

5

Tragedy, Comedy, Carnival, and History on Stage

❧ Caryl Emerson

"Tragedy plays on our emotions, it involves us and demands our sympathy for the protagonist; comedy appeals to our intellect, we observe critically and laugh at the victim. Yet comedy may be considered the more serious of the two because it has a greater power to disturb the audience's conventional attitudes, whereas tragedy … purifies …"[1]

"In the usual sense of the word, there is no meaning to comedy. Meaning is what comedy plays *with*."[2]

Between 1825 and 1830, inconsistently but suggestively, Pushkin referred to his *Boris Godunov* as a comedy, a tragedy, and a "Romantic tragedy."[3] The front cover of the 1831 edition did not help to clarify matters: *Boris Godunov, sochinenie* [*composition*]. How significant for Pushkin were these shifts of label? Or for that matter, dramatic genre in general?[4] At the beginning of the *Boris* year, January 1825, Pushkin's lycée friend Ivan Pushchin brought the poet a manuscript copy of Alexander Griboedov's *Gore ot uma* [*Woe from Wit*], a dazzling Russian variant on the French comedy of manners. Pushkin had compliments as well as criticisms on the play, but prefaced both by saying: "One must judge a dramatic writer by the laws which he acknowledges for himself."[5] What laws did Pushkin set for himself in his *Boris,* which he completed later that same year?

These questions resist a straightforward answer. Pushkin did indeed title his play a *komediia,* but today's connotations were not Pushkin's. In the pre-Petrine period, the term "comedy" did not have to designate a comic, lighthearted, or laughing text; it referred to events presented on stage through conversation.[6] By the early nineteenth century, the Russian term *komediia* had come to reflect a narrower European usage, which included the popular Shakespearean festive comedy, the Italian *commedia,* and the French *comédie,* as well as other non-tragic and non-epic staged works. But a Russian playwright still enjoyed considerable leeway along this terminological fault line. Pushkin, who was a master at juxtaposing the received genres of his time and always eager to exploit ambiguity, surely took advantage of all these overlapping meanings.

It is our thesis that Pushkin's gradual shift in nomenclature was palpable and significant. From 1825 to the end of the decade, "comedy" as an appellation gradually falls away; in Pushkin's references to his play, only the label "tragedy" remains. The present chapter steps back to ask how each of these two fundamental dramatic modes is experienced, coded in, juxtaposed to its opposite, and how expectations change when a playwright alters the proportion of one to the other within a single work. Among the most ancient distinctions between the lofty epic/tragic genres and the lowly comic ones is that epic and tragedy must bear responsibility: for founding a city, for realizing justice, for finding out enough about the world to assign cause and blame. It is emblematic of comedy that its characters do not shoulder these burdens. Comic heroes in all genres (Falstaff, Sancho Panza, Master Elbow, the Good Soldier Švejk) have the right to be inept as historical agents, indifferent to destiny, addicted to simple pleasures, cynical toward the workings of justice. In a drama that strives for a responsible representation of historical events, is it possible to combine tragic and comic worlds in a trustworthy way? For Pushkin, the comic had tasks to perform more serious than topical satire, that is, than the humiliation of a pompous public figure or a pretentious ideology. Nor was comic activity mere temporary distraction from a tragic denouement – what is often called "comic relief," a dramatic device handled skillfully by Shakespeare in his myth-based plots (*Hamlet, Macbeth, King Lear, Measure for Measure*) and in the delightfully comic-erotic scenes in his chronicle and history plays. Pushkin understood such relief, as well as the verbal wit essential to it, designing entire scenes in its spirit. But on balance, comic behavior in Pushkin is not especially therapeutic, neither for stage heroes nor for their audience. It becomes an historical agent.

The idea was radical. There were few precedents for "historically significant" comedic episodes on the nineteenth-century stage. A telling illustration can be found in the genesis of the opera *Boris Godunov,* some three decades after Pushkin's death. In July 1870, in between his two versions of *Boris,* Musorgsky played a portion of his newly-composed "scenes with peasants" to a musical gathering at Vladimir Stasov's estate, Pargolovo. It is unclear from Musorgsky's account precisely which scenes were performed, but most likely they included the opening mass chorus in the courtyard of Novodevichy Monastery. The composer's shockingly "Shakespearean" choral dramaturgy was surely in evidence: a stylized mass song or choral lament punctuated by cynical individualized voices in a sort of self-ironizing counterpoint. The effect was comic, but at the same time these peasants were passing irreverent judgment on power-makers in the Muscovite state – as occurs in Pushkin's equivalent scene. Such judgments were a potential historical force. That evening, Musorgsky communicated to Rimsky-Korsakov his bemused concern over the reception of those scenes. "I've been at Pargolovo twice and yesterday I played my *pranks* [*shalosti*] before a large audience," he wrote. "As regards the peasants in *Boris,* some found them to be *bouffe* (!), while others saw tragedy."[7] The exclamation mark is significant. Commoners crowded into a public square could have two meanings: they were either trivially festive (that is, festive without historical consequence) or else emblematic of the fixed fate of a people or a nation, carriers of the dis-tanced wisdom of a Greek tragic chorus. It was impermissible not to be told which convention applied. Musorgsky was well aware that he had given mixed signals, and that only tragedy carried with it the weight of historical respect. In historical drama, or in historical music-drama, a *serious* mixing of tragedy and comedy – for purposes more profound than comic relief or satire – could only create ambiguity about a nation's destiny and the power of its heroes to shape that destiny.

In addition to this genre confusion, there were more practical prob-lems. Throughout the nineteenth century, tragedy and comedy each had its own sphere of concerns, its own linguistic registers and stylistic norms. The internal architecture of the imperial theaters in the Russian Romantic period was not conducive to a flexible combination of these two modes. If ancient tragedy was designed for an arena stage or theater-in-the-round, and neoclassical tragedy – the special target of Pushkin's impatience – for the flat, deep box of the proscenium stage, then *Boris Godunov* was surely conceived in the spirit of the Elizabethan thrust or apron stage, with its several levels jutting exuberantly into audience space, making possible overlapping scenes of action and corners of inti-macy. As we know from Pushkin's disgruntled commentary, he did not consider the neoclassical imperial theaters of 1826 properly equipped to mount a dramatic spectacle such as *Boris.*[8] The popular stage perhaps—

but *Boris* was not vaudeville, operetta, or farce. It was thoughtful comedy, with the rapid pacing, simultaneous exits and entrances, radical refocusings of audience attention, and fluid linkage of scenes that are the trademarks of Pushkin as dramatist. Comedy is not only a genre. It is a terrain, a tempo, a worldview for processing events and responses to events that is intrinsically hostile to pomposity and heroic self-absorption. The comic spirit is generous but not, as a rule, thoughtful; it tends to ridicule any slowness in gesture or articulation. From early adolescence on, Pushkin felt very much at home in this world. For him, comedy cut across genre or period. Whereas he took constant potshots at neoclassical tragedy, he was enthusiastic about neoclassical verse comedy throughout his life, and among his earliest playwriting efforts at the Lycée was a five-act comedy.[9]

In recent times, literary-critical minds of the first order, such as Andrei Siniavsky in his *Strolls with Pushkin,* have made the comedic lightness, swiftness, and decentering of Pushkin's texts illustrative of all the values most precious to the poet: chance, gratitude, generosity, superstition, and a joyous surrender to fate.[10] Indeed, the comedic is so pervasive in Pushkin that it is difficult to isolate a single set of devices that the poet employed. L. I. Vol'pert opens her 1979 essay on Pushkin and eighteenth-century French comedy with this disclaimer: "To elucidate the meaning and place of the comedic genres in Pushkin's creative evolution is an important, as yet unresolved problem in our literary scholarship. Insufficient study of this question can be explained by the situation, at first glance paradoxical, that Pushkin wrote no single finished comedy, but his entire creative output is permeated by a vivid comedic quality."[11]

Pushkin did finish one full-length work in 1825 that he called a comedy. But as we have seen, the critical tradition has been more comfortable working with the later canonical text, analyzing it under an alternative label, a "Romantic [which is to say, *not* neoclassical] tragedy." Pushkin himself defended his play most often in this negative way, in terms of what it was not, stressing the originality and excitement made possible by a violation of the classical unities. For him, true Romanticism always involved an element of surprise, usually achieved by juxtaposing diverse perspectives at unexpected angles. A tragedy subjected to a "Romantic" impulse would make legitimate a looser plot, freer in form (as in Shakespeare's tragedies), more attentive to real dialogue and individualized psychology. For those relatively few critics who have taken the evolution of the play's hybrid genre seriously, tragedy routinely ends up in the defining position. But some have lingered more thoughtfully over the problem. A recent example is J. Douglas Clayton in his 2004 monograph, *Dimitry's Shade: A Reading of Alexander Pushkin's "Boris Godunov."*

Clayton notes that Pushkin's sense of the comedic was shared by three plays that defined the genre during his lifetime: Shakhovskoi's *The Waters of Lipetsk*, Griboedov's *Woe from Wit*, and Gogol's *Inspector General*.[12] In all three (as well as in the later, great comedies by Turgenev and Chekhov), the Western model for comedy is subverted. Love triangles are lopsided and unpredictable, the stage action does not end with marriage for the young couple, old age is not universally ridiculed before new life, and stasis (or a moment of shock) can substitute for consummation. "Russian comedies are very serious, 'dark' comedies, but it is precisely this generic innovation that distinguishes them within the world tradition," Clayton argues (32). He acknowledges "a shift in Pushkin's own perception of the work from when he completed it in Mikhailovskoe to when he finally received permission to print it," seeing in the playwright's increasing reference to his play as tragedy an assimilation to "Shakespeare's tradition" (45). These adjustments included shedding the blatant archaisms, reducing the unwieldy medieval title to the eponymous hero's name (as is the practice in Shakespeare's tragedies and historical dramas), and recasting the play uniformly in unrhymed iambic pentameter – or eliminating those scenes that did not fit that meter (45–46). All the same, many vital scenes in Pushkin's play remain as much Racinian as Shakespearean. Clayton concludes that the canonical *Boris* is on balance tragedic, not comedic, albeit a tragedy subjected to a potent Romantic-Shakespearean corrective.

There is a third and minor genre option for the play that does take the comedic very seriously indeed. It entered twentieth-century Pushkin scholarship in the wake of the world-wide explosion of critical interest in Bakhtin and carnival. One side effect of the carnival boom has been to refocus attention on the initial version of Pushkin's play. Can this new vision compete with the romantic and the tragic in accounting for the richness of Pushkin's *Komediia*?

"Boris Godunov" as Carnival: Pro and Contra

In the preceding chapter, Sergei Fomichev embraces both the enthusiasms and the vulnerabilities of the carnival thesis. The 1825 *Komediia*, he

argues, is set in a "laughing world," the realm of the carnivalesque. For
the carnival critic, the energy that Andrei Siniavsky sensed in Pushkin's
individual persona – his lightness, brightness, speed, the weightless
ethers of poetry against pedantry and self-pity – is manifest in certain
institutions of Russian medieval culture itself. To accomplish his reading, Fomichev relies on the findings of several eminent medieval scholars and folklorists: Dmitry Likhachev and Alexander Panchenko's *"The
World of Laughter" in Old Russia* (1976) and its expanded sequel with
Natalia Ponyrko, *Laughter in Old Russia* (1984).[13] Inspired by Bakhtin's
brilliant readings of sixteenth-century French public-square culture in
the novels of François Rabelais, this distinguished team sought – and
found – equivalently robust, progressive cultural forms in the Russian
late middle ages. Central among these were the irreverent *skomorokh* or
wandering minstrel, banned by the Orthodox Church for levity and
promiscuous music-making; the *yurodivyi* or holy fool, whose public
scandals are analyzed here less as feats of personal humility than as
provocative social spectacle (with bold political overtones); and the
lubok or comic-strip woodcut, so expressive of the common people's
anxiety and resilience in the face of catastrophic social change. The
ambivalent – or black – humor of such formidable pre-Petrine personalities as Ivan the Terrible and Archpriest Avvakum is shrewdly dissected.
The two volumes were a scholarly sensation. Carnival, it seemed, had
come home.

It was soon realized, however, that the Likhachev-Panchenko thesis,
for all its initial Bakhtinian impulse, had little in common with the
utopian mix of Western habitats and Slavic folklore that constitutes
Bakhtin's carnival study of Rabelais. The Rabelaisian "laughing world" is
intensely personalistic. Organic, fearless, affirmative toward the asymmetrical and grotesque body, this world is invested by Bakhtin with
incarnational, even eucharistic virtues. In contrast, the Likhachev-
Panchenko model displays far more structural constraint – and far fewer
opportunities for epiphany or unexpected spiritual gain. (In general,
official late-Soviet-era proponents of a medieval "laughing world"
reflect their materialist upbringing by muffling the religious intonations
of their subject matter, its redemptive and ecstatic sides, which would
have been unacceptable to Pushkin and Bakhtin – not to mention
Rabelais.) The Likhachev-Panchenko thesis is supra-personal in focus
and semiotic in an elegant binary way. It presents the medieval Russian
worldview as strictly dualistic.

"The universe is divided into a world that is real, organized, a world of culture – and a world that is not real, not organized, negative, a world of anti-culture," Likhachev writes in his opening chapter. "In the first world, there is prosperity and an ordered regularity to its sign system; in the second, beggary, famine, drunkenness, and the complete confusion of all meanings" (*Smekh*, 13). Residents of the second world do not have stable positions in it. They cannot, because this second world – called variously an "antiworld," an "outer / infernal world" [*mir kromeshnyi*], and a "world turned inside out" [*iznanochnyi mir*] – is not in itself real; it is only a fabrication, a semiotic inversion. Its most important function is to remind people of its opposite: "the tavern replaces a church, the prison courtyard replaces a monastery; drunkenness replaces ascetic feats. All signs mean something opposite to what they mean in the 'normal' world." The very fact of doubling or mirroring (the idea of an antiworld) is itself sensed as comic.

This bipolar model of the world, which distributes medieval Russian culture neatly (if rather too schematically) between sacred and demonic, is a curious mix of freedom and unfreedom, of optimism and despair. Evil in it is not radical or permanent, but transitory. The laughter of medieval texts is heard as intelligent, liberating, healthy, a carrier of strength. "Laughter was directed not at others," Likhachev insists, repeating a deeply Bakhtinian teaching about carnival, "but at oneself and at the situation being created within the work itself" (*Smekh*, 11). Everywhere emphasized in the 1984 book is the rebellious potential of laughing forms. Likhachev's chapter on "Laughter as Worldview" highlights the "Rebellion [*bunt*] of the outer world," whereas Panchenko's chapter on "Laughter as Spectacle" ends with "Holy Foolishness as social protest."

Since subversion and destabilization are as indispensable to postmodernist rhetoric as they were to reigning communist doctrine, the Likhachev-Panchenko paradigm caught on in a powerful way, both in the East and West. Among Russian classics, Pushkin's *Boris Godunov* proved especially attractive. Panchenko cites appreciatively Pushkin's remark that "drama was born on the popular square" (*Smekh*, 84). Note is made of the play's memorable medieval images: a holy fool, a poet-*skomorokh*, and an ambitious evil monk (the latter two figures occurring only in 1825). All are rebels. Of Nikolka the Iron Cap we read: "In Pushkin, the holy fool insulted by children is the bold and unpunished denouncer of the child-murderer Boris Godunov. If the *narod* in Pushkin's drama is silent, then the holy fool speaks for it – and speaks fearlessly" (*Smekh*, 116). Carnival protest and carnival courage are universal, but every culture embodies this energy in its own way. Thus is Belinsky's socially progressive reading of Pushkin's *narod bezmolvstvuet*, not only as nemesis but as political optimism, echoed 150 years later by Soviet medievalists, as part of the recurring effort to integrate Russian national history into the European fabric.

The Likhachev-Panchenko picture of a laughing, carnival-spirited Russian Middle Ages did not go uncontested. The most powerful resistance came from a source that might at first seem surprising, Yuri Lotman and the cultural semioticians of the Tartu School. Surprising, because much in the Likhachev model must have struck Lotman's group of pioneering theorists as quite correct: the binary nature of Russian traditional culture and the semiotic inflexibility of its worlds. Where the Tartu scholars had reservations was with the nature of medieval laughter and the benevolent, transient "irreality" of the infernal world. In an important review article in *Voprosy literatury* (1977), Lotman and his colleague Boris Uspensky respectfully laid out their objections to the Likhachev team.[14] They were disconcerted by the fact that the corpus of evidence was largely literary, in a culture where written records were scanty and distorted by taboo. They insisted that Bakhtin's glorification of ambivalent, open, participatory laughter in Rabelais – laughter that conquered fear and suspended human judgment by creating a sort of "purgatorial" space between two timeless absolutes – was not translatable into medieval Russian culture, which (as the Likhachev-Panchenko model itself suggested) distributed itself unambiguously between the sacred and the demonic. The public square was as much a place of tortures and executions as of festivities (as several scenes in Pushkin's *Boris Godunov* reflect). On this square, laughter was not perceived as liberating; it was blasphemy, the guffaw of Satan. Thus one could not say that for the medieval Russian subject, to laugh more meant to fear less. Such a confluence of attitudes could have occurred only late in the seventeenth century, under the influence of Western texts and practices. In traditional Muscovite consciousness, the behavior of holy fools was neither magic (a contractual relationship, reliable and comforting), nor was it comic or incipiently democratic; it was strange and specular, meant to strike terror or awe in the audience. In a cautionary footnote, Lotman and Uspensky warn against the faddish, mechanical extension of Bakhtin's ideas "into areas where their very application should be a subject of special investigation" (51).

Literary criticism routinely inherits the backwaters and tidal residue of theories that draw on the professional language of more strictly monitored disciplines. The debate over carnival was no exception. Long after sociologists had grown wary of it and historians had pointed out its inappropriateness to documented experience, the Bakhtinian carnival paradigm, as an interpretive tool for fiction, retained its popularity. Certain fictional texts were especially favored. Since Bakhtin had cited a scene from *Boris Godunov* in the final pages of the Rabelais book, the carnival resonance of those jester-monks, holy fools, and public-square crowds was easy to sustain. Any attempt to account for all the play's components under this rubric, however, confronts serious obstacles.

Exemplary of the difficulty is Sergei Fomichev's essay on Pushkin's "Komediia" from the mid-1990s, included in his *Prazdnik zhizni. Etiudy o Pushkine* (1995), where decades of uncertainty about the proportion of tragic to comic in Pushkin's play eventually came to rest on a noncommittal mean.[15] Freed from the ideological formulas of the communist era, Fomichev makes many astute observations. He notes the unruly abundance of characters and the diversity of literary forms in the 1825 version (its excess of heroes, its disregard for well-rounded dramatic episodes, the predominance of prose in the comic patches and the odd metrical choice for the "Evil Monk" scene). He resists any "heroic" Belinskian reading of the *narod,* citing all those places where the crowd, whether massed on stage or merely cohering in the imagination of its leaders, is shown to be undisciplined, ungrateful, and capricious in its political judgment (96–97). Citing Likhachev on "cultures of laughter," he remarks on the difficulty experienced by stage directors who try to bestow on these crowds anything like an historically leading role; the *narod*'s laughter sooner "returns the world to its original chaotic state" (97). Laughter, Fomichev claims, is the background noise [*smekhovoi fon*] for the entire play. It is healthy in a Bakhtinian sense: modest, decentering, indifferent to power. Although the people mock authority, they are wise enough to want none of it for themselves. "In Pushkin's drama it is the *narod* that embodies in itself this chaos, this Time of Trouble, this instinctive resistance to system," Fomichev writes (98). "In those instances when it is forced to subordinate itself to this system, it turns its laughter on itself." Into this anarchic and cheerfully self-deprecating context, Fomichev fits the two competing political figures, Boris and Dmitry. Tsar Boris is "genuinely tragic, strong, willful, sworn to the highest power but in violation of the moral law ... overcome by torments

of conscience and tragic guilt"; fate subjects him to a "cleansing catharsis" (100–101). Dmitry, on the other hand, serves the comedic principle.
As an emanation or specter from the antiworld, he has no tragic task.
The carnival *narod* – which is also without a task – is intuitively predis-
posed to elect this carnival king, an "historical phantom."

Through this lens, the politics between tsar, people, and pretender
is primarily symbolic. Fomichev values the person of Tsar Boris, but
largely as tragic misfit and antihero. When he touches upon real history
and real historical attitudes in the play, he treats them as potent but transitory metaphors, local color within a larger "comic instrumentation"
(95). In keeping with most prior scholarship on the play, Fomichev cares
less about history than Pushkin did. "'Long live Dimitrii Ivanovich!',"
Fomichev writes (95). "Could Pushkin have treated such a scene seriously? Of course not." Because the purpose of the present volume is to
argue for the integrity of the initial version, as well as for the seriousness
of Pushkin as historian and the accuracy of his vision, such dismissals
must be scrutinized carefully. Are Fomichev's two readings (1995, and
the essay in this volume) too swayed by the carnival mystique? Or, to
pose the question more broadly: perhaps carnival is not the best way to
make sense out of the comedic element in this play?

There are, it seems, at least three areas where carnival readings of *Boris
Godunov* fall short of accounting for the whole. First, a poetics of literary
carnival – inspired by Bakhtin's reading of Rabelais – does not have a
sophisticated, well-elaborated model of language. Communication during carnival, which can indeed be joyous and intense, takes place not as
much through words as through body gestures, most of them related to
the "lower bodily stratum" and involving orifices other than the eyes and
the mouth. What utterances there are tend to be short expletives, always
highly expressive and preferably obscene. This is dialogue, certainly, but
not the complex verbal dialogue that deserves analysis in the work of a
great poet. For this reason, carnival readings of *Boris Godunov* tend to
ground themselves in the larger worldview, in crude energetic move-
ments capped with some verbal device: a mildly shocking epithet, a comic
ditty, a perfectly timed insult. Some critics (following Bakhtin's methodology with Rabelais) ignore altogether the stylistic particulars of the text.
But surely the most overtly comic scenes in *Boris Godunov*, as in Shakespeare's plays, involve a graphic blend of both physical vitality *and* verbal
wit: the three languages speaking past each other in the hilarious
"mercenary" scene with Captains Margeret and Rosen, "A Plain near

Novgorod-Seversky," or, several scenes later, "Sevsk," where a Prisoner and a Pole exchange insults that are partly verbal, partly a threatening fist. Such comic routine, backed up with vigorous physical gesture, is authentic carnival – but linguistically it can exist in the play only as moments, not as the norm. The norm is narrative poetry, at a level both fluid and philosophical. As Grigory Vinokur observed in his classic essay on Pushkin's language, the remarkable accomplishment of *Boris Godunov* as stage drama is that "the poet in Pushkin constantly triumphs over the stylizer"; archaic written sources are transformed into "concrete-lyrical language" made up of utterances that living people, listening to one another, could actually exchange at normal tempo, within a sixteenth-century worldview and yet with the feel of Pushkin's verse-line.[16] Such a deployment of language is fully compatible with comedy. But it is not an essential part of the carnival world; in fact, it can even be an obstacle to it.

A second and related shortcoming of carnival readings is that they cannot deal satisfactorily with guilt. Carnival is not weighed down by the burden of memory, so essential for conscience; the fact that the present tense is sufficient for carnival is a major source of its strength and resilience. But what, then, is to be done with Tsar Boris? There is a respected, well-researched line in *Boris* scholarship which holds that the unfortunate tsar was not responsible for the death of Dmitry of Uglich – and certain contemporaries of Pushkin, most notably the historian Mikhail Pogodin, encouraged the poet to rethink his own "Karamzin-ian" assumptions on this score. If Tsar Boris had not ordered Dmitry's death nor indeed even wished it, he was nevertheless a beneficiary of that tragic event and this fact alone could generate guilt. However one disputes the historical options here, the "stain" on Boris's conscience and the agony it causes him (in both versions of the play) cannot be simply brushed away. Too much that matters flows from it. Those critics who identify the guilt of the tsar as the play's governing principle invariably turn the work into a full-scale tragedy, albeit of a special spiritualized sort. Olga Arans, for example, has read *Boris Godunov* as a "Christian tragedy" in which Pushkin investigates a startlingly new idea, the crime in thought, as an alternative to the classical crime of deed; such a transgression entails radically new modes of verification and punishment.[17] Lidiia Lotman, in a recent article on Biblical subtexts in *Boris Godunov*, suggests that Pushkin, in quest of a "tragedy of a new type," turned to the Old Testament story of King Saul as a parallel for Boris.[18] Saul's fate symbolized the inevitability of punishment – military defeat, loss of children, loss of kingdom – awaiting all who wield power, regardless of penance or good deeds. With King Saul as prototype, the poet could avoid condemning his Boris as a hypocrite (as did Karamzin) and examine his dilemma more compassionately. Such Boris-centered readings, which take seriously the capacity of drama to narrate a story without defaulting to a single moralizing voice, are also not the whole of Pushkin's truth. But they are an inseparable part of it – and the lessons they teach are elevated, not carnivalistically debased.

The previous two caveats prepare us for the most serious problem with carnival as an interpretive tool for Pushkin's drama. Carnival – and even more, "carnival laughter" – cannot be made historical. It too much resembles play, that is, human behavior outside the sphere of necessity and utility, in principle free from consequence. In his essay on "Bakhtin, Laughter, and Christian Culture," Sergei Averintsev intimates that Bakhtin's utopia of laughter can only be poor authority for any historically grounded project. Even if one assumes that the behavior of the medieval *narod* was driven by laughter (and here we have a choice between the open-optimistic Likhachev-Panchenko and the demonic-pessimistic Lotman-Uspensky), Averintsev reminds us that the Bakhtinian model defines laughter as transcendental, "not laughter as an empirical, concrete, palpable given, but as the hypostatized and highly idealized essence of laughter ..."[19] Averintsev speaks as a cultural historian, for whom Bakhtin's formulations about laughing cultures are elevated "to such heights of abstract universality that raising the question of verification becomes, of itself, impossible" (84). The problem to which he refers is one that conscientious Western historians of early modern Russia began to address forcefully in the 1990s. They were dismayed at the tendency of some experts in the social sciences, whose research area was Russia, to take the literary-spiritual mythographers as straight historical fact, defaulting (as one of their members has put it) to *The Brothers Karamazov* for their theology and to structuralism or semiotics for the manageable binary construct.[20]

Carnival, antiworld, and world-turned-inside-out offer a certain elegance of form, as do all binary theories. But *historical* drama as Pushkin understood it was obliged to achieve its symmetry by uncovering more complex mandates. In matters of state interest, Pushkin was a keen believer in historical necessity. In his annotations to the first book of the *Annals* of Tacitus, made for the most part during 1825, Pushkin defends (against the sardonic tone of the historian) the political murder of the young Agrippa Postumus by the Roman Emperor Tiberius – because Tiberius was a skilled statesman and because the Empire benefited for two decades from the deed. Pushkin's mood during the *Boris* year, as he outgrew the moralizing approach to history appropriate to Tacitus or Karamzin, is reflected in these annotations; the poet surely pondered the parallels between that Roman succession crisis in the year 14 and the reign of Boris Godunov (the same duplicitous reluctance to take the crown; eventually even a False Agrippa). Pushkin's "Machiavellian" position here has been variously interpreted by scholars.[21] But however it is read, a carnival view of history along Bakhtin's lines cannot accommodate such a vision of state or political necessity; indeed, carnival is the loophole out of such necessity.

Thus we return, on the far side of the carnival divide, to the larger question of comedy and tragedy. Like most comedies, the 1825 *Boris* is attentive to attractions and stresses between nonheroic persons in the social and domestic domain. But it has the potential and the intent of becoming something more: the representation of a historical period. Its comedic core is not just social, but highly politicized. Given Russia's politics during the 1590s–1610s, in the devastated wake of Ivan the Terrible, no part of its plot could culminate in a return to Nature or "a restoration of the natural order" after the usual fashion of festive comedies – that is, by retreating to gardens and forests. (The one nature-laden garden scene in *Boris,* the Pretender's tryst with Maryna, is a parody of such boy-gets-girl demystifications and culminations.) Nor can it default to those other comedic genre markers: the frivolous, the funny, the private, the low-born, the "happy end." History, and especially national history during a Time of Troubles, is manifestly serious, in the public eye, and full of unhappy ends.

Pushkin did not make light of that national history, nor could he have wished to do so. As Fomichev points out in chapter 4, the earliest plans for a Boris play from November 1824 contained almost no comic elements; the comedic entered the text in stages, as (among much else) a congenial way of handling causality and time. Pushkin desired to present history not as a reconstruction from a later period – the temporal privileging common to neoclassical tragedy and epic – but as a slice of experience sufficient unto itself, acting only on what it knows, free of "hints and allusions" to subsequent events. As he wrote testily in an unsent letter to the editors of *Moskovskii vestnik* several years later, "Thanks to the French, we cannot understand that a dramatist can fully renounce his own line of thought in order to transfer completely into the period he is describing."[22] Against the end-driven plot and the epic perspective, Pushkin sensed something comedic in the very workings of history when it was viewed "close up," in its own time. It is this possibility – the parallel dynamics of comedy and history, when a piece of the past is honestly represented in its own present – that Pushkin explores in his play, not the *escape* from history that comedy (and even more, its subset carnival) traditionally presumes and exploits.

Comedic and Tragic Expectations – and How a History Play Might Cope with Them

Let us review, in broad terms, what tragedy and comedy are conventionally expected to do.[23] The genre of tragedy implies a highborn but flawed hero, who fails in his struggle against some force or process of which he is ignorant (Fate, God, gods, an Absolute), thus instructing us in the limits of human action. There is nobility in this failure – whence the elevated, often formally-rhyming verse – but, for all our outer respect and even awe, we are not encouraged to become intimate with the doomed hero. Tragic theater promises aesthetic distance and discipline. Its struggles unfold within five compact acts, obedient to the unities of time and space. Similar to its kindred ancient high genre, the epic, tragedy is implicated in the fate of cities and nations. Thus if an unruly love plot intervenes, civic duty must triumph over Eros. Ideally, this Eros will be tamed by civic-minded duty. But the girl often dies before the desired taming can take place, because the survival of young girls is a fertile, forward-looking sign, a revival of hope and a failure of punitive discipline. Justice is bloody. For this reason, tragic drama is more comfortable with dead bodies than with potential brides. (Shakespeare's astonishing interweave of stereotypical tragic and comic situations, teetering them on the brink of one another while innocent lives are saved only by accident or at the last minute, is what so confounds us in his "comedy" *Measure for Measure,* and is surely what fascinated Pushkin about that play.)

How does tragedy cope with real history? If the fictional or mythical framework for tragedy accommodates an Oedipus, a Hamlet, a King Lear as the doomed hero who ends up maimed or dead with his constituency in disarray, what can be said of its kindred hybrid genre, *histor-*

ical tragedy? It would respect the same priorities, while working within a skeleton of recognizably real past events. Tragically dressed historical events tend to identify a limited number of heroes at the top, who are willing to assume (rightly or wrongly) political and moral responsibility. Actions take on a predetermined, perhaps even an overdetermined feel. The news might be bad – but for the audience, not especially surprising; we have been guided by omens. Our literacy in tragedy has to do with the surplus of knowledge that comes from knowing how events turned out and being able to read the signs. We, the crowd in the audience, know that Dmitry's entry into Moscow was not a glorious victory over the tyrant Boris but a brief interlude, a prelude to assassination and the Time of Troubles. The crowd on stage cannot know that. But when (as is common in stagings of *Boris Godunov,* both play and opera) such crowds on stage are treated like Greek choruses, or like that odd "Time, the Chorus" appearing halfway through Shakespeare's late romance *The Winter's Tale* as a device to move events along – they assume precisely such prophetic, precautionary authority. The drama then becomes historical tragedy.

What about comedy, the genre named for Comus, a Greek god of fertility? Comic drama restores the order of nature and thus emphasizes survival over punitive justice. It focuses not on the fate of nations but on the antics of the commons, whose chaotic rejuvenation in the face of repression or folly effectively destroys, or at least confuses, the linear unfolding that is natural to plots of retribution. Comedy's short memory – its inability to brood or nurture resentments over long periods of time, and the ready pleasure it takes in the processes of life – is one means for keeping itself open to the unexpected. Limited perspective is one of the secrets of comedic flexibility. For a fundamental wisdom of comedy, part of the modesty of its worldview, is that it is riveted to what is seen and known *now.* Thus in comedy, what seem like accidents of timing can compete successfully with the authority of omens; it is not stoic fortitude but the ability to respond to accidents creatively that becomes the most valued human quality. Retribution is not the only way to set things right. On occasion, evil acts can be diluted to insignificance or actually forgotten (forgiven). In the special sense that accrued to Dante's *Commedia* (called "Divine" after the sixteenth century), comedy came to imply excess and gratitude, that is, grace. However persistent our sins, and however appalling the journey, at the end we receive *more* of the good than we deserve.

Such, then, is one aspect of comedy: it implies a whole that is more than the sum of its available finished parts. When, in 1841, Honoré de Balzac entitled all his work (published novels as well as unrealized projects) *La Comédie Humaine,* he was respecting the devotion to individual detail (over two thousand characters) and the multiplicity of times, ages, and social class that is characteristic of comedic treatment. Comedy is gross: its energy overflows. We sense the comedic spirit in titles that cover a situation or a terrain rather than name a single historical hero ("Comedy About a True Calamity that Befell the State of Muscovy ..." rather than "Boris Godunov"), and yet, once inside the comedy, the scope of what can be glimpsed, heard, and grasped at any one time is often extremely limited. From an epic or tragedic perspective, such a localization of experience is hopelessly naïve. When it is our only source of information, a randomly individual point of view on a potentially world-historical event is sensed as an insult to history, and almost always as comic – like those waves of weeping and pleading that emanate from some distantly off-stage center and sweep progressively over the crowds near Novodevichy Monastery on the day that Boris accepts the crown. Access to the whole of any history would contaminate this sympathetic reaction, burdening it with consequence. In comedy, enthusiasm, dynamism, and survival are favored over a frozen moment laden with fatalistic symbolism. A boisterous cheer (even if deluded) would be more appropriate to the aroused crowd than a *narod bezmolvstvuet.*

If distance and awe are necessary to the effects of tragedy, then unpretentiousness, incongruity, and spontaneous response are keys to comedy. Its natural medium is not pity and terror, but laughter. Here, however, we confront a comedic paradox that must have thrilled the neoclassically inclined Pushkin. Comedy is indeed fertile, fast-paced, abundantly "overflowing" when measured against tragedy. But equally important is comedy's insistence on symmetry and proportionality. However hopeless the muddle in the middle, however often all hell breaks loose, the ending must restore the decorum and order appropriate to the social class or dominant worldview of the dramatic personages on stage. As life is reconciled with its imperfections, the original hierarchies are restored and reaffirmed. It is often remarked that the final moments of the 1825 *Boris Godunov* are intuitively symmetrical in this way. In the opening scenes, members of the nobility conspire darkly while the commoners, herded together and commanded to cheer by Shchelkalov from the Main Porch of Granovitaia Palace, obediently (and cynically) hail the aspirant to the throne, whoever it may be; at the end, this time in a murderous conspiracy, Mosalsky, also from a Kremlin palace porch, commands the crowd to welcome Dmitry Ivanovich with a cheer – which it obediently does. Such symmetrical behavior *is* comedic. But it would be a mistake to play the final cheer as manipulated or forced. At the beginning of the play, fixed precisely in Moscow, February 20, 1598, the people are reacting to what they know at that time and in that place: that the powerful Regent, the boyar Boris, is angling for the throne. He has long been at the helm, and they take his ascension as a given, merely wondering (as Prince Shuisky himself wonders in the bracketing scenes) how to adjust to this fact with the least pain and the maximum profit to themselves. The end is different. What the people now know (and all they know in 1605) is that Tsar Boris has been a tyrant for six years. Everything they have heard about Tsarevich Dmitry, whether triumphantly emerged from hiding or miraculously resurrected, promises a change for the better. Their cheer is not necessarily elicited from under the knout; it is open-ended, hopeful, and (as Pushkin was aware) historically accurate. Seen from within its own present and true to the rules of comedy, Dmitry's return to the throne of Moscow would restore the violated hierarchy and reaffirm the proper order of things. The *narod* was capable of both cynical acquiescence and genuine faith in a returning warrior prince. Those options were the energetic ones that the young Pushkin coded into his *komediia* in 1825, and it was symmetry with a difference, because in fact history does not repeat. Each moment of the present generates its own potential. Only later, at the turn of the decade and into the 1830s, do we find a grimmer verdict on popular energy, in the omitted chapter from Pushkin's novel about Pugachev, "The Captain's Daughter": "May the Lord save us from another such senseless and ruthless Russian rebellion!"[24]

These ruminations on comedic shapes in history suggest the possibility of a second hybrid form. Historical tragedy is familiar; but can there be *historical comedy*? If so, what might it look and sound like? It is no accident that Herbert Lindenberger's well-known study of historical drama, which sets out to explore the "characteristic shapes" that describe "relationships between drama and reality," divides its material into conspiracy, tyrant, and martyr plays: three manifestly somber, tragic categories.[25] Tragedy fits history more comfortably. To test the comedic-history hypothesis, one would have to take a piece of tragic history (say, Karamzin's account of the Fall of Boris) and recast it so as to reduce the distance, demote the language, focus on the present moment, refrain from prophetic authorial asides, allow intimate access to the loftiest heroes not only in their eloquent moments but also in their morbidly embarrassed ones, strive to make conspirators, tyrants, and martyrs look a bit ridiculous, and make the audience laugh. Most importantly, the playwright must make it seem as if chance events really mattered, perhaps even made all the difference. Making history comic is exciting – but there are immediate practical difficulties with it. In politically controlled cultures that care about art (and nineteenth-century Russia was one such culture), a canonized historical plot treated comedically could quickly become disrespectful, even subversive. The lightness and "presentness" of comedy can threaten teleological explanations in general, by questioning whether today's suffering and sacrifice can in fact be justified in the name of some future glory "waiting in the wings." Unlike tragedy, comedy does not trust wings. The future does not yet exist, no destined events yet fill it, and thus glory (or any other fate) cannot passively *wait*. Instead, comedy puts its trust in happy coincidence and in the boundless inventiveness and resilience of human beings flourishing in the now.

The strongest argument for historical comedy is probably Pushkin's belief in the potency of chance. His conviction that "chance is a tool of providence" sits squarely at the center of his paradoxical theory of history. A faith in the fortuitousness of events can coexist easily with all types of disaster and failure, as well as with the buoyancy that marks Pushkin's historical fiction, but it cannot be squared with the workings of neoclassical tragedy, or with most historical tragedy as it was practiced in Pushkin's era. That a momentous sequence of events "might have been otherwise" – Pushkin's favorite thought experiment – is not a truth that the winning side likes to hear. Chance and laughter are supposed to govern only lesser fates. For good reason, comedy on stage (vaudeville and "bouffe") was conventionally associated with the follies of nonhistorical private life, with the weaknesses that *unite* us. In contrast, tragedy depends for its sublime communicative moment on the ideologies that divide us, that elevate a cause and make it worth dying for. Or worthwhile slaying others.

Tragedies and Comedies of History

For all the risks involved, there is much to suggest that Pushkin wrote *Boris Godunov* in the spirit of historical comedy. The received image of the Time of Troubles, vivid in everyone's mind from Karamzin's volumes 10 and 11, was that of a tragic period, full of enemies and martyrs, prefigured to collapse ruinously so that the Romanov dynasty might rise gloriously from the ashes. Into this self-congratulatory, humorless narrative Pushkin inserted burlesque, parody, indecent wit, melancholic brooding at the wrong times (Boris's embittered monologues), and lighthearted reconciliation also at the wrong times. One example of the latter is the most perfect of the play's several historically grounded, comedically realized battle scenes, "Forest." The Pretender, soundly defeated, mourns only the loss of his horse – and his companion Gavrila Pushkin marvels at the way this youthful commander can fall asleep: "carefree as a child. / Providence watches over him, of course; / Well then, my friends, we'll not be downcast either." Such is an authentic comic response to defeat.

But Pushkin also provides, from the opening lines of the play on out, authentic proactive comic motivation: gossip, slander, rumor, cynical realism. As remarked earlier, these episodes occur not merely as comic relief from the "real" tragic plot but as an agent *in* that plot, as an instigator of genuine historical change. Such are the stock-in-trade but crucial figures of Varlaam and Misail, the comically-doubled buffoons of the Tavern Scene, as well as the melodramatic-gothic "Evil Monk" by the Monastery Wall. Whether such figures really existed as accomplices of the historical Pretender is of secondary importance. As we have seen, about the major lineaments of that biography Pushkin knew more than most, then and now. What matters is that the poet *writes comedy in,* seriously, coterminous with the tragic plot and at times even overwhelming it. Pushkin seems to have grasped that just because history is going nowhere is no reason to disbelieve the accidents, hilarities, and temptations of the present. On the contrary, the enthusiasms of the present (especially if short-lived and deceptive) are all the more compelling when they are deprived, as the present almost always is, of adequate context and perspective.

From memoirs and director's notes of that fateful year 1936, it would appear that the great theater director Vsevolod Meyerhold had attempted to stage his Jubilee *Boris Godunov* as historical comedy in precisely this sense.[26] The project was a revival of his attempted 1925–26 production with the Vakhtangov Theater, but now with incidental music commissioned from Sergei Prokofiev.[27] Throughout that summer and fall, Meyerhold rehearsed Pushkin's play. He was concerned at all points

to "return Pushkin to Pushkin" – that is, to recreate that sense of immediacy, intimacy, and risk that had been lost through the poet's canonization and the monumentalization of Musorgsky's opera. His company
worked most thoroughly on scene 5, in Pimen's cell, and on scene 8, in
the Tsar's chambers where Boris delivers his famous monologue. Apparently, Meyerhold, with Prokofiev's musical support, planned to include
at least one of the scenes written in 1825 and excluded in 1831: scene 6,
"Monastery Wall: Grigory and an evil monk."[28]

The Boris set was stripped down to its essentials, so that the actors
could move. Meyerhold's assistant at the Vakhtangov Theater, Boris
Zakhava, recalls the director protesting against the conventional stiff
portrayal of Pushkin's tsars and boyars, as if their furs and caftans had
"grown to their bodies; there seemed no way to undress them or to imagine them naked. 'We should be able to spy on Boris when he is taking a
bath!' Meyerhold exclaimed ..."[29] This desire to see heroes naked and
engaged in everyday bodily maintenance is, of course, a fundamental
mark of comedy. But Meyerhold went further. The play's most solemn
and self-pitying speeches were not allowed any space to flourish. A defining moment in the whole fabulous Meyerhold concept was the delivery
of Boris's famous monologue in scene 7, "I have attained the highest
power." His production team tracked down authentic lamentations and
wailings for the swarm of sorcerers, soothsayers, dwarfs, and hunch-
backs prancing around the stage as Boris readied himself for his famous
lines. "I was convinced that Meyerhold would find some way to get this
entire group offstage, and only then would Boris's speech begin,"
Zakhava recalls. "How great then was my surprise when in the very heat
of this bacchanal of sorcerers Meyerhold suddenly called out to
Shchukin: 'The speech! Start the speech!' Shchukin began, but of course
it was impossible to make out anything in all that confusion. No matter
how hard Shchukin tried to outshout the sorcerers, one could make out
only a couple of individual sentences of the entire text. But to our common surprise Meyerhold was apparently very satisfied" (98–99). Here
too, the device is pure comedy applied to the conceit of heroic Romantic
self-fashioning: dilute the hero, obstruct his lines with clatter, don't allow
his catalogue of complaints to be heard above the din of the present,
move the spotlight away. "Never mind, it will be all right," Zakhava
recalls Meyerhold saying, to the dismay of the actors' collective. "It's one
of Pushkin's unsuccessful speeches ..." (99).

Deflating the play's title role was only the beginning, however. Meyerhold also insisted on all the exquisite *timing* of comedy routine, especially in scenes involving the Pretender. He saw Grigory as something of a hooligan, in the positive sense: alert reflexes, good muscle tone, able to seize the moment like a healthy animal. One of the most patiently rehearsed episodes was Grigory's leap through the window in the Tavern Scene. This sequence of several seconds was choreographed as a single movement, well-known to slapstick: the Hostess pulls the tables toward her and clears the way, Grigory jumps through and out, the tables are pushed back, the guards crash into them and into each other (97). Even more remarkable was Meyerhold's Pimen. From the memoirs of Mikhail Sadovsky we learn that the Cell Scene was set not in some dim, low-vaulted dungeon ("such cells never existed anywhere but in the theater," Meyerhold remarked [100]); these monastery quarters were cozy, clean, bright, white-and-yellow, the well-equipped retreat of an experienced writer. Pimen was bustling about, full of energy and stories. "He has three dominant traits," Meyerhold observed, "intelligence, humor, and childishness. He has always written, he is writing at the moment, and he still has a great deal to write.... It isn't true that this is his 'final story'; he will always find something more to write about" (101). Here too, forward-looking comedy – whose dominant trait is a pleasure in the activities of the present – vanquishes backward-looking tragedy.

Meyerhold worked with the canonical 1831 text and everywhere referred to Pushkin's play as a tragedy. Although he blamed the censor for forcing Pushkin to replace the cheer to Dmitry with the more cautious *narod bezmolvstvuet,* he is on record saying, conventionally, that the change improved the play because it strengthened the people's role within it.[30] But the ending and the appellation notwithstanding (both were mandatory for Stalin-era Pushkin), Meyerhold's production, had it been allowed to ripen and open to the public, would have been a brilliant reading of Pushkin as author of historical comedy. Meyerhold sensed in the poet an absolutely original dramatic mind. And to get at that mind, his motto, apparently, was *Pushkin bez posrednikov* [Pushkin without intermediaries]. "We must play Pushkin, not Kliuchevsky," he constantly cautioned his actors and staff.[31] Meyerhold revered Pushkin not only as a great playwright but as a great (if untested) stage director. "In the text itself there is everything that the actor needs to know about the epoch." This attempt to realize Pushkin's genius for the stage was aborted because of Stalinist politics, not aesthetics. Meyerhold's *Boris Godunov* never opened to the public. Meyerhold's Theater was closed down a year later; its director was arrested and in February 1940, put to death.

It is still worth asking, however, whether Meyerhold's bold concept, which aimed to revivify a sluggish performance tradition and deautomatize reactions to the play, fully captures Pushkin's intent. It would seem that large parts of it do. What Pushkin hadn't liked in many staged plays of his time was exactly what Meyerhold didn't like about earlier productions of *Boris,* such as the Moscow Art Theater's production under Nemirovich-Danchenko: boring, predictable, heavy, the lines not spoken but recited in an ecstatic drone ("as soon as they get up on stage the words go all greasy, oily ... terribly greasy words," Meyerhold remarked of the actors' bad elocution habits).[32] Shakespeare's histories were riveting and real, Meyerhold believed, because the dialogue heard up front was not the sole focus of attention, "his background is continually in an uproar ..." And such was also appropriate for Russia's Time of Troubles. "What kind of play is *Boris Godunov?* the struggle of passions against the background of a stormy sea ..." (108–9).

But Meyerhold, too, shared the biases of his militantly secular time. He resisted (at least publicly) any hint that the religious dimension of the play mattered to Pushkin – whether in Pimen, in the Patriarch, or in Boris. For him, the play was fueled solely by a Machiavellian struggle for power. And Pushkin's astonishing capacity to sound like everyone's contemporary (and to make all who experience him feel more alive and intelligent for being within reach of his words) was understood by the great director quite conventionally, as a choice between poetry and history – in which one set of truths had to lose: "Since he was a thoroughly contemporary individual and interested not in history, but in somehow smuggling through history his own part in it, that is, to put in what led to the Decembrist uprising, we must read differently a few of the things he has included ..." (108).

Here, it seems, is the nub of the problem. Meyerhold resolved it in a strong way, as have several directors since, combining a bold, fast-paced comedic concept with various degrees of transparency to later politics and events. But there are drawbacks to such a solution. A comedy of history will do what comedic drama does best: make relationships modifiable in the present by relying on coincidence and chance. But what happens then to memory and conscience? To the pastness of the historical event and its autonomy in its own time? And to the fact (lying at the core of all tragedy) that the awful event has happened, is now over, and its consequences must be lived with and paid for? Pushkin was well aware of the challenge in combining history and drama on stage – a different order of challenge than his exercise in combining history and fictional prose (*The Captain's Daughter*), or history and verse (*Poltava*). In those latter hybrid genres, reception is more private, representation is less embodied. In contrast, drama is public performance. It was diminished, Pushkin felt, when the playwright performs like a lyric poet, distributing universalized bits of himself (however fascinating) to his characters; this was his problem with Byron's plays.[33] "What is necessary to a dramatist?" he asked in a jotting of 1830. "A philosophy, impartiality, the political acumen of an historian, insight, a lively imagination. No prejudices or preconceived ideas. *Freedom.*"[34]

What, then, was necessary to the historian? In her thoughtful study of Pushkin as historian, Svetlana Evdokimova suggests that for the poet-playwright, history and poetry are a complementarity. Each has its own "multiple perspectives and autonomous truths" that are not subject to any easy synthesis of oppositions.[35] "Pushkin does not privilege one kind of writing over the other. Neither poet nor historian, according to Pushkin, can portray the way things really happened.... The reconstruction of the whole truth requires the omniscience that neither the artist nor the historian can achieve" (27–28). What makes this statement ring true is its grasp of what we might call Pushkin's epistemological modesty, his willingness to discriminate between what can and cannot be known. Just because some future point of view, arbitrarily selected and conveniently frozen in place, happens to know how one open-ended moment of the past was eventually resolved, is no special mark of wisdom. The honest playwright must renounce all such privilege for his own arbitrarily-selected time of writing as well. But by the same token, Pushkin tolerated no collapse into historical nihilism. Although art on historical themes must not contradict known facts, it is still obliged to coordinate those themes and reflect them in an ordered way, if not in a mirror then in that beloved image from the final stanzas of *Evgenii Onegin*, a magic crystal or kaleidoscope. Historical events are like random fallings of chips during the turn of a kaleidoscopic wheel. Viewed through the funnel of art, these fallen chips are refracted and juxtaposed as patterned domains. The historical poet is this crystalline lens; he cannot intervene, but he must discern the pattern. Pushkin felt keenly the obligation of poets to embed the known within the unknown in a humble manner, so that the boundaries of each are respected. It was the lack of such humility that caused him to chafe against the excessive skepticism of Voltaire, and that prompted his surprisingly harsh criticism of the unfortunate Alexander Radishchev.[36]

In the 1820s, Pushkin did not often discuss his play in terms of dramatic genre, remaining instead within the boundaries of the then-current debate over Classical versus Romantic. He did, however, put a related question into the mouth of his friend Nikolai Raevsky in July 1825 (in a letter drafted but never sent): "Vous me demanderez: votre tragédie est-elle une tragédie de caractère ou de coutume? [a tragedy of character or "customs," the latter term designating fidelity to the particulars of a historical era]. J'ai choisi le genre le plus aisé, mais j'ai tâché de les unir tous deux."[37] It is not immediately obvious which genre was "easier," but the key here is that Pushkin was attempting to combine the two, to create a type of historical drama that had the immediacy of the present as well as the wisdom of the past. It would be a genre as yet unseen on the Russian (or French) stage. There wasn't a word for it. This new art form would have a powerful moral and educative effect, as befitted the public genre of drama. In that same letter drafted to Raevsky, Pushkin paid himself the rare self-compliment: "Je sens que mon âme s'est tout-à-fait développée, je puis créer."

Pushkin had ripened as a creator, but his audience had not. Much of what we know from Pushkin about his own genre experiments was elicited by his disappointment in others' response to them. Most likely the poet would have considered historical tragedy – assuming that it aimed to be true to history at all – a poor vehicle for portraying historical knowledge in an acceptably "modest" way. But a comedy of history would also not be sufficient to his purpose. As we have seen, Pushkin raised, through his historical personages and sets, concrete particulars and "autonomous truths" that he meant to be taken seriously in their own time: in the details and placements of the battle scenes; in Afanasy Pushkin drinking mead at Shuisky's house and talking dangerously about serfdom; in Tsar Boris speaking privately with Basmanov about abolishing *mestnichestvo*.[38] Pimen, too, was "not my invention," Pushkin noted in that same open letter from 1828. "In him I drew together those characteristics in our ancient chronicles which captivated me: the innocence of soul, the disarming humility, the almost child-like quality which is at the same time combined with wisdom, the pious devotion to the divine Right of the Tsar" (222). This image of Pimen is far from the sly, energetic, fidgety professional writer of Meyerhold's "de-pietized" production. That Pimen had been crafted of the same material as the exasperated Patriarch, the sassy crowd, the battlefield cacophony of mercenaries and Russian troops. But not every scene in *Boris Godunov* can be speeded up to the same degree of comic briskness and repartee. Some moments are clearly designed to be riveting, lofty, and tragedic: Pimen's reminiscences, the Patriarch's lengthy recitation of the miracle at Uglich to the Tsar's Council, the dying Boris's farewell to his son. Pushkin would doubtless have been mesmerized by Meyerhold's production. But one suspects a thoroughly comic presentation would have struck him as unbalanced. The balanced truth requires a juxtaposition of different modes. More likely, Pushkin's goal was neither historical tragedy nor historical comedy, but some intermediate construct, something approaching a tragicomedy of history.

Tragicomedy and the Real

The term "tragicomedy" or "tragedo-comedy" was known in Pushkin's era. "Mungrell Tragy-comedie" had been deplored in England as early as the 1580s, and Shakespeare was often accused of writing in this motley form, especially his later plays. Formal treatises on the genre were familiar in Italy from at least the early seventeenth century and in Russia from the early eighteenth.[39] Its identifying marks include the interspersing of comic scenes throughout what is otherwise a tragedy, a display of elevated protagonists in domestic or private settings, and an ending designed to evoke a muted audience response: not punitive toward individuals, not cathartic via pity and terror, but also not set up for the happy marriage. Rather than resolve in either direction, the end is compassionately suspended, sympathetic to the ambivalent, often compromised situation in which all parties find themselves. (Giovanni Guarini, the most important Renaissance apologist for tragicomedy, stressed the social advantages of such a moderate ending; by avoiding extremes, it educated the spectators away from either "excessive tragic melancholy or comic relaxation."[40]) In such endings – neither closed through the attainment of full knowledge, nor happy through romantic consummation or military victory – we would seem to approach the effect of Pushkin's original cheer on behalf of the Pretender Dmitry.

Pushkin's library contains no theoretical works on this mixed genre.

But the fondness Pushkin repeatedly expressed for Pierre Corneille, and especially for his innovative tragedy *Le Cid* (1636, initially called a tragicomedy), suggests that he admired precisely the French playwright's attempt to create a genuine "third type" of drama, one bold enough to abandon the straightjacket of neoclassical tragedy, leave uncertain the fate of the lovers, and yet not sacrifice highborn heroes, nobility, or lofty tone.[41] Tragicomedy (like Pushkin's own transitional label, "Romantic tragedy") encourages its audience to think in terms of the resilience of parts over the finality of ends, even when those parts are arranged in an orderly or symmetrical way. Like comedy proper, tragicomedy strives to restore balance to the represented world, but – and here we speak to the core of Pushkin as an historian – it holds open the possibility that there are other routes to balance than strong, definitive closure, whether of grief or of joy. Thus tragicomedy has a perpetually "modern" feel, something we sense acutely when Pushkin's treatment of history is measured against the later, and more conservative, playwrights in Russia's Age of Kukolnik.

"In its modern context it signals the final breakdown of the classical separation of high and low styles," writes John Orr in his *Tragicomedy and Contemporary Culture*. It is "a drama which is short, frail, explosive and bewildering. It balances comic repetition against tragic downfall," often calling into question "the conventions of the theatre itself."[42] Beckett, Pinter, Genet, and Shepard all share with Pushkin this eclectic spirit of the tragicomedic genres, and all those modern playwrights have exercised influence on twentieth-century productions of *Boris Godunov*. But tragicomedy alone is not enough. We now arrive at our final genre refinement. A tragicomedy *of history* would seem to face further challenges, especially when the playwright is concerned about how to register historical experience in an accurate, responsible way.

This subgenre, a tragicomedy of history, has received compelling treatment in recent decades by such accomplished critics as Paul Hernadi.[43] He observes that dramatizations of history in the tragicomedic mode are especially abundant in the immediate aftermath of times of trouble (the post-World War One and Two worlds). But his discussion, like John Orr's cited above, opens on a type of nay-saying that would sooner usurp than supplement the tasks of the historian. "In part no doubt as a backlash against nineteenth- and twentieth-century efforts to turn historiography into an objective and predictive or even quantifiable science," Hernadi writes, "some of the best historical plays of the last decades *conspicuously fictionalize history*" (10). Hernadi sets us up well to appreciate the complexities of Pushkin's genre-mixing experiment. Pushkin's 1825 play was as eclectic and radical for its time as any postcatastrophe modernist experiment. But it was written in an era, the 1820s, where the backlash and disillusionment were of quite a different sort. In Western Europe as well as in the Russian empire, historical writing had only recently parted company with the belletristic. Karamzin himself began as a poet who, in his twilight years, trained in the archives in order to turn the stories of the Russian past into a patriotically edifying bestseller.[44] The historiographical "efforts" toward scientificity that concern Hernadi had not yet taken place. There were no schools preaching historical truth as objective or quantifiable. But history as *prediction*, an idea anchored in the figural Christian tradition, was, during Pushkin's time, practiced in several genres. Pushkin's immediate source, Karamzin's Sentimentalist narrative, partook of such a tone at its loftiest moments, seeing in the Fall of Boris an "apostrophe to the future."

Pushkin was dissatisfied with the models of both historical writing and dramatic writing available to him in the 1820s. To combine the two in something like a tragicomedy of history would require not only a balance between repetition and linear collapse, and not only a mixing of high and low styles, but above all, discipline about the workings of time. How might a poet who wished *not* to "conspicuously fictionalize history" achieve a balance between the claims of patterning and the openness of chance? The poet in Pushkin saw patterns everywhere, and relished working within the strictest formal economy. But as an historian, he was suspicious of any patterning that might serve to close time down. For time works differently in the past and future. A past event can always be understood after the fact as a combination of realized plans and unexpected accident. But whatever pattern eventually emerges from this mix of calculation and chance must not be imposed upon the future, which remains open to shocks wholly unforeseen. This is the meaning (or one of the meanings) of Pushkin's famous remark in 1830 à propos of the French historian Guizot that "the human mind is not a prophet, but a conjecturer ... it cannot foresee chance – that powerful and instantaneous instrument of Providence."

As Evdokimova glosses these lines, Pushkin's problem with French Romanticist historiography was its obsession with system, and precisely systems presuming to predict (53–54). In her reading of Pushkin's view, such systems-thinking might work with European history, which was (or liked to believe it was) rational and progressive. But not with Russian history. Russia, explains Evdokimova, "demonstrated anything but progressive development." Because of the wide scope allowed its tyrants, its high degree of political centralization, and the rigid but still erratic and arbitrary nature of its governance, the principle of chance was far more potent in Russia and chance events more lethal. Like a belief in gambling, a belief in chance had acute behavioral consequences. Lengthy preparation and sensible planning seem superfluous; attention is forced on the absolute present. What sort of historical causality could be traced in societies such as this? "Pushkin," Evdokimova writes, "was incessantly preoccupied with the role chance plays in history and the way it should be incorporated in accounts of the past" (55).

If we follow Evdokimova's reading of Pushkin's intent, to expect laws or regularities to function in a state such as Russia was to fictionalize its history. Again, balances or patterns might emerge *after* the fact; with his keen poet's eye, Pushkin glimpsed them amidst the most awful chaos, in the Time of Troubles and later in Pugachev's Rebellion. But conventionally, such an impulse toward historical patterning, put to work in art, served tragedy.

In his fragment "On Tragedy," written while at work over his *komediia*, Pushkin remarked on the lack of verisimilitude in all dramatic genres, and in tragedy especially. He lamented the artificial impediment imposed by the classical unities and insisted that such strict constraints on time, space, and character could not gratify a serious audience; "Interest," he remarked archly, "is also a unity." And in the final line he noted enigmatically: "*smeshenie rodov kom. trag. – napriazhenie* [a mixing of the genres of comic and tragic – a tension]."[45] The plan, it would appear, was to provide his Romantic tragedy with the necessary tension (plot and character interest) by an admixture of the comic. Before turning in the following chapter to possible sources for this mixed vision of drama, it might be useful to review what could be called the "tragicomedic" competencies, and specifically those with the potential to free up Pushkin to be a *better* historian.

As a first move, tragicomedy vastly increases the repertory and subtlety of audience response. In place of the old dichotomy – stage heroes who, as Paul Hernadi puts it, are either "tragically hardened and consummated" or "comically softened and preserved" (46) – a whole spectrum becomes available that approaches the complexity of reactions we encounter in real life. "Besides laughing (comedy) and weeping (tragedy) and besides gaze (romance) and frown (satire)," Hernadi writes, "I see tragicomedy as capable of also integrating various combinations and degrees of cheer (festivity), sob (melodrama), jeer (farce), and throb (mystery)" (46). All those emotions are evoked in *Boris Godunov*, and especially acutely in its 1825 original. What is more, when fate and prediction are downplayed, the more unsentimental, Machiavellian aspects of Muscovite politics can be revealed in all their wit, eloquence, and savagery – that vein of Ivan the Terrible, which was so well developed in the latter years of the reign of Tsar Boris. "Neither legitimacy nor sin is accorded much importance by Machiavelli," Monika Greenleaf notes in her discussion of this dimension of *Boris Godunov*. "Pushkin's insights into the workings of realpolitik and political imposture in his own time suggested a demystified, and at the same time appropriately Renaissance, outlook on the strange careers of three of Russia's sixteenth-century tsars."[46]

Finally there is the question of love. In a tragedy, love is usually half the problem (the other half being politics or war); in most historical tragedy, there is a romantic subplot requiring the young lovers at some point to chose between Eros and Duty. Prompted perhaps by Voltaire, Pushkin was intrigued by the possibility of getting rid of this subplot altogether.[47] "A tragedy without love appealed to my imagination," he wrote to Nicholas Raevsky in 1829, preparing to send him a copy of the play.[48] To deprive a tragedy of its viable romantic subplot was a bold idea. But almost more outrageous for the time would be a *comedy* without love, which Pushkin, in 1825, strove to produce. In the *Komediia*, the scene "Maryna's Dressing Room" – struck out in 1830 – contained historically true information about the Pretender as well as a comic routine between mistress and maid recalling the sassy *soubrette* of French neoclassical comedy. There was, however, this all-telling difference: Rózia the maid (along with other flirtatious and savvy Poles) is trying to inject a little romance into the situation, while Maryna, purportedly the romantic lead, steadfastly repudiates it. Maryna Mniszech is composed entirely of politics and military glory. Pushkin was fascinated by her ambitious historical persona and wished to return to her in later compositions. For in her violation of erotic-dramatic expectations – canonical as regards the female side – he might well have seen the core of a new type of plot. Tragedies have romantic subplots; comedies are resolved by romantic union. Pushkin combines the two genres and permits true love to dissipate.

An enormous semantic space is opened up by this excision of love. A tragicomedy without love? What's left to talk about? Surely Pushkin would say (again echoing Voltaire), everything important to history: politics, conscience, loyalty, paternal responsibility, good governance, the suffering of the people, serfdom, civil war. These topics could be raised with less bombast and more seriousness in the open-ended comedic forms, which Pushkin was always careful not to reduce to parody. In his 1830 survey of Russian drama (in connection with Pogodin's historical play *Marfa Posadnitsa*) he remarked: "Let us note that high comedy [*vysokaia komediia*] is not based solely on laughter, but on development of character, and that it often approaches tragedy."[49]

We might assume, then, that in composing *Boris Godunov*, Pushkin was driven by the same delight in genre-mixing and code-switching that had been a trademark of his work since *Ruslan and Liudmila*. Part of the respect (often misplaced) that Pushkin bore toward his readers was the assumption that they would recognize the forms he started with, appreciate the work he had put in to alter those forms, and tolerate being in a state of "genre insecurity" – creative tension – for the duration of the work. Such tension, he must have hoped, could only heighten their interest and aesthetic pleasure. Was *Evgenii Onegin* a verse narrative or a novel? "The Queen of Spades" a supernatural gothic tale or a realistic spoof of one? The "Little Tragedies" really tragedies – or just lopped-off fifth acts? "Poltava" a history or a romance? "The Bronze Horseman" an ode to Peter the Great or a prosaic lament for the martyred little man? *Boris Godunov* a historical tragedy, a historical comedy, or a tragicomedy of history? In the case of this last masterpiece, experiencing the play correctly meant experiencing history correctly. Much was at stake for both these new aspects of Pushkin's professional development, now that the poet believed he had fully matured as a writer, and could create.

Notes

1. David L. Hirst, *Tragicomedy*, xi.

2. Robert I. Williams, *Comic Practice/Comic Response*, 55.

3. In an oft-cited letter to Viazemsky from mid-July 1825, Pushkin gleefully announced his "romantic tragedy," for which he would be "covered with kisses." The labels tragedy and comedy were already overlapping.

4. Pushkin tended to apply genre labels to a work according to his own perception of its form and content, not necessarily following the conventions established by its author or by critical tradition. In his 1833 drafts for *Andzhelo*, for example, he

referred to his source text, Shakespeare's comedy *Measure for Measure*, as a tragedy. See PS, 5: 435.

5. Pushkin to Alexander Bestuzhev, end of January 1825; see *Letters*, 200. As a point of comparison, it is worth noting that *Gore ot uma* was treated much more leniently in the pre-Decembrist climate of 1824 than was Pushkin's *Boris* two years later. Griboedov, a man with no independent wealth who served in the office of foreign affairs, returned to Perersburg in June 1824 on sick leave from diplomatic service in Tehran and Tiflis, in order to marshal his newly-composed drama through the censorship. As approval proceedings stretched out for months and then for a year, he gave dozens of unauthorized readings; finally the author permitted written copies to be made of his play. His friends organized a group of scribes – and by 1830, according to one estimate, there were 40,000 manuscript copies of the play in circulation throughout the empire. Thus *Woe from Wit* had successfully defied the censorship, on a scale unparalleled until the Soviet period, but at the cost of becoming public property and – of course – depriving its needy author of royalties and formal recognition. For this story, see Kelly, *Diplomacy and Murder in Tehran*, ch. 13, esp. 98–100.

6. See Fomichev's discussion of this point in chapter 4 of the present volume. For the classic study in English, see Simon Karlinsky, *Russian Drama from Its Beginnings to the Age of Pushkin*, 52. Until the end of the seventeenth century, Karlinsky writes, three words for designating stage plays were in general circulation (from Polish, German, Latin, and Italian roots): *deistvo* or *deistvie; akt;* and *komediia.*

7. Musorgsky to Nikolai Rimsky-Korsakov, 23 July 1870; see Leyda and Bertensonn, *The Musorgsky Reader,* 148.

8. See his draft article on *Boris Godunov* written in 1828 (intended for, but not sent to, the editor of *Moskovskii vestnik*): "Firmly believing that the obsolete forms of our theatre demand reform, I ordered my Tragedy according to the system of our Father Shakespeare ..." Pushkin then provocatively lists his departures from stale neoclassical unities and formulas. In Wolff, *Pushkin,* 220–23, esp. 221.

9. A. D. Illichevskii to P. N. Fuss, 16 January 1816: "Pushkin is now writing a comedy in 5 acts, under the title 'The Philosopher.' The plan is rather successful and the beginning, that is, the first act which so far is all that is written, promises something good; as regards the verses – what's there to say – and such an abundance of witty words! God only grant him patience and perseverance, which are rare qualities in young writers ..." Cited in Veresaev, *Pushkin v zhizni,* 1: 81.

10. "The calculating man in Pushkin's works is a despot, a rebel, Aleko. The usurper Boris Godunov. The petty thief Hermann. The calculating man, having calculated everything, stumbles and falls, never understanding why, because he is always dissatisfied (grumbles at fate). Pushkin relates in dozens of variations how opponents of fate are brought to their knees... There is something providential in Pushkin's consonances: his discourse, which has scattered in different directions without a backward glance, suddenly notices in amazement that it is surrounded, locked up by an agreement between fate and freedom." Abram Tertz (Andrei Sinyavsky), *Strolls with Pushkin,* 65–66.

11. L. I. Vol'pert, "Pushkin i frantsuzskaia komediia XVIII v.," 168–87, esp. 168.

12. J. Douglas Clayton, *Dimitry's Shade: A Reading of Alexander Pushkin's Boris Godunov*, ch. 2, "*Boris Godunov* and the Theatre," 31–32. Clayton's chapter contains an excellent discussion of Pushkin's interest in contemporary French debates over neoclassical versus Romantic drama (triggered by August von Schlegel's controversial writings on the subject) as well as a context for Pushkin's many abandoned prefaces to *Boris* in the "theatrical" or "dramatic manifesto," a polemical genre inspired by Victor Hugo (35–37). We find problematic, however, the larger thesis of Clayton's book: that by 1825 Pushkin's social and religious convictions were already conservative, and that this ideology is reflected in the play. Further page references in the text.

13. D. S. Likhachev, A. M. Panchenko, "*Smekhovoi mir*" *Drevnei Rusi* (1976); D. S. Likhachev, A. M. Panchenko, and N. V. Ponyrko, *Smekh v drevnei Rusi* (1984). Subsequent page references in the text are to the more recent volume, abbreviated *Smekh*.

14. Iu. Lotman and B. Uspenskii, "Novye aspekty izucheniia kul'tury Drevnei Rusi," 148–66. A translation (not wholly reliable) by N. F. C. Owen can be found in Ann Shukman, ed., *Ju. M. Lotman, B. A. Uspenskij: The Semiotics of Russian Culture*, 36–52. Page references in the text are to the English translation.

15. "Komediia o velikoi bede Moskovskomu Gosudarstvu, o tsare Borise i o Grishke Otrep'eve," in S. A. Fomichev, *Prazdnik zhizni. Etiudy o Pushkine*, 82–107. Further page references in the text.

16. G. O. Vinokur, "Iazyk 'Borisa Godunova,'" in Vinokur, *Kommentarii*, 350–87, esp. 368, 373.

17. O. P. Aranovskaia [Olga Arans], "O vine Borisa Godunova v tragedii Pushkina," 128–56.

18. L. Lotman (St. Petersburg), "Sud'by tsarei i tsarstv v Biblii i tragizm istorii v 'Borise Godunove,'" 101–8, esp. 101, 107. Saul is one of several Biblical object lessons on the near-impossibility of just rule for kings who are caught, as Tsar Boris was, between an exacting God or Prophet and an unruly People. Lotman is certainly correct in her intuition that the figure and fate of Boris (not of his victims or of his nation) is what anchors Pushkin's play to some type of tragedy, in both its versions; the fact that the changes in the text from 1825 to 1831 primarily involve scenes *not* featuring the eponymous hero reinforces this stable tragic core at the center of an originally comedic design.

19. Sergei Averintsev, "Bakhtin, Laughter, and Christian Culture," 84. Further page references in the text.

20. See the pioneering volume edited by Samuel H. Baron and Nancy Shields Kollmann, *Religion and Culture in Early Modern Russia and Ukraine*, editors' introduction ("Religion and Cultural Studies in Russia, Then and Now," 3–16). For a tactful cautionary word on the cultural semioticians as a source for historical thinking, here identified loosely as "structuralists" – see also David A. Frick, "Misrepresentations, Misunderstandings, and Silences," 149–68, esp. 152–54.

21. For an excellent survey by a classicist, see G. W. Bowersock, "The Roman Emperor as Russian Tsar: Tacitus and Pushkin," 130–47. On the difficult question of

Pushkin's punitive attitude toward Boris Godunov, so out of keeping with his sympathy toward Tiberius, see B. G. Reizov, "Pushkin, Tatsit, i 'Boris Godunov,'" 66–82, esp. 72–73. In defining the poet's sense of historical necessity, Reizov concludes that Pushkin punishes Boris Godunov not out of moral considerations but because he *fails;* his reign devolves into terror and bloodshed, so his criminal deed cannot be condoned.

22. "On Boris Godunov" [possible draft preface to the play, written 1828], in Wolff, *Pushkin,* 223.

23. Guidance here and later in this chapter has been provided by three excellent entries in *The New Princeton Encyclopedia of Poetry and Poetics* (Princeton: Princeton University Press, 1993): "Comedy" (224–28, by Timothy J. Reiss); "Tragedy" (1296–1302, by Timothy J. Reiss); and "Tragicomedy" (1302–3, by Robert L. Montgomery).

24. "Omitted chapter from 'The Captain's Daughter'" [1835–36], Appendix A in Paul Debreczeny, ed. *Alexander Pushkin: Complete Prose Fiction,* 450.

25. Herbert Lindenberger, *Historical Drama: The Relationship of Literature to Reality,* xi and ch. 2: "History and the Structure of Dramatic Action."

26. For commentary and a translation of Meyerhold's own notes to this production, see Paul Schmidt, ed., *Meyerhold at Work,* ch. 4 ("Meyerhold and Pushkin"), 81–140. The remark about theatrical language is from Schmidt, 82.

27. For a fine survey of this creative partnership, see A. Fevral'skii, "Prokof'ev i Meierkhol'd," 94–120. Discussion of *Boris Godunov* on 108–15. When Prokofiev is mentioned in the text, page references are to this article.

28. Here as with his 1936 incidental music to Alexander Tairov's (also aborted) Kamerny Theater stage performance of *Eugene Onegin,* Prokofiev strove to differentiate his incidental music from the canonized opera versions by Musorgsky and Tchaikovsky. Although some overlap in episodes could not be avoided, he concentrated on those scenes that his great nineteenth-century predecessors had not set to music. Some of Prokofiev's most effective music for Meyerhold was the evening at Shuisky's and the cacophonous battle scenes, which pitched Western orchestras against the howling of Russian regiments (Fevral'skii, "Prokof'ev," 110–11). Prokofiev's solution to *narod bezmolvstuet* was ingenious: to score a gradually intensifying hum (or groan) for chorus over the final several scenes, and then to abruptly cut it off.

29. "Meyerhold and Pushkin," reminiscences of Boris Zakhava, in Schmidt, *Meyerhold at Work,* 95. Further page references to this section included in the text.

30. "Pushkin was a student of Shakespeare, and this was sufficiently revolutionary for a theater burdened with the legacy of neoclassicism, but the spirit of his 'Boris Godunov' was even more revolutionary than the formal structure of the play. When, at the censor's order, he replaced the proclamation of the *narod* 'Long live Tsar Dimitrii Ivanovich!' with the well-known stage direction 'the people do not respond,' then he outwitted the censor, since he did not diminish, but strengthened the role of the *narod.*" "Meyerhold govorit (zapisi 1934–1939 godov)," in Aleksandr Gladkov, *Meierkhol'd,* 315.

31. "Piat' let s Meierkhol'dom," in Gladkov, *Meierkhol'd*, 165 (the discussion of *Boris Godunov*). Vasily Kliuchevsky (1841–1911) was a Russian historian renowned for his careful scholarship and beautiful prose style.

32. Boris Zakhava in Schmidt, *Meyerhold at Work*, 104. Subsequent page reference in text.

33. See Pushkin's draft commentary "On Byron's Plays," 1827, in Wolff, *Pushkin*, 209. Pushkin acknowledges that Byron himself understood this weakness in his dramatic writing and strove to overcome it.

34. "Notes on Popular Drama and on M. P. Pogodin's *Marfa Posadnitsa*" [1830, unpublished review], in Wolff, *Pushkin*, 264.

35. Svetlana Evdokimova, *Pushkin's Historical Imagination*, 14. Further page references given in the text.

36. In 1836, Pushkin wrote a review of *Journey from St. Petersburg to Moscow* intended (but not approved) for his journal *Sovremennik* (see "Alexander Radishchev," in Wolff, *Pushkin*, 390–91). "The whole of contemporary French philosophy is reflected in Radishchev: Voltaire's skepticism, Rousseau's philanthropy, Diderot's and Raynal's political cynicism; but all in an incoherent and twisted manner, as things seen through a distorting mirror.... Everybody read and forgot his book in spite of the fact that there are in it a few sensible ideas, a few well-intentioned assumptions, which it was quite unnecessary to dress up in abusive and bombastic phrases ..." This negative take on one of the heroes of the Russian revolutionary movement has caused progressive Pushkinists no end of worry. Some claim Pushkin was opportunistically echoing Catherine the Great's furious marginalia in 1793; others, that he was simply trying to return the banned author to a life in print, under guise of an acceptable (that is, condemnatory) review. The censor ultimately ruled that no mention of Radishchev in print was the safer policy. I would argue that Pushkin is not being especially "Aesopian" in his review, but that he genuinely considered Radishchev's melodramatic and presumptuous social criticism to be bad (inaccurate, unusable, ineffectual, unbeneficial) history.

37. Draft letter to N. N. Raevsky, second half of July 1825, in Wolff, *Pushkin*, 156.

38. It was Bulgarin's use of this last detail, among others, in his own historical novel *Dimitrii Samozvanets* that triggered Pushkin's accusations of plagiarism. Bulgarin could not have "seen" this historical reality himself. "All these are dramatic fictions and not traditions handed down by history," Pushkin noted with some irritation in his "Refutations to Criticism," a private list of complaints compiled in 1830. See Wolff, *Pushkin*, 254.

39. The phrase "mungrell Tragy-comedie" belongs to Sir Philip Sidney. For two good introductions to the complexity of the genre, see Hirst, *Tragicomedy*, and Nancy Klein Maguire, ed., *Renaissance Tragicomedy: Explorations in Genre and Politics*. The Italian playwright and theorist Giambattista Guarini published his *Compendio della Poesia Tragicomica* in 1601.

40. See R. L. M. (Robert L. Montgomery), entry on "Tragicomedy," *The New Princeton Encyclopedia of Poetry and Poetics*, 1302. Defenders of tragicomedy tend to

be suspicious of Aristotle's claim that tragic catharsis in fact settles the passions rather than inflames them.

41. *Le Cid* was the cause of a bitter literary debate in 1637, when it was attacked by Scudéry for its bad versification and violation of the unities; the French Academy had to step in and mediate (see Hirst, *Tragicomedy*, ch. 4, "French seventeenth-century tragicomedy," 48). Pushkin was of course knowledgeable about these debates. In his various passing comments on *Le Cid* he expresses sympathy and approval for the liberties taken by Corneille: "Voyez comme Corneille a bravement mené le Cid. Ha, vous voulez la règle des 24 heures?" (draft letter to N. N. Raevsky, July 1825, repeated in a draft preface to *Boris Godunov* in 1830, in Wolff, *Pushkin*, 155, 247); or in his 1828 comments on *Boris Godunov*, "Note that in Corneille you do not find allusions" (Wolff, *Pushkin*, 223). Corneille escapes criticism that Pushkin directs freely at Racine and Molière.

42. John Orr, *Tragicomedy and Contemporary Culture: Play and Performance from Beckett to Shepard*, 1.

43. Paul Hernadi, *Interpreting Events: Tragicomedies of History on the Modern Stage*. Further page references in the text.

44. In the Preface to his *History of the Russian State*, Karamzin specifically instructed the "simple citizen" to read history: it would "reconcile him with the imperfections of the visible order of things ... [and] console him during state disasters, giving witness to the fact that similar events had happened earlier, events that were even worse ..." From "Predislovie (K 'Istorii gosudarstva Rossiiskogo')," in N. M. Karamzin, *Predaniia vekov*, 31.

45. "Draft note on tragedy," in Wolff, *Pushkin*, 130, translation corrected. Wolff incorrectly renders the Russian *Interes – edinstvo*, as "Interest is All."

46. Monika Greenleaf, *Pushkin and Romantic Fashion: Fragment, Elegy, Orient, Irony*, 177. Greenleaf observes that Pushkin had "nothing but contempt" for the popular Romantic reading of "the allegedly Shakespearean tragicomedy," which "had become the vehicle for Romantic revolutionary heroes transforming their nations' destinies – often an unsubtle form of political allegory masquerading as history" (160). This was to misuse both drama and historical perspective.

47. For a persuasive discussion, see Brian James Baer, "Between Public and Private: Re-Figuring Politics in Pushkin's *Boris Godunov*," 25–44. Baer argues that Voltaire recommended merely omitting the romantic subplot from tragedy, whereas Pushkin, more boldly, proceeded to "lay it bare," exposing it as false and forcing it to serve political ends.

48. Pushkin to Nikolai Raevsky the Younger, 30 June or 30 July 1829; see *Letters*, 365; and our chapter 3, 128 n. 79.

49. "Notes on popular drama and on M. P. Pogodin's *Marfa Posadnitsa*," in Wolff, *Pushkin*, 265.

6

The Ebb and Flow of Influence: Muffling the Comedic in the Move toward Print

∾ CARYL EMERSON

"Returning to 'Boris Godunov,' I'd like to ask: what in the world is it good for? It can't go on stage, it's impossible to call it a narrative poem, a novel, a history in voices – or anything at all; for which of the human feelings does it hold any value or virtue? Who will want to read it, once the initial curiosity passes? I read it through today for the third time, and already skipped over a lot; and when I finished I thought: O! (a cipher)."

Pavel Katenin, 1 February 1836

Nowhere was Pushkin's behavior as provocative as in the realm of theater. This provocation attached both to his unruly, outspoken person in the theater stalls and to his aesthetic judgments. By 1817, the year Pushkin finished the Lycée, performance arts in the capitals functioned "not only as a theater, but as a club"; the theater was a forum to quarrel, hiss, cheer, create scandals, seduce, and debate art and politics.[1] The cutting edge of Russian culture was here. Memoirs of the period attest that the hotheaded Pushkin was a familiar figure, conversant with all dramatic camps from Shakhovskoi to Katenin, praising them in public, berating them in private, but aligning himself with none. Indeed, Pushkin found fault with almost *all* Russian performance practice of his time: tragedy, melodrama, vaudeville, historical and patriotic drama. His own ambitions in drama, which were considerable, encountered constant obstacles and left relatively modest fruit. As Fomichev has remarked, nowhere in Pushkin's work "is there so sharp a disproportion between the impressive quantity of creative plans (about 25) and the small number of realizations."[2]

It was suggested in chapter 2 that even the completed 1825 *Comedy* was in a sense an incomplete project, the first part of a trilogy. The complete historical cycle, culminating in the triumph of a new dynasty, would be fueled by ambition, social injustice, violent retribution, popular humor, pure chance – a daring set of causalities, unfit for both romantic and neoclassical modes of telling history. If Pushkin had imagined his trilogy as three serial chronicle plays on a Shakespearean model, then, as real history is crooked, progress through it also would be crooked and catch people by surprise. Arguably, the real protagonist of this larger historical arc would have been neither the beleaguered Boris, nor the progressive and wildly popular Dmitry, but the grimmer, more tenacious Prince Vasily Shuisky – schemer, flatterer, and court chameleon, who must be vanquished by the rising sun of the Romanovs.

In the first installment of this trilogy, Boris Godunov's fate is tragic and the Pretender's is Romantic. The partially concealed comedic ligature that survives them both is Shuisky. He is that deep well of plots and resilience, hampered by neither power nor love, innocent of the burdens of sincerity, who adjusts, twists, grasps the potentials of the moment, while never showing his hand – "un singulaire mélange d'audace, de souplesse et de force de caractère," as Pushkin remarked admiringly in a draft preface from 1828.[3] Through his person, we learn that History, which in Karamzin's view was the "Sacred Book of Nations," need not be moved forward by beneficent agents or preordained acts. Carriers of history can be petty, their alliances opportunistic or accidental. For one of the strategies of a "tragicomedy of history" is to stitch together the comically trivial and the tragically lofty so that the boundaries between them are blurred. Foreground and background change places. At any given time, the spectator cannot distinguish a genuinely historical agent from a purely local disruption distracting from that agency – because reality on stage is dynamic, not rhetorical or structural. It moves forward in rapid dialogue, glancing over its shoulder for possible spies. Just how crucial Prince Shuisky is to this type of dialogue is clear from the first ten scenes, which move from the closeted exchange between Shuisky and Vorotynsky (where the interlocutor is foolish), to the closeted exchange between Shuisky and Afanasy Pushkin (where the interlocutor is wise). In between, the "transitional rulers" Boris and Dmitry forge their identities and flag the causes that will trap them.

Shuisky is the perfect swing character. He is always at the right place, in the right mood, at the right time: a complainer and blackmailer with

Vorotynsky, a trustful and truth-telling friend to Pushkin, a sycophant with Tsar Boris, ever drawing stories out and launching them into circulation. A Iago who plots out of malice against his superiors, in himself he is pure energy, without any coherent positive program or principle. Unlike the harassed Boris who is always watching the clock, and also unlike the restless poetic Dmitry, Prince Shuisky is a rogue prince, at home everywhere because he looks out only for himself and has all the time in the world. His tools are toadying up, deception, and delay.[4] The last we see of Shuisky (scene 17), the boyars are congratulating him on his masterful management of the hallucinating tsar, who has just suffered through the Patriarch's account of miracles at Uglich. In the original order of scenes (where scene 18 was "The Square in front of the Cathedral, Moscow," not the comic polyphony of "A Plain near Novgorod-Seversky"), this pressure on Boris is uninterrupted and brutally sustained: as soon as Shuisky saves the day for the tsar, ritual humiliation can be administered by Nikolka the Iron-Cap. Only if Shuisky cannot undermine power will he deign to play up to it. Within the bounds of this first play, this strategy is marvelously successful: the dying Boris recommends Shuisky to his young son as a trustworthy advisor.

The present chapter is limited to the 1825 text and its 1831 derivative, without the fascinating penumbral possibilities of the unwritten trilogy. More narrowly, it will focus on those parts of the 1825 text that were eventually omitted or altered, as Pushkin (after some success publishing individual scenes) came to realize that his drama would not be printed in full as he had written it and would most likely not have sequels. Of special interest are the dramatic genres, both native and imported, that might have influenced these altered portions, for those resonances then disappear from the printed text of the play. In chapter 4 of this volume, Fomichev summarizes, in seven entries, the significant differences between the 1825 and 1831 texts. Our discussion of them will take place at the level of frames, scenes, and episodes rather than of individual words, punctuation, and orthography. For it would be foolhardy to attempt to explain all of Pushkin's adjustments, carried out over six years on several manuscript copies, as part of an integrated strategy. Vinokur's textology of the play, long taken as authoritative but rife with unsupported suppositions, shows the great difficulty of restoring the proper balance between censorship pressure, precautionary self-censorship, errors and eccentricities of the copyist, the well-meaning advice of friends, and Pushkin's own improvements and corrections.[5] Works revised under such pressures can be patched affairs, with crippling losses surviving alongside surprisingly vigorous new wholes. It is generally conceded that as revisions went forward the play became more "tragic" (in the Shakespearean sense). Many of its boldest historical insights were blunted, some of the cacophony standardized or smoothed out, and the comedic abundance of genres muffled. But these "disappeared" segments of the *Comedy* have rarely received integrated analysis.

This chapter will assume, first, that Pushkin was drawn to the generically diverse mode of comedy as that narrative form most true to his vision of historical causality. And second, it presumes that this initial comedy was to function, at least provisionally, within a larger trilogy that would end on triumph for the Romanovs. The result would be a patriotic chronicle that ultimately made peace, even glorious peace, with Russia's destiny, thus qualifying it for imperial patronage. But its means, its language, the breathtaking suspense of its scenes, its pace and political daring would be utterly unlike the stilted and servile tributes that made up traditional historical drama. After 1830, Pushkin put his whole painful "Time of Troubles" project to rest. He took up other genres (prose fiction, historical romance, history proper) to examine alternative crisis periods in the Russian past, especially Peter the Great and the rebel Pugachev. But the wisdom about the workings of history reflected in the 1825 play was never lost.

It is our thesis, further, that taken as a whole, the portions that Pushkin chose to omit are rather "scandalous" – politically, aesthetically, and in terms of a specifically Russian philosophy of history. It is no accident that the range of sources and allusions (the sheer scope of dramatic genres, quotations, poetic meters) is markedly broader in 1825 than in 1831. This scope was surely polemical. In the early 1820s, Pushkin understood the eclectic spirit of Romanticism as the poet's right to create an amalgam of imported and native models.[6] He was neither alone nor original in this crusade. As Douglas Clayton has shown, Pushkin was reflecting on Russian soil the French theater debates of the early 1820s, which peaked in Victor Hugo's use of Shakespeare as a weapon against neoclassicism in his preface to *Cromwell*.[7] Then 1825 intervened. And Clayton concludes: "If in France, the liberal revolution continued and romanticism was victorious in the theater, then in Russia, on the other hand, there was a swing toward greater conservatism, even reaction, and therefore much less favorable conditions for any theatrical reforms" (36).

Pushkin, however, went further than Hugo, and further than most of his fellow reformers of the stage. He was selective even about Shake-speare (both before and after his English was good enough to appreciate the Bard in the original) – in part because of his neoclassical intuitions, and also because Russian theater language was too undeveloped, too young and unstable, to permit any playwright merely to graft Shake-spearean devices onto it.[8] Pushkin would attempt more daring grafts on to a more primitive native trunk. For his eclectic brand of national Romanticism, he stylized aspects of a Russian medieval dramatic tradi-tion that had little equivalent in the more secular European debates. By the mid-1830s, Katenin's candid opinion of *Boris Godunov* (the epigraph to this chapter) stood as an index to the failure that Pushkin himself had predicted.[9]

Stimuli behind the "Komediia": A Provisional Accounting

With very great poets, it is more appropriate to speak of stimuli than of influence. What dramatic precedent might have stimulated Pushkin before 1825? As we have seen, source studies for *Boris* have been con-strained by several factors. First, scholars have tended to underestimate the extent to which Pushkin in 1825 was already a serious historian, with an informed, critical view of Karamzin and his methodology. Second, Pushkin's major statements on drama postdate the writing of *Boris* by several years (1827–30). And finally, Pushkin was specific about only a handful of direct inspirations for his Comedy: Karamzin's *History,* the ancient Russian chronicles, and "our father Shakespeare."[10]

Even those acknowledged stimuli must be handled carefully. Much ingenuity has gone into tracing episodes and lines borrowed from spe-cific Shakespeare plays, but the best students of this connection hasten to point out the profound differences. Chief among them are Pushkin's laconicism, his emotional and rhetorical constraint, his lack of titanic heroes, his reluctance to indulge supernatural effects such as witches and ghosts, and his willingness to let historical events stand unconnected and alone.[11] Structurally, "Shakespearism" in *Boris Godunov* owes less to the tragedies than to the chronicle plays. Pushkin was impressed by François Guizot's preface to his 1822 French edition of Shakespeare's plays, where the difference between the tragedies and historical chronicles is clearly laid out: scenes of a tragedy must link and explain, always keeping the fate of the hero in view, whereas chronicles and historical dramas need only stack up separate episodes and fill them with action.[12] For Pushkin, tragedy remained the least satisfying of the neoclassical genres dominant on the Russian stage. In turning to chronicles in 1824 – both Shakespeare's dramatized ones and the Russian chronicles quoted by Karamzin in the apparatus to his *History* – he was making one large integrated move *away* from the linear, elucidating, explanatory power of tragedy as conventionally defined.

In chapter 2 of the present study, Dunning broadened the range of sources and stimuli for the *Komediia* beyond the three that Pushkin overtly names. The poet surely knew of Schiller's revolutionary plays, including his *Demetrius* fragment (although the degree of familiarity has been debated).[13] Sumarokov, Kotzebue, and Ryleev were certainly familiar, if only as negative examples. Ancient Greek tragedy, with its political destinies worked out through successive plays, might have been an inspiration.[14] As an historian, Pushkin eagerly sought out both Russian chronicles and uncensored Western accounts that Karamzin had *not* fully incorporated into his narrative (especially Jacques Margeret). He researched his own family papers at Mikhailovskoe. But many questions of genesis remain.

For example, how well could Pushkin have known the history of Russian theater in the 1820s, from his reading or from friendly conversations? How many texts, now obscure, were so familiar to Pushkin's generation that it was superfluous to identify allusions to them? (In this regard, Simon Karlinsky's pioneering study *Russian Drama from Its Beginnings to the Age of Pushkin* remains a gold mine of restored subtexts.) Although the exiled Pushkin continually requested that books be sent to him by his brother and his friends, how many actually arrived? (Pushkin's own library dates only from 1826.) In addition to Corneille and Racine, did the Lycée curriculum in the 1810s introduce its students to Russian adaptations of Jesuit school drama? (Although pupils were forbidden to stage plays, the tradition might have been known: the teaching staff included a Jesuit before the Order was banned.) We know from the notes of Pushkin's classmates that Polish–Russian tensions were a theme in the introductory literary surveys in 1812–14, and that Feofan Prokopovich was on the reading list.[15]

Here documentation is incomplete, but we do have hints. In September 1825, already deep into his own play, Pushkin wrote to Pavel Katenin, an "archaist" poet: "Heed me, my dear, lock yourself in and get started on a romantic tragedy in eighteen acts (like Sophia Alekseevna's trage-

dies). You would accomplish a revolution in our literature ..."[16] Tsarevna
Sophia, Peter the Great's elder sister (d. 1704), did not write the play
Pushkin attributed to her, but this is of little account; Pushkin's advice to
Katenin, for all its bantering tone, betrays an awareness of domestic
experiments in drama and the need to supplement tame European bor-
rowings with something more interesting and uncouth. Several years
later (1830), as part of an unpublished review essay on Pogodin's historical drama *Marfa Posadnitsa*, Pushkin sketched out a history of European
drama and Russia's place in it.[17] He mentions there the mystery plays of
Dmitry of Rostov (d. 1709), who, together with Simeon Polotsky and
Feofan Prokopovich, constitute the triad responsible for the best Russian
school drama. From his few sentences on this era of Russian theater history, it is clear that Pushkin understood how, why, and for whom those
early Russian dramas were performed. However, the essay on Pogodin's
play is important in another way: it is a requiem for what Pushkin had
hoped his own *Boris Godunov* would do.

Pogodin's melodramatic, rather moralizing play about Novgorod's
resistance to Grand Prince Ivan III – a staple theme of the Russian theater – did not merit the warm appreciation that Pushkin gave it. Pushkin's generosity was probably motivated more by gratitude, personal
esteem, and editorial loyalty than by the virtues of the piece.[18] Indeed,
Pushkin's review is scarcely remembered for its remarks on *Marfa Posadnitsa* but only for its general argument, already touched upon by Fomichev. European drama was born on the public square. As a popular form,
its primary obligation has always been to please, entertain, and astonish.
(Pushkin noted: "The people demand strong sensations; for them even
executions are spectacles.") Thus not pale verisimilitude but the cruder
emotions – laughter, pity, terror, surprise – are essential to its success.
When "poets moved to court," drama grew more decorous and lowered
its voice. It took on problems of state, began to speak stiffly, trembled
before high officials. Style became more uniform and tedious. And in
both comedy and tragedy, Pushkin cautions, a monotony of technique is
fatal; if satiric laughter is all one hears, it grows weak, and even murders
and executions can become habitual. Because Shakespearean tragedy
remained outspoken and complexly motivated, it was to be preferred to
the court tragedies of Racine.

Closer to home, Pushkin's views become more original – and more
pessimistic. Dramatic art in Russia "was never a popular need." The first

theater companies imported from the West in the late seventeenth century did not attract an audience.[19] Sumarokov's "limp, frigid" imitations of neoclassical tragedy had no impact on popular taste. Russia still lacked a genuine national tragedy of her own. "Comedy has been more fortunate," Pushkin writes; "we have two dramatic satires" (Fonvizin's *The Minor* and Griboedov's *Woe from Wit*). Although in Pushkin's view "dramatic satire" was not the richest form of comedy, at least the language of those two comedies of manners was alive and performable; the obstacles to genuine Russian tragedy were far more severe. It would have to shed its servile tone, its haughty dialogue, its rigidity of form. Pushkin ends his sketch with a compassionate discussion of Pogodin's historical drama, which he considered an earnest attempt at "popular tragedy." By then, his own tragicomedy of history had languished four years in the censorship.

The present chapter is an expansion on these sentiments expressed by Pushkin in his essay on *Marfa Posadnitsa,* applying them speculatively to his own still-captive *Comedy.* Dunning, in his chapters 1 through 3, has scrutinized both the history *of Boris Godunov* and *Boris Godunov as* history. Here the focus shifts: from traces left by historical events to traces left by dramatic genres, that is, by past modes for capturing reality (including historical reality) on stage. Genres inevitably shape the events they describe – and Pushkin was unhappy with almost all the inherited modes. As he wrote in his essay on Pogodin's play, it is not the business of the dramatic poet "to excuse, condemn, or prompt"; he must be as "impartial as Fate." His task is to "express the people of the past, their minds, their prejudices." Such a task would be beyond the means of tragedy – shackled by a neoclassical poetics and by lofty moralizing diction – but conceivably was within the means of comedy, far more flexible, low-spoken, and free.

A play set in 1598–1605, however, should reflect pre-Petrine forms of freedom. In an early draft of his *Marfa Posadnitsa* essay, Pushkin speaks of public squares and village fairs alongside a reference to *vol'nost' misterii,* the freedom (or license) of the medieval mystery plays.[20] This will be our starting point. As we move down Fomichev's list of omitted passages and altered lines, we will highlight other dramatic genres (and in one case, songs) that might have stimulated Pushkin in 1825 – toward stylization, imitation, barbed or affectionate parody. In each case, traces of these native or assimilated texts, which contributed to the mesmerizing effect of Pushkin's maiden readings of the play in 1826, were later weakened or altogether erased.

The Archaic Comedic Frame: Traces of Seventeenth-Century School Drama and the Seditious Russian-Polish Connection

The *Comedy about Tsar Boris and Grishka Otrepiev* closes with the cumbersome phrase: "End of the comedy, in which the leading person is Tsar Boris Godunov. Glory be to the Father, and to the Son, and to the Holy Ghost, AMEN."[21] This mock-archaic title and pious closing prayer – the first and final entry on Fomichev's list – are textual dimensions that Pushkin always took seriously: titles and frames. Why might these medieval labels have been useful to Pushkin, who capriciously wrapped them around his radically modern-sounding play?[22] Such formulas were the province of that omnibus genre, Jesuit school drama, Russianized in the mid-seventeenth century and a formative influence on Russian historical drama.[23] Pushkin knew, of course, that school drama came to Russia from Poland-Lithuania, a culture that figures prominently in his own play and that signified, more abstractly, high free art – just as Muscovy signified pious chroniclers, holy fools, and a politically suspect caste of minstrels.

School drama, written in Latin as a showcase of humanist education, was central to the missionary aims of the Roman Catholic Church throughout the pre-Petrine period. As the genre spread eastward and gained an audience, Russian churchmen resolved to counter this Jesuit threat. School drama was co-opted by the Kievan Mohyla Academy, cast in a mix of Polonized Church Slavic and Ukrainian, and adapted to the didactic, panegyric purposes of the Russian Church. Those purposes proved difficult to control, however, given the popularity and wide dissemination of the plays. They were performed by amateurs in provincial seminaries to mark church holidays, as well as at the Muscovite court to welcome monarchs to the throne. Soviet research on these dramas – while acknowledging the backwardness of Russian theater vis-à-vis the West[24] – has emphasized their extremely loose structure and mongrelized, thus "progressive," form. Political harangues on contemporary topics were often inserted into a traditional cast of personified vice and virtue (Good, Evil, Fortune, Vengeance, Truth, Hope, Human Nature); extensive prose prologues and epilogues of a realistic texture coexisted with highly stylized "interludes" of dance, pantomime, ballet, chorus. The unmasking of false tsars was a popular theme of many school dramas, and often connected with Biblical prophecy.

In addition to Dmitry of Rostov's Nativity Play (*Komediia na den' Rozhdestva Khristova*), there are two additional works in this genre that the poet could have known. The first has a subtext relevant both to the Dmitry plot of illicit border-crossing and to Pushkin's own restlessness under police surveillance: Simeon Polotsky's *Comedy on the Parable of the Prodigal Son* [*Komidiia pritchi o bludnom syne*]. Well-known in Russia, Simeon's *Comedy* was published posthumously in 1685 and reprinted four times before the end of the century. This parable had been a special favorite with Polish Jesuits. But Simeon, Russia's first professional court poet, chose to emphasize in it not the usual Divine Grace but a topical scandal that had occurred during Tsar Alexis's reign – namely, the refusal of a group of young men to return home after being sent abroad to study. A similar "non-returnee" scandal had marked Boris Godunov's regency – a group of gifted young men were sent abroad to study and none came back, nor did their assigned companion-spies. In the sixth act of Simeon's *Comedy*, the repentant Prodigal Son delivers (in clumsy grammatical rhymes constructed under the influence of Polish fixed penultimate stress) a moralizing soliloquy on the ingratitude of such wayward young men. By the early nineteenth century, Polotsky's *Komidiia* had come to represent to Russian men of letters all that Peter the Great's reforms were to sweep away: the immobility of persons and the immobility of verse.

The second play, also with a strong allegorical dimension, is the tragicomedy *Vladimir* by Peter the Great's court poet, Feofan Prokopovich.[25] In it, the Christianization of Russia in the tenth century prefigures Peter's enlightened reforms, with pagan resistance presented as obscurantist and demonic-comic. Similar to Varlaam and Misail in Pushkin's play, the greedy scheming pagan priests in *Vladimir* are more than comic relief. Although cast against a schematic backdrop of Heaven and Hell, they develop into individuated personalities, witty and energetic, integrated into the main action as agents of history.[26] In a recent appreciation of *Vladimir* as a vehicle for a comic view of history, Marcia Morris has analyzed Prokopovich's play as a "tragicomedy of history" that, by means of comedic devices, embeds the dual perspectives necessary to a secular historian without trivializing the sacred mission of Prince Vladimir.[27] Could Pushkin have seen the same double-voiced potential in these early genre experiments of his native predecessors, in which comedy, improvisation and spontaneity are employed on behalf of imperial destiny? It is hard to say. The stilted stage language and mongrelized diction of school drama could not have impressed the poet. But when he recalled the political and comic tasks of this outmoded genre by choosing an archaic frame for his *Comedy*, playfully substituting Aleksashka Pushkin for the chronicler Palitsyn, Pushkin activated complex and affectionate associations.

There remains one detail of the 1825 frame deserving of attention: the Russian spelling of the word comedy itself.[28] Pushkin's manuscript contains two variants, *komediia* (in the title) and *komidiia* ["Konets komidii ..."] at the end. Scholarly discussion frequently standardizes the two spellings to -e-, but let us assume that the poet had a reason for differentiating them. The -e- of the *Komediia* – the play's opening note – recalls more Western genres: the Italian *commedia dell'arte,* the later French *comédie.* The line of development here is secular, from sixteenth-century humanist comedy up through Shakespeare, Voltaire, and the Enlightenment. A generic label on -e- announces a dramatic spectacle with stock comic characters as well as energetic improvisation, showcasing the virtues of live conversational form. As we remarked in chapter 5, in a special Russian turn on Western models, by the nineteenth century the best comedies were becoming unsentimental and ironic, boldly dispensing with true love or happy marriages at the end.[29]

And *komidiia*? The -i- spelling triggers a quite different, more somber and pious aura. An -i- vowel reflects Ukrainian-Polish orthography, of course, the conduit through which school drama reached Russia. Biblical allusions and Jesuit didacticism were the norm for this genre (recall Simeon Polotsky's *Komidiia pritchi o bludnom syne*). Indeed, everything about the word is more archaic and less satirical (there are resonances of "Proskomidiia," the introductory part of the Orthodox liturgy, which Pushkin certainly knew). And yet this near-native *komidiia* definitely possessed rich literary and comic potential. In his notes for an essay on Russian literature written in 1830, as he was again drafting prefaces for his *Boris*, Pushkin wistfully remarked how good it would be to look back "with curiosity and veneration" on Russia's "ancient monuments," noting the difference between the "naïve satire of the French *trouvers*" and the "sly mockery of our minstrels [*skomorokhov*], the public-square joke of a semi-religious mystery play and the conceits of our ancient comedy [*komidii*].[30] In the closing formula for his play, Pushkin brings together these various traditions of comedy, the more recently imported and the more homegrown, in a juxtaposition that stands as testimony to his genius for overlapping and confounding genres. *Konets komidii*, "End of the comedy," clearly echoes the Italian *"finita la commedia"* – but dragging, as it were, the more archaic and pious Russian *komidiia* into the brighter zone of Western satire.

The Three Omitted Scenes

Fomichev's second item – the dedication of the 1831 text to Karamzin and the absence of such tribute in 1825 – has been explicated thoroughly by Dunning in chapter 3. That gracious but late-breaking gesture was part of Pushkin's calculated bid for the status of Russia's premiere historian, a position also bid for by his enemies at court. As such, it belongs as much to the annals of Russian historiography and the Machiavellian intrigues of tsarist censorship as to the textual history of Pushkin's play. The tactical recasting of Karamzin from problematic interlocutor to revered dedicatee was reflected inside the play as well. But there is no scholarly consensus, and even less is there scholarly consistency, regarding the aesthetic wisdom of omitting the three scenes mentioned in Fomichev's third item.[31]

The status of scene 3, "Maiden's Field. Novodevichy Convent," was resolved by Soviet scholars in a straightforward, ideologically satisfying fashion. Pushkin shows the common people as disrespectful and irreverent; tsarist censors had therefore removed the scene; thus it must be restored. The first censor's report (December 1826) had indeed objected to the episode of the onion and the indifference of the populace ("is it seemly to thus interpret the people's feelings?").[32] Vinokur speculated that in 1829 Zhukovsky, to facilitate publication of this stalled work, crossed out all the "dangerous places" (230), including so large a chunk of scene 3 that "Pushkin apparently preferred to sacrifice the entire scene" (236) – even though by so doing he destroyed the two symmetrical cheers that book-ended the play. Such a reading of the evidence can be disputed. But since scene 3 has its source in Karamzin and is valued as a vigorous, if miniaturized, adaptation of a Shakespearean crowd scene to Russian terrain, it was the scene most easily reintegrated into the canonical text of *Boris*. "Maiden's Field" was published in 1841 and restored to the play irregularly throughout the nineteenth century, routinely in the twentieth.

What was lost in 1831 with the disappearance of that scene? Fomichev is surely correct to note that in the published version, the "comic tonality of a series of scenes was significantly muffled" and that the mass scenes (of which scene 3 is one) are invariably comic.[33] This comedic politics is also mildly subversive; the crowd's outer obedience contrasts with its pragmatic cynicism and inner freedom. (In chapter 4, Fomichev remarks on the comic-demonic resonances of this scene: the bogey-man [*buka*] that frightens children and the fact that the most important event, Boris's acceptance of the crown, takes place in the invisible distance, "beyond the border" of the stage, in unprotected space.[34]) More important from a genre perspective than this thematic play with the unclean force, however, is the fact that this scene, together with the even briefer preceding scene 2, realizes a formal device that will become standard for the treatment of time and space in the crowd scenes of the *Comedy*. Dialogue in such domains is both stylized (as when the *narod* speaks in a single voice) and cast in individualized, realistic vernacular. Scene 3 opens with random voices, each restricted in what it sees and hears: One, Another, a Third, Woman, One, Another, First, One. Church steeples, crosses, walls, and roofs are covered with people, but we experience the events on Maiden's Field one at a time, "on the ground," peering up from under, as if the spoken lines had been caught by a close-range microphone passed through the crowd. Within the almost neoclassical limits of "only two voices at a time," Pushkin manages to communicate a sense of density, chaotic variety, and vastness. To experience that constriction of focus inside a huge public event, the audience in the hall must locate itself not above or beyond the crowd but inside it, sharing its local, roaming point of view.

Just such an experience is choreographed by Pushkin in the middle of the scene, the popular mass wail as described by a witness about to be engulfed by it. "What is that sound?" "What sound? / The people wailing, sinking down like waves, / Row after row ... nearer ... nearer ... It's got / To us! On your knees!" To feel these lines properly means to be drawn into these waves, into the immediacy of their moment. In that carnival image so beloved by Bakhtin, the audience vaults over the footlights to participate in this "staged" campaign to move Boris toward yes. History is made by such participation, Pushkin would say, with people manipulated, randomly recruited and aroused, given to ludicrous gestures, acting by chance and without access to the larger picture. With the omission of the "Maiden's Field" scene (and the loss of the people's cheer at the end), this lesson in historical dynamics disappears. The plea Shchelkalov delivers from the Main Porch to a hushed and waiting crowd then abuts directly on Tsar Boris himself in the Kremlin Palace, newly crowned, addressing his boyars and patriarch. Power has been bestowed from the top down. Comedic history could never come to pass in that humorless, rhetorically distanced way, reminiscent of the moralizing tone of Karamzin's main narrative.

The status of the other two omitted scenes, "Monastery Wall" and "Maryna's Dressing Room," is more problematic. The simplest explanation offered for their omission has been the formal one: because most of the *Komediia* is written in unrhymed iambic pentameter with caesura after the second foot, and each of these omitted scenes departs markedly from that norm (scene 6 is in trochaic octometer, scene 13 in rhymed iambic lines of varying length), perhaps Pushkin, in his revisions, wished to standardize and thereby dignify the meters of the play. But authorial intention here is difficult to decipher.

The brief episode "Monastery Wall. Grigory and an Evil Monk" directly follows upon Pimen's lengthy, pious scene and is in striking contrast to it. In a sing-song octometric line, which suggests an elongated *chastushka,* the bored and trapped Grigory laments his monastic incarceration.[35] The *zloi chernets* [evil monk] who prompts this restless novice to pretendership is not identified. Is he a routine troublemaker? An agent of the Romanovs or their princely allies? (According to Karamzin and confirmed by later historians, monks from the Chudov Monastery were implicated in the plot to unseat Boris.) Or might he be some demonic tempter, a common enough apparition in monastic communities and a staple of Saints' Lives? Pushkin had acquainted himself with Goethe's *Faust* during his southern exile, and the earliest plan for his own "Faust" excerpt dates from 1825; perhaps the *zloi chernets* is the Devil, offering a Faustian pact?[36] Politically, psychologically, metrically, the scene is indeed anomalous. In 1828, two poets whom Pushkin highly respected, Adam Mickiewicz and Anton Delvig, recommended that it be dropped.[37] The scene was crossed out – we cannot be certain by whom – in a manuscript copy of the *Komediia* in 1829. But Baron Egor Rozen, who translated *Boris* into German between 1831 and 1833, was eager that it be retained. He claimed that Pushkin had excised it solely on the advice of poets who felt that its presence lessened the effect of Pimen's story, and insisted that Pushkin "intended to restore this scene in the second edition."[38] It is doubtful that an atheistic, cynically corrupt monastic scene like this could have passed the censor in any event (significantly, it was not published by Zhukovsky in 1841 together with the other two omitted scenes). Unlike the case of "Maiden's Field," however, censorship pressure and Karamzinian credentials for the episode have not worked in favor of its restoration. Rather, such deans of *Boris* scholarship as Vinokur have concluded that conflicting testimony can only mean the "absence of a direct sanction from the author" to reinstate the scene – and all the more so, Vinokur adds, since "this scene departs sharply from the general style of Pushkin's tragedy, and artistically is far weaker than the rest of the text of *Boris Godunov*" (244). Critical opinion has been firmly against the reinstallation of "Monastery Wall."

Against this consensus, we assume that Pushkin had a reason for writing scene 6 and would have liked to retain it. Vinokur and his likeminded predecessors are correct that within the "general style of a tragedy" the scene might well be inappropriate, both conceptually and in performance.[39] Within a comedy, however, priorities and potentials shift. Russian comedies were eclectic. As far back as Prokopovich's *Vladimir*, and in many school dramas, comedic, gothic, and melodramatic scenes added complexity and surprise to the otherwise linear unfolding of a didactic plot. Early on, comic patches served as forums where parallel explanations for events could be aired. For thus does national history get started: in rumor, legend, folk ditty, and lament, in sensational and demon-ridden narratives of popular reconstruction. Since Pushkin's *Comedy* was, among much else, an attempt to dramatize the workings of history, we might surmise that an anomalous scene like "Monastery Wall" was included to allow yet another genre the opportunity to explain a series of inexplicable events. The Chudov monk was real. But that historical fact intrudes into scene 6 with its demonized and rhythmic-folkloric envelope intact. We witness Dmitry's story marked by its mode of transmission. As Pushkin well understood, communicative genres could themselves have the force of historical documents.

At times, the *Komediia* approaches a catalogue of such genres. First Shuisky presents the Uglich story from within the zone of aristocratic court gossip. Then Pimen, that stylized chronicler, retells it from the perspective of monastic piety. The *zloi chernets* steps into Pushkin's play from a third genre, the Russian folk- or magic tale, with its own quasi-fantastical modes of causality and its ability to generate an external demonic agent to represent what is otherwise an inexpressible internal temptation. It was this psychological stratum, perhaps, that Meyerhold had in mind in mid-November 1937 when, rehearsing the Cell Scene, he remarked that he would like to include the "Monastery Wall" scene as well, but playing it as Grigory's dream.[40] "That's why the rhythm [of Pushkin's verse line] breaks down," Meyerhold remarked: a dream, as an altered state of consciousness, justifies the employment of a different meter. Although this metrically innovative idea was to die together with the entire production, Prokofiev, with his superb ear for rhythmic contrast, was very taken by the idea of Grigory singing his trochaic octometer lines in a sort of somnambulant trance. The scene feels folkloric, prelogical, reminiscent of those early Muscovite narratives in which dissatisfied young men dream of what the devil can bring and then suddenly hear his seductive, accommodating voice.

This intuition of "folkness" in the Pretender's story is not new. Irena Ronen, drawing on the folk typologies of Vladimir Propp, has examined the fairytale space of Dmitry's biography and all the ways it reflects a *volshebnaia skazka* [magic tale]: the "miraculous birth of the hero" out of sleep (in scene 5) and his descent back into sleep (at the end of scene 21, "Forest"); the border-crossings between "one's own" and "alien" domains; the trials set Dmitry by the evil avenging bride; and the mandatory but elusive reward of Kingdom and Marriage at the end.[41] Ronen accepts the 1831 text as canonical and thus mentions the "Monastery Wall" scene only in passing, as an episode "artistically alien to the texture of the whole work" (47). But she notes that the *zloi chernets* does neatly satisfy one of Propp's categories, the *otpravitel'-daritel'* (he who sends the hero off, having supplied him with a gift), an indispensable service that is then more weakly fulfilled by the Hostess at the Tavern on the border. In keeping with mainstream opinion, Ronen does not much like the Pretender and finds Pushkin's affectionate portrait of him unacceptable, except as the folkloric stylization of a clever and deceptive thief [*lovkii vor*]. "The historical Grigorii Otrepiev was a considerably less enchanting figure than Pushkin's Pretender," she writes (45). As we have seen, this view is flawed: Pushkin admired the historical Pretender, both his person and his policies, and knew a great deal about him from foreign sources. At the same time, however, Pushkin respected the power of native Russian folklore (and its premodern means of information transfer) to amplify Dmitry's virtues and pave the way for his political success. In this regard, what does the "Monastery Wall" scene supply to the overall texture and thematics of the *Comedy*, and why should we be sorry to lose it?

Three motifs introduced by Pushkin in scene 6 will eventually form a subversive subtext to the play. First is the principle of comedic doubles for more lofty clerical figures. There are two such elevated figures in the play, Pimen and the Patriarch – both serious presences attached to institutions, concerned to discharge their civic duties responsibly. But Pimen, the dissident chronicler, is obedient to God and would thus expose the renegade and tsaricide Tsar Boris; the Patriarch, royal beneficiary and bureaucrat, is obedient to his patron Boris and would protect him. The *zloi chernets*, prefiguring those rogue monks Varlaam and Misail in the Tavern scene, is craftier than both. It is impossible to say whom or what he serves – or whether, indeed, he is merely the externalized, incarnated sanction for an irresistible dream. This theme of the dream of freedom, seeded in the mind of the wretched novice Grigory by this rogue monk, will become the positive fantasy that fuels the play, in counterpart to the dark and guilt-laden fantasy of Tsar Boris. As has often been noted, Pushkin's own desperate maneuvering in the mid-1820s to break out of domestic exile and then out of Russia, the charade of his fake aneurysm, and his growing cynicism regarding the imperial reception of his play are echoed in the nervous, impeded border-crossings in the play, where the tools are chance, deception, and fairytale black magic.

Secondly, scene 6 reinforces the motif of monastery as prison. Pimen has just presented his end-of-life retreat as a higher freedom. If that scene 5 stands alone, the young novice attending on the old monk appears to us as a restless, but reasonably pious, good son; for the young Grigory in scene 6, however, life is nothing but *skuka* and *gore*, boredom and grief. The "Monastery Wall" that surrounds him is a wholly punitive structure. The theme resurfaces immediately in scene 7, when the Patriarch, in an irritated outburst, promises to exile the accursed Otrepiev "to Solovetsky for perpetual penance." (The historical Patriarch Iov, Tsar Boris's appointee, was well aware of this practice. By the early nineteenth century, this great and wealthy monastic retreat in the arctic Far North had long doubled as a political prison. It was Tsar Shuisky in 1606 who had exiled the first "state enemy" to the Solovetsky Islands – and one of Pushkin's close relatives, Pavel Isaakovich Gannibal, a general and veteran of the Napoleonic Wars, was sent to Solovki in 1826 for suspected complicity in the Decembrist revolt.[42])

A final sounding of this monastery-as-prison motif is in the song Var-laam begins to sing in scene 9, "A Tavern on the Lithuanian Border." This song – about a *chernets bedniak* [wretched monk] tonsured against his will, who begs a young beauty passing by his cell to enter, disrobe him, caress him, feel the beating of his heart – is identified by two consecutive lines at two different points in Varlaam's drunken repartée: "You walk past my cell, my dear one …" and "Where a fine young lad, against his will …" As we shall see below (the fifth item on Fomichev's list), Pushkin in 1831 replaced this text with another folk song, "Kak vo gorode bylo vo Kazani," an equally ribald but considerably less despairing variant on the same theme.[43] It would seem that Pushkin, in his revisions, strove to dampen this association of the monastic with the erotic and the incar-cerated, an ancient comedic alignment.

It remains to mention one last contribution of the "Monastery Wall" scene to the elusive character of the would-be Dmitry. As Dunning has demonstrated, Pushkin knew Jacques Margeret's history well and was alert to the Frenchman's assertion that the historical Dmitry had been identified as Grigory Otrepiev only by fiat, as a clumsy propaganda move on the part of Boris and then of the usurper Shuisky, without firm docu-mentary evidence.[44] In his play, Pushkin prudently respects Karamzin's state-approved biography for the pretender. But in the Evil Monk scene – in contrast to the preceding scene in Pimen's cell – the political motiva-tions so prominent in Karamzin's account are downplayed. Whether the Chudov monks are plotting, whether the Evil Monk is an agent of the Romanovs: this is of little concern to Grigory. Bored rather than ambi-tious, he is reduced to the loneliness and restlessness of the *chernets-molodets* of folksong fame who has been tonsured against his will and wants out. Any interruption in his dreary life – an attack by the khans, an attack by Lithuania – would bring equivalent relief. And the devil, whatever his political agenda, knows how to make use of such youthful appetites. Grigory sings of his own fate in the opening bars. Significantly, his conversation with the *chernets* is locked into the same rhythms, sug-gesting an event already accomplished and recorded in song. The initial seduction succeeds without any invocation of national responsibility, only a bitter private lament that turns daredevil on a casual bet. With this scene gone, the Pretender assumes a more sober and civic-minded image.

The final omitted scene, 13, "Maryna's Dressing Room," is the second of four Polish scenes (12–15), in effect a Polish Act at the epicenter of the original play. (If this boudoir scene feels familiar, that is because Musorgsky set it to music in his revised opera, rewriting most of its lines to give his prima donna – rather than her maid, as in Pushkin – something to sing.) The omission of this scene has been poorly explained. Vinokur, finding no evidence for why it was dropped, claims nevertheless that "one could scarcely doubt Pushkin was governed by purely artistic considerations" (244). Dunning puts forth a more plausible political argument in chapter 3, that the events of 1830 were highly unfavorable for Pushkin's publishing plans – the July Revolution in France, an uprising in Warsaw against Russian imperial rule, nervousness at home toward any liberationist rhetoric in writing on historical themes – and these factors alone would be sufficient to mandate a reduction in the Polish presence (scene 12 also took large cuts). Our focus will be on the logic of Dmitry's insurrectionary image as it evolves throughout the four scenes of the original Polish Act, and on the comedic resonances of "Maryna's Dressing Room," which then disappear from the play.

In the first Polish scene (12), the Pretender is at the peak of his game. He speaks with assurance to the Pater, to Gavrila Pushkin, to Kurbsky's son, to the Russian defector Khrushchov, to the cossack chieftain, to the rapturous poet, fulfilling the expectation of each: "All's in my favor, men and destiny." Throughout the next three scenes, this self-confidence steadily erodes. Evidence is not direct – for reputations are made by rumor and demeanor, not by deed – but it is precisely this indirectness that is deadly. Rózia the maid plants doubts in Maryna's mind about the Pretender's authenticity (scene 13). After a comic bridge scene of the older generation (scene 14), the Pretender is again center stage, but no longer articulate or magnanimous; waiting for Maryna at the Fountain, he is paralyzed and mute (scene 15). In the "Dressing Room" scene, Maryna had been distraught and unsure; now the insecurity is Dmitry's. He is speechless, scared, needy, all of which impels him toward doubting his assumed role and telling the truth. In an early draft, Pushkin had added a passage following "Monastery Wall" that introduces Grigory to these doubts (and to their resolution) while still on the domestic side of the border: "I'm here alone and everything is silent, / A chill spirit is blowing in my face ... / What is this? What does it mean? / Is it disaster [beda] for me? For Moscow? / It's disaster for you, devious Boris!"[45] In the 1825 text, these anxieties are all displaced on to the play's one love scene – which, tellingly, involves love only in its destructive, cynical, self-serving and self-revelatory aspects.

5. Early-seventeenth-century woodcut of Princess Maryna Mniszech. From D. A. Rovinskii, *Materialy dlia Russkoi Ikonografii*, part 2 (St. Petersburg, 1884). Courtesy of Houghton Library, Harvard University.

Pushkin was fascinated with Maryna's calculated, galvanizing cold-ness. It is no surprise that Maryna is not driven by love. At this stage, however, she is not even driven primarily by vanity or ambition. As we learn from Rózia, Maryna has had boundless opportunity to gratify both at far less risk. But it is risk – high-quality risk, and the risk-taking man – that attracts her. So what spurs her on is cognitive: "I must know every-thing." She wants to know not only if Dmitry commands the popular support necessary to carry through his campaign (here Rózia's gossip is devastating) but whether Dmitry, in the absence of such support, could generate it out of his own will. Until her interrogation pricks him to the quick, Dmitry is not certain of his own potential in this regard. It is only after her humiliation of him that he returns to the self-confident, brash warrior of the opening Polish scene. Maryna *does* make a man of him – at an excruciating cost. Without the rumor-mongering of Rózia's chatter, the Fountain scene reduces to a male-female duel in the Angelo-Isabella mode, intensely interesting to Pushkin psychologically but insufficient to motivate historical drama. For contrary to the dramatized histories of Shakespeare, where regime change is the stuff of conspiracy and palace coups, in Russian historical drama a successful pretender must be both *of* the people and sustained by *mnenie narodnoe,* "popular esteem."[46] To know the Pretender is to know how he allows himself to be known.

Yet there is more to "Maryna's Dressing Room" than this subtext. The *Komediia* is a collage of comic sites. With the excision of this scene, several levels of comedy drop out of the play, of which the most basic is of French origin. J. Thomas Shaw has shown in detail how the Polish scenes are the most "Westernized" segments of the play – thematically, erotically, musi-cally, and metrically.[47] The Russian counter-bride to the Polish princess, Tsarevna Ksenia, is roughly the same age as Maryna (perhaps even a bit older), but her companions in the *terem* are still her brother and her nurse. Maryna and her retinue are of a wholly other world. Scholars have noted the clear affinities between the maid Rózia and the *soubrette* of French *comédie,* which by Pushkin's time was a commonplace on the Rus-sian stage. As Karlinsky observes, "Pushkin was capable of depicting believable, realistically observed Russian serfs and peasants": Tatiana's nurse, Masha Mironova's maidservant. "But whenever he writes some-thing inspired by the tradition of the neoclassical verse comedy of the Shakhovskoy-Khmelnitsky-Griboedov type, we invariably get lively and witty soubrettes of the French and Russian comedic traditions who could not possibly have existed in actual Russian life."[48] Among the "impossibilities" Karlinsky lists are Liza Muromskaia's Nastia in "Baryshnia-Krest'ianka," Parasha in "Count Nulin," and Rózia in *Boris Godunov*.

The inclusion of Rózia in this list confirms the appropriateness of Pushkin's staffing of scene 13. If her type is unlikely in a provincial Belkin Tale or even in the Moscow of Griboedov's *Woe from Wit* (Sofia Pavlovna Famusova is attended by just such an impertinent maid, Lizanka), for that reason she is a fitting marker for *alien* cultural space in a Russian historical drama set in the early seventeenth century. The appearance, on Renaissance Polish soil, of this stock female figure from French comedy highlights the non-Russianness of the milieu. But Rózia and her mistress are merely a first-level comedic reminiscence, Pushkin's opening move, which he subjects to immediate parodic variation. As L. I. Volpert notes in her discussion of Pushkin and eighteenth-century French comedy, although the soubrette as a type was "maximally alien to Russian reality," it was difficult for Russian playwrights to do without her. The native *gornichnaia* had none of her skills – or duties. And thus, Vol'pert writes,

> for Russian writers of stage comedy in the first third of the century, the role of the female servant was rather complex. The comedic soubrette is an invention of the French stage, a purely national type. According to tradition she not only organizes the intrigue, but also, being an original sort of "psychologist and knower of the heart," she rules the feelings of her masters, is able on her own whim to "inflame" and "extinguish" love in their hearts.... the soubrette resorts to the vocabulary of comedic "psychology," and the "language mask" – the well-known "we" of the French soubrette (who appears to share with her mistress all her experiences) – becomes a source of the comic.[49]

Pushkin sensibly places his soubrette in Poland, where she belongs. But where, in scene 13, is the amatory intrigue, and where is this "we" of solidarity between mistress and maidservant? Pushkin's handling of such imported stereotypes is his final caprice in this triply comedic scene. Maryna's Rózia not only fails to secure the man for her mistress; her babble all but destroys their cautious courtship. While being dressed by her maid, Maryna hardly talks at all. This proud woman is not the sharing sort, and Rózia is comic precisely because she has no idea of the real desires that run the scene. Such inversions are appropriate, because Pushkin's Polish Act is an anti-love story, where the love object is indifferent and the lover sincere and therefore inept. The sassy soubrette is the conduit for rumors that, once tested in the Fountain scene, will persuade Dmitry to abandon love definitively for war.

Thus do these two omitted scenes, 6 and 13, supply Pushkin's play with two competing literary modalities: one Russian (a folk lament on the monastery as prison), the other markedly Western (chatter in the boudoir as a prelude to seduction). Both motivate the Pretender toward his glorious historical role. In the first, the *zloi chernets* responds to a complaint about *nevolia* [unfreedom] by prompting *volia* [will], wherever it might lead. "You will be tsar," he tells Grigory: but first you must wake up, leap out, and make your start over there. On Russian soil, as we learn in scene 12, even the best poets are despised as mere minstrels. In the omitted Polish scene, already "over there," the stock figures of French neoclassical comedy, amatory mistress and scheming maid, are parodied on several levels. Taken together with the episodes excised from scene 12, "Monastery Wall" and "Maryna's Dressing Room" deliver an ascetic message in this deeply unsentimental, politically astute play. Become whatever you want in that miraculous foreign land, but you must trust nothing, desire nothing, and keep moving. If you stop to take stock or insist on the truth, you will fail. If you succeed, however, you will take on the virtues of a comic hero, Pushkin's much-admired lighthearted "adventurer": the perfect listener who finds it easy to satisfy others because he needs so little for himself.

Excised Passages and Episodes

Fomichev draws our attention (chapter 4) to two segments of the *Komediia* that were cut from the 1831 edition: Ksenia's lament in verse that opens the terem scene (11, "The Tsar's Palace") and several excisions from the petitioners' dialogue surrounding the Pretender in the first Polish scene (12, "Cracow. Wiśniowiecki's House"). The disappearance of this initial lament (together with Ksenia's question to her brother: "Was the prince like his portrait?") weakens the folkloric image of the innocent widow-bride, set up in transparent opposition to the crafty Maryna in the Polish Act immediately to come. Over there, women manipulate and spurn; in Muscovy, the obedient bride does not see her betrothed. But even shorn of this lament, the opening of scene 11 (a dialogue between Ksenia and her nurse) remains a transcription of folk formulas on grief and how to deal with it. Whatever net loss there is in comic effect occurs chiefly through the potential such formulas have for self-parody. The excised lament is the sole stanzaic presentation of Ksenia's mourning; the exchange that follows between Ksenia and her *mamka*, while rhythmic and formulaic, is laid out in prose. In Pushkin as in Shakespeare, such switchings from verse to prose can have a comic and lowering effect – and Pushkin seemed to delight in lowering his stage conversations to prose precisely in those personages from whom prosaic expression is least expected (the Patriarch, for example, in his cameo appearance in scene 7). On such boundaries, the reader senses the edge between quoting, reciting, and spontaneous conversation.[50] As with the unusual octometric line in "Monastery Wall," a noticeably poetic formula brings an emotion to the surface by formally containing it, thereby distancing and gently mocking it.

More substantial to the plot are the cuts in the first Polish scene, "Cracow." Scene 12 opens on the Pretender welcoming to his side young Kurbsky, son of Ivan the Terrible's mortal enemy, and Sobański, a Polish nobleman. Catching sight of Russian dress, he then remarks: "these are men of ours" [*Eto nashi*] – Karela, a cossack, and Khrushchov, a defector from Moscow. Karela remains in the text, but most of Khrushchov's lines are cut. Dunning notes one likely reason: Khrushchov provides too honest an account of the groundswell of popular support for the Pretender ("… the people know / The Tsarevich has been saved. Your proclamation / Is widely read, and everyone expects you"), a fact of history that was unacceptable to the anti-Dmitry sentiments of Karamzin as well as to the reigning Romanov tsar, Nicholas I. Khrushchov also remarks on Boris's appalling cruelty, and on his failing health ("He's ill, can hardly drag himself about. / His end seems near."). The loss of Khrushchov's testimony has a two-pronged political effect. First, the inner politics of the scene is muffled, with less mention of the strong and potentially dangerous ties between Dmitry and the *narod*. Second, the outer politics that governed Pushkin's revisions in 1828–29 emerges more clearly. Without Khrushchov's preparatory comments, Boris's abrupt dying in scene 22 ("Moscow. The Tsar's Palace") comes as a shock. This unnatural and unexpected death takes on almost Karamzinian tones of moral predestination. At the peak of his reforming zeal, resolved to abolish *mestnichestvo* and modernize the Russian state, this forceful but anguished ruler, who might have been a Peter before his time, must pay for the crime of Uglich. Such enhanced resonance would be an appropriate tribute to the play's new dedicatee.

The second cut in scene 12, a brief stage aside between Gavrila Pushkin and Khrushchov, had to be deleted once the Russian defector disappeared from the scene. That exchange relates more to poetry than to history – but in fact these two realms are here boldly intertwined, which might have been one reason why Pushkin simply omitted the passage rather than redistribute its lines. The Pretender has graciously received some Latin verses from a Polish poet. While Dmitry is reading them, Khrushchov gestures to the poet and asks Pushkin: "Who's that?" On hearing the answer "A bard" [*piit*], Khrushchov fails to understand. Pushkin explains further: "In Russian – a scribbler of verse [*vershepisets*], or *minstrel* [*skomorokh*]." Some critics have found this ill-tempered remark by Pushkin's rebel ancestor on the status of poetry in Russia – a country without respect for its bards – too blatantly autobiographical and open to the charge of anachronism.[51] But the reference to *skomorokhi* and their minstrel art [*skomoroshestvo*], Russia's equivalent to medieval *Spielmänner* and *jongleurs,* rewards some examination of context.

Russian minstrels, extremely popular in the villages and towns, were considered bearers of paganism and thus routinely persecuted by the Orthodox Church, beginning in the late fifteenth century.[52] Some became itinerant brigands, others settled down into a professional caste, but two facts about them must have impressed Pushkin. First, there was a long history associating *skomorokhi* with the printed word (illuminated books often featured Slavic letters realized in the form of minstrels and jugglers, with their pliable, colorful, athletic bodies defying the monastic norm of a piety well-draped and immobile). Second, the comic irreverence of this caste came to represent uncontrolled laughter and unapproved merrymaking, musical as well as verbal. By the sixteenth century, such freethinking was formally criminalized; Maxim the Greek denounced the *skomorokhi* as tools of Satan, and those who enjoyed their company (or failed to denounce them) were liable to excommunication. With good reason did Likhachev and his fellow medievalists, populating their "world of laughter" with protest figures, raise to heroic status both *iurodstvo,* holy foolishness, and *skomoroshestvo.*

Why should we regret the loss of the image of "poet as *skomorokh*"? Although the reference might appear gratuitous in the "Cracow" setting, scene 12 is not the first time the presence of this persecuted folk profession is invoked. Fomichev has drawn our attention to Varlaam as *skomorokh* in chapter 4 of this book. In scene 9, "A Tavern on the Lithuanian Border," the tipsy Varlaam puts Grigory in his place with the proverb "a minstrel is no friend of a priest" [*skomorokh popu ne tovarishch*] – and, in an earlier proverb, Varlaam makes reference to a *gudok* and a *gusli,* the two stringed folk instruments most closely associated with *skomorosh-estvo* [the phrase is rendered by Antony Wood as "a rebeck or a rattle"]. Indeed, as J. Thomas Shaw has shown in his ingenious formal analysis of scene 9, the colorful utterances of the vagrant monk are less prose than they are a variety of spoken verse [*skazovyi stikh*], laden with the punning end-rhymes and dactylic rhythms characteristic of *skomorokh* speech.[53] Grigory is fully aware of the power of talking in *pogovorki* (popular sayings). He answers Varlaam's provocation about the *skomo-rokh* with a rhymed maxim of his own – "Drink your health, but watch yourself … See? I can do nice speaking too" – for here as at other moments in his career, Grigory's initial move to gain control over his situation is to assimilate others' speech patterns and turn them to his advantage (Shaw, 177). *Skomorokh*-talk, like a poet's talk, is an artificed code.

Such impious, unruly rhyming behavior was found offensive in the first censor's report of 1826. Varlaam's rogue completion of the proverb "Freedom for the free / and Paradise for the *drinker* [as opposed to *saved*]" was singled out for censure, with the comment that although the episode of the vagrant monks is found in Karamzin, "debauchery and drinking sprees ought not to be ennobled in poetry, especially as regards the calling of monks."[54] But is this comic duo really monastic? As we saw in the Evil Monk scene, a wide variety of persons and purposes can find refuge behind a "Monastery Wall." Varlaam's guiding appetites are wine, women, and song – especially wine – and there is a sense in which his entire behavior in the scene is an illicit performance, a play within a play, for which he expects to be compensated in donations of kopeks or drink. This performance is also a political diversion. Varlaam's most energetic rhyming, punning, and singing occur in the first half of the scene, where, as Shaw suggests, these *skomorokh*-like antics serve as a shield behind which Grigory discovers through the hostess "not only about the existence of the border control, but also how to escape across the border" (Shaw, 183). Varlaam is, of course, a profligate and a coward; as soon as the police enter the tavern and begin their interrogation, his extravagant minstrel-talk stops. His bawdy songs and rhymes switch to a lament about miserliness and hard times; by the end, oral rhymings recede as he mobilizes the minimal literacy at his disposal to save his life.

Important to remember about Varlaam is that his "spoken verse" is part of a continuum, which stretches from spontaneous prosaic conversation to embedded folk-sayings to *skomorokh* rhymings to actual folk-songs performed in real time on stage. We know that Pushkin researched carefully the song Varlaam was to sing in the Tavern scene. As with "Maryna's Dressing Room," this detail of Pushkin's play has been highlighted in the public mind through Musorgsky's boisterous setting in the opera ("Kak vo gorode bylo vo Kazani"). Unfortunately, Vladimir Stasov, who researched the matter for Musorgsky, identified the wrong song.[55] To understand the texture of Pushkin's scene, therefore, we must first forget Musorgsky's Varlaam. But we must also attend to the songs that Pushkin himself selected, for Varlaam sings a different text in 1831 from the one he sings in 1825. We now turn to Fomichev's fifth item, the song swap in the Tavern scene, to speculate on possible reasons and effects.

Varlaam's Song

Stage directions come with varying potential. It has long been debated, for example, whether the famous *narod bezmolvstvuet* of the 1831 text is meant to communicate as a line of print, read out loud or to oneself (a literary device appropriate to closet drama such as the "Little Tragedies"), or as a stage cue to be realized by the director. The musical stage direction has a somewhat different status than cues for other actions because its full realization requires a block of formally organized time. This can be the time of "background music," layered over (or under) the dramatic text, enhancing but not impeding its temporal flow. Or it can cue a pause in the dialogue and stage action, during which time a musical piece is actually performed. Sometimes the cue is "stylized," alluding to a performance but not putting the audience through it. Pushkin used several types of musical stage directions in his dramatic writings. In *The Stone Guest,* for example, the stage direction "She sings" is inserted so snugly into the middle of a line in scene 2 that the reader acknowledges Laura's performance of a song but otherwise doesn't miss a beat. In *Mozart and Salieri,* the directive for the blind musician's aria from *Don Giovanni* is worded in such a way that real time could be flexibly accommodated ("The fiddler plays an aria ... Mozart laughs"). But when Mozart, dying, asks Salieri to "listen to / My *Requiem,*" that musical event is outside of real time. The stage direction stipulates "He plays," but the entire composition is tucked into the space of a single line, at the end of which Salieri is already weeping in response to the cumulative effects of the music.

Varlaam's song in scene 9 is yet another sort of musical cue. It is texted music performed live on stage by a character whose words we know to be barbed and slyly shaped. The song begins only minutes into the scene, as soon as the hostess brings on wine. A stage direction specifies that "The monks drink; Varlaam strikes up a song: 'Ty prokhodish' dorogaia' i pr." ['You walk past my cell, my dear one', and so on.]. Several lines later, as per another stage cue – "'Gde nevolei dobryi molodets' i pr." ['Where a fine young lad, against his will,' and so on] – the already tipsy Varlaam delivers a second installment from the same song (its third line). He is, it would appear, drinking, singing, and talking all at the same time. The phrase "and so on" suggests that this sung story is ongoing on stage, a words-and-music performance on Varlaam's part for other characters – and for us. Since Pushkin goes to the trouble of providing, as stage cues at two different points, sequential lines from the same song, we might assume that he expected a stage director to incorporate the correct song into the production – and an attentive audience to recognize it as yet one more story circulating on stage. To realize properly Pushkin's intent, then, we must fill in the words of the song. What is Varlaam singing about?

Pushkin provided three different songs for Varlaam, one each for the manuscripts of 1825 and 1826 and a third for the printed text of 1831.[56] The 1826 substitution was a simple dance refrain, but the other two are folk narratives that speak in intriguing ways to the overall thematics of the play. Both belong to the widespread and irreverent category of "monkish" or "novice" song [monasheskaia-chernecheskaia pesnia]. By Pushkin's time, this song type had a firm plot skeleton and cast of characters.[57] One popular variant, sung to a round-dance or khorovod, opens on a monk, tonsured against his will, languishing in his cell; he either fantasizes a female visitor or "goes for a stroll" [zakhotelos' poguliati] to find one. The groups of women he sees en route are gradated in attractiveness: first old hags, then young wives, finally beautiful maidens – and as the temptation grows, the eager novice tosses back more (or all) of his cowl and monkish attire. Finally he throws his cassock on the ground ("Oh burn up, cell! Oh get lost, cassock! I've had it with saving myself!"). This is the plot of the song Varlaam sings in the 1831 text ("How it was in the town of Kazan'"), which Pushkin found in Novikov's Songbook of 1780. It recapitulates in caricature Grigory's career, from boredom behind the monastery wall through escape, a leap into freedom, and introduction to profane delights. While Grigory is whispering with the hostess about how to slip across the border, the drunken Varlaam is singing a variant of his biography, a song that ends with the gleeful novice's cry: "Isn't it time that a fine young lad like me got married, to one of these sweet pretty maids!"

With its exuberance and hint of liberation, this Kazan song suits well both Varlaam's sly, crude temperament and Grigory's restlessness in the Tavern scene. Its energy is pure comedy, moving from constraint to indulgence, celibacy to marriage. Pushkin left no record of the reasons why, for the 1831 edition, he replaced his original song with this boisterous substitute. Lidiia Lotman, in her 1996 commentary to *Boris Godunov*, suggests that the "motif of boredom and wild breaking-out [*motif skuki i zagula*]" in the 1831 song was more fitting to dissolute monk-tramps than the text Pushkin had originally chosen (BG 299–300). She reprints the original song, "Kak prokhodit dorogaia mimo kel'i" ["Whenever my dear one walks past my cell"], also found in Novikov's *Songbook*, noting that it had been composed by the well-known actor and theater personage F. G. Volkov and surmising that Pushkin, in his revisions, realized that this eighteenth-century songwriter could not be a vehicle for "the feelings of monks in the seventeenth century." In his 1993 edition of the *Komediia*, Fomichev also reprints the original song, although in a different version taken from Russia's first printed songbook, Mikhail Chulkov's collection of 1770–74.[58] Fomichev adds that this song was "probably also familiar to Pushkin in live performance." As one reason for its ultimate replacement he suggests that such a text was "impermissible at that time in print" – meaning, perhaps, that it was impermissible for a playwright even to allude to it in a stage direction. Since Pushkin provides only two early lines of this song as musical cues, and neither line accords precisely with either transcribed song variant, it is difficult to know which version of "Kak prokhodit mimo kel'i…" he had in mind. Both are more lyrical than the 1831 replacement. Both begin with an imprisoned monk, dreaming of a woman's caress. In both, the physical need for contact is urgent and explicit. But this clichéd opening scene then unfolds quite differently in each variant. The two denouements suggest alternative subtexts, each resonating with a larger theme in the *Komediia* – and perhaps in Pushkin's work as a whole.

In Fomichev's version, there is no liberation at the end, no casting away of the cowl. On the contrary, the temptress outside the cell becomes the monk's counselor, an intercessor who urges him toward reconciliation with his unfree fate. His text is as follows:

> Whenever my dear one walks past the cell,
> Past the cell where a poor novice is grieving,
> Where a fine fellow has been tonsured against his will,
> Where he is punished by his severe fate;
> He implores the beautiful maiden:
> Come, come to my cell, my beauty;
> Take off the kamelaukion from my head, my darling,
> And then take off my black cassock from me,
> Place your hands on my breast,
> Feel how my heart is trembling,
> Flushed with blood because of my rapid sighs,
> Look at my face covered with pallor
> All my life I've been shedding tears,
> Tormented over the joy of my past life;
> I beg forgiveness of my sins.
> Here I keep thinking about you, beautiful maidens.
> Touched by the elder's [starets's] words, the beautiful maiden
> Tried to calm the elder [starets] down, pleading with him to seek
>   salvation in his cell:
> Save yourself, you fine young fellow, in your cell,
> Forget this vain and frivolous life of ours.

What comes to mind in this strangely spiritualized song, which interweaves in reverie or hallucination the voices of a young monk, an elder monk [starets], and a young girl, is the image of Pimen in the Cell scene, a figure that moved and fascinated Pushkin as both a historical and literary type. The beautiful maiden's advice to the monk in this version of the 1825 song is, of course, Pimen's advice to Grigory, even though the plot of the play depends on Grigory finding that advice impossible to follow. And the song closes on that profoundly Pushkinian couple: a man tormented by his passions and an unapproachable, inaccessible beauty who counsels self-discipline and acceptance of fate.

The variant offered by Lidiia Lotman (the text she ascribes to the actor Volkov) is less mystifying, more secular, and linked directly to the problem of pretendership. The multiple identities and conflated ages of the trapped monk are explained as a perceptual error, a case of false identity. Can you not see who I really am? the young monk asks in despair. Do not my desires define me more clearly than my status or outer clothing? This text, unlike Fomichev's initial line but identical with Pushkin's stage direction, opens on a second-singular address. The song reads:

> You walk past my cell, my dear one,
> Past my cell, where a poor monk [*chernets*] is grieving,
> Where a fine fellow has been tonsured by force [*nasil'no*],
> Tell me, beautiful maiden, the whole truth,
> Have people gone completely blind,
> Why do they all call me elder [*starets*]?
> Take off the kamelaukion from my head, my darling,
> Take off from me, sweetie, my black cassock too,
> Feel how my heart is trembling,
> Flushed with blood because of my rapid sighs,
> Wipe the bitter tears from my rosy face,
> And once you've had a look at me, tell me, do I really resemble an elder
>   [*starets*],
> As a novice [*chernets*] I am sighing over you,
> All awash in bitter tears
> I am not pleading [with God for] forgiveness of my sins
> But pleading [with Him] that you will love my heart.

In both variants, love is unrequited. In both, the message is more somber than the reckless tale of liberation and lechery sung by Varlaam in 1831. Both variants of the original song are applicable to aspects of the Pretender's highly poetic life. The False Dmitry is no "fine young fellow" whose free, post-monastery future lies in marrying a "sweet pretty maid"; he will live out his dream, in which he climbs high, triumphs for a time, and is laughed down by the people on the public square. We are reminded of Douglas Clayton's remark that Russian comedies are problem comedies, serious and dark.[59] As such, they address the destinies of an environment, not just individual happiness. The tragicomedic in Pushkin's historical *Komediia* recalls a Divine Comedy of false quests and sought-after self-knowledge. In the fine details of the 1825 original, we glimpse the personified vices and virtues of a didactic school-drama *komidiia* as well as all the vastness implied by those various mock-medieval titles, which emphasize a domain and a disaster rather than a successful historical agent or a Romantic hero.

Reversed Order of Scenes in the Rush toward the End:
The People's Cheer, AMEN.

Pushkin's policy toward scenes, as toward stage directions, has long intrigued scholars. Early drafts were organized into parts and acts, but this framework was gradually abandoned. The fullest version of the play is a sequence of twenty-six unnumbered scenes, labeled according to place and occasionally, as in chronicle entries, by date. Each episode is complete in itself, but there is no real sense of a "curtain" between scenes. Episodes flow one into the other – which blurs them as bounded events and alerts us to the importance of historical clusters.

The ordering of the final third of the play apparently gave Pushkin some trouble.[60] In his list of changes, Fomichev notes as his sixth item the fact that scene 18 (the Holy Fool in front of St. Basil's) and 19 (the multi-lingual scene between Margeret and Rosen on the Plain near Novgorod-Seversky) switch places in the printed text. Dunning, in his chapter 3, has called this reversal confusing and without sense. It breaks up a cluster of three battle scenes disastrously unpropitious for the Pretender, diluting a career arc that begins with comic mercenaries during a rout (scene 19), moves through a comic prisoner-of-war interrogation (scene 20), and ends with total defeat, a comic and child-like default to Providence in the episode with the dying horse (scene 21). This triad of military follies does not distress the Pretender. Nor does it obstruct his victory. Resolving to fight afresh the next day, the False Dmitry falls back into the sleep from which he had emerged in Pimen's cell – and that is the last we see of him in the play.

Boris likewise has the trajectory of his fate "severed" by this switching of the scenes, but his weakness is too much consciousness, not too little. Among the more remarkable achievements of Pushkin as historian is his realization – attested to through numerous details in his play, usually in discussions between Tsar Boris, Shuisky, Basmanov – that Boris, while indeed a cruel and even Machiavellian ruler, acted as he did not out of maliciousness alone or desire for power, but simply so that the state could survive. The tragedy that Pushkin sensed (confirmed by recent historical research) was a geopolitical one, the tragedy of Russia's un-workable fiscal-military state.[61] In the *Komediia*, this larger disaster is embedded partly in the title, partly in the political clusters that dominate in the second half of the play. One such cluster especially marks Boris as trapped. In the original order of scenes, the confrontation with Nikolka the Iron Cap in front of St. Basil's follows immediately upon the Patri-arch's tale of miracles in Uglich (scene 17, "The Tsar's Council"): two suc-cessive humiliations by the most exalted and then the most humble members of the Orthodox hierarchy. Performed back to back, these episodes inevitably suggest a comic or even carnival doubling, just as the crowned Tsar Boris and Nikolka the Iron Cap are doubles. If the Pre-tender is undeterred by his defeats, forgets everything and falls asleep, then Boris can forget nothing – and he replicates his guilt at every step.

Boris disintegrates, condemned by deeds and rumors of deeds, and the Pretender rises on rumor's wave: the final scenes of the 1825 play celebrate the logic of this comedic development. Pushkin's play features the people as interesting and vibrant. That Pushkin could do so with integrity was in part due to the fact that a "pretender play" based on Russian history had more options than its Shakespearean or Schillerian counterpart. If the West had heresies, then Russia had pretenders – and they were not of the conniving royal court but of the people, acting in its name and arousing its passionate support.[62] It is for this reason that our study has set itself against the almost universal opinion that the *narod* on the square, ordered to shout "Long live Dimitry Ivanovich," does so in a cowardly or traumatized state. The populace is indeed shocked at the murder of the royal family. But it shouts its support all the same – since in fact the people are pleased to be rid of the tyrant Tsar Boris and his reign of terror, and have little reason to doubt the promises of this returning tsarevich. History, properly portrayed in historical drama, cannot be cut up into scenes or acts and then revisited from some later, arbitrary point in time. It stops in its own present.

In light of the above, how might we best understand *Konets komidii*, the end of the comedy? As Pushkin's wry verdict that history – especially Russian history – is farce, as that phrase in Italian so often suggests? As affectionate tribute to the worldview behind chronicles and school dra-mas, which saw human events as out of our control, but that persevered in art forms designed to instruct and console? Or as the drama of all Christian comedy, which Gavrila Pushkin comes to realize while wishing the Tsarevich "pleasant dreams" in the forest of his defeat: every day is sufficient unto its own evil, therefore worry not, and trust in Providence? There is no tradition of producing Pushkin's play in the comedic mode throughout – that is, without the portentous, tragically-inflected *narod bezmolvstvuet* and with some attempt to reflect the "Amen" at the end. One could argue, as we did in the Introduction to this study, that Musorgsky respected just such comic potential in the newly-composed mass scene for his revised *Boris Godunov*, the jubilant "Forest near Kromy." But even there, a tragicomedic note is sounded at the final moment: the stage clears and the Holy Fool enters alone, singing his thinly-orchestrated, prophetic lament. Had Pushkin completed his trilogy, we might have seen the people's impulses toward freedom, as well as our necessary submission to destiny, at last brought under a single structure.

Notes

1. Pushkin's relationship with the world of the imperial theaters is discussed by Zagorskii, *Pushkin i teatr*, chs. 2–5 (quote from page 47); unfortunately, his treatment of *Boris Godunov* (ch. 5) conflates the 1825 and 1831 versions and concentrates largely on the villainies of censorship and of Nicholas I. In its tone and political pieties, Zagorskii's book is a thoroughly Stalin-era study, but is valuable in its principled avoidance of stuffiness or reverence toward its subject. In fact, Zagorskii attacks "bourgeois Pushkinists" who insist on lacquering the image of the poet, citing copiously in his support from correspondence and memoirs (39–48) on Pushkin's rude, loud-mouthed behavior in theater halls. A similar portrait is drawn by T. J. Binyon in his *Pushkin: A Biography*, chs. 3–5, esp. pages 71–82.

2. S. Fomichev, "Dramaturgiia A. S. Pushkina," ch. 8 in *Istoriia russkoi dramaturgii (XVII – pervaia polovina XIX veka)*: 261–95, esp. 261.

3. This preface, dated 30 January 1829, was a revision of a letter to N. N. Raevsky written in July 1825. See Wolff, *Pushkin*, 245–47, esp. 246.

4. Survivors and manipulators need time. It was this realization, perhaps, that later in the century prompted A. K. Tolstoi, mimicking Pushkin's unrealized design but setting it one generation earlier, to structure his "large dramatic poem" of post–Ivan the Terrible history plays (1866–70) as a trilogy. For this later playwright, of course, Boris Godunov is the shady Shuisky figure, the force behind the throne in the first two plays (*The Death of Ivan the Terrible* and *Feodor Ioannovich*). Unlike both the historical and the Pushkinian Shuisky, however, Tolstoi's Boris, before becoming tsar, is earnest, rational, enlightened, a man who at every step strives to undo those cruel epithets about himself spoken by Shuisky in the first scene of Pushkin's play.

5. Vinokur, *Kommentarii*, parts 4, 5, and 6 (199–248). Vinokur concentrates on unwelcome censorship pressure, but, in keeping with the mainstream Soviet line, concludes that most of the changes Pushkin made were artistic improvements.

6. On this question of Pushkin's sources, Zagorskii provides a good contrast with the best book written on Russian drama in English, Simon Karlinsky's *Russian Drama from Its Beginnings to the Age of Pushkin*. Karlinsky's task is to combat the widespread prejudice that Russian literature began with Pushkin and that the eighteenth century was mere imitation; he thus emphasizes the richness of Russian theatrical life and the importance for Pushkin, in his narrative poems as well as in his works for the stage, of prior dramatic models (prose and verse comedy, tragedy, vaudeville). Understandably, Karlinsky does not much like *Boris Godunov*, to which he devotes only two pages (322–23); citing with approval both Mirsky and Nabokov, he considers it "on many levels an unsatisfactory play" (323). Karlinsky's dislike of the play lends additional credence to his excellent study, which celebrates the force and fertility of a dramatic tradition that Pushkin – while deeply engaged with it – was boldly trying to break.

7. See J. Douglas Clayton, *Dimitry's Shade: A Reading of Alexander Pushkin's "Boris Godunov,"* 33–37, esp. 36. Although the polemical Preface to *Cromwell* impressed Pushkin, Hugo's actual play did not, and Pushkin resented any comparison between the "absurdities" in that historical drama and his own *Boris Godunov* (see Pushkin's letter to Pletnev, 7 January 1831, and his 1836 essay reviewing Chateaubriand's translation of *Paradise Lost* (Wolff, *Pushkin*, 301; 453–57). Further page references to Clayton in the text.

8. For a succinct discussion free of Soviet-era clichés, see Janko Lavrin, *Pushkin and Russian Literature*, ch. 7, "Pushkin and Shakespeare," 140–60.

9. The epigraph is from Katenin in a letter dated 1 February 1836 to an unknown addressee, most likely V. Karatygin, cited in Zagorskii, *Pushkin i teatr*, 96. Pushkin thought highly of Katenin's judgment and was saddened by his verdict (see Wolff, *Pushkin*, 302).

10. From a passage destined for a preface, 1829–30. See Wolff, *Pushkin*, 247, but NB, for our purposes, her mistranslation in the sentence that follows "Ne smushchaemym nikakim svetskim vliianiem, Sheksp. ia podrazhal …" is translated by Wolff as "Untouched by any other influence I imitated Shakespeare …" The correct rendering of this phrase, an idea given several variant expressions in Pushkin's drafts (PS, 11: 140 and 385), is: "Not distracted by the influence of high [i.e., salon or court] society, I imitated Shakespeare …" Pushkin's reference, it would appear, is to his enforced isolation from St. Petersburg society at Mikhailovskoe, not his isolation from other or earlier influences on his play.

11. Two recent works in English provide excellent summaries and extensions of the best Russian scholarship: Catherine O'Neil, *With Shakespeare's Eyes: Pushkin's Creative Appropriation of Shakespeare*, esp. ch. 2, "Ghostly Fathers and Unthrifty Sons: Shakespeare and *Boris Godunov*"; and also Clayton, *Dimitry's Shade*, ch. 2, "Boris Godunov and the Theater," 30–53.

12. See S. Bondi, "Dramaturgiia Pushkina i russkaia dramaturgiia XIX veka," in *Pushkin: Rodonachal'nik novoi russkoi literatury*, 365–436, esp. 381.

13. See Zagorskii, *Pushkin i teatr*, 128. V. A. Rozov argues against; M. P. Alekseev argues for Pushkin's knowledge of Schiller's *Demetrius*.

14. On this topic see Irena Ronen, *Smyslovoi stroi tragedii Pushkina "Boris Godunov,"* ch. 5, "The Romantic Hero and the Traditions of Ancient Tragedy."

15. "Iz materialov Pushkinskogo Litseia," 325–26. I thank Igor Nemirovskii for this reference, and for his reasoned judgment on the Lycée curriculum.

16. Letter from Pushkin in Mikhailovskoe to Pavel Katenin, first half of September 1825. It was not Sophia but her sister Natalia who wrote plays; the play Pushkin had in mind was "A Comedy about St. Catherine." See Wolff, *Pushkin*, 253, 293.

17. "Notes on popular drama and on M. P. Pogodin's *Martha, the Governor's Wife*" [1830], in Wolff, *Pushkin*, 263–69.

18. See the excellent discussion by Feliks Raskol'nikov, "'Marfa Posadnitsa' M. Pogodina i istoricheskie vzgliady Pushkina," 3–15. Although Pushkin lauds the attempt at a popular tragedy, he gently reproaches Pogodin for presenting Ivan III as a stage villain with no redeeming features (repentance, a bad conscience, cruelty out of state necessity) – much the same argument that Pushkin makes against Tacitus's image of Tiberius.

19. Here Pushkin was correct: official Russian theater-going had a punitive aura to it. The first theater performances in the 1670s lasted up to ten hours without interruption. Early audiences for Peter the Great's state-sponsored German theater in the Kremlin had to be bribed to turn up. Catherine the Great made theater attendance compulsory for courtiers and visiting foreigners. In fact, it was not until the 1860s that Russian monarchs ceased requiring their subjects to attend a play (and arguably, Stalin revived the practice in the 1930s). See Karlinsky, *Russian Drama*, 47 ("[The company of Johann Kunst imported from Danzig] was the most unmitigated disaster in the history of Russian theater") and 63 (on Catherine I's punitive sentencing of courtiers to nine days of theatrical attendance). Also see A. N. Robinson, "Pervyi russkii teatr kak iavlenie evropeiskoi kul'tury," in his *Novye cherty v russkoi literature i iskusstve (XVII-nachalo XVIII v.)*: 8–27, esp. 11–13.

20. The phrase *vol'nost' mistirii* occurs in an early plan for the Pogodin article (see PS, 11: 419) and is reattached to the opening of the essay in Wolff, *Pushkin*, 263. On the possible influence of *vertep* (puppet shows of the Nativity) on *Boris,* see Popova, "Boris Godunov," 67–71.

21. Although Pushkin eventually settled on spelling the name "Godunov" consistently and correctly, the spelling "Gudunov" (and at times "Gudonov") in the two earliest manuscripts was part of a series of orthographical caprices. Vinokur, unsure whether this was a slip of the pen or a deliberate variant, remarked: "*Gudun* sounds more oriental." See Vinokur, *Kommentarii*, 198.

22. As Dunning suggests in chapter 2, it is one of literary history's ironies that Pushkin might have derived the idea for his title from an 1824 essay in *Ruskaia Taliia* by Nikolai Grech, "An historical survey of Russian theater before the beginning of the 19th century," which served also as the source for Bulgarin's Censor's Report, communicated to Pushkin by Count Benckendorff. The Grech essay mentions medieval dramas with identical formulas to the one Pushkin chose (i.e., "Comedy … in which the first person [komediia … v nei zhe pervaia persona]"). See Bulgarin, *Ruskaia Taliia*, 1–36.

23. See Mark J. Pomar, "The Roots of Russian Historical Drama: School Drama

and Ceremonial Spectacles," 113–24; see also the introductory discussion in Karlinsky, *Russian Drama*, 7–11.

24. Consider the opening paragraph of the Introduction to the famous "Zagreb collection" of five Russian school dramas, discovered in that Croatian city in 1921/22: "Old Russia knew neither theater nor dramaturgy. Popular oral drama and the performances of minstrels held sway in Russia at the time when in other countries, medieval mysteries and morality plays had long been snuffed out by the dramaturgy of the humanists and by school drama, and later by the plays of Shakespeare, Lope de Vega, Racine and Molière." I. M. Badalich and V. D. Kuz'mina, *Pamiatniki russkoi shkol'noi dramy XVIII veka (po zagrebskim spiskam)*, 3. Further generalizations on the genre are taken from the editors' discussion of these five dramas.

25. For an overview in English, see Karlinsky, *Russian Drama*, 24–29.

26. For two essays that address the vigor and unexpectedness of the low-born comic characters in school drama (shepherds, pagan priests, townsfolk), see A. S. Eleonskaia, "Komicheskoe v shkol'nykh p'esakh kontsa XVII-nachala XVIII v.," and A. S. Demin, "Teatr v khudozhestvennoi zhizni Rossii XVII v.," both in Robinson, ed., *Novye cherty v russkoi literature i iskusstve (XVII-nachalo XVIII v.)*: 73–87 and 28–61, esp. 37–38. Both essays are somewhat under the sway of the fashionable Likhachev-Bakhtin carnival thesis, but lose neither sobriety nor documentary rigor.

27. See Marcia Morris, "Feofan Prokopovich's *Vladimir* as a Vehicle for the Comic View of History in Early East-Slavonic Drama," 1–15.

28. For insight into the different resonances of *komediia* and *komidiia* (and for other discussions on the subtler points of Pushkin's two versions), I am indebted to my colleague Ksana Blank of Princeton University.

29. This point is made by Douglas Clayton in his *Dimitry's Shade*, 32: "Russian comedies, however, tend to be very different from the accepted Western pattern [i.e., two young lovers pitted against an older male figure who obstructs their union] ... Russian playwrights deliberately subvert the pattern by having the action not end with the marriage of the young couple." Among the masters in this "subversive" mode Clayton mentions Griboedov, Gogol, Turgenev, and Chekhov.

30. "Nabroski stat'i o russkoi literature" [1830], in PS, 11, 184. Translation in Wolff, *Pushkin*, 272 (adjusted). Pushkin then adds: "But unfortunately, we have no ancient literature. Only a dark steppe – and a single monument rises up on it: *The Lay of the Host of Igor.*"

31. Pushkin neither supervised the publication of his play nor read the galley proofs; wearied with two rejections, he had turned this task over to Zhukovsky and Pletnev before taking off for Arzrum. See Vinokur, *Kommentarii*, 239. Vinokur provides a history of the two manuscript variants (1825 and 1826) in "6. Pechatnyi tekst i osnovnaia redaktsiia tragediia" (235–48), with some modest speculation (not always persuasive) on Pushkin's motivations. Vinokur attributes to Zhukovsky changes that were more likely entered by cruder hands. Further page references to this section of Vinokur's discussion are included in the text.

32. This 1826 censor's report, first published in 1889, is reproduced in Vinokur,

Kommentarii, 212–16. The objection to scene 3 was the fourth in a list of six problem spots in the play. At the time, such a mild and modest intervention was perceived (by Viazemsky and others) as good fortune for the poet and a sign of royal favor (217). Further page references in the text.

33. Sergei Fomichev, "Neizvestnaia p'esa A. S. Pushkina," 236–49, esp. 246–47.

34. For more on demonic border-crossings in this play, see Ute Scholz, "Die Faszination des Bösen: Mythologische Teufelsanspielungen in Puškins 'Boris Godunov,'" 275–86, esp. 276–78.

35. "Grigory's song" – for the opening does resemble a folk song, albeit oddly transcribed – generated scholarly quarrels as early as the 1850s. "The metrical form of this excerpt, written in trochaic octometer, is unusual for tragedy, a point that has attracted the attention of A. I. Beletskii, but this metrical aspect of Grigory's song had long ago provoked a scholarly debate between Tikhonravov and Shevyrev. To approximate the structure of folk songs, it would be better to adopt the suggestion, proposed by the former [Tikhonravov], of dividing each verse line into two parts." See B. V. Varneke, "Istochniki i zamysel 'Borisa Godunova,'" 12–19, esp. 14, n. 2.

36. Varneke (n. 33) floats this hypothesis, but then utilizes it as a justification for Pushkin's eventual excision of the scene. Varneke argues that Pushkin's innate sense of his own native history "saved him from the temptation" to insert this link to Faust (Pushkin read the scene to Shevyrev, who, Varneke surmises, must also have recommended its omission); even Pushkin's genius could not succeed at "approximating Dmitry to the broad image of Faust." So the omitted scene "retains a purely historical significance," as "superfluous evidence of Goethe's influence on the original plan [*pervonachal'nyi zamysel*] of the tragedy" (14–15). From the perspective of the present study, much is dissatisfying about Varneke's mode of argument. The 1825 text was not the "original plan" but a finished play; it was still primarily a comedy rather than a tragedy and thus welcomed incongruous genres and reminiscences; and finally, there were, of course, native Russian variants of the Faust tale (*Savva Grudtsyn* and others), which must have intrigued Pushkin, with his intense curiosity about Russian assimilation of West European forms.

37. The great Polish poet Mickiewicz heard Pushkin read the play aloud at Lavalle's salon in St. Petersburg on 21 May 1828; presumably he advised Pushkin soon after. See Vinokur, *Kommentarii*, 224.

38. Pushkin did not live to see a second edition. Baron Rozen's full translation was not published, but this one scene did appear, at the end of Rozen's review essay on *Boris* that appeared in *Dorpater Jahrbücher*, preceded by this commentary: "In conclusion we wish to remark on one scene, which the author excluded at the advice of the Polish poet Mickiewicz and our own late Delvig, since in their opinion this scene weakened the impression made by Pimen's story. The writer of these lines holds to a completely different view, and considers that with the exclusion of this scene, the transition from that story to Otrepiev's flight is too abrupt ... Since the author intends to restore this scene in the second edition, he has permitted us to acquaint German readers with it in advance." (See G. Rosen, "Boris Godunov,"

257–58.). Upon hearing that Rozen had written an essay on his play, Pushkin revived his hopes of writing a preface – a theatrical manifesto – in response to it, much as he had cast his earlier draft prefaces as communications to Nikolai Raevsky. "I am thinking of writing a letter to you for the second edition, if you are willing, and setting forth in it my ideas and rules by which I was guided in composing my tragedy." See Pushkin's letter to Baron Rozen, October–first half of November 1831, in *Letters*, 534.

39. In his *Pushkin i teatr* (1940), Zagorskii, following the leads in Karamzin, interprets the "evil monk" in a thoroughly political fashion, as an agent of secular power – most likely the "offended princelings" who groomed Otrepiev for the throne. In his view, the scene contradicts Pushkin's larger plan for the tragedy, which was to develop not by "the will of individual persons but by the course of history." Thus the demonic subtext is tucked more subtly into Grigory's dream in the Cell scene, and scene 6 was omitted, which would have "led the spectator on to another plane, where it was unclear in whose interests the *chernets* was sent" (123).

40. A. Fevral'skii, "Prokofiev and Meierkhol'd," 94–120, esp. 109–20.

41. Ronen, *Smyslovoi stroi tragedii Pushkina 'Boris Godunov,'* ch. 2, "Kul'turno-geograficheskie antinomii: Rossiia i Pol'sha," 46–49. Further page references in the text.

42. I thank Chester Dunning for these details of Solovki during the sixteenth century. See also Roy R. Robson, *Solovki: The Story of Russia Told through Its Most Remarkable Islands* (Yale University Press, 2004), 153.

43. Both variants can be read profitably in counterpoint with the Pimen-Grigory "drama of generations," a theme dear to Pushkin: Pimen, after a boisterous life, rests in his "prison/retreat," grateful for a chance to write and to pray; Grigory, stalled at the beginning of his life, has no such patience.

44. See Dunning, "Rethinking the Canonical Text of Pushkin's *Boris Godunov*," 569–91, esp. 580–81; also Dunning, "Who Was Tsar Dmitrii?" 705–29, esp. 716–18.

45. PS, 7: 269–70.

46. See O'Neil, *Through Shakespeare's Eyes,* ch. 1, esp. section "The *Narod* and *Samozvanchestvo* (Pretenderhood) in Pushkin and Shakespeare," 62–66. O'Neil locates the bridge between Pushkin's *narod* and Shakespeare's history plays in the pretender Grigory, who knows how to "ride" the people like a horse – and also how to sympathize with its sufferings (56–60).

47. See J. Thomas Shaw, *Pushkin's Poetics of the Unexpected. The Nonrhymed Lines in the Rhymed Poetry and the Rhymed Lines in the Nonrhymed Poetry,* ch. 5, "Dramas: Boris Godunov: (2) Romeo and Juliet and 'Mniszek's Sonnet'," 191–219. Uniquely among Pushkin scholars, Shaw has examined "local color" as registered metrically and lexically in the "Western-Shakespearean" and "native-folkloric" segments of the play, attending especially to the embedded sonnet and abundant rhyme pairs of the Polish scenes, and to the *skazovyi stikh* or rhymed spoken verse of Varlaam in the Tavern scene. Working with the 1831 text, Shaw deals with three Polish scenes only – but Rózia's rhymed chatter fully reinforces his thesis.

48. Karlinsky, *Russian Drama*, 330–31.

49. Vol'pert, "Pushkin i frantsuzskaia komediia XVIII v.," 177.

50. L. S. Sidiakov, "Stikhi i proza v tekstakh Pushkina," 4–31, esp. 11–18 (on *Boris Godunov*). Sidiakov holds that Pushkin's switchings between verse and prose are often prepared for by intermediate steps, with calculated comic effects when lofty content is expressed in prose. In discussing Ksenia's lament, Sidiakov remarks: "In the first redaction of the tragedy [i.e., 1825], this scene opened with verse that imitates a text of folk poetry; thus, its beginning contrasted to the end of the preceding scene simultaneously with the switch of meter (trochaic trimeter) and subsequently, a transition to prose" (16, n. 21). Technically speaking, the passage is in trochaic dimeter with dactylic cadences (a standard means of folk stylization), but Sidiakov's general point holds nonetheless.

51. See Ronen, *Smyslovoi stroi*, 55: "Pushkin probably omitted this dialogue as an overly cutting and almost parodic expression of the role of a poet in contemporary society."

52. The best account in English remains Russell Zguta, *Russian Minstrels: A History of the Skomorokhi*, from which this general information is drawn (26–61).

53. See Shaw, *Pushkin's Poetics of the Unexpected*, ch. 4, "Dramas: Boris Godunov: (1) Varlaam's Rhymes in a 'Prose' Context," 175–90, esp. 176–84. Further page references in the text are to Shaw.

54. Quotation from Vinokur, *Kommentarii*, 214. In his notes, Shaw provides more details on Pushkin's sources for Varlaam's racy talk (the irreverent and unruly monks of nearby Sviatogorsky Monastery, and other anecdotes); see Shaw, *Pushkin's Poetics*, 312–13.

55. The epic Siege of Kazan song that Varlaam sings in the opera, while a brilliant piece of musical dramaturgy, is wholly inappropriate for these lecherous and drunken monastic tramps. For the relevant texts and sources in the folksong anthologies of the time, see Richard Taruskin, "Appendix: Folk Texts in *Boris Godunov*," in his *Musorgsky: Eight Essays and an Epilogue*, 291–99, esp. 291–93.

56. See Lidiia Lotman's commentary to Varlaam's song in "Notes to Pushkin's *Comedy*" in this book and BG, 299–301. Here as elsewhere in this study, I am indebted to Ksana Blank for her translations, intuitions, and insights about these multiple versions.

57. See the discussion and text (unfortunately, only of the 1831 replacement song, "Kak vo gorode, bylo vo Kazani") by V. Chernyshev, "Pesnia Varlaama," 127–29, and Nikolai Vinogradov's adjustment to this note a year later, "Eshche o pesne Varlaama (Popravka k zametke g. V. Chernysheva)," 65–67. N. Vinogradov corrects Chernyshev in his assumption that these rakish songs were not available in print; he finds seven variants of the Kazan' song in Sobolevskii's collection.

58. Fomichev, "Neizvestnaia p'esa A. S. Pushkina," 248–49. As his source in that essay, Fomichev notes only "sbornik Chulkova," but later confirmed the best citation for Varlaam's song in the fuller collection: *Novoe i polnoe sobranie rossiiskikh pesen, soderzhashchee v sebe pesni liubovnye, pastusheskie, shutlivye, prostonarodnye, kho-*

ral'nye, svadebnye, sviatochnye, s prisovokupleniem pesen iz raznykh rossiiskikh oper i komedii (Moscow: Universitetskaia tipografiia N. Novikova, 1780), Chast' 4, 133–34 (N 149).

59. Clayton, *Dimitry's Shade*, 32.

60. See S. Fomichev, "Tvorcheskaia istoriia p'esy," in BG, 123–34.

61. See RFCW, esp. chs. 1–3.

62. See N. Eidel'man, "Lzhe …", in his *Iz potaennoi istorii Rossii XVIII-XIX vekov*, 201–13, esp. 202–3.

Concluding Remarks

Boris Godunov and the Russian Literary Canon

∿ CARYL EMERSON AND CHESTER DUNNING

In the preceding chapters, we put forth a case for the 1825 *Komediia* as the canonical text of *Boris Godunov*. Our primary motivation has been respect for what we believe to be Pushkin's intent. But there is also our judgment that the original text is a better, more effective, historically more accurate play. Since the "canonical" *Boris* coalesced carelessly, inconsistently, and for political reasons during half a century, its status is suspect. What is at stake in these recuperation efforts? Are they worth it?

In closing this study, let us try briefly to address these questions. Canon formation in any country is a delicate process, dependent in part upon the inherent excellencies of a text, in part upon institutional support for it, and in part upon simple inertia. The Russian literary canon has reflected additional burdens. In the modern period it has known several levels of censorship (political, ecclesiastic, theatrical, self-); a heroic, salvational role for literature in the quest for national identity and authenticity; and the assumption (not wholly unfounded) that the greatest nineteenth-century writers tended to be dissidents or rebels. That paradigm was flipped only at the end of the century, when the state dropped its official hostility and suspicion toward writers and began to recruit them – indeed, to canonize them, in the strong sense of the word – as secular saints.[1]

Canons are agonistic. There is exclusivity and struggle built into them. As Frank Kermode wrote several decades ago, discussing institutional controls on interpretation through a "canonical" exemplar, the Catholic Church: "The desire to have a canon, more or less unchanging, and to protect it against charges of inauthenticity or low value (as the Church protected Hebrews, for example, against Luther) is an aspect of the necessary conservatism of a learned institution."[2] Institutions of literary study – academies with their tenuring procedures, scholarly journals, lay readerships – cannot, of course, discipline or punish with anything resembling ecclesiastical rigor. But even in the weaker and looser secular fields, Kermode points out, command of the canon creates a sense of guild competence, certifying us in ways we are loathe to put in question. Thus the literary canon is formed (and reformed) in the process of resisting "attacks upon it" (178). The "total license in regard to the canon" (Kermode's phrase), such as currently reigns in American literary studies, is an event of recent vintage, and one that would not have been tolerated under Russia's two previous Old Regimes.

There is, in addition, the centrality of Pushkin, not only to the Russian literary canon but to Russian literary consciousness. In a tradition so compact, so self-referential and reverent, texts quickly become icons. Even tiny parts of texts – such as the stage direction, *narod bezmolvstvuet* – can accumulate around themselves whole minor industries, passionate debates about the nature of ethical responsibility or historical truth. Our purpose in this study has not been to dislodge (even were it possible) the 1831 text, canonized in the Jubilee Edition of the Soviet era, together with its rich reception tradition. We have aimed, more modestly, to restore the original *Komediia* to a status more serious than the "minor initial variant" of a play that was published by its author six years after its composition. Optimally, the play could have two canonical versions. Both versions are masterpieces (although we argue that the one less assaulted by outside forces is the more masterful). Both are biographically as well as artistically significant. But this significance attaches to different junctures in Pushkin's brief, driven life.

The 1825 text, recited to fellow poets, confirmed Pushkin in his own eyes as politically daring, a rebel, and an outsider. He intended to tone down some of its indecently vigorous language in his refinements for print. The two subsequent plays in the dreamt-of trilogy would lead Russian theater-goers where no historical dramatist had yet taken them – to the glories of Empire and Romanov splendor, but without sentimentalizing the characters or concealing the costs. The 1831 text was produced as a result of other pressures and directed at other goals. The angry poet had aged. His favorite drama was now to be a weapon, the golden key to make him acceptable, more of an insider. This desire to serve his country, to edge out his unscrupulous competitors, to support his future family, and thus to adjust his text to political reality so that his own larger gifts might prosper should not, we feel, be branded as some shameful act of betrayal. Such morally burdened terms began to be widely applied to Russian writers only in the second half of the nineteenth century, when the canon of literary criticism came to be controlled by an intelligentsia deeply alien to Pushkin in most of its priorities and commitments.[3]

When there is a choice between a text the author wants to see in print and a text that the author – at the end of his rope and obliged to move on to other matters – "puts through to print," it would seem prudent to choose the less impeded variant. The *Komediia* deserves a better fate than it has so far enjoyed. Two hundred years after Pushkin's birth, and four hundred years after the triumphant entry into Moscow by the Pretender's troops (1605), it is time to put this daring play on stage as the brilliant young poet-historian originally intended. Alone in Mikhailovskoe in November 1825, Pushkin (as we know from a letter to Peter Viazemsky) clapped his hands with glee over the pleasure of bringing his Boris tale to completion. In a letter written several days later to Alexander Bestuzhev, Pushkin repeated his delight – "but it's terrifying to publish it."[4] If it was terrifying at the end of November 1825, how much more so for the poet one month later, after the uprising on Senate Square. A series of historical accidents with political consequences changed the life of the poet and the life of his play. The time has come to set this accident right.

Notes

1. See Jeffrey Brooks, "Russian Nationalism and Russian Literature: The Canonization of the Classics," 315–34. On Pushkin's role, see esp. 322–23.

2. Frank Kermode, "Institutional Control of Interpretation," ch. 8 in his *The Art of Telling*: 168–84, esp. 173. We thank William Mills Todd for bringing this and the Brooks essay to our attention.

3. The best brief text on Pushkin's posthumous relationship to the second half of his century remains D. S. Mirsky's classic essay "Pushkin," originally published in *The Slavonic Review*, II, No. 4, 1923, repr. in G. S. Smith, ed., *D. S. Mirsky: Uncollected*

Writings on Russian Literature (Berkeley, CA: Berkeley Slavic Specialties, col. 13, 1989): 118–31.

4. Pushkin to Viazemsky, about November 7, 1825, from Mikhailovskoe to Moscow, in *Letters,* 261; Pushkin to Bestuzhev, November 30, 1825, from Mikhailovskoe to Petersburg, in *Letters,* 264.

Comedy about Tsar Boris and Grishka Otrepiev

Translator's Preface

⌇ ANTONY WOOD

This translation is designed to be read aloud. I have aimed at discreetly modern diction and idiom, not too pointedly of the present day, and avoided archaisms except in the language of ecclesiastics. I see Pushkin's project as an exercise in realism. This seems to have been the impact made on those who heard his first readings of the *Komediia* in September and October 1826.[1] A wide variety of voices is heard in Pushkin's text – boyars and courtiers, the people, ecclesiastics high and low, military commanders and common soldiery, members of the tsar's family, regional supporters of the Pretender, a number of Polish characters – I have tried to bring out contrasted flavors and registers.

Pushkin's inspiration for verse drama came, of course, from the example of Shakespeare. In his draft preface dating from 1829 he writes: "The verse form I have used (iambic pentameter) has been generally adopted by the English and the Germans." However, in terms of prosody it was the French Alexandrine that he took as his model rather than the altogether freer Shakespearean pentameter: "I have retained the caesura after the second foot [*na vtoroi stope*] as in the French pentameter [Pushkin must mean the *middle* of the Alexandrine], and, I think, was mistaken in doing so, having thus voluntarily deprived my verse of its distinctive variety."[2] It is astonishing, however, how much variety Pushkin achieves in the blank verse of the *Komediia* even with this handicap.

It is hardly surprising that Pushkin's metrical model was French and not English. The stress pattern of both the Russian and the French languages is far more definite and defined than that of English, and English verse plays upon variety of stress, optional and indeterminate stress, and elisions to a much greater degree than is found in Russian and French verse.

I have done what I could to keep the architecture of Pushkin's lines and speeches. It would have been too constraining to keep the second-foot caesura throughout; if it came up naturally in English, well and good; if not, I didn't worry, having Pushkin's comment in mind. I have kept five metrical stresses in each line, but thought in terms of living speech and speech rhythms and tried to avoid the unnatural, mechanical, and deadening effect of perfect scansion. I have not hesitated (1) to reverse an iambic foot into a trochaic, (2) to prune off a weak syllable beginning a line, (3) to elide or (4) throw in an extra weak syllable in order to maintain natural English phraseology. I have not elided consistently in different occurrences of the same word. Here are some examples (metrical stress indicated by underlining, variation from strict scansion by bold):

(1) **Soldiers, merchants, traders** – all honest people
(2) **Will** you be so stubborn and so senseless
(3) The prayers and wailing of the people **of** Moscow
(4) The people **will** weep and wail a little more

The result is blank verse that reads with less metric regularity than Pushkin, but more regularly, I think, than is typical of English tradition.

Scansion in my translation is not always self-evident, sometimes depending on chosen emphasis, such as stress on the first syllable of a line (as in example 2 above), and will often be clarified by reading aloud. This is easiest to demonstrate from scene 6 ("Monastery Wall"), where Pushkin uses an unusual eight-foot trochaic line (octometer). He divides the line, with a central caesura, into two equal half-lines, which read like the trochaic tetrameter of his longer folk tales, except that this verse is unrhymed. I have rendered these lines as iambic (sometimes trochaic) heptameters with a caesura dividing the line freely into three- and four-foot units, and haven't minded surrounding the stresses with doubled weak syllables (i.e., varying iambic feet with anapests and dactyls):

[Ponimaesh'?]

Grigorii:
Net, niskol'ko.

Chernets:
                              ‖ Slushai, glupyi nash narod
Legkoveren: rad divit'sia‖ chudesam i novizne;

[Do you understand?]

Grigory:
Not at all.

Monk:
    Well, listen. Our people are stupid, ‖ they're
    easily taken in;
They're quick to believe in miracles – ‖ always wondering
    at some new thing.

A central problem of translating Russian verse into English is the great discrepancy between the polysyllabic Russian language and monosyllabic English.[3] Russian abounds in long sinuous words often extended by inflection to five or six syllables, but in English this number of syllables is rare except in the case of abstract nouns, whereas monosyllables are frequent. If verbal weight may be expressed in terms of "specific gravity," the English language might be said to have a higher specific gravity than Russian, the latter with its higher quantity of syllables, especially unstressed syllables. A phrase or passage in Russian will take up more syllabic "space" than its equivalent in English – even allowing for the greater number of words in English, boosted by the article. "*Ostanovilasia ona*," reads a line in *Eugene Onegin* (III.41.8, and again at V.11.14), "She stopped." To represent this phrase in English in the same metrical space as it occupies in Russian, words will have to be added, and this any translator who keeps the original metrical scheme is forced to do, producing padding and verbal inflation. *All* Pushkin's words are necessary and natural, however, and translation should aim at the same qualities.

Rather than try to make up for the syllabic shortfall of English by adding words, I have accepted a significant reduction in the overall line count. In translating blank verse, this approach is the equivalent of using a different meter from the original, with a shorter line, in translating lyric verse (as I have done with the lyric meters of scene 13 ["Palatine Mniszech's Castle, Sambor"], rendering hexameters as pentameters). Now, it has long been the prevailing view that English translation of

Russian verse should occupy exactly the same metrical space as the original – the same lyric metrical forms, and in nonstanzaic verse (e.g., blank verse) to as near as possible the same overall number of lines as in the original.[4] This notion seems to give inadequate consideration to the demands of *English as the target language.* Before the modern period, compression, precision, and economy – Pushkinian qualities – were usually more characteristic of English verse than looseness and prolixity. And these characteristics are underpinned on a purely physical level, as I have indicated, by the syllabic ratio of English as compared to Russian.

As I have said, I have tried to keep, as far as possible, the architecture of Pushkin's lines – in word order and placing, emphasis, balance, patterns of repetition, and rhyme where it occurs. Much of the time this is possible. But where it simply isn't, I have fitted Pushkin's lines into fewer in English. For example, Pimen's opening speech in scene 5 ("Night. A Cell in the Chudov Monastery") consists of 27 lines; my translation has 22½ lines – a reduction in the overall line count of 17 percent.[5] These four lines toward the end of the speech:

> *Teper' ono bezmolvno i spokoino,*
> *Ne mnogo lits mne pamiat' sokhranila,*
> *Ne mnogo slov dokhodiat do menia,*
> *A prochee pogiblo nevozvratno …*

become three in my translation:

> Now it is hushed and peaceful, few the faces
> I still recall, the voices still I hear,
> And all the rest is vanished utterly …

I can't keep up with Pushkin's long adjectives in the first line, but hold on to two key features of the passage: (1) the principle of repetition at the beginning of the second and third lines; and (2) the concentrated weight of the last two words of the last line, with their plethora of syllables (five in English against seven in the original).

Without this overall reduction of the line count – had I, in the passage just quoted, for example, contrived to keep Pushkin's two lines beginning "Ne mnogo" as two full lines in the translation – the consequent need to fill available metrical space with inessential words in English would have diluted the force of the key words in general verbal inflation, to use that bogy-phrase once more.[6]

Nevertheless, it must be admitted that a reductive process of any kind in translation does have its dangers, and the clash of priorities between the quest for poetry on the one hand and the demands of accuracy and completeness of meaning on the other did throw up problems of over-reduction in the preparation of this translation. However, the advice of two authors of this book, Professors Chester Dunning and Caryl Emerson, has helped me greatly in addressing these, and I should like to express my enormous gratitude to both for their knowledgeable, tough-minded but imaginative and sensitive critical scrutiny of successive drafts.

In the pronunciation of proper names, stress in this translation is as in Russian: Grigory, Kirill, Pimen, Sergey, Shestunov, Shuisky, Tsarevich, Tsarevna, Tsaritsa, Uglich, Vladimir, Vorotynsky. In tsars' names, however, the stress is anglicized: Boris, Ivan. If names are spoken in strict accordance with iambic meter, and every syllable is pronounced, stress will be broadly correct, though meter alone will not give the single main stress in the longer polysyllabic names.

Notes

1. See Mikhail Pogodin's reminiscence quoted in chapter 3 of this book.

2. Both quotations are taken from Wolff, *Pushkin*, 248.

3. I have explored this question in "The Carthorse, the Posthorse and Pegasus," 180, 185; "Can Pushkin Survive Translation?: Experiments in Lyric Verse," 206, 208; and in the Afterword to Pushkin, *The Bridegroom*, 60–61.

4. Joseph Brodsky is the classic modern proponent of the argument that verse meters are not to be changed in translation. On the other hand, Vladimir Nabokov, before coming to hold the view that translation of rhymed metrical verse was impossible, had no compunction about departing from original metrical forms in his translations of lyrics (see Nabokov, ed. and trans., *Pushkin, Lermontov, Tyutchev: Poems*, 9–11, 35–37), though his translations of Pushkin's blank verse in the same volume (12–35) conform more to the "prevailing view" I have mentioned in very nearly keeping pace with Pushkin's line count.

5. No other English version of this passage in translations of *Boris Godunov* I have examined reduces the line count to this extent. The line counts of those translations are as follows: C. E. Turner (1899) = 27, Alfred Hayes (1918) = 23+, Philip Barbour (1953) = 27, D. M. Thomas (1985) = 25, Alex Miller (1987) = 26, and Roger

Clarke (1999) = 27. See Pushkin, *Translations from Pushkin*, 200–201; idem, *Poems, Prose and Plays*, 342–43; idem, *Boris Godunov* (1953), 19–21; idem, *Boris Godunov* (1985), 22; idem, "Boris Godunov" (1987), 13; and idem, *Complete Works*, 6: 55–56.

6. In writing this preface, in order to test this statement I did my best to render Pushkin's four lines beginning "*Teper' ono bezmolvno*" as four in English:

> The past is hushed and peaceful to me now,
> Few are the faces that I call to mind,
> Few the voices that come down to me,
> And all the rest is vanished utterly …

The need to take up available metrical space to my mind induces an aesthetically inferior version. In the first line there is unnecessary and clumsy repetition of "past" (three lines back) for Pimen's gently flowing "*ono*" ("it"); in the expanded second and third lines there are too many shapeless monosyllables; and an unwanted rhyme has crept into the last two lines.

А. С. ПУШКИН

КОМЕДИЯ О ЦАРЕ БОРИСЕ И О ГРИШКЕ ОТРЕПЬЕВЕ. 1825.

Transcribed by Professor Sergei Aleksandrovich Fomichev from the original manuscript located in Institut russkoi literatury (Pushkinskii Dom) Rossiiskoi Akademii nauk (RAN), Rukopisnyi otdel, St. Petersburg; fond 244, opis' 1, No. 891, listy 1-51.

Alexander Pushkin

Comedy about Tsar Boris and Grishka Otrepiev (1825)

Translated by Antony Wood

Dramatis Personae

(Pushkin did not include a dramatis personae in the original manuscript of the *Komediia*)

BORIS GODUNOV, boyar, then Tsar of Muscovy
FEODOR, his son, the Tsarevich
KSENIA, his daughter, the Tsarevna
NURSE to Ksenia
PRINCE SHUISKY
PRINCE VOROTYNSKY
SEMYON GODUNOV
SHCHELKALOV, Secretary of the Council (Duma) of Boyars
BOY at Shuisky's house
AFANASY PUSHKIN
MARGERET, a French captain in the tsar's service
W. ROSEN, a German captain in the tsar's service
ROZHNOV, a Russian prisoner taken by the Pretender
BASMANOV, commander of the tsar's army
GRIGORY (GRISHKA) OTREPIEV, later THE PRETENDER DIMITRY

Supporters of the Pretender:

GAVRILA PUSHKIN
KURBSKY
FATHER CZERNIKOWSKI, a Jesuit
KHRUSHCHOV, a Russian noble
KARELA, a Cossack
SOBAŃSKI, a Polish gentleman
POET
MNISZECH, Palatine of Sambor
WIŚNIOWIECKI, Polish magnate
MARYNA, daughter of Mniszech
RÓZIA, maid to Maryna

Other characters:

PIMEN, monk and chronicler
EVIL MONK
PATRIARCH
FATHER SUPERIOR of the Chudov Monastery
VARLAAM, vagrant monk
MISAIL, vagrant monk
HOSTESS at a tavern on the Lithuanian border
FRONTIER GUARDS
HOLY FOOL
THE PEOPLE
Boyars; courtiers; Russian, German and Polish soldiers; Polish dancing couples; Tsaritsa; boys; boyars loyal to the Pretender (Mosalsky, Golitsyn, Molchanov, Sherefedinov); streltsy; guard at Godunov's house

[Сцена 1]

1598 года, 20 февраля

КРЕМЛЕВСКИЕ ПАЛАТЫ

КНЯЗЬЯ ШУЙСКИЙ И ВОРОТЫНСКИЙ.

Воротынский

Наряжены мы вместе город ведать,
Но, кажется, нам не за кем смотреть:
Москва пуста; вослед за патриархом
К монастырю пошел и весь народ.
Как думаешь, чем кончится тревога?

Шуйский

Чем кончится? Узнать не мудрено:
Народ еще повоет да поплачет,
Борис еще поморщится немного,
Что пьяница пред чаркою вина,
И наконец по милости своей
Принять венец смиренно согласится;
А там — а там он будет нами править
По-прежнему.

Воротынский

           Но месяц уж протек,
Как, затворясь в монастыре с сестрою,
Он, кажется, покинул всё мирское.
Ни патриарх, ни думные бояре
Склонить его доселе не могли;
Не внемлет он ни слезным увещаньям,
Ни их мольбам, ни воплю всей Москвы,
Ни голосу Великого Собора.
Его сестру напрасно умоляли
Благословить Бориса на державу;
Печальная монахиня-царица
Как он тверда, как он неумолима.

[Scene 1]

February 20, 1598[1]

PALACE IN THE KREMLIN[2]

Princes Shuisky and Vorotynsky.[3]

Vorotynsky
You and I have charge of Moscow, but
There's not a living soul in sight:[4] the people
Have followed the Patriarch to the monastery,
The city's empty.[5] How will this business end?
What do you think?

Shuisky
                Not difficult to guess:
The people will weep and wail a little more,
Boris will wear his frown a little more,
Just like a drunkard peering at his cup;
And out of boundless generosity,
Most humbly, he will take the crown at last;
And then – why then, he will proceed to rule us
Exactly as before.[6]

Vorotynsky
                A month has passed
Since, cloistered with his sister, he renounced
All worldly matters.[7] No one can shake his purpose,
Not Patriarch, not Council of the Boyars;[8]
He doesn't heed their tearful supplications,
The prayers and wailing of the people of Moscow,
The Great Assembly's voice.[9] They urged his sister
To give her blessing to him for the crown;
The nun-tsaritsa was implacable,
Boris's spirit must have hardened hers.[10]
What if cares of state have wearied him?
What if he'll not assume the vacant throne?

Знать, сам Борис сей дух в нее вселил;
Что ежели правитель в самом деле
Державными заботами наскучил
И на престол безвластный не взойдет?
Что скажешь ты?

                    Шуйский
                    Скажу, что понапрасну
Лилася кровь царевича-младенца;
Что если так, Димитрий мог бы жить.

                    Воротынский
Ужасное злодейство! Полно, точно ль
Царевича сгубил Борис?

                    Шуйский
                              А кто же?
Кто подкупал напрасно Чепчугова?
Кто подослал обоих Битяговских
С Качаловым? Я в Углич послан был
Исследовать на месте это дело:
Наехал я на свежие следы;
Весь город был свидетель злодеянья;
Все граждане согласно показали;
И, возвратясь, я мог единым словом
Изобличить сокрытого злодея.

                    Воротынский
Зачем же ты его не уничтожил?

                    Шуйский
Он, признаюсь, тогда меня смутил
Спокойствием, бесстыдностью нежданой,
Он мне в глаза смотрел как будто правый:
Расспрашивал, в подробности входил —
И перед ним я повторил нелепость,
Которую мне сам он нашептал.

                    Воротынский
Не чисто, князь.

What would you say to that?

Shuisky
                    I'd say, in that case,
Young Prince Dimitry's blood was shed for nothing;
Then the Tsarevich might as well have lived.[11]

Vorotynsky
A ghastly crime! But can one know his death
Was any of Boris's doing?

Shuisky
                    Who else's, now?
Who was it tried to pay off Chepchugov?[12]
Who sent the Bitiagovskys and Kachalov
On secret missions?[13] I was sent to Uglich
To make investigation of the matter:[14]
I found the trail still fresh; the assembled town
Had been a witness to that dreadful deed,
The people testified with single voice;[15]
I could have brought their verdict back to Moscow,
One word – the villain could have been unmasked.

Vorotynsky
Why did you not unmask him then and there?

Shuisky
He thoroughly confused me, I confess –
His calmness as he looked me in the eye,
His unexpected boldness, confidence,
Interrogating me on every detail –
All I could do before him was repeat
The absurdities he whispered in my ear.[16]

Vorotynsky
Shame on you, prince.

Шуйский
А что мне было делать?
Всё объявить Феодору? Но царь
На всё глядел очами Годунова,
Всему внимал ушами Годунова:
Пускай его уверил я во всем;
Борис тотчас его бы разуверил,
А там меня ж сослали б в заточенье
Да в добрый час, как дядю моего,
В глухой тюрьме тихонько б задавили.
Не хвастаюсь, а в случае, конечно,
Никая казнь меня не устрашит,
Я сам не трус, но также не глупец
И в петлю лезть не соглашуся даром.

Воротынский
Ужасное злодейство! Слушай, верно,
Губителя раскаянье тревожит:
Конечно, кровь невинного младенца
Ему ступить мешает на престол.

Шуйский
Перешагнет; Борис не так-то робок!
Какая честь для нас, для всей Руси!
Вчерашний раб, татарин, зять Малюты,
Зять палача и сам в душе палач,
Возьмет венец и бармы Мономаха…

Воротынский
Так, родом он незнатен; мы знатнее.

Шуйский
Да, кажется.

Воротынский
Ведь Шуйский, Воротынский…
Легко сказать, природные князья.

Шуйский
Природные, и Рюриковой крови.

Shuisky
But what was I to do?
Tell Feodor everything I knew? The Tsar
Saw all things through the eyes of Godunov,
Heard all things through the ears of Godunov:[17]
Even had I convinced him of it all,
Boris would very soon have unconvinced him,
I'd have been quietly put away, and then
In due course, like my uncle, put to death.[18]
I will not boast, but when the moment comes –
No punishment exists that frightens me.
I'm not a coward, nor am I a fool,
I wouldn't place a noose around my neck.

Vorotynsky
A ghastly crime! And now it seems to me,
Remorse disturbs the executioner:
The blood of infant innocence it is,
It surely is, that keeps him from the throne.[19]

Shuisky
That won't stop him; Boris is not so timid!
What honor to us all, to all of Russia!
A Tatar and an erstwhile slave,[20] Maliuta's
Son-in-law, he too at heart a hangman – [21]
To wear the cape and crown of Monomakh ...[22]

Vorotynsky
You're right, he isn't of the blood that we are.

Shuisky
Certainly not.

Vorotynsky
Shuisky, Vorotynsky ...
Names known to all as names of princes born.

Shuisky
And princes of the blood, of Riurik's blood.[23]

Воротынский

А слушай, князь, ведь мы б имели право
Наследовать Феодору.

Шуйский
                Да, боле,

Чем Годунов.

Воротынский
Ведь в самом деле!

Шуйский
                        Что ж?

Когда Борис хитрить не перестанет,
Давай народ искусно волновать,
Пускай они оставят Годунова,
Своих князей у них довольно, пусть
Себе в цари любого изберут.

Воротынский

Не мало нас наследников Варяга,
Да трудно нам тягаться с Годуновым:
Народ отвык в нас видеть древню отрасль
Воинственных властителей своих.
Уже давно лишились мы уделов,
Давно царям подручниками служим,
А он умел и страхом, и любовью,
И славою народ очаровать.

Шуйский
(глядит в окно)

Он смел, вот всё — а мы... Но полно. Видишь,
Народ идет, рассыпавшись, назад —
Пойдем скорей, узнаем, решено ли.

Vorotynsky
Each of us therefore has a right to claim
The throne.

Shuisky
More so than Godunov.

Vorotynsky
                    Indeed!

Shuisky
Well then, if Boris doesn't stop his foxing,
Let us employ our skills amongst the people,
And make them turn away from Godunov;[24]
The Russian people do not lack for princes,
So let them choose their tsar from one of them.

Vorotynsky
We heirs of the Varangians, strong in number,
Cannot compete with Boris Godunov:[25]
The people long ago stopped seeing in us
Their ancient line of warlike overlords,
We long ago gave up our appanages,
We are the underlings of Moscow's tsars;[26]
But Godunov inspires both fear and love,
And his renown has quite bewitched the people.[27]

Shuisky
(looks out of the window)
He's bold, that's all – while we … But that's enough.
The people are returning and dispersing –
We must be off to see how matters stand.

[Сцена 2]

КРАСНАЯ ПЛОЩАДЬ

НАРОД.

Один

Неумолим! Он от себя прогнал
Святителей, бояр и патриарха.
Они пред ним напрасно пали ниц;
Его страшит сияние престола.

Другой

О Боже мой, кто будет нами править?
О горе нам!

Третий

Да вот верховный дьяк
Выходит нам сказать решенье Думы.

Народ

Молчать! молчать! дьяк думный говорит;
Ш-ш — слушайте!

Щелкалов
(с Красного крыльца)

Собором положили
В последний раз отведать силу просьбы
Над скорбною правителя душой.
Заутра вновь святейший патриарх,
В Кремле отпев торжественно молебен,
Предшествуем хоругвями святыми,
С иконами Владимирской, Донской,
Воздвижется; а с ним синклит, бояре,
Да сонм дворян, да выборные люди,
И весь народ московский православный,
Мы все пойдем молить царицу вновь,
Да сжалится над сирою Москвою

[Scene 2]

RED SQUARE[28]

The people.[29]

First
He was implacable! The priests, the boyars,
The Patriarch – they all knelt down before him –
In vain; the dazzle of the throne unnerves him.

Second
Lord, who will it be to rule us now?
Woe to us!

Third
Here's the Duma Secretary.
He'll tell us what the boyars have decided.

People
Hush! Hush! The Duma Secretary is speaking.[30]
Shhh – Listen!

Shchelkalov
(standing on the Main Porch)[31]
The Assembly has resolved
To try, for one last time, the power of pleading
Upon our ruler's sad and suffering soul.[32]
Tomorrow the most holy Patriarch
Will lead a solemn prayer; and then set forth,
Preceded by the holy gonfalons
And icons of Vladimir and the Don,[33]
Accompanied by the boyars of the Council,
The magnates and select provincial gentry,[34]
And all the Christian populace of Moscow –
And go to the Tsaritsa, to implore her
To pity orphaned Moscow – give her blessing

И на венец благословит Бориса.
Идите же вы с Богом по домам,
Молитеся — да взыдет к небесам
Усердная молитва православных.

(Народ расходится.)

To Boris's accession to the throne.
Go to your homes with God, and let the prayers
Of all true Orthodox rise up to Heaven.

(The people disperse.)

[Сцена 3]

ДЕВИЧЬЕ ПОЛЕ.
НОВОДЕВИЧИЙ МОНАСТЫРЬ

НАРОД.

Один

Теперь они пошли к царице в келью,
Туда вошли Борис и патриарх
С толпой бояр.

Другой
Что слышно?

Третий
                           Всё еще
Упрямится; однако есть надежда.

Баба
(с ребенком)
Агу! не плачь, не плачь; вот бука, бука
Тебя возьмет! агу, агу!.. не плачь!

Один
Нельзя ли нам пробраться за ограду?

Другой
Нельзя. Куды! и в поле даже тесно,
Не только там. Легко ли? Вся Москва
Сперлася здесь; смотри: ограда, кровли,
Все ярусы соборной колокольни,
Главы церквей и самые кресты
Унизаны народом.

Первый
Право, любо!

[Scene 3]

MAIDEN'S FIELD. NOVODEVICHY CONVENT[35]

The people.

First
Now they're in the Tsaritsa's cell – Boris,
The Patriarch, the boyars.

Second
What's the news?

Third
He's still resisting; but they say there's hope.

Woman
(with an infant)
Stop crying! Stop crying! Here comes the bogeyman,
The bogeyman will get you! No more crying, now!

First
Can't we get through around the wall?

Second
We can't!
Maiden's Field is packed – all round the Convent.
Can't move a single step. The whole of Moscow –
All gathered here – look: all along the wall,
The roofs, all the way up the belfry, domes
And crosses too, everywhere thick with people!

Another
A sight to see!

Один

Что там за шум?

Другой

       Послушай! Что за шум?
Народ завыл, там падают, что волны,
За рядом ряд… еще… еще… Ну, брат,
Дошло до нас; скорее! на колени!

Народ
(на коленах. Вой и плач)

Ах, смилуйся, отец наш! властвуй нами!
Будь наш отец, наш царь!

Один
(тихо)
                 О чем мы плачем?

Другой

А как нам знать? то ведают бояре,
Не нам чета.

Баба
(с ребенком)
       Ну, что ж? как надо плакать,
Так и затих! вот я тебя! вот бука!
Плачь, баловень!

         (Бросает его обземь.
           Ребенок пищит.)

         Ну, то-то же.

Один
             Все плачут,
Заплачем, брат, и мы.

Другой
         Я силюсь, брат,
Да не могу.

First
What is that sound?

Second
Just listen!
The people wailing, sinking down like waves,
Row after row … nearer … nearer … It's got
To us! On your knees!

People
(on their knees; wailing and sobbing)
Father, have pity on us!
Rule over us! and be our Tsar, our Father![36]

First
(in a low voice)
Why are they weeping?

Second
How should we know? The boyars,
They'll know, it's not our business.

Woman
(with the infant)
Now what's this?
Just when you should be crying you go all quiet!
You'll catch it now! Here comes the bogeyman …
Now cry, you brat!

*(Throws the infant to the
ground; it yells.)*[37]

That's it.

First
We should be weeping –
Like everyone else.

Second
I'm trying, my friend, I can't.

Первый
Я также. Нет ли луку?
Потрем глаза.

Второй
Нет, я слюней помажу.
Что там еще?

Первый
Да кто их разберет?

Народ
Венец за ним! он царь! он согласился!
Борис наш царь! да здравствует Борис!

Another
The same with me. If only we had an onion
To rub our eyes with.

Second
Have to make do with spit.[38]
What's happening now?

Another
Can't make it out at all.

People
Boris accepts the crown! He has consented!
We have a tsar! Tsar Boris! Long live Boris![39]

[Сцена 4]

КРЕМЛЕВСКИЕ ПАЛАТЫ

БОРИС, ПАТРИАРХ, БОЯРЕ.

Борис
Ты, отче патриарх, вы все, бояре,
Обнажена моя душа пред вами:
Вы видели, что я приемлю власть
Великую со страхом и смиреньем.
Сколь тяжела обязанность моя!
Наследую могущим Иоаннам —
Наследую и ангелу-царю!..
О праведник! о мой отец державный!
Воззри с небес на слезы верных слуг
И ниспошли тому, кого любил ты,
Кого ты здесь столь дивно возвеличил,
Священное на власть благословенье:
Да правлю я во славе свой народ,
Да буду благ и праведен, как ты.
От вас я жду содействия, бояре.
Служите мне, как вы ему служили,
Когда труды я ваши разделял,
Не избранный еще народной волей.

Бояре
Не изменим присяге, нами данной.

Борис
Теперь пойдем, поклонимся гробам
Почиющих властителей России —
А там, сзывать весь наш народ на пир,
Всех, от вельмож до нищего слепца;
Всем вольный вход, все гости дорогие.

(Уходит, за ним и бояре.)

[Scene 4]

PALACE IN THE KREMLIN

Boris; Patriarch; boyars.

Boris
Most holy Father Patriarch, and boyars,
I lay my soul before you. You have seen
The trepidation and humility
With which I now accept the highest power;
And heavy is the burden! – I succeed
The mighty Ivans and the Angel-Tsar! ...[40]
O righteous one! O my most sovereign Father,
Look down upon the tears of those who serve you,
And from on high bestow on him you have loved,
Him that you have so wondrously exalted,
Your holy blessing for the tasks of rule:
And grant that I shall lead my people greatly,
Shall be benevolent and just, as you are.
Boyars, I count on your support. Serve me
As you served Feodor, when I shared your labors,
Before being chosen by the people's will.

Boyars
We'll not betray the oath that we have sworn.

Boris
Now let us go and pray before the tombs
Of former rulers of our land – and later
We'll bid our people join us in a feast;
Our doors shall be opened to all, from lord to beggar,
And all shall be our cherished guests.

(Exit, followed by the boyars.)

Воротынский
(останавливая Шуйского)
Ты угадал.

Шуйский
А что?

Воротынский
     Да здесь, намедни,
Ты помнишь?

Шуйский
   Нет, не помню ничего.

Воротынский
Когда народ ходил в Девичье поле,
Ты говорил —

Шуйский
    Теперь не время помнить,
Советую порой и забывать.
А впрочем, я злословием притворным
Тогда желал тебя лишь испытать,
Верней узнать твой тайный образ мыслей;
Но вот — народ приветствует царя —
Отсутствие мое заметить могут —
Иду за ним.

Воротынский
   Лукавый царедворец!

Vorotynsky
(stops Shuisky)

So you
Were right.

Shuisky
In what respect?

Vorotynsky
The other day
Here in this very room, you don't remember?

Shuisky
I don't remember anything at all.

Vorotynsky
All the people had gone to Maiden's Field ...
You said –

Shuisky
This is no time for reminiscing,
I would advise you rather to forget.
The fact is, I was testing you, my friend,
The better to discern your secret thoughts;
Here come the people, though, to greet their tsar.
My absence might be noticed and remarked on;
I'll go.

Vorotynsky
A perfect servant of the Tsar!

[Сцена 5]

1603 года

НОЧЬ.
КЕЛЬЯ В ЧУДОВОМ МОНАСТЫРЕ

ОТЕЦ ПИМЕН, ГРИГОРИЙ СПЯЩИЙ.

Пимен
(пишет перед лампадой)
Еще одно, последнее сказанье —
И летопись окончена моя,
Исполнен долг, завещанный от Бога
Мне, грешному. Недаром многих лет
Свидетелем Господь меня поставил
И книжному искусству вразумил;
Когда-нибудь монах трудолюбивый
Найдет мой труд усердный, безымянный,
Засветит он, как я, свою лампаду —
И, пыль веков от хартий отряхнув,
Правдивые сказанья перепишет,
Да ведают потомки православных
Земли родной минувшую судьбу,
Своих царей великих поминают
За их труды, за славу, за добро —
А за грехи, за темные деянья
Спасителя смиренно умоляют.
На старости я сызнова живу,
Минувшее проходит предо мною —
Давно ль оно неслось событий полно,
Волнуяся, как море-окиян?
Теперь оно безмолвно и спокойно,
Не много лиц мне память сохранила,
Не много слов доходят до меня,
А прочее погибло невозвратно…
Но близок день, лампада догорает —
Еще одно, последнее сказанье.

[Scene 5]

The year 1603[41]

NIGHT. A CELL IN THE CHUDOV MONASTERY[42]

Father Pimen;[43] *Grigory asleep.*[44]

Pimen
(writing by icon-lamp)
One record more, the last of all – and then
This chronicle of mine is done, fulfilled
The task that God has laid on me, a sinner.
Not in vain did God appoint me witness
To many years, and teach me bookish art;
Some far-off day another toiling monk
Will chance upon my zealous, nameless work,
Will light his lamp, as I have done, will shake
The dust of ages from these scrolls, and copy
The faithful record of my chronicle;
And thus the future sons of Orthodoxy
Shall learn their native land's past fate, recall
The labors of their tsars for good and glory,
Implore the Savior's mercy for their sins.
Now in old age I live my life anew,
The past unfolds before me – can it be long
Since, agitated as the stormy ocean
And heavy with events, it hastened by?
Now it is hushed and peaceful, few the faces
I still recall, the voices still I hear,
And all the rest is vanished utterly …
It's dawn, the lamp is low. One record more,
The last of all.

(Writes.)

(Пишет.)

Григорий
(пробуждается)
Всё тот же сон! возможно ль? в третий раз!
Проклятый сон!.. А всё перед лампадой
Старик сидит да пишет — и дремотой
Знать, во всю ночь он не смыкал очей.
Как я люблю его спокойный вид,
Когда, душой в минувшем погруженный,
Он летопись свою ведет; и часто
Я угадать хотел, о чем он пишет?
О темном ли владычестве татар?
О казнях ли свирепых Иоанна?
О бурном ли новогородском Вече?
О славе ли отечества? Напрасно.
Ни на челе высоком, ни во взорах
Нельзя прочесть его сокрытых дум;
Всё тот же вид смиренный, величавый.
Так точно дьяк в приказах поседелый
Спокойно зрит на правых и виновных,
Добру и злу внимая равнодушно,
Не ведая ни жалости, ни гнева.

Пимен
Проснулся, брат.

Григорий
Благослови меня,
Честный отец.

Пимен
Благослови Господь
Тебя и днесь и присно и вовеки.

Григорий
Ты всё писал и сном не позабылся,
А мой покой бесовское мечтанье
Тревожило, и враг меня мутил.

Grigory
(wakes)

Again that dream! – The third time!
That cursed dream! … And still the old man writes
By icon-lamp – he can't have slept at all.
How I love his tranquil air as, spirit
Sunk in the past, he writes his chronicle;
How often I have tried to guess his theme:
The terrible dominion of the Tatars?[45]
The savage executions loved by Ivan?[46]
The turbulence of citizens' assemblies
In Novgorod of old?[47] The glory of Rus?
In vain. His lofty brow cannot be read;
Always he wears a humble dignity.
With just such calm a government official,[48]
Grown grey in service, views the innocent
And guilty, lends his ear to good and ill
Impartially, not knowing pity or anger.

Pimen

You've woken, brother.

Grigory

Give me your blessing, Father.

Pimen

The Lord God bless you this day and ever after.

Grigory

You've written all night, you haven't slept. My peace
Was stolen by the Devil. I had a dream:
I dreamed I climbed a tower, and from a height

Мне снилося, что лестница крутая
Меня вела на башню; с высоты
Мне виделась Москва, что муравейник;
Внизу народ на площади кипел
И на меня указывал со смехом,
И стыдно мне и страшно становилось —
И, падая стремглав, я пробуждался…
И три раза мне снился тот же сон.
Не чудно ли?

Пимен
            Младая кровь играет;
Смиряй себя молитвой и постом,
И сны твои видений легких будут
Исполнены. Доныне — если я,
Невольною дремотой обессилен,
Не сотворю молитвы долгой к ночи —
Мой старый сон не тих и не безгрешен,
Мне чудятся то шумные пиры,
То ратный стан, то схватки боевые,
Безумные потехи юных лет!

Григорий
Как весело провел свою ты младость!
Ты воевал под башнями Казани,
Ты рать Литвы при Шуйском отражал,
Ты видел двор и роскошь Иоанна!
Счастлив! а я, от отроческих лет
По келиям скитаюсь, бедный инок!
Зачем и мне не тешиться в боях,
Не пировать за царскою трапезой?
Успел бы я, как ты, на старость лет
От суеты, от мира отложиться,
Произнести монашества обет
И в тихую обитель затвориться.

Пимен
Не сетуй, брат, что рано грешный свет
Покинул ты, что мало искушений

Saw Moscow all before me, like an ant-hill;
And on the square below the people swarmed,
And pointed fingers up at me and laughed;
I grew ashamed, afraid – I fell headlong,
And then awoke ... Three times I've dreamed that dream.
Strange.

Pimen
It is the play of youthful blood.
Subdue yourself by prayer and abstinence
And you shall dream of gentler things. If I, now,
Happen to fall asleep without saying prayers,
My aged sleep is never calm and sinless;
My dreams are dreams of riotous banqueting,
Of bivouacs and clashes in the field,
And all the mad diversions of my youth!

Grigory
What happiness – to spend one's youth as you did!
You fought beneath the bastions of Kazan,[49]
With Shuisky you repulsed the Lithuanians,[50]
You saw the luxury of Ivan's court!
O happiness! Whilst I have been a monk
From earliest youth, and trailed from cell to cell![51]
Why may not *I* participate in battle,
Sit with the Tsar at table? Then, like you,
Forsake the hurly-burly of the world
When old age comes upon me, take the vow,
And live within the still monastic fold?

Pimen
Brother, do not complain that you so soon
Gave up the sinful world, and that the Almighty

Послал тебе Всевышний. Верь ты мне:
Нас издали пленяет слава, роскошь
И женская лукавая любовь.
Я долго жил и многим насладился;
Но с той поры лишь ведаю блаженство,
Как в монастырь Господь меня привел.
Подумай, сын, ты о царях великих.
Кто выше их? Единый Бог. Кто смеет
Противу их? Никто. А что же? Часто
Златый венец тяжел им становился:
Они его меняли на клобук.
Царь Иоанн искал успокоенья
В подобии монашеских трудов.
Его дворец, любимцев гордых полный,
Монастыря вид новый принимал:
Кромешники в тафьях и власяницах
Послушными являлись чернецами,
А грозный царь игуменом смиренным.
Я видел здесь — вот в этой самой келье
(В ней жил тогда Кирилл многострадальный,
Муж праведный. Тогда уж и меня
Сподобил Бог уразуметь ничтожность
Мирских сует), здесь видел я царя,
Усталого от гневных дум и казней.
Задумчив, тих сидел меж нами Грозный,
Мы перед ним недвижимо стояли,
И тихо он беседу с нами вел.
Он говорил игумену и братье:
«Отцы мои, желанный день придет,
Предстану здесь алкающий спасенья.
Ты Никодим, ты Сергий, ты Кирилл,
Вы все — обет примите мой духовный:
Прииду к вам, преступник окаянный
И схимию честную восприму,
К стопам твоим, святый отец, припадши.»
Так говорил державный государь,
И сладко речь из уст его лилася —
И плакал он. А мы в слезах молились,
Да ниспошлет Господь любовь и мир

Sent you so few temptations. For believe me,
From far off, worldly glory and luxury,
And woman's cunning love, may captivate us.
Long have I lived, and much have I enjoyed;
But never did I know content, till God
Guided my steps to this our monastery.
Think now, my son, of all the mighty tsars.
Who stands above them? God alone. Who dare
Oppose them? None. And yet how often we see
The golden crown become a heavy burden
Whose wearer would exchange it for a cowl.[52]
In semblance of monastic toil Tsar Ivan
Sought peace; his palace, filled with haughty favorites,
Took on the aspect of a monastery;
Oprichniki, in skullcaps and hair-shirts,
Became devoted monks, the tsar himself,
The fearsome tsar, their meek and humble abbot.[53]
Here in this cell I once beheld the Tsar
(Kyrill the Long-Suffering was living here,
A righteous man.[54] Even then God blessed me too
With sight to see through worldly vanity) –
Here I beheld the Tsar, the Terrible,
Weary of angry deeds and executions.
He sat among us, and his thoughts roved free;
We stood before him motionless, and quietly
He spoke to us – the Abbot, all the monks:
"The longed-for day will come at last, good fathers,
And I shall come to you, my soul shall seek
Salvation. Nicodemus, Sergius, Kyrill –
All of you shall receive my soul's commitment:
Accursed sinner that I am, before you
I shall put on the habit of obedience,
Fall and embrace your feet, most holy father."[55]
So did our mighty ruler speak to us,
And speech flowed sweetly from his lips – he wept.
And we wept too, and prayed Almighty God
To take compassion on his storm-tossed soul.
And Ivan's son, Tsar Feodor? On the throne
He craved the eremitic life; he turned

Его душе страдающей и бурной.
А сын его Феодор? На престоле
Он воздыхал о мирном житие
Молчальника. Он царские чертоги
Преобратил в молитвенную келью;
Там тяжкие, державные печали
Святой души его не возмущали.
Бог возлюбил смирение царя,
И Русь при нем во славе безмятежной
Утешилась — а в час его кончины
Свершилося неслыханное чудо;
К его одру, царю едину зримый,
Явился муж необычайно светел,
И начал с ним беседовать Феодор
И называть великим патриархом.
И все кругом объяты были страхом,
Уразумев небесное виденье,
Зане святый владыка пред царем
Во храмине тогда не находился.
Когда же он преставился, палаты
Исполнились святым благоуханьем
И лик его как солнце просиял —
Уж не видать такого нам царя.
О страшное, невиданное горе!
Прогневали мы Бога, согрешили:
Владыкою себе цареубийцу
Мы нарекли.

                    Григорий
            Давно, честный отец,
Хотелось мне тебя спросить о смерти
Димитрия царевича; в то время
Ты, говорят, был в Угличе.

                    Пимен
                    Ох, помню!
Привел меня Бог видеть злое дело,
Кровавый грех. Тогда я в дальний Углич
На некое был послан послушанье,

The royal chambers into cells for prayer
Where all the cares of heavy sovereignty
Could not intrude upon his holy soul.
And God was pleased by such humility,
And Russia, while he ruled, took consolation,
Serene and glorious. When his end was near,
A miracle unheard-of came to pass.
At his bedside, to Feodor's eyes alone,
Appeared a man surpassing bright in radiance.
Feodor conversed with him, addressed him as
Great Patriarch. The court was sore afraid,
Knowing this for a heavenly visitation,
For in the chamber of the Tsar not one
Set eyes upon that Patriarch.[56] And when
Tsar Feodor breathed his last, in all the chambers
A holy fragrance hung;[57] his countenance
Shone like the sun.[58] No, such a tsar as this
We shall not look upon again. O sin
Unprecedented and most terrible!
We have provoked God's wrath: for we have named
A tsaricide our ruler.

Grigory
I have long wished,
Most holy father, to question you about
The death of Prince Dimitry, the Tsarevich;
I've heard you were at Uglich.

Pimen
Yes, indeed,
God made me witness to a bloody crime there.
I had been sent to Uglich on a duty,
I arrived at night. Next day, at the hour of Mass,

Пришел я в ночь. Наутро в час обедни
Вдруг слышу звон, ударили в набат,
Крик, шум. Бегут на двор царицы. Я
Спешу туда ж — а там уже весь город.
Гляжу: лежит зарезанный царевич;
Царица-мать в беспамятстве над ним,
Кормилица в отчаяньи рыдает,
А тут народ, остервенясь волочит
Безбожную предательницу-мамку...
Вдруг между их, свиреп, от злости бледен,
Является Иуда Битяговский.
«Вот, вот злодей!» — раздался общий вопль,
И вмиг его не стало. Тут народ
Вслед бросился бежавшим трем убийцам;
Укрывшихся злодеев захватили
И привели пред теплый труп младенца,
И чудо — вдруг мертвец затрепетал —
«Покайтеся!» народ им загремел,
И в ужасе под топором злодеи
Покаялись — и назвали Бориса.

Григорий

Каких был лет царевич убиенный?

Пимен

Да лет семи; ему бы ныне было
(Тому прошло уж десять лет... нет, больше:
Двенадцать лет) — он был бы твой ровесник
И царствовал; но Бог судил иное.
Сей повестью плачевной заключу
Я летопись мою; с тех пор я мало
Вникал в дела мирские. Брат Григорий,
Ты грамотой свой разум просветил,
Тебе свой труд передаю. В часы
Свободные от подвигов духовных
Описывай, не мудрствуя лукаво,
Всё то, чему свидетель в жизни будешь:
Войну и мир, управу государей,
Угодников святые чудеса,

I heard the sudden pealing of the tocsin,
Shouts, uproar from the court of the Tsaritsa.[59]
I hastened there – and found all Uglich gathered.
There the Tsarevich lay; his throat was slit;
His mother lay upon him in a swoon,
His nurse was wailing; furiously the people
Dragged off his other nurse, that godless traitor …[60]
Suddenly, in the crowd, appeared the face –
Pale with hate – of that Judas, Bitiagovsky.[61]
The cry went up all round: "There – there's the murderer!"
But on the instant he was off. The people
Rushed to pursue the three assassins,[62] caught them,
Brought them before the young boy's corpse, still warm;
And now, a miracle! – the body trembled.
"Confess!" the people howled; and terror-struck,
Beneath the axe, the three confessed – and Boris
Was named.[63]

Grigory
How old was the Tsarevich then?

Pimen
Seven, he would have been;[64] now he'd have been
(Ten years have passed since then – no, more, say twelve),
He would have been about your age … and tsar;[65]
But God did not decree it.
     This sad tale
Closes my chronicle; since those events
I've taken little notice of the world.
Brother Grigory, you have studied much;[66]
To you I hand my work. In those hours free
From spiritual discipline, you must describe
Unvarnished all you witness in this life:
The conduct of our rulers, war and peace,
The prodigies and portents of the heavens,
The holy miracles of saints … And now

Пророчества и знаменья небесны —
А мне пора, пора уж отдохнуть
И погасить лампаду… Но звонят
К заутрене… благослови, Господь,
Своих рабов!.. подай костыль, Григорий.

(Уходит.)

Григорий
Борис, Борис! всё пред тобой трепещет,
Никто тебе не смеет и напомнить
О жребии несчастного младенца, —
А между тем отшельник в темной келье
Здесь на тебя донос ужасный пишет:
И не уйдешь ты от суда мирского,
Как не уйдешь от Божьего суда.

It's time for me to rest, put out the light –
The matin-bell already. Bless, O Lord,
Thy servants! ... Give me, please, my staff, Grigory.

(Exit.)

Grigory
Boris, Boris! All your subjects tremble,
And none of them has dared recall to you
The lot of that unlucky boy ... But meanwhile,
In this forgotten cell, an anchorite
Has written a terrible indictment of you:
You'll not escape the judgement of the world,
You'll not escape the judgement too of God.

[Сцена 6]

ОГРАДА МОНАСТЫРСКАЯ

ГРИГОРИЙ И ЗЛОЙ ЧЕРНЕЦ.

Григорий

Что за скука, что за горе наше бедное житье!
День приходит, день проходит — видно, слышно всё одно:
Только видишь черны рясы, только слышишь колокол.
Днем, зевая, бродишь, бродишь; делать нечего — соснешь;
Ночью долгою до света всё не спится чернецу.
Сном забудешься, так душу грезы черные мутят;
Рад, что в колокол ударят, что разбудят костылем.
Нет, не вытерплю! нет мочи. Чрез ограду да бегом.
Мир велик: мне путь-дорога на четыре стороны,
Поминай как звали.

Чернец

Правда: ваше горькое житье,
Вы разгульные, лихие, молодые чернецы.

Григорий

Хоть бы хан опять нагрянул! хоть Литва бы поднялась!
Так и быть! пошел бы с ними переведаться мечом.
Что, когда бы наш царевич из могилы вдруг воскрес
И вскричал: "А где вы, дети, слуги верные мои?
Вы подите на Бориса, на злодея моего,
Изловите супостата, приведите мне его!.."

Чернец

Полно! не болтай пустого: мертвых нам не воскресить!
Нет, царевичу иное, видно, было суждено —
Но послушай: если дело затевать, так затевать…

[Scene 6]

MONASTERY WALL[67]

Grigory and an evil monk.[68]

Grigory

This wretched life of ours – how wearisome it is, how boring!
Days come, days go – you see and hear the same thing, all the time:
All you see – black cassocks; all you hear – the tolling bell.
By day you walk, and yawn, and yawn, and walk; there's nothing
     to do –
All you can do is doze; but then at night you toss and turn.
No sooner have you got to sleep, black dreams torment your soul;
You're glad to hear the bell at last, to be woken with a stick.
No – I can't endure any more of it! Over the wall, I'm off.
The world is wide, the road is open in any direction I please.
I'll vanish into thin air.

Monk

It's true, your lives are wearisome;
You may be monks – but you're young as well, high-spirited and
     untamed.

Grigory

If only the Khan attacked again, or Lithuania rose![69]
What an opportunity! I'd try my sword against them.
How would it be if our Tsarevich suddenly rose from the grave,
And he cried to us: "Where are you, lads? Where are my faithful
     followers?
Join me against Boris, help me against the criminal,
Capture that adversary of mine, and bring him here before me!"

Monk

Enough of this empty talk; how can we resurrect the dead?
No, the Tsarevich met with quite a different fate – listen:
If you think of doing something, do it …

Григорий

Что такое?

Чернец

Если б я был так же молод, как и ты,
Если б ус не пробивала уж лихая седина…
Понимаешь?

Григорий

Нет, нисколько.

Чернец

Слушай, глупый наш народ
Легковерен: рад дивиться чудесам и новизне;
А бояре в Годунове помнят равного себе;
Племя древнего Варяга и теперь любезно всем.
Ты царевичу ровесник… если ты хитер и тверд…
Понимаешь?

(Молчание.)

Григорий

Понимаю.

Чернец

Что же скажешь?

Григорий

Решено
Я — Димитрий, я — царевич.

Чернец

Дай мне руку: будешь царь.

Grigory
What do you mean?

Monk

If I were your age,
If my whiskers weren't already streaked with grey … Do you
   understand?

Grigory
Not at all.

Monk
Well, listen. Our people are stupid, they're easily taken in;
They're quick to believe in miracles – always wondering at some new
   thing.[70]
In Godunov the boyars remember an equal of themselves;
Even today the old Varangian line is loved by all.[71]
You're the same age as the Tsarevich[72] … If you are bold and
   cunning …
You understand?

Silence.

Grigory
I understand.

Monk
What do you say?

Grigory

Decided.
I am Dimitry, the Tsarevich.

Monk
My hand: you will be Tsar.

[Сцена 7]

ПАЛАТЫ ПАТРИАРХА

ПАТРИАРХ, ИГУМЕН ЧУДОВА МОНАСТЫРЯ.

Патриарх

И он убежал, отец игумен?

Игумен

Убежал, святый владыко. Вот уж тому третий день.

Патриарх

Пострел, окаянный! Да какого он роду?

Игумен

Из роду Отрепьевых, галицких боярских детей. Смолоду постригся неведомо где, жил в Суздале, в Ефимьевском монастыре, ушел оттуда, шатался по разным обителям, наконец пришел к моей чудовской братии, а я, видя, что он еще млад и неразумен, отдал его под начал отцу Пимену, старцу кроткому и смиренному; и был он весьма грамотен; читал наши летописи, сочинял каноны святым; но, знать, грамота далася ему не от Господа Бога...

Патриарх

Уж эти мне грамотеи! что еще выдумал! *буду царем на Москве!* Ах, он сосуд диавольский! Однако нечего царю и докладывать об этом; что тревожить отца-государя? Довольно будет объявить о побеге дьяку Смирнову или дьяку Ефимьеву; эдака ересь! *буду царем на Москве!..* Поймать, поймать врагоугодника да и сослать в Соловецкий на вечное покаяние. Ведь это ересь, отец игумен.

Игумен

Ересь, святый владыко, сущая ересь.

[Scene 7]

THE PATRIARCH'S PALACE

The Patriarch; Father Superior of the Chudov Monastery.

Patriarch

So he's run away, has he, father?

Father Superior

He has, my lord. Three days ago.[73]

Patriarch

The rogue! What's his family?

Father Superior

He's of the Otrepiev family, descendants of petty gentry from Galich.[74] Took his vows at an early age, not known where – lived for a time in Suzdal, Yefimiev Monastery – left it and wandered about from one place to another – in the fullness of time, came to our brotherhood here at Chudov,[75] and seeing how young and unwise he was, I put him in the hands of Father Pimen, an elder, a quiet and gentle one. He certainly had education; he read all our chronicles, he composed hymns to the saints; but such education could not have come to him from the Lord God –

Patriarch

I've had enough of the educated ones! Whatever will they think up next? *"I shall be Tsar in Moscow!"* He's an instrument of Satan! But there's no reason to report any of this to the Tsar – mustn't trouble the Sovereign Father. It will suffice to report his disappearance to Secretary Smirnov or Secretary Yefimiev. The heresy of it! *"I shall be Tsar in Moscow!"* We must catch him, we must, this creature of the Devil, and he must be sent to Solovetsky for perpetual penitence.[76] This is heresy, is it not, father?

Father Superior

Heresy indeed, Holy Father, outright heresy![77]

[Сцена 8]

ЦАРСКИЕ ПАЛАТЫ

ДВА СТОЛЬНИКА.

Первый
Где государь?

Второй
          В своей опочивальне
Он заперся с каким-то колдуном.

Первый
Так, вот его любимая беседа:
Кудесники, гадатели, колдуньи.—
Всё ворожит, что красная невеста.
Желал бы знать, о чем гадает он?

Второй
Вот он идет. Угодно ли спросить?

Первый
Как он угрюм!

          (Уходят.)

Царь
(входит)
          Достиг я высшей власти;
Шестой уж год я царствую спокойно.
Но счастья нет моей душе. Не так ли
Мы смолоду влюбляемся и алчем
Утех любви, но только утолим
Сердечный глад мгновенным обладаньем,

[Scene 8]

THE TSAR'S PALACE

Two courtiers.

First

Where is the Tsar?

Second

As usual, in his bedchamber;
He's closeted with some magician.

First

Yes,

His favorite company now: he only talks
To sorcerers, fortune-tellers and magicians;
He's always reading omens, like a bride.[78]
I'd like to know what this is all about.

Second

Here he comes. Is this the time to ask?

First

How grim

He looks!

(Exeunt.)

Tsar
(enters)

I have attained the highest power;
I have enjoyed six years of peaceful rule.
But in my heart I know no happiness.
Is this not the way we fell in love when young,
Thirsting for the joys of love, and slaking
Our heart's desire with momentary possession –

Уж охладев, скучаем и томимся?..
Напрасно мне кудесники сулят
Дни долгие, дни власти безмятежной —
Ни власть, ни жизнь меня не веселят;
Предчувствую небесный гром и горе.
Мне счастья нет. Я думал свой народ
В довольствии, во славе успокоить,
Щедротами любовь его снискать —
Но отложил пустое попеченье:
Живая власть для черни ненавистна.
Они любить умеют только мертвых —
Безумны мы, когда народный плеск
Иль ярый вопль тревожит сердце наше!
Бог насылал на землю нашу глад,
Народ завыл, в мученьях погибая;
Я отворил им житницы, я злато
Рассыпал им, я им сыскал работы —
Они ж меня, беснуясь, проклинали!
Пожарный огнь их домы истребил,
Я выстроил им новые жилища.
Они ж меня пожаром упрекали!
Вот черни суд: ищи ж ее любви.
В семье моей я мнил найти отраду,
Я дочь мою мнил осчастливить браком —
Как буря, смерть уносит жениха...
И тут молва лукаво нарекает
Виновником дочернего вдовства —
Меня, меня, несчастного отца!..
Кто ни умрет, я всех убийца тайный:
Я ускорил Феодора кончину,
Я отравил свою сестру царицу —
Монахиню смиренную... всё я!
Ах! чувствую: ничто не может нас
Среди мирских печалей успокоить;
Ничто, ничто... едина разве совесть.
Так, здравая, она восторжествует
Над злобою, над темной клеветою...
Но если в ней единое пятно,

But soon to cool, and grow oppressed and bored?[79]
In vain have all the soothsayers promised me
Long years, long tranquil years of power unchallenged;
For neither power nor life can gladden me:
I feel the thunder and the woe of Heaven.
There is no happiness for me. My people
I thought to offer glory and contentment,
To win their love with liberality;
But I have laid aside that fruitless task –
Living power is hateful to the mob,
Their love is given only to the dead:
We should be madmen if we were to let
The people's howls or plaudits move our heart.
God visited a famine on our land,
The people were in torment, wailing, dying;[80]
I opened granaries, I scattered gold,
I sought out work for them – they raged and cursed me![81]
Conflagration swallowed up their homes,
I built them new – they blamed me for the fire![82]
The rabble's judgement: who would seek its love!
I thought I might find solace in my family,
I thought to give my daughter joy in marriage –
And like a storm, death carries off the bridegroom![83]
Now evil rumor fastens on to *me*
As author of my daughter's widowhood,
Me, the unhappy father! … Whoever dies,
I am the secret murderer: Feodor too
I helped to his end; I poisoned my own sister,
The Nun-Tsaritsa … Always, I am blamed![84]
Ah! how I feel it: nothing gives us peace
Amidst the tribulations of this world;
Nothing, nothing … save, perhaps, only conscience.
When it is clear, it triumphs over evil,
The blackest calumny … But should one stain,
One single stain, just chance to appear upon it,
Then – woe betide us! Raging pestilence
Will burn the soul, and poison fill the heart,
Reproach assault the ears with hammer-blows,

Единое, случайно завелося;
Тогда — беда! Как язвой моровой,
Душа сгорит, нальется сердце ядом,
Как молотком, стучит в ушах упреком,
И всё тошнит, и голова кружится,
И мальчики кровавые в глазах…
И рад бежать, да некуда… ужасно!
Да, жалок тот, в ком совесть нечиста.

And spinning head, and rising nausea,
And blood-bathed boys appear before the eyes ...
How glad I'd be to flee – but where?[85] ... Horrible!
Oh, pity him whose conscience is unclean!

[Сцена 9]

КОРЧМА
НА ЛИТОВСКОЙ ГРАНИЦЕ

МИСАИЛ И ВАРЛААМ, БРОДЯГИ-ЧЕРНЕЦЫ;
ГРИГОРИЙ ОТРЕПЬЕВ, МИРЯНИНОМ; ХОЗЯЙКА.

Хозяйка
Чем-то мне вас потчевать, старцы честные?

Варлаам
Чем Бог пошлет, хозяюшка. Нет ли вина?

Хозяйка
Как не быть, отцы мои! сейчас вынесу.

(Уходит.)

Мисаил
Что ж ты закручинился, товарищ? Вот и граница литовская, до которой так хотелось тебе добраться.

Григорий
Пока не буду в Литве, до тех пор не буду спокоен.

Варлаам
Что тебе Литва так слюбилась? Вот мы, отец Мисаил да я грешный, как утекли из монастыря, так ни о чем уж и не думаем. Литва ли, Русь ли, что гудок, что гусли: всё нам равно, было бы вино… да вот и оно!..

Мисаил
Складно сказано, отец Варлаам.

Хозяйка
(входит)
Вот вам, отцы мои. Пейте на здоровье.

[Scene 9]

A TAVERN ON THE LITHUANIAN BORDER

Misail and Varlaam, vagrant monks; Grigory Otrepiev, dressed as a layman;[86] *hostess.*

Hostess

With what am I to regale you with, me good fathers?

Varlaam

Whatever God provides, my good lady. Would there be any vodka?[87]

Hostess

That there surely is, me fathers! I'll fetch you some at once.

(Exit.)

Misail

Why so gloomy, my friend? This is the Lithuanian border, that you were so eager to reach.

Grigory

I won't rest until I'm in Lithuania.

Varlaam

Why so fond of Lithuania? Now look at us, Misail and myself, sinner that I am – ever since we gave the monastery the slip we haven't had a care in the world. Russia or Lithuania, a rebeck or a rattle:[88] everything's fine as long as there's wine – and here comes mine![89]

Misail

Nicely spoken, Father Varlaam.

Hostess

(enters)

There you are, me good fathers. Drink yer 'ealth.

Мисаил
Спасибо, родная, Бог тебя благослови.

*(Монахи пьют; Варлаам затягивает
песню: «Ты проходишь дорогая»
и пр.)*

(Григорию)
Что же ты не подтягиваешь да и не потягиваешь?

Григорий
Не хочу.

Мисаил
Вольному воля…

Варлаам
А пьяному рай, отец Мисаил! Выпьем же чарочку за шинкарочку…

*(«Где неволей добрый молодец»
и пр.)*

Однако, отец Мисаил, когда я пью, так трезвых не люблю; ино дело пьянство, а иное чванство; хочешь жить, как мы, милости просим — нет, так убирайся, проваливай: скоморох попу не товарищ.

Григорий
Пей да про себя разумей, отец Варлаам! Видишь, и я порой складно говорить умею.

Варлаам
А что мне про себя разуметь?

Мисаил
Оставь его, отец Варлаам.

Misail

Thank you, my dear, and God bless you.

*(The monks drink; Varlaam begins a
song: "You walk past my cell, my dear
one," etc.)*[90]

(to Grigory)

Do you think it's wrong to sing along? Do you think it's daft to have a draft?

Grigory

I don't feel like it.

Misail

Freedom for the free –

Varlaam

– And Paradise for the drinker! That's it, Father Misail! And a toastess to the hostess! ..

*("Where a fine young lad, against his
will," etc.)*

But you know, Father Misail, your true-blue toper don't like 'em sober; enjoyin' a cup can't be stuck up. If you want to live like us, then God love you, we embrace you – if not, then off and away with you: a minstrel is no friend of a priest.[91]

Grigory

Drink your health, but watch yourself, Father Varlaam! See? I can do nice speaking too.

Varlaam

And why should I watch myself?

Misail

Leave him alone, Father Varlaam.

Варлаам

Да что он за постник? Сам же к нам навязался в товарищи, неведомо кто, неведомо откуда — да еще и спесивится; может быть, кобылу нюхал…

(Пьет и поет.)

Григорий
(хозяйке)

Куда ведет эта дорога?

Хозяйка

В Литву, мой кормилец, к Луёвым горам.

Григорий

А далече ли до Луёвых гор?

Хозяйка

Недалече, к вечеру можно бы туда поспеть, кабы не заставы царские да сторожевые приставы.

Григорий

Как, заставы! что это значит?

Хозяйка

Кто-то бежал из Москвы, а велено всех задерживать да осматривать.

Григорий
(про себя)

Вот тебе, бабушка, Юрьев день.

Варлаам

Эй, товарищ! да ты к хозяйке присуседился. Знать, не нужна тебе водка, а нужна молодка, дело, брат, дело! у всякого свой обычай; а у нас с отцом Мисаилом одна заботушка: пьем до донушка, выпьем, поворотим и в донушко поколотим.

Varlaam

What sort of a faster is he supposed to be? It was *him* that wanted to be friends with *us*, heaven knows who he is, heaven knows where he comes from – and the airs he puts on; perhaps he's sniffed out a mare …[92]

(Drinks and sings.)

Grigory
(to the hostess)

Where does this road lead?

Hostess

To Lithuania, me young master, to the Luyov 'ills.

Grigory

Is it far to the Luyov Hills?

Hostess

'tain't far, you could get there be nightfall, that's if you don't meet one of the Tsar's pickets or the frontier guards.[93]

Grigory

Pickets – what do you mean?

Hostess

Someone's run away from Moscow, and orders 'as gone out everyone's to be stopped and searched.[94]

Grigory
(to himself)

Now mother, here's Saint George's Day for you.[95]

Varlaam

Oho, my friend! Sweetening up our hostess, eh? You won't have wine and you won't have song, it's women for you, all the way. At 'er boy! Different strokes for different folks. Father Misail and me, we've just the one: drink up, and drink to the bottom o' the tankar'; turn 'er upside-down and spank 'er.[96]

Мисаил

Складно сказано, отец Варлаам…

Григорий

Да кого ж им надобно? Кто бежал из Москвы?

Хозяйка

А Господь его ведает, вор ли, разбойник — только здесь и добрым людям нынче прохода нет — а что из того будет? ничего; ни лысого беса не поймают: будто в Литву нет и другого пути, как столбовая дорога! Вот хоть отсюда свороти влево да бором иди по тропинке до часовни, что на Чеканском ручью, а там прямо через болото на Хлопино, а оттуда на Захарьево, а тут уж всякой мальчишка доведет до Луёвых гор. От этих приставов только и толку, что притесняют прохожих да обирают нас бедных. *(Слышен шум.)* Что там еще? ах, вот они, проклятые! дозором идут.

Григорий

Хозяйка! нет ли в избе другого угла?

Хозяйка

Нету, родимый. Рада бы сама спрятаться. Только слава, что дозором ходят, а подавай им и вина, и хлеба, и неведомо чего — чтоб им издохнуть, окаянным! чтоб им…

(Входят приставы.)

Пристав

Здорово, хозяйка!

Хозяйка

Добро пожаловать, гости дорогие, милости просим.

Один пристав
(другому)

Ба! да здесь попойка идет; будет чем поживиться.

(Монахам)

Вы что за люди?

Misail

Nicely spoken, Father Varlaam …

Grigory

But who do they want? Who's run away from Moscow?

Hostess

God only knows, some brigand or bandit or other – only now it's ordinary decent folk can't get through – and what'll come of it all? Nothing!
They won't catch nobody! As if the 'igh-road was the only way into Lithuania! Now what you 'ave to do, turn left from 'ere, take the footpath through
the pines[97] as far as the shrine by the stream at Chekansk, from there cross
straight over the marsh to Khlopino, then on to Zakharievo, and from
there any little boy will see you to the Luyov 'ills. All those guards are good
for is bullying travelers and shaking us poor folk down. *(A noise is heard
outside.)* What's that now? Ah, it's them again, damn them guards!

Grigory

Landlady! Would you have a little cubby-hole somewhere?

Hostess

No, me dear. I'd be glad to 'ide from 'em meself. It's only what they say,
that they're going on their rounds, but I 'ave to serve 'em vodka and bread
and God knows what – wish they'd drop dead, curse 'em! wish they'd …

(Enter guards.)

Guards

'ullo there, good 'ostess!

Hostess

Welcome, dear guests, you're very welcome.

One of the Guards
(to the other)

Aha! Some drinkin' goin' on 'ere. We'll make somethin' outa this.

(To the monks)

'oo are you then?

Варлаам

Мы Божии старцы, иноки смиренные, ходим по селениям да собираем милостыню христианскую на монастырь.

Пристав
(Григорию)

А ты?

Мисаил

Наш товарищ…

Григорий

Мирянин из пригорода; проводил старцев до рубежа, отселе иду восвояси.

Мисаил

Так ты раздумал…

Григорий
(тихо)

Молчи.

Пристав

Хозяйка, выставь-ка еще вина — а мы здесь со старцами попьем да побеседуем.

Другой пристав
(тихо)

Парень-то, кажется, гол, с него взять нечего; зато старцы…

Первый

Молчи, сейчас до них доберемся. — Что, отцы мои? каково промышляете?

Варлаам

Плохо, сыне, плохо! ныне христиане стали скупы; деньгу любят, деньгу прячут. Мало Богу дают. Прииде грех велий на языцы земнии. Все пустилися в торги, в мытарства; думают о мирском богатстве, не о спасении души. Ходишь, ходишь; молишь, молишь; иногда в три дни трех полушек не вымолишь. Такой грех! Пройдет неделя, другая, заглянешь в мошонку,

Varlaam

Elders of God, sire, just humble monks, just going about the villages collecting alms from Christian folk for our monastery.

Guard
(to Grigory)

And you?

Misail

He's our comrade –

Grigory

I'm a layman from the outskirts of the town. I've accompanied these monks to the border, and now I'm on my way home.

Misail

So you've changed your mind –

Grigory
(under his breath)

Be quiet!

Guard

Bring us some more vodka, m' lady. We'll 'ave a little drink and some conversation with the monks 'ere.

Second Guard
(in a low voice)

The boy don't look as if he 'as a kopek on 'im – but those monks …

First Guard

Shh! We're just coming to 'em now. – Well fathers, 'ow's business?

Varlaam

Poorly, good sirses, poorly! Christian folk these days are turned into misers; they're fond of their coppers, so they 'ide 'em away. Little do they give to the Lord. Great sin hath visited upon the tribes of the Earth. They have sunk unto trade and extortion; their minds are filled with Mammon, not salvation. You walk all day, you pray all day, and yea, some-

ан в ней так мало, что совестно в монастырь показаться; что делать? с горя и остальное пропьешь; беда да и только.— Ох плохо, знать, пришли наши последние времена...

Хозяйка
(плачет)

Господь помилуй и спаси!

(В продолжение Варлаамовой речи
первый пристав значительно
всматривается в Мисаила.)

Первый пристав

Алеха! при тебе ли царский указ?

Второй

При мне.

Первый

Подай-ка сюда.

Мисаил

Что ты на меня так пристально смотришь?

Первый пристав

А вот что: из Москвы бежал некоторый злой еретик, Гришка Отрепьев, слыхал ли ты это?

Мисаил

Не слыхал.

Пристав

Не слыхал? ладно. А того беглого еретика царь приказал изловить и повесить. Знаешь ли ты это?

times three days of praying don't bring you three quarter-kopeks.[98] Such sin! One week goes by, another week goes by, you look into your purse and find so little in it you're ashamed to show your face at the monastery. What can you do – you 'ave to drink the pittance you've got out of sheer grief. It's a calamity, so it is. – Verily, verily, poorly things are nowadays; the Last Days are upon us …[99]

Hostess
(weeping)

Lord have mercy on us and save us!

(During Varlaam's speech the first
guard has been staring at Misail.)

First Guard

Alyokha! You've got the Tsar's Decree, 'asn't you?

Second Guard

I've got it.

First Guard

Let's 'ave it then.

Misail

Why are you staring at me like that?

First Guard

I'll tell you why. Some wicked 'eretic 'as run away from Moscow – Otrepiev, 'e's called. 'aven't you 'eard?

Misail

No.

Guard

You 'aven't 'eard? Well, the Tsar has sent out a Decree for that wicked 'eretic to be captured and 'anged. Didn't you know?

Мисаил

Не знаю.

Пристав
(Варлааму)

Умеешь ли ты читать?

Варлаам

Смолоду знал, да разучился.

Пристав
(Мисаилу)

А ты?

Мисаил

Не умудрил господь.

Пристав

Так вот тебе царский указ.

Мисаил

На что мне его?

Пристав

Мне сдается, что этот беглый еретик, вор, мошенник — ты.

Мисаил

Я! помилуй! что ты?

Пристав

Постой! держи двери. Вот мы сейчас и справимся.

Хозяйка

Ах, они окаянные мучители! и старца-то в покое не оставят!

Пристав

Кто здесь грамотный?

Misail

No, I didn't.

Guard
(to Varlaam)

Can you read?

Varlaam

When I was young I could, but I've lost it all now.

Guard
(to Misail)

And what about you?

Misail

God didn't enlighten me.

Guard

'ere's the Tsar's Decree for you then.

Misail

What would I be doing with that?

Guard

I 'ave an idea that that runaway 'eretic, that criminal, that scoundrel –
is *you*.

Misail

Me? Lord have mercy! What's that you're saying!

Guard

Just a minute! Bolt the doors. We're goin' to get to the bottom o' this.

Hostess

Ah, these cursed tormentors! Won't even leave an old monk in peace!

Guard

Can anyone 'ere read?

Григорий
(выступает вперед)

Я грамотный.

Пристав

Вот на! А у кого же ты научился?

Григорий

У нашего пономаря.

Пристав
(дает ему указ)

Читай же вслух.

Григорий
(читает)

«Чюдова монастыря недостойный чернец Григорий, из роду Отрепьевых, впал в ересь и дерзнул, наученный диаволом, возмущать святую братию всякими соблазнами и беззакониями. А по справкам оказалось, отбежал он, окаянный Гришка, к границе литовской...»

Пристав
(Мисаилу)

Как же не ты?

Григорий

«И царь повелел изловить его...»

Пристав

И повесить.

Григорий

Тут не сказано *повесить*.

Пристав

Врешь: не всяко слово в строку пишется. Читай: изловить и повесить.

>   *Grigory*
>   *(steps forward)*

I can.

>   *Guard*

Aha! And 'oo taught you, might I ask?

>   *Grigory*

Our sexton.

>   *Guard*
>   *(handing him the Decree)*

Read this out then.

>   *Grigory*
>   *(reads)*

"The unworthy monk Grigory of the Chudov Monastery, from the Otrepiev family, has fallen into heresy and, instructed by the Devil, has had the audacity to distress the holy brotherhood by all manner of incitements and iniquities. According to reports, the accursed Grishka has fled from the said monastery and is making for the Lithuanian border –"

>   *Guard*
>   *(to Misail)*

So 'ow's this not you?

>   *Grigory*

"– and the Tsar decrees that he be seized –"

>   *Guard*

And 'anged.

>   *Grigory*

It doesn't say "hanged."

>   *Guard*

Oh yes it does. You 'ave to read between the lines as well.[100] Read it out proper: "Seized and 'anged."

Григорий

«И повесить. А лет ему вору Гришке от роду... *(смотря на Варлаама)* за 50. А росту он среднего, лоб имеет плешивый, бороду седую, брюхо толстое...»

(Все глядят на Варлаама.)

Пристав

Ребята! здесь Гришка! держите, вяжите его! Вот уж не думал, не гадал.

Варлаам
(вырывая бумагу)

Отстаньте, блядины дети! что я за Гришка? — как! 50 лет, борода седая, брюхо толстое! нет, брат! молод еще надо мною шутки шутить. Я давно не читывал и худо разбираю, а тут уж разберу, как дело до петли доходит. *(Читает по складам.)* «А лет е-му от-ро-ду...20.» — Что брат? где тут 50? видишь? 20.

Второй пристав

Да, помнится, двадцать. Так и нам было сказано.

Первый пристав
(Григорию)

Да ты, брат, видно забавник.

*(Во время чтения Григорий стоит
потупя голову, с рукою за пазухой.)*

Варлаам
(продолжает)

«А ростом он мал, грудь широкая, одна рука короче другой, глаза голубые, волоса рыжие, на щеке бородавка, на лбу другая.» Да это, друг, уж не ты ли?

Grigory

"... and hanged. The said criminal Grishka is ..." *(looking at Varlaam)* "over fifty years of age. He is of medium height, bald at the front, has a grey beard, a fat belly ..."

(Everyone looks at Varlaam.)

Guard

Lads! That's Grishka! 'old 'im! Tie 'im up! I wouldn't never 'ave thought it, never 'ave guessed it, no I wouldn't.

Varlaam
(snatches the Decree)

Just a minute, you sons of whores![101] What sort of Grishka am I? What did you say? Fifty years of age, grey beard, fat belly! All right, my young friend, you can make jokes about me if you like. It's a long time since I read anything, and I can hardly make it out, but I'll make it out this time, since it's the noose we're talking about. *(Reads out syllable by syllable:)* "And – he – is ... twenty – years of age." What's this, my friend? Where does it say fifty? Look here – "twenty."

Second Guard

Yes, I remember now, it *was* twenty. That's what they said.

First Guard
(to Grigory)

Now my friend, what are you playin' at?

*(During Varlaam's reading Grigory has
been standing with bowed head, his
hand tucked into his shirt.)*

Varlaam
(continues)

"He is short of stature, broad-chested, has one arm shorter than the other; eyes blue, hair ginger; he has a wart on one cheek and another on his forehead."[102] Now doesn't that sound more like you, my friend?

(Григорий вдруг вынимает кинжал;
все перед ним расступаются, он
бросается в окно.)

Приставы

Держи! держи!

(Все бегут в беспорядке.)

*(Grigory suddenly draws a dagger;
everyone backs away from him, he
makes a dash for the window.)*

Guards

'old 'im! 'old 'im!

(Everyone rushes about in confusion.)

[Сцена 10]

МОСКВА.
ДОМ ШУЙСКОГО

ШУЙСКИЙ, МНОЖЕСТВО ГОСТЕЙ. УЖИН.

Шуйский
Вина еще.

(Встает, за ним и все.)

Ну, гости дорогие,
Последний ковш! Читай молитву, мальчик.

Мальчик
Царю небес, везде и присно сущий,
Своих рабов молению внемли:
Помолимся о нашем государе,
Об избранном тобой, благочестивом
Всех христиан царе самодержавном.
Храни его в палатах, в поле ратном,
И на путях, и на одре ночлега.
Подай ему победу на враги,
Да славится он от моря до моря.
Да здравием цветет его семья,
Да осенят ея драгие ветви
Весь мир земной — а к нам, своим рабам,
Да будет он, как прежде, благодатен,
И милостив и долготерпелив,
Да мудрости его неистощимой
Проистекут источники на нас;
И, царскую на то воздвигнув чашу,
Мы молимся тебе, Царю небес.

Шуйский
(пьет)
Да здравствует великий государь!
Простите же вы, гости дорогие;

[Scene 10]

MOSCOW. SHUISKY'S HOUSE

Shuisky; a number of guests. Supper.

Shuisky

More wine.

(Rises to his feet, followed by the rest.)

Dear guests, a last cup! – Boy, the prayer.

Boy

O Lord, which art in all things, everywhere,
Now hear Thy servant's prayer. Let us pray
For him Thou chose to rule us Christian people,
Our noble and devout Tsar-Autocrat.
Preserve him in his palace, on the field,
And in his journeying, by day and night.
And grant him victory over all his foes,
And may his glory reach from sea to sea,
His family flourish, may its precious branches
Provide a sure protection for the world;
May he bestow his mercy and his patience
On us his humble servants, now and always,
And may the wellsprings of his wisdom flow
Without surcease upon us. Let us raise
The royal cup: our prayer come unto Thee,
O Lord of Heaven.[103]

Shuisky
(drinks)

Long live our noble sovereign!
Farewell, dear guests; I thank you for your kindness,

Благодарю, что вы моей хлеб-солью
Не презрели. Простите, добрый сон.

(Гости уходят, он провожает их
до дверей.)

Пушкин

Насилу убрались; ну, князь Василий Иванович, я уж думал, что нам не
удастся и переговорить.

Шуйский
(слугам)
Вы что рот разинули? Всё бы вам господ
подслушивать.—
Сбирайте со стола да ступайте вон.— Что такое,
Афанасий Михайлович?

Пушкин
Чудеса да и только.
Племянник мой, Гаврила Пушкин, мне
Из Кракова гонца прислал сегодня.

Шуйский
Ну.

Пушкин
Странную племянник пишет новость.
Сын Грозного... постой.

(Идет к дверям и осматривает.)

Державный отрок,
По манию Бориса убиенный...

Шуйский
Да это уж не ново.

Пушкин
Погоди:
Димитрий жив.

Not to have spurned my hospitality.
Farewell to you, a pleasant night to all.

(Exeunt guests; Shuisky
accompanies them to the door.)

Afanasy Mikhailovich Pushkin[104]
At last they're gone. Well now, Prince Vasily Ivanovich, I was beginning
to think we should never have a chance to talk together.

Shuisky
(to the servants)
What are you gaping at? Eavesdrop on your masters, that's all you'd ever
do if you could.[105] – Clear the table and be off with you. – What is it,
Afanasy Mikhailovich?

Pushkin
Miracles, that's all one can say.
Today a courier came to me from Cracow –
Sent by my nephew there, Gavrila Pushkin.[106]

Shuisky
Well?

Pushkin
My nephew sends the strangest news.
Ivan the Terrible's son ...

(Goes to the door and looks about.)

His son and heir,
Murdered at Boris Godunov's behest –

Shuisky
Hardly news.

Pushkin
Dimitry is alive.

Шуйский

Вот-на! какая весть!
Царевич жив! ну подлинно чудесно.
И только-то?

Пушкин

Послушай до конца.
Кто б ни был он, спасенный ли царевич,
Иль некий дух во образе его,
Иль смелый плут, бесстыдный самозванец,
Но только там Димитрий появился.

Шуйский

Не может быть.

Пушкин

Его сам Пушкин видел,
Как приезжал впервой он во дворец
И сквозь ряды литовских панов прямо
Шел в тайную палату короля.

Шуйский

Кто же он такой? откуда он?

Пушкин

Не знают.
Известно то, что он слугою был
У Вишневецкого, что на одре болезни
Открылся он духовному отцу,
Что гордый пан, его проведав тайну,
Ходил за ним, поднял его с одра
И с ним потом уехал к Сигизмунду.

Шуйский

Что ж говорят об этом удальце?

Пушкин

Да слышно, он умен, приветлив, ловок,
По нраву всем. Московских беглецов

Shuisky

Well now, that's news! Dimitry is alive?
A miracle indeed! What else do you know?

Pushkin

Let me finish. Whoever he might be,
The real Tsarevich come to us alive,
Some spirit in the shape of the Tsarevich,
Or simply an arrant rogue, a shameless pretender –
The plain fact is, Dimitry has appeared.

Shuisky

Impossible!

Pushkin

Pushkin saw him himself,
Arriving at the royal court; he strode
Straight through the ranks of Lithuanian nobles
Into the private chambers of the King.[107]

Shuisky

Who is he? Where does he come from?

Pushkin

No one knows.
All that is known is that he was a servant
To Wiśniowiecki, whom, upon his sickbed,
He told of many things; the haughty prince,
Learning the young man's secret, cared for him
And set him on his feet again, and took him
To Cracow to the court of King Sigismund.[108]

Shuisky

What do they say of this audacious fellow?

Pushkin

That he's extremely clever, cunning, charming,
Everyone likes him. He has quite bewitched

Обворожил. Латинские попы
С ним заодно. Король его ласкает,
И говорят, помогу обещал.

Шуйский
Всё это, брат, такая кутерьма,
Что голова кругом пойдет невольно.
Сомненья нет, что это самозванец,
Но, признаюсь, опасность не мала.
Весть важная! и если до народа
Она дойдет, то быть грозе великой.

Пушкин
Такой грозе, что вряд царю Борису
Сдержать венец на умной голове.
И поделом ему! он правит нами,
Как царь Иван (не к ночи будь помянут).
Что пользы в том, что явных казней нет,
Что на колу кровавом, всенародно
Мы не поем канонов Иисусу,
Что нас не жгут на площади, а царь
Своим жезлом не подгребает углей?
Уверены ль мы в бедной жизни нашей?
Нас каждый день опала ожидает,
Тюрьма, Сибирь, клобук иль кандалы,
А там — в глуши голодна смерть иль петля.
Знатнейшие меж нами роды — где?
Где Сицкие князья, где Шестуновы,
Романовы, отечества надежда?
Заточены, замучены в изгнаньи.
Дай срок: тебе такая ж будет участь.
Легко ль, скажи! мы дома, как Литвой,
Осаждены неверными рабами;
Всё языки, готовые продать,
Правительством подкупленные воры.
Зависим мы от первого холопа,
Которого захочем наказать.
Вот — Юрьев день задумал уничтожить.
Не властны мы в поместиях своих.

The Moscow émigrés. The Jesuits
Are close to him. He's favored by the King –
It's said the King has promised him his help.[109]

Shuisky

My friend, all this confusion makes one's head spin.
No doubt of it, the man is an impostor;
The danger, though, is none the less for that.
The news you bring is grave, and should it reach
The people, we shall have a mighty storm.

Pushkin

And such a storm, our tsar may find it hard
To keep the crown upon his clever head.
Well, serve him right! He rules us like Tsar Ivan
(Whose name should never be pronounced at night).
What if we have no public executions?
What if, before the people's eyes, we sing
No hymns to Jesus on the bloodied stake?
What if we're not being burned on the public square,
On coals the Tsar himself stokes with his rod?
Can we be certain of our wretched lives?
Disgrace awaits us where we least expect it,
Prison, Siberia, fetters or the cowl,
A lonely death by hanging or starvation.
Where are the most illustrious families now?[110]
Where are the Sitskys, Shestunovs, Romanovs –
The hope of all our land? In dungeons, or
In exile.[111] We are sure to share their fate.
What lives we live! Our treacherous servants
Lay siege to us in our homes like Lithuanians;
Every tongue is ready to betray us,
The government buys every brigand's ear.
We're at the mercy of the lowliest bondsman
We're going to punish with good cause.[112] And now ...
Now he abolishes Saint George's Day.
We are not masters of our own estates.
You can't dismiss an idler! Like it or not,

Не смей согнать ленивца! Рад не рад,
Корми его; не смей переманить
Работника! — Не то, в Приказ холопий.
Ну, слыхано ль хоть при царе Иване
Такое зло? А легче ли народу?
Спроси его. Попробуй самозванец
Им посулить старинный Юрьев день,
Так и пойдет потеха.

                    Шуйский
                    Прав ты, Пушкин.
Но знаешь ли? Об этом обо всем
Мы помолчим до времени.

                    Пушкин
                         Вестимо,
Знай про себя. Ты человек разумной;
Всегда с тобой беседовать я рад,
И если что меня подчас тревожит,
Не вытерплю, чтоб не сказать тебе.
К тому ж твой мед да бархатное пиво
Сегодня так язык мне развязали...
Прощай же, князь.

                    Шуйский
                    Прощай, брат, до свиданья.

(Провожает Пушкина.)

He's yours to feed.[113] And lure away a peasant –
You'll have the Slaves' Commission after you.[114]
I ask you, even in the reign of Ivan,
Whoever saw such things? And are the people
Happier? Ask them.[115] Should the Pretender promise
The restoration of Saint George's Day –
Then the fun will begin.[116]

Shuisky
　　　　Pushkin – you're right.
But listen: not a word of any of this
Until the moment comes.

Pushkin
　　　　Of course, agreed:
We'll keep this to ourselves. A man of reason.
I'm always glad to have a talk with you.
And meanwhile, should I hear disturbing news,
I shall not fail to tell you. How your mead
And velvet ale untied my tongue this evening …
Good-night, prince.

Shuisky
　　　　Till we meet again, my friend.

(Sees Pushkin out.)

[Сцена 11]

ЦАРСКИЕ ПАЛАТЫ

ЦАРЕВИЧ ЧЕРТИТ ГЕОГРАФИЧЕСКУЮ КАРТУ.
ЦАРЕВНА, МАМКА ЦАРЕВНЫ.

Ксения
(держит портрет)
Что ж уста твои
Не промолвили,
Очи ясные
Не проглянули?
Аль уста твои
Затворилися,
Очи ясные
Закатилися?..

Братец — а братец! скажи: королевич похож был на мой образок?

Феодор
Я говорю тебе, что похож.

Ксения
(целует портрет)
Милый мой жених, прекрасный королевич, не мне ты достался, не своей невесте — а темной могилке, на чужой сторонке. Никогда не утешусь, вечно по тебе буду плакать.

Мамка
И, царевна! девица плачет, что роса падет; взойдет солнце, росу высушит. Будет у тебя другой жених и прекрасный, и приветливый. Полюбишь его, дитя наше ненаглядное, забудешь Ивана-королевича.

Ксения
Нет, мамушка, я и мертвому буду ему верна.

[Scene 11]

THE TSAR'S PALACE

The Tsarevich, drawing a map; Tsarevna; Tsarevna's nurse.[117]

Ksenia
(holding a cameo portrait)
Why don't your lips
Speak to me,
Your bright eyes
Look at me?
Or have your lips
Closed for ever,
Your bright eyes
Set for ever?

Brother – brother! Tell me: was the prince like his portrait?[118]

Feodor
As I've been telling you, he was.

Ksenia
(kisses the portrait)
My dear bridegroom, my handsome prince, you were not given to me, your bride, but to a dark grave in the foreign quarter.[119] I shall never be consoled, I shall weep for you forever.

Nurse
Now Tsarevna! A young girl's tears are like the fallen dew; the sun comes up and the dew dries.[120] You'll have another bridegroom, and he will be handsome and charming too. You will be in love with him, precious child, you'll soon forget your prince.

Ksenia
No, Nurse, even though he has died, I shall be true to him.

(Входит Борис.)

Царь

Что, Ксения? что, милая моя?
В невестах уж печальная вдовица!
Всё плачешь ты о мертвом женихе.
Дитя мое! судьба мне не сулила
Виновником быть вашего блаженства.
Я, может быть, прогневал небеса
И счастие твое не мог устроить.
Безвинная, зачем же ты страдаешь? —
А ты, мой сын, чем занят? Это что?

Феодор

Чертеж земли московской; наше царство
Из края в край. Вот видишь: тут Москва,
Тут Новгород, тут Астрахань. Вот море,
Вот пермские дремучие леса,
А вот Сибирь.

Царь

         А это что такое
Узором здесь виется?

Феодор

         Это Волга.

Царь

Как хорошо! вот сладкий плод ученья!
Как с облаков ты можешь обозреть
Всё царство вдруг: границы, грады, реки.
Учись, мой сын: наука сокращает
Нам опыты быстротекущей жизни —
Когда-нибудь, и скоро, может быть,
Все области, которые ты ныне
Изобразил так хитро на бумаге,
Все под руку достанутся твою —
Учись, мой сын, и легче, и яснее
Державный труд ты будешь постигать.

(Enter Boris.)

Tsar

My Ksenia, dearest daughter, so unhappy?
No sooner a bride, already a mourning widow!
Fate, my child, has not ordained that I
Should be the originator of your bliss.
Perhaps I have provoked the wrath of God,
And therefore cannot find you happiness.
O innocence! Why is it you that suffers? –
And you, my son, what are you doing? What's this?

Feodor

A map of Muscovy: it shows our country
From end to end. There's Moscow – Astrakhan –
Novgorod – there, the dark, dense woods of Perm –
The sea – Siberia.[121]

Tsar

What is this that makes
A winding pattern?

Feodor

That's the Volga.

Tsar

Good!
Learning's sweet fruits! As from the clouds above,
You look upon the whole of our dominions,
The cities and the rivers and the frontiers.
Study, my son, study; for learning hastens
Experience, that consumer of our life –
Some time, and soon perhaps, the regions
You have so skillfully drawn on paper here
Shall all be in your hands. Study, my son,
The tasks of rule will then be easier for you.

(Входит Семен Годунов.)

Вот Годунов идет ко мне с докладом.

(Ксении)

Душа моя, поди в свою светлицу;
Прости, мой друг. Утешь тебя Господь.

(Ксения с мамкою уходит.)

Что скажешь мне, Семен Ильич?

       Семен Годунов
                Сегодня
Ко мне, чем свет, дворецкий князь-Василья
И Пушкина слуга пришли с доносом.

       Царь
Ну.

       Семен Годунов
    Пушкина слуга донес сперва,
Что поутру вчера к ним в дом приехал
Из Кракова гонец — и через час
Без грамоты отослан был обратно.

       Царь
Гонца схватить.

       Семен Годунов
        Уж послано в догоню.

       Царь
О Шуйском что?

       Семен Годунов
        Вечор он угощал
Своих друзей, обоих Милославских,
Бутурлиных, Михайла Салтыкова,
Да Пушкина — да несколько других;
А разошлись уж поздно. Только Пушкин

(Enter Semyon Godunov.)[122]

Here's Godunov with news for me.

(to Ksenia)

My darling,
Go to your room. God grant you consolation.

(Exeunt Ksenia and the nurse.)

Well now, Semyon Ilyich?[123]

Semyon Godunov
At dawn today
Pushkin's man and Shuisky's came to my house.

Tsar

Well?

Semyon Godunov
Pushkin's man reported first: a courier
Arrived from Cracow yesterday, and left
Their house within the hour with no word back.

Tsar

Take him.

Semyon Godunov
We're after him already, Sire.

Tsar

And Shuisky? …

Semyon Godunov
Yesterday he entertained
Some friends – the Miloslavskys, Saltykov,
Pushkin and the Buturlins, with some others;[124]
They didn't leave till late. But Pushkin stayed
And talked alone with him.

Наедине с хозяином остался
И долго с ним беседовал еще. —

Царь

Сейчас послать за Шуйским.

Семен Годунов

                                        Государь,
Он здесь уже.

Царь

            Позвать его сюда.

            (Годунов уходит.)

Царь

Сношения с Литвою! это что?..
Противен мне род Пушкиных мятежный,
А Шуйскому не должно доверять:
Уклончивый, но смелый и лукавый...

            (Входит Шуйский.)

Мне нужно, князь, с тобою говорить.
Но кажется — ты сам пришел за делом:
И выслушать хочу тебя сперва.

Шуйский

Так, государь: мой долг тебе поведать
Весть важную.

Царь

            Я слушаю тебя.

Шуйский
            (тихо указывая на Феодора)
Но, государь...

Царь

                    Царевич может знать,
Что ведает князь Шуйский. Говори.

Tsar
> Fetch Shuisky.

Semyon Godunov
> > > Sire,
He's come already.

Tsar
> Call him here at once.

(Exit Semyon Godunov.)

Dealings with Lithuania![125] What is this?
How I hate this rebel clan of Pushkins;[126]
And Shuisky too I cannot fully trust –
He's slippery, but courageous, shrewd …

(Enter Shuisky.)

> > > > Now prince,
I have a matter to discuss with you.
But you, it seems, have come with business: first
I'll hear what you've to say.

Shuisky
> > It is my duty
To bring you, Sire, important news.

Tsar
> > > That is …?

Shuisky
(in a low voice, pointing to Feodor)
Sire …

Tsar
> The Tsarevich has a right to know
What Shuisky knows.

Шуйский
Царь, из Литвы пришла нам весть…

Царь

                                        Не та ли,
Что Пушкину привез вечор гонец.

Шуйский
Всё знает он! — Я думал, государь,
Что ты еще не ведаешь сей тайны.

Царь
Нет нужды, князь; хочу сообразить
Известия; иначе не узнаем
Мы истины.

Шуйский
                        Я знаю только то,
Что в Кракове явился самозванец
И что король и паны за него.

Царь
Что ж говорят? Кто этот самозванец?

Шуйский
Не ведаю.

Царь
                Но… чем опасен он?

Шуйский
Конечно, царь: сильна твоя держава,
Ты милостью, раденьем и щедротой
Усыновил сердца своих рабов.
Но знаешь сам: бессмысленная чернь
Изменчива, мятежна, суеверна,
Легко пустой надежде предана,
Мгновенному внушению послушна,

Shuisky
I hear from Lithuania –

Tsar
Through Pushkin's courier – yesterday?

Shuisky
          – He knows
Everything! – Sire, I really didn't think
That news had reached you yet.

Tsar
        No matter, prince.
I like to have my news from different sources;
How else find out the truth?

Shuisky
        I only know –
In Cracow, a pretender has appeared;
The King and the nobility are for him.[127]

Tsar
What is this rumor? Who is this pretender?

Shuisky
Sire, I don't know.

Tsar
     How is he dangerous, though …?

Shuisky
Your realm is mighty, Sire, your subjects' hearts
Are won by your munificence and mercy.
But as you know too well, the senseless mob
Is superstitious, fickle and rebellious,
Often attached to insubstantial goals,
Responsive to the passions of the season,
Deaf and indifferent to the voice of reason,

Для истины глуха и равнодушна,
А баснями питается она.
Ей нравится бесстыдная отвага.
Так если сей неведомый бродяга
Литовскую границу перейдет,
К нему толпу безумцев привлечет
Димитрия воскреснувшее имя.

Царь

Димитрия!.. как? этого младенца!
Димитрия!… Царевич, удались.

Шуйский

Он покраснел: быть буре!..

Феодор

Государь,

Дозволишь ли…

Царь

Нельзя, мой сын, поди.

(Феодор уходит.)

Димитрия!..

Шуйский

Он ничего не знал.

Царь

Послушай, князь: взять меры сей же час;
Чтоб от Литвы Россия оградилась
Заставами: чтоб ни одна душа
Не перешла за эту грань; чтоб заяц
Не прибежал из Польши к нам; чтоб ворон
Не прилетел из Кракова. Ступай.

Шуйский

Иду.

Ready to feed its mind on fairy-tales.
It relishes a bold and brazen game.
So if the unknown vagabond should cross
From Lithuania, he'll collect the dross
Drawn by Dimitry's resurrected name.

Tsar

Dimitry, did you say ... the boy ... Dimitry!
Leave us at once, Tsarevich.

Shuisky
                              How he flushed!
A storm is brewing ...

Feodor
                    But Sire –

Tsar
                              Go now, my son.

(Exit Feodor.)

Dimitry! ...

Shuisky
– Ah, so then he didn't know.

Tsar
You must take measures, prince, immediately:
Muscovy must be sealed from Lithuania
By guards and barriers. Not a single soul
Must cross that border; not a single hare
Must get to us from Poland, not a raven
From Cracow. Act now.[128]

Shuisky
                    Sire, I shall.

Царь

Постой. Не правда ль, эта весть
Затейлива? Слыхал ли ты когда,
Чтоб мертвые из гроба выходили
Допрашивать царей, царей законных,
Назначенных, избранных всенародно,
Увенчанных великим патриархом?
Смешно? а? что? что ж не смеешься ты?

Шуйский

Я, государь?..

Царь

Послушай, князь Василий:
Как я узнал, что отрока сего...
Что отрок сей лишился как-то жизни,
Ты послан был на следствие; теперь
Тебя крестом и Богом заклинаю,
По совести мне правду объяви:
Узнал ли ты убитого младенца
И не было ль подмена? Отвечай.

Шуйский

Клянусь тебе...

Царь

Нет, Шуйский, не клянись,
Но отвечай: то был царевич?

Шуйский

Он.

Царь

Подумай, князь. Я милость обещаю,
Прошедшей лжи опалою напрасной
Не накажу. Но если ты теперь
Со мной хитришь, то головою сына
Клянусь — тебя постигнет злая казнь:
Такая казнь, что царь Иван Васильич
От ужаса во гробе содрогнется.

Tsar

No, wait.
Perhaps – what do you think – this news is false?
Whoever heard of corpses leaving graves
To question tsars, rightful and lawful tsars,
Named and chosen by the assembled people,
Crowned by the holy Patriarch himself?
Laughable, is it not? Why aren't you laughing?

Shuisky

Why should I laugh?

Tsar

Now listen, Prince Vasily:
The moment that I heard the boy had been …
Had somehow lost his life, I called for you
And sent you to investigate the matter.[129]
Now I conjure you by the Cross, by God,
Speak truly: did you recognize the corpse?
Could there have been a substitution? Answer.

Shuisky

I swear –

Tsar

No oaths, I'll have a simple answer:
Was it the body of the Tsarevich?

Shuisky

Yes.[130]

Tsar

Consider carefully, prince. I shall be lenient,
You'll suffer no unnecessary disgrace
For past deceits. But now, if you deceive me,
I swear to you upon the head of Feodor –
You'll die, and by such fearful execution
That even Ivan's bones shall shake with horror.

Шуйский

Не казнь страшна; страшна твоя немилость:
Перед тобой дерзну ли я лукавить?
И мог ли я так слепо обмануться,
Что не узнал Димитрия? Три дня
Я труп его в соборе посещал,
Всем Угличем туда сопровожденный.
Вокруг его тринадцать тел лежало,
Растерзанных народом, и по ним
Уж тление приметно проступало,
Но детский лик царевича был ясен,
И свеж, и тих, как будто усыпленный;
Глубокая не запекалась язва,
Черты ж лица совсем не изменились.
Нет, государь, сомненья нет: Димитрий
Во гробе спит.

Царь

Довольно; удались.

(Шуйский уходит.)

Ух, тяжело!.. дай дух переведу…
Я чувствовал: вся кровь моя в лицо
Мне кинулась — и тяжко опускалась…
Так вот зачем тринадцать лет мне сряду
Всё снилося убитое дитя!
Да, да — вот что! теперь я понимаю.
Но кто же он, мой грозный супостат?
Кто на меня? Пустое имя, тень —
Ужели тень сорвет с меня порфиру,
Иль звук лишит детей моих наследства?
Безумец я! чего ж я испугался?
На призрак сей подуй — и нет его.
Так решено: не окажу я страха —
Но презирать не должно ничего…
Ох, тяжела ты, шапка Мономаха!

Shuisky

It isn't death I fear, but your displeasure;
How, in your presence, would I dare deceive?
And could I have denied my very eyes –
Not recognized Dimitry? Several times
I went to the cathedral, to his body,
Accompanied by all Uglich. There I saw
The bodies of thirteen the crowd had lynched,
In which decay was visible already,
But the Tsarevich's young face was fresh,
Clear and serene, as if he were asleep;
His wound still gaped, his features were unaltered.[131]
Impossible to doubt: Dimitry, Sire,
Rests in his grave.

Tsar
Enough now. Go.

(Exit Shuisky.)

                                    How hard
To bear this! I must catch my breath … I felt it –
Blood rushed to my face, then painfully drained away …
So this is why my dreams, for thirteen years,
Have been of nothing but a murdered child!
Yes, yes – I see now! Now I understand. –
But what is he, this fearful adversary?
An empty name, a shade … And shall a shade –
A sound, remove the purple from my back,
Deprive my children of their patrimony?
Madman! What is there here to frighten me?
Blow on this phantom … it will disappear.
It is decided: I shall show no fear –
But neither shall I cease to watch and mark …
Ah, heavy is the cap of Monomakh![132]

[Сцена 12]

КРАКОВ.
ДОМ ВИШНЕВЕЦКОГО

САМОЗВАНЕЦ И PATER ЧЕРНИКОВСКИЙ.

Самозванец
Нет, мой отец, не будет затруднений;
Я знаю дух народа моего;
В нем набожность не знает исступленья:
Ему священ пример царя его.
Всегда, к тому ж, терпимость равнодушна.
Ручаюсь я, что прежде двух годов
Весь мой народ и вся восточна церковь
Признают власть наместника Петра.

Pater
Вспомоществуй тебе святый Игнатий,
Когда придут иные времена.
А между тем небесной благодати
Таи в душе, царевич, семена.
Притворствовать пред оглашенным светом
Нам иногда духовный долг велит;
Твои слова, деянья судят люди,
Намеренья единый видит Бог.

Самозванец
Amen. Кто там?

(Входит слуга.)

Сказать: мы принимаем.

*(Отворяются двери; входит толпа
русских и поляков.)*

Товарищи! мы выступаем завтра
Из Кракова. Я, Мнишек, у тебя
Остановлюсь в Санборе на три дня.

[Scene 12]

CRACOW. WIŚNIOWIECKI'S HOUSE

The Pretender; Father Czernikowski.[133]

Pretender
Father, I see no difficulties at all.
I am acquainted with my people's nature;
Their faith is not expressed in zealotry,
The example of their tsar is sacred to them.
And tolerance, need I say, is even-handed.
In less than two years' time, I vouch to you,
All my people, all the Eastern Church
Will be obedient to the throne of Peter.[134]

Father Czernikowski
The holy Saint Ignatius grant you succor
In times to come.[135] Meanwhile conceal, Tsarevich,
The seeds of heaven's bliss within your soul.
Spiritual duty may at times bid us
Dissemble to the uninitiated;
Your fellow men assess your words and deeds,
But God alone perceives your true intent.

Pretender
Amen. Who's there?

(Enter a servant.)

Tell them we shall receive them.

*(The doors are opened; enter a
throng of Russians and Poles.)*

My friends, tomorrow we'll set forth from Cracow.
And Mniszech, I shall stay three days with you
In Sambor.[136] Your hospitable demesne

Я знаю: твой гостеприимный замок
И пышностью блистает благородной
И славится хозяйкой молодой —
Прелестную Марину я надеюсь
Увидеть там. — А вы, мои друзья,
Литва и Русь, вы, братские знамена
Поднявшие на общего врага,
На моего коварного злодея,
Сыны славян, я скоро поведу
В желанный бой дружины ваши грозны. —
Но между вас я вижу новы лица.

Гаврила Пушкин
Они пришли у милости твоей
Просить меча и службы.

Самозванец
                         Рад вам, дети.
Ко мне, друзья. — Но кто, скажи мне, Пушкин,
Красавец сей?

Пушкин
Князь Курбский.

Самозванец
                              Имя громко!

(Курбскому)

Ты родственник казанскому герою?

Курбский
Я сын его.

Самозванец
Он жив еще?

Курбский
                  Нет, умер.

Not only abounds in every kind of splendor;
It also glories in a fine young hostess –
I long to see the beautiful Maryna.[137]
And you, my comrades, Lithuania, Russia,
Your banners joined against the common foe,
Against that evil adversary of mine:
Sons of the Slavs, I'll lead your mighty ranks
Into the battle you have long desired.
– I see new faces here.

             Gavrila Pushkin[138]
                  They seek your bounty;
They ask for arms and service.

             Pretender
                       They shall have them.
You'd best join me, my lads. But tell me, Pushkin,
Who is that stalwart?

             Pushkin
Kurbsky.

             Pretender
                       That great name!

        (to Kurbsky)

A kinsman of the hero of Kazan?[139]

             Kurbsky

I am his son.[140]

             Pretender
Is he alive still?

             Kurbsky
                  No.

Самозванец
Великий ум! муж битвы и совета!
Но с той поры, когда являлся он,
Своих обид ожесточенный мститель,
С литовцами под ветхий город Ольгин,
Молва об нем умолкла.

Курбский
          Мой отец
В Волынии провел остаток жизни,
В поместиях, дарованных ему
Баторием. Уединен и тих,
В науках он искал себе отрады;
Но мирный труд его не утешал:
Он юности своей отчизну помнил
И до конца по ней он тосковал.

Самозванец
Несчастный вождь! как ярко просиял
Восход его шумящей, бурной жизни.
Я радуюсь, великородный витязь,
Что кровь его с отечеством мирится.
Вины отцов не должно вспоминать;
Мир гробу их! приближься, Курбский. Руку!
— Не странно ли? сын Курбского ведет
На трон, кого? да — сына Иоанна…
Всё за меня: и люди и судьба.—
Ты кто такой?

Поляк
Собаньский, шляхтич вольный.

Самозванец
Хвала и честь тебе, свободы чадо!
Вперед ему треть жалованья выдать.—
Но эти кто? я узнаю на них
Земли родной одежду. Это наши.

Pretender
A noble mind, in battle and in council![141]
Since, with his Lithuanians, he avenged
His wrongs outside the ancient city of Pskov,
We haven't heard of him.[142]

Kurbsky
                My father spent
The last years of his life in solitude,
On lands Báthory gave him in Volynia.[143]
He gave himself to scientific studies,
But peaceful work could not afford him solace:
He never forgot the country of his youth,
He languished for his homeland to the end.[144]

Pretender
Unhappy prince! How brilliant was the sunrise
Of his resounding and tempestuous life.
My noble knight, what happiness to me
To see his blood and homeland reconciled.
Our fathers' sins should not be called to mind;
Peace to their graves! Now Kurbsky, come, your hand.
Is it not strange? Whom should the son of Kurbsky
Lead to the throne – whom but the son of Ivan …
All's in my favor, men and destiny.
– And you?

Pole
Sobański, of the free nobility.[145]

Pretender
All praise and honor to you, son of freedom!
One-third advance on this month's pay to him.
– And who are these? I recognize their dress,
Our country's. These are men of ours.

Хрущов
(бьет челом)
Так, государь, отец наш. Мы твои
Усердные, гонимые холопья.
Мы из Москвы, опальные, бежали
К тебе, наш царь, мы за тебя готовы
Главами лечь, да будут наши трупы
На царской трон ступенями тебе.

Самозванец
Мужайтеся, безвинные страдальцы, —
Лишь дайте мне добраться до Москвы,
А там уже Борис со мной и с вами
Расплатится. Что ж нового в Москве?

Хрущов
Всё тихо там еще. Но уж народ
Спасение царевича проведал.
Уж грамоту твою везде читают.
Все ждут тебя. Недавно двух бояр
Борис казнил за то, что за столом
Они твое здоровье тайно пили.

Самозванец
О добрые, несчастные бояре!
Но кровь за кровь! и горе Годунову!
Что говорят о нем?

Хрущов
          Он удалился
В печальные свои палаты. Грозен
И мрачен он. Ждут казней. Но недуг
Его грызет. Борис едва влачится,
И думают, его последний час
Уж недалек.

Самозванец
          Как враг великодушный,
Борису я желаю смерти скорой;

                    Khrushchov[146]
                 (making obeisance)
                                    Yes, Sire,
Your dedicated, persecuted bondsmen,
Outlawed from Moscow. We have fled the gallows
To give our lives for you, our rightful Tsar –
Our corpses are the stairway to your throne.[147]

                    Pretender
Take courage, innocents! Once I reach Moscow,
Boris shall answer to both you and me.
What news is there from Moscow?[148]

                    Khrushchov
                              For the moment
Everything's quiet there – though the people know
The Tsarevich has been saved. Your proclamation
Is widely read, and everyone expects you.
Two boyars drank your health the other day –
Immediate execution.[149]

                    Pretender
                    Poor, brave boyars!
But blood for blood! and death to Godunov!
What are they saying of him?

                    Khrushchov
                              He has withdrawn
Into his gloomy palace. He is grim;
More executions are expected. But
He's ill, can hardly drag himself about.
His end seems near.[150]

                    Pretender
                    I am magnanimous:
I wish him speedy death; for otherwise

Не то беда злодею. А кого
Наследником наречь намерен он?

Хрущов
Он замыслов своих не объявляет,
Но кажется, что молодого сына,
Феодора — он прочит нам в цари.

Самозванец
В расчетах он, быть может, ошибется.
Ты кто?

Карела
Казак. К тебе я с Дона послан
От вольных войск, от храбрых атаманов,
Узреть твои царевы ясны очи
И кланяться тебе их головами.

Самозванец
Я знал донцов. Не сомневался видеть
В своих рядах казачьи бунчуки.
Благодарим Донское наше войско.
Мы ведаем, что ныне казаки
Неправедно притеснены, гонимы;
Но если Бог поможет нам вступить
На трон отцов, то мы по старине
Пожалуем наш верный вольный Дон.

Поэт
*(приближается, кланяясь низко и
хватая Гришку за полу)*
Великий принц, светлейший королевич!

Самозванец
Что хочешь ты?

It will go hard with him – the scoundrel! Who, though,
Does he intend to name as his successor?

Khrushchov
He hasn't yet declared his choice. I think,
However, he will name his young son, Feodor.

Pretender
Perhaps he'll be mistaken in his reckoning.
And who are you?

Karela
                    A Cossack, sent from the Don,
From the free warriors, from the valiant atamans,
To gaze upon your shining royal eyes,
And swear, on all our heads, undying loyalty.[151]

Pretender
I know the people of the Don, I expected
We'd see their horsetail banners in our ranks.
You soldiers of the Don, our gratitude.
We know too well the unjust persecution
The Cossacks suffer at the present time;[152]
If God should help us to our rightful throne,
The free and faithful Don shall be rewarded.

Poet
*(approaches and bows low, seizing
the hem of Grishka's garment)*[153]
O mighty Prince, illustrious Korolevich![154]

Pretender
What is your wish?

Поэт
(подает ему бумагу)
            Примите благосклонно
Сей бедный плод усердного труда.

Самозванец
Что вижу я? Латинские стихи!
Стократ священ союз меча и лиры,
Единый лавр их дружно обвивает.
Родился я под небом полунощным,
Но мне знаком латинской Музы голос,
И я люблю парнасские цветы.

(читает про себя)

Хрущов
(тихо Пушкину)
Кто сей?

Пушкин
      Пиит.

Хрущов
      Какое ж это званье?

Пушкин
Как бы сказать? по-русски — виршеписец
Иль скоморох.

Самозванец
      Прекрасные стихи!
Я верую в пророчества пиитов.
Нет, не вотще в их пламенной груди
Кипит восторг: благословится подвиг,
Его ж они прославили заране!
Приближься, друг. В мое воспоминанье
Прими сей дар.

(Дает ему перстень.)

      Когда со мной свершится

Poet
(giving him a page of manuscript)
Your favor in accepting
This meager fruit of dedicated toil.

Pretender
What have we here? Verses in Latin script!
Sacred a hundredfold the laureled union
Of sword and lyre.[155] I was born under midnight skies,
But know the language of the Latin muse,
And dearly love the flowers of Parnassus.[156]

(Reads to himself.)

Khrushchov[157]
(in a low voice to Pushkin)
Who's that?

Pushkin
A bard.

Khrushchov
What's that?

Pushkin
How shall I say?
In Russian – scribbler of verses, or a minstrel.

Pretender
Excellent verses! I believe in bards'
Prophecies. Not in vain does passion burn
Within their fiery breasts: blest is the deed
That, in foretelling, they have glorified!
Come here, my friend. Accept this gift in memory
Of me.

(Gives the poet a ring.)

When Fate's commandment is fulfilled,
When I put on my forebears' crown and mantle,

Судьбы завет, когда корону предков
Надену я, надеюсь вновь услышать
Твой сладкий глас, твой вдохновенный гимн.
Musa gloriam coronat, gloria que musam.
Итак, друзья, до завтра, до свиданья.

Все
В поход, в поход! Да здравствует Димитрий,
Да здравствует великий князь московский!

I'll hear once more the sweetness of your anthem.
Musa gloriam coronat, gloria que musam.[158]
And so, my friends, until we meet tomorrow.

All

To arms, to arms! To battle! To the field!
Hail Dimitry! Hail, Grand Prince of Moscow!

ЗАМОК ВОЕВОДЫ МНИШКА
В САНБОРЕ

Уборная Марины

МАРИНА, РУЗЯ УБИРАЕТ ЕЕ, СЛУЖАНКИ.

Марина
(перед зеркалом)
Ну что ж? готово ли? нельзя ли поспешить?

Рузя
Позвольте: наперед решите выбор трудной:
Что вы наденете, жемчужную ли нить
Иль полумесяц изумрудной?

Марина
Алмазный мой венец.

Рузя
Прекрасно! помните? его вы надевали,
Когда изволили вы ездить во дворец.
На бале, говорят, как солнце, вы блистали.
Мужчины ахали, красавицы шептали...
В то время, кажется, вас видел в первый раз
Хоткевич молодой, что после застрелился.
     А точно, говорят: на вас
     Кто ни взглянул, тут и влюбился.

Марина
Нельзя ли поскорей.

Рузя
        Сейчас.
Сегодня ваш отец надеется на вас.

[Scene 13]

PALATINE MNISZECH'S CASTLE, SAMBOR[159]

Maryna's Dressing Room

Maryna; Rózia dressing her; maidservants.

Maryna
(in front of a mirror)
Haven't you finished yet? Quickly, come here!

Rózia
We have to make a difficult decision:
And that is – what are you to wear?
Emeralds or pearls for this occasion?

Maryna
My diamond coronet.

Rózia
That will be excellent!
Do you remember? You put it on
For the ball you went to at the Palace.
They say you shone that evening like the sun.
Sighs from the men, all the court beauties jealous …
The young Chodkiewicz saw you there, it's said,
Who later put a bullet through his head.[160]
They never need a second chance,
They fall in love at half a glance.

Maryna
Can't you hurry.

Rózia
We won't be long.
Today your father has high hopes of you.

Царевич видел вас недаром,
Не мог он утаить восторга своего,
Уж ранен он; так надобно его
Сразить решительным ударом.
А точно, панна, он влюблен.
Вот месяц, как оставя Краков,
Забыв войну, московской трон,
В гостях у нас пирует он
И бесит русских и поляков.
Ах, Боже мой! дождусь ли дня?..
Не правда ли? когда в свою столицу
Димитрий повезет московскую царицу,
Вы не оставите меня?

Марина

Ты разве думаешь — царицей буду я?

Рузя

А кто ж, когда не вы? кто смеет красотою
Равняться здесь с моею госпожою?
Род Мнишков — ничьему еще не уступал;
Умом — превыше вы похвал...
Счастлив, кого ваш взор вниманья удостоит,
Кто сердца вашего любовь себе присвоит —
Кто б ни был он, хоть наш король
Или французский королевич —
Не только нищий ваш царевич,
Бог весть какой, Бог весть отколь.

Марина

Он точно царский сын и признан целым светом.

Рузя

А всё ж он был прошедшею зимой
У Вишневецкого слугой.

Марина

Скрывался он.

Now, the Tsarevich … You have made a strong
   Impression on him – he's wounded – so
   Now you must strike the final blow.
In love he'll be, my lady – see if I'm wrong.[161]
It's been a month he's not been seen in Cracow,
   But feasting here within our walls,
   Forgetting war, the throne of Moscow,
Maddening both the Russians and the Poles.
   Ah! Shall I live to see the day –
   The day when Moscow's Tsar Dimitry
Makes you Tsaritsa – then you'll not, I pray,
Forget me?

Maryna
I, you really think – Tsaritsa?

Rózia
Who, if not you? For beauty, who will dare
Claim mention in the same breath as my mistress?
What family is superior to the Mniszechs?
For intellect, you are beyond compare …[162]
Fortunate, he your eye has set apart,
He you honor with your noble heart –
   Whether it be the Polish King,
   Whether it be the French Dauphin –
   Or only your poor Tsarevich, come
   From God knows where, and known to none.

Maryna
He is the son of a tsar – the whole world knows.[163]

Rózia
He was a servant, though, last year,
Employed in Wiśniowiecki's house.

Maryna
He was hiding.

Рузя

Не спорю я об этом —
А только знаете ли вы,
Что говорят о нем в народе?
Что будто он дьячок, бежавший из Москвы,
Известный плут в своем приходе.

Марина

Какие глупости!

Рузя

О, я не верю им —
Я только говорю, что должен он, конечно,
Благословлять еще судьбу, когда сердечно
Вы предпочли его другим.

Служанка
(вбегает)

Уж гости съехались.

Марина

Вот видишь: ты до света
Готова пустяки болтать,
А между тем я не одета…

Рузя

Сейчас, готово всё.

(Служанки суетятся.)

Марина
Мне должно всё узнать.

Rózia
So it would appear.
But what the people say, I fear,
Is this: that he's a runaway priest,
That he's a well-known rogue, our guest –
From Moscow.

Maryna
What stupidities!

Rózia
You mustn't think I credit this –
I'm only saying he ought to bless his lot
Now that you have given him your heart.

Maidservant
(running in)
The guests are here!

Maryna
I'll hear your chattering
Till dawn, and never a moment's rest,
And meanwhile, I am still not dressed …

Rózia
We won't be long.

(The maidservants bustle about.)

Maryna
I must know everything.

[Сцена 14]

РЯД ОСВЕЩЕННЫХ КОМНАТ. МУЗЫКА

ВИШНЕВЕЦКИЙ, МНИШЕК.

Мнишек
Он говорит с одной моей Мариной,
Мариною одною занят он...
А дело-то на свадьбу страх похоже;
Ну — думал ты, признайся, Вишневецкий,
Что дочь моя царицей будет? а?

Вишневецкий
Да, чудеса... и думал ли ты, Мнишек,
Что мой слуга взойдет на трон московской?

Мнишек
А какова, скажи, моя Марина?
Я только ей промолвил: ну, смотри!
Не упускай Димитрия!.. и вот
Всё кончено. Уж он в ее сетях.—
Идет, идет... И с панною Мариной!

*(Музыка играет польской.
Самозванец идет с Мариною
в первой паре.)*

*Марина
(тихо Димитрию)*
Да, ввечеру, в одиннадцать часов,
В аллее лип, я завтра у фонтана.

(Расходятся. Другая пара.)

Кавалер
Что в ней нашел Димитрий?

[Scene 14]

SUITE OF ILLUMINATED ROOMS. MUSIC

Wiśniowiecki; Mniszech.[164]

Mniszech
He speaks to no-one here but my Maryna,
He's interested in no-one but Maryna ...
Begins to look uncommonly like a wedding;
Now tell me, Wiśniowiecki, would you have thought –
My daughter, as Tsaritsa? Would you now?

Wiśniowiecki
A miracle ... Would you have imagined, Mniszech,
My servant sitting on the throne of Moscow?[165]

Mniszech
But what do you say to my Maryna, eh?
I only said to her: "Now keep a watch-out!
You mustn't let Dimitry get away!"
And what do you know, she's caught him. It's decided.[166]

*(A polonaise is played. The Pretender and
Maryna form a first pair.)*

Maryna
(in a low voice to Dimitry)
Tomorrow, at eleven in the evening,
The fountain in the avenue of limes.

(They separate. Second pair.)

Gentleman
What does Dimitry see in her?

Дама
Как! она
Красавица.

Кавалер
Да, мраморная нимфа:
Глаза, уста без жизни, без улыбки…

(Новая пара.)

Дама
Он не красив, но вид его приятен,
И царская порода в нем видна.

(Новая пара.)

Дама
Когда ж поход?

Кавалер
Когда велит царевич,
Готовы мы; но видно, панна Мнишек
С Димитрием задержит нас в плену.

Дама
Приятный плен.

Кавалер
Конечно, если вы…

(Расходятся. Комнаты пустеют.)

Мнишек
Мы, старики, уж нынче не танцуем,
Мазурки гром не подзывает нас,
Прелестных рук не жмем и не цалуем —
Ох, не забыл старинных я проказ!
Теперь не то, не то, что прежде было:
И молодежь, ей-ей,— не так смела,

Lady

                    But she's

A beauty!

Gentleman

        Yes indeed, a marble nymph:

Her eyes and lips are lifeless, never a smile …

(Next pair.)

Lady

He isn't handsome, but his looks are pleasing …

One clearly sees the royal line in him.[167]

(Next pair.)

Lady

When do you march?

Gentleman

                When the Tsarevich orders.

We're ready now; it seems, though, Panna Mniszech

Is holding us and Dmitry prisoners here.

Lady

Such sweet captivity.

Gentleman

        Ah yes, if you …

(They separate. The rooms empty.)

Mniszech

Old men like us no longer join the dance;

The sound of the mazurka cannot thrill

Greybeards, we do not squeeze, or kiss, soft hands …

Ah, memories of those times are with me still!

Now things are different, youth is not so bold,

Nor beauty so light-hearted as we knew it –

И красота не так уж весела —
Признайся, друг: всё как-то приуныло.
Оставим их; пойдем, товарищ мой,
Венгерского, обросшую травой,
Велим открыть бутылку вековую,
Да в уголку потянем-ка вдвоем
Душистый ток, струю, как жир, густую,
А между тем посудим кой о чем.
Пойдем же, брат.

       Вишневецкий
       И дело, друг, пойдем.

I think we must acknowledge that the world
Is now a duller place; we'll leave them to it.
I would propose we don't stay here, my friend,
A moment more; we'll see if we can find
An old Hungarian vintage, moss-encrusted,
And in some corner, just the two of us,
We'll pour the rich, fat, fragrant stream and taste it,
And talk together.[168]

Wiśniowiecki
Let us, dear comrade, yes.

[Сцена 15]

НОЧЬ. САД. ФОНТАН

Самозванец
(входит)

Вот и фонтан; она сюда придет.
Я, кажется, рожден не боязливым;
Перед собой вблизи видал я смерть,
Пред смертию душа не содрогалась.
Мне вечная неволя угрожала,
За мной гнались — я духом не смутился
И дерзостью неволи избежал.
Но что ж теперь теснит мое дыханье?
Что значит сей неодолимый трепет?
Иль это дрожь желаний напряженных?
Нет — это страх. Чего же я боюсь?
Не знаю сам. День целый ожидал
Я тайного свидания с Мариной,
Обдумывал всё то, что ей скажу,
Как обольщу ее надменный ум,
Как назову московскою царицей, —
Но час настал — и ничего не помню.
Не нахожу затверженных речей;
Любовь мутит мое воображенье...
Но что-то вдруг мелькнуло... шорох... тише...
Нет, это свет обманчивой луны,
И прошумел здесь ветерок.

Марина
(входит)
                    Царевич!

Самозванец
Она!.. Вся кровь во мне остановилась.

[Scene 15]

NIGHT. GARDEN. FOUNTAIN[169]

Pretender
(enters)
The fountain – this is where she'll come. It seems
I've been without the sense of fear from birth;
Often I have been face to face with death,
And death has never made my spirit quail.
A lifelong dungeon I have seen before me,
I have been hunted – I have never faltered,
I have preserved my liberty by daring.
What, therefore, can this be that stops my breath,
This trembling that I cannot overcome?
Perhaps the shiver of suppressed desire?
No – it is fear. All day I have awaited
This rendezvous in secret with Maryna,
And weighed with care what I shall say to her,
And how I shall beguile her haughty mind,
How I shall call her Muscovy's Tsaritsa –
And now the hour has come – and all forgotten,
The words I have repeated and rehearsed;
For love fills every corner of my mind …[170]
Ah, something flashed that way … I heard a rustling …
No, nothing but the moonlight playing its tricks,
The whispering of the breeze.

Maryna
(enters)
　　　　　Tsarevich!

Pretender
　　　　　　　　　　She …

She stops my blood.

Марина

Димитрий! Вы?

Самозванец

Волшебный, сладкий голос!

(Идет к ней)

Ты ль наконец? Тебя ли вижу я,
Одну со мной, под сенью тихой ночи?
Как медленно катился скучный день!
Как медленно заря вечерня гасла!
Как долго ждал во мраке я ночном!

Марина

Часы бегут, и дорого мне время —
Я здесь тебе назначила свиданье
Не для того, чтоб слушать нежны речи
Любовника. Слова не нужны. Верю,
Что любишь ты; но слушай: я решилась
С твоей судьбой и бурной, и неверной
Соединить судьбу мою; то вправе
Я требовать, Димитрий, одного:
Я требую, чтоб ты души своей
Мне тайные открыл теперь надежды,
Намеренья и даже опасенья —
Чтоб об руку с тобой могла я смело
Пуститься в жизнь — не с детской слепотой,
Не как раба желаний легких мужа,
Наложница безмолвная твоя —
Но как тебя достойная супруга,
Помощница московского царя.

Самозванец

О, дай забыть хоть на единый час
Моей судьбы заботы и тревоги!
Забудь сама, что видишь пред собой
Царевича. Марина! зри во мне
Любовника, избранного тобою,
Счастливого твоим единым взором —

Maryna
Dimitry – is that you?

Pretender
Her voice, sweet magic!

(Approaches her.)

Do I really see you,
Alone with me, in night's soft shades? How slowly
The empty day has limped its weary length!
How slow the dying of the day's last light!
How long I have waited in the dark of night!

Maryna
My time is short and precious – my intention
Was not to hear a lover's tender speeches.
I trust you love me; why waste words? – With your
Tempestuous and uncertain destiny
I am resolved to join my own: Dimitry,
I ask one thing – reveal your heart to me,
With all its secret hopes, intents and fears.
I will go forward hand in hand with you
Boldly, not with the blindness of a child,
Not as slave to a husband's lightest wish,
Not as a concubine who does not speak –
But as a fitting consort at your side,
The helpmeet of the Tsar of Muscovy.[171]

Pretender
Oh let us put aside, just for an hour,
The cares and troubles of my destiny!
Forget, Maryna, that you see before you
Dimitry the Tsarevich. See in me
The lover you have chosen, who can now
Be filled with joy by a single glance from you –

О, выслушай моления любви,
Дай высказать всё то, чем сердце полно.

    Марина

Не время, князь. Ты медлишь — и меж тем
Приверженность твоих клевретов стынет,
Час от часу опасность и труды
Становятся опасней и труднее,
Уж носятся сомнительные слухи,
Уж новизна сменяет новизну;
А Годунов свои приемлет меры…

    Самозванец

Что Годунов? во власти ли Бориса
Твоя любовь, одно мое блаженство?
Нет, нет. Теперь гляжу я равнодушно
На трон его, на царственную власть.
Твоя любовь… что без нее мне жизнь,
И славы блеск, и русская держава?
В глухой степи, в землянке бедной — ты,
Ты заменишь мне царскую корону,
Твоя любовь…

    Марина
      Стыдись; не забывай
Высокого, святого назначенья:
Тебе твой сан дороже должен быть
Всех радостей, всех обольщений жизни,
Его ни с чем не можешь ты равнять.
Не юноше кипящему, безумно
Плененному моею красотой,
Знай: отдаю торжественно я руку
Наследнику московского престола,
Царевичу, спасенному судьбой.

    Самозванец

Не мучь меня, прелестная Марина,
Не говори, что сан, а не меня
Избрала ты. Марина! ты не знаешь,

Let me recite the fervent prayer of love,
And speak of what it is that fills my heart!

Maryna
This is not the time, prince. While you dally,
The loyalty of your followers is fast cooling,
From hour to hour your difficulties and dangers
Become more difficult and dangerous still;
Rumors abound, events crowd on events,
And Godunov will soon be taking steps –

Pretender
Why do you speak of Godunov? Your love, then,
My bliss on earth, is in the power of Boris ...?
No. I have come to look indifferently
Upon his throne, upon a tsar's dominion.
For what is life to me without your love,
What is the luster of fame, the throne of Russia?
In some mud hut out on the steppe, your love
Will be the equal of my crown, your love –

Maryna
For shame! Your high and sacred destiny,
Your crown, should be a dearer thing to you
Than all life's happinesses, life's temptations;
To nothing, then, in life should you compare it.
No, not the callow captive of my beauty,
But he whom fate has favored, the Tsarevich,
He who shall sit upon the throne of Moscow
Shall be the one to whom I give my hand.

Pretender
Don't torment me, my beautiful Maryna,
Don't say you chose my status, and not me!
You wound my heart – you cannot know how sorely ...

Как больно тем ты сердце мне язвишь —
Как! ежели… о страшное сомненье! —
Скажи: когда не царское рожденье
Назначила слепая мне судьба;
Когда б я был не Иоаннов сын,
Не сей давно забытый миром отрок:
Тогда б… тогда б любила ль ты меня?..

              Марина
Димитрий ты и быть иным не можешь;
Другого мне любить нельзя.

              Самозванец
                      Нет! полно:
Я не хочу делиться с мертвецом
Любовницей, ему принадлежащей.
Нет, полно мне притворствовать! скажу
Всю истину; так знай же: твой Димитрий
Давно погиб, зарыт — и не воскреснет;
А хочешь ли ты знать, кто я таков?
Изволь; скажу: я бедный черноризец;
Монашеской неволею скучая,
Под клобуком, свой замысел отважный
Обдумал я, готовил миру чудо —
И наконец из келии бежал
К украинцам, в их буйные курени,
Владеть конем и саблей научился;
Явился к вам; Димитрием назвался
И поляков безмозглых обманул.
Что скажешь ты, надменная Марина?
Довольна ль ты признанием моим?
Что ж ты молчишь?

              Марина
              О стыд! о горе мне!

(Молчание.)

But what if ... dreadful doubt! – what if blind fate
Had never had me born Tsarevich, had
Never had me born the son of Ivan,
That boy the world has long ago forgotten:
Then ... say – would you have loved me then?

Maryna
                                                    You are
Dimitry, and you cannot be another;
I could not love another.

Pretender
                    There, enough:
I will not share my loved one with a corpse.
No more dissembling, now the truth: Dimitry
Was dead and buried long ago; he'll not
Come back to life. You'll ask, then – who am I?
I'll tell you who I am – a wretched monk.
Grown weary of monastical confinement,
I hatched a bold design beneath the cowl,
A miracle to put before the world –
I left my cell at last to make my home
The riotous encampments of Ukrainians;[172]
I trained myself to master steed and saber,[173]
Appeared before you, named myself Dimitry,
And duped the brainless Poles. My proud Maryna,
Is my confession to your taste? You're silent?

Maryna
Oh shame and woe!

(Silence.)

Самозванец
(a parte)

Куда завлек меня порыв досады!
С таким трудом устроенное счастье
Я, может быть, навеки погубил.
Что сделал я, безумец? — Вижу, вижу:
Стыдишься ты не княжеской любви.
Так вымолви ж мне роковое слово;
В твоих руках теперь моя судьба,
Реши: я жду.

(Бросается на колена.)

Марина
          Встань, бедный самозванец.
Не мнишь ли ты коленопреклоненьем,
Как девочке доверчивой и слабой,
Тщеславное мне сердце умилить?
Ошибся, друг: у ног своих видала
Я рыцарей и графов благородных;
Но их мольбы я хладно отвергала
Не для того, чтоб беглого монаха...

Самозванец

Не презирай младого самозванца;
В нем доблести таятся, может быть,
Достойные московского престола,
Достойные руки твоей бесценной...

Марина
Достойные позорной петли, дерзкий!

Самозванец
Виновен я; гордыней обуянный,
Обманывал я Бога и царей,
Я миру лгал; но не тебе, Марина,
Меня казнить; я прав перед тобою.
Нет, я не мог обманывать тебя.
Ты мне была единственной святыней,

Pretender
(aside)
One moment of vexation …
The happiness I've labored to construct
Collapses all around me … and for ever?
What have I done? A madman!
                                        – Now I see,
Unprincely love is shameful to you. Then
Pronounce the word that is my destiny;
Decide. Your word …

(Falls on his knees.)

Maryna
                    Wretched pretender, rise!
Surely you cannot think your bended knee,
As if before some meek and trustful maiden,
Will move my lofty heart? You are mistaken.
Many a noble knight bent low before me
Has had his pleas received with cold dismissal.
Do you imagine that a runaway monk –

Pretender
Do not pour scorn upon a young pretender;
There lies in him, perhaps, a virtue worthy
Of Moscow's throne, and of your priceless hand –

Maryna
The noose more likely! Bare-faced insolence!

Pretender
Yes, I am guilty; urged by boundless pride,
I have deceived God, Tsar, and all the world.
You have no cause, however, to condemn me,
For I have been, Maryna, true to you.
You I could not deceive; before my shrine
I could not, and I cannot now dissemble,

Пред ней же я притворствовать не смел.
Любовь, любовь ревнивая, слепая,
Одна любовь принудила меня
Всё высказать.

Марина
　　Чем хвалится безумец!
Кто требовал признанья твоего?
Уж если ты, бродяга безымянный,
Мог ослепить чудесно два народа,
Так должен уж по крайней мере ты
Достоин быть успеха своего
И свой обман отважный обеспечить
Упорною, глубокой, вечной тайной.
Могу ль, скажи, предаться я тебе,
Могу ль, забыв свой род и стыд девичий,
Соединить судьбу мою с твоею,
Когда ты сам с такою простотой,
Так ветрено позор свой обличаешь?
Он из любви со мною проболтался!
Дивлюся: как перед моим отцом
Из дружбы ты доселе не открылся,
От радости пред нашим королем,
Или еще пред паном Вишневецким
Из верного усердия слуги.

Самозванец
Клянусь тебе, что сердца моего
Ты вымучить одна могла признанье.
Клянусь тебе, что никогда, нигде,
Ни в пиршестве за чашею безумства,
Ни в дружеском, заветном разговоре,
Ни под ножом, ни в муках истязаний
Сих тяжких тайн не выдаст мой язык.

Марина
Клянешься ты! итак, должна я верить —
О верю я! — но чем, нельзя ль узнать,
Клянешься ты? не именем ли Бога,

Love – blind, jealous love has spurred me on
To tell you all.

Maryna
What does this madman boast of?
Who asked you for confessions? A vagabond
Who blinds two nations with a miracle –
You should have proved the equal of your exploit
And lent your bold success the solid ground
Of deep and everlasting secrecy.
How can I devote myself to you,
Forsake my lineage and my modesty,
How can I join my destiny with yours –
So thoughtlessly you air your own disgrace!
For love of me the stripling wags his tongue!
I wonder that your friendship with my father
Hasn't induced you to confide in him,
Your rapture hasn't sent you to the King –
You haven't told your master Wiśniowiecki
As promptly as a loyal servant should have.

Pretender
I swear to you – you are the only one
To wring confession from this heart. I swear
That never again – in feasting's cup of folly,
In the most intimate exchange of friendship,
Never beneath the knife, upon the rack –
Shall these grave secrets pass my lips again.

Maryna
You swear, and so I must believe you! But
Tell me by what you swear: the name of God,
As might the adopted son of Jesuits?

Как набожный приимыш езуитов?
Иль честию, как витязь благородный,
Иль, может быть, единым царским словом,
Как царский сын? не так ли? говори.

Димитрий
(гордо)

Тень Грозного меня усыновила,
Димитрием из гроба нарекла,
Вокруг меня народы возмутила
И в жертву мне Бориса обрекла —
Царевич я. Довольно, стыдно мне
Пред гордою полячкой унижаться. —
Прощай навек. Игра войны кровавой,
Судьбы моей обширные заботы
Тоску любви, надеюсь, заглушат —
О как тебя я стану ненавидеть,
Когда пройдет постыдный страсти жар!
Теперь иду — погибель иль венец
Мою главу в России ожидает,
Найду ли смерть, как воин в битве честной
Иль как злодей на плахе площадной,
Не будешь ты подругою моею,
Моей судьбы не разделишь со мною;
Но — может быть, ты будешь сожалеть
Об участи, отвергнутой тобою.

Марина

А если я твой дерзостный обман
Заранее пред всеми обнаружу?

Самозванец

Не мнишь ли ты, что я тебя боюсь?
Что более поверят польской деве,
Чем русскому царевичу? — Но знай,
Что ни король, ни папа, ни вельможи —
Не думают о правде слов моих.
Димитрий я иль нет — что им за дело?
Но я предлог раздоров и войны.

Or on your honor as a noble knight?
Or simply by the royal word, the Tsar's,
Since you are a Tsarevich? Not so? Tell me.

Dimitry
(proudly)
The shade of Ivan has adopted me,
Given me the name Dimitry from the tomb,
Aroused the peoples on behalf of me,
Made me the instrument of Boris's doom –
I am the Tsarevich. Enough – how shameful
To bow before a puffed-up Polishwoman.
– For ever, then, farewell. War's bloody sport,
The myriad burdens of my destiny
Will numb the pains of love – how I shall hate you
When once the heat of shameful passion cools!
I'll go now – whether destruction or the crown
Awaits me in Russia, death as an honest warrior
Or criminal upon the public block,
Consort you shall never be of mine,
You shall not share my destiny; one day
You'll rue the lot that you have cast away.

Maryna
And what if I unmask before the world
The brazen impudence of your deceit?

Pretender
Surely you don't imagine *I* fear *you*?
A Polish maid, you think, to be believed
Rather than the Tsarevich of the Russias?
Listen – no king, no pope, no magnate, cares
One whit if what I say is true or not,
Whether or not I really am Dimitry;
I am the pretext for dissent and war,

Им это лишь и нужно, и тебя,
Мятежница! поверь, молчать заставят.
Прощай.

Марина

Постой, царевич. Наконец
Я слышу речь не мальчика, но мужа.
С тобою, князь — она меня мирит.
Безумный твой порыв я забываю
И вижу вновь Димитрия. Но — слушай.
Пора, пора! проснись, не медли боле;
Веди полки скорее на Москву —
Очисти Кремль, садись на трон московский,
Тогда за мной шли брачного посла;
Но — слышит Бог — пока твоя нога
Не оперлась на тронные ступени,
Пока тобой не свержен Годунов,
Любви речей не буду слушать я.

(Уходит.)

Самозванец

Нет — легче мне сражаться с Годуновым
Или хитрить с придворным езуитом,
Чем с женщиной — черт с ними: мочи нет.
И путает, и вьется, и ползет,
Скользит из рук, шипит, грозит и жалит.
Змея! змея! — Недаром я дрожал.
Она меня чуть-чуть не погубила.
Но решено: заутра двину рать.

And that is all the world requires of me.
Should you oppose me – you will soon be silenced.
Farewell.

Maryna
No, stay, Tsarevich. Now I hear
The accents of a man and not a boy –
They win me to you now, and I forget
That madman's outburst, now once more I see
Dimitry. Listen to me – It's time, it's time!
You must delay no more, you must arise
And straightway lead your regiments to Moscow.
Clear the Kremlin, take the throne of Moscow,
Then have a nuptial emissary sent to me.
God is my witness that until your foot
Rests on the steps by which you'll mount the throne,
Until I hear that Godunov is toppled,
I'll close my ears to all your words of love.

(Exit.)

Pretender
Easier far to fight with Godunov
Or tussle with a Jesuit at court
Than with a woman – devil take them all!
They'll crawl and wriggle, writhe and weave confusion,
Slip through your fingers, threaten, hiss, and bite.
Serpents! Not surprising that I trembled.
She brought me to the very brink of ruin …
It's settled now. My army moves at dawn.

[Сцена 16]

1604, 16 октября

ГРАНИЦА ЛИТОВСКАЯ

КНЯЗЬ КУРБСКИЙ И САМОЗВАНЕЦ, ОБА ВЕРХАМИ.
ПОЛКИ ПРИБЛИЖАЮТСЯ К ГРАНИЦЕ.

Курбский
(прискакав первый)
Вот, вот она! вот русская граница!
Святая Русь, Отечество! я твой!
Чужбины прах с презреньем отряхаю
С моих одежд — пью жадно воздух новый:
Он мне родной!.. теперь твоя душа,
О мой отец, утешится и в гробе
Опальные возрадуются кости! —
Блеснул опять наследственный наш меч,
Сей славный меч, гроза Казани темной,
Сей добрый меч, слуга царей московских!
В своем пиру теперь он загулял
За своего надёжу-государя!..

Самозванец
(едет тихо с поникшей головой)
Как счастлив он! как чистая душа
В нем радостью и славой разыгралась!
О витязь мой! завидую тебе.
Сын Курбского, воспитанный в изгнаньи,
Забыв отцом снесенные обиды,
Его вину за гробом искупив —
Ты кровь излить за сына Иоанна
Готовишься; законного царя
Ты возвратить отечеству… ты прав,
Душа твоя должна пылать весельем.

[Scene 16]

October 16, 1604[174]

THE LITHUANIAN BORDER

Prince Kurbsky and the Pretender, both on horseback.
Their forces are approaching the border.

Kurbsky
(gallops up first)
Here – here it is at last! The Russian frontier!
Holy Rus, our Fatherland![175] I am yours!
Contemptuously I rid these clothes of mine
Of foreign dust – and drink in sweet fresh air:
My native air! ... Your restless soul, my father,
Your bones so long disgraced, can now rejoice!
The ancestral sword has once again flashed forth,
That glorious sword, the conqueror of Kazan,
That faithful sword, the servant of our Tsars![176]
Now it shall hold a feast-day of its own
In honor of the sovereign of its hopes!

Pretender
(riding slowly with bowed head)
How happy he is! His spotless soul runs high
And overflows with jubilance and glory!
My bold, brave hero, how I envy you:
The son of Kurbsky, raised in banishment,
The wrongs your father suffered all forgotten,
His honor now redeemed beyond the grave – [177]
And you prepare yourself to shed your blood
For Ivan's son, to see the lawful Tsar
Restored at last to Russia ... Yes, you are right,
Well may your soul be lit with happiness.

Курбский

Ужель и ты не веселишься духом?
Вот наша Русь: она твоя, царевич.
Там ждут тебя сердца твоих людей:
Твоя Москва, твой Кремль, твоя держава.

Самозванец

Кровь русская, о Курбский, потечет —
Вы за царя подъяли меч, вы чисты.
Я ж вас веду на братьев; я Литву
Позвал на Русь, я в красную Москву
Кажу врагам заветную дорогу!..
Но пусть мой грех падет не на меня —
А на тебя, Борис-цареубийца! —
Вперед!

Курбский
Вперед! и горе Годунову!

*(Скачут. Полки переходят
через границу.)*

Kurbsky

How can your spirit not be uplifted too?
Before us lies our Rus – Tsarevich, yours.
The hearts of all your people wait for you;
Your Moscow, and your Kremlin, and your throne.

Pretender

First, Kurbsky, Russian blood will have to flow!
You draw sword for your tsar, you are pure in heart.
I lead you against your kin, the Lithuanians
Against the Russians, show your enemies
The sacred road that leads to holy Moscow! ...
Let, though, my sin not lie upon *my* head,
But on the tsaricide's – on Godunov's!
Forward!

Kurbsky

Forward! And woe to Godunov!

*(They gallop off. The Pretender's
forces cross the border.)*

ЦАРСКАЯ ДУМА

ЦАРЬ, ПАТРИАРХ И БОЯРЕ.

Царь

Возможно ли? Расстрига, беглый инок
На нас ведет злодейские дружины,
Дерзает нам писать угрозы! Полно,
Пора смирить безумца! — Поезжайте
Ты, Трубецкой, и ты, Басманов: помочь
Нужна моим усердным воеводам.
Бунтовщиком Чернигов осажден.
Спасайте град и граждан.

Басманов

              Государь,
Трех месяцев отныне не пройдет,
И замолчит и слух о самозванце;
Его в Москву мы привезем, как зверя
Заморского, в железной клети. Богом
Тебе клянусь.

    (Уходит с Трубецким.)

Царь

          Мне свейский государь
Через послов союз свой предложил;
Но не нужна нам чуждая помога;
Своих людей у нас довольно ратных,
Чтоб отразить изменников и ляха.
Я отказал. Щелкалов! разослать
Во все концы указы к воеводам,
Чтоб на коня садились и людей
По старине на службу высылали —
В монастырях подобно отобрать
Служителей причетных. В прежни годы,

[Scene 17]

THE TSAR'S COUNCIL[178]

The Tsar; Patriarch; boyars.

Tsar
How can this be? An unfrocked, runaway monk
Collects a horde of ruffians, sets them on us
And dares to write us threats![179] I'll have no more,
Time to humble this madman! You, Trubetskoy –
Basmanov, go; my generals need your help.
Chernìgov is surrounded. You must save
The city and its people.[180]

Basmanov
　　　　　　　Sire, three months
From now – rumors will cease of this pretender;
He'll be in Moscow in an iron cage,
He'll be displayed like some exotic beast.
I swear to God.

(Exit with Trubetskoy.)

Tsar
　　　　　　The King of Sweden's envoys
Have offered us alliance; but we need
No foreign help, we have men of our own
To put to flight the traitors and the Poles.
I have declined.[181] Shchelkalov![182] Send out orders
To voivodes everywhere to mount their horses
And as in days of old, raise men for service – [183]
And monks from all the monasteries as well.
When danger used to threaten Russia, even
Hermits went off to battle – now, however,
We'll not disturb them; they shall pray for us:[184]

Когда бедой отечеству грозило,
Отшельники на битву сами шли —
Но не хотим тревожить ныне их;
Пусть молятся за нас они — таков
Указ царя и приговор боярский.
Теперь вопрос мы важный разрешим:
Вы знаете, что наглый самозванец
Коварные промчал повсюду слухи;
Повсюду им разосланные письма
Посеяли тревогу и сомненье;
На площадях мятежный бродит шепот,
Умы кипят... их нужно остудить —
Предупредить желал бы казни я,
Но чем и как? решим теперь. Ты первый,
Святый отец, свою поведай мысль.

Патриарх

Благослови, Всевышний, поселивший
Дух милости и кроткого терпенья
В душе твоей, великий государь;
Ты грешнику погибели не хочешь,
Ты тихо ждешь — да пройдет заблужденье:
Оно пройдет, и солнце правды вечной
Всех озарит.
         Твой верный богомолец,
В делах мирских не мудрый судия,
Дерзает днесь подать тебе свой голос.
     Бесовский сын, расстрига окаянный,
Прослыть умел Димитрием в народе;
Он именем царевича, как ризой
Украденной, бесстыдно облачился:
Но стоит лишь ее раздрать — и сам
Он наготой своею посрамится.
     Сам Бог на то нам средство посылает:
Знай, государь; тому прошло шесть лет —
В тот самый год, когда тебя господь
Благословил на царскую державу —
В вечерний час ко мне пришел однажды
Простой пастух, уже маститый старец,

The Tsar's decree and boyars' resolution.[185]
Now an important matter must be settled.
An insolent pretender, as you know,
Has sown the seeds of doubt and discontent
By sending open letters everywhere;
Restlessness is rife on public squares,
And minds are in a ferment ... we must cool them.
I would avoid resort to executions,
But how?[186] We must decide the question. First,
You, holy father, let us know your mind.

Patriarch

May the Almighty bless us, who has breathed
The spirit of humility and tolerance,
O great and noble sovereign, into your soul;
You do not seek destruction of a sinner,
But quietly wait and let the error pass –
For pass it will, the eternal sun of truth
Shall then illumine all.
                      Your godly servant,
An unwise judge in matters of the world,
Will now presume to offer you his thoughts.
   A cursed unfrocked monk, son of the Devil,
Now passes with the people for Dimitry;
Shamelessly, like a stolen chasuble,
He has put on the mantle of Tsarevich –
But if it be removed, then he himself
Will be ashamed at his own nakedness.[187]
   The remedy is sent by God himself:
Hear, sire. Six years ago, the year that God
Conferred the powers of tsar on you, one evening
A venerable old man, a simple shepherd,
Came and told me of a miraculous secret.
   "When I was young," said he, "I lost my sight,

И чудную поведал он мне тайну.

  «В младых летах, — сказал он, — я ослеп
И с той поры не знал ни дня, ни ночи
До старости: напрасно я лечился
И зелием и тайным нашептаньем;
Напрасно я ходил на поклоненье
В обители к великим чудотворцам;
Напрасно я из кладязей святых
Кропил водой целебной темны очи;
Не посылал Господь мне исцеленья.
Вот наконец утратил я надежду,
И к тьме своей привык, и даже сны
Мне виданных вещей уж не являли,
А снилися мне только звуки. Раз
В глубоком сне, я слышу, детский голос
Мне говорит: "Встань, дедушка, поди
Ты в Углич-град, в собор Преображенья;
Там помолись ты над моей могилкой,
Бог милостив — и я тебя прощу."
— Но кто же ты? — спросил я детский голос.
"Царевич я Димитрий. Царь небесный
Приял меня в лик ангелов своих
И я теперь великий чудотворец! —
Иди, старик." — Проснулся я и думал:
Что ж? Может быть, и в самом деле Бог
Мне позднее дарует исцеленье.
Пойду — и в путь отправился далекий.
Вот Углича достиг я, прихожу
В святый собор, и слушаю обедню,
И, разгорясь душой усердной, плачу
Так сладостно, как будто слепота
Из глаз моих слезами вытекала.
Когда народ стал выходить, я внуку
Сказал: "Иван, веди меня на гроб
Царевича Димитрия." И мальчик
Повел меня — и только перед гробом
Я тихую молитву сотворил,
Глаза мои прозрели; я увидел

And from that time knew neither night nor day
Up to old age: in vain I sought a cure
In herbs, in secret charms and incantations,
Bowed low before the greatest miracle-workers,
And bathed my sightless eyes in healing waters;
God did not will that I should see again.
And in the end I lost all hope, accustomed
To life in darkness; even in my dreams
Things visible did not appear to me,
Only sounds did I dream. Once, in deep sleep
I heard a child's voice say to me: 'Arise,
Go to the town of Uglich, to the Cathedral
Of the Transfiguration; pray at my tomb there –
God is merciful; I shall forgive you.'
'Who are you?' I asked the voice that spoke to me.
'I am Dimitry, the Tsarevich. God
Appointed me among his host of angels;
I am a worker of great miracles!
Go forth, old man.' – And I awoke, and thought:
Why, then, should I not? For God may heal me.
And off I set upon my lengthy journey.
I reached the town, and entered the cathedral,
Heard Mass, and in the fervor of my soul
Wept joyously, as if my lifelong blindness
Were flowing from my eyes with my warm tears.
After Mass, I said to my grandson, 'Ivan,
Take me to the grave of the Tsarevich
Dimitry.' There he led me; at the tomb
I spoke a quiet prayer: my eyes were opened,
I saw God's light, my grandson, and the tomb."
That is the story, sire, the old man told me.

> *(General consternation. During the*
> *remainder of the Patriarch's speech*
> *Boris wipes his face several times*
> *with a handkerchief.)*

Thereupon I sent enquirers out to Uglich;
It was confirmed that many sufferers found

И Божий свет, и внука, и могилку.»
Вот, государь, что мне поведал старец.

*(Общее смущение. В продолжение сей
речи Борис несколько раз отирает
лицо платком.)*

Я посылал тогда нарочно в Углич,
И сведано, что многие страдальцы
Спасение подобно обретали
У гробовой царевича доски.

  Вот мой совет: во Кремль святые мощи
Перенести, поставить их в соборе
Архангельском; народ увидит ясно
Тогда обман безбожного злодея,
И мощь бесов исчезнет яко прах.

(Молчание.)

Князь Шуйский
Святый отец, кто ведает пути
Всевышнего? Не мне его судить.
Нетленный сон и силу чудотворства
Он может дать младенческим останкам,
Но надлежит народную молву
Исследовать прилежно и бесстрастно;
А в бурные ль смятений времена
Нам помышлять о столь великом деле?
Не скажут ли, что мы святыню дерзко
В делах мирских орудием творим?
Народ и так колеблется безумно,
И так уж есть довольно шумных толков:
Умы людей не время волновать
Нежданною, столь важной новизною.

  Сам вижу я: необходимо слух,
Рассеянный расстригой, уничтожить;
Но есть на то иные средства — проще.—
Так, государь — когда изволишь ты,
Я сам явлюсь на площади народной,
Уговорю, усовещу безумство
И злой обман бродяги обнаружу.

Deliverance at the tomb of the Tsarevich.[188]
     This then, I counsel: bring the saintly relics
To Moscow, to the Kremlin; place them in
The Cathedral of the Archangel; the people
Shall see that godless villain brought to shame,
His devil's powers will vanish as the dust.[189]

(Silence.)

Prince Shuisky
Holy Father, who knows the Almighty's ways?
He may confer upon a child's remains
Miraculous powers and undecaying sleep,
But we should carefully and dispassionately
Investigate all rumors from the people –
And in the present stormy, troubled times
Can we give due thought to such a matter?
It will be said we crudely turn a shrine
Into a tool for secular affairs.
The people's mood swings wildly as it is,
There's quite enough unruly talk already;
Now is no time to agitate the people
With such momentous sudden news as this.[190]
     I see, of course, we must without delay
Destroy the claims this unfrocked monk is making;
But other means are possible, and simpler.
Sire, if you will give me leave, I shall myself
Go out upon the public square and speak,
Turn people's minds and consciences from madness,
And make them see this vagrant's black deception.[191]

Царь

Да будет так! Владыко патриарх,
Прошу тебя пожаловать в палату:
Сегодня мне нужна твоя беседа.

(Уходит. За ним и все бояре.)

Один боярин
(тихо другому)

Заметил ты, как государь бледнел
И крупный пот с лица его закапал?

Другой

Я — признаюсь — не смел поднять очей,
Не смел вздохнуть, не только шевельнуться.

Первый боярин

А выручил князь Шуйский. Молодец!

Tsar
So be it! My Lord Patriarch, I ask you,
Come to my palace, I must talk with you.

(Exit, followed by all the boyars.)

One Boyar
(in a low voice to another)
Did you see the Tsar turn pale just now,
Did you see his face break out in a sweat?

Second Boyar
I must confess I didn't dare to look,
I didn't dare draw breath, or move a muscle.[192]

First Boyar
Prince Shuisky saved the day. All praise to Shuisky!

[Сцена 18]

ПЛОЩАДЬ
ПЕРЕД СОБОРОМ В МОСКВЕ

НАРОД.

Один
Скоро ли царь выйдет из собора?

Другой
Обедня кончилась; теперь идет молебствие.

Первый
Что? уж проклинали *того*?

Другой
Я стоял на паперти и слышал, как диакон завопил: Гришка Отрепьев — Анафема!

Первый
Пускай себе проклинают; царевичу дела нет до Отрепьева.

Другой
А царевичу поют теперь вечную память.

Первый
Вечную память живому! Вот ужо им будет, безбожникам.

Третий
Чу! шум. Не царь ли?

Четвертый
Нет; это юродивый.

[Scene 18]

SQUARE IN FRONT OF THE CATHEDRAL, MOSCOW[193]

The people.

One of the Crowd
When is the Tsar going to come out of the Cathedral?

A Second
Mass is over; it's prayers now.

First
What's that? 'ave they pronounced the curse on '*im* yet?

Second
I was standing on the porch and I heard the Deacon shout: "Grishka Otrepiev – he shall be Anathema!"

First
They can curse 'im 's much as they like – the Tsarevich ain't got nothin' to do with Otrepiev.[194]

Second
Now they're chanting eternal remembrance for the Tsarevich.

First
Eternal remembrance for the living! They'll catch it for that, the godless scoundrels.

Third
Shhh! There's a noise. It might be the Tsar.

Fourth
No, it's the holy fool.

(Входит Юродивый в железной
шапке, обвешенный веригами,
окруженный мальчишками.)

Мальчишки
Николка, Николка — железный колпак!.. тр-р-р-р-р...

Старуха
Отвяжитесь, бесенята, от блаженного. — Помолись, Николка, за меня грешную.

Юродивый
Дай, дай, дай копеечку.

Старуха
Вот тебе копеечка; помяни же меня.

Юродивый
(садится на землю и поет)
Месяц едет,
Котенок плачет,
Юродивый, вставай,
Бай, бай, бай...
Богу помолися! —

(Мальчишки окружают его снова.)

Один из них
Здравствуй, Николка; что же ты шапки не снимаешь?
(Щелкает его по железной шапке.) Эк она звонит!

Юродивый
А у меня копеечка есть.

Мальчишка
Неправда! ну покажи.

(Вырывает копеечку и убегает.)

*(Enter holy fool wearing an iron cap
hung with chains, surrounded by boys.)*

Boys

Nikolka, Nikolka – Iron-cap![195] ... Tr-r-r-r ...

Old Woman

Leave the blessed one alone, you little devils. – Pray for me, Nikolka,
pray for a sinner.

Holy Fool

Give me a kopek, a kopek, a kopek.

Old Woman

'ere's a kopek for you. Remember me in your prayers.

Holy Fool

(Sits down on the ground and sings.)
The moon shines bright
The cat wails loud,
Arise, holy fool,
Hush-a-bye ...
And pray to God![196]

(The boys gather round him again.)

A Boy

Good day, Nikolka! Why don't you take your cap off?

(Taps the fool's iron cap.)

Ooh, what a sound!

Holy Fool

I've got a kopek.

Boy

Not true! Let's see it, then.

(Snatches the kopek and runs away.)

Юродивый
(плачет)
Взяли мою копеечку; обижают Николку!

Народ
Царь, царь идет.

(Царь выходит из собора.
Боярин впереди раздает нищим
милостыню. Бояре.)

Юродивый
Борис, Борис! Николку дети обижают.

Царь
Подать ему милостыню. О чем он плачет?

Юродивый
Николку маленькие дети обижают... Вели их зарезать, как зарезал ты маленького царевича.

Бояре
Поди прочь, дурак! схватите дурака!

Царь
Оставьте его. Молись за меня, юродивый.

(Уходит.)

Юродивый
(ему вслед)
Нет, нет! нельзя молиться за царя Ирода — Богородица не велит.

Holy Fool
(weeping)
They've taken my kopek; they've insulted Nikolka!

People
The Tsar – the Tsar is coming.

*(The Tsar comes out of the Cathedral. A
boyar walks in front of him distributing
alms to the beggars. Other boyars
follow.)*

Holy Fool
Boris! Boris! The children have insulted Nikolka!

Tsar
Give him alms. Why is he weeping?

Holy Fool
The little children have insulted Nikolka … Have their throats cut, as
you cut the young Tsarevich's.

Boyars
Away with you, old fool! Seize the fool!

Tsar
Leave him alone. Pray for me, blessed fool.

(Exit.)

Holy Fool
(after him)
No, no! No-one must pray for King Herod –[197] The Mother of God
forbids it.

[Сцена 19]

21 декабря

РАВНИНА
БЛИЗ НОВГОРОДА-СЕВЕРСКОГО

БИТВА.

Воины
(бегут в беспорядке)
Беда, беда! Царевич! Ляхи! Вот они! вот они!

(Входят капитаны Маржерет и
Вальтер Розен.)

Маржерет
Куда, куда? Allons... пошоль назад!

Один из беглецов
Сам *пошоль*, коли есть охота, проклятый басурман.

Маржерет
Quoi? quoi?

Другой
Ква! ква! тебе любо заморскому ворону квакать на русского царевича; а мы ведь православные.

Маржерет
Qu'est-ce à dire *pravoslavni*?.. Sacrés gueux, maudites canailles! Mordieu, mein herr, j'enrage: on dirait que ça n'a pas de bras pour frapper, ça n'a que des jambes pour foutre le camp.

В. Розен
Es ist Schande.

[Scene 19]

December 21, 1604

A PLAIN NEAR NOVGOROD-SĔVERSKY[198]

A Battle.[199]

Soldiers
(running in disorder)
Disaster! Disaster! The Tsarevich! The Poles! They're coming! They're coming![200]

(Enter Captains Margeret and
Walter Rosen.)[201]

Margeret
Where do you zink you're off to? *Allons* ... Beck wiz you!

Fleeing Soldier
Beck with yourself, if you want to, damned infidel![202]

Margeret
Quoi? Quoi?[203]

Another Soldier
Kwa! Kwa! All very well for a foreign crow like you to go croaking at the Russian Tsarevich.[204] We're Orthodox, we are.

Margeret
Qu'est-ce à dire "Orthodoxe"? ... Sacrés gueux, maudites canailles! Mordieu, mein herr, j'enrage: on dirait que ça n'a pas de bras pour frapper, ça n'a que des jambes pour foutre le camp.[205]

W. Rosen
Es ist Schande.[206]

Маржерет

Ventre-saint-gris! Je ne bouge plus d'un pas – puisque le vin est tiré, il faut le boire. Qu'en dites-vous, mein herr?

В. Розен

Sie haben Recht.

Маржерет

Tudieu, il y fait chaud! Ce diable de Samozvanetz, comme ils l'appellent, est un bougre qui a du poil au cul. Qu'en pensez-vous, mein herr?

В. Розен

Oh, ja!

Маржерет

Hé! voyez donc, voyez donc! L'action s'engage sur les derrières de l'ennemi. Ce doit être le brave Basmanoff, qui aurait fait une sortie.

В. Розен

Ich glaube das.

(Входят немцы.)

Маржерет

Ha, ha! voici nos Allemands. – Messieurs!.. Mein herr, dites leur donc de se rallier et, sacrebleu, chargeons!

В. Розен

Sehr gut. Halt!

(Немцы строятся.)

Marsch!

Немцы
(идут)

Hilf Gott!

(Русские снова бегут.)

Margeret

*Ventre-saint-gris! Je ne bouge plus d'un pas – puisque le vin est tiré, il
faut le boire. Qu'en dites-vous, mein herr?*[207]

W. Rosen

Sie haben Recht.[208]

Margeret

*Tudieu! Il y fait chaud! Ce diable de "Pre-tend-er," comme ils l'appellent,
est un bougre qui a du poil au cul. Qu'en pensez-vous, mein herr?*[209]

W. Rosen

Oh, ja!

Margeret

*Hé! voyez donc, voyez donc! L'action s'engage sur les derrières de l'en-
nemi. Ce doit être le brave Basmanoff, qui aurait fait une sortie.*[210]

W. Rosen

Ich glaube das.[211]

(Enter Germans.)

Margeret

*Ha, ha! Voici nos Allemands. – Messieurs! ... Mein herr, dites leur donc
de se rallier et, sacrebleu, chargeons!*[212]

W. Rosen

Sehr gut. Halt![213]

(The Germans fall into line.)

Marsch!

Germans
(marching)

Hilf Gott![214]

(Again the Russians flee.)

Ляхи

Победа! победа! Слава царю Димитрию.

Димитрий
(верхом)

Ударить отбой! мы победили. Довольно; щадите русскую кровь. Отбой!

(Трубят, бьют барабаны.)

Poles

Victory! Victory! Long live Tsar Dimitry![215]

Dimitry
(on horseback)

Sound cease-fire! Victory is ours. Enough; we must spare Russian blood. Cease fire![216]

(Trumpets and drums.)

[Сцена 20]

СЕВСК

САМОЗВАНЕЦ, ОКРУЖЕННЫЙ СВОИМИ.

Самозванец
Где пленный?

Лях
Здесь.

Самозванец
　　　　Позвать его ко мне.

(Входит русский пленник.)
Кто ты?

Пленник
Рожнов, московский дворянин.

Самозванец
Давно ли ты на службе?

Пленник
　　　　С месяц будет.

Самозванец
Не совестно, Рожнов, что на меня
Ты поднял меч?

Пленник
　　　　Как быть, не наша воля.

Самозванец
Сражался ты под Северским?

Пленник
　　　　　　Я прибыл
Недели две по битве — из Москвы.

[Scene 20]

SEVSK[217]

The Pretender, surrounded by his men.

Pretender
Where is the prisoner?

Pole
Here.

Pretender
Bring him to me.

(Enter a Russian prisoner.)

Your name?

Prisoner
Rozhnov, a nobleman, from Moscow.[218]

Pretender
Have you served long?

Prisoner
About a month.

Pretender
Aren't you
Ashamed, Rozhnov, to raise your sword against me?

Prisoner
Not *my* choice.

Pretender
Did you fight at Sèversky?

Prisoner
I came two weeks before that.

Самозванец

Что Годунов?

Пленник

    Он очень был встревожен
Потерею сражения и раной
Мстиславского, и Шуйского послал
Начальствовать над войском.

Самозванец

        А зачем?
Он отозвал Басманова в Москву?

Пленник

Царь наградил его заслуги честью
И золотом. Басманов в царской Думе
Теперь сидит.

Самозванец

    Он в войске был нужнее.
Ну что в Москве?

Пленник

    Всё, слава Богу, тихо.

Самозванец

Что? ждут меня?

Пленник

    Бог знает; о тебе
Там говорить не слишком нынче смеют.
Кому язык отрежут, а кому
И голову — такая, право, притча!
Что день, то казнь. Тюрьмы битком набиты.
На площади, где человека три
Сойдутся — глядь — лазутчик уж и вьется,
А государь досужною порою
Доносчиков допрашивает сам.
Как раз беда; так лучше уж молчать.

Pretender

Godunov, now –

How do things stand with him?

Prisoner

He is most alarmed

By his defeat, and seeing Mstislavsky wounded –

Shuisky is now commander of the Army.[219]

Pretender

Why did he call Basmanov back to Moscow?

Prisoner

The Tsar has honored and rewarded him

For service in the field, and now Basmanov

Sits in the Council.[220]

Pretender

He would be more use

With the army.[221] So then, how are things in Moscow?

Prisoner

All quiet, thank God.

Pretender

Are they expecting me?

Prisoner

God knows! No-one dares speak of you in Moscow.

It's tongues out here, and heads off there – what times!

Every day an execution. The prisons

Are crammed. Three people gathered in a square –

Lo and behold – they find a spy amongst them;

Godunov is always with informers,

Interrogating them himself in private.

What times, what troubles – best not speak of them.[222]

Самозванец
Завидна жизнь Борисовых людей!
Ну, войско что?

        Пленник
      Что с ним? одето, сыто,
Довольно всем.

      Самозванец
      Да много ли его?

       Пленник
Бог ведает.

      Самозванец
      А будет тысяч тридцать?

      Пленник
Да наберешь и тысяч пятьдесят.

     (Самозванец задумывается.
   Окружающие смотрят друг на
        друга.)

      Самозванец
Ну! обо мне как судят в вашем стане?

       Пленник
А говорят о милости твоей,
Что ты, дескать (будь не во гнев), и вор,
А молодец.

      Самозванец
      (смеясь)
     Так это я на деле
Им докажу: друзья, не станем ждать
Мы Шуйского; я поздравляю вас:
На завтра бой.

      (Уходит.)

Pretender
Life under Godunov – most enviable!
And what about his army?

Prisoner
Dressed and fed,
Happy enough.[223]

Pretender
How many men?

Prisoner
Who knows?

Pretender
Thirty thousand maybe?

Prisoner
No – nearer fifty.[224]

*(The Pretender is silent. Those
around him exchange glances.)*

Pretender
What opinion do your men have of me?

Prisoner
They talk of your charity; it's also said –
Don't be angry with me! – that you're a brigand,
But still an excellent fellow.[225]

Pretender
(laughing)
I'll prove it then.
We'll not wait here for Shuisky; God be with you –
Tomorrow we take the field.

(Exit.)

Все
Да здравствует Димитрий!

Лях
На завтра бой! их тысяч пятьдесят,
А нас всего едва ль пятнадцать тысяч.
С ума сошел.

Другой
Пустое, друг: поляк
Один пятьсот москалей вызвать может.

Пленник
Да, вызовешь. А как дойдет до драки,
Так убежишь от одного, хвастун.

Лях
Когда б ты был при сабле, дерзкий пленник,
То я тебя

(указывая на свою саблю)

вот этим бы смирил.

Пленник
Наш брат русак без сабли обойдется:
Не хочешь ли вот этого

(показывая кулак),

безмозглый!

*(Лях гордо смотрит на него и
молча отходит. Все смеются.)*

All
Long live Dimitry!

Pole
We take the field tomorrow! Fifty thousand
Of them – fifteen of us. He's lost his wits!²²⁶[226]

A Second Pole
And so have you, my friend: have you forgotten –
One Pole can challenge fifty Muscovites.

Prisoner
Challenge them, yes. But when it comes to fighting
You'd run away from one, you popinjay.

First Pole
If only you had your saber at this moment –
I'd cut you down to size,

(*pointing to his own saber*)

you insolent fellow!

Prisoner
A Russian soldier doesn't need a saber:
Just try a taste of this,

(*showing his fist*)

you brainless clod!

(*The Pole gives him a haughty look
and walks away without a word.
Everyone bursts out laughing.*)

[Сцена 21]

ЛЕС

ЛЖЕДИМИТРИЙ, ПУШКИН.

*(В отдалении лежит конь
издыхающий.)*

Лжедимитрий
Мой бедный конь! как бодро поскакал
Сегодня он в последнее сраженье
И, раненый, как быстро нес меня.
Мой бедный друг!

Пушкин
(про себя)
                    Ну вот о чем жалеет?
Об лошади! когда всё наше войско
Побито в прах!

Самозванец
                    Послушай, может быть,
От раны он лишь только заморился
И отдохнет.

Пушкин
Куда! он издыхает.

Самозванец
(идет к своему коню)
Мой бедный конь!.. что делать? снять узду
Да отстегнуть подпругу. Пусть на воле
Издохнет он.

*(Разнуздывает и расседлывает
коня. Входят несколько ляхов.)*
Здорово, господа.

[Scene 21]

FOREST

The False Dimitry; Gavrila Pushkin.
A dying horse in the background.

The False Dimitry
My poor, poor horse! How gallantly he galloped
Today and, wounded as he was, how swiftly
He carried me! My poor, poor friend!

Pushkin
(to himself)
                                        His horse
He grieves for – when our army is destroyed![227]

Pretender
Perhaps he's only exhausted from his wound,
And resting.

Pushkin
Not at all! The horse is dying.

Pretender
(goes to his horse)
Poor horse ... What can I do? Take off the bridle,
Undo the saddle-girth, and let him die
In freedom.[228]

*(Unbridles and unsaddles the
horse. Enter some Poles.)*

Gentlemen, good evening. Why,

Что ж Курбского не вижу между вами?
Я видел, как сегодня в тучу боя
Он врезался; тьмы сабель молодца,
Что зыбкие колосья, облепили,
Но меч его всех выше подымался,
А грозный клик все клики заглушал.
Где ж витязь мой?

Лях
Он лег на поле смерти.

Самозванец
Честь храброму и мир его душе!
Как мало нас от битвы уцелело.
Изменники! злодеи-запорожцы,
Проклятые! вы, вы сгубили нас —
Не выдержать и трех минут отпора!
Я их ужо! десятого повешу,
Разбойники! —

Пушкин
Кто там ни виноват,
Но всё-таки мы начисто разбиты,
Истреблены.

Самозванец
А дело было наше;
Я было смял передовую рать —
Да немцы нас порядком отразили;
А молодцы! ей-богу, молодцы,
Люблю за то — из них — уж непременно
Составлю я почетную дружину.

Пушкин
А где-то нам сегодня ночевать?

Самозванец
Да здесь в лесу. Чем это не ночлег?

I don't see Kurbsky: tell me where he is.
I saw him cut his way, not long ago,
Into the thick of the enemy, surrounded
By countless sabers, like a field of corn;
His saber, though, was raised above the rest,
His mighty war-cry drowned out all the others.
Where is my warrior?

Pole
On the field of death.

Pretender
All honor to the brave – peace to his soul!
How few of us survive today. Damn you!
You Zaporozhian traitors! It was you
Who caused our downfall – couldn't hold three minutes![229]
I'll teach them! Every tenth one of them shall hang.
Scoundrels![230]

Pushkin
Whoever's fault it is, we're beaten,
Destroyed.

Pretender
The field was ours; I all but smashed
Their front – but then the Germans beat us back.[231]
Brave lads, by God, brave lads! I truly love them –
My guard of honor shall be raised from them.[232]

Pushkin
Where are we going to spend the night?

Pretender
The forest.
This is our bivouac. Where else do you think?

Чем свет, мы в путь; к обеду будем в Рыльске.
Спокойна ночь.

(Ложится, кладет седло под
голову и засыпает.)

Пушкин

Приятный сон, царевич.
Разбитый в прах, спасаяся побегом,
Беспечен он, как мирное дитя:
Хранит его, конечно, провиденье;
И мы, друзья, не станем унывать.

We're off at dawn; we'll be in Rylsk by midday.[233]
Good-night.

(Lies down on the ground, places his saddle
under his head and goes to sleep.)

Pushkin
I wish you pleasant dreams, Tsarevich ...
A grave defeat, he flees to save his life –
And see, he's carefree as a child.
Providence watches over him, of course;
Well then, my friends, we'll not be downcast either.

МОСКВА.
ЦАРСКИЕ ПАЛАТЫ

БОРИС, БАСМАНОВ.

Царь

Он побежден, какая польза в том?
Мы тщетною победой увенчались.
Он вновь собрал рассеянное войско
И нам со стен Путивля угрожает —
Что делают меж тем герои наши?
Стоят у Кром, где кучка казаков
Смеются им из-под гнилой ограды.
Вот слава! нет, я ими недоволен,
Пошлю тебя начальствовать над ними;
Не род, а ум поставлю в воеводы;
Пускай их спесь о местничестве тужит;
Пора презреть мне ропот знатной черни
И гибельный обычай уничтожить.

Басманов

Ах, государь, стократ благословен
Тот будет день, когда Разрядны книги
С раздорами, с гордыней родословной
Пожрет огонь.

Царь

    День этот недалек;
Лишь дай сперва смятение народа
Мне усмирить.

Басманов

    Что на него смотреть;
Всегда народ к смятенью тайно склонен:
Так борзый конь грызет свои бразды;
На власть отца так отрок негодует;

[Scene 22]

MOSCOW. THE TSAR'S PALACE

Boris; Basmanov.

Tsar
We've beaten him, but what's the use of that?
Our victory is fruitless – he has rallied
And now he's well defended in Putivl.[234]
Meanwhile, what are our heroes doing for us? –
Tied down at Kromy by a band of Cossacks
Mocking them from behind a crumbling wall.[235]
There's glory for you! I am displeased with them.
Basmanov, I appoint you their commander;[236]
I would have brains, not breeding, in my generals.
The vanities of Precedence must go;
It is time to spurn the noble rabble's protests
And do away with this pernicious custom.[237]

Basmanov
Sire, blessed a hundred times the day on which
The Registers of Military Commands,
With all their rivalries and pride of lineage,
Are burnt![238]

Tsar
                Soon now. But first I must pacify
The people.[239]

Basmanov
                Sire, I see no cause for worry;
Unrest will always simmer in the people;
Always the fiery steed will chew the bit,
Always the son resent his father's power –

Но что ж? конем спокойно всадник правит,
И отроком отец повелевает.

Царь

Конь иногда сбивает седока,
Сын у отца не вечно в полной воле.
Лишь строгостью мы можем неусыпной
Сдержать народ. Так думал Иоанн,
Смиритель бурь, разумный самодержец,
Так думал и — его свирепый внук.
Нет, милости не чувствует народ:
Твори добро — не скажет он спасибо;
Грабь и казни — тебе не будет хуже.

(Входит боярин.)

Что?

Боярин

Привели гостей иноплеменных.

Царь

Иду принять; Басманов, погоди.
Останься здесь: с тобой еще мне нужно
Поговорить.

(Уходит.)

Басманов

Высокий дух державный.
Дай Бог ему с Отрепьевым проклятым
Управиться, и много, много он
Еще добра в России сотворит.
Мысль важная в уме его родилась.
Не надобно ей дать остыть. Какое
Мне поприще откроется, когда
Он сломит рог боярству родовому!
Соперников во брани я не знаю;
У царского престола стану первый…
И может быть… Но что за чудный шум?

What of it? The horseman will control his horse,
The father will prevail upon the son.

Tsar

But then the horse will sometimes throw its rider,
The son not always do his father's bidding.
Only by unremitting vigilance
Can we restrain the people. So thought Ivan,
Calmer of storms, cool-headed autocrat;
Such was the view of his ferocious grandson.[240]
No, mercy the people never feel or notice:
Do them good – they'll never thank you for it,
Rob, execute – they'll not think worse of you.[241]

(Enter a boyar.)

What do you want?

Boyar
Sire, foreign visitors.

Tsar

I shall receive them, then. Basmanov, wait;
I need to talk to you.

(Exit.)

Basmanov
Great sovereign spirit!

Pray God he rids us of that cursed Otrepiev:
From what he sows, much good will come for Russia.
A high idea has ripened in his mind;
It must not die. What avenues shall be mine
When he has clipped the wings of ancient lineage!
I have no rival on the field of battle;
I shall stand nearest to the throne … perhaps …[242]
What is that noise?

(Тревога. Бояре, придворные
служители в беспорядке бегут,
встречаются и шепчутся.)

Один
За лекарем!

Другой
Скорее к патриарху.

Третий
Царевича, царевича зовет!

Четвертый
Духовника!

Басманов
Что сделалось такое?

Пятый
Царь занемог.

Шестой
Царь умирает.

Басманов
                    Боже!

Пятый
На троне он сидел и вдруг упал —
Кровь хлынула из уст и из ушей.

(Царя выносят на стуле; всё царское
семейство, все бояре.)

*(Alarm. Boyars and attendants
run about in confusion and
whisper together.)*

First
Call the physician!

Second
No –

The Patriarch!

Third
He called for the Tsarevich!
For the Tsarevich!

Fourth
Send for a priest!

Basmanov
What's happened?

Fifth
The Tsar is sick.

Sixth
The Tsar is dying.

Basmanov
God!

Fifth
He was seated on the throne, and then he fell –
And blood came gushing from his mouth and ears.[243]

*(The Tsar is brought in on a chair,
accompanied by all his family and
boyars.)*

Царь

Подите все — оставьте одного
Царевича со мною.

(Все удаляются.)

Умираю;

Обнимемся, прощай, мой сын: сейчас
Ты царствовать начнешь... о Боже, Боже!
Сейчас явлюсь перед тобой — и душу
Мне некогда очистить покаяньем.
Но чувствую — мой сын, ты мне дороже
Душевного спасенья... так и быть!
Я подданным рожден и умереть
Мне подданным во мраке б надлежало;
Но я достиг верховной власти... чем?
Не спрашивай. Довольно: ты невинен,
Ты царствовать теперь по праву станешь,
Я, я за всё один отвечу Богу...
О милый сын, не обольщайся ложно,
Не ослепляй себя ты добровольно —
В дни бурные державу ты приемлешь:
Опасен он, сей чудный самозванец,
Он именем ужасным ополчен...
Я, с давних лет в правленьи искушенный,
Мог удержать смятенье и мятеж;
Передо мной они дрожали в страхе;
Возвысить глас измена не дерзала —
Но ты, младой, неопытный властитель,
Как управлять ты будешь под грозой,
Тушить мятеж, опутывать измену?
Но Бог велик! Он умудряет юность,
Он слабости дарует силу... слушай:
Советника, во-первых, избери
Надежного, холодных, зрелых лет,
Любимого народом — а в боярах
Почтенного породой или славой —
Хоть Шуйского. Для войска нынче нужен
Искусный вождь: Басманова пошли
И с твердостью снеси боярский ропот.

Tsar
Leave me with the Tsarevich.

(Exeunt all.)

I am dying;
Let us embrace. Farewell, my son: your reign
Will soon begin ... O God! I stand before you
With all my sins upon my soul. However,
I feel, my son, you are more dear to me
Than spiritual salvation ...[244] Then so be it!
A subject I was born, and should by rights
Have died a subject, in obscurity;
But I attained the highest power ... How –
Do not ask. Enough now; you are innocent,
And you shall reign by right. I, I alone
Shall answer to the Almighty for the past ...
Do not, my dear son, cherish falsity,
Do not give way to wilful self-delusion –
Your reign begins in days of tribulation:
From nowhere springs a perilous pretender,
Armed with that most terrible of names ...[245]
Long practiced in the art of government,
I have learned to quell rebellion and disorder;
They quaked before me; treason dared not speak –
But you, a boy, an inexperienced ruler,
How will you govern, if disaster strikes?
How outwit treason, how put down rebellion?
But God is mighty, and He teaches wisdom,
Weakness He turns to strength ... Listen. First, choose
A wise adviser, whom you trust, of ripe
And sober years, loved by the people, respected
For blood or reputation by the boyars –
Shuisky, say.[246] Next, our army in the field
Needs an able commander: send Basmanov,
And do not heed the protests of the boyars.[247]
You've sat with me in Council since your boyhood,
The ways of governance are known to you.
Do not change established forms of things,
For custom is the soul of government.

Ты с малых лет сидел со мною в Думе,
Ты знаешь ход державного правленья;
Не изменяй теченья дел. Привычка —
Душа держав. Я ныне должен был
Восстановить опалы, казни — можешь
Их отменить; тебя благословят,
Как твоего благословляли дядю,
Когда престол он Грозного приял.
Со временем и понемногу снова
Затягивай державные бразды.
Теперь ослабь, из рук не выпуская…
Будь милостив, доступен к иноземцам,
Доверчиво их службу принимай.
Со строгостью храни устав церковный;
Будь молчалив; не должен царский голос
На воздухе теряться по-пустому;
Как звон святой, он должен лишь вещать
Велику скорбь или великий праздник.
О милый сын, ты входишь в те лета,
Когда нам кровь волнует женский лик.
Храни, храни святую чистоту
Невинности и гордую стыдливость:
Кто чувствами в порочных наслажденьях
В младые дни привыкнул утопать,
Тот, возмужав, угрюм и кровожаден,
И ум его безвременно темнеет.
В семье своей будь завсегда главою;
Мать почитай — но властвуй сам собою —
Ты муж и царь — люби свою сестру,
Ты ей один хранитель остаешься.

Феодор
(на коленях)

Нет, нет — живи и царствуй долговечно:
Народ и мы погибли без тебя.

Царь

Всё кончено — глаза мои темнеют,
Я чувствую могильный хлад…

I was compelled to bring back banishment
And execution – now you can repeal them;
Then the people will bless you, as they blessed
Your uncle when he ascended Ivan's throne.
In time, draw tight the reins of government;
For now, relax them, but never let them go …
Pay foreigners attention and respect,
Give them trust, and accept their services.[248]
Strictly observe the statutes of the Church.
Be sparing of your words – the sovereign's voice
Should not be wasted on the empty air;
Like a cathedral bell, it should announce
Tidings of great sorrow or great joy.
Dear son, you are on the threshold of those years
In which our blood is roused by woman's beauty.
Preserve, preserve the blessed purity
Of innocence, the pride of modesty;
He who in youth has learnt to drown his feelings
In sinful pleasures, grows in adulthood
Morose and bloodthirsty, his mind soon darkens.[249]
Always be the master in your family;
Honor your mother – but hold sway yourself;[250]
For you are man and tsar. Cherish your sister,
Henceforth her sole protector will be you.[251]

Feodor falls on his knees.

Feodor
No – you will live and reign for many years:
For us – the people – all is lost without you.

Tsar
All is finished, all I see is darkness,
I feel the coldness of the grave …

(Входят патриарх, святители, за
ним все бояре. Царицу ведут под
руки, царевна рыдает.)

Кто там?
А! схимия… святое постриженье…
Ударил час, в монахи царь идет —
И темный гроб моею будет кельей…
Повремени, владыко патриарх,
Я царь еще: внемлите вы, бояре:
Се тот, кому приказываю царство;
Целуйте крест Феодору… Басманов,
Друзья мои… при гробе вас молю
Ему служить усердием и правдой!
Он так еще и млад, и непорочен.
Клянетесь ли?

Бояре
Клянемся.

Царь
Я доволен.
Простите ж мне соблазны и грехи
И вольные и тайные обиды…
Святый отец, приближься, я готов.

(Начинается обряд пострижения.
Женщин в обмороке выносят.)

(Enter the Patriarch and priests,
followed by all the boyars; the tsaritsa,
supported under each arm; the
Tsarevna, sobbing.)

Who's there? ...
I take the habit of the strictest order ...
Now the ritual cutting of the hair ...
The hour has come, the Tsar becomes a monk – [252]
The grave will be my cell ... Lord Patriarch,
Wait a little, I rule still as your Tsar;
And boyars, hear me now: I designate
Your future sovereign. Kiss the Cross to Feodor ...
Basmanov, friends: on the threshold of the grave
I ask you – serve him zealously and truly!
He is so young and innocent of the world.
You swear?

Boyars
We swear.[253]

Tsar
So be it. I am content.
Forgive me all my sins and weaknesses,
Wrongs I have done, with and without intent ...
Come to me, holy father, I am ready.

(The ritual cutting of the Tsar's
hair begins. Women are carried
out in a faint.)

[Сцена 23]

СТАВКА

БАСМАНОВ ВВОДИТ ПУШКИНА.

Басманов
Войди сюда и говори свободно.
Итак, тебя ко мне он посылает?

Пушкин
Тебе свою он дружбу предлагает
И первый сан по нем в московском царстве.

Басманов
Но я и так Феодором высоко
Уж вознесен. Начальствую над войском,
Он для меня презрел и чин разрядный,
И гнев бояр — я присягал ему.

Пушкин
Ты присягал наследнику престола
Законному; но если жив другой,
Законнейший?..

Басманов
                    Послушай, Пушкин, полно,
Пустого мне не говори; я знаю,
Кто он такой.

Пушкин
                    Россия и Литва
Димитрием давно его признали,
Но, впрочем, я за это не стою.
Быть может, он Димитрий настоящий,
Быть может, он и самозванец. Только
Я ведаю, что рано или поздно
Ему Москву уступит сын Борисов.

[Scene 23]

FIELD HEADQUARTERS[254]

Basmanov enters with Pushkin.

Basmanov
You can speak freely. So, he sent you to me?

Pushkin
He offers you not only friendship, but
The highest rank when he is Tsar of Moscow.[255]

Basmanov
Feodor has already honored me.
I am commander of his troops; for me
He disregarded rules of precedence,
The boyars' anger – I am sworn to him.[256]

Pushkin
Sworn to the successor to the throne
By lawful right. But what if someone else,
With greater lawful right –

Basmanov
                                    Pushkin, enough,
Don't try me with this nonsense; I am aware
Who this man is.

Pushkin
                                    Russia and Lithuania
Affirmed him as Dimitry long ago,
However, I shall not insist on it.[257]
Perhaps he really is the true Dimitry,
Perhaps he's only a pretender. All
I know is this: Boris's son and heir
Is bound to yield him Moscow in the end.

Басманов

Пока стою за юного царя,
Дотоле он престола не оставит;
Полков у нас довольно, слава Богу!
Победою я их одушевлю,
А вы, кого против меня пошлете?
Не казака ль Карелу? али Мнишка?
Да много ль вас, всего-то восемь тысяч.

Пушкин

Ошибся ты: и тех не наберешь —
Я сам скажу, что войско наше дрянь,
Что казаки лишь только селы грабят,
Что поляки лишь хвастают да пьют,
А русские... да что и говорить...
Перед тобой не стану я лукавить;
Но знаешь ли, чем мы сильны, Басманов?
Не войском, нет, не польскою помогой,
А мнением; да! мнением народным.
Димитрия ты помнишь торжество
И мирные его завоеванья,
Когда везде без выстрела ему
Послушные сдавались города,
А воевод упрямых чернь вязала?
Ты видел сам, охотно ль ваши рати
Сражались с ним; когда же? при Борисе!
А нынче ль?.. нет, Басманов, поздно спорить
И раздувать холодный пепел брани:
Со всем твоим умом и твердой волей
Не устоишь; не лучше ли тебе
Дать первому пример благоразумной,
Димитрия царем провозгласить
И тем ему навеки удружить?
Как думаешь?

Басманов
Узнаете вы завтра.

Basmanov

But our young tsar will not give up the throne
While I stand by him. We have regiments
Enough, thank God, and under me they'll be
Victorious – Who can you, though, put against me?
A handful of Cossacks like Karela? Mniszech?[258]
How many men – eight thousand at the most?[259]

Pushkin

Not even that. Our army is a rabble.
The Cossacks just destroy the villages,
The Poles just brag and drink – and then the Russians,
The less one says of them … I'll not deceive you …[260]
Where *our* strength lies, I'll tell you now, Basmanov:
Not in our numbers, not our Polish allies,
But in esteem – in popular esteem![261]
Don't you remember when Dimitry triumphed,
His bloodless conquests, how the cities yielded
Without a shot? How voivodes who resisted
Were bound and handed over to the people?[262]
You saw your army loath to fight against him;
And when was that? When Boris ruled! But now?
Too late to be against him now, Basmanov,
One cannot stir cold ashes into flame;
With all your brilliance, all your strength of will,
You cannot stop him; better far to be
The first to set a sensible example,
Proclaim Dimitry Tsar, and win him to you
For life. What do you think?

Basmanov
　　　You'll know tomorrow.

Пушкин

Решись.

Басманов

Прощай.

Пушкин
Подумай же, Басманов.

(Уходит.)

Басманов
Он прав, он прав; везде измена зреет —
Что делать мне? Ужели буду ждать,
Чтоб и меня бунтовщики связали
И выдали Отрепьеву? Не лучше ль
Предупредить разрыв потока бурный
И самому... Но изменить присяге!
Но заслужить бесчестье в род и род!
Доверенность младого венценосца
Предательством ужасным заплатить —
Опальному изгнаннику легко
Обдумывать мятеж и заговор —
Но мне ли, мне ль, любимцу государя...
Но смерть... но власть... но бедствия народны...

(Задумывается.)

Сюда! кто там?

(Свищет.)

Коня! трубите сбор.

Pushkin

Decide.

Basmanov

Goodbye.

Pushkin

Think carefully now, Basmanov.

(Exit.)

Basmanov

He is right, he is right; betrayal everywhere –
Am I to wait till rebels tie me up
And hand me over to Otrepiev?[263] Best
Anticipate the storm ... But then – my oath!
To earn dishonor down the generations ...
Repay the young tsar's trust with treachery!
All very well for exiles in disgrace
To hatch rebellion and conspiracy – [264]
But how could I, the favorite of the Tsar ...
But death ... but power ... the suffering of the people ...

(Falls into thought.)

Is anyone there?

(Whistles.)

Bring me my horse! Sound muster.

[Сцена 24]

ЛОБНОЕ МЕСТО

ПУШКИН ИДЕТ, ОКРУЖЕННЫЙ НАРОДОМ.

Народ
Царевич нам боярина послал.
Послушаем, что скажет нам боярин.
Послушаем.

Пушкин
(на амвоне)
Московские граждане,
Вам кланяться царевич приказал.

(Кланяется.)

Вы знаете, как промысел небесный
Царевича от рук убийцы спас;
Он шел казнить злодея своего,
Но Божий суд уж поразил Бориса.
Димитрию Россия покорилась;
Басманов сам с раскаяньем усердным
Свои полки привел ему к присяге.
Он к вам идет с любовию и с миром.
В угоду ли семейству Годуновых
Подымете вы руку на царя
Законного, на внука Мономаха.

Народ
Вестимо, нет.

Пушкин
Московские граждане!
Мир ведает, сколь много вы терпели
Под властию жестокого пришельца:
Опалу, казнь, бесчестие, налоги,

[Scene 24]

PLACE OF EXECUTIONS[265]

Enter Pushkin, surrounded by a crowd.[266]

People
Here comes a boyar, sent by the Tsarevich.
Let's hear now what the boyar has to tell us.
Let's hear him!

Pushkin
(on a rostrum)
First, good citizens of Moscow,
I bow to you, as the Tsarevich bade me.

(Bows.)

You all know how the hand of Providence
Delivered the Tsarevich from foul death.
Just as he marched to levy retribution
Upon his would-be executioner,
The Judgement of the Lord struck Boris down.
Russia has submitted to Dimitry;
Basmanov too, sincere in his repentance,
Has sworn allegiance, with his army, to him.[267]
Dimitry comes in love and peace to you.
Would you prefer the house of Godunov,
And raise your hand against the lawful Tsar,
Against the flesh and blood of Monomakh?

People
We would not – never!

Pushkin
Citizens of Moscow!
The world well knows how much you have endured
During the reign of that cruel interloper:
Disgrace, dishonor, levies, executions,

И труд, и глад — всё испытали вы.
Димитрий же вас жаловать намерен,
Бояр, дворян, людей приказных, ратных,
Гостей, купцов — и весь честной народ.
Вы ль станете упрямиться безумно
И милостей кичливо убегать?
Но он идет на царственный престол
Своих отцов — в сопровожденьи грозном.
Не гневайте ж царя и бойтесь Бога.
Целуйте крест законному владыке;
Смиритеся, немедленно пошлите
К Димитрию во стан митрополита,
Бояр, дьяков и выборных людей,
Да бьют челом отцу и государю.

(Сходит. Шум народный.)

Народ

Что толковать? Боярин правду молвил.
Да здравствует Димитрий наш отец.

Мужик на амвоне

Народ, народ! в Кремль! в царские палаты!
Ступай! связать Борисова щенка!

Народ
(несется толпою)

Вязать! вязать! Да здравствует Димитрий!
Да гибнет род Бориса Годунова!

Hard labor, famine – what have you not suffered!
Dimitry will bestow his grace upon you,
On boyars, nobles, servants of the Tsar,
Soldiers, merchants, traders – all honest people.
Will you be so stubborn and so senseless –
And spurn his generosity? Dimitry,
Escorted by his formidable army,
Is marching to his throne, his forebears' throne!
Do not provoke the anger of the Tsar.
Fear God, bow down before your lawful ruler,
Kiss the cross to him; send to Dimitry
The Metropolitan and all the boyars,
Your honored men and officers of state,
To bow before your Father and your Tsar.[268]

(Exit. The people are abuzz.)

People
What's left to say? The boyar speaks the truth.
Dimitry is our Tsar. Long live our Father!

Peasant on the rostrum
Everyone to the Kremlin! The Tsar's palace!
Forward! We'll take that whelp of Godunov's![269]

People
(surging forward)
We'll bind him! drown him! Long live Tsar Dimitry!
Death to Godunov! Death to his breed![270]

[Сцена 25]

КРЕМЛЬ. ДОМ БОРИСОВ.
СТРАЖА У КРЫЛЬЦА

ФЕОДОР ПОД ОКНОМ.

Нищий
Дайте милостыню, Христа ради!

Стража
Поди прочь, не велено говорить с заключенными.

Феодор
Поди, старик, я беднее тебя, ты на воле.

(Ксения под покрывалом подходит
также к окну.)

Один из народа
Брат да сестра! бедные дети, что пташки в клетке.

Другой
Есть о ком жалеть? Проклятое племя!

Первый
Отец был злодей, а детки невинны.

Другой
Яблоко от яблони недалеко падает.

Ксения
Братец, братец, кажется, к нам бояре идут.

Феодор
Это Голицын, Мосальский. Другие мне незнакомы.

Ксения
Ах, братец, сердце замирает!

[Scene 25]

THE KREMLIN. HOUSE OF THE GODUNOVS

Guard on the porch. Feodor at the window.

Beggar
Give me a kopek, in Christ's name.

Guard
Off with you. It's forbidden to talk to the prisoners.

Feodor
Go away, old man, I am poorer than you are, you are free.

*(Ksenia, veiled, also appears at
the window.)*

One of the People
Brother and sister! Poor children, they're like two little birds in a cage.

A Second
There's a pair to feel sorry for! Cursed breed!

First
Their father was a villain, but the children are innocent.

Second
An apple doesn't fall far from the tree.

Ksenia
Brother dear, I think the boyars are coming.

Feodor
It's Golitsyn and Mosalsky. I don't know the others.[271]

Ksenia
Dear brother, my heart has stopped!

(Голицын, Мосальский, Молчанов и
Шерефединов. За ними трое
стрельцов.)

Народ
Расступитесь, расступитесь. Бояре идут.

(Они входят в дом.)

Один из народа
Зачем они пришли?

Другой
А верно, приводить к присяге Феодора Годунова.

Третий
В самом деле? — слышишь, какой в доме шум! Тревога, дерутся...

Народ
Взойдем! — двери заперты — слышишь? визг! Это женский голос — крики замолкли — шум продолжается.

(Отворяются двери. Мосальский
является на крыльце.)

Мосальский
Народ! Мария Годунова и сын ее Феодор отравили себя ядом. Мы видели их мертвые трупы.

(Народ в ужасе молчит.)

Что ж вы молчите? кричите: да здравствует царь Димитрий Иванович!

Народ
Да здравствует царь Димитрий Иванович!

7 ноября
1825

(Enter Golitsyn, Mosalsky, Molchanov
and Sherefedinov, followed by three
streltsy.)[272]

People
Make way, make way for the boyars.

(They enter the house.)

One of the People
What have they come for?

A Second
Most likely to fetch Feodor Godunov to take the oath.

A Third
Really? – Listen to the noise from inside the house! What an uproar – there's a struggle going on ...[273]

People
Let's go up! – The doors are locked. – Can you hear? Screaming! – That's a woman's voice – the screaming's stopped. – There's still a noise going on.

(The doors open.
Mosalsky appears on the porch.)

Mosalsky
People! Maria Godunova and her son Feodor have taken poison. We have seen their dead bodies.[274]

(The people are silent in horror.)[275]

Why are you silent? Shout: "Long live Tsar Dimitry Ivanovich!"

People
Long live Tsar Dimitry Ivanovich![276]

November 7, 1825

Конец комидии,
в ней же первая персона
царь Борис Годунов.

Слава Отцу и Сыну и Святому Духу,
АМИНЬ.

End of the comedy,
in which the leading person is Tsar Boris Godunov.

Glory be to the Father, and to the Son, and to the Holy Ghost,
AMEN.

Notes to Pushkin's *Comedy*

     Chester Dunning with Lidiia Lotman
and Antony Wood

One of the main purposes of this book is to help readers appreciate young Alexander Pushkin as an historian, not just as a playwright. As noted in chapter 2, Pushkin worked very hard to make his *Comedy* historically accurate. Not only did he carefully consult many sources, but he also demonstrated remarkable historical insight into the events and characters of Russia's Time of Troubles. As pointed out in chapter 3, Pushkin also had a rather sophisticated audience in mind for his subversive play: "historically conscious" theatergoers who had read about the Time of Troubles and could appreciate his *Comedy*'s "good jokes and delicate allusions to the history of the time." In fact, Pushkin's great care to use correct historical terminology in his play would have satisfied even the fussiest historians of his era, and they were undoubtedly part of his intended audience. But what may have been obvious to educated Russians in the early nineteenth century is, unfortunately, not always easy for twenty-first century readers to comprehend. For that reason, the following annotation is designed primarily to demonstrate Pushkin's precise use of historical terminology, the extraordinary accuracy of his historical references, and his deep understanding of early modern Russian history. Up-to-date historical information is also provided to help the reader understand the confusing and frequently misinterpreted period in which Pushkin's play is set and to show just how remarkably shrewd and intuitive the poet-historian really was. Partly because of Musorgsky's famous opera and partly because of the weakness of past scholarship concerning Pushkin's intentions in writing *Boris Godunov,* the second half of his play – which is primarily concerned with the Pretender Dmitry's military campaign – has been underappreciated. It is hoped that the annotation of those brilliant later scenes provided here will help readers rediscover them as an important part of Pushkin's *Comedy about Tsar Boris and Grishka Otrepiev.*

1. In early January 1598, Tsar Feodor Ivanovich (r. 1584–98) – the son of Tsar Ivan IV ("the Terrible") – died without an heir, ending the only ruling dynasty Moscow had ever known. His death triggered the Time of Troubles (*Smuta*), a horrific decade and a half of political struggle, famine, civil war, and foreign intervention that nearly destroyed Russia before ending with the establishment of the Romanov dynasty in 1613. When the mentally retarded Tsar Feodor died, his brother-in-law, Boris Godunov (1552–1605), who had been Feodor's regent and the effective ruler of Russia for more than a decade, maneuvered to succeed him. In the face of stubborn aristocratic opposition and widely circulating rumors that he was a tsaricide, however, Godunov was forced to play a cautious game. He repeatedly denied any interest in becoming tsar and retreated to the Novodevichy Monastery in the Moscow suburbs. Godunov's supporters then arranged for a huge procession of Muscovites to go to the monastery on February 20, 1598, in order to beg Boris to take the throne. See Skrynnikov, "Boris Godunov's Struggle," 325–53.

2. The Kremlin – Moscow's walled citadel and seat of government – housed the official premises of the tsar and his family, several cathedrals and churches, and many ornate buildings where bureaucrats worked, state functions were held, foreign ambassadors were received, and the tsar's boyar council (or boyar duma) sat.

3. The Shuiskys and Vorotynskys were high-born princes by birth. Prince Vasily Shuisky had been a leading boyar (aristocratic servitor) at the court of Tsar Feodor and was a potentially strong claimant to the throne. Although generally represented as an opponent of Boris Godunov, Shuisky made no attempt to claim the vacant throne in 1598, and he may actually have tried to help Godunov's cause somewhat among his fellow boyars. (One of Shuisky's brothers was related to Godunov by marriage.) The Shuisky clan probably reasoned that Boris was an unstoppable candidate for tsar, but they may also have been cowed by the murder of leading members of their family who had openly opposed Godunov while he was Tsar Feodor's regent. The Vorotynsky princes had also opposed Godunov during Feodor's reign, and – as a result – they too

suffered exile and intermittent persecution. See RFCW, 62–63, 92, 210; BG, 256.

4. During extraordinary occasions such as interregnums and sieges, members of the boyar council routinely took turns acting as highly visible commanders of Moscow's police force and its defenses, thereby helping to reassure the capital's population and maintain order.

5. Patriarch Iov (Job) was the first patriarch of the Russian Orthodox Church, elevated from the rank of metropolitan to that supreme spiritual office in 1589 thanks to the efforts of his close friend, Boris Godunov. In 1598, Patriarch Iov became Godunov's most active supporter in his struggle for the throne. He personally organized the procession to Novodevichy Monastery to beg Boris to accept the crown. See Skrynnikov, *Boris Godunov,* chapters 4 and 9; idem, "Boris Godunov's Struggle."

6. As the brother of Tsaritsa Irina (Tsar Feodor's wife), Boris Godunov became the effective ruler of Russia by the late 1580s, even before being named regent. As regent, he amassed enormous power and influence and also became one of the richest men in the country. Godunov was strongly supported by members of the clergy, bureaucrats, and the bulk of the gentry, but he had many jealous rivals among high-born princes who considered themselves more worthy of the throne than Boris, whose father had been a mere provincial cavalryman. See RFCW, 60–72.

7. Boris Godunov's sister, Tsaritsa Irina (widow of Tsar Feodor), had been named co-ruler by her husband in the 1590s, which gave her an authentic claim to the throne in 1598. Patriarch Iov proclaimed that Tsar Feodor had intended that Irina rule after him, and the Russian people quickly swore allegiance to her. Within just a few days, however, Irina became a nun, entered Novodevichy Monastery, and renounced the throne in favor of the boyar council. She nevertheless continued to work behind the scenes to promote her brother's candidacy. Boris Godunov soon joined his sister at the convent, where he publicly threatened to become a monk if people continued to pressure him to take the throne. See RFCW, 92; Thyrêt, *Between God and Tsar,* chapter 3.

8. The boyar council (or duma) was the principal advisory body assisting the tsar in ruling Russia. Composed of aristocratic servitors who had been promoted into its ranks, the boyar council acted as an informal, quasi-legislative body and military council. It handled important affairs of state and many judicial and administrative matters. Its members also acted as heads of various bureaucratic offices, governors of

towns, and commanders of the tsar's military forces. A majority of boyars supported Boris Godunov as tsar in 1598, but a vocal minority resisted his enthronement. In order to overcome that opposition, Boris continued to stay at Novodevichy Monastery and repeatedly refused to consider taking the throne. In the meantime, the boyar council announced its intention to convene a *zemskii sobor* (Assembly of the Land) to choose a new tsar. Created by Tsar Ivan IV (r. 1547–84) as a sounding board composed of various social strata and convened at the government's pleasure, the Assembly of the Land had no independent power, but it could become a significant player in the unprecedented task of choosing a new tsar. Godunov prevented the convening of a true Assembly of the Land at this time because he could not yet control the outcome of an election. See Skrynnikov, "Boris Godunov's Struggle."

9. Pushkin's terminology here is precise and accurate. "Great Assembly" is a reference to the unprecedented convocation of church officials and other Godunov supporters that was organized by Patriarch Iov at this time in order to bypass the boyar council in choosing Boris as the new tsar. Surviving documents refer to this assembly as a "Consecrated Council" (*dukhovnyi sobor;* i.e., a Church Council convened to elect a tsar), but later Godunov propaganda represented it as a truly representative *zemskii sobor* or Assembly of the Land – something that has confused many historians writing on the subject. The hand-picked and politically reliable "Great Assembly" dutifully chose Godunov as tsar, but its decision did not initially receive the support of the boyar council. That disappointing development forced Boris temporarily to reject his "election" and to remain at Novodevichy Monastery. See Skrynnikov, *Boris Godunov,* chapter 9; idem, "Boris Godunov's Struggle," 331–37.

10. Boris Godunov's sister did want him to become tsar, but she could not pass the crown directly to her brother because of the opposition of some powerful boyars. Instead, she publicly supported Boris's clever strategy: to appear to be extremely reluctant to take the throne until Patriarch Iov and thousands of Muscovites had assembled before Novodevichy Monastery and loudly, repeatedly demanded that Boris become tsar or else face excommunication for failing to do his patriotic and sacred duty.

11. The reference is to Tsarevich Dmitry Ivanovich, Ivan the Terrible's youngest son (by his seventh wife, Maria Nagaia), who was born in 1582. After Tsar Ivan's death and a failed coup d'état in favor of little Dmitry, the Nagoi clan was disgraced and exiled from court. Dmitry and his

mother were sent to Uglich where they were kept under surveillance. Tsarevich Dmitry supposedly died in Uglich on May 15, 1591, from a self-inflicted wound that occurred during an epileptic seizure while he was playing knife toss. Boris Godunov's opponents claimed that Dmitry's death was not accidental – that instead the regent had ordered the murder of the tsarevich in order to clear a path to the throne for himself. Pushkin credited that accusation as did most Russian historians before the twentieth century. Today, many scholars doubt that Godunov had anything to do with the Uglich tragedy, but the potent accusation that he was a tsaricide resurfaced in 1598 as his opponents tried desperately to stop him from becoming tsar. See RFCW, 61–67; Skrynnikov, *Boris Godunov*, chapter 6.

12. According to the extremely unreliable *New Chronicle* (composed in the early years of Tsar Mikhail's reign and reflecting the official Romanov interpretation of the Time of Troubles), a man named Nikifor Chepchugov was asked to join in Boris Godunov's assassination plot against Tsarevich Dmitry but refused to participate (see PSRL, 14: 40). Karamzin used the *New Chronicle* extensively in composing his *History of the Russian State*, and Pushkin also consulted it while composing his play.

13. Secretary (*d'iak*) Mikhail Bitiagovsky was the crown official at Uglich who had been appointed by Boris Godunov shortly before Tsarevich Dmitry's death. He was accused by the Nagoi clan of treating the exiled Tsaritsa Maria and other members of the family unfairly and of directing his own son, Danilo Bitiagovsky, and his nephew, Nikita Kachalov, to murder Tsarevich Dmitry on May 15, 1591. See PSRL, 14: 40–42; Klein, *Uglicheskoe sledstvennoe delo; Russkaia istoricheskaia biblioteka* [hereafter cited as RIB], 13: col. 7.

14. After hearing conflicting reports about Dmitry's death, Tsar Feodor sent an investigating commission to Uglich to determine what had actually happened. Prince Vasily Shuisky was chosen to be the highest ranking member of that commission in order to reassure people that Boris Godunov would not be able to influence its conclusions. The commission, including Shuisky, eventually exonerated Godunov and declared that Dmitry had accidentally killed himself. However, rumors of the tsarevich's murder spread widely, and the Shuisky clan may well have been involved in circulating those rumors. See Vernadsky, "Death of Tsarevich Dimitry," 1–19; Perrie, *Pretenders*, 52–53.

15. The population of Uglich was incited by the Nagoi clan to kill the

alleged murderers of Tsarevich Dmitry – Mikhail and Danilo Bitiagovsky and Nikita Kachalov – and to tell the Uglich investigating commission a carefully scripted story of how the assassins had carried out the crime. That testimony was filled with contradictions and was not credible to the commissioners. Eventually, many of the townspeople of Uglich were exiled to Pelym in Siberia as punishment for their actions. See PSRL, 14: 42; Vernadsky, "The Death of Tsarevich Dimitry."

16. Boris Godunov tried hard to still the charge of tsaricide leveled against him by his enemies, but here Pushkin has Shuisky remembering the events of 1591 in a self-serving way. In fact, perhaps as a reward for presiding over the Uglich investigating commission's conclusion that Dmitry's death had been accidental, Vasily Shuisky's status and influence at court rose after 1591, and he managed to stay out of trouble. In addition, his brother, Dmitry Shuisky, was promoted to the rank of boyar in 1591 and was even allowed to marry a relative of the regent, undoubtedly with Boris's approval. See RFCW, 67, 92.

17. Tsar Feodor did indeed trust his brother-in-law who ruled in his name. The tsar took the regent's side in virtually all of Boris Godunov's conflicts with other aristocrats. See RFCW, 61–62.

18. The reference is to Prince Ivan Petrovich Shuisky, who attempted to supplant Boris Godunov at court in 1586 by staging a riot in Moscow and orchestrating a demand by several lords (including Prince Vorotynsky) that Tsar Feodor divorce Boris's sister, the "barren" Tsaritsa Irina. Tsar Feodor, however, loved his wife and authorized Boris Godunov to suppress the opposition. Ivan Shuisky and his son Andrei were disgraced and sent into exile, where they died mysteriously – perhaps murdered by Godunov agents. Their deaths thrust Vasily Shuisky into the limelight as the leader of the Shuisky clan. Although Pushkin knew that Ivan Shuisky was Vasily's uncle, many historians mistakenly identified him as Vasily's father. See RFCW, 62; Skrynnikov, *Boris Godunov*, 32–34.

19. Although most scholars today doubt that Boris Godunov had anything to do with Tsarevich Dmitry's death, rumors that he was a tsaricide definitely affected how he conducted his struggle for the throne. Recent attempts to link Godunov to the Uglich tragedy are based on unreliable sources; see Zimin, "Smert' tsarevicha Dimitriia," 92–111; Perrie, "Jerome Horsey's Account," 28–49; and RFCW, 66–67.

20. The Godunov clan itself encouraged the false belief that Boris was descended from a Tatar (Mongol) emir named Chet-murza who joined Muscovite service in the fourteenth century. When Boris Godunov's

high-born aristocratic enemies unfairly accused him of being a former slave, what they really meant was that he was lowborn. In fact, Godunov's ancestors had been boyars at the court of the grand princes of Moscow, but family fortunes had waned by the sixteenth century; Boris's father was a low-ranking provincial gentry cavalryman. Boris's uncle, Dmitry Godunov, brought Boris and his sister Irina to the court of Ivan the Terrible, where they became close friends of Ivan's son Feodor. Tsar Ivan seems to have considered the Godunov children to be members of his own family, and he eventually agreed to the marriage of Feodor and Irina. Young Boris Godunov was allowed to marry the daughter of one of Tsar Ivan's principal advisers, the notorious Maliuta Skuratov. See Skrynnikov, *Boris Godunov*, 1–7; RFCW, 60–61.

21. Boris Godunov's father-in-law, Grigory Lukianovich Skuratov-Belsky (Maliuta Skuratov), had been an active member of Tsar Ivan's dreaded *oprichnina* (a state within the state, under the tsar's direct control) and gradually emerged as its all-powerful boss. Boris Godunov and his uncle Dmitry both served in the *oprichnina*. Much of the terror and bloodshed associated with the *oprichnina* was blamed on the hated Skuratov, who forged a political alliance at court with Dmitry Godunov. That alliance in 1570 led to Boris Godunov's marriage, at age eighteen, to Skuratov's daughter, Maria.

22. The ancient cap of Monomakh is a beautiful ceremonial crown, one of several the grand princes and tsars could wear. It is decorated with precious stones and trimmed with sable. According to legend, it had been a gift to Grand Prince Vladimir Monomakh of Kiev (r. 1113–25) from the Byzantine Emperor Constantine IX "Monomachus" (1053–1125), along with a shoulder-cape (or short robe) adorned with medallions of gold, enamel, and precious stones. Grand Prince Vladimir assumed the name "Monomakh" as a symbolic claim for his own dynasty's right to succeed the Byzantine emperors, but there is still no agreement among scholars about the actual origins of these "gifts."

23. The princely families of Muscovy with the highest status were those (such as the Shuiskys) who could trace their ancestors back to Riurik, the semi-mythical ninth-century founder of Russia's ruling dynasty.

24. Pushkin's characterization of Shuisky as a sly troublemaker is accurate, but the historical Vasily Shuisky carefully avoided being associated with opposition to Boris Godunov in 1598. Instead, Godunov's principal rival at the time was Feodor Romanov, future patriarch of the

Russian Orthodox Church and father of Mikhail, founder of the Romanov dynasty in 1613.

25. "Varangians" was the old Russian name for Scandinavians and other North Europeans. According to legend, the Varangians (led by Prince Riurik) were invited by the Slavs to rule over them in the year 862.

26. These "appanages" were the inherited estates of the ancient Russian princes that were gradually eliminated by the grand princes and early tsars of Muscovy. Those high-born princes were eventually forced to compete for status, power, and influence at court with men of lesser birth. All boyars were required to live in Moscow and to attend the tsar for many hours each day. Thanks in large part to Ivan the Terrible's self-serving propaganda and terror campaigns, by the late sixteenth century these aristocrats had come to be regarded by many ordinary Russians as greedy exploiters of their social inferiors and as potential traitors to the realm. See Perrie, "Popular Image," 275–86.

27. Vorotynsky's words have a double meaning. On the one hand, a political opponent of Godunov acknowledges the services performed by Boris as regent, his popularity and personal charm (noted by his contemporaries), and his capable rule; on the other hand, the root meaning of the word "bewitch" indicates that Vorotynsky sees in Boris's influence over many people signs of enchantment or sorcery. (A number of Boris's opponents actually accused him of sorcery.) As regent, Boris Godunov managed to gain the strong support of most of the Orthodox Church hierarchy, the bulk of the gentry cavalry force, and much of the bureaucracy. Nevertheless, he was actually hated by many ordinary Russians for enserfing the peasants by "temporarily" suspending their right to move on St. George's Day, for overtaxing the townspeople and binding them to their places of residence, and for curbing cossack freedom on Russia's southern frontier. See RFCW, chapters 4–6; Dunning, "Who Was Tsar Dmitrii," 722–23.

28. Red Square is the large, bustling city square located northeast of and adjacent to Moscow's Kremlin. In addition to shopping and gossiping, crowds of Muscovites gathered there to hear official proclamations.

29. *Narod*, the common people – peasants, townsfolk, low status clerics, soldiers, and other ordinary subjects.

30. The Duma Secretary (*dumnyi d'iak*) was the secretary of the boyar council (or boyar duma). He had lower status than the boyars but was still a member of the ruling elite and was often able to influence the agenda of council meetings and to shape the final language of council

decrees or instructions. The Duma Secretary in 1598 was Vasily Shchelkalov, who had succeeded his brother to the post in 1594. According to a
contemporary, Shchelkalov – a renowned speaker – appeared before the
people during the interregnum and urged them to swear an oath of obedience to the boyar council. See Skrynnikov, *Boris Godunov*, 90.

31. The "Main Porch" was an elevated platform at the top of the "Red
Stairs," the formal entry to the Granovitaia Palace (Palace of Facets). The
Palace of Facets, which contained the throne room, was designed by Ital-
ian architects for Grand Prince Ivan III in the late fifteenth century.

32. "Assembly" here refers to the extraordinary convocation of church
officials, bureaucrats, and others gathered by Patriarch Iov to "elect"
Boris Godunov as tsar. See note 9.

33. These were two of the most famous of all Russian icons. One of
them was known as "Our Lady of Vladimir," a wooden icon of the
Madonna and Child dating back at least to the twelfth century. It was
supposedly brought by boat from Constantinople to Kiev before 1155;
sometime later (after 1169), it was transferred by Prince Andrei Bogo-
liubsky from Kiev to the new "capital" of Russia, Vladimir (in Suzdal
province). The other icon mentioned here was known as the Holy Virgin
of the Don. It had been a gift from the cossacks (part-time mercenary
soldiers and bandits who lived on the steppe) to Grand Prince Dmitry
(Donskoi) and accompanied his army to the battle of Kulikovo Field in
1380. In 1591, the Holy Virgin of the Don was brought out from its resting
place to protect the Russian army that successfully defended Moscow
against a Crimean Tatar attack.

34. Pushkin's use of historical terminology here is very precise. He
refers to the *sinklit,* the old Russian term for boyar council, and to the
vybornye dvoriane, the top rung of the provincial gentry who were chosen for three years of service in Moscow and then usually rotated back to
their home provinces.

35. Maiden's Field was located on the outskirts of Moscow near the
wealthy Novodevichy Monastery (or New Maiden's Convent), which was
founded in 1524. Both Boris Godunov and his sister, Tsaritsa Irina (the
nun Aleksandra), resided in Novodevichy Monastery during the interregnum. This scene ("Devich'e pole. Novodevichii monastyr'") was
excluded from the first printed edition of *Boris Godunov.* It was also
excluded from many subsequent editions until the Stalin era, when it was
finally restored and included in the canonical text of the play. The scene
was first published in 1841, in the first official posthumous edition of

Pushkin's works edited by Vasily Zhukovsky; see Pushkin, *Sochineniia Aleksandra Pushkina*, 9: 193–95; and our chapters 1 and 6.

36. Muscovites really did gather in large numbers to loudly wail and beg Boris Godunov to become tsar. See Timofeev, *Vremennik*, 53.

37. Pushkin borrows this incident from Karamzin; see Karamzin, *Istoriia* (1892), 10: 139–40 and note 397.

38. Boris Godunov's enemies claimed that his agents forced the crowd to shout in favor of him by using threats of fines and beatings. Karamzin mentioned unenthusiastic people rubbing their eyes with saliva in order to appear to be supportive of the new tsar, but Pushkin took the idea for generating fake tears by means of an onion directly from the chronicle that Karamzin had consulted. See RIB, 13: cols. 14–15; Karamzin, *Istoriia*, 10: note 397; Brody, *Demetrius Legend*, 241–42.

39. This is essentially accurate. Godunov did try to assume the throne at this point, but continuing boyar resistance forced him to maneuver for many more weeks against his opponents. He finally succeeded in overcoming his enemies by means of a convenient (and greatly exaggerated) military threat to Moscow posed by the Crimean Tatars. No Crimean army actually invaded Russia, but on the "campaign" Boris played the part of the kindly, fair, and generous ruler, and he was quickly accepted as commander-in-chief (i.e., as tsar) by the boyars. He was eventually crowned as tsar on September 1, 1598. See Skrynnikov, "Boris Godunov's Struggle."

40. These references are to Grand Prince Ivan III (r. 1462–1505), the "gatherer" (unifier) of Russia; Tsar Ivan IV (the Terrible), who founded the Russian Empire by conquering the Volga khanates of Kazan and Astrakhan during the 1550s; and Ivan the Terrible's feebleminded son, Tsar Feodor, who was extremely pious and loved to ring church bells. Feodor Ivanovich was beloved by the Russian people and considered to be a saint by some of them.

41. Pushkin's literary purpose led him to place this scene in 1603. The monk Grishka Otrepiev actually fled to Poland-Lithuania in 1602. See RFCW, 126; Briggs, *Alexander Pushkin*, 166; and our chapter 4.

42. The Chudov Monastery (or the Miracles Monastery) was an elite monastery (also the oldest) located in the Moscow Kremlin, literally across the street from Boris Godunov's quarters. According to legend, the Chudov Monastery was founded in the fourteenth century by Metropolitan Aleksei to commemorate the "miraculous" healing of a Mongol khan's wife; it was dismantled only in 1929.

43. Father Pimen is a fictional character probably based on a monk named Pimen who, according to Karamzin, accompanied Grishka Otrepiev across the border to Lithuania. But Pimen had several historical prototypes. Pushkin actually tried to enter into the way of thinking and the language of the period by reading Russian chronicles. His image of Pimen embodied several historical figures found in those chronicles, not so much in content as in characteristic style, language, thought process, and judgement of events. See Karamzin, *Istoriia* (1892), 11: 76 and note 199; Emerson, *Boris Godunov*, 123–24; BG, 274–76.

44. Grigory (Grishka) Otrepiev was a monk at the Chudov Monastery. According to convention, Otrepiev ran away to Poland-Lithuania where he assumed the identity of the dead Tsarevich Dmitry. Many historians, including Karamzin, accepted that identification. (See, for example, Skrynnikov, *Samozvantsy;* and Perrie, *Pretenders.*) Recently, however, that long-held view of the identity of the Pretender Dmitry has been challenged. See RFCW, chapter 8; Dunning, "Who Was Tsar Dmitrii."

45. A reference to the "Tatar Yoke," the conquest and domination of Russia by the Mongol Golden Horde from approximately 1240 to 1480.

46. A reference to Ivan the Terrible's notoriously cruel punishments of his enemies, especially during the period of the dreaded *oprichnina*. Starting in the 1560s, Tsar Ivan IV turned executions and torture into public spectacles. Well-known politicians, prelates, aristocrats, and famous army commanders – all were executed in cruel and humiliating ways; wives, children, and servants were also executed. In 1570, thousands of Novgorodians were tortured and executed en masse; and citizens along with their wives and children were drowned in the Volkhov River by the thousand. Similar public punishments occurred in Moscow and elsewhere. See BG, 277; Skrynnikov, *Ivan the Terrible.*

47. Novgorod's ancient, democratic popular assembly, known as the *veche,* debated and voted on major issues such as war, peace, and taxes. For much of the rich and independent city's history, all Novgorodian officials were elected by the *veche,* but an oligarchy of aristocrats and merchants gradually gained considerable power. Novgorod's *veche* was officially abolished in 1478 when the city was conquered by Grand Prince Ivan III. Interest in medieval Novgorod grew rapidly in late eighteenth-century Russia, especially with the appearance of Yakov Kniazhnin's play *Vadim of Novgorod,* which was seen by many as a tribute to ancient freedom. See BG, 277–78; Pushkin, *Boris Godunov* (1965), 124.

48. Pushkin uses the term *d'iak* ("secretary") here – a Russian official

who would now be called a bureaucrat or civil servant. Hundreds of them served in the *prikazy*, departments of state that administered particular governmental operations (such as foreign affairs) or specific provinces (such as Siberia). Although inferior socially to the aristocrats, the *d'iaki* had relatively high status and received salaries and land allotments from the tsar.

49. A reference to Tsar Ivan IV's successful campaign against the khanate of Kazan (a remnant of the Golden Horde) in 1552, which ended with a siege of the city of Kazan. The city's mighty fortifications were finally breached after Russian miners dug tunnels under them, filled the tunnels with many barrels of gunpowder, and then ignited the powder.

50. The reference here is to Ivan Petrovich Shuisky, not Vasily Shuisky. During the last years of Tsar Ivan IV's unsuccessful Livonian War (1558–83), Russia faced invasion by armies of Poland-Lithuania led by the legendary King Stefan Báthory (r. 1576–86). (Poland and Lithuania had formally joined together in the Union of Lublin in 1569.) In 1581–82, however, Prince Ivan Petrovich Shuisky, one of the tsar's best generals, presided over the long and successful defense of strategically located Pskov. That Russian "victory" helped convince Báthory to end the war.

51. As a teenager, Yury Bogdanovich Otrepiev was tonsured as the monk Grigory (Grishka) and wandered for several months from monastery to monastery before entering the elite Chudov Monastery in Moscow's Kremlin. See RIB, 13: cols. 638–39; PSRL, 14: 59; PSRL, 34: 111; Skrynnikov, *Boris Godunov*, 131–35.

52. Several Russian grand princes and tsars besides Ivan the Terrible chose to become monks on their deathbeds, symbolically leaving behind the sins they had committed as rulers.

53. Ivan the Terrible's dreaded *oprichnina* was loosely organized as a monastic regime, with Ivan himself playing the role of abbot. (The hated *oprichniki* even dressed in black clothing.) Ivan chose three hundred *oprichniki*, allegedly the most wicked, and turned them into his "brotherhood." In their imitation monastery, located in the settlement (*sloboda*) of Aleksandrovskaia, bloody punishments and acts of sadistic violence against the local population were accompanied by prayers and mock religious ceremonies. Some scholars regard the *oprichnina* as Ivan's conscious (or unconscious) parody of a monastery and monastic life. See BG, 279–80; Hunt, "Ivan IV's Mythology," 769–809.

54. This passage in Pimen's speech is based on letters written by Ivan the Terrible to the father superior and monks of the Kirillo-Belozersky

Monastery and Ivan's letter to Father Superior Kozma of 1578. Karamzin's *History* contains a detailed account by Ivan of his conversations with the monks, his expectation of becoming a monk himself, and his repentance and self-abasement before the father superior. Pushkin transfers the events that Ivan recalled from the Kirillo-Belozersky Monastery to the Chudov Monastery. See Karamzin, *Istoriia* (1892), 9: 34–87; BG, 280.

55. Pushkin reproduces not only the content of Tsar Ivan's account but also its phraseology. See BG, 280.

56. This part of Pimen's speech echoes Karamzin, who (citing the Nikonov Chronicle) briefly retold the legend of Tsar Feodor's deathbed vision of a "man of light" in clerical dress – an angel. But Pushkin includes in Pimen's lines details from the Nikonov Chronicle not contained in Karamzin's *History*. See *Russkaia letopis'*, 8: 54; Gorodetskii, *Dramaturgiia*, 181; BG, 280–81.

57. According to medieval Russian folklore, the bodies of saints were supposed to give off fragrant smells instead of the stench of rotting flesh. See Possevino, *Moscovia*, 58.

58. Solar imagery associated with tsars was meant to evoke images of Jesus Christ. See Perrie, *Pretenders*, 66.

59. A reference to Tsaritsa Maria Nagaia, widow of Ivan the Terrible.

60. According to the unreliable *New Chronicle*, Tsarevich Dmitry's governess, Vasilisa Volokhova, was drawn into the assassination plot along with her son Osip. See PSRL, 14: 40–41.

61. This reference is probably to Mikhail Bitiagovsky, Boris Godunov's hand-picked administrator of Uglich, but legend suggests that it may be to Bitiagovsky's son Danilo.

62. According to legend, the three assassins were the boys Danilo Bitiagovsky, Nikita Kachalov, and Osip Volokhov. See notes 13, 15, and 60.

63. So powerful was the historical image of Boris Godunov as a tsaricide that Pushkin – writing when he did – could not have known that there were, in fact, no confessions of murder made after the Uglich tragedy, and none of the suspects ever identified Boris Godunov as the mastermind behind the alleged assassination.

64. Tsarevich Dmitry, born in October 1582, was actually eight years old in May 1591.

65. Although some scholars still believe that Tsarevich Dmitry would automatically have become tsar after Tsar Feodor's death, this is not at all clear. Dmitry was the son of Ivan the Terrible's seventh wife, a marriage which was considered to be uncanonical by the Russian Orthodox

Church. By contrast, Feodor's widow, Tsaritsa Irina, had been named co-ruler by her husband and had a real claim to the throne. See Thyrêt, *Between God and Tsar*, 103–7; RFCW, 66.

66. The monk Grigory Otrepiev was intelligent and highly literate. He even managed to become a trusted secretary of Patriarch Iov before fleeing to Lithuania in 1602. See Margeret, *Russian Empire*, 81; RIB, 13: cols. 17–19, 639, 933; PSRL, 14: 59; RFCW, 125–26.

67. Pushkin wrote the Russian text of this scene ("Ograda monastyrskaia") in trochaic octometer, with a caesura dividing the line into two equal halves – making each line virtually two trochaic tetrameters strung together. The "folk" ring of Pushkin's meter comes from his use of trochaic tetrameter, and the double tetrameter aptly expresses the weary monotony of monastic life about which Grigory is complaining. This scene was excluded from the first published edition of *Boris Godunov* and from most subsequent editions and translations. The first published version of it appeared as a note to Egor Rozen's German review of *Boris Godunov;* see *Dorpat Jahrbücher für Litteratur, Statistik und Kunst, besonders Russlands*, 1831, no. 1: 56–58. A Russian translation of Rozen's German version of the scene appeared in the journal *Literaturnye Pribavleniia k Russkomu Invalidu*, 1834, no. 2: 23. In the late nineteenth and early twentieth centuries, Peter O. Morozov argued passionately in favor of the *Komediia* as the canonical text of *Boris Godunov*, but he was always careful to exclude this controversial scene from the main text of the play, offering it instead as an appendix. See Pushkin, *Sochineniia i pis'ma*, 3: 355–57, 631, 637; and our chapters 1 and 6.

68. Pushkin's evil monk ("zloi chernets") is based upon an "evil monk" ("zloi inok") found in Karamzin's *History;* see Karamzin, *Istoriia* (1892), 11: 75. According to Karamzin, however, the real source of Otrepiev's plot to assume the identity of Tsarevich Dmitry was Catholic Poland, not "evil" monks of the Chudov Monastery. On the other hand, a leading historian of early modern Russia, Ruslan Skrynnikov, has recently identified the Chudov monks as the most likely source of the pretender scheme; see Skrynnikov, *Rossiia v nachale XVII v.*, 97.

69. The khan of the Crimean Tatars (a remnant of the Golden Horde), who was a vassal of the Turkish sultan, often waged war against Russia in the sixteenth century. In 1571, a Crimean Tatar army managed to reach Moscow and burn much of the city, returning to Crimea with more than 100,000 Russian prisoners. Pushkin's reference to Lithuania is to the grand principality of Lithuania, the junior partner of Poland and

an ancient antagonist of Muscovy. Lithuania was formally joined to Poland in 1569 in the Union of Lublin, and the new country was called the Polish-Lithuanian Republic or Poland-Lithuania.

70. Popular belief in miracles among the already superstitious Russians grew rapidly during the late sixteenth and early seventeenth centuries. Dmitry's apparently miraculous escape from Uglich seemed to prove to many Russians that God was on his side and that Boris Godunov was a usurper. Thus, Boris Godunov suffered from a "miraculous" conflation of two incompatible myths: that he was a tsaricide, and that the real Dmitry still lived. In the context of the manifest cruelties of his reign, such belief patterns proved inflammatory. See RFCW, chapter 7.

71. A reference to the descendants of Riurik (the semi-mythical founder of Kievan Rus) who ruled Russia from the ninth century until the death of Tsar Feodor in 1598. The shock of the extinction of that old ruling dynasty and the consequent loss of God's grace was regarded by contemporaries as one of the main causes of Russia's horrific Time of Troubles (1598–1613). The accession of an unpopular "boyar-tsar," Boris Godunov, was an innovation that did not settle well with many Russians; after all, boyars were supposed to advise tsars, not become tsars. Thus the Pretender Dmitry's "miraculous" appearance in Poland-Lithuania ("proving" that the sacred old dynasty had not died out) stirred fanatical support for his cause among the disgruntled subjects of Tsar Boris. See RFCW, 90–93, 115–18.

72. Tsarevich Dmitry was born in 1582. In order to "prove" that Grigory Otrepiev had assumed the identity of Dmitry, propagandists of Tsar Boris claimed that he was the same age as the tsarevich, and many historians dutifully wrote that down; but there are contemporary sources claiming that Otrepiev was several years older than Dmitry. See RFCW, 130.

73. The flight of several "monks" (including Grishka Otrepiev) from Moscow to the Lithuanian border that so upset Tsar Boris and Patriarch Iov actually occurred in 1602, not 1603 as Pushkin has it here. See note 41.

74. Galich, a town northeast of Kostroma, was the home of the Otrepiev family.

75. Propagandists in the Time of Troubles and during the early years of the Romanov dynasty manufactured many different stories about the teenage years of Yury Bogdanovich Otrepiev, the future monk Grigory. Some claimed that he became a monk voluntarily; others stated that he was tonsured as punishment for wickedness. One version has the teen-

ager Yury disobeying his parents, running away from home, and falling into heresy – for which he was forcibly tonsured. Another version has Yury voluntarily becoming a monk at age fourteen. In any case, the young man did wander from monastery to monastery for several months or years before his widowed mother and other relatives pulled strings to get him accepted into the prestigious Chudov (or Miracles) Monastery in Moscow, where his grandfather (Elizary Zamiatin) was a monk. See RFCW, 125–26; Dunning, "Who Was Tsar Dmitrii," 712; BG, 287.

76. Patriarch Iov and his propagandists fabricated the story that while he was a monk, Grishka Otrepiev had dabbled in the black arts and disavowed God. It was claimed that the Church had condemned Otrepiev to exile and confinement in the remote northern Solovetsky Monastery (located on the Solovki Islands in the White Sea), but that he somehow managed to escape to Lithuania instead. According to legend, another relative of Otrepiev, a secretary named Efimiev, helped the young monk and two companions (including the priest Varlaam) flee the country. See Skrynnikov, *Rossia v nachale XVII v.*, 83, 88, 91–92; BG, 287–88.

77. By claiming that the Pretender Dmitry was really a runaway monk who had become a heretic and tool of Satan, Patriarch Iov and Tsar Boris were trying to prevent Dmitry's potential supporters from rallying to him by conjuring the most wicked image available in early modern Russia.

78. Tsar Boris believed in magic and sorcery. But there was a cynical, Machiavellian side to his belief: like Ivan the Terrible before him, Godunov also used accusations of witchcraft to destroy his political opponents. See Skrynnikov, *Boris Godunov*, 107–9; Purchas, *Hakluytus Posthumus*, 14: 162; Palitsyn, *Skazanie*, 252–53; Zguta, "Witchcraft Trials," 1192–93; BG, 288–89.

79. This passage in Tsar Boris's monologue drew a virulent attack from Pushkin's hated literary rival, Faddei Bulgarin, who – in a review of a German translation of *Boris Godunov* – saw it as a violation of historical verisimilitude: "We are sure that German critics will sometimes be more charitable to the author than educated Russian readers who are familiar with Russian history. Thus, for example, it will not seem odd to the Germans that a devout Russian tsar of the seventeenth century, an exemplary husband and father, well known for his moral purity, should amid the torments of conscience compare his lot with amatory consolations.... In the seventeenth century, after the reign of the pious Feodor Ivanovich, in circles from which the female sex was excluded, 'momentary possessions' were unknown or scarcely thought of." (See *Severnaia*

pchela, 1831, no. 266, 2–4; BG, 290.) Bulgarin conveniently forgot to mention that Boris Godunov grew up at the court of Ivan the Terrible, scarcely known for its strict morality, and that he had been an *oprichnik* in his youth. Pushkin, on the other hand, places an enumeration of all the slanderous rumors circulating about Godunov in the mouth of Boris himself, who is here engaged in a dialogue with his own conscience. Alone with his thoughts, Boris is apparently sincere; he does not deny his part in the death of Tsarevich Dmitry. But he insistently speaks of that act of regicide as if it were his only serious crime, completely ignoring the many other victims of his bloody rise to power or his attacks on several boyar families after he became tsar – crimes that many contemporaries believed had triggered the Time of Troubles.

80. Owing to severe weather and successive crop failures, Russia endured its worst famine during Boris Godunov's reign. Between 1601 and 1604, up to one third of the population of Russia perished. See RFCW, chapter 6.

81. Tsar Boris did try to provide famine relief to Russian town dwellers, but there was nothing he could do about the starvation of millions of peasants in the countryside. In Moscow and elsewhere, bread and small amounts of money were widely distributed to the hungry. Unfortunately, news of those relief measures attracted tens of thousands more people to Moscow where they overwhelmed the relief efforts of church and state. As a result, more than 100,000 people died in Moscow during the famine; Tsar Boris paid for a shroud for every one of them. Despite his generosity, Godunov, widely regarded as a usurper, was blamed by many of his subjects for provoking God's anger and punishment of Russia in the form of the famine. In fact, many of his subjects came to suspect that Tsar Boris was in league with Satan. Such sentiment greatly aided the Pretender Dmitry's cause. See RFCW, chapter 6.

82. In May 1591, following the death of Tsarevich Dmitry in Uglich, there was a huge fire in Moscow. An extensive area of the city was burned down, including many wooden buildings, shops, and stalls. Boris Godunov commissioned and paid for stone buildings to replace the old wooden ones, earning much praise from Moscow merchants. Enemies of Godunov who accused him of responsibility for the tsarevich's death also blamed him for starting the fire in order to distract Tsar Feodor and prevent him from traveling to Uglich to investigate Dmitry's death. There is no truth to that allegation. Boris did not set fire to Moscow, and Feodor never contemplated going to Uglich; but the regent's enemies spread

these lies far and wide. A government investigation of the fire eventually produced arsonists who claimed to have been employed by the Nagoi clan. Many people were as skeptical of that explanation as they were of Godunov's supposed innocence in the death of Dmitry. See Margeret, *Russian Empire,* 17–18; BG, 295–96.

83. Tsar Boris tried hard to arrange foreign marriages for his children. Ksenia was betrothed to the Danish Duke Johan, brother of King Kristian IV. The handsome and intelligent Johan was joyfully and lavishly received in Moscow, where he made a very good impression at court. When Johan fell ill, Boris visited him, assigned his own doctors to care for the duke, and offered a huge reward for his cure. Johan's death caused great unhappiness in the Godunov household. See Margeret, *Russian Empire,* 59–60; BG, 296–97.

84. Boris Godunov's enemies blamed him for – among other crimes – the deaths of Tsar Ivan IV, Tsarevich Dmitry, Tsar Feodor, and even his own sister. Many people were inclined to believe those wild accusations because Boris already stood accused of being responsible for the mysterious (and convenient) deaths of several of his political enemies. See RFCW, 60–67, 94–96; Perrie, *Pretenders,* 140–42; Skrynnikov, *Ivan the Terrible,* 198; Karamzin, *Istoriia* (1892), 11: 87 and note 235; BG, 297–98.

85. After Tsar Boris died in April 1605, wild rumors circulated that he was not dead but had secretly fled the country to England or Sweden. See Massa, *Short History,* 106–7.

86. In 1602, in the midst of the terrible famine in Russia, a small group of "monks," including the future Pretender Dmitry, fled from Moscow to Poland-Lithuania. Grishka Otrepiev was definitely one of those runaways, and Tsar Boris Godunov's government quickly identified him as the person who assumed the identity of Dmitry. The monks Misail Povadin and Varlaam Yatsky also accompanied Otrepiev across the border, and Varlaam helped convince Polish authorities that Dmitry was genuine. After Tsar Dmitry's assassination in 1606, however, Varlaam testified that the dead ruler was really Grishka Otrepiev. There are many good reasons to doubt that testimony, but it convinced generations of historians that Otrepiev and Tsar Dmitry were one and the same person. See RFCW, chapter 8; Dunning, "Who Was Tsar Dmitrii," 713–15.

87. The Russian word *vino* used here sometimes refers to wine and sometimes to vodka. State-licensed taverns generally served kvas (weak beer), mead, and vodka during the early seventeenth century. Wine is seldom mentioned in sources concerning the taverns. During the great

famine, however, distillation of spirits was temporarily forbidden in order to preserve precious grain for flour and bread. See Smith Christian, *Bread and Salt,* passim; Bushkovitch, "Taxation," 397.

88. The rather obscure terms in the proverbial Russian phrase Pushkin uses here (meaning "a matter of indifference"), *gudok* and *gusli,* refer to ancient musical instruments closely associated with the *skomorokhi* – wandering minstrels who were linked with Russia's pagan past and with witchcraft and sorcery. A *gudok* was a three-stringed viol or rebeck, and *gusli* a multi-stringed instrument similar to a psaltery or zither. See Zguta, *Russian Minstrels,* 3, 4, 5, 28, 48, 105–7.

89. Varlaam's rhyming prose seems to grow straight out of Russian folk idiom, which is rich in rhymed sayings. While composing his *Comedy,* Pushkin paid considerable attention to folk elaborations, and folk-style rhyming exuberance is evident in other works he wrote at the time – for example, the ballad *Zhenikh* ["The Bridegroom"] (1825).

90. The song "You walk past my cell, my dear one" was composed by F. G. Volkov, a well-known eighteenth-century actor and theater man. It was first published by N. I. Novikov in 1772. For unknown reasons, Pushkin changed the song Varlaam sang to "Once in the city of Kazan" for the 1831 edition of *Boris Godunov.* (That song had also been published by Novikov.) Musorgsky later misinterpreted "Once in the city of Kazan," which is really about a young monk yearning for adventure, as a martial song concerning Ivan the Terrible's conquest of Kazan in 1552. See BG, 299–301; and Taruskin, *Musorgsky,* 291–99.

91. Minstrels were very popular among the Russian people; they were also feared and respected as magicians. Minstrels were loudly denounced as tools of Satan by the Russian Orthodox Church in the sixteenth and seventeenth centuries. See Zguta, *Russian Minstrels,* 4–5, 8–11, 29–30, 60–61, 110.

92. Varlaam's line here ("perhaps he's sniffed out a mare") has long puzzled scholars and translators. The Russian phrase ("mozhet byt', kobylu niukhal") has been translated as "he might be a flogged criminal" or "maybe he has even been flogged at a whipping post"; see, for example, Pushkin, *Complete Works,* 6: 71; and idem, *Boris Godunov* (1953), 39. It is possible that this line is a reference to a whipping post or to a whip made of horse hair sometimes used to administer floggings. But the translator has chosen the phrase's more usual meaning which makes as much, if not more, sense in this scene.

93. During the famine years Tsar Boris closed Russia's western border, in part at least to prevent the spread of deadly diseases from Lithuania. See Koretskii, "Golod," 230.

94. It has been incorrectly claimed that no effort was made to stop the flight of these "monks" (see, for example, Skrynnikov, *Boris Godunov*, 140). In fact, Pushkin has it historically right. Tsar Boris and Patriarch Iov made strenuous efforts to prevent the escape of the future Pretender Dmitry; they specifically issued orders to stop "two traitors" from crossing the border. See RIB, 13: col. 21; Margeret, *Russian Empire*, 81–82; Koretskii, "Novoe o krest'ianskom zakreposhchenii," 143–44.

95. The reference here to St. George's Day has been grossly misunderstood, but Pushkin knew exactly what the term meant. Starting in 1497, the movement of Russian peasants wishing to leave the estates of their lords was restricted to a two-week period around St. George's Day (November 26). In the 1590s, Boris Godunov "temporarily" suspended the St. George's Day privilege in order to preserve the state's tax base and the dwindling labor force of the Russian gentry. The result was the de facto enserfment of millions of Russian peasants. During the famine years, however, Tsar Boris was forced to allow the transfer of some peasants from one estate to another in order to relieve massive suffering. Many people at the time incorrectly thought he had restored the St. George's Day privilege of peasant departure, and as a result there was a chaotic movement of large numbers of peasants. That greatly upset many struggling lords and resulted in considerable violence and coercion in order to prevent the loss of critically important peasant labor. As soon as the famine ended, Tsar Boris quickly restored his "temporary" prohibition against peasant departure – in effect restoring serfdom. See RFCW, 67–68, 100–102.

96. According to Pushkin's friend A. N. Vulf, the source of Varlaam's witticism was a favorite saying of Iona, the father superior of the Sviato-gorsk Monastery, who was given the task of spying on Pushkin at Mikhailovskoe: "Our Foma / Drinks to the bottom, / Drinks it all and turns it over, / Then drubs it the bottom." According to Pushkin's friend Ivan Pushchin, Pushkin plied Iona with liquor and pretended to be reading *Lives of the Saints* when the monk came to check up on the dangerous young exile. See Veresaev, *Pushkin*, 1: 263; Vatsuro, *A. S. Pushkin*, 1: 109, 414; Cooke and Dunning, "Tempting Fate," 48; BG, 301.

97. At this point in the text of the first edition of *The Uncensored Boris*

Godunov, Sergei Fomichev incorrectly transcribed Puchkin's original *da borom* ("through the pines") as *da brodom* ("cross the ford"). The editors regret this error.

98. The old Russian coin that Pushkin mentions here, the *polushka*, was a silver quarter-kopek that was already rare by the end of the sixteenth century.

99. Varlaam's attempt to speak Church Slavonic, done to impress the guards, is beyond his capabilities. For example, at the beginning of this speech he uses an incorrect vocative (*syne* instead of *synu*) and two lines further on the nominative form *iazytsy zemnii* instead of an accusative. The translation attempts to match his mangled style.

100. "You 'ave to read between the lines as well." The literal meaning of this statement refers to the diacritic *titlo*, written above (or below) the line in old Russian manuscripts, and gives body to the guard's metaphor.

101. Pushkin used the phrase *bliadiny deti* or "sons of whores" in the original version of his *Comedy*, but it was tamed down in published editions of *Boris Godunov* to *sukiny deti*, "sons of bitches." See PS, 7: 36; BG, 51, 301–2.

102. Although Karamzin described Otrepiev in very similar terms, the list of physical characteristics mentioned here was actually derived from an accurate contemporary description of Tsar Dmitry that Pushkin himself read in Margeret's *Estat de l'Empire de Russie*. See BG, 302; Margeret, *Russian Empire*, 75.

103. Tsar Boris had a prayer honoring himself composed and ordered that it be recited on all occasions, official and private. Karamzin included the prayer in his *History* as evidence of Boris's tyranny. Pushkin's shorter version omits the most offensively sycophantic expressions contained in the original. See Karamzin, *Istoriia* (1892), 11: 57–58 and note 138; BG, 302.

104. Afanasy Mikhailovich Pushkin is an invented character, in whom Alexander Pushkin offers a composite image of some of his real ancestors who were opponents of Tsar Boris. It has been claimed that Afanasy was modeled after Evstafy Mikhailovich Pushkin, who served at court for twenty-five years before being promoted into the boyar council (or duma) in 1598. But *dumnyi dvorianin* Evstafy Pushkin had already been disgraced by Tsar Boris and sent into Siberian exile in 1601. His brother Ivan M. Pushkin replaced him on the boyar council and may actually have been the prototype for Afanasy Pushkin. See Skrynnikov, "Boris Godunov i predki Pushkina," 133; BG, 303–4.

105. Tsar Boris did reward servants for reporting suspicious activities on the part of their masters. Such reports sometimes led to exile, confiscation of property, or even execution. Vasily Shuisky's brother Ivan was accused of witchcraft by one of his slaves and expelled from the boyar council by Tsar Boris. Other members of the family were also harassed by Godunov, but the Shuiskys avoided any further charges of treason and, at least publicly, remained loyal to Tsar Boris. See Margeret, *Russian Empire*, 60; RIB, 13: col. 1279; Zolkiewski, *Expedition*, 42–43; Skrynnikov, *Boris Godunov*, 107.

106. Gavrila Grigorevich Pushkin (d. 1638) was a prominent figure during the Time of Troubles. He married a wealthy relative of Ivan the Terrible's sixth wife and thereby obtained a fine estate in the late sixteenth century. Alexander Pushkin's poetic license allowed him to place Gavrila Pushkin in Poland-Lithuania at this point. In fact, during the Pretender Dmitry's campaign for the throne, Gavrila surrendered to Dmitry early on and was immediately employed by him. Pushkin rode to Moscow and, on June 1, 1605, read Dmitry's proclamation to the residents of the capital who were assembled on Red Square. Pushkin's dramatic speech immediately triggered the rebellion that overthrew the Godunov dynasty. Later in the Time of Troubles, Gavrila served as an infantry commander helping to defend Moscow. In 1613, he was one of several Pushkins who participated in the election and coronation of Tsar Mikhail Romanov. After the Time of Troubles, Gavrila sat on Tsar Mikhail's boyar council and briefly served as an ambassador. Alexander Pushkin's research in his family papers also uncovered Gavrila Pushkin's involvement in the burning of an entire town as punishment for supporting the wrong faction during the final, chaotic phase of the Troubles. (Unfortunately, such brutal actions were not uncommon at that time.) The great poet admired his ancestor as a man "of great talent, a military commander, courtier, and above all a conspirator" against Boris Godunov. See *Letters*, 366; RFCW, 194; Skrynnikov, "Boris Godunov i predki Pushkina," 132–33; BG, 304.

107. After many delays, during the summer of 1604 the Pretender Dmitry was granted a private audience with King Sigismund (Zygmunt) III of Poland-Lithuania (r. 1587–1632). He was seeking recognition and support for his planned military campaign to gain the Russian throne, but the king was unsure of the identity of the pretender and genuinely feared reprisal from Tsar Boris if he publicly supported Dmitry's claims.

During their meeting, Sigismund made very stiff demands for territorial concessions once Dmitry became tsar in return for nothing more than informal recognition and extremely limited support. See RFCW, 134–37.

108. Prince Adam Wiśniowiecki (Vishnevetsky), a member of a rich and powerful Ukrainian family and a distant relative of Ivan the Terrible, was the "discoverer" of the Pretender Dmitry in Poland-Lithuania. It was he who brought Dmitry to the attention of Jerzy Mniszech and other powerful Polish lords. Prince Adam was involved in a bitter dispute with Tsar Boris at the time he took up Dmitry's cause. According to Prince Adam's letter to King Sigismund, Dmitry revealed his true identity to him in 1603. A number of sources claim that the Pretender had been employed as a servant in the Wiśniowiecki household before revealing his "true" identity. The Romanov-influenced *New Chronicle* claimed that Otrepiev cleverly feigned dying before revealing his "true" identity to a priest and then to Prince Adam. See RFCW, 132–34; Perrie, *Pretenders*, 37–41; PSRL, 14: 60.

109. The Pretender's exemplary behavior while living in Poland-Lithuania and the arrival of many Russians eager to testify to Polish authorities that they recognized him as the true son of Ivan the Terrible made a strong impression on many Poles. The Pretender's willingness to secretly convert to Catholicism also made a strong impression at the Polish court. King Sigismund and the Jesuits concluded that he might well be the true Dmitry, but the king was nevertheless extremely reluctant to provide him with any public support. While the Jesuits actively took up Dmitry's cause in the hope of converting the Russian people to Catholicism, the king offered only paltry financial support. Sigismund's most important contribution to the Pretender's cause was simply to look the other way while Dmitry raised a small army in order to invade Russia. See RFCW, chapter 8.

110. As a ruler, Tsar Boris was relatively mild by comparison with his mentor, Ivan the Terrible. Tsar Ivan's horrifying public torture and execution of suspected traitors gave way to more subtle and secret methods of eliminating opponents. Nonetheless, many boyar families felt the heavy hand of Godunov's increasingly paranoid regime, especially after reports of the miraculous survival of Tsarevich Dmitry began to circulate in Moscow. From then on, according to a contemporary, "there was nothing but torturing and racking every day because of this." See RFCW, 90–96; Margeret, *Russian Empire*, 60.

111. As a young man, Boris Godunov successfully feuded with mem-

bers of the princely Sitsky and Shestunov clans. Shortly after becoming tsar, he struck at several other leading aristocratic families, especially the Romanovs. In 1600, fearing that they planned to move against his dynasty, Godunov purged the Romanovs from court. Family members were exiled to remote locations, their estates were confiscated, and their military retainers were dispersed. Feodor Romanov, the leader of the clan, was forcibly tonsured, becoming the monk (and future Patriarch of the Russian Orthodox Church) Filaret. Two of Filaret's exiled younger brothers died soon thereafter under mysterious circumstances. See BG, 306–7; RFCW, 95–96.

112. Tsar Boris revived Ivan the Terrible's destructive tactic of encouraging the denunciation of political foes by their relatives, associates, servants, and even slaves. For example, slaves helped manufacture charges against the Shuiskys and the Romanovs. This greatly embittered many aristocrats who saw it as a grave threat to Russia's social hierarchy. Such ruthless measures apparently drove Godunov's remaining aristocratic opponents together in a secret alliance against him – an alliance that soon placed its hopes on the "resurrected" Tsarevich Dmitry. See RFCW, 94–96; Margeret, *Russian Empire*, 60–61.

113. This aristocratic lament accurately reflects the ambivalence of Russian boyars about the elimination of the St. George's Day privilege of peasant departure. That drastic measure favored the gentry and – among other things – was intended to stop the common aristocratic practice of enticing (or even stealing) peasants away from the estates of the tsar's struggling cavalrymen. In spite of Boris Godunov's attempt to protect the interests of the gentry against aristocratic predation, however, it remained a chronic problem until at least 1649. Pushkin may also have intended this passage to be ironic. During the great famine, many greedy lords callously dismissed from their service peasants and slaves they no longer needed and did not wish to feed. The result was extreme misery and many deaths from starvation. See Hellie, *Enserfment*, chapters 3, 5–8; Skrynnikov, *Boris Godunov*, chapter 8; RFCW, chapters 4 and 6.

114. The Slavery Chancellery (*Prikaz kholopii*). Until the late sixteenth century, there were several types of slavery in Russia. But in 1597, Boris eliminated the often-used tax dodge of short-term "contract slavery" and arranged for short-term slaves to be converted to hereditary slaves (i.e., slaves for life). Peter the Great finally abolished slavery in the early eighteenth century; by then it was no longer needed because the legal status of Russian serfs had declined to virtually the same degraded status

as chattel slaves. See Hellie, *Slavery,* 39–40, 50–53, 62, 326–27, 331, 697; RFCW, 69–70.

115. Many Russians blamed Boris Godunov personally for enserfing the peasants. He was also unpopular for binding and overtaxing towns-men, for turning short-term contract slavery into real slavery, and for harassing the cossacks (part-time mercenary soldiers and bandits who lived on the steppe) on Russia's southern frontier. In fact, the end result of Godunov's drastic measures to shore up state finances and the tsar's military forces was the alienation of millions of Russians. See RFCW, 67–72, 109–22, 138–43.

116. As discussed in our chapter 2, working from the books available to him while living in internal exile, Pushkin came up with the original idea that the Pretender Dmitry's campaign for the throne was tremen-dously aided by the Russian people's expectation that Dmitry would abolish serfdom (by restoring the St. George's Day right of peasant movement). Thus, in startling contrast to Karamzin's semi-official *His-tory of the Russian State,* Pushkin's play contains the first written claim that Dmitry's popular support was dependent – at least in part – upon his promise to abolish serfdom. Tsar Nicholas's censors were quick to recognize the potential danger of this passage in the play and argued strenuously against its publication. In later generations, Marxist scholars frequently (but incorrectly) claimed that the Pretender Dmitry's prom-ise to abolish serfdom was the main reason for the popular uprisings that helped put him on the throne. See Dunning, "Rethinking," 581–82; RFCW, introduction and chapter 7; Gorodetskii, *Tragediia,* 33–43, 69–70.

117. Both of Tsar Boris Godunov's children – his daughter, Ksenia (1582–1622), and his son, Feodor (1589–1605) – were described by con-temporaries as very bright, extremely well-educated, and handsome.

118. Ksenia's opening lines and Feodor's line of response were omitted from the 1831 published edition of *Boris Godunov* and from most subse-quent editions. The excluded lines demonstrate that Ksenia Godunova, like all royal women of Muscovy, lived in relative seclusion in separate living quarters. Elite Muscovite women were not supposed to be seen by any men except their relatives, and they were not even allowed to meet their future husbands in person until the day of their wedding. See Koll-mann, "The Seclusion of Elite Women," 170–87; and our chapter 6.

119. As noted above, Tsar Boris arranged for the marriage of Ksenia to Duke Johan, the handsome younger brother of King Kristian IV of Den-mark. Duke Johan was very well received in Moscow but died suddenly

(allegedly of overindulgence but possibly poisoned) before meeting his intended bride. He was buried in the Lutheran church graveyard located in the Livonian-German suburb of Moscow. See Margeret, *Russian Empire*, 59–60.

120. The source of the nurse's words is a song about a slain warrior quoted by Karamzin among his examples of popular poems which "in their truth of feeling and linguistic boldness, if not entirely in their style then in their spirit, are closer to the sixteenth century than to the eighteenth." The song (probably composed in the early eighteenth century) contains these words: "The wife weeps as the dew falls / The sun rises and dries the dew." See Karamzin, *Istoriia,* 10: 159; BG, 309–10.

121. Pushkin the historian is excellent here. Feodor Borisovich (1589–1605) received a very good education, and his father made sure that he was well prepared to rule after him. Although Tsar Boris's enemies circulated rumors that young Feodor was weak and feeble-minded, the handsome and robust tsarevich was impressive. Among other things, Feodor was deeply interested in cartography. According to some sources, he personally drew a fine map of Russia. Some scholars doubt that, claiming instead that he briefly studied cartography under the guidance of the Dutch map-maker Hessel Herrits, hired by Tsar Boris, and was probably allowed to help finish one of his maps. Whatever the case, Herrits's famous map of Russia (first published in 1614 and republished many times) contains an inset map of Moscow attributed to Feodor Borisovich Godunov. The representation of Siberia on Feodor Borisovich's map would have been of considerable interest to Tsar Boris, who continued Ivan the Terrible's conquest and annexation of Siberia and was responsible for the construction of several important Siberian towns – including Tomsk.

122. The sinister Semyon Nikitich Godunov, Boris Godunov's uncle, was the head of Tsar Boris's secret police. He was greatly feared even by aristocrats and high-born princes and was probably the most hated man in Russia at the dawn of the seventeenth century.

123. This is one of the few historical mistakes Pushkin made in writing his *Comedy;* Semyon Godunov's patronymic was Nikitich, not Ilyich. Pushkin himself corrected this error before *Boris Godunov* was published. See Vinokur, *Kommentarii,* 239.

124. Pushkin includes in this fictionalized list of guests visiting Vasily Shuisky the names of persons actually persecuted by Boris Godunov as well as those who were rumored to have been conspirators working

secretly for the Pretender Dmitry. The Buturlins had been persecuted by Godunov in the late sixteenth century. Nevertheless, I. M. Buturlin became one of Tsar Boris's best generals, although he did not participate in the campaign against the Pretender Dmitry. Members of the Pushkin clan were also persecuted by Godunov, and some of them became active supporters of Dmitry. The *New Chronicle* openly accused Mikhail G. Saltykov of treachery and responsibility for the failure of Tsar Boris' siege of Dmitry's army at Kromy. The minor princely Miloslavsky clan was not involved in intrigue during the Time of Troubles and only became powerful at court by marrying into the Romanov family in the seventeenth century. However, members of the Miloslavsky clan were widely believed to have been active supporters and fomenters of the streltsy (musketeer) rebellion in 1682, which temporarily blocked the rise of Peter the Great's family at court. See PSRL, 14: 64; Margeret, *Russian Empire*, 66, 159–60 note 224; Pavlov, *Gosudarev dvor*, 133 note 58; RFCW, 62–63, 156, 185, 194.

125. The reference is to Poland-Lithuania, united since 1569.

126. This declaration has often been taken by scholars (including the renowned historian S. B. Veselovsky) as nothing more than poetic license and a certain boastful family pride – completely without basis in historical records. Recently, however, a leading historian of early modern Russia, Ruslan Skrynnikov, looked closely at Pushkin family records and found plenty of evidence that the Pushkins had often been rebels and troublemakers. In fact, more than one member of the ancient family ended up being exiled to Siberia. See Veselovskii, *Issledovaniia*, 107–12; BG, 311; Skrynnikov, "Boris Godunov i predki Pushkina," 131–33.

127. King Sigismund III provided Dmitry with very limited support, primarily by turning a blind eye to the organization of the Pretender's small army. Some self-serving Polish lords also supported Dmitry, and a few of them became directly involved in his campaign for the Russian throne. Nevertheless, most Polish nobles remained openly skeptical about the identity of "Tsarevich Dmitry" and strongly cautioned against formal recognition of him or any involvement in his war against Tsar Boris's Russian Empire. See RFCW, 124, 132–37; Barbour, *Dimitry*, chapter 2.

128. Despite the skepticism of some historians, Russia's western border really was closed and guards were posted specifically to prevent the escape of the Pretender Dmitry. See RIB, 13: col. 21; Margeret, *Russian Empire*, 81–82.

129. In 1591, Tsar Feodor Ivanovich and Patriarch Iov – not Boris

Godunov – ordered Vasily Shuisky to lead the investigation into the mysterious death of Tsarevich Dmitry in Uglich. Shuisky was chosen precisely because he was a high born prince whose family had actively opposed the rise of Godunov and had suffered as a consequence. It was hoped that whatever conclusion Shuisky's commission reached would therefore not be dismissed simply as a whitewash orchestrated by the all-powerful regent. See Vernadsky, *Tsardom*, 1: 194–95; Skrynnikov, *Boris Godunov*, 53; RFCW, 64–65.

130. The untrustworthy Vasily Shuisky changed his story many times. In fact, members of the Uglich commission were unable to state with certainty that the body they were shown by the Nagoi clan was that of the real tsarevich. See RFCW, 132; Barbour, *Dimitry*, 323–24.

131. Pushkin moves testimony of Tsarevich Dmitry's unspoiled body back about fifteen years. In 1606, after Vasily Shuisky orchestrated the assassination of Tsar Dmitry and seized the throne, he sent a delegation to Uglich to retrieve the remains of Tsarevich Dmitry in order to "prove" that the real Dmitry had died in 1591. This was done primarily to counter the potent rumor that Tsar Dmitry had escaped assassination and would soon return to seek revenge against the usurper Shuisky. In Uglich, Shuisky's agents had trouble locating the tsarevich's grave. Eventually, they conveniently "discovered" the unspoiled remains of a boy identified as the tsarevich (who was either killed for the purpose or had just died). Shuisky's agents claimed that, when discovered, the body of Tsarevich Dmitry was "miraculously preserved" and gave off sweet smells; in other words, the martyred child was a saint. Soon, reports were widely circulated that the body of the tsarevich miraculously cured many ill or dying people who touched his casket. The remains of "St. Dmitry" were transported to Moscow and interred in a Kremlin cathedral. See RFCW, 245–48.

132. By the seventeenth century, the term "cap of Monomakh" came to mean the imperial crown of Russia. "Heavy is the cap of Monomakh" became a common Russian term for weighty problems. See BG, 312.

133. Pater Czernikowski is a character loosely based upon the real Jesuit priest, Nicholas Czyrzowski (spelled "Chernikovskii" in Karamzin's *History*) who accompanied the Pretender Dmitry on his campaign for the Russian throne and hoped to persuade him, once he became tsar, to convert Russia to Catholicism. See Karamzin, *Istoriia* (1892), 11: note 240; Santich, *Missio Moscovitica*, 113–16, 122–30, 136–37, 140–42.

134. "Eastern Church" refers to the Eastern Orthodox Christian

Church or to the Russian Orthodox Church. (For unknown reasons, Pushkin's reference to the "Eastern Church" was changed to "Northern Church" in the 1831 edition of *Boris Godunov*.) While living in Poland-Lithuania and seeking support for his campaign for the Russian throne, the Pretender Dmitry secretly converted to Catholicism and made vague promises to church officials and to King Sigismund about eventually bringing the Russian Orthodox Church under the spiritual leadership of the Pope. Dmitry's enemies claimed that he wished to destroy the Russian Orthodox Church, and many historians came to believe that wild claim because of Dmitry's secret (probably insincere) conversion to Catholicism. In fact, once he was on the throne, Tsar Dmitry made no effort to overthrow the Russian Orthodox Church, kept his contact with Catholics (especially the Jesuits) to a minimum, and ended up greatly frustrating Polish Catholic officials. See RFCW, 123–24, 131, 135–36, 198, 206–7, 213, 227–33.

135. St. Ignatius (Ignatius Loyola) founded the Society of Jesus (the Jesuits) in the sixteenth century.

136. Palatine Jerzy Mniszech was a powerful Catholic Polish lord (commander of both Sambor and Lvov) who became the Pretender Dmitry's champion in Poland-Lithuania. Mniszech helped him raise a small army and briefly served as its commander-in-chief during Dmitry's invasion of Russia in 1604. Pushkin spells Sambor incorrectly as "Sanbor"; in this he was probably confused by one of Jerzy Mniszech's official titles – Palatine of Sandomierz. See Barbour, *Dimitry*, 20.

137. The Pretender Dmitry fell in love with Palatine Jerzy Mniszech's daughter, Maryna (1588–1614).

138. Gavrila Pushkin, one of Alexander Pushkin's ancestors, surrendered to Dmitry during his invasion of Russia (and not while the Pretender was still in Poland, as Pushkin has it in the play). As noted earlier, Dmitry put the young man to work immediately, and Gavrila Pushkin ended up playing a major role in the surrender of Moscow to Dmitry.

139. Andrei Kurbsky (c. 1528–83) was a heroic participant in the siege of Kazan in 1552. At one time a close friend of Tsar Ivan the Terrible, he defected to Poland-Lithuania in 1564 (during the Livonian War). He then supposedly exchanged many letters with Tsar Ivan in which the aristocrat chided his former friend for tyranny, for ignoring the recommendations of his advisers, and for grossly mistreating his nobles. See Fennell, *Correspondence*.

140. This is a fictional character. Andrei Kurbsky did remarry while living in exile, and his last wife bore him a son (Dmitry) and a daughter shortly before his death in 1583. But Dmitry Kurbsky did not participate in the events of Russia's Time of Troubles. Pushkin may have been inspired to include a Kurbsky in his play by reading Boris M. Fedorov's serialized novel *Kniaz' Kurbskii* (1825), or by reading an article about Andrei Kurbsky written by K. F. Kalaidovich and published in *Severnyi Arkhiv*, 1824, no. 19: 1–6. See Meilakh, *Pushkin i ego epokha*, 560; BG, 314–15.

141. Andrei Kurbsky had been one of Ivan the Terrible's principal advisers during the early years of his reign. In 1562, during the Livonian War, Tsar Ivan appointed the able Prince Kurbsky as one of the main commanders of the Russian army fighting in Livonia. In 1564, Kurbsky defected to Poland-Lithuania, where he lived in exile until his death in 1583. See Skrynnikov, *Ivan the Terrible*, 46–48, 70–77, 79–86.

142. Pushkin uses the term "Saint Olga's city" to mean the town of Pskov, near which St. Vladimir's grandmother Olga was born. Pushkin's reference here is to Polish military operations near Pskov in 1581. The Pretender Dmitry's statement that Kurbsky avenged the wrongs done to him by Ivan the Terrible by fighting *against* the Russian army marks Pushkin's radical departure from the semi-official portrayal of the "traitor" Kurbsky found in Karamzin's *History*. See BG, 315–16.

143. Stefan Báthory was the king of Poland whose military victories finally forced Ivan the Terrible to end the long and unsuccessful Livonian War. Volynia was a rich, agricultural province of western Ukraine.

144. Historical opinion on Andrei Kurbsky is divided. On the one hand, he is alleged to have been a fine scholar and to have written much while living in exile, including an exchange of letters with Ivan the Terrible and a book-length history of Ivan's reign – sources frequently cited by historians. But on the other hand, the Harvard scholar Edward Keenan doubted that Kurbsky was even literate, let alone one of the most astonishingly well-educated Russians of the sixteenth century. According to Keenan, the writings attributed to Kurbsky were seventeenth-century forgeries. See Fennell, *Correspondence*; idem, *Prince A. M. Kurbsky's History*; Skrynnikov, *Ivan the Terrible*, 47; Keenan, *Kurbskii-Groznyi Apocrypha*.

145. Here Pushkin uses the term "free *Szlachta*," which means Polish gentry – who were indeed free-born, especially in comparison to Russian cavalrymen of that era.

146. Pushkin modifies historical facts here. Peter Khrushchov was actually a nobleman trusted by Tsar Boris and sent by him to try persuading the Don cossacks not to support the Pretender Dmitry. The cossacks, who hated Godunov and championed Dmitry's cause, tied Khrushchov up and delivered him to the Pretender in Poland-Lithuania. Much to everyone's surprise, Khrushchov did a great service to Dmitry's cause by "recognizing" him as the true tsarevich (because of Dmitry's facial characteristics that were similar to those of Ivan the Terrible). The Pretender pardoned Khrushchov and learned from him that many Russians awaited the return of the "true tsar" Dmitry. See *Sobranie gosudarstvennykh gramot i dogovorov* [hereafer cited as SGGD] 2: 173–78; Perrie, *Pretenders*, 59–61.

147. As just noted, Khrushchov had not been a supporter of Dmitry, had not been persecuted by Tsar Boris, and did not flee from Moscow. On the other hand, hundreds of other disgruntled Russians of all social classes (especially the cossacks) did flock to Dmitry's banner when his proclamations were secretly read in many Russian towns and villages. Those recruits formed a significant part of Dmitry's small invasion army, and many more Russians joined Dmitry's army after it crossed the border. See RFCW, 137.

148. This line of the Pretender's and the dialogue with Khrushchov following it were omitted from the 1831 published edition of *Boris Godunov* and most subsequent versions of the play. The deletion of Khrushchov's statement that the Russian people believe in the Pretender and await his return as well as Khrushchov's statement that Tsar Boris is gravely ill and has withdrawn from public view had a serious impact on the play – making the Pretender a less attractive character and making Boris's death seem much more sudden and dramatic. See our chapter 6.

149. Although frequently reported by historians, this is actually a legend. Tsar Boris did not execute two boyars for toasting the health of Dmitry. Nevertheless, he did suspect (rightly) that some boyars were involved in the pretender episode, and several people of lesser rank were arrested, tortured, and put to death as traitors for being sympathetic to Dmitry or for distributing his proclamations to the Russian people urging them to overthrow the usurper Godunov. See RFCW, 124–25.

150. Tsar Boris, who had long been in poor health, did actually become seriously ill again during Dmitry's campaign for the throne. As news of Dmitry's progress arrived at court, Boris withdrew from almost

all public appearances and hid in his Kremlin palace. See RFCW, 180; Skrynnikov, *Boris Godunov*, 151.

151. The Pretender Dmitry made strenuous efforts to appeal to Russian cossacks. Due in part to cossack hatred of Boris Godunov for his frontier policy, he was very successful. In November 1603, the Don cossacks sent ataman (chieftain) Andrei Karela and others to Lithuania to cement their alliance with Dmitry and to make war plans. Karela, a very brave and able man, subsequently became one of Dmitry's most important military commanders (see notes 235 and 258). See RFCW, 134, 175–76, 178–79, 187–88.

152. Boris Godunov as regent and then as tsar made strenuous efforts to gain control over the cossacks. His southern frontier fortress construction program was intended – at least in part – to eliminate cossack freedom, and his agents harassed cossacks who did not cooperate. During the famine, Tsar Boris' government even withheld grain from hungry, uncooperative cossacks. By the time of the Pretender Dmitry's appearance, Godunov was bitterly hated by most Russian cossacks. See Dunning, "Cossacks," 59–64.

153. This is the only stage direction in the play in which Grigory Otrepiev is called "Grishka." Lidiia Lotman has speculated on the reasons why Pushkin chose to use his diminutive name at this point in the play; see BG, 317.

154. *Korolevich* means son of a king. The Russian word for king (*korol'*) was derived not from Polish but directly from Old High German *Karl* – after Karl der Grosse or Carolus Magnus (Charlemagne).

155. The Pretender's improvised line ("… the laureled union / Of sword and lyre") is reminiscent of an emblem – a picture with a motto or verses, allegorically suggesting some moral truth. Emblems were popular in Russian schools, and Pushkin was probably familiar with the famous anthology of symbolic pictures and emblems *Simvoli i Emblemata* that was published during Peter the Great's reign and republished in 1788 and again in 1811. There were a number of favorite motifs in those symbolic pictures and emblems, the lyre and sword among them. See BG, 319–20.

156. The Pretender Dmitry briefly studied Latin at some point, although he made many mistakes in writing it. Captain Margeret, the head of Tsar Dmitry's bodyguard, wrote the following: "However, it is very certain that he spoke no Latin. I can testify to that. He knew even

less how to read and write it, which I can show by the poor manner in which he signed his name." See Margeret, *Russian Empire*, 85.

157. This exchange between Khrushchov and Pushkin, which reveals the complete ignorance in seventeenth-century Russia of the meaning of the word "bard" as well as a bard's role at a royal court, was omitted from the 1831 edition of *Boris Godunov*.

158. "The muse crowns glory, and glory – the muse." The Latin aphorism here may spell out the symbolic meaning of the earlier emblem, "the laureled union / Of sword and lyre." See BG, 319–20.

159. Pushkin wrote the Russian text of this scene ("Zamok voevody Mnishka v Sanbore: Ubornaia Mariny") in freely alternating iambic meters, mostly hexameters and tetrameters, with occasional pentameters and a single trimeter. The metrical form and light conversational tone are reminiscent of Griboedov's brilliant verse comedy *Woe from Wit* (with which Pushkin was acquainted at the time he wrote his *Comedy*). This scene was excluded from the first published edition of *Boris Godunov* (1831) and from many subsequent editions. The text of the scene was first published in 1841 in the first official posthumous edition of *Sochineniia Aleksandra Pushkina* (9: 196–99). Peter Morozov restored it to the main text of *Komediia* in his many editions of Pushkin's works, and Musorgsky drew on it for the revised version of his opera *Boris Godunov* (see Emerson and Oldani, *Modest Musorgsky*, 53–55, 210–16; and our chapters 1 and 6). As noted earlier, Pushkin misspells "Sambor" as "Sanbor." Dmitry frequently visited Mniszech's home in Sambor (in Galicia) while the latter was helping him raise an army for his campaign against Boris Godunov. Pushkin uses the Russian title *voevoda* (commander or military governor) for Mniszech, but his actual title was a somewhat loftier one, "palatine."

160. The Chodkiewicz family were among the leading aristocrats of Poland-Lithuania. One of them, Commander (Hetman) Jan Karol Chodkiewicz, became notorious for his bloody campaigns in Russia during the period of Polish intervention in the Time of Troubles.

161. The Pretender Dmitry really did fall in love with Maryna Mniszech while staying at her father's castle. Palatine Jerzy Mniszech took advantage of that infatuation and maneuvered successfully to have his daughter betrothed to the future tsar.

162. Maryna's reputation for intelligence, ambition, and cunning was strong during her own lifetime. Pushkin became very interested in her, and so did his main literary rival, Faddei Bulgarin. It has occasionally

been claimed that Bulgarin's interpretation of Maryna, published in 1824, influenced Pushkin's play. See Mucha, "Samozwańcza," 529–36.

163. The deletion of this scene from the 1831 edition of *Boris Godunov* – and especially the loss of this line by Maryna indicating her belief in Dmitry's claim as well as widespread popular belief that he really *was* the son of Ivan the Terrible – parallels the deletion from the play of similar comments by Khrushchov in the scene immediately preceding this one, "Cracow. Wiśniowiecki's House." These omissions produced a different image of Maryna (as well as the Pretender's relationship to the Russian people) in the published versions of *Boris Godunov* compared to Pushkin's original *Comedy*, thus subtly altering the politics of the play. See our chapters 1 and 6.

164. Both Prince Adam Wiśniowiecki and Palatine Jerzy Mniszech became deeply involved in the affair of the Russian Pretender. While Wiśniowiecki had a personal grudge against Tsar Boris, Mniszech's motivation had more to do with greed and a desperate desire to get out of debt.

165. Several versions of the "discovery" of the Pretender Dmitry in Poland-Lithuania circulated during the Time of Troubles. According to Conrad Bussow, a Saxon mercenary in Russia at the time, Dmitry was living in disguise as Prince Adam Wiśniowiecki's valet when he tearfully revealed his true identity to Prince Adam after the latter boxed his ears for some minor offense. See Bussow, *Disturbed State*, 28–29; PSRL, 14: 60; Perrie, *Pretenders*, 37–41.

166. When Jerzy Mniszech secured the Pretender Dmitry's pledge to marry his daughter once he became tsar, Mniszech received as part of the bargain a written promise from Dmitry to pay him a huge sum of money and to cede valuable territory on Russia's western frontier to his future father-in-law. When Mniszech deserted Dmitry's army after only a few months of campaigning, however, he broke his own part of the bargain. See SGGD, 2: 161–62, 166; Skrynnikov, *Rossiia v nachale XVII v.*, 122, 124–26.

167. The Pretender Dmitry was indeed not very impressive physically. He was beardless, somewhat short in stature, and very muscular – with one arm slightly shorter than the other; he had a dark complexion with a large wart near his nose under his right eye. Several sources claim that Dmitry's obvious good breeding (his education, eloquence, noble bearing and manner, as well as his uncalloused hands) helped convince King Sigismund and the Jesuits that he really was Tsarevich Dmitry. See

Margeret, *Russian Empire*, 70, 75, 88: Pierling, *La Russie et le Saint-Siège*, 3: 49–50, 434–35; Barbour, *Dimitry*, 32–44; RFCW, 131.

168. The American Pushkin scholar J. Thomas Shaw has offered the ingenious hypothesis that this 14-line speech of Mniszech's is in fact a sonnet, albeit of irregular rhyme scheme, included by Pushkin in his dramatic text on the model of the sonnet with which Shakespeare closed Act I of *Romeo and Juliet*, a play that Pushkin considered as exemplifying the style of the Italian Renaissance. Following Shakespeare's example, Pushkin sets out to reproduce the style of his material – the refined culture of seventeenth-century Poland – in this speech, a Polish magnate's "sonnet." (See Shaw, "Romeo and Juliet," 1–35.) The sonnet-like form of Mniszech's speech is also reminiscent of a speech by the Pretender Dmitry found in Lope de Vega's famous play *El Gran duque de Moscovia y emperador persequido* (1617). See Pushkin, *Boris Godunov* (1953), 186 note 88; Brody, *Demetrius Legend*, 52–140.

169. Contemporaneous critics almost universally attacked this scene. The dramatic art of its laconic speeches and the characterization of Maryna and the Pretender presented here were not well understood. A major reason for this problem was the omission of scene 13 ("Maryna's Dressing Room") and Khrushchov's speech in scene 12 from the published edition of *Boris Godunov* – resulting in a less attractive Pretender and turning Maryna into a more calculating and ambitious character. In real life, however, Maryna proved to be bold and courageous as well as ambitious. Pushkin was fascinated by her and planned to return to "Tsaritsa Maryna" in a future play that was never written. In an early draft for a preface to *Boris Godunov*, Pushkin wrote: "A tragedy without love appealed to my imagination. But apart from the fact that love entered greatly into the romantic and passionate character of my adventurer, I have rendered Dmitry enamored of Maryna in order to better reveal her unusual character. It is only sketched out by Karamzin." See BG, 322–23; *Letters*, 365; and our chapters 1 and 6.

170. The Pretender Dmitry was betrothed to Maryna Mniszech before launching his invasion of Russia, and by all accounts his passion was sincere. Once on the throne, Tsar Dmitry rejected all attempts by his advisors and Russian Orthodox church officials to dissuade him from marrying the Catholic Polish princess.

171. Maryna Mniszech was made of sterner stuff than most Polish princesses. After her marriage to Tsar Dmitry in the spring of 1606 and his assassination immediately thereafter, Maryna was held captive by the

usurper Tsar Vasily Shuisky for more than a year. In 1608, she was allowed to return home to Poland, but instead she joined the rebel camp of the "second false Dmitry," who was then fighting against Shuisky. Maryna publicly recognized the obvious impostor as her husband and soon produced an "heir," little Ivan Dmitrievich (also known as the "little brigand"). After the second false Dmitry's death, Maryna and Ivan – aided by cossacks led by Ivan Zarutsky – continued to struggle for the Russian throne for several years. Maryna and her son were eventually captured by forces loyal to Russia's new tsar, Mikhail Romanov, and they were put to death in 1614. See Perrie, *Pretenders*, 109–10, 183–86, 198–99, 201–3, 206–11, 215–29.

172. The Pretender Dmitry maintained good relations with Ukrainian cossacks, who had a history of supporting pretenders to the throne in Moldavia and elsewhere in Eastern Europe. In 1603, Prince Adam Wiśniowiecki, who had strong ties to Ukrainian cossacks, felt confident enough in Dmitry's ability to plead his own case that he sent him to negotiate directly with the Zaporozhian cossacks (soldiers from the famous cossack community located on the lower Dnieper River in Ukraine) for military assistance. Dmitry was honorably and favorably received by them. For all of these reasons, some contemporaries and later historians came to believe that the Pretender was originally a low-born cossack. See PSRL, 14: 60; Longworth, *Cossacks*, 77; Skrynnikov, *Boris Godunov*, 145–47; Mérimée, *Épisode*, 293–97, 301–5; Pokrovsky, *Brief History*, 1: 73, 76.

173. Tsar Dmitry was extremely strong and agile; he was also an excellent horseman and a skilled warrior. More than one person has asked how and where a runaway monk could have gained such martial training. See RFCW, 123–24, 131.

174. The date of this scene (October 16, 1604) was taken directly from Karamzin's *History*, but Karamzin was in error. On October 13, 1604, Dmitry's small invasion army (less than 5,000 men) launched his campaign for the throne by crossing the border from Poland-Lithuania into Severia (or Seversk), a remote region of southwestern Russia – very far from the main roads to Moscow that were heavily guarded by sturdy fortresses and well armed garrisons loyal to Boris Godunov. See RFCW, chapter 9.

175. Here Pushkin playfully puts one of Prince Andrei Kurbsky's original ideas into the mouth of his fictional son. In fact, the term "Holy Rus" or Holy Russia appeared for the first time in writings attributed to

Andrei Kurbsky. See RFCW, 474–76, 590 note 87; Cherniavsky, "Holy Russia," 617–37.

176. Andrei Kurbsky and his brother Roman were indeed heroes of the siege and capture of Kazan in 1552. See Fennell, *Prince Kurbsky's History*, 58–75.

177. Here again Pushkin's praise of Prince Kurbsky and his criticism of Tsar Ivan IV for mistreating the hero of Kazan contrasts sharply with Karamzin's semi-official criticism of Kurbsky as a "traitor."

178. As noted earlier, the tsar was advised by an informal boyar council known in the early modern period as the *sinklit*. Historians later referred to it as the "boyar duma" (or boyar council) and incorrectly claimed that it had legal powers that to some extent counterbalanced the power of the ruler. Edward Keenan has claimed that the boyars really ruled Russia in the name of the tsar and that autocracy itself was a convenient fiction masking oligarchic rule. That view has been strongly challenged by several other scholars. See Keenan, "Muscovite Political Folkways," 115–81; and Crummey, "Silence of Muscovy," 157–64.

179. The Pretender Dmitry sent many "cunning" letters and manifestos to towns and villages throughout southwestern Russia (and even to Moscow) in which he pleaded his case and urged the Russians to reject the usurper Boris Godunov. Those letters stirred up the frontier provinces and provoked sympathy for Dmitry in the capital. Dmitry also sent letters directly to Tsar Boris and Patriarch Iov, offering them clemency if they would end their resistance and recognize him as tsar. See SGGD, 2: 173–75; *Sbornik Imperatorskago Russkago Istoricheskago Obshchestva*, vol. 137: 243, 248, 260; Purchas, *Hakluytus Posthumus*, 14: 160; Massa, *Short History*, 88; Koretskii, "Novoe o krest'ianskom zakreposhchenii," 145–46; RFCW, 137, 138, 174, 198; Crummey, *Formation*, 216–17.

180. The Pretender Dmitry's invasion force quickly captured the ancient frontier town of Chernigov, thanks primarily to a rebellion of its townspeople and soldiers who tied up their commanders and enthusiastically opened the gates to Dmitry's troops. Peter F. Basmanov was one of Tsar Boris' best generals; at the time of Dmitry's invasion he was one of the commanders of the fortress of Novgorod-Seversky and was not in Moscow. Basmanov and boyar Nikita R. Trubetskoi received urgent orders from Tsar Boris to prevent the capture of Chernigov, but their relief force did not reach that town in time. The quick-thinking Basmanov immediately retreated to Novgorod-Seversky and prepared it to withstand a siege by Dmitry's army. See RFCW, 144–46.

181. In anticipation of Dmitry's invasion, Tsar Boris signed a treaty with King Karl IX of Sweden in August 1604 – at least in part to prevent the possibility of a two-front war. During the negotiations, Karl offered to send military forces to aid Tsar Boris, but the confident Godunov turned him down. See RFCW, 143; BG, 325.

182. This mention of Vasily Shchelkalov is anachronistic; he was no longer Duma Secretary. By this time, Afanasy Ivanovich Vlasiev held the post. Shchelkalov had been ousted from that sensitive job in 1600. Push-kin may have been inadvertently in error, or assuming poetic license, or intending this anachronistic reference to Shchelkalov to be ironic, since sources available to him indicated that the Shchelkalovs actually helped rescue Tsarevich Dmitry from Boris Godunov's assassins in Uglich in 1591. See PSRL, 14: 60; Skrynnikov, *Boris Godunov*, 108; BG, 326.

183. "Voivode" (Russian: *voevoda*) means commander or military governor. After the Pretender Dmitry gained a foothold on Russian soil and a few towns had surrendered to him, Tsar Boris issued an emergency order for the immediate mobilization of all available military forces. Boyars, gentry, ordinary soldiers, and all other men trained in fighting were required – on pain of death – to report to Moscow within two weeks. The mobilization actually took several weeks, but it did yield a large army. See RFCW, 150–57.

184. It is true that in some earlier national emergencies in Muscovy all available men, including monks, were expected to fight. However, that custom eventually gave way to a requirement that monasteries provide peasant recruits for such tasks as road clearing and bridge and fortifica-tion construction. Monasteries also supported the tsar's military opera-tions with, for example, horses and carts. See Margeret, *Russian Empire*, 47; Massa, *Short History*, 74.

185. Here Pushkin is using the customary formulaic language for decrees issued by the tsar in conjunction with his boyar advisors.

186. Rumors about the progress of the Pretender Dmitry's forces and a continuing barrage of "seductive" letters from Dmitry to the Russian people stirred up sympathy for the Pretender in many places, including Moscow. The head of Tsar Boris's secret police, his uncle Semyon Godu-nov, responded by spying on just about everyone and by liberal use of denunciations, executions, and torture. At the outset of his reign, Tsar Boris had pledged to make peace with his political opponents, but he broke that promise as early as 1599. In response to the Pretender Dmitry's challenge, Godunov authorized a dramatic increase in "racking and

torturing." See Margeret, *Russian Empire*, 60–61; Massa, *Short History*, 55–56, 59, 91–92; Skrynnikov, *Rossiia v nachale XVII v.*, 179–81.

187. Patriarch Iov, a close ally of Boris Godunov, launched a full-scale propaganda assault against the Pretender Dmitry, denouncing him as the runaway monk Grishka Otrepiev and asserting that he was a tool of Satan. Iov falsely asserted that the Church had been forced to condemn Otrepiev to life imprisonment for dabbling in the black arts. See RFCW, 125–27.

188. As noted earlier, the idea of the martyred Tsarevich Dmitry as a miracle worker was actually not put forward during the Pretender's invasion of Russia. Instead, it was created as the centerpiece of a clever propaganda campaign launched by the usurper Vasily Shuisky after Tsar Dmitry's assassination in order to "prove" that the dead tsar had been an impostor and that the real Dmitry had died in 1591. Phoney reports of miracles occurring at the site were sent to Moscow in an attempt to quiet down the unrest caused by Tsar Dmitry's assassination and to prevent the appearance of yet another Pretender Dmitry. The ploy turned out to be only partially successful. According to his friend Ivan Pushchin, Pushkin himself read the *Saints' Calendar* (*Chet'i Minei*) that contained accounts of the miracles associated with "St. Dmitry" and Tsar Boris's horrified reaction to news of the miracles. See RFCW, 245–48; Vatsuro, *A. S. Pushkin*, 1: 109.

189. In 1606, Tsar Vasilii Shuisky ordered the transfer of the "miraculously preserved" body of Tsarevich Dmitry from Uglich to Moscow. Miracles were staged along the way in an attempt to prove that the martyred boy was a saint. Many Muscovites saw through this cynical ploy, however, and on the day Dmitry's casket arrived in Moscow Shuisky was briefly in danger of being stoned to death by the crowd gathered to watch the spectacle. The body of "Saint Dmitry" was quickly taken into the Kremlin and placed in the Cathedral of the Archangel. Additional miracles were proclaimed over the next few days, but the stench of the decaying body in Tsarevich Dmitry's casket soon forced church officials to close the cathedral and quietly inter "Saint Dmitry." See Margeret, *Russian Empire*, 74; Massa, *Short History*, 160–61; Bussow, *Disturbed State*, 85–86.

190. This speech by Vasily Shuisky is one of Pushkin's little jokes buried in the play. Far from objecting to the idea of making use of such a "momentous novelty," Shuisky himself "crudely" turned Tsarevich Dmitry into "Saint Dmitry" in 1606.

191. After Boris Godunov's death, Tsar Feodor Borisovich recalled Vasily Shuisky from his position as an army commander fighting against the Pretender Dmitry. Upon his arrival in Moscow, Shuisky did try to calm the restive crowds in Red Square by publicly declaring that the real Tsarevich Dmitry had died in 1591 and that he, Shuisky, had seen the boy's body in his coffin in Uglich. Massa, *Short History*, 97; BG, 327.

192. This particular boyar may have been shocked by witnessing Tsar Boris's suffering and near collapse, but boyars were also raised from childhood to regard the tsar with such awe that it was difficult to get them to speak up even during council meetings when they were supposed to offer advice to the tsar. See Margeret, *Russian Empire*, 69–70.

193. In the first published version of *Boris Godunov* (1831) and subsequent editions of the play, the location of this scene was switched from before to after scene 19 ("A Plain Near Novgorod-Seversky"). See our chapters 1 and 6.

194. Patriarch Iov did have Grishka Otrepiev condemned by the Russian Orthodox Church. As part of the propaganda war against the Pretender Dmitry, he also produced several very seedy and unimpressive "witnesses" who claimed that Otrepiev had sacrilegiously assumed the identity of Tsarevich Dmitry. Few people were persuaded by the patriarch's clumsy tactics, however, and support for the Pretender continued to grow rapidly throughout Russia. See RFCW, 126–27.

195. The *iurodivyi* (or "fool in Christ") was held in awe by both peasants and tsars in early modern Russia. Some holy fools were undoubtedly charlatans, but others were sincere men and women of faith. Spiritual descendants of the hermits of the early Christian East, holy fools strove for "Christian humility through self-humiliation." They often wore an iron collar or chains and walked around naked even in winter. Their severe mode of life and dire prophecies made the rich and powerful uncomfortable. "Beggars and princes alike felt the sting of their tongues." A famous Russian holy fool, Nikolka of Pskov, was a contemporary of Ivan the Terrible, and his role as a jester of the Lord (or "divinely inspired clown") allowed him "to play the prophet with impunity." During Ivan's reign, the holy fools Vasily and Nikolka both confronted and criticized the tsar to his face and "lived to tell the tale." Nikolka is specifically credited with saving Pskov from being sacked shortly after Novgorod was devastated on Ivan's orders in 1570. Standing before the gates of Pskov, Nikolka denounced Tsar Ivan as "a devourer of Christian flesh" and demanded that he "leave Pskov in peace." "Ivan's stunned silence" before

Nikolka and his decision not to sack Pskov reflected the deep respect Russians had for holy fools. Pushkin actively sought information about Nikolka and other holy fools while writing his play, and Karamzin obliged by sending him a work about Nikolka. Pushkin transfers Nikolka forward in time to the Time of Troubles; Nikolka actually died in 1576. See Crummey, *Formation*, 128–29; Likhachev and Panchenko, "*Smekhovoi mir*" *drevnei Rusi*, 93–182; Berry and Crummey, *Rude and Barbarous Kingdom*, 219–20, 268–69; BG, 331; *Letters*, 247, 254, 267.

196. Nikolka's nonsensical lines in this scene were transformed into a model folk melody – and into a dire prediction of political and social apocalypse – by Musorgsky in his various settings of the *iurodivy*'s laments to music.

197. Herod was the king of Judea who ordered all boys in Bethlehem two years of age and under to be slain in order to dispose of Jesus; Herod considered him to be a pretender to his own throne after soothsayers foretold that this child would become King of Judea, a leader who would "save the nation" of Israel (Matthew 2: 6–7, 13, 16–18).

198. The bulk of this scene is spoken in French (and a little German), accurately representing the participation of foreign mercenaries in Tsar Boris's army. Pushkin probably intended to remind his audience that French and German soldiers had fought on Russian soil long before Napoleon's invasion in 1812. The irony of a *French* officer commanding part of the tsar's army undoubtedly also appealed to the playwright. Pushkin attached great significance to this scene, a piece of coarse military prose which achieves vivid comic effect through the mingling of three languages in the midst of a chaotic battle. For the imperial theater audience this was a dazzling display of languages they knew. For the less well educated audience, another interpretation "programmed" by Pushkin was possible – the perception of a clash of forces as a spectacle of Babeldom. See BG, 327.

199. After Tsar Boris's brilliant and energetic commander, Peter Basmanov, failed to prevent the surrender of Chernigov to the Pretender Dmitry's forces, he hastily retreated to the fortress of Novgorod-Seversky (in southwestern Russia). Basmanov quickly fortified the town and reinforced its garrison. The town's strategic importance also prompted the tsar's commanders to concentrate a large army nearby in order to prevent Dmitry from threatening Russia's heartland. On December 21, 1604, Tsar Boris's large army (which outnumbered Dmitry's army by

three to one) engaged the Pretender Dmitry's forces in a three-hour battle fought within sight of Novgorod-Seversky. See RFCW, chapter 9.

200. Because of the timidity of Tsar Boris's commanders, Dmitry's forces were able to seize the initiative early in the battle. Three Polish cavalry companies made a lightning-quick strike against the enemy's right wing regiment. It wavered and began to retreat in disorder into the main regiment, which in turn began to waver and retreat. During all this time the tsar's commanders made no effort to turn the tide of battle against the small attacking force. See RFCW, 160.

201. Captain Jacques Margeret, who entered Russian military service in 1600 after serving King Henri IV of France, shared overall command of Tsar Boris's 2,500 Western mercenary troops with Walther von Rosen, a Livonian German. The bulk of their forces consisted of Germans, Livonians, and Poles, with small numbers of Swedes, Danes, Greeks, Flemings, Dutch, French, English, and Scots as well. After Dmitry became tsar, Margeret entered his service and became captain of the tsar's foreign bodyguard. A few months after Tsar Dmitry's assassination, Margeret received permission from Tsar Vasily Shuisky to return to France, where Henri IV immediately commanded him to write a book about Russia. Margeret's *Estat de l'Empire de Russie et Grand Duché de Moscovie*, published in 1607, was the first printed French account of Russia. It is an extremely important source for reconstructing early modern Russian history and has been used extensively by historians ever since the eighteenth century. Margeret's book was frequently cited by Karamzin and had a significant impact on Pushkin's sympathetic interpretation of Tsar Dmitry. See RFCW, 154, 160, 165; Dunning, "Use and Abuse," 357–80; and Margeret, *Russian Empire*.

202. The fleeing soldier's taunt of Captain Margeret as an "infidel" (*basurman*) was probably influenced by Pushkin's own memories of the popular reaction to Napoleon's occupation of Moscow in 1812. According to Alexander Martin, contemporary sources reveal that anti-French propaganda "was so effective that Muscovites talked about fighting against the *basurman*, the 'infidel,' a term that evoked past wars against 'unclean' Tatars and Ottomans and may have had particular resonance among a population to whom the Muslim East, as much if not more than Europe, remained the 'other' whose presence shaped their own identity." See Martin, "Moscow," 480.

203. Translation: "What, what?"

204. This passage contains a pun; in Russian *kvakat'* means to croak. The pun was made even more pronounced in the 1831 edition of *Boris Godunov* – and virtually all subsequent editions – by the substitution of the phrase "liagushka zamorskaia" ("foreign frog") for the more menacing "zamorskii voron" ("foreign crow") found in Pushkin's *Komediia*.

205. Here and subsequently, dramatically translated by Antony Wood: "What is zis 'Orthodox'? ... Damned rascals, cursed scum! Damnation, *mein 'err*, it meks me furious: you'd zink zey 'ad no arms to fight wiz, only legs to run away wiz." Somewhat less colloquially translated, "One might have said the Russians had no arms to strike with,…" is the most famous phrase in Captain Margeret's book, *Estat de l'Empire de Russie*. Margeret's colorful but honest observation about the inactivity of the tsar's army while it was under attack during the battle before Novgorod-Seversky was later embellished by Karamzin and Pushkin so that not only did the tsar's troops have no arms to strike with, they had only legs to run away. See Margeret, *Russian Empire*, 62, 155 note 203; and Karamzin, *Istoriia* (1892), 11: 98–99 and note 274.

206. Translation: "It is a disgrace."

207. Translation: "… By God, I no move one single step from 'ere. Since ze bottle is opened, you 'ave to drink. What you say, *mein 'err*?" The well known French colloquial expression Pushkin uses here ("Ventre-saint-gris") dates from the sixteenth century and has been attributed to Margeret's first employer, King Henri IV; see Robert, *Dictionnaire*, 1886.

208. Translation: "You hef right."

209. Translation: "My God, it ees getting 'ot 'ere! Zees devil of a 'Pretend-er', az zey call 'im, 'e's a fellow wiz a wild 'air up 'iz arse. What you zink, *mein 'err*?" A large proportion of Pushkin's intended audience had a good enough knowledge of French to be able to understand the obscenity of Margeret's swearing, which may have reminded many of them of the shockingly coarse language used by French soldiers in Napoleon's army during the occupation of Moscow in 1812 (see Martin, "Moscow," 477–78). Pushkin was well aware that including this crude utterance by the French captain would make his play "unfit for the ladies" and unacceptable to tsarist censors (see *Letters*, 261, 308). In fact, this passage was specifically cited by tsarist censors as unacceptable (see Lemke, *Nikolaevskie zhandarmy*, 608; Reitblat, *Vidok Figliarin*, 94; Gozenpud, "Iz istorii," 255). During Pushkin's unsuccessful effort to gain permission to publish *Komediia* during the late 1820s, he stubbornly

resisted altering the play. Nevertheless, he did offer to revise this particular passage, but the alternative he proposed was equally offensive to the tsar's censors, albeit for a different reason (see our chapter 3).

210. Translation: "Hé! Look zere, look zere! Zere is action in ze enemy's beck side. Zat must be ze brave Basmanoff 'oo 'as made a sortie." Peter Basmanov tried to assist the tsar's army during the battle before Novgorod-Seversky. He ordered the continuous bombardment of Dmitry's forces by all of Novgorod-Seversky's artillery, and he dispatched frequent sorties to harass and tie down Dmitry's forces and to capture enemy supplies. Basmanov's efforts were remarkably successful, but the senior commanders of Tsar Boris' army failed to take advantage of the opportunity provided by him and quickly lost the initiative to Dmitry's forces. See RFCW, 159.

211. Translation: "Zo zink I."

212. Translation: "A-ha! 'ere come our Germans! – *Messieurs!* ... *Mein* 'err, tell zem to fall into line and, damnation, we shall mek a charge!" In fact, Captain Margeret did not order his mercenary troops to charge at the Pretender Dmitry's attacking forces during the battle before Novgorod-Seversky. He did, however, do exactly that at a critical point during the battle of Dobrynichi in January 1605. According to eyewitnesses, Margeret's decisive actions on that occasion saved the day for the tsar's army, for which he was profusely thanked and rewarded by Tsar Boris. See Margeret, *Russian Empire*, 156–57 note 212; Bussow, *Disturbed State*, 40.

213. Translation: "Very good. Halt!"

214. Translation: "*Gott* help us!" This phrase is a direct quotation from the Saxon mercenary Conrad Bussow's eyewitness account of the battle of Dobrynichi. Karamzin's inclusion of this passage in his *History of the Russian State* inspired Pushkin to include it in his play, although Pushkin moved it to the battle of Novgorod-Seversky. See Bussow, *Disturbed State*, 40; Karamzin, *Istoriia* (1892), 11: 102 and notes 283–84.

215. After a confusing three-hour battle before Novgorod-Seversky (during which the commander of Tsar Boris's army, Prince Feodor Mstislavsky, was thrown from his horse, wounded, and very nearly captured), the tsar's army retreated, leaving Dmitry's forces holding the field and able to declare victory. News of that victory spread like wildfire and convinced many more Russians to join the cause of the "true tsar" Dmitry. See RFCW, 160–61.

216. During the battle before Novgorod-Seversky, the Pretender Dmitry personally inspired courage in his troops, and his bravery was noted by several contemporaries. Pushkin's portrayal of his open aversion to spilling any more of the blood of his future subjects than absolutely necessary is historically accurate. That strategy helped Dmitry's cause tremendously. See RFCW, 121, 144–45, 160–61.

217. One of the first regions of southwestern Russia to rise against Tsar Boris in support of the Pretender Dmitry was the huge, fertile Komaritsk district inhabited by relatively rich and fiercely independent peasants. In the Komaritsk district, the town of Sevsk enthusiastically joined Dmitry's cause and sent him its recently deposed pro-Godunov military governors as prisoners. After the Novgorod-Seversky battle in December, Dmitry's army retired to the friendly Komaritsk district and set up their winter headquarters about ten kilometers from Sevsk. See RFCW, 149, 161–63.

218. This is an imaginary character, but Rozhnov was in fact the name of distant relatives of the Pushkins. See Veselovskii, *Issledovaniia*, 62–63, 91, 98, 102.

219. Tsar Boris was, of course, shocked and disappointed by the defeat of his army in the battle before Novgorod-Seversky and by the continued existence (and growth) of Dmitry's military forces. Godunov tried to hide the defeat from his people; he staged a fake "victory" parade in Moscow and sent congratulations to the wounded Prince Mstislavsky for his courageous efforts. In January 1605, large numbers of reinforcements were sent to bolster the tsar's army in preparation for an advance against the Pretender Dmitry's forces. The prestigious Prince Vasily Shuisky was appointed as Mstislavsky's second-in-command at this time; he did not replace Mstislavsky as senior commander – as Pushkin has it. Instead, with Shuisky's assistance, the wounded but extremely proud commander was able to stay in the field for the next battle. See RFCW, 161, 164–65.

220. Pyotr Basmanov stubbornly defended Novgorod-Seversky against Dmitry's forces before, during, and after Mstislavsky's army was defeated. Dmitry reluctantly lifted the siege of the town on December 28, 1604, and withdrew his army into the Komaritsk district. Basmanov was then recalled to Moscow by Tsar Boris, who showered gifts on him for the heroic defense of Novgorod-Seversky – just about the only thing Godunov had to celebrate at that point. An authentic victory parade for the popular Basmanov was followed by his promotion to the rank of

boyar. Never before had a military commander been so honored by a tsar. Basmanov soon emerged as a leading figure in the ailing and beleaguered tsar's court. See RFCW, 161, 179–80.

221. Basmanov did not wish to remain at court in Moscow. His talents were desperately needed on the front line against Dmitry (a wisdom that Pushkin here puts into Dmitry's mouth), and Basmanov begged to be allowed to rejoin the military campaign as senior commander. Unfortunately for Tsar Boris, more prestigious aristocrats who were jealous of Basmanov prevented him from receiving such a commission. Instead, he remained in Moscow until after Tsar Boris died in April 1605. See Massa, *Short History*, 91, 97; Purchas, *Hakluytus Posthumus*, 14: 142.

222. At this unhappy time in Moscow, the sinister Semyon Godunov's agents spied on almost everyone and managed to terrorize the general population. Torture, death, and excommunication awaited anyone even remotely suspected of harboring sympathy for Dmitry. See Margeret, *Russian Empire*, 60–61; Purchas, *Hakluytus Posthumus*, 14: 160; Massa, *Short History*, 55–56, 73; Skrynnikov, *Boris Godunov*, 149–51.

223. This may be one of Pushkin's jokes buried in the play. Tsar Boris's army was far from being well fed, well dressed, or happy at this time. In general, Russian soldiers mustered for winter campaigns were not prepared for prolonged military operations or sieges. Sympathy for the Pretender Dmitry began to surface within the ranks of those grumbling, ill-clad, hungry men huddled in their tents, standing guard, or out on patrol during the winter months. See RFCW, 150–57, 164–65, 179–80.

224. By January 1605, Mstislavsky's army received reinforcements from far and wide in preparation for the next battle against Dmitry's forces. The tsar's army in the field (including slaves and recruits) stood at approximately 40,000 men. Dmitry's army at this time was growing daily, but it still contained no more than 15,000 men. See Bussow, *Disturbed State*, 40; and RFCW, 162–65.

225. News of the Pretender Dmitry's valor, his mild treatment of prisoners, his distaste for spilling blood unnecessarily, his unwillingness to allow his soldiers to loot surrendering towns, and his exceptionally kind treatment of the local population wherever he went caused many people to flock to his banner. It also stirred sympathy for him in the tsar's army. See RFCW, 121, 137, 144–45, 148, 160–64.

226. On the eve of the battle of Dobrynichi (January 21, 1605), the Pretender Dmitry's few remaining Polish officers argued strongly against risking open confrontation with Mstislavsky's much larger army; they

urged Dmitry to be more cautious or even to negotiate with the tsar's commanders. Overconfident after the Novgorod-Seversky battle, however, Dmitry listened instead to his cossack atamans (chieftains), who favored an immediate attack. It proved to be a very costly decision. See RFCW, 165.

227. Dmitry's army was defeated at the battle of Dobrynichi (January 21, 1605) and forced to flee. During the disorderly retreat Dmitry himself barely escaped capture. His horse was shot out from under him, and only the quick thinking and bravery of Dmitry's new ally, the Putivl commander Vasily M. Mosalsky, saved him from certain death. Dmitry lost all of his artillery and nearly all his infantry in the battle. Thousands of his soldiers were killed or captured, and most of the captives were immediately put to death by Tsar Boris's forces. See Massa, *Short History,* 84; Bussow, *Disturbed State,* 40–41; RFCW, 167–68.

228. Contemporaries testified to the Pretender Dmitry's great riding skill, love of horses, and ability to choose the best steed. In contrast to most other early modern Russian rulers, Dmitry did not like traveling in a carriage and preferred to ride on horseback. See Margeret, *Russian Empire,* 86–87; Bussow, *Disturbed State,* 52; Skrynnikov, *Samozvantsy,* 188.

229. After the battle of Dobrynichi, Dmitry's Polish officers falsely blamed the catastrophe on the Zaporozhian cossacks. The Poles claimed that the cossacks had been frightened by great clouds of smoke drifting across the battlefield and run away. For a while, at least, Dmitry was inclined to believe the Poles and blamed his cossack infantry for fleeing the battlefield. In reality, however, it was Dmitry's Polish cavalry who were the first to turn back in confusion. See Margeret, *Russian Empire,* 63; and RFCW, 167.

230. Dmitry did not hang any Zaporozhian cossacks or any other soldiers after the battle of Dobrynichi.

231. Pushkin is historically correct here. At the outset of the battle of Dobrynichi, Dmitry's Polish cavalry led a furious attack on the right wing of the tsar's army, trying to repeat the successful tactic they had used in the battle before Novgorod-Seversky. This time, however, in anticipation of such a move, Captain Margeret and others lined up three hundred cannon and 10,000 infantrymen armed with harquebuses to protect the right flank of the tsar's army. Just as Dmitry's forces approached them at top speed, the tsar's forces let loose a general volley. Not only did that kill many of Dmitry's men, but it so startled and unnerved his cavalry that they turned back in confusion, causing great

disorder as they retreated right into Dmitry's other advancing cavalry units. The result was chaos and a hasty, disorderly retreat from the battlefield. Dmitry's fleeing soldiers were then hotly pursued for several kilometers by Margeret's foreign cavalry, who cut down as many rebels as possible. See RFCW, 165–67.

232. After Tsar Boris's death and the surrender of his army to the Pretender Dmitry, many of the foreign mercenaries who had fought bravely against Dmitry did indeed ask to join his service. Rather than scolding them, Dmitry praised their steadfastness to the oath they had sworn to the Godunov dynasty and their skill and valor. He formally accepted them into his service and admonished them to show the same zeal for him that they had shown for the Godunovs. In this way, Captain Margeret entered Dmitry's service and retained his position as commander of the tsar's foreign troops. A few months later, Margeret organized some of his Western mercenaries into a new bodyguard for Tsar Dmitry. See Bussow, *Disturbed State*, 44, 49; Massa, *Short History*, 100; Margeret, *Russian Empire*, xviii, 69; and RFCW, 198–99.

233. After the disaster at Dobrynichi, Dmitry retreated south to the town of Rylsk (located about 70 kilometers northeast of stone-walled Putivl, Dmitry's temporary "capital"). Tsar Boris's army followed him so slowly that it lost the initiative gained from the great victory at Dobrynichi. This allowed Dmitry not only to survive but to reorganize his forces for his next offensive. See RFCW, 171–74.

234. According to legend, the Pretender Dmitry was in such despair after the disaster at Dobrynichi that he planned to flee to Poland, only to be upbraided by the citizens of Putivl, who threatened to turn him over to Tsar Boris if he did not stay in Russia and continue his campaign for the throne. In fact, Dmitry remained very active at this time, and thousands of Russians continued to flock to his banner. In Putivl, he formed a war council, raised a large sum of money, rebuilt his military forces, and began calling himself "Tsar Dmitry" instead of "Tsarevich Dmitry." According to a contemporary, he "took courage again" and "put a fine army back in the field." See Massa, *Short History*, 86; and RFCW, 173–74.

235. Located in southwestern Russia, the strategically located fortress of Kromy guarded the route to Moscow. (This fortress has become famous as the site of the final scene of Musorgsky's revised version of his opera *Boris Godunov*, 1872.) During Dmitry's invasion, the inhabitants of Kromy rebelled against Tsar Boris, forcing the tsar's commanders to send a small army to besiege that important town while Godunov's main

army engaged Dmitry's forces. After the battle of Dobrynichi, the army besieging Kromy was immediately strengthened with more men and artillery. Nonetheless, the stubborn rebels – reinforced by several hundred Don cossacks who managed to break through the siege camp with fresh supplies – continued to hold out and to inflict severe casualties on the tsar's siege army. The energetic and heroic defense of Kromy was led by cossack ataman Andrei Karela, whose cossacks frequently mocked their besiegers, calling them poor soldiers and traitors to the true tsar. Karela supposedly even had naked women appear on the ramparts of the destroyed fortress to hurl gross insults at the frustrated besiegers and to sing satirical ditties about Tsar Boris's commanders. By spring 1605, the tsar's siege army, pushed to the limit by hunger and exposure to cold weather, was exhausted and demoralized. See Massa, *Short History*, 88–89; RFCW, 164, 172–73, 175–79.

236. Tsar Boris did not appoint Basmanov as commander of his siege army, in spite of repeated requests by the hero of Novgorod-Seversky to be sent back to active service. The frustrated Basmanov recognized the grave danger to Tsar Boris posed by the failing siege of Kromy, but he was forced to remain on the sidelines while less skillful commanders of higher birth conducted the campaign. Basmanov was finally dispatched from Moscow as one of the new commanders of the Kromy siege army only after Tsar Boris's sudden death in April 1605. See RFCW, 180, 182.

237. Tsar Boris is referring to *mestnichestvo,* the precedence-ranking system of Muscovy whereby administrative, court, and military appointments were made according to family background rather than individual merit. This imaginary conversation between Godunov and Basmanov was important to Pushkin; it embodies his independent historical insight in artistic form. He therefore found the use of this passage by Bulgarin (in his novel *Dimitrii Samozvanets*) a particularly offensive act of plagiarism. See Pushkin, *Sochineniia A. S. Pushkina* (Morozov, 1887), 3: 84; TL, 3: 108; Gozenpud, "Iz istorii," 268; Simmons, *Pushkin,* 272; Binyon, *Pushkin,* 314; and BG, 335–36.

238. The *mestnichestvo* records were not finally burned until 1682, during the reign of Tsar Feodor Alekseevich. According to a leading authority on the subject, Nancy Shields Kollmann, "Precedence was abolished in 1682 when the clan-based elite had been so transformed in membership and attitude that the system of reckoning hierarchy by clan heritage had become antiquated." See Kollmann, *By Honor Bound,* 250.

239. In spite of the Pretender Dmitry's setback at the battle of Dobry-

nichi, during late winter and early spring 1605 many more Russians joined his cause, and enthusiasm for Dmitry grew rapidly – even in Moscow. See RFCW, 179–82.

240. Ivan the "calmer of storms" was Grand Prince Ivan III ("the Great") who ruled from 1462 to 1505; his "ferocious grandson" was Tsar Ivan IV ("the Terrible") who ruled from 1547 to 1584.

241. This speech by Tsar Boris (like his monologue "I have attained the highest power" in scene 8) contains arguments similar to those found in Machiavelli's writings, especially chapter 17 of *The Prince* – entitled "Cruelty and compassion; and whether it is better to be loved than feared, or the reverse." Machiavelli concludes that "it is far better to be feared than loved if you cannot be both." See BG, 336; Greenleaf, *Pushkin*, 175–79.

242. Basmanov became a favorite at the court of Tsar Boris thanks to his military skill and popularity. His ambition, however, was frustrated by jealous rivals who had higher status based on genealogy. Pushkin was correct to portray Basmanov as a foe of the old *mestnichestvo* system of precedence. In fact, the poet was well aware that it was a *mestnichestvo* dispute among Russian commanders that eventually prompted Basmanov to betray the Godunov dynasty in favor of the Pretender Dmitry. See RFCW, 180, 182–84, 190.

243. By early spring 1605, Tsar Boris had been gravely ill for a long time. Even so, his sudden death on April 13 came as a shock to everyone. Rumors circulated that he had committed suicide or had been poisoned, but he probably died of natural causes. See Margeret, *Russian Empire*, 64; Purchas, *Hakluytus Posthumus*, 14: 147, 160; Barbour, *Dimitry*, 108–9; and RFCW, 181.

244. These lines echo the last words Shakespeare gives to the dying king in *Henry IV (part II):* "God knows, my son, / By what by-paths and indirect crook'd ways / I met this crown." See BG, 338.

245. This section of Boris's dying speech is full of echoes from Karamzin's official account of Boris Godunov's inner repentance and end – but here spoken as advice by a dying monarch in luminous control of his past. (See Karamzin, *Istoriia* [1892], 10: 134; 11: 89; and BG, 338.) It is part of Pushkin's plan for this "tragicomedy of history" to bring the tormented ruler to a sense of social reality only when the larger political picture makes such wisdom impossible to implement. See our chapter 5.

246. Immediately following the death of Tsar Boris, the new tsar Feodor Borisovich recalled to Moscow his two senior commanders, Feodor

Mstislavsky and Vasily Shuisky. The main reason for their recall was probably the need for the stabilizing influence of the two most prestigious boyars in disorderly Moscow and at court. See Massa, *Short History*, 97; and RFCW, 182.

247. Following the plans of his dying father, one of the first decisions made by Tsar Feodor Borisovich was to dispatch newly-promoted boyar Pyotr Basmanov to the tsar's siege camp before Kromy in order to administer the oath of loyalty to the army and to help bring the siege to a successful conclusion. Although Basmanov was one of Russia's ablest military officers, he was forced to serve – nominally at least – as deputy commander instead of commander-in-chief because of his relatively low *mestnichestvo* status. Nevertheless, almost as soon as he arrived in the siege camp, Basmanov's position as deputy commander was challenged by jealous rivals with better pedigrees. Unfortunately, Tsar Feodor's court gave in to the pressure of aristocrats who disliked the ambitious "upstart." The extremely proud Basmanov was quickly demoted, and a less able but more prestigious boyar was appointed deputy commander of the tsar's army. That decision by the new tsar and his advisors proved to be fatal for the Godunov dynasty. Basmanov became so angry at his humiliation that he immediately got involved in an already developing conspiracy to transfer the army's loyalty to the Pretender Dmitry. See Skrynnikov, *Boris Godunov*, 151–52; and RFCW, 182–83.

248. Tsar Boris, like Ivan the Terrible before him, welcomed into his service foreigners with useful skills or knowledge. See Platonov, *Moscow and the West*, 1–48.

249. Here Pushkin reconstructs the moral and psychological insights that Godunov might have gained at the court of Ivan the Terrible. See BG, 339–40.

250. Tsar Feodor Borisovich's mother, Tsaritsa Maria (daughter of *oprichnina* boss Maliuta Skuratov), was very unpopular. Almost as sinister as her father, Maria's "malignant" influence at the court of her son was resented by many Russians and helped undermine elite and popular support for the Godunov dynasty. Curiously, Pushkin appeared not at all interested in the powerful female personality of this matriarch, restricting his attention to the two brides, East and West (Ksenia and Maryna). See RFCW, 180, 181, 183.

251. The fate of Ksenia Borisovna was indeed precarious, but probably not as dire as legend later described it. According to Tsar Vasily Shuisky's propagandists, Ksenia was raped by Tsar Dmitry soon after he

came to power. Many historians accepted that slander at face value, and Sumarokov's *Dimitrii Samozvanets* (written in 1771) portrays Ksenia as a principal rival of the evil Pretender. Pushkin was a good enough historian to doubt this particularly outrageous charge against Dmitry. See *Letters*, 366; Baer, "Between Public and Private," 29.

252. Like Ivan the Terrible before him, Tsar Boris became a monk on his deathbed.

253. In spite of their solemn promise to the dying Tsar Boris, many aristocrats at court began to work secretly on behalf of the Pretender Dmitry. During the popular rebellion in Moscow which abruptly ended the Godunov dynasty on June 1, 1605, boyar support for Tsar Feodor simply evaporated; not a single one of them was willing to fight for Boris Godunov's son. See RFCW, 182, 192–96.

254. This scene takes place in the tsar's siege camp before rebel-held Kromy.

255. Basmanov did become one of Tsar Dmitry's favorites after the Godunovs were overthrown. For that reason, he was falsely accused by his enemies of corresponding with the Pretender Dmitry and of masterminding the plot to transfer the army's loyalty to him. There is no evidence that Gavrila Pushkin ever visited the siege camp to try to persuade Basmanov to switch sides, but Dmitry's agents did maintain secret contact with conspirators in the tsar's army. See RFCW, 183–84.

256. Basmanov remained loyal to Tsar Feodor Borisovich until he was suddenly demoted from his position as deputy commander of the tsar's army to make way for boyar prince Andrei Teliatevsky. According to a contemporary source, upon learning of his demotion Basmanov "wept for an hour," claiming that he preferred death to dishonor; he then joined the conspiracy against the Godunov dynasty. See Perrie, *Pretenders*, 72; and RFCW, 183.

257. This passage was probably influenced by a contemporary source used by Karamzin and other scholars to "prove" that the Pretender Dmitry was an impostor. The Saxon mercenary Conrad Bussow claimed that Basmanov, while he was Tsar Dmitry's favorite, admitted to the low-ranking foreign soldier that Tsar Dmitry was not really the son of Ivan the Terrible, although still worthy to wear the crown. In fact, it is extremely unlikely that Basmanov committed lese majesty in a conversation with a foreign soldier. See Bussow, *Disturbed State*, 82; and RFCW, 513 note 9.

258. Ataman Karela and his men were largely responsible for the heroic

defense of the ruined fortress of Kromy, and Karela was deeply involved in the successful plot to transfer the allegiance of the tsar's siege army to the Pretender Dmitry. Dmitry's future father-in-law, Jerzy Mniszech, had originally served as commander-in-chief of Dmitry's invasion force, but he deserted Dmitry at the beginning of January 1605 and returned home to Poland-Lithuania. See RFCW, 162, 175–79, 187.

259. Historians, including Karamzin, painted a false picture of a down-and-out pretender who was on the ropes and only saved by the sudden death of Tsar Boris. In fact, by the spring of 1605 Dmitry had recovered from the disaster at Dobrynichi and was able to "put a fine army back into the field." By then his military forces had rebounded to more than 12,000 men, including about half of all the Don cossacks and most of the Russian frontier commanders and their garrisons, whose task it had been to stop his invasion. See Massa, *Short History,* 86; Bussow, *Disturbed State,* 41–44; Margeret, *Russian Empire,* 66–67; and RFCW, 174, 179, 190.

260. This grossly inaccurate characterization of cossacks and Polish troops in Dmitry's army reflects Karamzin's prejudice against them, not their actual military value. The exceptionally stubborn and competent cossacks were largely responsible for Dmitry's success. In addition, Dmitry strictly prohibited the looting and destruction of towns and villages by his troops. That helped his cause among the Russian people, but it caused grumbling among his booty-hunting Polish troops, many of whom soon deserted him. Far from being a mere rabble in arms, by spring 1605 Dmitry's growing army was a potent threat to the Godunov dynasty. See RFCW, 144–45, 161, 162, 174, 179.

261. This is absolutely correct historically; Dmitry's campaign for the throne was greatly assisted by popular uprisings in his name and by his reputation for mercy and kindness. This particular phrase of Pushkin's has served as the basis for numerous interpretations of his play in which the thesis of the people's perspicacity – condemning Tsar Boris's crimes and rising against his regime – became axiomatic. At the same time, the very word *mnenie* (meaning "opinion" or "esteem") relates to the verb *mnit'* (meaning "to think," but also "to suppose erroneously") and to the nouns *somnenie* ("doubt") and *mnitel'nost'* ("mistrustfulness"), creating an aureola of associations giving rise to the idea of error. See BG, 343–44.

262. During the Pretender Dmitry's invasion, many towns and garrisons rebelled against their own commanders who remained loyal to Tsar Boris. Some hated commanders were killed by their own soldiers or

by townsmen before the gates were opened to Dmitry's forces, but most of them joined their men in swearing an oath to Tsar Dmitry and were, to their great surprise, immediately accepted into his service. See RFCW, 144, 147–49, 170; PSRL, 14: 61–62; PSRL, 31: 150; RIB, 1: col. 369; RIB, 13: cols. 571–72, 724; Margeret, *Russian Empire*, 61; Massa, *Short History*, 73; Bussow, *Disturbed State*, 37; Purchas, *Hakluytus Posthumus*, 14: 159–60.

263. During the rebellion of the tsar's siege army, some Russian commanders were tied up by the rebels and handed over to the Pretender Dmitry's forces. One of the principal conspirators, Vasily Golitsyn, panicked during the insurrection and ordered his slaves to tie him up so he would not look like a traitor if the rebellion failed. See PSRL, 14: 64; and RFCW, 188.

264. Russian aristocratic families who had been harassed and exiled by Tsar Boris – including the Romanovs and Nagois – were probably responsible for the appearance of "Tsarevich Dmitry" in Poland-Lithuania. See RFCW, 124–25.

265. *Lobnoe mesto* – a circular, elevated stone platform located outside the Kremlin wall on Red Square not far from St. Basil's Cathedral. Tsars and boyars occasionally appeared before the people on *lobnoe mesto*. It was also where tsarist decrees were read to the inhabitants of Moscow and where, from time to time, executions took place.

266. By the end of May 1605, Tsar Feodor Borisovich had lost most of his army and half of his country to the Pretender Dmitry. On the morning of June 1, 1605, Gavrila Pushkin boldly entered Moscow to read Dmitry's proclamation to the city's anxious population. Pushkin was accompanied by many Russians from the capital's suburbs and encountered no resistance from Godunov supporters as he made his way to Red Square. There thousands of Muscovites gathered to hear Pushkin speak, and the crowd proved to be far from hostile to Dmitry's courier. Previous couriers sent to Moscow by Dmitry had been killed or imprisoned. See RFCW, 193–94.

267. Basmanov and other commanders at Kromy led a successful rebellion of the tsar's army against the Godunov dynasty on May 7, 1605. The army then swore an oath of loyalty to "Tsar Dmitry," after which many towns and regions quickly joined the insurrection. A large number of Tsar Feodor Borisovich's former commanders then rushed to join Dmitry's service. He allowed most of them to retain their high positions and privileges. See RFCW, 183–92.

268. Pushkin accurately paraphrases the Pretender Dmitry's conciliatory proclamation that Gavrila Pushkin read aloud to the assembled people on Red Square. Note that Pushkin was also aware that Patriarch Iov was not included in the list of officials invited to pay homage to Dmitry, who was camped near the capital by this time. (Iov had been a close friend of Boris Godunov and one of the Pretender Dmitry's greatest foes.) Instead, the Muscovites were invited to send the metropolitan, the second highest ranking church official. The "traitor" Iov was removed from office, roughed up, and banished to a remote monastery before Dmitry entered Moscow. See Massa, *Short History*, 104; Purchas, *Hakluytus Posthumus*, 14: 148–49; and RFCW, 194, 198.

269. During the Moscow rebellion on June 1, 1605, supporters of the Pretender Dmitry invaded the Kremlin, plundered the Godunov clan's palaces, and arrested Tsar Feodor Borisovich and his mother. The palace guard fled; nowhere did any guards, courtiers, troops, or boyars put up any resistance to the rebels – a clear indication that the Godunovs had lost control of the Kremlin itself as well as the capital. See PSRL, 14: 65; PSRL, 34: 204; Bussow, *Disturbed State*, 46; Massa, *Short History*, 105; Margeret, *Russian Empire*, 67; and RFCW, 195.

270. The Pretender Dmitry's request that the uprising be bloodless was generally honored. Relatives and high-profile supporters of the Godunovs were arrested but not killed, and their homes were looted. The only serious casualties were among the rebels themselves, of whom more than fifty died of over-drinking or fighting with one another over the spoils. See RFCW, 194–96.

271. As soon as the rebellion in Moscow quieted down, the boyars formally deposed Tsar Feodor Borisovich and proclaimed their support for Tsar Dmitry. Dmitry received this good news in his camp near Moscow and sent a delegation headed by Vasily Golitsyn and Peter Basmanov (two of the principal organizers of the rebellion of the tsar's army at Kromy) to receive the Muscovites' oath of allegiance to the new tsar and to prepare the capital for Tsar Dmitry's triumphal entry. As soon as the delegation arrived in Moscow, Golitsyn went to the Godunov palace and personally presided over the assassination of Feodor Borisovich and his mother. Golitsyn may have been accompanied by Prince Vasily M. Mosalsky, one of the commanders of Putivl who led that city's rebellion against Tsar Boris Godunov and subsequently became an important courtier of the Pretender Dmitry. It was Mosalsky who saved Dmitry

from certain death after the battle of Dobrynichi. See PSRL, 14: 66; and RFCW, 197.

272. According to the *New Chronicle*, the assassins Golitsyn and Mosalsky were assisted by Andrei Sherefedinov (a bureaucrat) and Mikhail Molchanov, an educated courtier who became a favorite of Tsar Dmitry. Dmitry's enemies later claimed that it was Molchanov's participation in the assassination of Feodor Borisovich that caused Dmitry to warm to him. (See PSRL, 14: 66; and RFCW, 204.) The "streltsy" involved in the assassination were Russian infantrymen (similar to musketeers).

273. Young Tsar Feodor Borisovich put up a good struggle before he was killed. He grappled with the assassins, kicking and screaming for help. Once the streltsy had him pinned down, one of the lords reached up under Feodor's robe "and seized him foully, with the grip of hands hardened to the use of battleaxes." Feodor roared with pain, struggled for a few more minutes, and then began to beg for a quick death. One of the assassins raised "a great stick and smote him about the shoulders." The noise of the prolonged struggle attracted a sizeable crowd, but no one attempted to intervene. See PSRL, 14: 66; Barbour, *Dimitry*, 126–27.

274. Feodor Borisovich and his mother were eventually strangled to death with rope, but it was falsely announced that they had committed suicide by taking poison. Although Dmitry's enemies claimed that the new tsar personally ordered the assassination of the Godunovs, there is no evidence to substantiate that charge. In fact, the bloodthirsty Golitsyn was quite capable of acting on his own, but Dmitry was probably relieved to have his rival eliminated before he entered Moscow. Ksenia Godunova was arrested and later forced to become a nun. See Bussow, *Disturbed State*, 47–48; Margeret, *Russian Empire*, 67; and RFCW, 197, 201.

275. There is no evidence that anyone mourned the passing of Feodor Borisovich and his hated mother. The remarkably passive response of the public to the news of their deaths (and the people's simultaneous celebration of Dmitry's triumph) was a clear sign that the Godunov dynasty had been delegitimized in the eyes of many Russians. No one had been willing to defend Tsar Feodor Borisovich during the rebellion of Moscow, and his assassination did not trigger a public outcry or even so much as a hint of popular resistance to the new regime. This was in remarkable contrast to the general reaction to Tsar Dmitry's assassination a year later – which triggered a civil war that raged for many years and nearly destroyed Russia. See RFCW, 197.

276. At the end of the *Komediia,* Pushkin accurately recorded the reaction of the *narod* to the accession of Tsar Dmitry. During his triumphal entry into Moscow, Tsar Dmitry was greeted by deafening shouts of joy and praise as "the true sun shining over Russia." When he entered the Kremlin accompanied by the bishops and boyars, hundreds of bells pealed and the crowd shouted, "Long live our Dimitry Ivanovich, Tsar of all the Russias." (See Bussow, *Disturbed State,* 49–50; Massa, *Short History,* 109–10; Purchas, *Hakluytus Posthumus,* 14: 161; and RFCW, 199.) The dramatic and historically correct final line of Pushkin's play was altered in the published version of *Boris Godunov* to the historically inaccurate but famous (and politically correct) phrase, "The people remain silent." The 1831 edition was also appropriately dedicated to Karamzin, whose ideology the play now much more closely resembled.

Bibliography

Abreviations

BG	Pushkin, *Boris Godunov: Tragediia*
Letters	Pushkin, *The Letters of Alexander Pushkin*
MERSH	*The Modern Encyclopedia of Russian and Soviet History*
PD	Institut russkoi literatury (Pushkinskii Dom) RAN. Rukopisnyi otdel
PS	Pushkin, *Polnoe sobranie sochinenii* (1937–59)
PSRL	*Polnoe sobranie russkikh letopisei*
RFCW	Dunning, *Russia's First Civil War*
RIB	*Russkaia istoricheskaia biblioteka*
SGGD	*Sobranie gosudarstvennykh gramot i dogovorov*
TL	Tsiavlovskii and Tarkhova, *Letopis' zhizni i tvorchestva Aleksandra Pushkina*

Archival Sources

Institut russkoi literatury (Pushkinskii Dom) Rossiiskoi Akademii Nauk (Institute of Russian Literature [Pushkin House] of the Russian Academy of Sciences).
Rukopisnyi otdel (Manuscript Division), St. Petersburg:
fond 244 (A. S. Pushkin fond),
opis' 1 (A. S. Pushkin's manuscripts),
No. 73, listy 1–10b (preliminary title of *Komediia*);
No. 302 (rough draft of a letter to Nicholas Raevsky [1829]);

No. 835 (Vtoraia masonskaia tetrad'),
   list 41 (a drawing of Karamzin among other drawings by Pushkin);
   listy 44–46, 470b-50, 520b, 55–56 (rough draft of first five scenes of
   Komediia);
No. 891, listy 1–51 (fair copy of *Komediia*);
opis' 16, No. 10, listy 10–17 (Third Section censor's report on *Komediia* [1826]);
opis' 25 (Lyceum materials related to A. S. Pushkin),
   No. 368 (A. M. Gorchakov's summary of lectures in Russian history).
Rossiiskii gosudarstvennyi istoricheskii arkhiv (Russian State Historical Archive),
St. Petersburg: Fondy Ministerstva narodnogo prosveshcheniia,
   fond 772 (Central directorate of censorship, 1828–1862),
      opis' 1, delo No. 2209 (Buturlin committee's secret report to Count S. S.
      Uvarov, 29 January 1849).

Published Primary and Secondary Sources

Abramkin, V. M. "Pushkin v dramaticheskoi tsenzure (1828–1917)." *Literaturnyi arkhiv: materialy po istorii literatury i obshchestvennogo dvizheniia,* vol. 1 (1938): 230–59.

Abramovich, G. V. *Kniaz'ia Shuiskie i Rossiiskii tron.* Leningrad: Izdatel'stvo Leningradskogo universiteta, 1991.

Alekseev, M. P. "A. S. Pushkin." In Alekseev, ed., *Shekspir i russkaia kul'tura,* 162–200.

———. "Boris Godunov i Dmitrii Samozvanets v zapadnoevropeiskoi dramy." In Derzhavin, ed., *"Boris Godunov" A. S. Pushkina,* 81–124.

———. *Ocherki istorii Ispano-Russkikh literaturnykh otnoshenii XVI-XIX vv.* Leningrad: Izd-vo Leningradskogo universiteta, 1964.

———. *Pushkin: Sravnitel'no-istoricheskie issledovaniia.* Leningrad: Nauka, 1984.

———. "Remarka Pushkina 'Narod bezmolvstvuet' v 'Borise Godunove.'" *Russkaia literatura,* no. 2 (1967): 36–58.

———, ed. *Shekspir i russkaia kul'tura.* Moscow-Leningrad: Nauka, 1965.

Annenkov, P. V. *The Extraordinary Decade: Literary Memoirs.* Ann Arbor: University of Michigan Press, 1968.

———. *Pushkin v Aleksandrovskuiu epokhu.* Minsk: Limarius, 1998.

———. *P. V. Annenkov i ego druz'ia.* St. Petersburg: Izd. A. S. Suvorina, 1892.

———. *Vospominaniia i kriticheskie ocherki: sobranie statei i zametok, 1849–1868 gg.* 3 vols. St. Petersburg: M. M. Stasiulovich, 1877–81.

Aranovskaia, O. P. "O vine Borisa Godunova v tragedii Pushkina." *Vestnik russkogo khristianskogo dvizheniia,* no. 143 (1984, iv): 128–56.

Arinshtein, L. M. "K istorii vysylki Pushkina iz Odessy: Legendy i fakty." In *Pushkin. Issledovaniia i materialy,* vol. 10: 286–304. Leningrad: Nauka, 1982.

Arkhangel'skii, A. N. "Poet – Istoriia – Vlast' ('Boris Godunov' A. S. Pushkina)." In *Pushkin i sovremennaia kul'tura,* 123–37. Moscow: Nauka, 1996.

Arkhangel'skii, K. P. "Problema stseny v dramakh Pushkina (1830–1930)." *Trudy Dal'nevostochnogo pedagogicheskogo instituta,* series 7, no. 1/6 (1930): 5–16.

Ashukin, N. S. *Pushkinskaia Moskva.* St. Petersburg: Akademicheskii proekt, 1998.

Averintsev, Sergei. "Bakhtin, Laughter, and Christian Culture." In Susan Felch and Paul J. Contino, eds., *Bakhtin and Religion: A Feeling for Faith,* 79–95. Evanston: Northwestern University Press, 2001.

Avrich, Paul. *Russian Rebels, 1600–1800.* New York: Norton, 1972.

Badalich, I. M., and V. D. Kuz'mina. *Pamiatniki russkoi shkol'noi dramy XVIII veka (po zagrebskim spiskam).* Moscow: Nauka, 1968.

Baer, Brian James. "Between Public and Private: Re-Figuring Politics in Pushkin's *Boris Godunov.*" *Pushkin Review/Pushkinskii vestnik* 2 (1999): 25–44.

Bakhtin, M. M. *Estetika slovesnogo tvorchestva.* Moscow: Iskusstvo, 1979.

———. *Rabelais and His World.* Translated by Hélène Iswolsky. Bloomington: Indiana University Press, 1984.

———. *Speech Genres and Other Late Essays.* Translated by Vern W. McGee. Edited by Caryl Emerson and Michael Holquist. Austin: University of Texas Press, 1976.

———. *Tvorchestvo Fransua Rable i narodnaia kul'tura srednevekov'ia i Renessansa.* Moscow: Khudozhestvennaia literatura, 1965.

Balashov, N. I. "'Boris Godunov' Pushkina: Osnovy dramaticheskoi struktury." *Literatury i iazyka* 39, no. 3 (1980): 205–18.

Barbour, Philip. *Dimitry Called the Pretender.* Boston: Houghton Mifflin, 1966.

Baron, Samuel H., and Nancy Shields Kollmann, eds. *Religion and Culture in Early Modern Russia and Ukraine.* De Kalb: Northern Illinois University Press, 1997.

Barsukov, Nikolai. *Zhizn' i trudy M. P. Pogodina.* 22 vols. St. Petersburg: Tip. M. M. Stasiulevicha, 1888–1910.

[Bartenev, P. I.] "Iz pisem A. F. Voeikova k B. M. Perevoshchikovu." *Russkii Arkhiv,* 1890, kniga 3, No. 9: 89–94.

Bayley, John. *Pushkin: A Comparative Commentary.* Cambridge: Cambridge University Press, 1971.

Bazilevich, K. V. "*Boris Godunov* v izobrazhenii Pushkina." *Istoricheskie zapiski* 1 (1937): 29–54.

Belinskii, V. G. *O drame i teatre.* 2 vols. Moscow: Iskusstvo, 1983.

———. *Sochineniia Aleksandra Pushkina.* Moscow: Detgiz, 1961.

———. *Stat'i V. G. Belinskago ob A. S. Pushkine.* Moscow: Tip. T-va I. D. Sytina, 1899.

Belkin, A. A. *Russkii dramaticheskii teatr.* Moscow: Prosveshchenie, 1976.

Berry, Lloyd, and Robert O. Crummey, eds. *Rude and Barbarous Kingdom: Russia in the Accounts of Sixteenth-Century English Voyagers.* Madison: University of Wisconsin Press, 1968.

Bethea, David. "The [Hi]story of the Village Gorjuxino: In Praise of Pushkin's Folly." *Slavic and East European Journal* 28, no. 3 (1984): 291–309.

———. "Pushkin: From Byron to Shakespeare." In Neil Cornwall, ed., *The Routledge Companion to Russian Literature,* 74–88. London and New York, 2001.

———. "Pushkin's Pretenders: From the Poet in Society to the Poet in History."

In Peter Rollberg, ed., *And Meaning for a Life Entire: Festschrift for Charles A. Moser...*, 61–74. Columbus, OH: Slavica, 1997.

———, ed. *Pushkin Today.* Bloomington: Indiana University Press, 1993.

———. *Realizing Metaphors: Alexander Pushkin and the Life of the Poet.* Madison: University of Wisconsin Press, 1998.

Billington, James H. *The Icon and the Axe: An Interpretive History of Russian Culture.* New York: Knopf, 1966.

Binyon, T. J. *Pushkin: A Biography.* London: HarperCollins, 2002.

Bitsilli, P. "Pushkin i Nikolai I." *Moskovskii Pushkinist* 3 (1996): 314–22.

Black, J. L., ed. *Essays on Karamzin: Russian Man-of-Letters, Political Thinker, Historian, 1766–1826.* The Hague and Paris: Mouton, 1975.

———. *Nicholas Karamzin and Russian Society in the Nineteenth Century.* Toronto: University of Toronto Press, 1975.

———. "The *Primechanija:* Karamzin as a 'Scientific' Historian of Russia." In Black, ed., *Essays,* 127–47.

Blagoi, D. D. *Masterstvo Pushkina.* Moscow: Sovetskii pisatel', 1955.

———. *Ot Kantemira do nashikh dnei.* 2 vols. Moscow: Khudozhestvennaia literatura, 1972–73.

———. *Sotsiologiia tvorchestva Pushkina: etiudy.* Moscow: Izd-vo Federatsiia, 1929.

———. *Tvorcheskii put' Pushkina (1813–1826).* Moscow and Leningrad: Izd. AN SSSR, 1950.

———. *Tvorcheskii put' Pushkina (1826–1830).* Moscow: Sovetskii pisatel', 1967.

Blake, Elizabeth Ann. "F. M. Dostoevskii's Dialogue with the Time of Troubles Narratives: Reading the Russo-Polish Tensions of the 1860s through the Lens of History." Ph.D. diss., Ohio State University, 2001.

Blok, G. P. *Pushkin v rabote nad istoricheskimi istochnikami.* Moscow: Izd-vo Akademii nauk SSSR, 1949.

Bocharov, S. G. *Siuzhety russkoi literatury.* Moscow: Iazyk russkoi kul'tury, 1999.

Bochkarev, V. A. *Russkaia istoricheskaia dramaturgiia perioda podgotovki vosstaniia dekabristov (1816–1825 gg.).* [*Uchenye zapiski,* no. 56.] Kyibyshev: Kyibyshevskii gos. ped. instituta imeni V. V. Kyibysheva, 1968.

———. *Tragediia A. S. Pushkina 'Boris Godunov' i otechestvennaia literaturnaia traditsiia.* Samara: Izd-vo Sam GPI, 1993.

Bogaevskaia, K. "Pervye chteniia 'Borisa Godunova.'" *Nauka i zhizn'* 11 (1972): 46–47.

Bondi, S. M. "Dramaticheskie proizvedeniia Pushkina." In A. S. Pushkin, *Polnoe sobranie sochinenii v desiati tomakh,* vol. 4, 480–515. Moscow: Izd. AN SSSR, 1975.

———. "Dramaturgiia Pushkina i russkaia dramaturgiia XIX veka." In *Pushkin: Rodonachal'nik novoi russkoi literatury,* 365–436

———. *O Pushkine: stat'i i issledovanie.* Moscow: Khudozhestvennaia literatura, 1978.

Bowersock, G. W. "The Roman Emperor as Russian Tsar: Tacitus and Pushkin." *Proceedings of the American Philosophical Society* 143, no. 1 (March 1999): 130–47.

Brandenberger, David. "'The People's Poet': Russocentric Populism during the USSR's Official 1937 Pushkin Commemoration." *Russian History* 26, no. 1 (Spring 1999): 65–73.

Briggs, Anthony D. P. *Alexander Pushkin: A Critical Study.* London: Croom Helm, 1983.

——. "The Hidden Forces of Unification in *Boris Godunov.*" *New Zealand Slavonic Journal,* no. 1 (1974): 43–54.

Brodskii, N. L., and V. V. Golubkov, eds. *Pushkin v shkole: sbornik statei.* Moscow: Izdatel'stvo Akademii pedogicheskikh nauk RSFSR, 1951.

Brody, Ervin C. *The Demetrius Legend and Its Treatment in the Age of the Baroque.* Cranbury, NJ: Farleigh Dickenson University Press, 1972.

——. "Pushkin's 'Boris Godunov': The First Modern Russian Historical Drama." *The Modern Language Review* 72, no. 4 (October 1977): 857–75.

——. "Schiller's 'Demetrius' and Pushkin's 'Boris Godunov': A Contemporary Interpretation." *Neohelican Review* 1, nos. 3–4 (Fall-Winter 1984): 241–94.

Brok, G. *Pushkin v rabote nad istoricheskimi istochnikami.* Moscow and Leningrad: Izd. AN SSSR, 1949.

Brooks, Jeffrey. "Russian Nationalism and Russian Literature: The Canonization of the Classics." In Ivo Banac, John G. Ackerman, and Roman Szporluk, eds., *Nation and Ideology: Essays in Honor of Wayne S. Vucinich,* 315–34. New York: Columbia University Press, 1981.

Brown, William Edward. *A History of Russian Literature of the Romantic Period.* 4 vols. Ann Arbor: Ardis, 1986.

Brun-Zejmis, Julia. "Chaadaev and Pushkin." Ph.D. diss., University of Texas at Austin, 1973.

Budgen, David. "Pushkin and Chaadaev: The History of a Friendship." In Richard Freeborn and Jane Grayson, eds., *Ideology in Russian Literature,* 7–46. New York: St. Martin's Press, 1990.

Bulgarin, Faddei. *Dimitrii Samozvanets, Istoricheskii roman.* 4 vols. 2nd ed. St. Petersburg: Tip. A. Smirdina, 1830.

——. "Marina Mnishek, supruga Dimitriia Samozvantsa." *Severnyi arkhiv,* 1824, no. 1: 1–13; no. 2: 59–73; no. 20: 55–77; no. 21: 111–37.

——, ed. *Ruskaia Taliia: podarok liubiteliam i liubitel'nitsam otechestvennago teatra na 1825 god.* St. Petersburg: Tip. N. Grecha, 1825.

Bushkovitch, Paul. "Taxation, Tax Farming, and Merchants in Sixteenth-Century Russia." *Slavic Review* 37, no. 3 (1978): 381–98.

Bussow, Conrad. *The Disturbed State of the Russian Realm.* Translated and edited by G. Edward Orchard. Montreal: McGill-Queen's University Press, 1994.

Chereiskii, L. *Pushkin i ego okruzhenie.* 2nd ed. Leningrad: Nauka, 1988.

Cherepnin, L. V. "Istoriia v tvorchestve A. S. Pushkina." *Voprosy istorii,* no. 9 (1963): 25–44.

Cherniavsky, Michael. "Holy Russia: A Study in the History of an Idea." *American Historical Review* 63 (April 1958): 617–37.

Chernyshev, V. "Pesnia Varlaama." In *Pushkin i ego sovremenniki,* vyp. V, 127–29. St. Petersburg: Imperatorskaia akademiia nauk, 1907.

Chkheidze, Anna. *"Istoriia Pugacheva" A. S. Pushkina.* Tbilisi: Izd. SSR Gruzii, 1963.

Chukovskii, K. I. *Dnevnik.* 2 vols. Moscow: Sovremennyi pisatel', 1991–94.

Clayton, J. Douglas. *Dimitry's Shade: A Reading of Alexander Pushkin's* Boris Godunov. Evanston: Northwestern University Press, 2004.

Cooke, Brett, and Chester Dunning. "Tempting Fate: Defiance and Subversion in the Writing of *Boris Godunov.*" *Pushkin Review/Pushinskii vestnik* 3 (2000): 43–63.

Cross, Anthony Glenn. *N. M. Karamzin: A Study of His Literary Career, 1783–1803.* Carbondale: Southern Illinois University Press, 1971.

Crummey, Robert O. *The Formation of Muscovy, 1304–1613.* London: Longman, 1987.

———. "The Silence of Muscovy." *The Russian Review* 46, no. 2 (1987): 157–64.

Custine, Astolphe, marquis de. *Letters from Russia.* London: Penguin Books, 1991.

Davydov, Sergei. "Pushkin's Easter Triptych." In Bethea, ed., *Pushkin Today,* 38–58.

Debreczeny, Paul, ed. *Alexander Pushkin: Complete Prose Fiction.* Stanford: Stanford University Press, 1983.

———. "*Boris Godunov* at the Taganka: A Note on a Non-Performance." *Slavonic and East European Journal* 28, no.1 (Spring 1984): 99–101.

———. *The Other Pushkin: A Study of Alexander Pushkin's Prose Fiction.* Stanford: Stanford University Press, 1983.

———. *Social Functions of Literature: Alexander Pushkin and Russian Culture.* Stanford: Stanford University Press, 1997.

Dela III-go otdeleniia sobstvennoi ego imperatorskogo velichestva kantseliarii ob Aleksandre Sergeeviche Pushkine. St. Petersburg: Izd. I. Balashova, 1906.

Del'vig, A. I. *Polveka russkoi zhizni: vospominaniia A. I Del'viga, 1820–1870.* 2 vols. Moscow: Academia, 1930.

Derzhavin, K. N., ed. *"Boris Godunov" A. S. Pushkina: sbornik statei.* Leningrad: Gosudarstvennyi akademicheskii teatr dramy, 1936.

Dinega, Alyssa. "Ambiguity as Agent in Pushkin's and Shakespeare's Historical Tragedies." *Slavic Review* 55, no. 3 (Fall 1996): 525–51.

"Dnevnik Samuila Maskevicha, byvshago v Rossii vo vremia Vtorago Samozvantsa, nazyvaemago Tushinskim Vorom." *Severnyi arkhiv,* 1825, no. 1: 3–20; no. 2: 109–33; no. 3: 221–41; no. 7: 117–36; no. 8: 217–45.

Doldobanov, G. I., and A. A. Makarov. *Khronika zhizni i tvorchestva A. S. Pushkina v trekh tomakh, 1826–1837.* 3 vols. Moscow: RAN, 2000.

Dolinin, Alexander. "Historicism or Providentialism? Pushkin's *History of Pugachev* in the Context of French Romantic Historiography." *Slavic Review* 58, no. 2 (Summer 1999): 291–308.

———. *Russkie pisateli XIX veka o Pushkine.* Leningrad: Khudozh. lit-ra, 1938.

Donchin, Georgette. "Pushkin." In Richard Freeborn, ed., *Russian Literary Attitudes from Pushkin to Solzhenitsyn,* 19–38. London: Macmillan, 1976.

Drevniaia Rossiiskaia Vivliofika. 2nd ed. 20 vols. Edited by N. Novikov. Moscow: Tip. Kompanii Tipograficheskoi, 1788–91.

Driver, Sam. *Pushkin: Literature and Social Ideas.* New York: Columbia University Press, 1989.

Dunning, Chester. "Cossacks and the Southern Frontier in the Time of Troubles." *Russian History* 19 (1992): 57–74.

————. "Rethinking the Canonical Text of Pushkin's *Boris Godunov*." *The Russian Review* 60, no. 4 (October 2001): 569–91.

————. *Russia's First Civil War: The Time of Troubles and the Founding of the Romanov Dynasty.* University Park: Penn State Press, 2001.

————. "The Use and Abuse of the First Printed French Account of Russia." *Russian History* 10, part 3 (1983): 357–80.

————. "Who Was Tsar Dmitrii?" *Slavic Review* 60, no. 4 (Winter 2001): 705–29.

Dyck, J. W. "Deceit and Conviction in the False Demetrius: Schiller – Pushkin – Hebbel." In *Probleme der Komparatistik und Interpretation*, 96–110. Bonn: Bouvier, 1978.

Dymshits, A. L., ed. *Pushkin v vospominaniiakh sovremennikov.* [Leningrad]: Gos. izd-vo khudozh. lit-ry, 1950.

Edmonds, Robin. *Pushkin: The Man and His Age.* New York: St. Martin's Press, 1994.

Eidel'man, Natan. *Iz potaennoi istorii Rossii XVIII-XIX vekov.* Moscow: Vysshaia shkola, 1993.

————. *Pushkin, istoriia i sovremennost' v khudozhestvennom soznanii poeta.* Moscow: Sovetskii pisatel', 1984.

————. *Stat'i o Pushkine.* Moscow: Novoe literaturnoe obozrenie, 2000.

Emerson, Caryl. *Boris Godunov: Transpositions of a Russian Theme.* Bloomington: Indiana University Press, 1986.

————. "Pretenders to History: Four Plays for Undoing Pushkin's *Boris Godunov*." *Slavic Review* 44, no. 2 (Summer 1985): 257–79.

————. "Pushkin, Literary Criticism, and Creativity in Closed Places." *New Literary History* 29, no. 4 (Autumn 1998): 653–72.

————. "'The Queen of Spades' and the Open End." In Bethea, ed., *Pushkin Today,* 31–37.

Emerson, Caryl, and Robert William Oldani. *Modest Musorgsky and Boris Godunov: Myths, Realities, Reconsiderations.* Cambridge: Cambridge University Press, 1994.

Engel'gardt, B. N. "Istorizm Pushkina." In Vengerov, ed., *Istoriko-literaturnyi sbornik,* 2: 58–75.

Entsiklopedicheskii slovar'. 82 vols. St. Petersburg: F. A. Brokgauz, I. A. Efron, 1890–1904.

Ershoff, G. "Prizhiznennaia izvestnost' Pushkina v Germanii." *Vremennik Pushkinskoi komissii* 21 (1987): 68–78.

Etkind, Efim. "'Sei ratnik, vol'nost'iu venchannyi': Grishka Otrep'ev, imperator Napoleon, marshal Nei, i drugie." *Revue des études slaves* 59 (1987): 55–62.

Evdokimova, Svetlana. *Pushkin's Historical Imagination.* New Haven: Yale University Press, 1999.

Fedorov, Boris M. *Kniaz' Kurbskii; istoricheskii roman iz sobytii XVI veka.* St. Petersburg: V tip. Imp. akademii nauk, 1843.

Feinberg, Il'ia. *Chitaia tetradi Pushkina.* Moscow: Sovetskii pisatel', 1985.

Feinstein, Elaine. *Pushkin: A Biography.* Hopewell, NJ: Ecco Press, 1999.

Fel'dman, O. M. *Sud'ba dramaturgii Pushkina.* Moscow: Iskusstvo, 1975.

Fennell, John, ed. *The Correspondence Between Prince A. M. Kurbsky and Tsar Ivan IV of Russia 1564–1579*. Cambridge: Cambridge University Press, 1963.

———, ed. *Prince A. M. Kurbsky's History of Ivan IV*. Cambridge: Cambridge University Press, 1965.

———. "Pushkin." In Harold Bloom, ed., *Alexander Pushkin: Modern Critical Views*, 73–116. New York: Chelsea House, 1987.

Fevral'skii, A. "Prokof'ev i Meierkhol'd." In *Sergei Prokofiev: Stat'i i materialy*, 2nd ed., 94–120. Moscow: Muzyka, 1965.

Filippova, N. F. *Narodnaia drama A. S. Pushkina 'Boris Godunov.'* Moscow: Kniga, 1972.

Filonov, Andrei. *Boris Godunov A. S. Pushkina: Opyt razbora so storony istoricheskoi i esteticheskoi*. St. Petersburg: Tip. Glazunova, 1899.

Fischer, Rudolf. "Schiller und Puschkin." *Weimarer Beiträge* 3 [*Zeitschrift für Deutsche Literaturgeschichte*]: 603–11. Weimar: Arion Verlag, 1960.

Flynn, James T. "S. S. Uvarov's 'Liberal' Years." *Jahrbücher für Geschichte Osteuropas* 20, no. 4 (1972): 481–91.

Fomichev, S. A. "Dramaturgiia A. S. Pushkina." In *Istoriia russkoi dramaturgii: XVII – pervaia polovina XIX veka*, 261–95.

———. "Neizvestnaia p'esa A. S. Pushkina." In Pushkin, *Komediia*, 236–49.

———. *Prazdnik zhizni: Etiudy o Pushkine*. St. Petersburg: Nauka, 1995.

———. "Zvezda plenitel'nogo schast'ia." *Russkaia rech'*, no. 2 (1993): 3–7.

Foote, I. P. "The St. Petersburg Censorship Committee, 1828–1905." *Oxford Slavonic Papers*, new series, 24 (1991): 60–120.

Frick, David A. "Misrepresentations, Misunderstandings, and Silences: Problems of Seventeenth-Century Ruthenian and Muscovite Cultural History." In Baron and Kollmann, eds., *Religion and Culture in Early Modern Russia and Ukraine*, 149–68.

Gasparov, Boris, Robert P. Hughes, and Irina Paperno, eds. *Cultural Mythologies of Russian Modernism: From the Golden Age to the Silver Age*. Berkeley: University of California Press, 1992.

Geichenko, S. S. *U lukomor'ia: rasskazyvaet khranitel' Pushkinskogo zapovednika*. 3rd ed. Leningrad: Lenizdat, 1977.

Gennadi, Grigorii, ed. *Prilozheniia k sochineniiam A. S. Pushkina*. St. Petersburg: Izd. Ia. A. Isakova, 1860.

Gifford, Henry. "Shakespearean Elements in *Boris Godunov*." *Slavonic and East European Review* 26 (1947–48): 152–60.

Gillel'son, M. I. *Molodoi Pushkin i arzamasskoe bratstvo*. Leningrad: Nauka, 1974.

———. *Ot arzamasskogo bratstva k pushkinskomu krugu pisatelei*. Leningrad: Nauka, 1977.

Gippius, V. "Pushkin v bor'be s Bulgarinym v 1830–1831 gg." *A. S. Pushkin: Vremennik pushkinskoi komissii* 6 (1941): 235–55.

Gladkov, Aleksandr. *Meierkhol'd*. Moscow: STD RSFSR, 1990.

Golovin, V. V. *Russkaia kolybel'naia pesnia v fol'klore i v literature*. Åbo: Åbo Akademis Förlag, 2000.

Gordin, A. M. *Pushkin v Mikhailovskom*. Leningrad: Lenizdat, 1989.

Gorodetskii, B. P. "'Boris Godunov' v tvorchestve Pushkina." In Derzhavin, ed., *"Boris Godunov" A. S. Pushkina*, 7–41.

―――. *Dramaturgiia Pushkina*. Moscow: AN SSSR, 1953.

―――. "Kto zhe byl tsenzorom 'Borisa Godunova' v 1826 godu?" *Russkaia literatura*, no. 4 (1967): 109–19.

―――. *Tragediia A. S. Pushkina 'Boris Godunov.' Kommentarii.* Leningrad: Prosveshchenie, 1969.

Gorodetskii, B. P., N. V. Izmailov, and B. S. Meilakh, eds. *Pushkin: Itogi i problemy izucheniia.* Moscow: Nauka, 1966.

Gozenpud, A. A. "Iz istorii literaturno-obshchestvennoi bor'by 20kh-30kh godov XIX v. ('Boris Godunov' i 'Dmitrii Samozvanets')." In *Pushkin: Issledovaniia i materialy*, vol. 6, 252–75. Leningrad: Nauka, 1969.

―――. "O stsenichnosti i teatral'noi sud'be *Borisa Godunova*." In *Pushkin: Issledovaniia i materialy*, vol. 5: 339–56. Leningrad: Nauka, 1967.

Granovskaia, N. "Iurodivyi v tragedii Pushkina." *Russkaia literatura*, no. 2 (1964): 92–94.

Great Soviet Encyclopedia. 3rd ed. Vol. 27. New York: Macmillan, 1981.

Grech, N. I. *Zapiski o moei zhizni*. Edited by E. G. Kapustina. Moscow: Kniga, 1990.

Greenleaf, Monika. *Pushkin and Romantic Fashion: Fragment, Elegy, Orient, Irony.* Stanford: Stanford University Press, 1994.

―――. "Tynianov, Pushkin and the Fragment: Through the Lens of Montage." In Gasparov, Hughes, and Paperno, eds., *Cultural Mythologies*, 264–92.

Grekov, V. D. "Istoricheskie vozzreniia Pushkina." *Istoricheskie zapiski*, no. 1 (1937): 3–28.

Grinchenko, N. A. "Istoriia tsenzurnykh uchrezhdenii v Rossii v pervoi polovine XIX veka." In *Tsenzura v Rossii: Istoriia i sovremennost': Sbornik nauchnykh trudov*, part 1, 15–46. St. Petersburg: Rossiiskaia Natsional'naia Biblioteka, 2001.

Grossman, Leonid. *Dostoevskii*. Moscow: Molodaia gvardiia, 1962.

Grushkin, A. *K voprosu o klassovoi sushchnosti Pushkinskogo tvorchestva.* [Leningrad]: Gos. izd. khudozhestvennoi lit., 1931.

Gukovskii, G. A. *Pushkin i problemy realisticheskogo stila.* Moscow: Izd-vo khudozh. lit-ry, 1957.

Gurevich, A. M. "Istoriia i sovremennost' v 'Borise Godunove.'" *Izvestiia Akademii nauk SSSR. Seriia literatury i iazyka* 43, no. 3 (1984): 204–14.

Helfant, Ian M. "Pushkin's Ironic Performance as a Gambler." *Slavic Review* 58, no. 2 (1999): 371–92.

Hellie, Richard. *Enserfment and Military Change in Muscovy*. Chicago: University of Chicago Press, 1971.

―――. *Slavery in Russia, 1450–1725*. Chicago: University of Chicago Press, 1982.

Hernadi, Paul. *Interpreting Events: Tragicomedies of History on the Modern Stage*. Ithaca: Cornell University Press, 1985.

Hirst, David L. *Tragicomedy*. London and New York: Methuen, 1984.

Holborn, Hajo. *A History of Modern Germany, 1648–1840*. New York: Alfred A. Knopf, 1964.

Hollingsworth, Barry. "Arzamas: Portrait of a Literary Society." *Slavonic and East European Review* 44 (1966): 306–26.

Horowitz, Brian. "Thus Spoke *Moskovskii Pushkinist*: Aleksandr Pushkin in Contemporary Russian Scholarship." *Slavic Review* 58, no. 2 (Summer 1999): 434–39.

Hunt, Priscilla. "Ivan IV's Mythology of Kingship." *Slavic Review* 52, no. 4 (Winter 1993): 769–809.

Iakovlev, A. "Bezumnoe molchanie." In *Sbornik statei, posviashchennykh Vasiliiu Osipovichu Kliuchevskomu*, 651–78. Moscow: S. P. Iakovlev, 1909.

Istoriia russkogo dramaticheskogo teatra. 7 vols. Edited by Iu. Dmitriev and E. Kholodov. Moscow: Iskusstvo, 1977–87.

Istoriia russkoi dramaturgii: XVII – pervaia polovina XIX veka. Edited by Iu. Gerasimov, L. M. Lotman, and F. Ia. Priima. Leningrad: Nauka, 1982.

Izmailov, N. V. "Pushkin i semeistvo Karamzinykh." In *Pushkin v pis'makh Karamzinykh 1836–1837 godov*, 11–48. Moscow and Leningrad: Izd. AN SSSR, 1960.

"Iz materialov Pushkinskogo Litseia." In *Pushkin: Issledovaniia i materialy*, vol. 8, 306–45. Leningrad: Nauka, 1989.

Jackson, Robert Louis. *Dostoevsky's Quest for Form*. New Haven: Yale University Press, 1966.

Kahn, Andrew. "The New Academy Pushkin: Toward a Definitive Text." *Slavic Review* 58, no. 2 (Summer 1999): 428–33.

Karamzin, Nikolai Mikhailovich. *Istoriia gosudarstva Rossiiskago*. 12 vols. 1st ed. St. Petersburg: Voennaia tip. Glav. shtaba, 1816–29.

———. *Istoriia gosudarstva Rossiiskago*. 12 vols. 2nd ed., with corrections. St. Petersburg: Tip. N. Grecha, 1818–29.

———. *Istoriia gosudarstva Rossiiskago*. 12 vols. St. Petersburg: Izdanie Evr. Evdokimova, 1892.

———. *Pis'ma N. M. Karamzina k I. I. Dmitrievu*. St. Petersburg: V tip. Imp. akademii nauk, 1866.

———. *Predaniia vekov*. Edited by G. P. Makagonenko. Moscow: Pravda, 1987.

Karlinsky, Simon. *Russian Drama from Its Beginnings to the Age of Pushkin*. Berkeley: University of California Press, 1985.

Katenin, P. A. "Neustanovlennomu litsu." *Literaturnoe nasledstvo* 58 (1952): 101–2.

Keenan, Edward L. *The Kurbskii-Groznyi Apocrypha: The Seventeenth-Century Genesis of the "Correspondence" Attributed to Prince A. M. Kurbskii and Tsar Ivan IV*. Cambridge, MA: Harvard University Press, 1971.

———. "Muscovite Political Folkways." *The Russian Review* 45, no. 2 (1986): 115–81.

Kelly, Laurence. *Diplomacy and Murder in Tehran: Alexander Griboyedov and Imperial Russia's Mission to the Shah of Persia*. London and New York: I. B. Tauris, 2002.

Kermode, Frank. *The Art of Telling*. Cambridge, MA: Harvard University Press, 1983.

Khokhlenko, Iu. I. *Skazaniia o predkakh Pushkina*. Moscow: "Academiia," 2000.

Khomiakov, A. S. *Stikhotvoreniia i dramy*. Leningrad: Sov. pisatel', 1969.

Kireevskii, I. V. *Polnoe sobranie sochinenii*. 2 vols. Moscow: Tip. Imp. Moskovskago Universiteta, 1911.

Klein, V., ed., *Uglicheskoe sledstvennoe delo o smerti tsarevicha Dimitriia 15-go maia 1591 goda.* Moscow: Arkheologicheskii institut, 1913.

Kochetkova, Natalya. *Nikolay Karamzin.* Boston: Twayne, 1975.

Koepnick, Thomas Louis. "The Journalistic Careers of F. V. Bulgarin and N. I. Grech: Publicism and Politics in Tsarist Russia, 1812–1859." Ph.D. diss., Ohio State University, 1976.

Koliupanov, N. P. *Biografiia Aleksandra Ivanovicha Kosheleva.* 2 vols. Moscow: O. F. Koshelovoi, 1889–92.

Kollmann, Nancy Shields. *By Honor Bound: State and Society in Early Modern Russia.* Ithaca: Cornell University Press, 1999.

———. "The Seclusion of Elite Women in Muscovy." *Russian History* 10, part. 2 (1983); 170–87.

Koretskii, V. I. "Golod 1601–1603 gg. v Rossii i tserkov." In *Voprosy istorii religii i ateizma. Sbornik statei,* vol. 7: 218–56. Moscow: Izd. AN SSSR, 1959.

———. "Novoe o krest'ianskom zakreposhchenii i vosstanie I. I. Bolotnikova." *Voprosy istorii,* no. 5 (1971): 130–52.

Kornblatt, Judith Deutsch. *The Cossack Hero in Russian Literature: A Study in Cultural Mythology.* Madison: University of Wisconsin Press, 1992.

Kostka, Edmund. *Schiller in Russian Literature.* Philadelphia: University of Pennsylvania Press, 1965.

Kotliarevskii, N. A. *Literaturnye napravleniia Aleksandrovskoi epokhi.* St. Petersburg: Tip. M. M. Stasiulevicha, 1913.

Kozlov, V. P. "Polemika vokrug 'Istorii gosudarstva Rossiiskogo' N. M. Karamzina v otechestvennoi periodike (1818–1830 gg.)." *Istoriia SSSR,* no. 5 (1984): 88–102.

Krasukhin, G. G. *Pushkin – Boldino, 1833: Novoe prochtenie.* Moscow: Flinta, 1977.

Kropf, David Glenn. *Authorship as Alchemy: Subversive Writing in Pushkin, Scott, and Hoffmann.* Stanford: Stanford University Press, 1994.

Kunin, V. V., ed. *Zhizn' Pushkina: Perepiska, Vospominaniia, Dnevniki: rasskazannaia im samim i ego sovremennikami.* 2 vols. Moscow: Pravda, 1987.

Lacombe, Jacques. *Histoire des revolutions de l'empire de Russie.* Amsterdam: Aux depens de la compagnie, 1760.

Lavrin, Janko. *A Panorama of Russian Literature.* London: University of London Press, 1973.

———. *Pushkin and Russian Literature.* New York: Russell and Russell, 1947.

Leach, Robert, and Victor Borovsky, eds. *A History of Russian Theatre.* Cambridge: Cambridge University Press, 1999.

Lednicki, Venceslas. *Pouchkine et la Pologne: A propos de la trilogie antipolonaise de Pouchkine.* Paris: Libraire Ernest Leroux, 1928.

Lemke, M. K. *Nikolaevskie zhandarmy i literatura 1826–1855 gg.* St. Petersburg: S. V. Bunin, 1908.

———. *Ocherki po istorii russkoi tsenzury i zhurnalistiki XIX stoletiia.* St. Petersburg: Trud, 1904.

Letopis' o mnogikh miatezhakh i o razorenii Moskovskago gosudarstva …. St. Petersburg, 1788.

Levesque, Pierre Charles. *Histoire de Russie.* 5 vols. Paris: Debure l'aîné, 1782.

Levin, Iu. D. "Literatura dekabristskogo napravleniia." In M. P. Alekseev, ed., *Shekspir i russkaia kul'tura,* 129–62.

———. "Nekotorye voprosy Shekspirizma Pushkina." In *Pushkin: Issledovaniia i materialy,* vol. 7: 58–85. Leningrad: Nauka, 1974.

———. *Shekspir i russkaia literatura XIX veka.* Leningrad: Nauka, 1988.

Levitt, Marcus C. "Pushkin in 1899." In Gasparov, Hughes, and Paperno, eds., *Cultural Mythology,* 183–203.

———. *Russian Literary Politics and the Pushkin Celebration of 1880.* Ithaca: Cornell University Press, 1989.

Levkovich, Ia. L. "Kavkazskii dnevnik Pushkina." In *Pushkin: Issledovaniia i materialy,* vol. 11: 5–26. Leningrad: Nauka, 1983.

Leyda, Jay, and Sergei Bertensson, eds. *The Musorgsky Reader.* New York: Da Capo Press, 1970.

Likhachev, D. S., and A. M. Panchenko. *"Smekhovoi mir" drevnei Rusi.* Leningrad: Nauka, 1976.

Likhachev, D. S., A. M. Panchenko, and N. V. Ponyrko. *Smekh v drevnei Rusi.* Leningrad: Nauka, 1984.

Lincoln, W. Bruce. *Between Heaven and Hell: The Story of a Thousand Years of Artistic Life in Russia.* New York: Penguin Books, 1998.

———. *Nicholas I: Emperor and Autocrat of All the Russias.* Bloomington: Indiana University Press, 1978.

Lindenberger, Herbert. *Historical Drama: The Relationship of Literature to Reality.* Chicago: University of Chicago Press, 1975.

Listov, V. S. "Pushkin i pol'skoe vosstanie 1830–1831 gg." *Moskovskii Pushkinist* 6 (1999): 285–91.

Listov, V. S., and N. A. Tarkhova. "K istorii remarki 'Narod bezmolvstvuet' v 'Borise Godunove.'" In *Vremennik Pushkinskoi komissii. 1979,* 96–102. Leningrad: Nauka, 1982.

Litvinenko, N. *Pushkin i teatr: Formirovanie teatral'nykh vozzrenii.* Moscow: Iskusstvo, 1974.

Lobanova, E. F. *Mikhailovskaia biblioteka Pushkina: Popytka rekonstruktsii kataloga.* Moscow: MtsNTI, 1997.

Longworth, Philip. *The Cossacks.* London: Constable, 1969.

Lotman, Iurii. *Aleksandr Sergeevich Pushkin: Biografiia pisatelia.* 2nd ed. Leningrad: Prosveshchenie, 1983.

———. *Pushkin: Biografiia pisatelia.* St. Petersburg: Iskusstvo-SPB, 1995.

Lotman, Iu., and B. Uspenskii. "Novye aspekty izucheniia kul'tury Drevnei Rusi." *Voprosy literatury* 3 (1977): 148–66.

Lotman, Lidiia M. "Eshche raz o 'mnenii narodnom' v 'Borise Godunove' A. S. Pushkina." *Trudy Otdela drevnerusskoi literatury* 50 (1966): 160–70.

———. "Sud'by tsarei i tsarstv v Biblii i tragizm istorii v 'Borise Godunove.'" In S. Schwarzband and D. Segal, eds., *Koran i Bibliia v tvorchestve A. S. Pushkina,* 101–108. Jerusalem: Hebrew University of Jerusalem, 2000.

Luzianina, L. N. "'Istoriia Gosudarstva Rossiiskogo' N. M. Karamzina i tragediia Pushkina 'Boris Godunov.'" *Russkaia literatura*, no. 1 (1971): 45–57.

Lysenkova, E. I. "O probleme tragicheskogo kharaktera v dramaticheskom fragmente Shillera 'Demetrius' i tragediia Pushkina 'Boris Godunov.'" In *Problemy sovremennogo pushkinovedeniia*, 59–69. Leningrad: Gos. ped. inst. im. A. I. Gertsena, 1986.

Maguire, Nancy Klein, ed. *Renaissance Tragicomedy: Explorations in Genre and Politics*. New York: AMS Press, 1987.

Maikov, L. *Pamiati Leonida Nikolaevicha Maikova*. St. Petersburg: Tip. Imperatorskoi akademii nauk, 1902.

———. *Pushkin: Biograficheskie materialy i istoriko-literaturnye ocherki*. St. Petersburg: Izdanie L. F. Panteleva, 1899.

Malia, Martin. *Alexander Herzen and the Birth of Russian Socialism*. New York: Grosset and Dunlap, 1965.

Mal'tsev, M. I. *Tema krest'ianskogo vosstaniia v tvorchestve A. S. Pushkina*. Cheboksary: Chebashkoe gos. izd-vo, 1960.

Margeret, Jacques. *Estat de l'Empire de Russie et Grand Duché de Moscovie*. 3rd ed. Edited by Julius Klaproth. Paris: De l'impr. de Fain, 1821.

———. *Istoricheskiia zapiski ....* Translated and edited by N. G. Ustrialov. Moscow: Tip. Lazarevykh vostochnykh iazykov, 1830.

———. *The Russian Empire and Grand Duchy of Muscovy: A 17th-Century French Account*. Translated and edited by Chester Dunning. Pittsburgh: Pittsburgh University Press, 1983.

———. *Sostoianie Rossiiskoi Derzhavy i Velikago Kniazhestva Moskovskago*. Translated and edited by N. G. Ustrialov. St. Petersburg: Tip. Glavnago Upravleniia Putei Soobshcheniia, 1830.

Martin, Alexander M. "The Response of the Population of Moscow to the Napoleonic Occupation of 1812." In Eric Lohr and Marshall Poe, eds., *The Military and Society in Russia: 1450–1917*, 469–89. Leiden and Boston, MA: Brill, 2002.

———. *Romantics, Reformers, Reactionaries: Russian Conservative Thought and Politics in the Reign of Alexander I*. DeKalb: Northern Illinois University Press, 1997.

Martinson, Deborah A., ed. *Literary Journals in Imperial Russia*. Cambridge: Cambridge University Press, 1997.

Massa, Isaac. *A Short History of the Muscovite Wars*. Translated and edited by G. Edward Orchard. Toronto: University of Toronto Press, 1982.

Mavrodin, V. V. "Soviet Historical Literature on the Peasant Wars in Russia." *Soviet Studies in History* 1 (Fall 1962): 43–63.

Mazur, T. P., and N. N. Malov. "Novye materialy o Pushkine." *Prometei* 10 (1973): 237–40.

McNally, Raymond T. *Chaadayev and His Friends*. Tallahassee, FL: Diplomatic Press, 1971.

Meilakh, Boris. *A. S. Pushkin: Ocherk zhizni i tvorchestva*. Moscow and Leningrad: AN SSSR, 1961.

————. *Pushkin i ego epokha.* Moscow: Gos. izd. khudozh. lit-ry, 1958.

Mérimée, Prosper. *Épisode de l'histoire de Russie – Les Faux Démétrius.* Paris: Calman-Lévy, 1889.

Mikhailova, N. I. "K istochnikam remarki 'narod bezmolvstvuet' v 'Borise Godunove.'" In *Vremennik Pushkinskoi kommissii,* no. 20, 150–53. Leningrad: Nauka, 1986.

Mikkelson, Gerald E. "The *Narod* as a *Dramatis Persona* in Pushkin's *Boris Godunov.*" In Jane Gary Harris, ed., *American Contributions to the Tenth International Congress of Slavists...Sofia, September 1988: Literature,* 273–82. Columbus, OH: Slavica, 1988.

Mirsky, D. S. *A History of Russian Literature.* New York: Knopf, 1966.

————. *Pushkin.* New York: E. P. Dutton, 1963.

Mocha, Frank. "Polish and Russian Sources of *Boris Godunov.*" *Polish Review* 25, no. 2 (1980): 45–51.

The Modern Encyclopedia of Russian and Soviet History. 55 vols. Ed. Joseph Wieczynski. Gulf Breeze, FL: Academic International Press, 1976–93.

Modzalevskii, B. L. *Biblioteka A. S. Pushkina.* St. Petersburg: Tipografiia Imperatorskoi Akademii Nauk, 1910.

————. *Pushkin.* Leningrad: Priboi, 1929.

————. *Pushkin i ego sovremenniki. Izbrannye trudy (1898–1928).* St. Petersburg: Iskusstvo-SPB, 1999.

————. *Pushkin pod tainym nazdorom.* Petrograd: Parfenon, 1922.

Monas, Sidney. "Šiškov, Bulgarin, and the Russian Censorship." *Harvard Slavic Studies* 4 (1957): 127–47.

————. *The Third Section: Police and Society under Nicholas I.* Cambridge, MA: Harvard University Press, 1961.

Mordovchenko, N. N. *Russkaia kritika pervoi chetverti XIX veka.* Moscow: Izd-vo Akademii nauk SSSR, 1959.

Morris, Marcia. "Feofan Prokopovich's *Vladimir* as a Vehicle for the Comic View of History in Early East-Slavonic Drama." *Australian Slavonic and East European Studies* 10, no. 1 (1996): 1–15.

Moss, Kevin. "The Last Word in Fiction: On Significant Lies in *Boris Godunov.*" *Slavic and East European Journal* 32 (Summer 1988): 187–97.

Mucha, Bogusław. "Samozwańcza Caryca Maryna Mniszchowna w ocenie Aleksandra Puszkina." *Slavia Orientalis* 37, no. 4 (1988): 529–36.

Nabokov, Vladimir, ed. *Pushkin, Lermontov, Tyutchev: Poems.* London: Lindsay Drummond, 1947.

Nakhimovsky, A. D., and A. S. Nakhimovsky, eds. *The Semiotics of Russian Cultural History.* Ithaca, NY: Cornell University Press, 1985.

Nechkina, M. V. *A. S. Griboedov i dekabristy.* Moscow: Khudozh. lit-ra, 1947.

Nepomniashchii, V., ed. *Poeziia i sud'ba: Stat'i i zametki o Pushkine.* Moscow: Sovetskii pisatel', 1983.

Nikitenko, A. V. *The Diary of a Russian Censor.* Translated by Helen Saltz Jacobson. Amherst: University of Massachusetts Press, 1975.

————. *Dnevnik.* 3 vols. [Leningrad]: Gos. izdatel'stvo khudozh. lit., 1955.

"O 'Borise Godunove,' sochinenii Aleksandra Pushkina. Razgovor pomeshchika i uchitelia rossiiskoi slovesnosti." *Russkaia starina* 68, no. 2 (1890): 445–55.

Ocherki po istorii russkoi zhurnalistiki i kritiki. 2 vols. Leningrad: Leningradskii gosudarstvennyi universitet imeni A. A. Zhdanova, 1950–65.

Onegin, A. F., ed. *Neizdannyi Pushkin.* Moscow and Petrograd: Gos. izd-vo, 1923.

O'Neil, Catherine. *With Shakespeare's Eyes: Pushkin's Creative Appropriation of Shakespeare.* Newark, DE: University of Delaware Press, 2003.

Orlov, P. A. "Tragediia Pushkina 'Boris Godunov' i 'Istoriia gosudarstva Rossiiskogo' Karamzina." *Filologicheskie nauki* 6/126 (1981): 3–10.

Orr, John. *Tragicomedy and Contemporary Culture: Play and Performance from Beckett to Shepard.* London: Macmillan, 1991.

Osterwald, Birgit. *Das Demetrius-Thema in der russischen und deutschen Literatur.* Münster: Aschendorff, 1982.

Ovchinnikov, R. V. *Pushkin v rabote nad arkhivnymi dokumentami ("Istoriia Pugacheva").* Leningrad: Nauka, 1969.

Ovchinnikova, S. T. *Pushkin v Moskve: letopis' zhizni A. S. Pushkina s dekabria 1830 g. po 15 maia 1831 g.* Moscow: Sov. Rossiia, 1984.

Palitsyn, Avraamii. *Skazanie ob osade Troitsko-Sergieva monastyria ot Poliakov i Litvy, i o byvshikh potom v Rossii miatezhakh, sochinennoe odnago zh Troitskago monastyria kelarem Avraamiem Palitsynym.* Moscow: Mosk. tip., 1784.

Palmer, Alan. *Alexander I.* New York: Harper and Row, 1974.

Pavlov, A. P. *Gosudarev dvor i politicheskaia bor'ba pri Borise Godunove (1584–1605 gg.).* St. Petersburg: Nauka, 1992.

Pavlov-Sil'vanskii, N. P. "Narod i tsar' v tragedii Pushkina." In N. P. Pavlov-Sil'vanskii, *Sochineniia,* vol. 2: 289–303. St. Petersburg: Tip. M. M. Stasiulevicha, 1910.

Perrie, Maureen. "Jerome Horsey's Account of the Events of May 1591." *Oxford Slavonic Papers,* new series, vol. 13 (1980): 28–49.

————. "The Popular Image of Ivan the Terrible." *Slavonic and East European Review* 56 (April 1978): 275–86.

————. *Pretenders and Popular Monarchism in Early Modern Russia: The False Tsars of the Time of Troubles.* Cambridge: Cambridge University Press, 1995.

Peterson, Otto P. *Schiller in Russland, 1785–1805.* New York: Verlag von A. Bruderhausen, 1934.

Pierling, Paul. *La Russie et le Saint-Siège: Études diplomatiques.* 3 vols. Paris: Plon, Nourrit, 1896–1901.

Pipes, Richard. "Karamzin's Conception of the Monarchy." In Black, ed., *Essays,* 105–26.

————, ed. *Karamzin's Memoir on Ancient and Modern Russia.* New York: Atheneum, 1966.

Platon (Metropolitan of Moscow). *Kratkaia Tserkovnaia Rossiiskaia istoriia.* 2 vols. 2nd ed. Moscow: V Sinodal'noi tip., 1823.

Platonov, S. F. *Boris Godunov.* Translated by L. Rex Pyles. Gulf Breeze, FL: Academic International Press, 1973.

————. *Moscow and the West*. Translated by Joseph Wieczynski. Hattiesburg, MS: Academic International Press, 1972.

Pogodin, M. P. *Istoriia v litsakh o Dimitrie Samozvantse*. Moscow: Universitetskaia tip., 1835.

————. *Istoriia v litsakh o tsare Borise Fedoroviche Godunove*. Moscow: V tip. gazety "Russkii," 1868.

————. *Istoriko-kriticheskie otryvki*. Moscow: Tip. Avgusta Semena, 1846.

————. *Nikolai Mikhailovich Karamzin, po ego sochineniiam, pis'mam i otzyvam sovremennikov*. 2 vols. Moscow: Tip. A. I. Mamontova, 1866.

————. "Smert' tsaria Borisa Feodorovicha Godunova." *Sovremennik* 5, no. 1 (1837): 247–78.

Pokrovskii, M. N. "Pushkin i rimskie istoriki." In *Sbornik statei, posviashchennykh Vasiliiu Osipovichu Kliuchevskomu*, 478–86. Moscow: Pechatnia S. P. Iakovleva, 1909.

————. *Brief History of Russia*. 2 vols. New York: International Publishers, 1933.

Polnoe sobranie russkikh letopisei. 40 vols. St. Petersburg/Leningrad and Moscow: Arkheograficheskaia komissiia, Nauka, and Arkheograficheskii tsentr, 1843–1995.

Pomar, Mark G. "The Roots of Russian Historical Drama: School Drama and Ceremonial Spectacles." *Russian Language Journal*, nos. 121–122 (1981): 113–24.

————. "Russian Historical Drama of the Early 19th Century." Ph.D. diss., Columbia University, 1978.

Popova, I. L. "'Boris Godunov': Misteriinye korni naradnoi dramy." *Moskovskii Pushkinist* 7 (2000): 65–73.

Possevino, Antonio. *The Moscovia*. Translated by Hugh Graham. Pittsburgh: Pittsburgh University Press, 1977.

Purchas, Samuel. *Hakluytus Posthumus, or Purchas His Pilgrimes*. 20 vols. Glasgow: MacLehose, 1905–7.

Pushkin, A. S. *Boris Godunov*. St. Petersburg: Tip. Departmenta narodnago prosveshcheniia, 1831.

————. *Boris Godunov*. Translated by Philip L. Barbour. New York: Columbia University Press, 1953.

————. *Boris Godunov*. Edited by Victor Terras. Chicago: Russian Language Specialties, 1965.

————. *Boris Godunov*. Translated by D. M. Thomas. Leamington Spa, U. K.: Sixth Chamber Press, 1985.

————. "Boris Godunov." Translated by Alex Miller. *Soviet Literature*, no. 1 (1987) [*Alexander Pushkin, 1799–1837*]: 6–68.

————. *Boris Godunov: Tragediia*. Edited by S. A. Fomichev and Lidiia Lotman. St. Petersburg: Akademicheskii proekt, 1996.

————. *The Bridegroom: with "Count Nulin" and "The Tale of the Golden Cockerel."* Translated by Antony Wood. London: Angel Books, 2002.

————. *The Complete Collection of Drawings*. Edited by S. A. Fomichev. Moscow: Voskresen'e, 1999.

———. *The Complete Works of Alexander Pushkin.* 15 vols. Norfolk, U. K.: Milner and Company, 1999.

———. *The Critical Prose of Alexander Pushkin.* Translated and edited by Carl R. Proffer. Bloomington: Indiana University Press, 1969.

———. *The History of Pugachev.* Translated by Earl Sampson. London: Phoenix Press, 1983.

———. *Komediia o tsare Borise i o Grishke Otrep'eve.* Edited by Sergei Fomichev. Paris and St. Petersburg: Izd. Grzhebina, 1993.

———. *The Letters of Alexander Pushkin.* Translated and edited by J. Thomas Shaw. Madison: University of Wisconsin Press, 1967.

———. *The Poems, Prose and Plays of Alexander Pushkin.* Edited by Avrahm Yarmolinsky. New York: Modern Library, 1936.

———. *Polnoe sobranie sochinenii.* 17 vols. Edited by Maksim Gor'kii et al. Moscow: Izd. AN SSSR, 1937–59.

———. *Rabochie tetradi.* 8 vols. Facsimile edition edited by Ernest Hall and S. A. Fomichev. St. Petersburg and London: RAN (Pushkinskii Dom), St. Petersburg Partnership Consortium, 1995–97.

———. *Sochineniia Aleksandra Pushkina.* 11 vols. in 6 books. St. Petersburg: V tipografii ekspeditsii zagotovleniia gosudarstvennykh bumag (vols. 1–8), V tipografii I. Glazunova i Ko. (vols. 9–11), 1838–41.

———. *Sochineniia A. S. Pushkina.* 6 vols. Edited by Grigorii N. Gennadi. St. Petersburg: Izd. Ia. A. Isakova, 1859.

———. *Sochineniia A. S. Pushkina.* 7 vols. in 3 books. Edited by P. O. Morozov. St. Petersburg: Izd. Obshchestva dlia posobiia nuzhdaiushchimsia i uchenym, 1887.

———. *Sochineniia A. S. Pushkina.* 3rd ed. 10 vols. St. Petersburg: Izdanie A. S. Suvorina, 1887.

———. *Sochineniia A. S. Pushkina: Polnoe sobranie v odnom tome.* 6th ed. Edited by P.V. Smirnitskii. Moscow: A. S. Panafinoi, 1909.

———. *Sochineniia i pis'ma A. S. Pushkina.* 8 vols. Edited by P. O. Morozov. St. Petersburg: Prosveshchenie, 1903–1906.

———. *Sochineniia; polnoe sobranie s biografiei napisannoi A. Skabichevskim…* 10 vols. in 5 books. Edited by A. M. Skabicheskii. St. Petersburg: Obshchestvennaia pol'za, 1891.

———. *Sochineniia Pushkina.* 7 vols. Edited by P. V. Annenkov. St. Petersburg: Izdanie P. V. Annenkova, 1855–57.

———. *Translations from Pushkin.* Translated by Charles Edward Turner. London: Sampson Low, Marston and Co., 1899.

Pushkin i ego sovremenniki: materialy i izsledovaniia. vyp. XXIII–XXIV. Petrograd: Imperatorskaia akademiia nauk, 1916.

Pushkin: Rodonachal'nik novoi russkoi literatury. Edited by D. D. Blagoi and V. Ia. Kirpotin. Moscow and Leningrad: Akademiia nauk, 1941.

Pypin, A. N. *Religioznye dvizheniia pri Aleksandre I.* Petrograd: Ogni, 1916.

Rabinovich, M. B. "'Boris Godunov' Pushkina, 'Istoriia' Karamzina i letopisi." In Brodskii and Golubkov, eds., *Pushkin v shkole,* 307–17.

Raskol'nikov, Feliks. "'Boris Godunov' v svete istoricheskikh vozzrenii Pushkina." In Robert A. Maguire and Alan Timberlake, eds., *American Contributions to the Twelfth International Congress of Slavists: Cracow, August-September 1998: Literature. Linguistics. Poetics,* 157–68. Bloomington: Slavica, 1998.

———. "'Marfa Posadnitsa' M. Pogodina i istoricheskie vzgliady Pushkina." *Russkaia literatura,* no. 1 (2003): 3–15.

Rassadin, S. B. *Dramaturg Pushkin: Poetika idei evoliutsiia.* Moscow: Iskusstvo, 1977.

Reitblat, A. I., ed. *Vidok Figliarin: Pis'ma i agenturnye zapiski F. V. Bulgarina v III otdelenie.* Moscow: Novoe literaturnoe obozrenie, 1998.

Reizov, B. G. "Pushkin, Tatsit i 'Boris Godunov.'" In B. G. Reizov, *Iz istorii evropeiskoi literatur,* 66–82. Leningrad: Leningradskii gosudarstvennyi universitet, 1970.

Riasanovsky, Nicholas. *The Image of Peter the Great in Russian History and Thought.* New York: Oxford University Press, 1985.

———. *Nicholas I and Official Nationality in Russia, 1825–1855.* Berkeley: University of California Press, 1967.

Richmond, Steven. "'The Conditions of the Contemporary': The Censors and Censoring of Soviet Theater, 1923–1927." *Russian History* 27, no. 1 (Spring 2000): 1–56.

Robert, Paul. *Dictionnaire alphabétique et analogique de la langue française.* Paris: Société du nouveau littré, 1973.

Robinson, A. N., ed. *Novye cherty v russkoi literature i iskusstve (XVII-nachalo XVIII v.).* Moscow: Nauka, 1976.

Ronen, Irena. *Smyslovoi stroi tragedii Pushkina "Boris Godunov."* Moscow: ITs-Garant, 1997.

Rosen, G. "'Boris Godunov.'" In *Pushkin v prizhiznennoi kritike 1831–1833,* edited by E. O. Larionova, 249–59. St. Petersburg: Institut Russkoi literatury, 2003.

Rothe, Hans. "Karamzin and His Heritage: History of a Legend." In Black, ed., *Essays,* 148–90.

Rowland, Daniel. "The Problem of Advice in Muscovite Tales about the Time of Troubles." *Russian History* 6, no. 2 (1979): 259–83.

Russkaia istoricheskaia biblioteka. 2nd ed. 39 vols. St. Petersburg-Leningrad, 1872–1927.

Russkaia letopis' po Nikonovu spisku. 8 vols. St. Petersburg: Pri imperatorskoi akademii nauk, 1767–92.

Ruud, Charles A. *Fighting Words: Imperial Censorship and the Russian Press, 1804–1906.* Toronto: University of Toronto Press, 1982.

Rybinskii, V. S. *Sbornik statei ob A. S. Pushkine po povodu stoletniago iubileia.* Kiev: Kievskoe pedagogicheskoe obshchestvo, 1899.

Rzadkiewicz, Chester M. "N. A. Polevoi's 'Moscow Telegraph' and the Journal Wars of 1825–1834." In Martinson, ed., *Literary Journals,* 64–87.

Rzhevsky, Nicholas. "Adapting Drama to the Stage: Liubimov's *Boris Godunov.*" *Slavic and East European Arts* 3, no. 1 (Winter/Spring 1985): 171–76.

Sakharov, A. N. *Aleksandr I.* Moscow: Nauka, 1998.

Sakulin, P. N. *Pushkin i Radishchev; novoe reshenie starogo voprosa.* Moscow: Al'tiona, 1920.

Sanders, Thomas, ed. *Historiography of Imperial Russia: The Profession and Writing of History in a Multinational State.* Armonk, NY: M. E. Sharpe, 1999.

Sandler, Stephanie. *Distant Pleasures: Alexander Pushkin and the Writing of Exile.* Stanford: Stanford University Press, 1989.

———. "Introduction." *Slavic Review* 58, no. 2 (Summer 1999): 283–90.

———. "The Problem of History in Pushkin: Poet, Pretender, Tsar." Ph.D. diss., Yale University, 1981.

———. "Solitude and Soliloquy in *Boris Godunov.*" In Bethea, ed., *Pushkin Today,* 171–84.

Santich, Jan Joseph. *Missio Moscovitica: The Role of the Jesuits in the Westernization of Russia, 1582–1689.* New York: Peter Lang, 1995.

Sbornik Imperatorskago Russkago Istoricheskago Obshchestva. Vol. 137. Published as *Pamiatniki diplomaticheskikh snoshenii Moskovskago gosudarstva s Pol'sko-Litovskim gosudarstvom,* book IV. Edited by S. A. Belokurov. Moscow, 1912.

Schapiro, Leonard. *Rationalism and Nationalism in Russian Nineteenth-Century Political Thought.* New Haven: Yale University Press, 1967.

Schiller, Friedrich. *Early Dramas and Romances.* Translated by Henry George Bohn and Theodore Martin. London: G. Bell, 1833.

———. *Oeuvres dramatiques de F. Schiller, traduite de l'allemand.* 6 vols. Paris: Chez Ladvocat, 1821.

———. *Sämmtliche Werke.* 2nd ed. 12 vols. Stuttgart and Tübingen, 1818–19.

Schmidt, Paul, ed. *Meyerhold at Work.* Austin: University of Texas Press, 1980.

Scholz, Ute. "Die Faszination des Bösen: Mythologische Teufelsanspielungen in Puškins 'Boris Godunov.'" *Die Welt der Slaven* 48 (2003): 275–86.

Schönle, Andreas. *Authenticity and Fiction in the Russian Literary Journey, 1790–1840.* Cambridge, MA: Harvard University Press, 2000.

Serman, I. Z. "Paradoxes of the Popular Mind in Pushkin's *Boris Godunov.*" *Slavonic and East European Review* 64, no. 1 (January 1986): 25–39.

———. "Pushkin i russkaia istoricheskaia drama 1830-kh godov." In *Pushkin: Issledovaniia i materialy,* vol. 6: 118–49. Leningrad: Nauka, 1969.

Shaw, J. Thomas. *Pushkin's Poetics of the Unexpected. The Nonrhymed Lines in the Rhymed Poetry and the Rhymed Lines in the Nonrhymed Poetry.* Columbus, OH: Slavica, 1993.

———. "Romeo and Juliet, Local Color, and Mniszek's Sonnet in *Boris Godunov.*" *Slavic and East European Journal* 35, no. 1 (Spring 1991): 1–35.

Shchegolev, P. E. *Duel i smert Pushkina.* 5th ed. St. Petersburg: Akademicheskii proekt, 1999.

Shcherbakova, M. N. *Pushkin i sovremenniki: stranitsy teatral'noi istorii.* St. Petersburg: Sankt-Peterburgskii Tsentr istorii idei, 1999.

Shcherbatov, M. M. *Istoriia rossiiskaia ot drevneishikh vremen.* 7 vols. St. Petersburg: Pri Imp. Akademii nauk, 1770–91.

———. *Kratkaia povest' o byvshikh v Rossii samozvantsakh.* 2nd edition. St. Petersburg, 1778.

Shervinsky, S. V. "Stage Directions in Pushkin's *Boris Godunov.*" *Soviet Studies in Literature* 8 (Spring 1972): 141–58.

Shevyrev, S. P. "Rasskazy o Pushkine." In Vatsuro, ed., *A. S. Pushkin v vospominaniiakh sovremennikov,* 2: 37–47.

Shmidt, S. O. "G. O. Vinokur i akademicheskoe izdanie pushkinskogo 'Borisa Godunova.'" In Vinokur, *Kommentarii,* 6–35.

Shmurlo, E. F. "Etiudy o Pushkine. Rol' Karamzina v sozdanii Pushkinskogo 'Borisa Godunova.'" In *Pushkinskii sbornik,* 5–40. Prague: Tip. Politika Praga, 1929.

Shukman, Ann, ed. *Ju. M. Lotman, B. A. Uspenskij: The Semiotics of Russian Culture.* Ann Arbor: Michigan Slavic Contributions (No. 11), 1984.

Sidiakov, L. S. "Stikhi i proza v tekstakh Pushkina." In *Pushkinskii sbornik* 2: 4–31. Riga: Uchenye zapiski Latviiskogo gosudarstvennogo universiteta, Otdel LGU im. Petra Struchki, 1974.

Simmons, Ernest J. *Pushkin.* Cambridge: Cambridge University Press, 1937.

Skrynnikov, R. G. *Boris Godunov.* Translated by Hugh Graham. Gulf Breeze, FL: Academic International Press, 1982.

———. "Boris Godunov i predki Pushkina." *Russkaia literatura,* no. 2 (1974): 131–33.

———. "Boris Godunov's Struggle for the Throne." *Canadian-American Slavic Studies* 11 (1977): 325–53.

———. *Ivan the Terrible.* Translated by Hugh Graham. Gulf Breeze, FL: Academic International Press, 1975.

———. *Rossiia v nachale XVII v. "Smuta."* Moscow: Mysl', 1988.

———. *Samozvantsy v Rossii v nachale XVII v.: Grigorii Otrep'ev.* Novosibirsk: Nauka, 1987.

———. *The Time of Troubles: Russia in Crisis, 1604–1618.* Translated by Hugh Graham. Gulf Breeze, FL: Academic International Press, 1988.

Skvoznikov, V. D. *Pushkin. Istoricheskaia mysl' poeta.* Moscow: Nasledie, 1999.

Slater, Wendy. "The Patriots' Pushkin." *Slavic Review* 58, no. 2 (Summer 1999): 407–27.

Slonimskii, A. L. "'Boris Godunov' i dramaturgiia 20-kh godov XIX v." In Derzhavin, ed., *"Boris Godunov" A. S. Pushkina,* 43–77.

Smith, R. E. F., and David Christian. *Bread and Salt: A Social and Economic History of Food and Drink in Russia.* Cambridge: Cambridge University Press, 1984.

Sobranie gosudarstvennykh gramot i dogovorov. 5 vols. St. Petersburg: Tip. N. S. Vsevolozhskago, 1813–94.

Solov'ev, Sergei M. "Obzor sobytii russkoi istorii ot konchiny tsaria Feodora Ioannovicha do vstupleniia na prestol doma Romanovykh." *Sovremennik,* no. 8 (1849), part 2: 1–36.

———. *Sobranie sochinenii Sergeia Mikhailovicha Solov'eva.* St. Petersburg: Izd. Tovarishchestva "Obshchestvennaia Pol'za," 1900.

Soloviev, Alexander V. *Holy Russia: The History of a Religious-Social Idea.* The Hague: Mouton, 1959.

Squire, P. S. *The Third Department.* Cambridge: Cambridge University Press, 1968.

Stark, V. P. "Pushkin i semeinye predaniia ego roda." In Virolainen, ed., *Legendy i mify o Pushkine*, 65–83.

Strakhov, Nikolai. "Glavnoe sokrovishche nashei literatury." In N. Strakhov, *Zametki o Pushkine i drugikh poetakh*, 17–34. St. Petersburg: Tip. brat. Panteleevykh, 1888.

Stroganov, M. V. "Eshche raz o remarke 'Narod bezmolvstvuet.'" In *Vremennik Pushkinskoi komissii*, no. 23, 126–29. Leningrad: Nauka, 1989.

Sukhomlinov, M. I. *Izsledovaniia i stat'i po russkoi literature i prosveshcheniiu*. 2 vols. St. Petersburg: Izd. A. S. Suvorina, 1889.

Sumarokov, A. P. *Selected Tragedies of A. P. Sumarokov*. Translated by Richard Fortune and Raymond Fortune. Evanston: Northwestern University Press, 1970.

Tarle, E. V. "Pushkin kak istorik." *Novyi mir*, no. 9 (1963): 211–20.

Taruskin, Richard. *Musorgsky: Eight Essays and an Epilogue*. Princeton: Princeton University Press, 1993.

Tatarinova, L. E. *Zhurnal "Moskovskii Telegraf" (1825–1834)*. Moscow: Izdatel'stvo moskovskogo universiteta, 1959.

Tatishchev, V. N. *Istoriia Rossiiskaia*. 7 vols. Moscow: Nauka, 1962–68.

Teplov, A. "Ateisticheskaia tema v 'Borise Godunove.'" In *Pushkinskii sbornik*, 21–32. Pskov: Pskovskii gosudarstvennyi pedegogicheskii institut, 1962.

Terras, Victor. *Belinskij and Russian Literary Criticism*. Madison: University of Wisconsin Press, 1974.

———. *A History of Russian Literature*. New Haven: Yale University Press, 1991.

———. "Pushkin and Romanticism." In Andrej Kodjak, Krystyna Pomorska, and Kiril Taranovski, eds., *Alexander Puškin: Symposium II*, 49–59. Columbus, OH: Slavica, 1980.

Tertz, Abram (Andrei Sinyavsky). *Strolls with Pushkin*. Translated by Catharine Theimer Nepomnyashchy and Slava I. Yastremski. New Haven: Yale University Press, 1993.

Thompson, Ewa M. *Understanding Russia: The Holy Fool in Russian Culture*. New York: University Press of America, 1987.

Thyrêt, Isolde. *Between God and Tsar: Religious Symbolism and the Royal Women of Muscovite Russia*. DeKalb: Northern Illinois University Press, 2001.

Timofeev, Ivan. *Vremennik Ivana Timofeeva*. Moscow-Leningrad: Izd. AN SSSR, 1951.

Todd III, William Mills. *Fiction and Society in the Age of Pushkin*. Cambridge, MA: Harvard University Press, 1986.

———, ed. *Literature and Society in Imperial Russia, 1800–1914*. Stanford: Stanford University Press, 1978.

———. "Periodicals in the Literary Life of the Early Nineteenth Century." In Martinson, ed., *Literary Journals*, 37–63.

Toibin, I. "'Istoriia Gosudarstva Rossiiskogo' N. M. Karamzina v tvorcheskoi zhizni Pushkina." *Russkaia literatura*, no. 4 (1966): 37–48.

Tomashevskii, Boris. "Primechaniia." In A. S. Pushkin, *Polnoe sobranie sochinenii v desiati tomakh*, 4th ed., vol. 5, 485–521. Leningrad: Nauka, 1978.

———. *Pushkin*. 2 vols. Moscow-Leningrad: Izd. AN SSSR, 1956–61.

Tsiavlovskii, M. A., ed. *Letopis' zhizni i tvorchestva A. S. Pushkina, 1799–1826.* 2d ed. Leningrad: Nauka, 1991.

Tsiavlovskii, M. A., and N. A. Tarkhova, eds. *Letopis' zhizni i tvorchestva Aleksandra Pushkina.* 4 vols. Moscow: Izdatel'stvo Slovo, 1999.

Tsvetaeva, Marina. *A Captive Spirit: Selected Prose.* London: Virago, 1983.

Turbin, V. N. "Kharaktery samozvantsev v tvorchestve Pushkina." In V. N. Turbin, *Nezadolgo do vodoleia: Sbornik statei,* 63–88. Moscow: Radiks, 1994.

Turgenev, A. I., ed. *Historica Russiae monumenta, ex antiquis exteranum gentium archivis et bibliothecis depromta, ab A. J. Turgenevio.* 2 vols. St. Petersburg: Typis Eduardi Pratzi, 1841–42.

Tynianov, Iurii. *Pushkin i ego sovremenniki.* Moscow: Nauka, 1969.

Umbrashko, K. B. *M. P. Pogodin: Chelovek. Istorik. Publitsist.* Moscow: RAN, 1999.

Ustrialov, Nikolai, ed. *Skazaniia sovremennikov o Dmitrii Samozvantse.* 5 vols. St. Petersburg: Tip. Imp. rossiiskoi akademii, 1831–34.

Varneke, B. V. "Istochniki i zamysel 'Borisa Godunova.'" In M. P. Alekseev, ed., *Pushkin: Stat'i i materialy,* 12–19. Odessa: Odesskii dom uchenykh Pushkinskaia komissiia, 1925.

Vatsuro, V., ed. *A. S. Pushkin v vospominaniiakh sovremennikov.* 2 vols. Moscow: Khudozhestvennaia literatura, 1985.

———. "Istoricheskaia tragediia i romanticheskaia drama 1830-kh godov." In *Istoriia russkoi dramaturgii: XVII-pervaia polovina XIX veka,* 327–67.

———. "Podvig chestnogo cheloveka." *Prometei* 5 (1968): 8–51.

———. *Pushkinskaia pora.* St. Petersburg: Akademicheskii proekt, 2000.

Vatsuro, V. E., and A. L. Ospovata, eds. *"Arzamas": Sbornik v dvukh knigakh.* 2 vols. Moscow: Khudozhestvennaia literatura, 1994.

Vengerov, S. A., ed. *Pushkinist: Istoriko-literaturnyi sbornik.* 4 vols. Petrograd: Tip. A. F. Dresslera, 1914–22.

Veresaev, V. *Pushkin v zhizni; sistematicheskii svod podlinnykh svidetel'stv sovremennikov.* 2 vols. 6th ed. Moscow: Sovetskii pisatel', 1936.

Verkhovskii, N. P. "Zapadnoevropeiskaia istoricheskaia drama i 'Boris Godunov' Pushkina." In V. M. Zhirmunskii, ed., *Zapadnyi sbornik,* 187–226. Leningrad: Izd. AN SSSR, 1937.

Vernadsky, George. "The Death of Tsarevich Dimitry: A Reconsideration of the Case." *Oxford Slavonic Papers* 5 (1954): 1–19.

———. *Russian Historiography: A History.* Belmont: Nordland, 1978.

———. *Tsardom of Moscow, 1547–1682.* 2 vols. New Haven: Yale University Press, 1969.

Veselovskii, S. B. *Issledovaniia po istorii klassa sluzhilykh zemlevladel'tsev.* Moscow: Nauka, 1969.

Viazemskii, Petr A. *Polnoe sobranie sochinenii kniazia P. A. Viazemskago.* 12 vols. St. Petersburg: Izd. grafa S. D. Sheremeteva, 1878–96.

Vickery, Walter N. *Alexander Pushkin.* New York: Twayne, 1970.

———. *Alexander Pushkin, Revised Edition.* New York: Twayne, 1992.

Vinogradov, A. K. *Merime v pis'makh k Sobolevskomu.* Moscow: Moskovskoe khudozhestvennoe izdat., 1928.

Vinogradov, N. "Eshche o pesne Varlaama (Popravka k zametke g. V. Chernysheva)." In *Pushkin i ego sovremenniki,* vyp. VII , 65–67. St. Petersburg: Imperatorskaia akademiia nauk, 1908.

Vinokur, G. O. "Kommentarii [k *Borisu Godunovu*]." In *Polnoe sobranie sochinenii A. S. Pushkina,* vol. 7 (*Dramaticheskie proizvedeniia*), 385–505. Moscow: Izdatel'stvo Akademii nauk, SSSR, 1935.

———. *Kommentarii k "Borisu Godunovu" A. S. Pushkina.* Moscow: Labirint, 1999.

———. "Kto byl tsenzorom 'Borisa Godunova'?" *Pushkin: Vremennik Pushkinskoi Komissii* 1 (1935): 203–14.

———. *Stat'i o Pushkine.* Moscow: Labirint, 1999.

Virolainen, M. N., ed. *Legendy i mify o Pushkine.* St. Petersburg: Akademicheskii proekt, 1994.

Vlasova, Z. I. *Skomorokhi i fol'klor.* St. Petersburg: Izd-vo Aleteiia, 2001.

Volk, S. S. *Istoricheskie vzgliady dekabristov.* Moscow: Izd-vo Akademii nauk SSSR, 1958.

Vol'pert, L. I. "Druzheskaia perepiska Pushkina Mikhailovskogo perioda (sentiabr' 1824 g.–dekabr' 1825 g.)." In E. A. Maimin, ed., *Pushkinskii sbornik: Sbornik nauchnykh trudov,* 49–62. Leningrad: Leningradskii gosudarstvennyi universitet, 1977.

———. "Pushkin i frantsuzskaia komediia XVIII v." *Pushkin: Issledovanie i materialy* 9 (1979): 168–87.

Vorob'eva, N. N. *Printsip istorizma v izobrazhenii kharaktera: Klassicheskaia traditsiia i sovetskaia literatura.* Moscow: Nauka, 1978.

Vyskochkov, L. V. *Imperator Nikolai I: Chelovek i gosudar'.* St. Petersburg: Izd. S.-Peterburgskogo universiteta, 2001.

Whittaker, Cynthia H. *The Origins of Modern Russian Education: An Intellectual Biography of Sergei Uvarov, 1786–1855.* DeKalb: Northern Illinois University Press, 1984.

Wiese, Benno von. *Friedrich Schiller.* Stuttgart: Metzlersche Verlagsbuchhandlung, 1963.

Williams, Robert I. *Comic Practice/Comic Response.* Newark, DE: University of Delaware Press, 1993.

Wirtschafter, Elise Kimerling. *The Play of Ideas in Russian Enlightenment Theater.* DeKalb: Northern Illinois University Press, 2003.

Wolff, Tatiana A. *Pushkin on Literature.* Evanston: Northwestern University Press, 1998.

———. "Shakespeare's Influence on Pushkin's Dramatic Work." *Shakespeare Survey* 5 (1952): 93–105.

Wood, Antony. "Can Pushkin Survive Translation?: Experiments in Lyric Verse." *Modern Poetry in Translation* [King's College London], vol. 15 (1999): 205–26.

———. "The Carthorse, the Posthorse and Pegasus." In A. D. P. Briggs, ed., *Pushkin: A Celebration of Russia's Best-Loved Writer,* 179–88. London: Hazar Publishing, 1999.

Yefimov, Igor. "A Duel with the Tsar." *The Russian Review* 58, no. 4 (October 1999): 574–90.

Zaborov, P. R. "Shekspir i russkii preromantizm – N. M. Karamzin." In Alekseev, ed., *Shekspir i russkaia kul'tura*, 70–80.

Zagorskii, M. B. *Pushkin i teatr.* Moscow and Leningrad: Gos. izd. Iskusstvo, 1940.

Zel'dovich, M. G., and L. Ia. Livshits, eds. *Russkaia literatura XIX veka: Khrestomatiia kriticheskikh materialov.* Moscow: Vysshaia shkola, 1975.

Zguta, Russell. *Russian Minstrels: A History of the Skomorokhi.* Oxford: Clarendon Press, 1978.

———. "Witchcraft Trials in Seventeenth-Century Russia." *American Historical Review* 82 (1977): 1187–1207.

Zimin, A. A. "Smert' tsarevicha Dimitriia i Boris Godunov." *Voprosy istorii,* 1978, no. 9: 92–111.

Ziolkowski, Margaret. *Hagiography and Modern Russian Literature.* Princeton: Princeton University Press, 1988.

Zolkiewski, Stanislas. *Expedition to Moscow.* Translated by J. Giertych. London: Polonica, 1959.

Zorin, Andrei. *Kormia dvuglavogo orla– : literatura i gosudarstvennaia ideologiia v Rossii v poslednei treti XVIII-pervoi treti XIX veka.* Moscow: Novoe literaturnoe obozrenie, 2001.

Index

Aeschylus, 77

Alekseev, Mikhail, 118, 121

Alexander I, Tsar, 25, 26; Arzamas Society of Obscure People and, 57; exile of Pushkin by, 51; Karamzin's work condemned by, 57; Pushkin's relationship with, 53, 58, 73; as tsaricide, 73, 140

Alexander II, Tsar, 28

Andzhelo (Pushkin), 186–87n4

Annals (Tacitus), 168–69

Annenkov, Pavel V., 28, 125, 155n19

Arans, Olga, 167

Aristotle, 38, 190n40

Arzamas Society of Obscure People, 55–56, 57, 96, 107

atheism, 43, 58, 112, 118

audience: author's expectations of, 186, 494n198; compulsory attendance of theater, 227n19; as dramatic participant, 19; hybrid genres and, 180, 184–85; Pushkin's contemporaries as intended, 14, 76, 98, 142–43, 454; revision to accommodate reading, 154; tragicomedy and, 184–85

authorial intention, 6, 40; gene and,

157–58; generic expectation and, 157–58; manuscript evidence of, 29; "Monastery Wall" scene and, 205–6; notebooks, Pushkin's working, as evidence of, 136–37, 145, 156n32; Pushkin's reluctance to revise *Komediia*, 153; revisions and, 33, 35, 194; trilogy planned by Pushkin, 77–80, 99, 103, 234

autocracy, 57; *Komediia* as opposed to serfdom, 98; Pushkin's attitude toward, 42–43; Pushkin's opposition to, 53, 55, 58, 73, 74, 98

Averintsev, Sergei, 168

Bakhtin, Mikhail, 13–14, 141, 162–65, 168, 204–5

Balzac, Honoré de, 172

Basmanov, Pyotr F., 65, 124, 490n180, 494n199, 498–99nn220–21, 502n236, 503n242, 504n247, 505nn255–57, 507n267, 508–9n271

Bayley, John, 64

Beletskii, A. I., 229n35

Belinskii, Vissarion, 9, 11, 12, 27, 164

Belkin, Anatoly, 147

535

PUBLICATIONS OF THE WISCONSIN CENTER
FOR PUSHKIN STUDIES

David Bethea, Alexander Dolinin
Series Editors

Realizing Metaphors: Alexander Pushkin and the Life of the Poet
David M. Bethea

The Pushkin Handbook
Edited by David M. Bethea

*The Uncensored Boris Godunov: The Case for Pushkin's Original Comedy,
with Annotated Text and Translation*
Chester Dunning with Caryl Emerson, Sergei Fomichev, Lidiia Lotman,
and Antony Wood

Alexander Pushkin's Little Tragedies: *The Poetics of Brevity*
Edited by Svetlana Evdokimova

Pushkin's Tatiana
Olga Hasty

The Imperial Sublime: A Russian Poetics of Empire
Harsha Ram

Pushkin and the Genres of Madness: The Masterpieces of 1833
Gary Rosenshield